THE MAN FROM HALIFAX

P.B. WAITE

The Man from Halifax
SIR JOHN THOMPSON
PRIME MINISTER

UNIVERSITY OF TORONTO PRESS
Toronto Buffalo London

© University of Toronto Press 1985
Toronto Buffalo London
Printed in Canada
ISBN 0-8020-5659-8

Design: William Rueter RCA

Canadian Cataloguing in Publication Data

Waite, P.B. (Peter Busby), 1922–
  The man from Halifax

Bibliography: p.
Includes index.
ISBN 0-8020-5659-8

1. Thompson, John S.D. (John Sparrow David), Sir,
1844–1894. 2. Prime ministers – Canada –
Biography. 3. Canada – Politics and government –
1867–1896.* 4. Nova Scotia – Politics and
government – 1867–1896.* I. Title

FC526.T48W34 1985   971.05′5   c84-099257-2
F1033.T48W34 1985

This book has been published with the help of a grant from the Social Science
Federation of Canada, using funds provided by the Social Sciences and
Humanities Research Council of Canada. Publication has also been assisted by the
Canada Council and Ontario Arts Council under their block grant programs.

Contents

Preface

One day in 1949 an erect old man came to the Public Archives in Ottawa, to the old stone building on Sussex Drive that had been the Archives since 1912. He asked to see the dominion archivist, Dr Kaye Lamb, newly appointed from the University of British Columbia. 'A Mr Thompson to see you,' Kaye Lamb's secretary said. 'I want to give you my father's papers,' the man remarked. Lamb was mystified and groped for the visitor's identity. Then he remembered. The man was Colonel John Thompson, economy control director during the war, whom he had seen in the Rideau Club. The papers Thompson meant were obviously those of Sir John S.D. Thompson, prime minister of Canada from 1892 to 1894.

There certainly were papers – some thirty trunks of them, down in the basement of the Rideau Club, whither Thompson had brought them from Toronto some years before. They were almost untouched. They had been boxed up after Sir John's death and conveyed to Toronto, where Lady Annie Thompson, the widow, had gone to live with her children. There they stayed, year in and year out. She had occasion to dip into them now and then, but that ended when she died in April 1913. Around 1921 Joseph A. Thompson, the colonel's younger brother, offered to sort out the papers, but the family objected and the matter was dropped. Colonel John, the oldest in the family, resisted attempts to open them up, to sort them, or to prune them. In 1948 some of the papers were taken out by one of the nieces and typed copies made. One letter of Sir John's to his wife in 1887, critical of Sir John A. Macdonald, disappeared at this point. It may have been family pressures of this kind that persuaded the old colonel to put his father's papers in the Public Archives of Canada.

The Thompson Papers have thus survived almost intact. They do not appear to have been gone through systematically until they came to the archives. Families can have nasty ways of dealing with papers, especially where family honour is concerned, a subject they interpret with latitude. Historians call this process 'laundering.' The Tupper Papers were not just laundered, they were starched, in order to provide posterity with a proper picture of Sir Charles Tupper. There are gaps in the Thompson Papers, but they are gaps that any collection of papers is subject to when the owner is changing houses, moving to Ottawa, or just cleaning up. And they are rich. They include the papers of Sir John Thompson's father, a fascinating Irishman who came to Halifax in 1827, as well as those of Lady Annie Thompson. In the latter are many letters between Thompson and herself. She insisted that whenever he was away from home he write to her every day, and he followed the injunction however busy he was. She did the same. It is the greatest husband-and-wife correspondence of any of the prime ministers. Altogether the Thompson Papers, father's and son's, take up over three hundred boxes in the Public Archives of Canada.

This book has been a long time in the making. Serious work began in 1974, and although other work has supervened from time to time, Thompson has been my main study. The debts incurred have been many. Dalhousie University has been generous with leave and requests for short-term funding for research; the Social Sciences and Humanities Research Council has given me leave fellowships and research grants. There are more personal debts. Murray Beck, now Professor Emeritus at Dalhousie, has read and commented on all the Nova Scotian chapters. John Willis, formerly of the University of Toronto and the Dalhousie law schools, has read chapters where I deal with Thompson's law. Lovell Clark, of the University of Manitoba, has read the chapters from 1891. They have corrected errors and made valuable suggestions. The manuscript required excisions where the historian was getting in the way of the biographer; Professors Beck and Willis, and one of the readers for the University of Toronto Press, at different stages, suggested cuts in order that Thompson could stand freer of the history in which he was partly submerged. The manuscript went to the University of Toronto Press in June 1983, as I was leaving for Australia, and the decision to publish was already in hand when I returned in December. No author could ask for more. Gerry Hallowell, history editor at the Press, has been especially gracious.

I should like also to thank numerous colleagues for suggestions they have made. Dr Kaye Lamb, formerly dominion archivist, has given me the story of Colonel Thompson bringing the Thompson Papers. H.R. Banks of Barrington, Nova Scotia, has donated some valuable Thompson letters. Professor Craig Brown of the University of Toronto has sent me useful sidelights on Thompson from the memoirs of Harold Daly. Allan Dunlop, assistant archivist of Nova Scotia, has been particularly helpful. The staff of the Public Archives of Canada have willingly met repeated calls on their time. Roger Tassé, deputy minister of justice, and Michael Tyrrell, chief of records, have given me permission to use certain departmental files.

A special thanks must go to Dr Eric Sams, of Sanderstead, Surrey, England, for his work on Thompson's shorthand. It had proved difficult to crack. It was an early nineteenth-century shorthand, but there were some seventy or so different methods even then, and no one I consulted in Canada could solve it. When working at the British Library in June 1978 I consulted Mrs Ann Payne, then assistant keeper of the Manuscript Room. She could not solve it but she knew someone who might – Dr Sams, who had done work in cryptography. He solved the Thompson shorthand in twenty-four hours. All students of Thompson, especially myself, have reason to be grateful to him. It proved to be an 1823 shorthand devised by J. Dodge and published in Providence, Rhode Island. Almost certainly J.S. Thompson learned it after he arrived in Halifax in 1827. That it was efficacious there can be no doubt, since both father and son used it extensively in court and legislative reporting.

Bette Tetreault and Nancy Martin typed several chapters of the manuscript, and Mary Wyman did several hundred pages of nearly perfect copy just when I needed it in June 1983. The final manuscript was edited for the University of Toronto Press by Diane Mew, who went through it with a fine comb, pulling out tangles. She may not have succeeded in smoothing it all – authors retain the right to be spiky once in a while; but the book has greatly benefited from her strong sense of narrative line and relevance of argument. She is a rare editor.

My wife and daughters will be delighted to see Thompson within the covers of a book rather than scattered through one whole room of the house, and to find the author more accessible.

P.B.W.
Halifax, Nova Scotia
April 1984

The young John David Thompson in 1859, about the time he was attending the
Free Church Academy at Halifax

Thompson in 1867, the year of his father's death, when, at the age of twenty-two, he was already practising law in Halifax

Thompson aged thirty-four, the young attorney general of Nova Scotia

Annie Affleck about the time of her marriage to Thompson in 1870

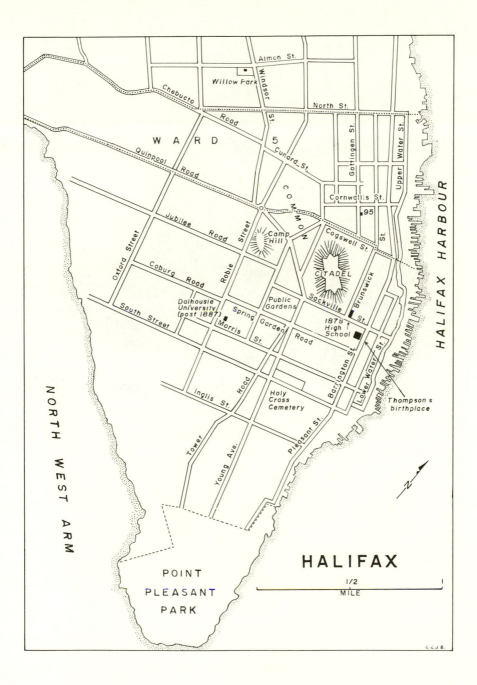

Almon St.

Willow Park

Windsor St.

Chebucto

Road

North St.

WARD 5

Quinpool Road

Gottingen St.

Upper Water St.

Cunard St.

COMMON

Cornwallis St.

95

Jubilee Road

Street

Camp.
Hill

Cogswell St.

Oxford Street

Coburg Road

Roble

CITADEL

Brunswick St.

South Street

Dalhousie
University
(post 1887)

Spring

Garden

Public
Gardens

Sackville

Morris

St.

Road

1878
High
School

Barrington St.

Lower Water St.

Inglis St.

Road

Holy
Cross
Cemetery

Pleasant St.

Thompson's
birthplace

Tower

Young Ave.

NORTH WEST ARM

HALIFAX HARBOUR

N

POINT
PLEASANT
PARK

HALIFAX

1/2
MILE

1

C.C.J.B.

View of Halifax from the Citadel, 1890

Intercolonial Railway Station, Halifax, built in the 1870s

Willow Park, the Thompson home in Halifax until the family moved to Ottawa in 1888; probably taken in the late 1870s

Bishop John Cameron, bishop of Antigonish, Thompson's friend and mentor throughout his political life

J.J.C. Abbott, prime minister following
the death of Sir John Macdonald
until November 1892

Sir Charles Tupper, 'the ram
of Cumberland County'

D'Alton McCarthy, Conservative MP
from Simcoe County, Ontario

George Foster, minister of finance in
Thompson's administration

Thompson in 1891, minister of justice in the Macdonald government

The Thompson boys: John (left) aged eighteen, and Joe, aged sixteen, in 1890

Frances (Frankie), the youngest, in 1893, eleven years old

Helena in 1895, aged seventeen

The eldest daughter, Mary Aloysia (Babe), in 1890, aged fourteen

Sir John Thompson in 1894, the year of his death

Lady Thompson, photographed in Paris in 1893

'Once we were snap-shotted in the middle of a hearty laugh ...':
left to right Mackenzie Bowell, Frankie, Sir John Thompson, unknown
woman, Joe (on the ground), Helena, Annie, Senator Sanford, Faith
Fenton of the *Empire* (?), Muriel Sanford (?), John T.C. Thompson

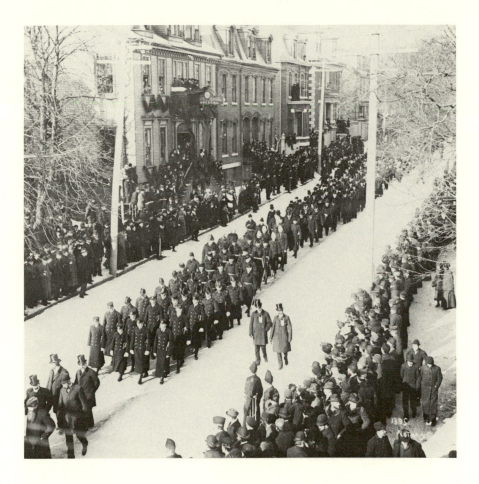

Thompson's funeral, 3 January 1895; the funeral cortège passes along
Barrington Street, Halifax

PART ONE

HALIFAX BOY AND LAWYER, 1845–1877

1

J.S. Thompson Comes to Halifax

John David Thompson was born on 10 November 1845 in a little wooden house that stood, until 1983, at 5 Argyle Street in the heart of Halifax. He was the seventh and the last child of Charlotte and John Sparrow Thompson.[1] The Thompson family were not well off. The old, narrow, three-story house was rented, and it was crowded with seven children from age fifteen down to the new baby. The father of this brood, John Sparrow Thompson, was a hard-working editor and part-time teacher, who added to his thin living by being a shorthand reporter. He kept all three careers going. He needed every one.

John Sparrow Thompson had been born about 1796 in Waterford, Ireland, and had come to Halifax in 1827, when he was thirty-two years old. He was not by any means the Irish immigrant of the 1840s, driven from Ireland by famine and desperation; he was driven rather by ambition, knowledge of his own worth, and belief in a better future. He was not Roman Catholic but was descended from one of a number of Waterford families who had been converted to Methodism by the sojourn there of John Wesley between 1747 and 1753.

William Thompson, the grandfather, was a wool dyer. The earliest record of him is 20 December 1789, when he married Mary Sparrow in Trinity Church, Waterford. The Sparrows were probably of Quaker origin.[2] John Sparrow Thompson left Waterford about 1818 when he was twenty-two, to try his fortune in London. It did not come easily.

Financial difficulties and other vicissitudes in his eight years in London made him think seriously, in 1826, of America. 'I have not allowed (thank God) adverse circumstances to break my spirits and sink my *Character*. Heaven and my own heart only knows, what pecuniary difficulties, what calumnies and maddening torture I have experienced.'[3] What these were is not known; but by the end of 1826 or early in 1827 Thompson had determined to leave for North America. He promised his family to stay away four years and then return. He sailed from England in the *Osprey* in the spring of 1827 and arrived in Halifax, Nova Scotia, in May.

Halifax in the late 1820s was a wooden town, nearly surrounded by sea, with some fourteen thousand inhabitants and a military and naval population adding another 15 per cent. Halifax's chocolate-brown houses were painted that way but were also stained with the smoke of coal fires; the dormer windows, perched out on the roofs like bluff Scottish eyebrows, had been watching life go by in the narrow, dirty streets for nearly a century. Chimneys and chimney-pots marked the climb of the houses up the hill toward the great counterscarp of the Citadel that crowned the city. There were some stone buildings, though much less common than in Scottish, English, or French towns. There was the handsome Government House for the governor that Sir John Wentworth had succeeded in wheedling out of the Assembly some twenty years before, built opposite the fields tht opened south of Spring Garden Road. There was Province House, the home of the Executive Council, Court, and Assembly, begun in 1812. And there were a few solid merchants' houses, unpretentious after the Halifax fashion, like the Henry House, made of the ironstone that was underneath the Halifax peninsula. Such houses were cornered, sometimes faced, with the granite that was a few miles to south and west. Around the city lay the sea, the forest, and countless lakes and ponds.

Halifax had never been chosen for its agricultural potential. As Sam Slick would say, the country around Halifax would starve a rabbit. Woods and lakes, sea and stone, of that there was plenty and indubitably part of Halifax's charm; but its population could not eat charm. Halifax was built to console Boston for the return of Louisbourg to the French in the 1748 Treaty of Aix-la-Chapelle and it cost the British government a pretty packet. Edmund Burke burst out in 1780: 'Good God! What sums the nursing of that ill-thriven, hard-visaged, and ill-favoured brat has cost to this wittol nation!'[4]

By the 1830s, with the Annapolis valley to feed it and a plump garrison to provide it with balls, pageants, and husbands, Halifax had grown and prospered. Its population in 1836 was 14,422; by 1851 it had reached 20,749, and the 1871 census reported a population of 29,582. Its wharfs, warehouses, and banks, following each other in that order, had spread along the harbour. Garrisons and ships had to be supplied with food, liquor, women. Not all of that was good quality, and the garrison made periodic incursions upon Halifax, but on the whole Halifax took its garrison, its trollops, and its fighting with equanimity mixed with occasional exasperation.[5]

Manners and morals were partly dictated by the garrison, the navy, and the governor, as well as by the local population. As late as the 1830s Sunday was not only for religion but for business and pleasure. On Sunday morning the fish market and green produce market were open; grocers generally stayed open until 10 a.m. After church, at 12:30 or so, it was customary for gentlemen to visit friends, where wine and cake would be set out on sideboards, and amiable conversation would go on until the dinner hour at 3 p.m. At dinner a great deal of claret was consumed, especially by the officers and the wealthier class of Halifax; when the ladies retired after dinner, and the port or madeira was passed around, it was not uncommon for men to fill each of three glasses. Drinking was not confined to the upper classes. Fire companies, militia companies, Freemasons, indeed nearly all associations expected to have strong drink available at their meetings. As one Haligonian said, 'Nothing could be done without it.'[6] Even choir practices had to be lubricated with punch; singing was thirsty business!

Halifax, like other British North American towns, lived and ate and drank and sinned and died amid conditions we would find primitive, if not offensive. Public institutions were meagre if they existed at all. One of the first acts of the legislature of Nova Scotia, in 1759, had been to establish a House of Correction, sometimes called the Work House, or Poor House, a refuge for those who could not earn their living. The nature of the incapacity was almost immaterial; it could be owing to lack of work, illness, infirmity, or even, in the early history of Halifax, lunacy.[7]

The poorhouse child, like those that Oliver Twist knew, was sullen, suspicious, and discontented. Most of the children on the street tended to run wild and were, of course, without education.[8] They came for the most part from wretched homes, ill supplied with water, ventilation, or morals. There was no sewage system but outdoor privies or cesspools wherever there was room. As late as the 1860s none were allowed to be connected with the public sewer, which was only concerned with the drainage of water.[9] In the downtown Halifax lots, usually fifty feet by sixty, there would be twenty-five feet or so behind the house where tenements were constructed. 'I ask any of my fellow citizens,' said the rector of St Paul's 'to walk into one or more of them about 11 a.m. in the month of August ... The reek is something terrible.' He spoke from hard personal experience in those houses and streets, ministering to the sick and dying:

The streets are made the receptacle ... for all the dirt that may be brought out of an over-crowded house. Go where you will through Barrack, Albemarle, and Grafton streets, you will see slatternly women, and half-grown girls emptying all sorts of vessels, with every species of foulness, into the gutter ... vegetable matter – such as potato peelings, cabbage leaves, turnips, onions, in various stages of putrefaction form little heaps here and there. Dead dogs, cats, and rats, abound by way of variety, some disembowelled, some with the brains dashed out ... A damp, cloudy day, succeeded by a bright and cloudless one, is the proper day for a walk through one of these streets. The vapour literally ascends in clouds ... and one goes home with the temptation ... to resort to rum.[10]

Autumn and winter were in this respect more tolerable. November in Halifax was a time of year when the city, like many another town in British North America, began to batten down for the winter, put on its storm doors and windows, and lay in its supplies. Ungainly colliers beat their way up the harbour against the pitiless November north-easters, their weather-stained brown sails, brown masts, and stiff white rigging sharply contrasted against the grey, white-flecked, driving sea. Ashore, Halifax sidewalks tended to be monopolized by heaps of shiny black coal from Sydney or Pictou. Carts trundled round the streets laden with potatoes, green cabbages, purple and gold turnips, all reminding the populace that November was now upon them. By mid-November already harbingers of Christmas would be appearing at the grocers. 'Swift winged "fruiters" land their cargoes of fruit and golden sherry. Grocers displayed yellow heaps of oranges and lemons, amber skinned figs, and luscious layers of raisins.'[11] And there was the November rain and sleet, the dark, drenching, bitter weather that cut Halifax's inhabitants to the bone.

John Sparrow Thompson adapted well to Halifax and within a year was thanking providence that he was not only free but respectable in this new and strange land. He wrote his elder brother William in May 1828, the first anniversary of his arrival in Nova Scotia, that he had just a week since drunk tea with the editor of the leading newspaper in Halifax.[12] This was young Joseph Howe, aged twenty-four, who had taken over the *Nova Scotian* six months before. They were to remain, Thompson and Howe, friends for the rest of their lives.

Thompson had not intended to stay in Halifax, but hoped to get enough money together and go on to the United States. It was never to come to that. There were two good reasons: he came to like Halifax, and he married. He wrote home in May 1829, two years out from Ireland, the immigrant who had landed on his feet and had great hopes for the future:

I am more respectably situated than I could at all expect to be in that time – I keep a school, conduct a newspaper, and other matters, which in a short time will pay me well. The climate agrees with me and the people are very kind, Halifax seems already like a kind of second home ... Halifax is a pretty place, the winters long and severe, the summers very warm, living is about as cheap as at home. House rent, and firing high, I pay for three rooms £26 a year. I have great reason indeed of thankfulness that I left home when I did, my prospects here are good, I earn what I get easily, and may have five hours of every day to myself ... Charlotte reads a small portion of your Thomas à Kempis, for me, every morning.[13]

Charlotte was his bride of two months. Her name was Charlotte Pottinger and she had come to Halifax from Pictou. The Pottingers were Scottish, emigrating in 1804 from Kirkwall, in the Orkneys north of the Pentland Firth. It is not known how Charlotte and John Sparrow Thompson met. They were of different religions, she Presbyterian, he Methodist, and were married in Brunswick Street Methodist Church on 24 March 1829. There were to be seven children of this marriage; the first, Mary, born in 1830 and named after Thompson's mother, Mary Sparrow; then Jane in 1832, William in 1834, Charlotte Jr in 1836, Joseph in 1838, Elizabeth in 1842, and finally John David in 1845.

John Sparrow Thompson was an affectionate father, not indulgent but generous and open. His Methodism freighted little prejudice, and he sought to stamp out bigotry when he saw it in his children. He loved the outdoors. One of the delights of Halifax was its lakes and woods and sea; as Thompson said of the beach at Point Pleasant, it was a joy to see 'the wood nymph hand in hand with the mermaid ... the sporting breakers ... tumbling headmost and as if laughing in ecstacy, running in among the weeds and shells at our feet.'[14] That side of Thompson was remarked upon by all who knew him. Letters to him from friends were full of reminiscences of walks, swims, or sailing in and around Halifax harbour.

Thompson's school teaching and his shorthand were not enough to satisfy his ambition. His friendship with Howe, and his experience as assistant editor on Howe's paper, the *Nova Scotian*, was the background for his assumption of the editorship of a literary venture that started in June 1830, the *Halifax Monthly Magazine*. Thompson had a strong belief in encouraging native Nova Scotian talent. To aspiring local poets, who frequently preferred the inflated to the substantial, Thompson offered good advice: 'Simplicity and strength cover a multitude of sins in poetry.'[15] The aim of a literary journal, Thompson believed, was not just to amuse but to instruct and improve. He had certain clear precepts. He believed all men equal in the sight of God and himself. He hated rank. He hated having to ingratiate himself with others; he hated to insinuate his worth, as it were, among either friends, merchants, or the reading public. If people wanted to read him and would pay him a competence, that was all he asked. Intelligence, industry, charity, these pre-eminent virtues J.S. Thompson had: suppliant he was not. He was also candid, sometimes too much so. He was apt to call a spade a spade, and this intellectual honesty was to endear him to discerning friends like Howe.

This did not prevent differences of opinion between Howe and Thompson, in particular about temperance. Thompson wrote to his friend:

You smiled at my sensitiveness, the other evening, on the subject of ardent spirits, but it is no laughing matter with me – the responsibility presses so *overwhelmingly* ... I may be called unwise, for this hurts myself, but I would not wish to have that wisdom would stifle the plain dictates of conscience.[16]

Howe felt it necessary to rein his friend in, and with some good advice:

You are tormenting yourself with a false view of the whole case, and are about to rush headlong into a warfare with the whole state of society around you, for no sufficient reason, and with the certainty of sacrificing the very means in your hands of promoting the cause you espouse.[17]

Important as temperance and other strong moral principles were to Thompson, literary judgments were just as much so. He defended Byron in a long article in the *Halifax Monthly Magazine* in September 1830. Byron's morality was, said Thompson, nearly irrelevant. Towering over such considerations was Byron's poetry, his 'scorn of mere rank, and his misanthropic contempt for the great world.'[18] What mattered were Byron's literary qualities, not his morals.

In 1833 the *Halifax Monthly Magazine* folded; there were not enough subscribers to carry it. Thompson had to fall back on his two other resources, school teaching and shorthand. By 1840, after other unsuccessful experiments, it was clear that Thompson could not manage the business side of publishing. A trenchant and able editor, a good judge of quality in others, fearless and straightforward, he lacked the grubby persistence essential for business – the need to dun old subscribers for payment, to scrounge for new ones, to cajole advertisers into using his space and paying for it.

In the autumn of 1840 Howe entered the coalition government that was formed under Lord Falkland. One result of Howe's influence was Thompson's appointment, early in 1843, as Queen's Printer. He received a regular salary from the government in return for editing the *Royal Gazette*. But Howe and his two Reform colleagues resigned from the Council in December 1843, and Thompson's career as Queen's Printer did not long survive the resignation of his friend. He refused to print the kind of articles the Tory majority of the Council wanted, and in February 1844 Thompson too resigned.[19]

That resignation was not easy. Thompson was now nearly fifty years old. He had a wife and six children dependent upon him. Many people would have swallowed their principles and stayed in office. His brother Joseph wrote him from Ireland consoling him:

Yes better to leave the field honourable in the estimation of friend and partisan than wage War (no matter how great the spoils) at the expense of the faintest reproach of conscience, or the withdrawing of the smile from the approving monitor within.[20]

There spoke the Methodist conscience! J.S. Thompson wrote to his nephew in Ireland in 1845 explaining his position, an honest, hard-working man, fighting his way in a difficult but still interesting world.

I have, dear William, had a series of difficulties in business; – again and again, and again, reckoning up and starting afresh, causes labour and loss ... I have had care, loss, disappointment, labour, years lapsed to little worldly profit, – but yet, thank Providence, my picture of life is not all dark ... a large and dutiful family has been given to me, and been spared to me – I have been enabled to rear children who may be of much more use in the world than I have been ...[21]

Three months after this letter was written, John David Thompson was born in the little wooden house in Argyle Street.

2

Father and Son

John David Thompson was the child of aging parents. By the time he was old enough to have a remembered sense of his world his father was fifty-five, his mother forty-nine. If that helped to give him his quiet nature it would not be surprising. So his father described him in 1853: 'John the youngest, has been noted for his comeliness and good manners. He is a shrewd demure little fellow, engaged at this moment, beside me, with first lessons on the flagolet.'[1]

It was in these years that Thompson at last got out of rented quarters. In June of 1851, when John David was five years old, his father gave up the house at 5 Argyle Street, and bought a house at Gottingen and Prince William streets, for £500. It was promptly mortgaged for £420.[2]

The Gottingen Street house was to remain with the Thompson family for the next twenty years. It was a typical Halifax house, like that in Argyle Street, two stories and an attic, shingled, with the sloping roof agreeably broken with a three-paned dormer window that leaned out over the roof curious to see the street below.[3] On a sixty by sixty-seven-foot lot, it was a narrow, economical house for narrow, economical circumstances.

It would be an exaggeration to say that J.S. Thompson lived in poverty; but he had, materially speaking, a close enough life. He never had in these years much more than £5 beyond immediate necessities. His own description to Howe is doubtless accurate, for Howe had been in his house often enough. 'I lived,' he said, 'with much economy, consistent with due decensy [sic].'[4] Frugality gets it right. Nevertheless Thompson radiated charm, and his home too. One of his young friends, W.A. Hendry, long afterward remembered the hearth of J.S. Thompson:

It was his delight to gather a few select friends about him generally at his own house, perhaps to read a paper of his own or more frequently the production of one of his guests, to be followed by a free discussion ... On such occasions Thompson would shine to great advantage. He was a close thinker as well as an extensive reader ... As a social companion Thompson was delightful ... simple and frolicsome as a child, his conversation being constantly enlivened with true Irish wit.[5]

There were domestic tragedies; before John David was old enough to remember, two of his sisters died. Jane, aged fifteen, died in November 1847. Eight months later, his eldest sister, Mary, died of dropsy at the age of eighteen. These deaths shook his father as much as any calamity he ever sustained. Thompson loved his children; he was devoted to them in the present and they carried his hopes for the future.[6] The deaths of Mary and Jane strengthened his fundamental conviction, which John David was to mark, that neither goods nor money was the measure of a man's happiness nor any test of his worth.[7]

John David's eldest brother, William, was eighteen years old in 1853 when he was appointed, doubtless through Howe's instrumentality, deputy-surveyor of crown lands in Lunenburg County. The title was grander than the salary, which gave little more than a maintenance. William was ambitious and restless, but for the moment settled into his job. Charlotte, now the eldest sister, was nearly seventeen, 'a plain steady girl, with aptitude for music and drawing,' according to her father;[8] but in a household of growing children, from John David aged eight upward, and with the mother not apparently in robust health, Charlotte's time was taken up with housework. Music and drawing had to be left aside. Charlotte's was the fate of many older girls in such families. Some of them were tied down by domestic drudgery for years. Charlotte was to have fourteen more years of it until she married in 1867. Elizabeth (or Bessie, as everyone called her) was eleven years old, 'a fine simple promising child,' adored by her father. She is the only one of John David's brothers and sisters of whom we have a photograph. She was to be the most long-lived of them all. John David's immediate older brother, Joseph, was just finishing study at the Free Church Academy, and his career was the immediate concern of his father.

In 1857 young Joseph Thompson tried to join the Orange Order. Prior to this time what anti-Catholicism there had been in Nova Scotia was more ceremonial than actual. Roman Catholics had to watch a Guy Fawkes' Day every year. In Halifax there was a bonfire on the Grand Parade in the evening of every November the Fifth, when the pope was burnt in effigy amid much cheering. It did not signify much. Indeed, in 1822 Nova Scotia was the first of the British North American colonies to remove the impediments against Roman Catholics holding office. By the 1851 census, the Roman Catholic population of Nova Scotia was 69,000 in a total of 277,000, or 25 per cent. In neither the 1861 nor the 1871 census did it increase much above 26 per cent. Nova Scotia had not had a tithe of the religious agitation that had shaken colonial societies in Newfoundland, Prince Edward Island, New Brunswick, and the Canadas in the 1850s. It was probably not because Nova Scotians were more tolerant; the type of Roman Catholic they encountered was different. The Acadian French were at the western end of Nova Scotia and at Arichat and Cheticamp in the east; they kept to themselves and in political terms did not count. The Scotch Roman Catholics in Antigonish County and in Cape Breton had been there long enough to be accepted. They even occasionally elected Protestants to represent them in the legislature. The Irish who came to Nova Scotia had come mainly to Halifax, arriving before the great hunger of the 1840s had sent the mass of starving, penniless, disease-stricken humanity to British North America. By the 1850s the Irish in Nova Scotia had become established, some as tradesmen and entrepreneurs, their Catholicism pretty much an accepted part of Halifax life.

Nevertheless, there were some primitive prejudices in existence. The Irish workmen building the railway from Halifax to Windsor in 1856 were not very tender souls, and the railway also employed some fairly tough Protestants. There was a riot at Gourlay's shanty in May 1856, caused by Protestants taunting Roman Catholics. The latter responded as best they knew how – they beat up their Protestant tormentors. The Irish workmen were charged, but when they came up for trial, in December 1856, the mixed jury split and no convictions were made. This was the immediate cause of the anger of Joseph Howe. Goaded into a fight with the Irish Catholics of Halifax, he ended up by offending all Catholics. It was a blunder politically, as the Liberals, who had won the election of 1855, now in February 1857 found out. When the Nova Scotia Assembly met, their Catholic supporters promptly deserted them for the Conservatives. This brought down William Young's Liberal government and put the Conservative party under J.W. Johnston in power. Howe had dark thoughts of leading a Protestant crusade.

The Orange Order had never been strong in Nova Scotia. The first lodge was founded in Halifax in 1847, and there were eight in the province by 1850. But in the late 1850s it began to feel its oats; incorporated in 1857 it had twenty-one lodges by 1862.[9] Among its new acolytes was Joseph Thompson, aged eighteen, a Methodist like the rest of his family. His father objected vigorously. From the earliest days of his Irish childhood, Thompson said, the Orange Order had been spoken of disparagingly by Catholics and Protestants alike. To be an Orangeman had been in Thompson's experience a sign of 'uncharitable bigotry.' Roman Catholicism should not be opposed by such sordid means as those associated with the Orange Order, the main results of which had been resistance by the Order's opponents and dissipation by its adherents. It was stupid, indeed wrong, to be insulting to Roman Catholics.

Many of these are good persons – I have found them as true and friendly as any others – and while opposed to their religious views, I would think a studied insult to them every way unwarrantable ...
    Do not estrange yourself from the family. We want yr. counsel and company. You may so estrange yourself & may cause sorrow to your Mother & me & regret to yr. brothers & sisters – or you may be a consolation & comfort to us all. May the Almighty guide you to choose the better and happr. path.[10]

John David and his two brothers were in the Sons of Temperance movement along with their father. They took part in more than one parade that celebrated the transcendent virtues of cold water. But enthusiasm for cold water was to die soon in William. He had proved adept in his work as deputy-surveyor in Lunenburg County. Surveying, however, meant field work during the day and paper work in the evening. It was the latter that proved to be William's undoing. His uncertain business practices and gregariousness he acquired from his father; these, combined with drink, were to prove altogether unsettling. The manly art of surveying led to other manly arts: William's books got into arrears and by the end of four years were in a tangle. Young William believed his problem was only catching up with arrears of paper work; but in 1859 he was dismissed from his position, an investigation started, and his father was asked for the amount of a bond he had signed in 1853.
    It was a terrible shock to the old man. There is little indication of how much money was involved, but it was at least £400, and likely nearer £700. That is about $35,000 in 1980s money. Fraud was alleged, but it was probably plain bad management. His father was confident that when the details were sorted out, there would be little to be paid. But there was also little to pay with. Thompson's August 1859 letter to the attorney general of Nova Scotia, now J.W. Johnston, is sad reading from a proud man, sixty-three years of age:

I need not say how much I have tried to prevent the difficulty, and how bitterly I have lamented it ... Within a few years I have met with disappointments and loss, and have been trying, with industry and economy, to meet daily absolute requirements. I have no monied means beyond what I describe, and no other property except a little furniture, &c., and a kind of nominal ownership of the house which I occupy, as Mr. Binton, Secretary of the Building Society is aware. If that were sold, it might deprive my family of a valuable refuge, without, perhaps, realizing £50, beyond encumbrances.[11]

Nevertheless the house was sold on 1 June 1860, and at a loss. Details are not clear; the family continued to live there, probably leasing from the architect to whom they had sold it.[12] The young witness of the sale signed himself J.S.D. Thompson. John David began to use his father's middle name, Sparrow, in his own name from about this time and so signed himself from 1860 onward.

William Thompson had been ready and anxious to redeem his character, but that was not going to be easy in the small community of Nova Scotia. The government service was closed against him. Finally, he left Halifax on 3 December 1859 for South Africa. The last letter from him in the J.S. Thompson Papers was from Cape Town, dated 20 February 1860, announcing his arrival.[13]

In February 1860 the Nova Scotian Assembly voted out the Conservatives and brought back the Liberals. William Young, the Liberal premier, appointed himself chief justice of Nova Scotia, and in August 1860 Joseph Howe became premier of his native province. J.S. Thompson was made reporter to the Assembly for the 1860 session.

Early in 1861 Howe's government appointed J.S. Thompson superintendent of the Money Order Department of the Nova Scotia Post Office. From that time on his income was at long last secure. A stipend of £200 a year – roughly $12,000 at 1980s levels – was not a great deal, but for Thompson it was enough. The office was not exacting; attention, punctuality, neatness were the essential virtues. None Thompson considered pre-eminent, not as against independence, integrity, and intellectual vitality; but he could summon them up. Now it might not be possible for him to take a couple of hours off today and make them up tomorrow. On hot days he had been wont to walk down to De Wolfe's wharf and take a plunge in the harbour when it was too humid to write or think.[14]

Thompson was now sixty-six. Life's uncertainties he had felt at an early age and they had not ended with his arrival in the new world. His friend W.M. Brown was struck by Thompson's remark, 'Is not life a fitful fever to us all?'[15] His brother Joseph in Ireland was writing elegiac letters about the days of their youth, morning days Joseph called them, about old houses, old rooms, and the ruins of memory that lived in them.[16] Thompson too had his elegiac moods. Martin Griffin, a boyhood chum of

John David's, tells how old Thompson loved to recite Whittier, and did it very well, especially 'My Playmate,' which had so many echoes of Thompson's lost Irish days.[17] For he was never to return to Ireland, never to see his Irish relations again. John David always kept a special place for Waterford and Ireland in his heart because of 'all the sadness I used to see in my father's face when he spoke of it.'[18]

Philosophical, at times pensive, Thompson was; gloomy he was not. He liked life, and there was a spring to his mind. He was ever ready with his hat and coat, ready to collect young John and the dog to go for a hike. Sometimes this was to Cole Harbour, twelve miles from Halifax on the Dartmouth side of the harbour; sometimes it would be across the harbour to sit over a fire on the beach at Tuft's Cove to enjoy the breeze on a warm summer's evening. W.M. Brown recalled a walk to Cole Harbour:

'The smoky currents' of vapour winding round the hillsides – and lake and meadow in the shadowy distance. The shades of evening too as we returned, meeting the villagers going home in their carts; – when the world without was lost to view, the beauties and treasures of the intellectual world were brought forth – old and new – familiar and strange, provoking laughter, or awaking a sigh. 'Who so happy as we?' we thought, if we did not speak it and we parted with the resolve to have another pleasant ramble.[19]

Or the two families, the Thompsons and the Browns, would go sailing together, John David at his favourite perch in the bow looking down into the clear water. 'I was made happier if that could be,' wrote Brown, 'by seeing your young people and mine so happy together, and yourself, at the helm, looked pleased "all over your face".'[20]

There were lots of stories between them.[21] Brown and Thompson would argue politics; Brown was indifferent about politics but Thompson certainly was not. Thompson insisted that a man's duty as citizen required that he study politics. Brown wrote, 'I could listen to your bursts of indignation against some wrong doer, and wait to hear you afterwards express sympathy for the wicked fool, notwithstanding his offences ... I have to thank God for that He hath thrown you in my way.'[22]

What remained especially in Brown's mind was young John David, at thirteen or fourteen, sitting quietly in the bow of the sailboat or walking beside the two men, listening earnestly to their talk, smiling when they were uproarious, as they frequently were.

There are few recollections of John David in these years. A British officer's son recalled how about 1853 John David, a bright, curly-headed eight-year-old, recited at Temperance Hall to great applause Caroline

Norton's poem from the 1830s, 'Bingen on the Rhine,' about a young German soldier in the French Foreign Legion, dying far from home: 'A soldier of the Legion lay dying in Algiers; / There was lack of woman's nursing, there was dearth of woman's tears ...'

Other information about John David's boyhood is thin. He attended the Royal Acadian School, George and Argyle streets, in the mid-1850s. His father was teaching there for a time, and would call the boys to order by banging on a heavy brass bell that stood on the desk. Old Thompson drilled them in recitations, and was especially concerned that they made the proper gestures and pauses when the school put on performances. Then the walls of Acadian's makeshift stage would be hung with spruce boughs and flags; there John David recited another of his father's favourite poems, Thomas Campbell's 'Battle of the Baltic,' written shortly after the battle of Copenhagen in 1801:

> Of Nelson and the North
> Sing the glorious day's renown,
> When to battle fierce came forth
> All the might of Denmark's crown ...[23]

He attended briefly, probably between 1859 and 1860, the Free Church Academy, a sort of grammar school founded in 1845 by the Presbyterians. It used the Dalhousie College building. (From 1844 to 1863 Dalhousie was a ghost, a building without students or professors.)

All too soon John David was forced to work by the ineluctable necessities of family life. By September 1860, when he was nearly fifteen, he was at work in the law office of Nepean Clarke, clerk of the sessions. More than that, he seems to have been relied upon by his father to help keep the family going when his father was away. Joseph was now a clerk and may have helped, but the one surviving letter from this period suggests how much the old man relied on John David. J.S. Thompson was in Truro in October 1860 as reporter for the session of the Supreme Court, presided over by Chief Justice William Young:

My dear John,

    ... I had rather a busy week, up to Saturday evening, chiefly in a tedious case of disputed land. The Chief Justice got on well and smoothly; Mr. Johnston was at the bar as Chief Council [Counsel] in the chief case, but evinced nothing but courtesy for his successful rival on the bench.

    ... I will be wanted in Pictou, next week, if a certain case comes on for trial; if so I may remain in Pictou for the week, altho I feel anxious about home ...

Write me by tomorrow's post, saying how affairs are at home, whether I am wanted there &c. Give my love to Mother, Charlotte, Bessy, Joe. Any news from William? ... State any particulars which may be suggested to your mind, as of any interest or consequence. I have perused but one Halifax paper since I left home.
Your loving father,
J.S. Thompson[24]

This letter assumes some maturity in young John, but it is still addressed to *Master* J.S.D. Thompson, at the office of Nepean Clarke. It is clear that John David was taking on some of his father's responsibilities.

By 1864 his father's work at the Post Office became more difficult for him; in the evenings after work at the law office, John David would go over to his father's office in the old Dalhousie College building and try to finish up what his father had been unable to do. John David's day was already long. A lawyer's apprentice had work of monumental dullness: copying out voluminous writs, elaborate arguments and pleadings, on long pieces of heavy lawyer's paper – the kind of work a typist would do in a tenth of the time. Thompson's handwriting had a certain copybook clarity: small, neat, without flourishes.

After early experience in Nepean Clarke's office, John David became articled in 1861 to Henry Pryor. Pryor was a well-to-do lawyer, the son of a loyalist merchant from New York. Like many wealthy men in Halifax, he took his duties as citizen seriously, serving three times as mayor, in 1849–50, 1853–5, and 1857–9. He was justice of the peace for Halifax County – one of the few lawyers who was – and in May 1867 was made stipendiary magistrate, a post he was to hold until 1883. Pryor's office was thus not a bad place for Thompson, however dull the work. There was a diversified legal business and Thompson could study law in whatever time he had available. He studied it with rare thoroughness, the way his father had taught him, with a ready mastery of detail. Pryor was no intellectual giant, but it made little difference to young Thompson what sort of a teacher he had, so long as he had access to a decent collection of law books.[25] There is evidence that Pryor found Thompson too shy, too bookish, perhaps too scrupulous. 'Thompson,' said Pryor once in a moment of annoyance, 'you will never be able to earn your salt.'[26] If by that Pryor meant wealth, he came closer to the truth than usual with such predictions.

The bar examinations were not difficult and on 25 July 1865, J.S.D. Thompson was admitted to the bar of Nova Scotia. He was nineteen years old. He had, of course, to set up his own practice. Early years as a fledgling professional are usually hard and it was fortunate that he had acquired mastery of his father's shorthand system. If worse came to worst, he used to say, he could always turn to and make a living with that. In fact he did. In the 1867 spring session of the Nova Scotia Assembly, the last one before confederation, he was John G. Bourinot's assistant in reporting debates.[27]

Thompson was, almost certainly, an anti-confederate between 1864 and 1869. There is no evidence to contradict the statement of Lawrence Power, clerk of the Assembly from 1867 to 1877, that Thompson was opposed to confederation and remained so until Howe joined the Macdonald government in 1869.[28] Thompson and his friends enjoyed the discomfiture of the confederationists. This diary entry for 1 July 1867 reflects their sentiments:

Our first day as Canada. The Union of the Colonies was celebrated in a very lame manner although I suppose the Confeds, will trumpet it in the most graphic manner – the bells rung or toll'd just as you please a few weak guns were fired ... Something they called a procession consisting of a representative of each of the trades and professions – all the Senators and the Band ... the day was very warm and dusty.[29]

A few months later, on 21 October 1867, Thompson's father died, after a short illness, in the house at 95 Gottingen Street. Thompson was left with full responsibility for the family and little to discharge it with, save the labour of hands and brain. There was no insurance, so far as is known. His mother and his sister Elizabeth had somehow to be provided for. Charlotte, his other sister, a few months earlier had married Daniel Sargent, a widower from Barrington, in Shelburne County. John David's brother William was in South Africa. His other brother, Joseph, was gone. In May 1865 Joseph had married Emma Hamilton, a Halifax girl; then, late in 1866, he had emigrated to Galveston, Texas, with his wife. There the young couple ran into an epidemic of yellow fever in the summer of 1867. On 2 August Joseph wrote to John David with some sang froid, 'Give our best love to all and in case of the worst we shall say good-bye. Your bro. Joe.'[30] Within a month both were dead.

Thus in October 1867, at nearly twenty-two, John David was left with the house to keep going and two women to support. That was what was left of the strivings, the hopes, the ambitions, of John Sparrow Thompson, the Irish immigrant who had come to Halifax forty years before.

Yet was it so small? Caring little about making money, believing all his life that the mind was man's real kingdom, J.S. Thompson was fearless, intelligent, charming, vigorous. He was not forgotten. His pensive, lean face still catches at passers-by out of the dark portrait by William Valentine.[31] He was unfitted for public life; so carefully did he balance the rights and wrongs of major issues that he could hardly decide upon them. In private, he was sure-footed, firm, sometimes even obstinate. His great passion in life was literature; the only book in the nineteenth century about Nova Scotian poetry was written by J.S. Thompson, published in 1862.[32] Those who knew him trusted his judgment and were much influenced, sometimes debilitated, by it. John Bell, later Halifax's city auditor, used to come away from a literary session at the house on Gottingen Street smarting from Thompson's merciless corrections. Bell had to admit that Thompson was right, that it was only his own 'thinskinnedness' – Thompson's word – that made the criticism so hard to endure.[33] Nothing could induce old J.S. Thompson to praise what he believed was faulty. His sincerity had in it a hardness that could be uncomfortable. He reminds one of Gregers Werle in Ibsen's *The Wild Duck*, pulling away the very illusions that made life bearable.[34] John David had ample occasion to observe how his father's friends had sometimes to pay a price for such rugged sincerity. But he had loved, admired his father: J.S. Thompson's great legacy of independence, integrity, and industry were to be carried over into John David's strong, coherent, and untrammelled mind.

3

The Courting of Annie Affleck

John David never seems to have been close to his mother; what he may have felt about her as a child is unknown. For all their richness, the Thompson Papers contain not a single letter to or from his mother. Charlotte Pottinger Thompson must remain unknown in default of evidence. She may have been chronically ill; if so, it was for a long time, since she died only in 1887. Conclusions must be highly tentative. But the apparent coldness of their relationship is difficult to explain on any other ground than that certain events of Thompson's early maturity permanently estranged him from his mother.

After his father's death, Thompson began what can be described as a quest for certainties. For all its charm, the Thompson home had frequently lacked material certainties. By the time Thompson had started to work himself, he could see how the receipt of a regular income from the Post Office had made his father more comfortable. Routine though the work was, it had brought in £50 every quarter after 1861. There was a lesson in it. Being a lawyer, as Thompson had become in 1865, did not guarantee a livelihood. Thompson's friend, Martin Griffin, discovered after being admitted to the bar that it was good to be in the newspaper business.[1] Beyond trying to earn his living in a crowded profession, Thompson knew where he was going, what he wanted to be. To be a judge was for young Thompson the summit of his profession; it required qualities that both he and his father cherished – knowledge, probity, and intellectual vigour. It was his ambition the moment he got his feet in a law office. He had only delight in the prospect of becoming what Sir John A. Macdonald was to call 'a legal monk.'[2]

His quest for certainty was to take him, however, further than that. He was restless and dissatisfied with the Methodist religion. He had been devoted enough; he attended with his family the Brunswick Street

Methodist Church, where his mother and father had been married in 1829; he had been taught, and had himself taught, in the Sunday school where he had been a star pupil. Indeed, his old Sunday school teacher remained his spiritual mother for the rest of his life.[3] Thompson was probably never attracted to the emotional manifestations of Methodism: the steamy confessions of sin, the passionate abjuring of evil, the golden catharsis that promised everything. These had not been what held his father either. Old J.S. Thompson liked Methodism's levelling, republican honesty, its absence of class, its instinct to measure a man by what he was rather than by what he appeared to be. It was to J.S. Thompson a plain-clothes religion, affirming the fundamental truth that all men were equal in the sight of God.

But for John David the Methodist faith may have been unsatisfying metaphysically. The religious upheavals of the 1840s and 1850s within the Church of England about the church and its doctrines, the revival of Roman Catholicism in Britain and in British North America, stirred his search for some towering theology, some better articulated eschatology than the simplicities that Methodism provided. About the time of his father's death John David began to attend the Church of England and the Roman Catholic church, to listen to sermons, to read religion, to search actively for the true faith. In this search he met the sophisticated, intelligent, courageous Roman Catholic archbishop of Halifax, Thomas Connolly.

Connolly was Irish, born in Cork in 1814. He studied in Rome for the priesthood, and had come to Nova Scotia in 1842 as secretary to Bishop Walsh, who had been appointed bishop of Halifax. In 1852 Connolly was made bishop of Saint John, New Brunswick, when Halifax itself was elevated into the archdiocese. When Archbishop Walsh died in 1858, Connolly succeeded him. In 1867 and 1868 Archbishop Connolly preached a series of sermons in St Mary's Cathedral on the foundations and doctrines of the church. These sermons and the man himself strongly influenced young Thompson. He was not yet a Roman Catholic, but, like so much else he did, he was carefully surveying the ground. Thompson was not the only one influenced by Connolly's high courage and strong mind. Connolly made a signal impression at the Vatican Council in Rome in 1869–70, where he spoke out strongly against the proposed doctrine of papal infallibility.[4] It was this sort of courage that attracted Thompson, and he was undeniably drawn to Connolly and the Roman Catholic faith over the more obvious, socially easier, claims of the Church of England. Nor was Thompson's conversion sudden. The manner of it was characteristic:

I had been attending the Church of England and Roman Catholic services exclusively for upwards of four years, and reading all of the controversy I could get my hands on, and finally yielded only when to believe and not to profess appeared to be wretched cowardice.[5]

Thompson's favourite character in history was Sir Thomas More.[6] It suggests the bent of his mind: he was not seeking *a* church but *the* church.

It was said that a young Catholic girl, Annie Affleck, had much to do with Thompson's conversion. He refuted this. He was making up his mind about the change before he met her and he only became a Roman Catholic nine months after he married her. 'I did not want it to appear as though I had "turned" in order to be married.'[7] Castell Hopkins, whose 1895 biography of Thompson had the family imprimatur, stated:

It is indeed understood that they never discussed religious matters, either before or after marriage, until he announced his intention of becoming a Roman Catholic. During their engagement, Mr. Thompson would frequently meet her at the church door and walk home, but he seldom or never attended the services with her.[8]

Annie Affleck was born in Halifax on 26 June 1845, the daughter of Captain James Affleck and Catherine Saunders. Her mother was born in Newfoundland; her father came from Berwick, in the north of England, in 1840. His two step-brothers emigrated to Barbados and established a successful plantation there, one that Captain James Affleck, as he became, visited on voyages south from Halifax.[9] On 24 July 1844, James Affleck married Catherine Saunders. They had eight children, of whom Annie was the eldest, and Frances, born 1863, the youngest.[10]

Annie was not well educated, but she was possessed of a quick and vivacious intelligence. She was an attractive young woman; she was also moody, loving wild weather, reminding one of Catherine Linton in *Wuthering Heights*. Annie was often a creature of her own impulses, and sometimes she was a victim of them, swung upon the great swells of her own exhilaration and depression. She had pride and independence without the physical resources for them, trapped between her emotions and her physical reality. Too often the latter conditioned the former. She was sometimes unwell and hated herself for being so. She feared becoming, as she put it, 'a useless mope,' neither useful in this world nor prepared for the next.[11]

Our first view of her is in June 1867 just at her twenty-second birthday. The first entry in her diary records that Thompson took her to a cricket match. It was Thompson's advent on the scene, about November 1866, a few months before the diary opened, that created a crisis with another young man called O'Flaherty. Nothing is known of him, but the ending of the affair reveals something of Annie. She and Thompson were out walking and met the rival, who bowed. 'He has had the best of it he acted his part well and now I suppose enjoys his revenge but let him get now out of my mind altogether and he that I would of once dared anything for.' That sense of daring marks Annie Affleck. She was high-spirited and unafraid; she was, after all, a sea captain's daughter. She did not yet give O'Flaherty his *congé*, but by late September 1867 that affair was virtually over.[12]

The courtship with Thompson proceeded apace. From July 1867 onward he was at Annie's five or six evenings a week. It was not always easy. They argued, Annie admitted, 'about wifely submission.' Submissive she was not. One has the impression of a fierce young nature only partly controlled by good manners and social custom. The subject of woman's role in marriage continued to arise. Whatever answers Annie may have given, Thompson continued to come and they continued to talk. They would sit around the house chatting, then go walking around the common. In those years and after, the common was the favourite resort for the poor and working classes of the city after work was over, especially in the summer and autumn.[13] Young and old would be there, old men watching grandchildren play, or young lovers like Thompson and Annie Affleck discussing their lives or debating, as they did frequently, 'work and a woman's position.' But it was not all fencing. Wednesday, 4 September 1867:

T called for me about 1/2 past 3 and we arrived in the [railway] cars at Bedford about 20 minutes to 5 ... We walked on the rail track down along to a dear little brook by the shore for about an hour. I felt real happy for a time kind of away from the world and troubles ... home just at 8 o'clock I need hardly say we talked the evening away.

Thompson began teaching her French; he was also teaching her shorthand, and by September Annie began to use it in her diary. It is from Annie's shorthand that one begins to understand something of their relationship.

The reasons why Thompson appealed to Annie is a natural question and is not susceptible of an easy answer. Annie was bold, original, and spirited; Thompson was quiet and controlled. She needed a flywheel to control her centrifugal forces; he enjoyed the refreshing vigour of them.

Annie in her own family felt a little helpless, and this was compounded by her being from time to time unwell. As the eldest daughter, much may have been expected of her. She was frequently cross and irritable. 'T. in. I did some French and *fought*.'[14] Thompson had his emotions disciplined but he was not a cold fish. He gave the impression of a powerful furnace whose coals were well banked but where an alteration of dampers and draughts could produce a raging fire. Nor was he dull; Annie did not enjoy dull people, any more than she could tolerate undisciplined ones. Thompson loved to tease and he had a vigorous sense of humour. More than that, Thompson seemed to be a man Annie could lean on in the business of living she found so hard. He gave her peace. She was soothed by his patience, caught by his kindness. 'How could I live without it now?' she asked herself on 8 September. A few days later she confided in shorthand, 'I kissed Thompson tonight. Heaven help me if I am doing wrong. I can't live without some kindness.'[15]

Courting was not easy with Annie's parents, three brothers, and two sisters around. 'Joey' (Annie's sister Johanna) was now twenty, the youngest sister, Frances, was only four; her brothers were fifteen, thirteen and eleven years of age. But sometimes Joey would be out or go upstairs. As Annie put it on 9 October, 'Thompson is in and Joey is out.' That night they talked for a while, then Thompson drew her to him, kissed her, and told her how much he cared for her. 'Ring or no ring,' wrote Annie in shorthand, 'it was pleasant, pleasant, to be petted ... lonesome I would be without him now.' There were times when she positively needed to be cajoled, or petted as she used to say. 'I felt horribly dissatisfied with myself and everyone else all day a kind of an uncomfortable independent reckless sort of mood. He kissed me, petted me, and talked it off.' In the midst of this came Thompson's father's final illness and death. Then it was Annie who reached out in sympathy. 'Poor child,' she wrote on 23 October, 'he is tired and worn out. His father is to be buried tomorrow.'[16]

When she knew she was being contrary or cross Annie wondered how Thompson's patience could last. Increasingly as November came, she found herself lonely when he was away or could not call. Is it me, she asked herself, or merely passion, that makes me so lonesome for him?[17] 'I shudder to think of having to get over liking him if ever I should have to.'

There was a similar ambiguity in their quarrels. One evening she refused to coaxed out of a bad mood, and Thompson left. She was unhappy, thinking that Thompson might believe she was really nothing to him, that he could live just as well, if not better, without her. The following day she spent sewing and reading the biography of Lord Bacon. Thompson came in after supper, and it was Annie who made up the quarrel, to her own surprise. 'I sat in his arms, and laid my head on his shoulder and felt glad to feel that I was not alone.'[18] That was 10 December. Christmas eve they spent talking by the fire; Annie remarked on the quiet content she felt and how she had thought that she would never feel that way with anyone:

... I felt that I was dear to him, and is he not as dear to me? He fastened a little chain around my neck to remember this Christmas Eve. I would remember it too ... Whatever my future Christmas Eves may be like this one, at last, after all the bitter trials of this year, troubles that my spirits almost broke under, hard and bitter, but they are in the past now. I am quieter and happier and thank God after all this Christmas Eve was the most peaceful and happy of all that I have spent. God guard him and I along into the dark future, be it long or short.[19]

She was still unwell from time to time; 27 December she spent staring morosely into the fire not even willing to read. Thompson did not come – something had held him up – but her impression of her world without him is fascinating:

I felt as if I were all alone in the world, the cold chill shiver of lonesomeness went over me. I tried to battle it off and to read but I could not ... and felt again all the long lonesome nights that I have spent ... wondering what I was sent into the world for ... I know that I am silly, that he would have been in tonight if he could and still I could not content myself to sit and read. I suppose as I am I must be; I cannot alter my nature now.[20]

Annie's New Year's eve was the summit of her year 1867, and she surveyed the long, difficult road she had come:

[Thompson is] the only one that cares for me in truth; for that I am content ... if he is to be in in the evening when he kisses me and tells me that I am all to him I feel happy, and when he goes I only think that tomorrow evening I will see him again for now I live for him I am trying to be content for him ... Who would have thought that this night last year, that before he came to be all to me that he was to make me contented with life and that I would look up to anybody ...
                                        Annie Affleck
Halifax, December 31st, just upon the stroke of 12 o'clock, back room in Starr Street.[21]

So ends Annie's diary. One is admitted to her private world in future only through her letters to and from Thompson.

As Annie's commitment to Thompson grew, so also did her mother's hesitations and her sister Joey's. The cause of the Affleck unease was probably Thompson's religion. It grew so uncomfortable that Thompson's letters and notes had to be smuggled in.[22] There was not yet any question of their marrying; Thompson was the sole support of his mother and sister and Annie had no money. She may even have worked for a while in a shop in the later 1860s to help her family.[23]

Of all the letters and notes that Thompson sent to Annie before they were married (in 1886 Annie had a whole box of them), nothing survives but one letter, of 3 December 1869. It was written from Barrington, in Shelburne County, where Thompson was visiting his sister Charlotte and brother-in-law, Daniel Sargent. This letter is written in longhand and shorthand, an example of Thompson's maturing style at the age of twenty-four:

Dear Annie,

I suppose it is very bold of me to write again and your Ma & Joey will be cross but I will be there soon I hope to apologize in person. Barrington is like a perpetual Sunday – the people are very nice and all very good. It seems strange though how they all live for you see no one going about and even those that keep shop only seem to be there for about an hour a day. Two or three vessels have run ashore in honor of my arrival to their own great personal inconvenience and the embarrasment [sic] of their owners. See what it is to make a sensation. With love to all, I remain, Yours, JSDT.

What follows in shorthand reveals, what is so often in Thompson concealed, the volcano underneath. It is at least four times the length of the longhand version:

My own baby dear,

Yesterday morning the first thing after breakfast I went up to the Way Office to see if the mail had come ... presently a wagon stopped at the house ... but no letters and I felt just as if I had not a friend in the world. But soon afterwards Dan'l came in with my darling's letters in his hand. My heart jumped up to the ceiling but I put them into my pocket until I could kiss them all four before reading them. My own pet there never were such darling notes written before. They made me so happy and I laughed over them and kissed them and prayed for Annie when I went to bed ... And I thought about her in the long black dress with that pretty frill for her shoulders ... Now ... your ugly coward boy that nobody likes but Annie and that nobody ever did like but Annie, is far away ... but he is counting the hours till he will be back to number 15 [Gottingen Street, the Affleck house] ... I hope dear pet

they did not make a fuss at home about my writing ... I wish I could give you a kiss
now and get a box on my ears and then a hug and a kiss and be called your darling.

Thompson found in Annie the first woman who really cared for him.
That she was beautiful and spirited was perhaps beside that more
fundamental consideration. Thompson threw himself into his relationship with Annie with an assiduity and a determination remarkable even
for a lover.

There was also that revealing phrase in shorthand, 'your ugly coward
boy that nobody likes but Annie.' It suggests a shy, lonely young man, who
had grown up close to his father and now, two years after his father's
death, was already distant from his mother. Perhaps Annie was beginning
to take on the mistress-mother role, one that was to suggest itself more
strongly later. The word 'coward' has to be interpreted carefully.
Thompson always appeared well mettled, capable of defending himself.
But it is possible to suggest the 'shrewd demure little fellow' that his father
observed at the age of eight had by the age of twenty-four developed
armour strong enough to protect, even hide, a real self more tender and
vulnerable than appearances would suggest. This interpretation puts a
great deal of weight upon one word, especially when that word is
represented only by the shorthand $\curlyvee$, that is, cwrd. But some of
Annie's letters suggest strongly that this is right, that it is important to
remember the 'slight and rather delicate youth, with a shy and timid
manner ... utterly devoid of anything like conceit or self assertion,' as
Hopkins put it, behind the man.[24]

Thompson met difficulties in his own home as well as in Annie's. The
steadily developing intimacy between them made both families unhappy;
probably Thompson's family was the more unhappy of the two, since
Thompson was the sole support of his mother and sister. By 1870,
however, their affair had gone on for three years, years in which it was
increasingly obvious that there was no prospect of their being separated
from each other. Sometime in the late spring of 1870, perhaps when
Annie's sea captain father was home, Annie's family consented to their
marriage.

Archbishop Connolly, who could have arranged all the dispensations,
was in Rome at the Vatican Council. An episcopal dispensation was
indisputably necessary, since Thompson was still a Methodist. Canon
Patrick Power of St Mary's Cathedral gave Annie's mother letters to the
Bishop of Portland, Maine, asking him to authorize the ceremony, letters
that Annie Affleck and her mother brought with them to Portland at the

end of June 1870, by steamer from Halifax. Bishop David William Bacon authorized the marriage, with the power of *ecclesia aeterna* sweeping away obstacles.[25] In the parlour of the bishop's palace on Congress Street, Portland, on Tuesday, 5 July 1870, Annie Affleck and John Sparrow David Thompson were married by Father R.J. deRose.

Nothing else about the wedding is known. They stopped in Saint John on the way home,[26] then probably travelled by boat to Windsor, and thence to Halifax by train. The newlyweds moved in with Thompson's mother and his sister Elizabeth in the old family home at 95 Gottingen Street. The first Dominion census in 1871 recorded the four of them there, Thompson and his three women; Annie gave her age as twenty-three (she was twenty-five); Thompson's mother and sister gave their true ages and declared their religion as Methodist. Thompson significantly gave his religion as Protestant.[27]

It was about the last stage of his quest for certainties. For at least three years he had brooded over the decision to become a Roman Catholic. That it was not an easy decision goes without saying. One of his favourite thinking walks was around Point Pleasant; it was (and is) a Halifax custom on fine days in summer or winter. One day early in 1871, on one of these ruminative walks, Thompson asked a friend who was with him, 'If I become a Roman Catholic, is it likely that my Protestant clients will desert me?'[28] The answer is not known. It would probably have made no difference; Thompson's question was rhetorical, prompted by his desire to apprehend realities, not by his unwillingness to take the risk. He was well aware of risks. He said to another friend, 'I have everything to lose from a worldly standpoint by this step I am about to take.'[29] Nevertheless, on 21 April 1871, in St Mary's Cathedral, he was baptized a Roman Catholic with the name of John David Thompson, as he had been baptized in the Methodist church twenty-four years before.[30] One of his new godparents was Archbishop Thomas Connolly.

Thompson's biographer, Castell Hopkins, asserted that Thompson's popularity in Halifax grew after his change of religion, because of the visible demonstration of the courage required to make it.[31] But at the time Thompson felt he was risking the prospect of material comforts for his wife, himself, and his future family. 'In fact,' Thompson said many years later, 'I believed that day of my baptism was the day that closed my chances of professional advancement or any other.'[32] George Johnson, a friend since school-days, remembered how Thompson ruminated about the consequences. 'Never mind,' said Thompson, half to himself, 'I know stenography and can scratch a living ... even though it be a poor one.'

Some of his friends were sure he had made a wrong turn. Jeremiah Northrup, an old friend of Thompson's father and of Howe, and vice-president of the Merchant's Bank, said to George Johnson, 'George, John Thompson has never yet to my knowledge put his foot down without being sure of his ground. But this time he has made a mistake.' But he had not; his clients respected him and stuck by him. 'You don't know,' Thompson said to Johnson, 'how much I love my old Methodist friends. Do you know that not one of them left me? I did not lose a single client of them that I had.'[33]

Thompson was not wealthy, but one ought not to exaggerate his poverty. If he started life with heavy burdens to carry, he was carrying them. He was never so poor that he could not go to the theatre when something good was in town. He and Martin Griffin were both attracted to the theatre, and they were fond of the great English actor, Charles James Mathews, who came to Halifax on his third and last North American tour.[34] The old Theatre Royal, at the corner of Spring Garden Road and Queen Street, saw much of Thompson and Griffin in the years prior to Thompson's marriage.

Martin Griffin was a close friend who shared Thompson's confidences and difficulties. Griffin had come to Halifax from Newfoundland with his family when he was seven. He was a Roman Catholic, educated at St Mary's College, and called to the bar in Halifax in 1868. Griffin found it hard to make a living, and having some literary flair, he became editor of a Halifax paper that was Roman Catholic in sympathy, the Halifax *Evening Express*. At the end of 1874 the *Express* was allowed to fold and in January 1875 the Halifax *Morning Herald* was formed, with Thompson on the board of directors and Griffin as its editor.[35]

Griffin was really responsible for the astonishing success of the *Herald*. He had a wicked pen and a temper as short as he was. He loved combat almost for its own sake, for its adrenalin, its sense of victories won, however evanescent the victories were. As one of the rival papers said, Griffin always had on his war paint, he was always 'brandishing his tomahawk, and feeling for his scalping knife.'[36]

Thompson's law practice developed steadily, if slowly. As long as his father was alive he was able to contribute to the household and still have a little money left over. In September 1867, just before his father's last illness, he had bought a small property at the corner of Argyle and Buckingham streets at an estate sale. Thompson paid £1,080 for it, and took a mortgage of £850. The assumption is either that he had £230 available for the purpose or had succeeded in borrowing all or part that amount.[37] Undoubtedly his father's death the next month severely inhibited further savings. His equity after nearly five years, in 1872, was still only $2,300 (£575).

On 1 April 1869 Thompson was taken on as a partner by a Halifax lawyer named Joseph Coombes. Coombes was made attorney in 1863 and admitted to the bar in May 1864. He had already some skill in court, succeeding in one famous breach-of-promise case before Justice Des-Barres. In these sorts of cases, and in many others, Thompson was behind the scenes in the back office of the little firm at 12 Bedford Row. By 1871 Thompson was beginning to appear in court, and in April of that year an equal division of the profits was arranged, supplanting the two-third/one-third arrangement of 1869.[38]

A partnership is like a marriage: each partner is jointly and severally responsible for the debts of the other. In Thompson's partnership with Coombes, however, it was agreed that the clients that they each had had prior to their partnership would continue to be their independent concerns. It was just as well. Coombes and Thompson were not suited to each other; an old family friend of Thompson's, John Bell, described Coombes as 'a blusterly low bred attorney without character and means, but abounding in impudence.'[39] Whatever the cause, the Thompson–Coombes partnership was dissolved in August 1873. Sometime after that Coombes, guilty of some irregularities in the administration of a client's affairs, was forced to quit Halifax, ending eventually in Guysborough. Thompson carried on his law practice alone until 1878.

Thompson had other strings to his bow. In 1868 J.G. Bourinot had gone to Ottawa as reporter to the House of Commons, and Thompson succeeded him as reporter to the Nova Scotia Assembly. He was paid on contract, at a price based on the government's (and his) assumption that the post-confederation sessions of the legislature would be much shorter. In 1868 it was the other way round, the heaviest session in several years. It was not a very remunerative first contract![40] The reporting of debates in Thompson's hands was deftly done, straightforward and compact, without the rotund style Bourinot had affected. Martin Griffin recalled how he and Thompson would sit up at night working on the proofs of those interminable debates. Thompson hated to have to be down at the law office at ten after a midnight working session like that. He was never to be an enthusiast for early rising.[41]

On one occasion an important member of the Assembly had been too indulgent drinking wine at dinner, and his speech afterward in the Assembly was voluble but nearly incomprehensible. What appeared in the debates was a lucid column, neatly directed at the question before the House. The MLA went to Thompson and told him, 'I never had a more accurate and satisfactory report of any speech.'[42]

Before going over to the House, Thompson usually went to Wilson's, a little restaurant on Hollis Street around the corner from his office in Bedford Row, and lunched on mutton pie and a cup of tea. His meal later became a package of coconut caramels, his favourite. He was eating unwisely. One illustration of this occurred a few years later, during what was known in Halifax legal lore as 'the run on the docket.' Mr Justice J.W. Ritchie was presiding at the Supreme Court on Spring Garden Road. The case being argued at 12:45 looked as if it would continue into the afternoon; lawyers with cases pending betook themselves to lunch. But the case ended suddenly, so Justice Ritchie called for the next case. No lawyer. Another case was called. No lawyer. Thirty-two more cases were called, one by one. By this time the news had got to the lawyers' offices on Hollis Street, and Thompson came steaming up the hill past St Mary's to the courthouse. There he met his law clerk, Benjamin Russell. 'I informed him,' said Russell, 'that he was too late and saved him from the danger of collapse, which might more easily have taken place in his case then in some others.'[43] Thompson was even then eating too well, as the 1879 portrait of him shows.

Thompson had taken the twenty-year-old Benjamin Russell into his office in 1869 to help him with the Assembly debates. His father was Nathaniel Russell, a Dartmouth fish merchant and lobster canner. The elder Russell was also a justice of the peace in Dartmouth and was frequently called to preside over the infinite variety of small court cases that were the JP's lot. One morning as Russell was dressing for court, when he knew a request for a filiation order was coming up, his daughter said to him, 'Father, whom are you getting all dressed up today for?' 'Oh, my dear,' said Nathaniel Russell, 'nothing but whores and bastards.'[44] Perhaps as a result of these salty asides from his father, young Benjamin grew up with a taste for law, and used his work as reporter to subsidize study for the bar. He was admitted in 1872, but continued as reporter to the Assembly after Thompson gave it up in 1873, until 1883. He then became a professor of law at the new Dalhousie Law School. All his life Russell was to remember Thompson, a friendship, he said, 'unbroken by a single misunderstanding.' They worked together side by side on the debates for four years, though both men were out of harmony with the government that they so faithfully served. 'It was never supposed,' wrote Russell to Thompson in 1880, 'that we were not faithful and impartial reporters, or that the character of the reports would have been improved by ... filling the place with a less skillful but more sympathetic officer.'[45]

By 1872, with reporting bringing in income and his law practice with Coombes growing, Thompson was able to consider buying a house. The Gottingen Street house was crowded, even though there were no children. In 1871 Annie had given birth to a baby girl, after a difficult first pregnancy; Annie had not been well, the baby was unusually large, and through the whole afternoon of 3 September 1871 her situation was critical. Finally the baby was born but could not survive the trauma and died in half an hour. That Annie was alive and safe was a vast relief to Thompson even with the loss of his first child.[46] In May 1872, when Annie was three months pregnant with her second baby, Thompson bought the house called Willow Park. The house was the central section of what had once been a much larger property that had originally belonged to John Young, 'Agricola' as he was called, after the letters he published in 1822 urging Nova Scotians to make their farming more scientific. After Young's death the property had passed to Colonel B.H. Hornsby, a Civil War veteran from the South, who cut the estate into lots and began to sell them. Thompson bought the original Young house and its immediate grounds at the southwest corner of Windsor and Almon for $12,000, a very ambitious purchase. His down payment consisted of the property he had bought downtown in 1867; for the balance of $9,400, Colonel Hornsby gave Annie Thompson and J.S.D. Thompson jointly a mortgage at 6 per cent.[47]

Thompson and Annie called their home Willow Park, as the district itself came to be called, and it was to remain theirs for all their married life. It was a commodious frame house, two stories, with big chimneys at each end. It had a fine bold front with a large main-floor veranda, reached from the ground by a flight of a dozen stairs. The roof leaked from time to time and inconveniently into the parlour; they never succeeded in quite remedying that. On cold nights in winter the nails of the house would contract with a snap that would sometimes keep Annie awake. It did not have indoor plumbing; the w.c. seems to have been in an attached building, probably heated. The house was on a big lot, over three hundred feet square, about two acres; it had a barn, a front field, and a back field; and every July the hay was cut. (The hay concession they rented out.) They kept hens. They had mice from time to time, Annie complaining once that she was quite lonesome without the patter of their feet after the Thompsons had acquired a big black cat.[48] They had strawberry beds, some large trees – willows, perhaps – and enough frogs in the field to make choruses on summer evenings. Across Windsor Street was Hornsby's Nursery, with a large, glass hot-house that did not improve the view; but to the west and north there were plenty of fields still farmed. It was about a mile and a half to Thompson's modest law office downtown, and about half that distance to the old house on Gottingen Street where Thompson's mother still lived.

Thompson's second child was safely born at Willow Park on 20 October 1872, and was christened a few days later by Archbishop Connolly with the archbishop's own name, John Thomas Connolly Thompson. The god-parents were Annie's brother and sister, James and Johanna Affleck, the latter now Sister Mary Helena with the Sisters of Charity at Mount St Vincent.[49] None of Thompson's children were to bear names of his side of the family.

By this time Thompson's friends had been urging him to stand for alderman. At the civic election of October 1871, the year before the birth of his son, Thompson was elected by the Catholic and Protestant ratepayers of Ward 5 to the city council of Halifax. He was not quite twenty-six years old.

4

The Halifax of Alderman Thompson

Disraeli used to say that every young man with political ambitions ought to start by getting his feet wet in local politics. Civic issues were sharp, the problems immediate, the taxes real, and the benefits and defects of city government laid out visibly. City politics could be savage; issues were close to home, narrow, and direct, and partisans often exigeant and obstreperous. It threw into relief a man's quality, honest or mendacious, strong or weak, capable or incapable.

On 13 September 1871 some seventy-eight electors in Ward 5 asked Thompson to stand for election, an invitation he accepted three days later. In the civic election of 1871, held on Monday, 2 October, Thompson won, 299 votes to 237, the second-largest majority of the six new aldermen.[1] Sworn into office on the following day, he would remain alderman of Ward 5 for six years, being re-elected by acclamation in 1874.

The main characteristics of Halifax's civic structure were laid down in 1841, with a consolidation of its charter in 1864. Halifax was governed by a mayor and eighteen aldermen for its six wards. Six aldermen were elected for each year. The mayor was elected separately for a one-year term; re-election was common.

Halifax's wards had remained unchanged since 1841. Inevitably, by 1871 the population was distributed very unevenly; Thompson's Ward 5 was the largest, containing one-third of the city's population. It was a slice of Halifax from sea to sea, from the harbour on the east to the Arm on the west, enclosed by Quinpool Road and Cogswell Street on the south, and Chebucto Road and North Street on the north. It was expanding rapidly in the early 1870s and there was considerable speculation in real estate. In order to encourage sales in his lots Colonel Hornsby in 1873 established a special omnibus to take residents the mile and a half into the city. It took thirty minutes to go from Willow Park to the downtown post office, the fare eight cents. Thompson took it frequently. The bus was drawn by two strong horses; coming out from town, a third horse was added to help haul the heavy yellow machine up the hill to Gottingen Street. The bus lasted until 1895 when it was absorbed into the city's new electric tramway system.[2]

Halifax had still much of its old character. The city streets had been lit by gas since 1849; the gas company had the quaint but inconvenient habit of turning off the street lights on nights of the full moon. This arrangement would last until electricity came in 1886.[3] Most Halifax streets were still unpaved; in spring and summer, dust could blow in clouds for two or three days at a time. A shower of rain would bring the dust to a temporary end. Buildings that had not been seen for several days suddenly became visible. There were watercarts whose job it was to slake the streets; the complaints always were that they never mastered the ubiquitous dust.

Halifax's sewers emptied into its sea inlets, the harbour and the North-West Arm. (They still do.) The original sewers had been designed to carry off water. The old pipes were crude stone or earthenware ones, subject to breakage since they were buried in the ironstone rock of the Halifax peninsula. The city hall maps were inaccurate. In 1873 E.H. Keating, Halifax's first city engineer, came out with a hard-hitting report: 'Many [sewers] are not two feet below the surface. They are to be found everywhere and anywhere but where they ought to be, ... When wanted no one knows where they are, unless occasionally some old inhabitant.'[4]

New sewers were urgent as water closets began to replace the privy. By the 1870s most of the newer houses were installing them and they were slowly appearing in old ones. There was a good deal of makeshift in these arrangements; even in the new suburb of Willow Park, a surface drain carried sewage down to the harbour. Halifax's sewers had a reputation as far as Saint John, New Brunswick, where a writer complained of the smells exhaled by the gratings in Halifax streets.[5]

Locals were casual about what they put out in the streets. Shopkeepers cleaned out Saturday night, leaving the result to be collected from the street; the noses of the church-goers on Sunday morning would be 'regaled with bouquet de squash pourri, together with triple extract of rotten cheese.' No doubt some of the forty-six hundred unregistered dogs loose in the city would solve the problem before the city did.[6]

There were the beggars, old drunks, and young children, the last the hardest to ignore. Was it good or bad to give money to half-naked children that solicited it? On 7 March 1877 three children, the youngest a girl of four, were brought before the stipendiary magistrate charged with begging. They were sent home and the parents sought out. The father was a workman with fairly constant work; it was the mother who forced the children to beg, in order to buy gin.[7]

Gin was a versatile substance. Thompson was amused at the story reported in Griffin's *Evening Express*. A horse and cart were on Market Wharf waiting to load potatoes from a schooner. Somehow the horse fell off the wharf, between the schooner and the piling. A boat had to be brought around to lead the frightened horse. This took some time; then it was discovered that there was no place for the poor beast to land and it had to be swum to the schooner slip at Queen's Wharf, some two hundred yards away. It was somehow got ashore. 'The horse was exhausted,' said the *Evening Express*, 'but was liberally supplied with gin and it revived.'[8]

Wharves were treacherous but other parts of town were scarcely less so. There were numerous complaints at city council about the condition of the Grand Parade. Built and levelled in the Duke of Kent's time in Halifax, between 1794 and 1800, the Grand Parade belied its name, being the receptable of all manner of city rubbish, material and human. The ownership of the Parade was disputed between Dalhousie College, which occupied its north end, and the city. Neither would spend money fixing it up; there it was, with crumbling, dangerous walls, a broken-down wooden railing, a standing reproach to the city and a menace to its citizens.

The city council that governed Halifax in Thompson's time had earned the sobriquet of the 'Bear Garden.' Personal quarrels, with the inevitable cliques and rancour, sometimes produced close votes, or ties that the mayor had to break.[9] There were regular meetings of council every fortnight, and numerous special ones. During the first six months of Thompson's incumbency as alderman, there was a council meeting a week. Calls to meetings did not always produce a quorum, for aldermen had their own professional work to do and they received no remuneration. The *Halifax Express* urged that aldermen be paid; many Halifax aldermen were fully equal to members of the Legislative Assembly, and therefore entitled to be paid.[10] It had no effect.

The duties of alderman did not merely comprehend attendance at city council. Thompson had to serve on several committees, struck each year: the Laws and Privileges Committee, the City Prison Committee, and several ad hoc committees thrown in. The city council together with the city medical officer functioned as the civic Board of Health. In May 1873, during a smallpox epidemic, it decided to vaccinate some four thousand

Haligonians at city expense.[11] There were also boards to which aldermen were appointed, the most important of which was the Halifax Board of School Commissioners. On top of everything else, an alderman, while in office, was a justice of the peace.

Thompson's first move was characteristic of him: legal housekeeping. He liked to clean up, codify, render clarity out of confusion. Here his object was the confusion of laws surrounding the city's charter. The chairman of the Laws and Privileges Committee, Lawrence Power, proposed in November 1871 that the laws and by-laws of the city be revised. By mid-December he and Thompson had a draft ready. It ran into difficulties. A motion to abandon the whole scheme was narrowly defeated in March 1872, and Thompson, recognizing the inevitable, proposed instead that they confine themselves to a few simple amendments. Even so, that passed only with the casting vote of the mayor. One result was the creation of the Board of Works, on which was to fall the burden of maintaining the streets.[12]

Thompson returned to the issue in the autumn of 1872. He proposed that Ward 5 be split into two, in view of the gross under-representation of its people on city council. This move was struck down by a vote of ten to seven. The Committee on Laws and Privileges was again given the job of revising the charter.[13] Two things emerged. The new consolidation of the city's charter was printed in 1873, under the editorship of Power and Thompson. Secondly, the province authorized the appointment of a new city auditor. Thompson and Power both felt that it was essential to make a beginning on straightening out the city's tangled accounts. In December 1874 the auditor was appointed by the usual method – open vote in council.

Approval of city officials was always by open vote; it had been laid down that way in the charter. There were seven candidates for city auditor, two aldermen among them: William Taylor, chairman of the Board of Works, who received no votes at all from his colleagues; and Alderman C.C. Vaux, who got special permission from council to vote for himself! The result was a tie between Vaux (who had, indeed, voted for himself), and John Bell. The mayor gave the casting vote for Bell, who was sworn into office on 2 January 1875. He was then fifty-eight years old; he was to remain in office for another twenty-seven years, dying in it in 1901.[14]

The tangle in the city's accounts was aggravated by some problems peculiar to Halifax. A substantial proportion of Halifax property was owned by government – the imperial government, the Dominion government, the Nova Scotian government – none of whom paid taxes or any funds in lieu of taxes. Thus the full burden of supporting the city fell upon its private citizens. When Thompson first took his seat on council Halifax's debt was over one million dollars. As a result of the development of the water system, the sewer system, and the erection of a new city hall, it would reach two million by 1891.[15]

Halifax's estimated expenses for the year 1 May 1872 to 30 April 1873 were $110,000. City receipts included an anticipated $12,000 from liquor and auction licences, and $3,500 from police court fines. Citizens were assessed for the balance. Added to that were assessments for institutions and payments authorized by provincial law, the most important of which was $50,000 to the Board of School Commissioners, as well as an additional $10,000 for the Commissioners for Poor; these items in effect doubled the original assessment.[16]

It was anything but easy to keep expenditure within revenue. The main cause was non-payment of taxes.[17] The rule was that occupiers of property were liable for its taxes. This meant that tenants had to pay the taxes on houses they rented. It also meant that the city could not sell such property for non-payment. By 1872 unpaid taxes reached $37,000, nearly 40 per cent of the current budget. They would be $200,000 a decade later, when finally the city was given power to force owners to pay. Thus in the 1870s the city was pinched to make ends meet. John Bell confided to his diary:

As usual the Press and citizens are down upon the Aldermen for waste and extravagance. I confess I do not see much of either. The expenses are narrowly watched and no alderman or official has any opportunity for misappropriation. The citizens are very inconsiderate. They are constantly urging upon the City Council the necessity for this that and the other improvement – and are most impatient if not gratified in their wishes, but they seem to forget that improvements cost money, and that the money must come from their own pockets.[18]

Thompson's city council lived a narrow existence, pressed by a public wanting more water mains, more sewers, better streets, better law and order, and unwilling to pay enough for them. The city hall reflected that too; council met in an 1810 brick court house at the bottom of George Street. The chamber had been the old ballroom, and rain now leaked in upon the aldermen in their deliberations; sewage seeped into the basement, where the police cells were. There was talk of change, of making repairs, and some new brick cells were added in 1870. But the overwhelming need was for a new city hall.[19]

Thompson was in the middle of the struggle for it. In March 1874 council agreed that the best place for the new city hall was at the south end of the Grand Parade. Thompson proposed that $100,000 be established for it and this package – for it was a compromise of several elements – passed council. It then went to the Nova Scotia legislature for enactment into law.[20]

The legislature usually got seven or eight Halifax bills every year. Although it might appear that the province kept the Corporation of Halifax in leading strings, the truth was the other way around. Members of both houses from outside Halifax rubber-stamped Halifax legislation, relying on the integrity of the Halifax members. But neither House relished doing it, and the bill for the new city hall, after passing the Assembly, ran into opposition in the Legislative Council. The Council was stirred up by the congregation of St Paul's Anglican Church, a church that faced the south end of the Grand Parade, who did not want to find themselves staring at the walls of a new city hall just outside their doors. Nor was Dalhousie College at the north end of the Parade pleased with the prospect. The upshot was that the Grand Parade site was blocked by a neat squeeze play. Thompson then proposed, and had unanimously accepted, a new site one-third of a mile farther north and coincidentally in his own ward. This site proved unpopular, and despite the agreement of city council, the proposal failed.[21]

Thompson had wanted the Grand Parade site. But though he lost this battle, in a way it could be said that he won the war. For after a decade-long struggle, the city finally purchased Dalhousie College in 1886. The building was razed and the stones used for the foundation of the new city hall that opened in 1890. It was on the Grand Parade after all.

Thompson and city council had other more immediate issues on their agenda. One of the most inconvenient was the temperance movement. In Nova Scotia the temperance movement was strong in Protestant counties, weak in Catholic ones and in Halifax. In 1872 a large petition asked that city council reduce the number of liquor licences it authorized yearly. Thompson seconded council's reply: that however desirable a reduction in liquor licences might be, excessive drinking could not be corrected by that means. He never believed that the evils of drunkenness could be solved by legislating liquor out of existence. The issue surfaced in 1873 in the Nova Scotia Assembly in a more insidious form. A bill would have made it obligatory to refuse a liquor licence when one-third of the ratepayers of the district petitioned against it. Thompson opposed this on the principle that it had never been before the Halifax City Council. A compromise in 1874 was suggested by Thompson, and passed, whereby all liquor licences be recommended by a two-thirds majority of the city's Liquor Licence Committee, and that an approving petition be forthcoming from a majority of the ratepayers of the district concerned. So the Halifax drinkers survived. The bar hours were generous, from 7 a.m. to 9 p.m. every day except Sunday. The irony was that after all the effort and struggle the number of licences issued annually by Halifax was the same as before.[22]

Liquor had a good deal to do with the population of Halifax's city prison. Thompson's first report as chairman of the City Prisons Committee, presented in March 1874, showed that half of the offences of the 506 persons admitted to prison during 1872–3 were for drunkenness, men and women alike. (Women amounted to over one-quarter of the prisoners.)[23] Though tolerant, Thompson found it easy to resist being charitable to prisoners who, if given the benefit of it, would only relapse. There was pressure in late 1875 from Mayor Richey to release a woman prisoner, Letitia O'Connell, on the ground that she had reformed. Thompson opposed her release:

I feel justified by my observation in saying that a strict and rigorous execution of the sentences imposed on such persons as this woman is essential not only for the well being of the City but for the discipline of the Prison. The class of unfortunate persons to which she belongs is numerous and very hard to deal with – the conduct of several of them while frequenting the Park and Judge Ritchie's woods which adjoin the Park was a great public nuisance last summer and the woman O'Connell is almost the first that the police had been able to bring to justice.

Nothing is more common in my experience of the Prison than for such a woman to endeavor by the most artful pretences to get the term of their imprisonment shortened. They invariably profess an intention to reform – frequently feign illness in order that they may be sent to the Hospital from which they can effect their escape.[24]

Thompson had other duties as chairman of the Prisons Committee. At Christmas he would entertain the governor, the guards, and perhaps even some of the inmates at Rockhead Prison. A letter in the *Halifax Evening Reporter* in March 1876 accused him of lavishing seventy dollars of the city's money in thus treating prison officials. Thompson had an intense pride and did not answer such unworthy charges. All he would say in council was that he spent seven dollars of the city's money. The rest was his own.

Point Pleasant Park, where Letitia O'Connell had too well demonstrated her charms, was 186 acres of woods at the tip of the Halifax peninsula, surrounded by the sea on three sides. The acquisition of this splendid site by Halifax was partly owing to Lord Dufferin who, as governor general of Canada from 1872 to 1878, was also instrumental in saving the walls of Quebec. Negotiations started in 1866 between Lord Dufferin, then parliamentary under-secretary of state for war, and Sir Charles Hastings Doyle, general officer commanding the British troops in North America. It was offered to the city in 1866 on a 999-year lease. Nova Scotia passed an act in 1866 allowing Halifax to accept it, but nothing was done. It might have been left that way had not Hastings Doyle been lieutenant-governor from 1867 to 1873. Newspapers pressed the matter from time to time, but it was only in March of 1873 that the Halifax City Council, under pressure from Thompson and other aldermen, drew up appropriate draft legislation.

Chapter 12 of the Statutes of Nova Scotia of 1873 established a board of park directors, composed of the mayor, six aldermen and four citizens. Thompson was named as one of the directors of the park, and three days later, when the new directors met for the first time, they appointed Sir William Young as chairman and Thompson as secretary. The city, dilatory to the last, would not pay out money; Sir William Young out of his own pocket paid $3,000 to get work started, and got the money back from the city only in February 1874 when some six miles of new roads had been made and the park fairly launched.[25] It was a place Thompson had known as a child and young man; many of his decisions were made in walks there. In many ways, even more than the Citadel, Point Pleasant was the British government's happiest legacy in Halifax. Thompson did much to help establish it.

The Public Gardens in the centre of town were also brought under public control by the energetic and purposive city council of the 1870s. The Nova Scotia Horticultural Society in the 1830s had acquired a portion of the South Common that fronted Spring Garden Road on a 999-year lease. They had made it into a handsome garden, open to the public for paid admission. By 1874 the society was in debt. They could not sell their land for building lots (a great temptation) since the land was held on conditions. The going price was $15,000 and the legislation enabling city council to buy it went through in 1875. By 1880, with the city spending $2,000 a year on their development, the Public Gardens, as they were now called, had become the pride of Halifax.[26]

There was another issue that Thompson faced, more difficult than liquor licences, parks, or a new city hall: Catholic and Protestant schools in Halifax. Since 1865 they had lived in amicable, uncomplicated promiscuity, side by side. To some that comfortable method was grotesquely out of place in the 1870s; the issue was to dominate Thompson's later years on city council. Schools – ordinary, everyday schools: were they to be Protestant, Catholic, or neither?

In Nova Scotia Roman Catholics made up only 25 per cent of the population and they were spread unevenly across the province by accidents of settlement. In Halifax they had prospered; they had absorbed the immigrant waves of the 1840s and by the 1870s, at about 40 per cent of the Halifax population, were an accepted part of its life. The second mayor of Halifax, in 1842, Edward Kenny, was a Roman Catholic; so was Stephen Tobin, 1867–70, and James Duggan, 1872–3. The later custom of alternating mayors between Protestant and Catholic was developing by the end of the century. In Halifax the two religions had, despite some setbacks, developed traditions of living together.

In Nova Scotia free public education had been brought into existence in 1864 by the determination of the provincial secretary and premier, Charles Tupper. The legislation was embodied in two acts in 1864 and 1865 (which really have to be read together), consolidated in 1873.

There were peculiarities in the Nova Scotian school system, partly owing to Tupper's wish to have it accommodate the Roman Catholics. Foremost among these peculiarities was the proposed Council of Public Instruction which, according to the 1864–5 act, was to be none other than the provincial cabinet. To no one else would be entrusted the delicate, essentially political task of balancing Catholic and Protestant. The cabinet also appointed all of the seven Boards of School Commissioners for the province. Thus proper representation of both religions would be ensured through appointment by cabinet, in ways that election of such commissioners could not. Archbishop Connolly accepted it, and his sensible attitude did much to ease the possibility of a major conflict between the Catholics and the government, which Tupper had good reason to avoid.[27]

Tupper's legislation required the great proportion of the school costs to be borne by local taxes. In Halifax the legislative grant amounted to only 12 per cent of the school budget. It was this insistence on major local taxation for school support that roused the ire of Nova Scotians. Nevertheless, the Nova Scotian educational system had arrived and it stayed. Each of the Boards of School Commissioners, except Halifax city, arranged their own school districts. Halifax was a special case; its Board of School Commissioners did the work both of commissioners nd of trustees.

It had no officials elected by the public at large. Its twelve-member board had six members appointed by cabinet and six members appointed by Halifax city council, one for each of Halifax's six wards.

The acts of 1864 and 1865 turned over the operation of Halifax primary schools to the Board of School Commissioners. In Halifax there were three free Catholic schools already in operation, and the acceptance of Roman Catholic views was essential to the school system's success. These Catholic schools were merged into the new system without being deprived of their essential character. What the board effectively asserted was a right of control over teachers. Through the good will of the archbishop the board acquired the Catholic schools given to it virtually rent free. Only a few Protestant schools were so generous.

The Halifax school system thus grew up in an atmosphere of accommodation between Roman Catholics and Protestants. There was no separate school system in the province; instead there were local accommodations to local realities. The Halifax arrangements typified that spirit. There would be a common curriculum; the control of the qualifications of teachers lay with the Board of School Commissioners, as did appointments and firings. It was understood that there would be Catholic teachers for Catholic schools. The hours were the same; the Roman Catholic children stayed after 3:30 p.m., the normal ending of the school day, for religious instruction, while the Protestant children went happily out to play. Taxes were paid by all ratepayers alike.

Thompson was elected by city council to the Board of School Commissioners on 1 November 1873 and would be re-elected annually for five years. When he joined the board in 1873 there were eighteen schools under its jurisdiction and some ninety teachers. Four of the schools, and thirty of the teachers, were Roman Catholic. Thompson found a vast range of minor problems to deal with: premises (arrangements for removing ashes from the furnaces and 'night soil' from the outhouses); replacement of teachers who were ill, or who wanted leave of absence; or dismissals. J.A. Smith of Albro Street School, a teacher for thirty years and the highest paid in the school next to the principal ($56.66 per month), was found drunk on the streets on Good Friday, 1874. There was a long hearing. Smith made excuses: the smell on his breath was not liquor but camphorated spirits he was taking as medicine; he was dizzy not drunk. But the witnesses were specific and Smith was fired. In defence of the board it has to be said that Nova Scotia school law was insistent on this point.[28]

The accommodations with Archbishop Connolly were shown in the way

Dutch Village School was admitted to the system in 1874. The school was run by the Sisters of Charity, an American order founded in 1813 and brought to Halifax from New York by Archbishop Walsh in 1849.[29] The archbishop offered the school to the board at a nominal rent, one dollar a year for seven years, on condition that the teachers in Dutch Village School remain there until the board decided otherwise.

Archbishop Connolly and John Thompson had been close personally for some years. It was a curious friendship; Thompson, his manner contained, his emotions controlled; the archbishop a big, open, friendly Irishman with fluency and vigour. Connolly had a rich vocabulary mixed with a good deal of blarney, and he was pleasantly seasoned with a taste for the good things of life. He had capacity to discern greatness in others and to reach out for it. Like some bishops, he enjoyed a good table and good company, and not least the acquaintance and the conversation of the rich, influential, and powerful. He could be stern with his flock, but he had an instinctive generosity of spirit that went a long way to explain his popularity in Halifax. He enjoyed Protestants at his table as much as, perhaps more than, Catholics, in his unpretending, story-and-half, frame 'palace' at the corner of Spring Garden Road and Barrington Street.

Connolly never made a secret of his political predilections. In the federal election of 1872 he had openly supported Tupper and Sir John A. Macdonald and was bitterly attacked by the Liberal *Morning Chronicle* because he did. He replied openly in the *Halifax Evening Reporter*:

In appealling to the press, rather than to the Pulpit as I always did, no undue advantage was taken of any man, Catholic or Protestant. My letters were even a peaceful and honorable challenge to all my fellow citizens ... in becoming an Archbishop he [Connolly] never ceased to be a man, and to have all a man's rights, except those he voluntarily renounced in his consecration ... As Catholics they [the members of my diocese] are bound to follow my teachings in faith and morals; as citizens ... the world knows they are free as the air they breathe. I have never asked or even wished my Priests or my people to give up their manhood.[30]

With this kind of refreshing openness, it is not surprising that the Catholic archbishop was popular with Catholics and Protestants alike.

Upon this idyllic scene came outside issues. A raging controversy had been going on in New Brunswick ever since the New Brunswick School Act of 1871 abolished such easy accommodations, and it was getting worse. (Two men were killed in the Caraquet riots in January 1875.) The ideas, especially the Protestant ones, engendered by this controversy could not be kept on the north side of Missiguash River – the isthmus boundary between New Brunswick and Nova Scotia.

There was a riot in Antigonish County in 1873. Charles Chiniquy was a former Catholic priest turned Presbyterian minister, and his favourite subject was the wickedness of the Roman Catholic church. Chiniquy specialized in riots. In July 1873, at the invitation of local Presbyterians, he was billed to speak in Antigonish on Acadian missions. He did not get to that part of his speech, for he began with his customary denunciation of the Roman Catholics. With a population 85 per cent Catholic, Antigonish was dangerous country for so inflammatory a speaker. Before Chiniquy was finished the church was surrounded by some two to three hundred furious Scotch Catholics, and the Protestants treated themselves to a general *sauve qui peut*. The Pictou Presbyterian Synod pressed for a government inquiry. This was held under a Halifax county court judge, J.W. Johnston, a Baptist. Johnston's judiciousness overcame his Protestantism, and the Catholic magistrates of Antigonish were absolved from not having suppressed the riot.[31]

By 1874 the movement had developed other ramifications. Some Protestants who had heretofore paid little attention to the educational condition of Halifax began to make noises about the inefficiency of the school system. Their list was long but their charges were basically four: extravagent expenditures; lack of a high school; glaring inefficiency in the schools; and improper partiality toward the Roman Catholics.[32] They did not go to the Board of School Commissioners with these charges, something that Protestant members of the board were not slow to point out; instead they called a public meeting at Temperance Hall, Friday evening, 20 February 1874. It was well attended, with Mayor John Sinclair, a Protestant, in the chair. But it was the high school question, not Protestantism, that was the main focus of citizen interest. James Thomson, the chairman of the School Board, said that the only reason why there was no high school was because the citizens of Halifax were opposed. As for a proposal to *elect* the Board of School Commissioners, he could not accept that. Elections would create ill-feeling instead of the harmony at present. The meeting was insistent. A motion was put forward by Rev. John Lathern of the Wesleyan Methodists and Rev. G.M. Grant of the Presbyterians that Halifax citizens should elect their own school commissioners, that a high school should be founded, and that, to push for both, the Halifax School Association should be established. The motion was accepted.[33]

Behind the move for the election of school commissioners unquestionably lay some anti-Roman Catholic feeling, sometimes open, sometimes masquerading as non-denominational fairness. One Dartmouth man protested his non-denominational feelings so vehemently that he reminded one newspaper of the logic of the Chinaman who remarked to the American, 'What for Amelican man kick Chinaman? Amelican man and Chinaman all one same brother, *hate nigger, hate injun*.'[34] Grant was not anti-Catholic. He said that if the High School Association were anti-Catholic in character, he would have no part of it.[35]

The school issue then surfaced in the legislature. A draft act was put forward to force the election of the school commissioners, and it was done without the approval of Halifax City Council. Council objected vigorously. On 9 April 1874 Alderman Thompson moved,

That the Council cannot view with approval a measure which is designed to take away from this body the control which it now exercises over the management of the public schools, and the expenditure of school moneys ... and that his Worship the Mayor be requested to address to the Chairman of the Committee of the House of Assembly on Education, an energetic remonstrance against the Bill now on the table.

Five days later Thompson's resolution passed city council, twelve to three.[36]

The bill to force the issue was at the committee stage over at the Legislative Assembly and some strong medicine was dished out. Lathern, the Wesleyan Methodist, said that Halifax schools were in a deplorable state, so bad that taxpayers were taking their children out of school. This statement was vigorously denied by two Halifax aldermen present, Vaux and Thompson, who challenged the reverend gentleman to prove his assertions. The following day, a Presbyterian divine, Rev. C. Bruce Pitblado, the real *deus ex machina* behind the bill, came on the scene and gave the legislative committee 'a mad gallop through good sense, good temper ... and over the common proprieties of discussion.'[37] Grant at once abandoned support of the Protestants after hearing the savagery of Pitblado; the Protestant cause was being ruined by the excesses of its friends.

In the Assembly the government drew back. In Committee of the Whole, the provincial secretary, W.B. Vail, who came from New Brunswick, spoke feelingly of the problems there:

In New Brunswick they had violence and quarrels and religious strife; and the position in that province was a warning to Nova Scotia ... The Government and the

Council of Public Instruction had endeavoured to make the school law work as popularly and smoothly as possible, and they had succeeded so well that they felt that there was not the slightest reason for the change asked for.[38]

The bill to elect school commissioners was killed by the Assembly on 5 May 1874 by a decisive vote of nineteen to four.[39]

The Halifax School Association, finding interest in alleged weaknesses of the Halifax school system feeble, turned its energies to getting a new high school. For the Protestant cry had been largely answered by facts. The Halifax School Board answered the charge of extravagance; as for partiality to Roman Catholics, the board was decisive. All teachers, Protestant and Catholic, took the same examinations; they were licensed, paid, dismissed, by the same authority; schools were all supervised equally.

The issue was now the high school. There was an amiable meeting between the Halifax School Association and the school board in February 1876, one so successful that Thompson, now vice-chairman of the board, moved a vote of thanks to the association for their efforts in promoting a new high school.[40] The board had money set aside for building the school, and in January 1877 the draft of the 'Act for the establishment of a High School' was agreed to and sent to the legislature for its April session. Twenty boys annually were to be admitted free, after competitive examination; tuition fees were set at forty dollars a year for other boys, provided they met admission requirements. The high school would admit girls in 1885.

An attractive site became available at the corner of Brunswick and Sackville streets. After long discussion a motion to acquire the site was adopted, Thompson supporting it. The board moved quickly to obtain the four properties required, a site about 113 feet by 135 feet, for $7,500.[41] Architects were hired, plans drawn up, and on 17 July 1878 the cornerstone was laid by the Grand Master of the Masons of Nova Scotia, J.W. Laurie. The new high school opened its doors six months later. The building still stands, handsome as ever, brick on a granite foundation, and in 1984 occupied, appropriately, by the very body that had created it, the Board of School Commissioners of Halifax.

One further issue arose in 1876 to test the effectiveness of the Halifax school compromise. What was, really, the power of the archbishop where Catholic teachers were concerned? In the actual appointment of teachers, he had no power; that was the prerogative of the board. The question really concerned his nominating power. A committee was struck of two Protestants and one Catholic – Thompson – and asked to report.

As long as the board retained its right to appoint, its right to fire, its right to judge the qualifications of the teachers it hired, it cannot be said, Thompson argued, 'that this right of nomination [of the Archbishop's] makes these schools "separate" in the ordinary acceptation of the term.' The archbishop's power to nominate was necessary for the Catholics; the quality of Catholic teachers was important since they did have religious instruction to give, and without that the schools ceased to be useful to Catholic ratepayers. Thompson concluded that the archbishop's nominating power was the key to everything that had been achieved in the Halifax system. 'Should the Board insist on abrogating its contract with the Archbishop, I fear that the harmony which has existed in educational matters in past years will be at an end.'[42]

Before the board could take up Thompson's argument, Archbishop Connolly was dead. He had been taken ill on 22 July 1876, and died five days later of 'congestion of the brain,' probably a cerebral haemorrhage. The Halifax school compromise owed much to him. Among those who most mourned his death was Rev. G.M. Grant of St Matthews Presbyterian Church not a hundred yards from the bishop's residence. Grant's words say much:

And many to-day think of the late Dr. Connolly, not as the self-denying priest, or the Archbishop abundant in labors, but as the man who has long deserved well of this city ... He was a wise man – rich in saving, common sense. He was a man of peace – ever seeking to build bridges rather than dig ditches between men of differing creeds. He was a great man, with eye that discerned any flash of greatness in others.[43]

The full argument on the archbishop's nominating power came in mid-August at the Board of School Commissioners. The religious lines were sharply drawn. A majority report abolishing any right of nomination passed, six to three. Had it been left there, the history of Halifax schools might have been different. Alderman Bremner, a Protestant, then proposed a compromise close to Thompson's: the archbishop's nominating power would simply be translated over to the Catholic members of the school board. This carried six to one, Protestants and Catholics alike voting for it, and one Protestant voting against it.

There was some protest locally from the *Halifax Evening Reporter*, a self-constituted protector of Protestants. The board's decision, the *Reporter* said, was an 'atrocious blunder,' it legalized denominational schools. 'What law in Nova Scotia authorizes the Halifax School Board to mark off a number of schools, label them Protestant ...?' But the *Reporter*'s arguments fell on stony soil. One critic replied quite sensibly:

It is bootless to denounce the 'resolution' as tending to sectarianize our schools ... It does not do so; *that* has been done long ago. *Our schools,* ever since the existing law began to come into effect in Halifax, *have been sectarian to a certain extent –* illegally, perhaps, but none the less certainly.[44]

In May 1878 Thompson was made chairman, a position he was to hold until October 1878. His report to the superintendent of education for Nova Scotia, as of 31 October 1878, showed a most satisfactory state of affairs. The issue of Catholic versus Protestant schools had been met and largely settled. There were 101 students already enrolled for the new high school soon to open; the school system as a whole had 5,300 students, an increase of 25 per cent since 1873, over one-sixth of the city's total population, almost exactly divided between girls and boys.[45]

Thompson now gave up his last position in civic affairs. He had only just turned thirty-three years of age, but he had had a tough apprenticeship in civic politics. It was a useful introduction to a larger world. Thompson was sufficiently popular by 1877 that it was averred he could have been elected mayor had he been willing to stand. It would be difficult to point out, said the Halifax *Morning Herald* on 2 November 1878, watching him step onward to a new stage of his career, 'an Alderman who, in so short a time, secured so high a place in public esteem, for ability, for probity, for unfailing courtesy and unflagging attention.' It was these very qualities had already made him a success at the bar.

5

Practising Law

The law is an exacting mistress; she does not take kindly to easy familarities. Even from the best she exacts a long and demanding apprenticeship. Law requires a mind that readily grasps detail. Attention to detail becomes for some an end in itself; some lawyers simply stop there, dedicated to, and dessicated by, an unending landscape of fact. One is reminded of Dickens's *Jarndyce* v. *Jarndyce*: the only man who had succeeded in knowing even part of that vast cause was called Mr Tangle. Or Palmerston's *jeu d'esprit* on the Schleswig-Holstein question: 'There's only three people who know anything about the Schleswig-Holstein question. There's the Danish King and he's dead; there's a German professor and he's gone mad; and there's me, and I've forgotten.'

Great lawyers, however, map these vast landscapes as they go. Thompson was such a one. He had a way of seeing the configurations of legal terrain. Not only that; he had two qualities rarely found together: he was amazingly quick at assimilating facts and he had a powerful persistence for getting at them. He could thus cover a great deal of ground in a short time. He was a formidable lawyer. He distrusted others who were slipshod in their application to the problems before them. Thompson liked to be sure of his ground. He liked to have all the facts of a case go through his own head. He disliked summaries or digests; they had no ring of reality to them. Someone else's gloss simply would not do. But, though he assimilated detail with awesome ease, the bent of his mind was not toward detail but toward the clarity that emerged on the other side, engendered by the ancient inductive process so characteristic of English law, when the particulars had been absorbed and intellectually systematized.

The development of Thompson's practice before the courts and his growing reputation at the bar are well attested by the Supreme Court cases reported in the mid and late 1870s. There were a dozen or so

Halifax lawyers whose names appear with surprising frequency in the Supreme Court reports, Thompson's among them. These reports are about the only source we have for the development of Thompson's practice; Thompson's legal papers disappeared in a fire at his old firm in 1885.[1]

Another source for information on Thompson's law practice are records of land and property purchases and sales. Of all the records kept in nineteenth-century Nova Scotia the best preserved are records of this kind. The difficulty here is in sorting out which purchases were carried out on Thompson's own behalf and which were made on behalf of clients. A mortgage was a common form of investment before stock markets and brokers made other forms of investment convenient and practicable. A lawyer's business did not merely consist of taking clients' briefs in civil and occasionally criminal cases, but included a great range of transactions in the buying, selling, and administration of property. A lawyer acted as agent or trustee for estates, as a repository of wills, as counsellor for companies and corporations new and old. A great many of Thompson's land transactions are thus recorded, both buying and selling, but without those burnt-up books of his, it is impossible to sort them out.

Thompson himself was never a businessman but, like many lawyers, he began to be connected with business. He was never to be wealthy, but he had a number of early business connections which, if they did not bring him great financial reward, did bring him familarity with the ways of business. As early as 1872 he appears in the incorporating acts of various ventures. The most important of these was the Spring Hill and Parrsboro Coal and Railway Company, a group formed to bring coal from Springhill to Parrsboro, a pretty port on the north shore of Minas Basin. Thompson was elected director of the company in February 1875. It was not for long. The difficulty is not clear; one element was a call on the directors for a loan to the company of several hundred dollars, with which Thompson refused to comply. This gave umbrage to the president, Robert Reed of Saint John, New Brunswick. Thompson could write strong letters:

I admit ... that my declining that request was a reason why I should tender my resignation, but why, in addition to resigning I should receive from Mr. Reed a lecture on the duties on a Director I cannot understand ... you will do me the favor of mentioning to Mr. Reed that I shall feel honored by his replying to my letters only when they are addressed to him.[2]

Thompson had toughness and persistence which may have come from his Scottish mother, of whom we know so little. But he had a lively sense of humour that came from his Irish father. He had a nice wit, though it often had an edge of sarcasm to it. As when he was out on one of the many Halifax Barristers' Society junkets at a country inn on the St Margaret's Bay Road with his friend Samuel Rigby. Rigby was a huge man in all departments. He had even to order his hats from England since nothing in Halifax fitted him. It was 1879; everyone knew that Rigby was thinking of the bench. Rigby was sitting beside Thompson when Rigby's chair began audibly to creak under his massive weight. Thompson looked at him. 'Well, Rigby,' said Thompson, 'it is clear that only the Bench can be depended upon to hold you securely!'[3]

Not that the bench was much of a prize. The salary was not large, the judges were not usually well off, and some of those on the Nova Scotia Supreme Court were not that competent either. Of the seven Supreme Court judges, three had been appointed before confederation. The chief justice, Sir William Young, had been appointed to the Court in 1860; in 1875 he was seventy-six years old and showing it. He had developed a bad habit of hearing clients' grievances against a lawyer, directing the clients to make their complaint in full court, and all without sworn proof. That was ended, according to N.H. Meagher, one of Thompson's younger colleagues and a Catholic, through the action of Thompson:

When one of such complaints was being made before the full Court, Sir William presiding, Mr. Thompson after consulting me inquired if the complainant, who was a woman, was moving for process to enforce her grievance, and was told she was not. He insisted the proceedings was altogether irregular, and his view was concurred in by Ritchie E.J. [equity judge] and Wilkins, J. and the practice was never repeated.[4]

J.W. Ritchie was unquestionably able, and had been made equity judge in 1873, having been on the Court since 1870. L.M. Wilkins had been on the Court since 1856, and was quite undistinguished. The other judges were Jonathan McCully, appointed by Sir John A. Macdonald in 1870; Hugh McDonald, appointed by Macdonald government on 5 November 1873, the day the government fell; W.F. DesBarres, a member of the Court since 1848, one of the early appointments to the bench under responsible government, and no great credit to the system of government that appointed him. Henry Smith was appointed by Alexander Mackenzie in January 1875. It was said in November 1874 that Smith had his judge's commission already in his pocket. He was, as the sharp and unfriendly Griffin of the *Evening Express* noted, neglecting his duties as attorney general 'in order that he might not supply, by his incompetence at the Bar during the session of the Court, a strong and untimely evidence of his unfitness for the Bench.'[5] Wallace Graham, who became Thompson's law partner in 1878, claimed in 1887 that there was only one decent judge on the whole Supreme Court of Nova Scotia, meaning R.L. Weatherbe.[6] Even Weatherbe, whom Mackenzie appointed at the last minute in October 1878, horrified the Supreme Court of Canada with the unorthodoxy of his decisions. He was a kind of devil's advocate on the Nova Scotia Supreme Court; it was argued that more injustice would be done if he were not there.[7] These were the men Thompson faced in the old Court House in Spring Garden Road; idiosyncratic, at times crotchety, some no doubt vulgar, unwell, lazy. Even the best of them had decided peculiarities. Generally they were old-fashioned. Thompson's recollection was what uphill work it had been arguing before judges with such anachronistic ideas.[8]

Thompson's first reported case came in 1875, *Mader et al.* v. *Jones.* Jones had agreed to buy some $1,100 worth of dried herring in barrels from Mader and others. Jones inspected four of the barrels, found them good, and shipped all 260 barrels to Boston, all branded Gulf Herring No. 1. When the barrels were opened in Boston only the four inspected barrels had good herring. Jones refused to pay. Action was brought by Mader before Chief Justice Young in November 1874 to recover the $1,100. It was a jury trial and the jury found that the fish had not been fraudulently packed, but neither were they merchantable. Judgment was given for Mader, in the amount of $350. Jones still felt cheated, and refused to pay the $350. He retained Thompson and N.H. Meagher, just admitted to the bar in 1872, to ask the full bench to set aside the judgment and order a new trial. At the hearing in July 1875, the lawyer for Mader *et al.*, Thompson's friend Rigby, argued that the labels on the barrels, 'Gulf Herring No. 1,' constituted no guarantee of what was inside them. Thompson replied that there were a number of cases to the contrary. A purchaser who in good faith bought dried herring labelled as No. 1 should certainly not have to pay for them if they were not up to standard, even if he had opportunity for inspection. And as to inspection, Thompson said, 'It is essential in the interests of trade as well as of morality that when a foreign merchant comes into our markets ... his rights should be protected, and the good faith of our business transactions vindicated.'

Justice McCully wrote the opinion of the Court on 11 August 1875, sustaining Thompson fully: '... the facts are so strong, and the [earlier] verdict so unsatisfactory, there seems to be no alternative but a new trial to secure justice.'[9]

McCully was not always so sensible. On one occasion before him

Thompson had set up a plea of insanity for a criminal and wanted to read the jury some relevant points from a medical book. McCully said Thompson couldn't read it since it was not a law book! Thompson simply laid the book down and repeated the passage from memory.[10]

One picturesque case Thompson argued was the affair of the Wickwire dike, in *Wickwire et al.* v. *Gould et al.* Gould owned a dike at Grand Pré that protected rich marsh meadows from the sea. About 1835 a much bigger dike was built by Wickwire outside of the Gould dike and which gave it extra protection. For this privilege it was agreed that Gould would pay £19 a year from 1848 onward. Then came the great Saxby gale of October 1869, which broke through the Wickwire dike and destroyed a substantial part of it. For two years the outer dike was left unrepaired and by the time it was fixed, the restoration was very expensive. Wickwire insisted on a wholly new scale of charges to pay for the repairs. Gould said no. The trial in 1878 revealed Thompson, Gould's lawyer, willing to challenge even the chief justice on points of law and evidence. The court reporter summarized the exchange:

YOUNG C.J.: The Saxby storm adds a new element to the equities of the case.
THOMPSON: No. It does not. All the witnesses swear that the new dyke is of no more benefit to them than the old one. The only new element is the increased expenses of the building of the new dyke, which conferred no new benefit to our dyke.[11]

Judgment by Justice McDonald on 10 December 1878 sustained Thompson's clients. It was an illustration of Thompson's mind: the clarity that emerged once he had mastered the facts.

A difficult business question was the Oakes affair. In 1873 the Halifax City Council planned to construct a major brick sewer across the North Common. A dispute arose between the city, represented by its engineer, Edward Keating, and the contractor, Oakes. At the Supreme Court, after a long and sometimes brilliant argument by both sides, Chief Justice Young struck down Oakes's claim on a technicality.[12] Thompson was Oakes's counsel. He was also an alderman. The *Morning Chronicle*, before the decision in the Court was given, accused Thompson of being on both sides in the Oakes case, on the plaintiff's side as Oakes's counsel, and on the defendant's as alderman.[13] That was absurd, Thompson said. Aldermen cannot be the defenders in law for the city. Its legal defender was the recorder, the city's law officer. And it was not a little curious, he noted, that no one had any complaint on this subject until the *Chronicle* 'deemed it expedient, for political purposes, to make an attack on my character.'[14] Oakes and Thompson were ultimately vindicated. The narrow, technical view of the chief justice was not shared by the Supreme Court of Canada, whither Thompson took the Oakes case in 1879 and won.[15]

In May 1877 Thompson's talents were recognized in an unexpected way, by Americans. Under the Treaty of Washington of 1871, the United States had been given the right to fish the Canadian and Newfoundland inshore fisheries, in return for a similar privilege within United States' territorial waters as far south as 39°N. But American waters were not much use for fish, and it was agreed that there would be an arbitration for the difference. What were the Canadian fisheries worth, over and above these American concessions, for a period of ten years? What was the value of the American right of transshipment, of use of Canadian ports? There were the questions to be decided by a commission of three, one British, one American, and a neutral chairman.

Getting the commission appointed was not easy. The British wanted Maurice Delfosse, the Belgian minister at Washington, as chairman, but Hamilton Fish, President Grant's secretary of state, did not like him. The British were stubborn, so early in 1877, for the sake of British–American amity, Fish finally agreed to Delfosse. The American commissioner was a fisheries expert from Massachusetts, christened Ensign H. Kellogg, the choice of senators from Maine and Massachusetts. Sir Alexander Galt was the choice of the British and Canadians. This was all a fait accompli when Rutherford Hayes became president on 4 March 1877. His secretary of state was from Massachusetts and New York, an able lawyer by the name of W.H. Evarts. It was arranged that the arbitration would take place at Halifax, beginning in June 1877, where the three-man tribunal would hear argument from both sides. The British–Canadian side was headed by the agent, Francis (later Sir Francis) Ford, a career diplomat, and with an array of Canadian counsel (all Liberals) appointed by Alexander Mackenzie: Joseph Doutre, Montreal; S.R. Thompson, Saint John; L.H. Davies, Charlottetown; R.L. Weatherbe, Halifax; and also William Whiteway, of St John's. The American agent was Dwight Foster of Boston, a former attorney general of Massachusetts. There were only two American lawyers, Richard Dana, Jr, author of *Two Years Before the Mast*, and W.H. Trescott.

The Americans badly needed a Canadian lawyer to help them. Thompson was asked in May 1877; the fee offered was $250 in gold.[16] Thompson was duly introduced to the commission on 30 July by Dwight

Foster. There was no publicity for Thompson in this enterprise; he made no speeches. But he had much to do with the preparation of the American case, expecially from the Canadian sources that the Americans felt were so important. An Edward Blake speech (he was minister of justice until 7 June 1877) on the fisheries question was, for example, sent from Boston to Halifax, for Thompson to study.[17]

The Fisheries Arbitration Commission occupied the Legislative Council chamber in Province House, Halifax, sitting every week day from 12 noon to 4 p.m. from August to November 1877. It was by no means unpleasant in the sunny red chamber. There was a tray of decanters on the sideboard, with Newfoundland port, Spanish sherry, ale, claret, and soda water. The three members of the commission sat in high chairs on one side of the council table, and the six British counsel and the three American sat around it. The British–Canadians presented their side of the argument first. Rules were casual; no objection was made to hearsay testimony or to leading questions. Witnesses could be cross-examined by the American lawyers, usually Foster and Dana. The evidence presented each day was printed and available the next.

Much of the information about the work of the commission comes from Richard Dana. It is only a sidelight on Thompson's work, but it reveals much about the character of Thompson's Halifax and its society as Americans saw it. The Americans brought their families to Halifax and made a summer (and autumn) of it. To a civilized Bostonian like Dana, Halifax was an agreeable place and he set out to enjoy it. The climate was not as hot as Boston, and at night especially there was a fragrant sea breeze. Dana's description of Point Pleasant and the North-West Arm suggests Haligonians were not wrong in cherishing both:

They have a park of pines, larches and spruces on the bank of the harbor, which is a pretty and unique feature of the town. Then the N.W. Arm, as it is called, is a great beauty. It is an arm of the sea, which stretches 5 or 6 miles into the country from the harbour ... not over half a mile wide, all of pure sea water, with a small and gentle tide, the banks are very high sloping and well wooded with evergreens (nothing else seeming to grow well here), and on this Arm a large part of the wealthier people live, in very handsome residences, each having its boat house and bathing house. There is no marsh, or flats, or reef, or sunk rock, but all is clear as an inland lake.[18]

Dana's own routine was to breakfast at 7 a.m., ride horseback at 8 for an hour, then meet with his fellow lawyers and Thompson until 11 a.m. After

4 p.m., when the work of the commission was over, calls were returned, dinner was at 6, unless there were invitations which were indeed innumerable.[19] Dana was amused with Haligonians' religious habits; Halifax seemed to him populated by strict church-goers, and at every dinner 'grace is said by the master of the house before sitting down.'

It was clear to Dana that Sir Alexander Galt was the major influence on the commission. Delfosse, the chairman, was intelligent and well-meaning, but he had had no experience in deliberative or judicial assemblies. Galt was adroit, clear-headed, and knew precisely where he was going. He anticipated good results, and said so to Alexander Mackenzie, the prime minister. Mackenzie wrote back that if it was successful it would 'justify me in insisting that we know our neighbors & our business better than any Englishman.'[20] Galt also had no qualms about making political rather than judicial decisions. He was not a lawyer in any case. The Americans liked him with his English–Canadian ways, but his capacity to charm Delfosse made Americans uneasy. This was the more so since Ensign Kellogg, the American commissioner, was such an ass. Kellogg drank too much and he was wholly unfitted in brains and manners to represent the United States, especially against a man as magnetic as Galt. On one occasion Kellogg was so drunk that he addressed Sir Alexander as 'Sir Ruggerdandy,' the best he could manage![21]

Kellogg in the tribunal was as bad as Kellogg in society. The American case was made well; its effectiveness was weakened desperately by Kellogg's failure as a member of the tribunal. The Americans lost in the end and lost badly partly because Delfosse was disgusted with Kellogg; it was by no means clear that Kellogg could follow argument even from his own side. The British and Canadians demanded $14.8 million, reckoning the American privileges of buying bait, procuring supplies, and trans-shipping cargoes in with the value of the inshore fisheries. The tribunal ruled out fringe issues and Galt then suggested a more realistic figure of $6.5 million. Americans had argued that there should be either no award at all or at the most $500,000. Delfosse suggested a compromise of $4.5 million on condition that Kellogg accept it. But Kellogg, with no arguments, no suggestions, opposed all compensation. In the face of that continual no, Delfosse felt it legitimate to move $1 million closer to Galt's figure. That was how the $5.5 million was arrived at.[22] The award was paid with a good deal of grumbling in 1878. Dwight Foster wrote Thompson from Boston early in 1878 to say that it was by no means certain that Congress would pay the award; 'but it is very certain that if it does there will be no reciprocity with Canada for many years to come.'[23]

That prediction turned out accurate enough. Foster also handsomely offered Thompson $750 in place of the original $250.

The money was useful but the experience Thompson gained was more valuable. In Dwight Foster Thompson discovered a great store of information and experience, and Thompson accepted Foster's invitation to come and see him in Boston in 1883 when he and some colleagues decided to establish the Dalhousie Law School. And in the larger sense, this experience at international arbitrations was to be immensely valuable at Washington in 1887, and at the Bering Sea arbitration in Paris in 1893.

Thompson's activities were by no means confined to Halifax. From early 1870s, as lawyer for the archdiocese of Halifax, for the archbishop, and for other clients, Thompson spent several days at a time out of town, in Saint John, Amherst, Guysborough, Kentville, as law cases came up. For example, he was in Saint John in December 1872 on business for the archbishop connected with a local will. Saint John seemed to Thompson a bustling place, more so than when he had last seen it two years before. New brick buildings were going up rapidly, which he found were being heated to suffocation. Thompson was impressed with the local court, the judge being young, able, and sensible. Thompson felt inclined to invite him to Nova Scotia!

He hated being away from home and complained of being lonesome at night, but was sleeping with his usual consistency. Sundays were long. Not even two services in the Saint John Cathedral consoled him. Besides, it was painted 'with the most miserable want of taste I ever saw displayed in any public place.' As for Annie, she was as lonely as he was. Thompson was writing in September 1874 from Amherst, about a second new baby:

... and please God as soon as little Joe is weaned we will go right off for about 3 or 4 weeks and be 'just married' again. I was ever so glad about letter. I was glad even that you cried about me but you poor pet when I came to the part where you said the house looked so big and the children so little I had to laugh right out.[24]

Thompson added in shorthand, 'Kiss the little fellow for me and tell them how much I love you. Your own Grunty.' It was one of several names Thompson used to sign himself. Annie also called him 'Torry,' sometimes with two r's, sometimes one, and neither probably having anything to do with politics. And so the little family would wait for him. 'Poor Joe,' Annie wrote in July 1876, when Thompson was up in Guysborough in the heat, 'has not missed an evening running down to the gate when the bus comes. I wish that you could see the baby with a handkerchief on her head out under the trees.'[25]

This was the third baby, a girl, Mary Aloysia, 'Babe' as she came to be called, born in March 1876, named after Sister Mary Aloysia Holden, of the Sisters of Charity at Mount St Vincent. Another girl, Mary Helena, was born two years later in March 1878. The house was a busy place. 'I am constantly worried with the thought of how you are plagued with the children,' Thompson ruminated. Annie wrote to him in September 1878 at Antigonish, how all the children got 'in bed with me last night and they were awake long before day break throwing boots at one another and sitting on my head.' Babe woke up one morning and wanted to know 'if you would be home by the time that she was ten years old.' Babe was then five.[26]

They were a precious tribe. One day all four of them were in the garden with every coal-oil lamp chimney in the house trying to make a telephone system! Annie wrote, a little desperately, 'Childie dear if you only knew how much we all are like orphans when you are away from us you would try and take care of yourself. Just think for a moment what would become of us without you.'[27]

Annie was not without assistance. There was a girl to help around the house; also her sister Frances (Fan) who in 1877 was fourteen years old. She lived a mile or so away on Gottingen Street with Annie's mother. Annie was also inflicted with a Thompson relation now and then. None of Thompson's family seem to have cherished Annie – they may have assumed, despite everything Thompson said, that Annie had made him into a Catholic. Perhaps they could not forgive that. It is possible that Annie did not like them. 'I am going to say something that I fear will annoy you,' Thompson wrote from Guysborough in July 1876, 'I got a letter from Daniel yesterday in which he said it was probable that Charlotte would come up this summer. She has been very sick.'[28]

On the back of this letter is written in Annie's hand, 'Torry's letters, 1876.' She saved them. She had an uncommon sense of the worth of her husband. She seemed rarely to look at his life in the short term; she had her sights on distant horizons. Thompson was the other way – bookish, lacking capacity or will to be importunate, hating to ask for favours, content with the status quo. Annie was never quite satisfied, and it was a major point of difference between them. Thompson had the gumption to recognize his own instincts for what they were, conservative, pedestrian, unadventurous. Before big decisions in his life he discovered a reservoir of pusillanimity disconcertingly large, as if he were positively dreading change, wanting only to cleave to what he had. Annie was bolder, more reckless, altogether a high-mettled creature. Thompson listened to her counsel, knowing that often her boldness was justified.

Thompson, with few relatives of his own, was surrounded with hers. She had three brothers and two sisters. One brother was drowned skating on the North-West Arm in 1873. Another brother died in Londonderry, Nova Scotia, in 1878, perhaps in a mining accident; the third brother, Peter Affleck, was something of a family problem; Thompson was still sending twenty-five dollars a month to him in the 1890s. The Affleck girls were better. Johanna, two years younger than Annie, joined the Sisters of Charity. Fan, the youngest sister, was always the closest to Annie. Besides her brothers and sisters, Annie had her aunts and cousins. Her mother, Catherine Saunders Affleck, had three sisters; all had married locally. Alice Saunders married Captain John Pugh, merchant and MLA, and there were five children there. Another aunt, Joanna Saunders, married William Devine, a Newfoundlander and cooper, and there were seven children. A third sister, Mary Saunders, married a local shopkeeper, James Kearney, where there were also seven children. Annie had thus seventeen first cousins locally. Altogether, Thompson, whose own family had rather melted away, found himself very much part of a large and generous range of his wife's relatives.

There is little evidence of close family ties on the Thompson side. On his mother's side, only David Pottinger, his cousin, was in any way close and he lived in Moncton. Thompson's mother had left Halifax in the early 1870s and gone to live with the Pottingers. Thompson's brother Joseph was dead; William was in South Africa; his sister Elizabeth seemed to be with his mother, although she eventually went to Barrington to live with Thompson's other sister, Charlotte. Perhaps the estrangement, for that is what it seemed to be, was religious at bottom; Thompson had drifted away from early moorings and it showed.

Thompson's letters to Annie, and hers back to him, show an uxorious husband who depended upon his wife, leaned on her, listened to her, vegetated without her, who was, as Thompson said, like Charles II of Spain without his queen – disagreeable, restless, and dangerous. Thompson could lose his temper with Annie or be impatient with her; he had his jokes about punishing her if she did not do what he said, that all wives needed a good beating now and then to keep them up to the mark. They were family jokes. But he had a temper. In 1879 he had suddenly to go to Truro on law business, and sent for a valise for overnight. The valise came with a razor and shaving things, a nightgown (pajamas only became common after the turn of the century), a tooth brush (they seem to have been used in the 1870s), and, important in Nova Scotia, a rubber rain coat: but there was no letter from Annie. 'I suppose you are so tired of my being cross and crabbed at home that you did not care to write,' Thompson wrote from the train. 'Never mind pet, I will not be so bad any more.'[29]

It was owing to Annie that Thompson became involved in the affairs of Mount St Vincent. Annie's sister Johanna became Sister Mary Helena; her first cousin, Ann Devine, became Sister May Pius; her old friend, Mary Holden, became Sister Mary Aloysia, all three Sisters of Charity. Annie's youngest sister, Fan, went to school at Mount St Vincent – it was called the Mount and still is – and Annie's own daughters, as they grew, would go to the Mount too. The Sisters of Charity had come to Halifax in 1849. In 1856 they separated from the New York sisters, were given the right to a mother house, and the right to open a novitiate. Their original duty was to teach poor children and orphans. The order became a great favourite of Archbishop Connolly's. He had a country house near Bedford Basin and it was the scene of many a pleasant party. Connolly was a good hand at the fiddle; the sisters played piano; there were cakes and wine. It was said that when Archbishop Connolly was feeling melancholy, he would hoist a signal from the roof of his country house, and in due course some sisters would arrive from the Mount to sing and play to him.[30] It was all cheerful and innocent; ascetic it was not.

In 1873, through the agency of John Thompson, the Sisters of Charity bought a substantial addition to their property at Rockingham, where, aided by the good offices of the archbishop, they put up a mother house and offered a boarding school for girls. Mount St Vincent expanded; it was situated on a handsome hillside on the shores of Bedford Basin, four miles from the centre of the city. They now put up a large building for $35,000 (it stood until a fire in 1951). The Sisters of Charity advertised for students in 1874 and got them, at $120 a year, board and tuition. Care would be taken, they said, of the religious training of Catholic students, and there would be 'no tampering whatever' with the religious principles of Protestants.[31]

There was another order in Halifax, the Ladies of the Sacred Heart, who had come about the same time. They had been brought to Halifax for the purpose of educating upper-class Catholic girls, and they ran a boarding school of good reputation in the centre of Halifax. They rather resented Mount St Vincent, and they found a supporter and protector in Michael Hannan, the vicar-general of the diocese.

When the death of the Archbishop Connolly in 1876 was followed by the consecration of Archbishop Michael Hannan, a flutter of alarm went through Mount St Vincent. Michael Hannan had been vicar-general of the Halifax archdiocese since the mid-1860s, and had served for several years on the Board of School Commissioners. He was hard-headed, apt to be exercised on the subject of his own authority, and was pushed off the school board in 1873 by Archbishop Connolly because he was too intractable. Nor was he the obvious choice for archbishop of Halifax. The first person nominated had been Bishop Cameron of Antigonish. It was said in Rome that Pius IX, being old, feeble, and in bad health, left the management of appointments of cardinals and archbishops to others, and that, plus influences (not specified) which Hannan was able to bring to bear, gave him the archbishopric.[32]

A quarrel developed between two strong-minded people, the new archbishop and a new mother superior at Mount St Vincent, Mother Mary Francis Maguire, elected in December 1876. That the Roman Catholic church is a monolithic organization, cunningly contrived, run with autocracy and unanimity, is a Protestant myth. Like all institutions, the church has to deal with ambition, greed, hypocrisy, among its own people as well as that in the world. The church had become skilled at handling such questions in its eighteen hundred years of experience with wickedness and waywardness. Its skill is illustrated in the Mount St Vincent affair.

Mother Mary Francis was a Halifax girl, of an Irish father and a German Lutheran mother. She had courage, capacity, and toughness, joined to some vindictiveness. The Sisters of Charity needed sprucing up and she was prepared to do it. The rule of the Mount was that the administration of the Sisters of Charity should be confined largely within its own walls. That did not exclude 'the essential supervision and control of the Archbishop.' What those words meant was not important under the benevolent rule of Archbishop Connolly, but it mattered very much when Michael Hannan came along. When a bishop called to his own diocese an institution from another, there was, as Bishop Cameron put it to Thompson, 'a kind of tacit contract by which he is obliged to respect its fundamental constitutions.'[33]

The reform of the Sisters of Charity was something Hannan believed he should undertake, not believing them capable of reforming themselves. The sisters preferred to handle that exercise on their own. But not all the sisters accepted gracefully Mother Mary Francis's corrections, nor did the mother superior accept benignly their resistance. The refractory sisters, a small minority, then turned to the archbishop for support, and he was more than ready to give it.

The quarrel finally broke into the open at Mount St Vincent's graduation exercises for 1879. The archbishop sent a peremptory note –

one without even salutation – that, by his order, there would be no public graduation exercises at Mount St Vincent that year, and that no lay person should be allowed to attend. Mother Mary Francis refused to accept this. On Saturday, 4 July 1879, the exercises duly went forward, with various Catholic dignitaries present, including a number of the local Catholic clergy; music was played by the girls, and 'French drama' acted. Fan Affleck appeared in both.[34]

This threw the gauntlet down in earnest. The sisters now had recourse to legal advice from Thompson, and almost certainly private ecclesiastical advice from Thompson's friend, Bishop Cameron of Antigonish. The result was that on 12 September 1879, two sisters, Mary de Sales Dwyer, and Mary Aloysia Holden, left Halifax secretly by train for Rimouski. There, at Pointe au Père, they boarded ship for England en route for Rome. The archbishop knew of it only when they had left. They were in Liverpool by 22 September, and in Rome a week later. They were attractive women and knew it, and like many such, found the world accommodating and pleasant.[35]

Rome was to be so, too, but as usual the church took its time. Everyone in ecclesiastical Rome disappeared around 1 October for two months' holiday. Mgr. Kirby, of the Irish College, befriended them. He was a kind gentleman who, as it turned out, was too gentle; he hated quarrels and was a friend only in time of peace. The sisters would need tougher metal, and found an ecclesiastical lawyer, Mgr. Fortini, who was well established with connections at the Propaganda.

The sisters' accusations were several, but the burden of them was a series of ruses by Dr Hannan to undermine the authority of the mother superior, including use of the confessional. This was especially insidious since many of the priests in the diocese supported Hannan's attempt to bring the sisters under control. Mgr. Fortini said he would need substantiation of all the sisters' statements against the archbishop. He also wanted, if possible, a petition signed by influential Catholics in Halifax praising the work of the Sisters of Charity.[36] All influential support helped, the two sisters wrote Thompson. 'As a consequence, the Seal of the Attorney-General has been our strength,' and they added with charming naïveté that the seals of the premier and the lieutenant-governor would help them too.[37]

The advice and support of Bishop Cameron was obtained. The sisters, he wrote Thompson in January 1880, will have to be prepared not only to present their own accusations against the archbishop, but to meet minutely his countercharges. Archbishop Hannan had good reason to know well what was going on at Mount St Vincent; the sisters had all along, Cameron said, 'spies in their camp and traitors in their citadel.' Hannan knew, in other words, the worst that could be brought against them. Cardinal Simeoni, of the Propaganda, would be a fair and just arbitrator, but, said Cameron writing to Thompson,

... he needs all the evidence which the Sisters can bring forward to their own defence, in order to be in a position to do them ample justice. Their litigation being with their Archbishop, they must not forget that they have terrible odds against them, and that they must look only to the evidence they will adduce of his guilt and their own innocence for a favorable verdict.[38]

At this point, January 1880, Archbishop J.J. Lynch of Toronto moved noisily and visibly into the Halifax affair. Lynch had been in Rome in October 1879, and as he was leaving for Canada, Cardinal Simeoni said to him, 'If you can find out *secretly* and *quietly* anything about this trouble in Nova Scotia let me know.'[39] Without any delicacy or prior warning he descended upon the sisters in Halifax saying that he had been commissioned to investigate the affair. The sisters hurriedly despatched a cable to Rome to check that. In the meantime they sent a firm reply to Lynch, who was staying with Hannan at St Mary's. It was a reply that bore the marks of Thompson's legal hand and Cameron's counsel. The sisters declined respectfully to enter into the matter. Lynch then asked, could he come and interrogate the sisters? This was accompanied by a minatory letter from Archbishop Hannan.[40] The sisters, a little desperate by now, cabled Sister Mary Aloysia in Rome: 'Lynch says Cardinal Prefect authorized him and that he will apply for further authority. Stop him.'[41] They did exactly that. Thompson was cabled in code that Cardinal Simeoni had ordered Lynch to stop the investigation. This was on 24 January 1880.

Lynch made a long report to Rome, somewhat grieved at being called off after having travelled all the way from Toronto. He included in his report some singular rumours, including one about Sister Mary Aloysia, that she was so forward as to take frequent sea baths in company not with a nun but with a married lady of the city (probably Annie Affleck Thompson).[42] Cameron gave excellent advice after the débâcle created by Archbishop Lynch, writing to Thompson, his Halifax secret agent:

In writing to Rome, however, let nothing unkind or disrespectful be said concerning the poor old man of Toronto; for it is all too probable that advantage has been taken of his dotage, and that he has been duped by the low knavery of others whose interest required that he should be misled.[43]

Furthermore, Cameron added a month later, be very cautious about using the name of Cameron. Some of the sisters boasted that the bishop of Arichat is fighting their battle against the archbishop. That, said Bishop Cameron, can do no one any good. On the other hand, Cameron feared little from Rome:

Rome is my country; and it so happens that it would be a dangerous undertaking for even an Archbishop to challenge me there. I say this, simply because I believe it to be a fact, not from any miserable vanity.[44]

In the end the sisters won. In April 1880 Leo XIII took the Sisters of Charity of Halifax from the control of Archbishop Hannan and placed them under the protection of Bishop Cameron. Archbishop Hannan came within an inch of losing his diocese altogether. The sisters glowed with triumph; they wanted the decision of the pope published for the world to see. The secretary at the Propaganda was wiser and older. 'The Conquerors can afford to be very humble and quiet,' he said.[45]

As Thompson had predicted, the archbishop's own acts had recoiled against him. The Italians, so good at intrigue themselves, were adept at recognizing it. Thompson had taken the whole responsibility as a lay Catholic lawyer; he had won others over and had persuaded the sisters they were right. They brought him a gold medallion from Rome; Thompson had staked his reputation for them and they were grateful.[46]

It will not be the least of your meritorious acts when you appear before God, to have helped our little barque from sinking[;] you have been laboring with no one less than a Divine Pilot surely, or it would long ere this have gone down, for you know well how many and great storms it has encountered[.] Sister says that she supposes the House will soon reopen, and she wants you to take care of yourself and that the work of the day ought to be sufficient without staying in town and doing the work of others at night – Be sure and obey her –[47]

That was in January 1880. It was easier said than done. Thompson had been the main pulling power in the Mount St Vincent affair, and he had become, by 1880, in the government of Nova Scotia, not only its attorney general but the mainspring of its strength and vigour.

PART TWO

POLITICIAN, ATTORNEY GENERAL, AND JUDGE, 1877–1885

6

Getting Elected for Antigonish

The Legislative Assembly of Nova Scotia after 1867 was composed of thirty-eight representatives for Nova Scotia's eighteen counties. Each had two members, except Pictou and Halifax counties, which had three. The Assembly had its rivalries and its traditions; before confederation it was regarded as treason to move from one political party to another. But confederation acted like a winnowing fan, and the new pattern of politics, confederates and anti-confederates, gradually became, by the mid 1870s, the struggle of the ins and the outs. The anti-confederate premier after 1867 was William Annand, the principal owner of the Liberal newspaper, the Halifax *Morning Chronicle*. In May 1875 Annand accepted an appointment, offered by Prime Minister Alexander Mackenzie, as agent general for Canada in London.[1] This left the Liberal government of Nova Scotia without a leader. The best Annand's colleagues could do was to bring in P.C. Hill, an adept and reputedly wealthy Conservative and president of the Halifax Banking Company. Hill became premier and provincial secretary in an ostensibly non-party government. The *Halifax Evening Reporter* tried to make the idea acceptable, but it did not wash with the Nova Scotian public. Hill was regarded as a renegade Conservative flying Liberal colours. His regime survived, barely holding its own amid the economic difficulties common to Canada and the United States in the later 1870s, and amid the attacks of an aggressive Conservative opposition.

By this time Thompson was a Conservative. He had been a follower of Howe through Howe's anti-confederate motions. When Howe joined the Conservative government of Sir John A. Macdonald as part of the settlement of 1869, he carried Thompson with him. Thompson's conversion to Catholicism in 1871 brought him still closer to the Conservatives; their tradition of tolerance toward Roman Catholics, symbolized by the good relations between Tupper and Archbishop Connolly, suited Thompson well.

The Conservatives offered something else; the gradual evolution of what Tupper called, as early as 1869, the 'national policy.' By this Tupper meant economic nationalism and a pan-Canadian mutual dependence – selling Nova Scotian coal in Ontario, Ontario wheat in Nova Scotia. Tupper developed the idea more fully in 1870;[2] its full form, as a protective tariff, appeared in the 1874 federal election, and had become Conservative policy by 1876. It was a vigorous and attractive alternative to reciprocity with the United States. Tupper could point to the success of his policy in Cumberland and Pictou counties, where rail links to eastern Canada now carried their iron and coal to New Brunswick, Quebec, and Ontario. The ideas from it whetted the appetites of industrialists in Amherst, New Glasgow, and Halifax.

The real Conservative weakness had been the Nova Scotian dislike of confederation, something that had savaged their party from 1867 to 1871; but by the mid-1870s the National Policy began to draw support, and had brought Thompson into the ranks of provincial Conservatives. They were led by Simon Holmes, a Pictou lawyer and newspaperman, and by Douglas Woodworth, of Kentville in the Annapolis valley, and by the newly created Halifax *Morning Herald*. The group around the *Herald* were Conservative businessmen and lawyers: W.J. Almon, T.E. Kenny, James MacDonald, J.J. Stewart, and Robert Sedgewick.

Most Nova Scotians, Thompson included, assumed there was no distinction between federal and provincial parties, and that it was neither possible nor desirable to make one. Charles Tupper thought of himself as the overall leader of Nova Scotia Conservatives, federal and provincial, but though MP for Cumberland, he was then living in Toronto and the overall leadership devolved largely upon James MacDonald, the MP from Pictou. It was Jim MacDonald's view that recapturing Nova Scotia for the federal Conservatives depended upon making inroads at the provincial level, specifically the next provincial election. He did not know when that would be – the last had been December 1874 – but a provincial Conservative victory was vital. MacDonald consulted Senator William Miller of Arichat. We need new blood, he wrote. J.S.D. Thompson would be an excellent man; is there a Catholic constituency in eastern Nova Scotia that he might stand for? Richmond County and Cape Breton County, both on Cape Breton Island, were Catholic; so was Antigonish on the mainland. MacDonald added a postscript: 'This is written without Thompson's knowledge or consent.'[3]

The inner group at the Halifax *Morning Herald* were close to Thompson, literally as well as politically: Thompson's office was at 12 Bedford Row; J.J. Stewart, Stewart's brother Douglas, and his brother-in-law, Robert Sedgewick, were at number 14. J.J. Stewart came from Cumberland County, and had been a former school principal in Amherst. In 1878 Stewart became the *Herald*'s editor, a paper he wrote, then ruled, until his death in 1907. He was a quiet, unobtrusive editor, but in ability, influence, and management he was in every way exceptional. About mid-October 1877, this *Herald* group took Thompson in hand to persuade him to stand for provincial politics. Thompson had no consuming urge to go into politics: his practice was going well, he had more than enough to do. It was put to him that his political apprenticeship, as alderman, had been over 1 October 1877, and his school board work would end in a year's time. Thompson still did not like the idea. Jim MacDonald said many years later that Thompson's career 'appeared to be rather thrust upon him than sought for by him ... he acceded to the persuasion of his friends without enthusiasm, if not with reluctance.'[4] For one thing, Thompson would not be able to stand for Halifax, a mixed constituency that he would possibly have accepted with some degree of cheerfulness. Worsening relations with Archbishop Hannan over Mount St Vincent made him impossible as a Catholic candidate in Halifax. He did not like campaigning. He had campaigned only once, in his first aldermanic election in September 1871 and that had been on home ground. He did not relish a hard political fight on unknown territory.

The seat in Antigonish had become vacant when J.J. MacKinnon, elected in the 1874 provincial election as an Independent, had resigned in July 1877 over an issue significant in Antigonish – patronage. Antigonish County occupies the forty miles between Pictou County and the Strait of Canso. The county faces the Gulf of St Lawrence, its back thirty-five miles inland on the divide that separates the waters that flow to the Gulf from those that flow to the Atlantic. It is a county of rolling hills, its woods and farms aslant to the sea; over on the west side of the county, against the Pictou County line, the hills run up to nine hundred feet, sending their trout streams eastward to the lower lands along the Gulf shore.

Antigonish had its beginning when Highland soldiers settled there after the American Revolution, but by 1820 its character was determined by the men who came from the western isles of Scotland, and from Lochaber and Inverness, as the names in the county still show. Many had the Gaelic; though English became the language of business, even that was salted with the lilt of Gaelic. Indeed, the 1841 school legislation of

Nova Scotia allowed instruction in any of the four languages of Nova Scotian immigrants, French, English, German, or Gaelic.

The main occupation of Antigonishers was what they had done for centuries in Scotland, raise cattle, sheep, and pigs. They were farmers only in the sense of farming to eat; their wants were few, their traditions had always been raising stock, and providing for the wants of the stock and themselves. They lived frugally; they were not imbued with the driving industry of their Presbyterian neighbours in Pictou County. Outside observers judged Antigonishers as 'too easily satisfied with the bare existence that even indolence can procure in this country.'[5]

Antigonish grew more slowly than the rest of Nova Scotia. Its population, across the four censuses from 1851 to 1881 went from 13,500 to only 18,000. There is one other feature of the Antigonish population. It was overwhelmingly Roman Catholic – 87 per cent in 1881. The Roman Catholics were both Scottish and Acadian, the proportion being three to one.

This was the county that Senator Miller in Arichat was thinking of for Thompson. He talked to Bishop Cameron, the newly installed bishop, who lived in Arichat. Antigonish would require delicate handling. Father Ronald Macdonald of Pictou town believed that if they wished to put Thompson into the constituency they should begin by making it a lay movement. Thompson should come up and give a lecture or two on the German persecutions at St Francis Xavier College in Antigonish village. (Thompson had recently given two lectures in Halifax on Bismarck's persecution of the German Catholics – the *Kulturkampf* – to the Catholic Temperance Society.) Thompson's talents displayed, a draft Thompson movement could be devised. An unopposed election was to be aimed at.

It was not so simple. Antigonish locals were averse to bringing in an outsider; they wanted a local man for the by-election. Let Thompson try in the general election to come in 1878. But Senator Miller in Arichat was unhappy with this. No matter when Thompson chose to come, there would always be a local group ready to oppose him; waiting would simply make election more difficult. One hard fight at the beginning and it would all be over, next year included.[6]

Thompson was persuaded to go only with difficulty, but once persuaded he made as sure as possible of his ground. He wrote J.J. MacKinnon, the recently resigned MLA, that he had only now, 6 November 1877, decided to yield to the solicitations – he might have called them importunities – of his friends. Would MacKinnon have any objections to Thompson's running? The letter is a good example of

Thompson's courtesy and solicitude:

The time has come now however when I must ask you to let me know what your views are on the whole question – more especially as today a rumor is current that you are opposed to my coming in to the county. I think you will accept my statement that we were all under the impression that you were not going to run as absolving me from any charge of want of courtesy or of seeking to interfere with your prospects. I supposed indeed that I could count on your cordial support if our friends thought it well that I should run this election but it is possible that I may have overlooked some considerations.

MacKinnon seems to have been encouraging and Thompson indulged the hope that he might be returned unopposed. That hope was soon blasted. On 17 November 1877 Thompson received his invitation to come to Antigonish; he replied by telegram that he was coming at once. Within an hour he had news back: Angus McGillivray was in the field, the strongest man in the county. Thompson might as well stay home; there was 'no use for you to offer.' Thompson came anyway. He arrived in Antigonish on 21 November, having had to walk the horses most of the way from New Glasgow owing to the wretched condition of the roads.[7]

The situation in Antigonish seemed as hopeless as the roads. There were now two other candidates in the field. One was Joseph McDonald, a local farmer, the government's candidate. The most serious rival was McGillivray, a local lawyer, well connected, and, like Thompson, determined to run against the government. 'There is no chance here whatever,' a discouraged Thompson wrote to Annie that night; for all the exertions of Dr Cameron, there seemed to be no give anywhere. Not a soul moved. The field on Thompson's side was almost deserted. 'We might as well be running the election in Japan for all the information we get,' he wrote Senator Miller. The 'we' was Thompson, Simon Holmes, and J.J. Stewart. They could not even get a copy of the electoral lists, telegraphed for long ago. For the moment the Halifax Liberal papers left Thompson alone, uncertain what to do. The *Morning Herald*, with Martin Griffin at his best, commented:

It is amusing to see how they walk round Mr. Thompson, as it were, watching him with angry eagerness, afraid to rush at him, at a loss what to say about him, in terror lest they should say or do something foolish, and yet most heartily wishing and impatiently waiting for an opportunity to hold as it were a bloody assize on his prospects and his reputation.[8]

J.J. MacKinnon was well disposed but powerless. John Cameron McKinnon, a local doctor and a nephew of Bishop Cameron, was on McGillivray's side. Dr McKinnon cheerfully spread the rumour that Thompson had renounced the election when he knew Thompson was coming.[9]

Nothing stayed in place. Nothing was where the party workers in Halifax and Arichat said it should be. It was going to be a nasty uphill battle; was it worth fighting at all? Thompson showed a bold front 'so as to bluff rather than be bluffed,' but he saw no sense in the election, wasting time, labour, and money for no gain to himself or the party. Further, if the clergy were asked to throw their influence on the losing side, they would lose credibility too. Father Gillis, the parish priest in Antigonish, saw no hope and told Bishop Cameron so. At last Bishop Cameron said to Miller in Arichat, 'What shall we do?'

Miller believed the watchword would have to be, 'No surrender.' The bishop would have to play a strong card: persuade McGillivray to withdraw.[10] Cameron disliked doing it, but agreed to try. McGillivray persisted in running but was nervous; he suggested to Thompson that if Thompson withdrew in 1877, McGillivray would make way in 1878. Thompson could not accept that. So it went on, like a poker game between Thompson, McGillivray, and Joe McDonald, each playing a hand and each keeping up a bold front. Some good meetings in mid-week in the smaller villages of the county encouraged Thompson a little. He did not expect to win; he would be content if he lost by only three hundred votes. 'The enemy,' he wrote Annie, 'boast of 1000 but I think I will bear it well and I am sure it will shorten purgatory, for the torture of the last week has been something I have never conceived.' Campaigning in this strange constituency was, he said, 'like crossing the Atlantic in a dorey.'[11]

Nomination day was Thursday, 27 November. It was a fine day and there was a crowd of about one thousand – the largest since 1867, so it was said. It was so large that it could not be held inside the court house, but was moved to the open air in front of Pushie's general store. Joseph McDonald, a government candidate, very critical of lawyers and especially those from out of town, asked to be supported because he was a good local farmer. Angus McGillivray did not speak; he had withdrawn that morning, announcing the fact in a reluctant telegram to the bishop. Thompson addressed the crowd, thinking all the time, as he said, of Annie and the babies, fighting for his votes. He impressed the Antigonish *Casket*. It said you could print his speeches as they stood, so lucid were they. He held his audience; friend and foe alike paid attention.[12]

Nomination day was thus a success, and for the first time Thompson began to feel he might not lose. But he warned Annie, 'I do not think I will leave you on an errand of this kind again.'[13] He was unused to the constant strain and was tired and homesick to boot. Annie's letters both sustained and demoralized him. They spoke so much of home; before going to a meeting at Pomquet Forks, he made the mistake of reading two of them. He burst into tears. But he also read the *Morning Chronicle*'s attack on him, so like the sterling character he was, he went to the meeting and made a good speech by giving the *Chronicle* a rough time.'[14]

The *Chronicle* had said the Conservatives were engaged in a desperate attempt to foist a total stranger on Antigonish County, a cheap device by a political clique in Halifax, aided by the bishop of Arichat. As for Thompson, the *Chronicle* did not wish to disparage his talents, but this remarkable gentleman had placed himself wholly at the disposal of the American government; *'in return for American gold he gave the benefit of his local knowledge to a foreign power.'*[15] It was said in Halifax, remarked the *Chronicle*, turning the knife a little further, that the Americans had difficulty finding a lawyer sufficiently unpatriotic to do their work, that even James MacDonald, not overly fastidious in such matters, had refused. The *Herald* replied that Thompson's transactions with the Americans were no more than a business transaction between client and counsel. Besides, were the Americans so devilish?

People brought the incendiary Americans to their homes; people dined with them, and drank their wine; people danced with their daughters and paid honor to their wives; the Lieutenant Governor gave them a room, and the use of the Library; the British agents gave them every facility ... and all these people, all this time, were permitted ... to go on their treasonable career.[16]

The *Halifax Evening Reporter* thought Antigonish lucky to get a candidate like Thompson, a man 'of unblemished character, of great ability, and of rising fame.' Measures that come before the Assembly would undergo a painstaking examination from 'a keen, clear-headed, honest man.'[17]

The by-election was held Tuesday, 4 December 1877. The day before the *Chronicle* conceded that they expected Thompson to be elected. By some unknown means, it hinted darkly, the bishop of Arichat was procured and McGillivray induced to withdraw; so slyly was this done that it was announced only on nomination day, too late to reorganize the campaign. The results bore out the *Chronicle*'s fears: Antigonish County gave a majority of 1,053 to 536 for Thompson over McDonald. Thompson carried every polling station but two.[18]

It was the aphorism of J.W. Longley, a young Liberal in Halifax, that the new member for Antigonish was 'the member for Bishop Cameron.'[19] An Antigonish Liberal claimed that it was quite useless for any man, however strong, to try to carry Antigonish against the influence used in Thompson's favour. 'It would be just as well for the Bishop to elect his man off-hand himself, as the late election was only a farce.'[20] These charges were not quite true. In 1871 and 1872 W.A. Henry, who had represented Antigonish from 1847 to 1867, had the 'influences' on his behalf and could not win the seat either provincially or federally. He was a Protestant, of course, and perhaps the influences were not as enthusiastic about him as about Thompson. On the other hand, Daniel McDonald, Thompson's fellow member from Antigonish, had been elected in 1867, 1871, and 1874 notwithstanding the fact that the influences were against him.[21]

It was true, however, that Bishop Cameron had told his clergy where his sympathies lay. Thompson won the Antigonish by-election partly on his own merits, partly on the strength of Bishop Cameron's intervention, and partly on the dissatisfaction in Antigonish with the existing government of P.C. Hill.

Thompson was introduced to the Nova Scotia legislature on 21 February 1878. It was a place he knew well; after all, he had reported its debates from 1867 until 1872 and in the process had mastered its style and procedures. The Assembly met in a modest and unpretending chamber on the north side of Province House, a room of greys and northernness. On the opposite end the Legislative Council luxuriated in the south room with sunshine and red carpets. Thompson had come into the oldest legislative assembly in Canada, one hundred and twenty years of law-making, and it had some characteristic traditions. Hats were still worn, except when addressing the Speaker; most of them were plug hats (North American slang for top hats), considered nearly indispensable to the dress of the local lawgiver. That suggests a polite, decorous place; the Nova Scotia Assembly was neither. It was rough and ready, like others in the Atlantic provinces, rather coarse-grained, salty, intimate. It could be bad-tempered; there was a long and nasty quarrel between D.B. Wood-worth, MLA for Kings, and the Annand government that ended in a court action that went to the Supreme Court of Canada. It could be appealled to by men of good sense and real capacity; but it preferred its arguments ad hominem.

The major issue in the 1878 session was the Eastern Extension railway being built from New Glasgow to the Strait of Canso. Two-thirds of the railway was in Antigonish County. It had created trouble for the Hill government and it fairly landed on Thompson. It was the story of the Prince Edward Island railway over again: wrong estimates, false quantities, engineers that certified wrongly, the general chicanery attendant upon too many North American railway enterprises. There were also some real problems. Nova Scotia had a small population, frequently intractable terrain, and not enough money to do what the government and the people wanted to have done.

Private enterprise had not been readily attracted to Nova Scotia. Nova Scotia's railways of 1867 were built for and contracted by the government, paid for by its people. There were three main parts: Halifax to Truro; Truro eastward to Pictou; and Halifax to Windsor; they were all taken over by the new Dominion government as part of the Intercolonial system. The difficult Truro to Moncton section was opened in 1872, and the rest completed in 1876. Prime Minister Mackenzie's experience with the government building of the Intercolonial showed that a strong hand was necessary; the Dominion wanted to undertake no more railways in Nova Scotia.

There were two lines of consuming interest to Nova Scotians: one was from Windsor to Yarmouth through the Annapolis valley; the Windsor–Annapolis section was opened for traffic in 1873. There would be problems completing it to Yarmouth. The second was in the east, one that all the MLAs from the counties east of Colchester were anxious for: the Eastern Extension, from New Glasgow to the Strait of Canso, and beyond to Sydney and Louisburg in Cape Breton.

Premier Annand was anxious to get the Eastern Extension started. The government of Nova Scotia had no wish to build the railway as a government work; the lessons of the Intercolonial had not been lost on them either. They wanted the railway built, and run, by a private company. But the Eastern Extension was not very promising terrain for profits; bait was needed to entice private companies in.

The bait was the forty-mile Pictou branch, Truro to Pictou, well enough built by Sandford Fleming for Premier Charles Tupper just before confederation. In 1874 it was one of the most profitable sections of the Intercolonial, and yet not really part of its main line. Prime Minister Alexander Mackenzie was willing to get rid of the Pictou branch in order to cut down on the range of Intercolonial commitments. Premier Annand, and his successor P.C. Hill, considered offers in 1875 and 1876. One was from Harry Abbott of Montreal, the younger brother of J.J.C. Abbott. He and his associates would build and maintain the railway from New Glasgow to the Strait of Canso, supply and maintain the steam ferry service across the strait, in return for 150,000 acres of crown land and $7,945 per mile.

This the Nova Scotian government closed with. Security was deposited; the company engineer, Charles Gregory, was ready to lay out the route in detail; and after some hitches at the Dominion government's end the Nova Scotian contract with Harry Abbott was signed on 31 October 1876.[22]

Gregory set to work and in 1877 the construction of the right-of-way went forward rapidly. It was to be ready for laying track by December 1878. Then, at the end of October 1877, Gregory abruptly stopped work. He claimed he had not received payment for work already done. In the mêlée some of the subcontractors got out of town with money that had been paid to them, a good deal of which was owing to labourers. It was a mess. Some three to four hundred labourers, mostly in Antigonish County, asked loudly where their wages were, wages for work they had done and perhaps for some they had not done. Some $3,000 was alleged to be owing to labourers and storekeepers in Havre Boucher alone.

The Hill government claimed that it was no business of theirs. If subcontractors ran off with money for wages, it was not the fault of the government.[23] The railway company said the same. When the by-election in Antigonish came along the government promised fifty cents on the dollar to the labourers, presuming that men so paid would vote for Joseph McDonald. The alacrity of the government ceased when Thompson's victory was announced.

Thompson promised investigation and adjudication of all these claims. He made no sweeping promises; he aimed at fairness all round. To the common sense of the ordinary man this course may have commended itself; indeed, Thompson later won approval from both the labourers and the railway company for his judiciousness. It was to be a characteristic note. He did not like promising what he could not perform.

Eastern Extension surfaced, inevitably, in the legislature. The session of 1878 would be the last before a provincial general election and the Conservatives hit the government hard. D.B. Woodworth roundly asserted – Woodworth had a vicious fluency of speech – that whenever Premier Hill walked across the floor of the Assembly you could hear the gold of Harry Abbott jingling in his pocket. In one of the rare examples of Milton in provincial debates, Woodworth got off a long passage from *Paradise Lost*, how from the incestuous embrace of Sin and Satan there sprang the government of P.C. Hill![24]

Unlike his Conservative colleagues, Thompson made no such sweeping accusations about Harry Abbott or Charles Gregory. For one thing Charles Tupper had told him they were friends of the party, and for another he should try to resolve differences between the two. 'I know of no one,' said Tupper, 'to whom they could better apply than yourself to bring about that result upon fair and just terms.'[25] In the Assembly Thompson simply laid out the case. He took the view that the work of subcontractors in default could be measured by a competent engineer against which to test and establish the claims of the labourers. After the investigation by the official Labourers' Claims Committee had begun, Harry Abbott rallied around and agreed that the unpaid claims would form a charge against the Halifax and Cape Breton Railway Company. The quid pro quo was the reasonable request that the validity of the company's charter be established.[26]

The committee's report came to the House on 3 April. It was a subject on which Thompson felt a good deal of warmth but as usual he reined himself in. The committee had acted independently of politics in trying to come to an equitable adjustment, and he would emulate that example. Thompson reminded the attorney general that the government was dealing with a company that had no valid existence. The committee asked, not that any unfair advantage be taken of this legal defect, but that in dealing with such a company money be kept 'in the Treasury to meet any liability which the legislature should decide they must assume.'[27]

The government member from Guysborough, Otto Weeks, was prepared to move the adoption of this report without the restraining clause that the committee wanted; but he discovered that the sentiment of the House was so strongly in favour of Thompson and the committee that Weeks abandoned the attempt and the report was accepted without dissent.

After the Assembly's show of reasonableness about the Eastern Extension railway, it soon reverted to a condition more appropriate to the imminence of a general election. On 4 April 1878 the arrival of the messenger calling the House to hear the prorogation speech interrupted a nasty, personal debate.[28] Five months later, the dissolution of the Assembly was proclaimed.

7

Attorney General of Nova Scotia

Thompson was thirty-three years old now; less than middle height at five foot seven, he was heavy set, and already weighed 180 pounds or so. The effect of Wilson's coconut caramels and other splendours was showing at a waistcoat already ample. This ripeness of appearance was emphasized by a wide mouth and full lips, and a well-shaped nose with flaring nostrils. He had heavy eyebrows, brown eyes, and a high broad forehead topped by a mass of dark curly hair, with sideburns in front of ears that lay neat and close to his head. He was not handsome; if you saw him on the street, especially if he had on a top hat, he looked like a country butcher dressed for a wedding. That at least was the impression Professor Archibald MacMechan of Dalhousie had. But MacMechan also remarked what a difference taking off that hat made to his appearance; he seemed a different person, 'his clean white, intellectual forehead transformed his entire aspect ... All the refinement of the face lay in the forehead.'[1]

Thompson had a look of controlled sensuality, not too far from the truth. Those who did not know him were not aware of it, but he had a lively temper, an acute sensibility, a natural modesty, a powerful intelligence; this parallelogram of forces was held in balance under high tension. The forces were strong but the balance was controlled by a mighty will. He was an intensely nervous man, though you would have had a hard time to find it out. He did not reveal himself easily; he detested the shallow arts by which men make themselves popular.[2] Confidence, he believed, was a plant of slow growth and had to be earned gradually. He himself never seemed to be in a hurry, never seemed to be too busy to give his attention to whatever was in front of him, yet he despatched an enormous amount of business, quickly, quietly, without obvious effort.

He had something of the apparent repose of great minds; if anything, he gave to some, perhaps many who did not know him, an impression of coldness and reserve. An intimate friend said of him, 'His self-repression was not due to coldness of feeling, or want of sensitiveness; it was a consequence of his mental and moral discipline by which he had brought ... all his passions into subjection to his conscience.'[3] But he had also wit and was quick to appreciate it in others. Those who knew him knew well that laugh that came from the very marrow of him. One of the saddest aspects of Victorian photography was that until the 1890s it was impossible to photograph people smiling. There is only one of Thompson in existence, and his whole face is transformed.

He liked his creature comforts. He liked a good table, and tended to compare dinners he was given with the splendid table he had enjoyed at Archbishop Connolly's.[4] Unlike his father, he was not averse to rum or whisky, and came, as Haligonians usually did, to a taste for claret. He liked a mild cigar, especially after dinner. He liked hot baths after a long, hard day, though before running hot water that was a luxury. In these early days at Willow Park, Annie used to bathe him, pouring jugs of hot water over him as he sat in a big galvanized iron tub. He loved children, and he would pay attention to them and try to understand what they had to say. His correspondence is full of letters to his children. All of this and other domestic comforts he missed sadly when he was away. He wrote from Antigonish in June 1878,

I will be home on Thursday night unless I telegraph to the contrary. Then I hope I may rest until the call to arms. The call to your arms on Thursday night will be a more welcome sound even than that. With many kisses for you and the babies, I remain, Your own, JSDT.

He made it clear in this letter that he was ready to leave politics just as soon as Annie would allow him. All politics did for him was to make him tired, bilious, and homesick. He was run down with begging applications for jobs. He was appalled by these, a taste of worse to come. 'Naples is not a circumstance to this place for mendicancy and the worst of it is that the lazaroni here will be the masters in a few weeks more,' he wrote. He wanted a promise from Annie that the next election would be his last.[5]

The provincial general election was called for 17 September 1878, the same day as the federal one. It was arranged deliberately. The Hill government knew they were in trouble – Thompson's victory the previous December had been a symptom of that – but they believed that Alexander Mackenzie and the Liberals at Ottawa would certainly win the federal election, and that the closer they were to the federal Liberals' coattails, the better.

In Antigonish there were continuous rumours that someone would run against Thompson. C.B. Whidden was one possibility (he would be elected to the seat in 1882); Archibald A. McGillivray was another, encouraged by a small local coterie. The arrangement for Antigonish that suited Bishop Cameron was for Angus McGillivray, the Liberal, and Thompson, the Conservative, to run for the two seats of Antigonish County; but Archibald A. McGillivray had other ideas. Archibald A., the nephew of Big Archie McGillivray, was a curious character, brassy, greedy, untrustworthy, and quite unabashed about all of it. He resented arrangements made without his prior consent and wanted to push Thompson out. Finally, with ill grace, he consented to withdraw but only after Bishop Cameron told his uncle in plain language to get him to retire, if he (Archibald A.) valued the bishop's friendship. 'Now,' said Archie, 'I cannot act in opposition to the wish of my Bishop ... Although at the same time I deny the right he has to dictate who shall and who shall not be a candidate for Legislative honours.' That was not the end of it. Archie kept saying people did not want him to withdraw, that the bishop did not really like Angus McGillivray; finally a few telegrams held the squirming Archie down.[6] Thompson was in Antigonish in early September of 1878, trying to control it and rather enjoying some of it. He found the countryside attractive, a land, as he described it, 'flowing with rum and whiskey – cards and fiddles.'[7] Much of the whisky was homemade.

On nomination day there were no other candidates, so Thompson and Angus McGillivray were in by acclamation. Senator Miller had been right in 1877; one hard fight had done it.

For the Hill government the policy of riding on an expected Mackenzie federal victory was a disaster. Neither Hill nor many others had imagined a Mackenzie defeat. But of the twenty-one Nova Scotian seats in the Dominion House of Commons, the Conservatives under Sir John A. Macdonald swept in with fourteen seats, their best showing since confederation. At the provincial level it was an even more decided victory with thirty Conservatives elected for the thirty-eight seats in the Assembly. Hill and three others of his cabinet were personally defeated. The victories at both the federal and provincial level, to say nothing of their extent, came as a stunning surprise. Father Daly in Windsor wrote to Thompson,

I don't think that the most sanguine Conservative in his wildest dreams could have expected so complete a wiping out of both governments. I need not tell you how greatly I rejoice for *your sake personally* and I expect to see you Attorney General. I do think you ought [?] to insist on that – You know you might have been it long ago if you could have imitated Hill. He must feel badly ... How proud the poor Arch. would be, were he alive now.[8]

No doubt the archbishop would have been proud. But as to actually being attorney general, Thompson hesitated, worried about the responsibilities of the office and the effect on his law practice. The office carried a salary of only $1,600 a year, and his practice was just starting to become prosperous. Martin Griffin at the *Morning Herald* was appalled that Thompson might refuse the attorney generalship. It would be madness, Griffin said; Charles Townshend of Amherst wants to be attorney general, and wants you to be deputy minister. 'This,' said Griffin, 'will stir up the very devil in our party. Pray act with firmness and be the leader you really ought to be.' It was easy for Griffin to talk. He did not have to fight elections. An MLA taking salaried office under the crown had to be confirmed by his constituents in a by-election. So Thompson would have to have yet another election at Antigonish if he took the office of attorney general. His third in eleven months! Father Gerroir, the parish priest at Havre Boucher, told Thompson he ought to 'keep number one in view always, if you do not, rest assured that the generality of others will not.'[9] Keeping number one in view was something Thompson was not always capable of doing. He had no hard carapace to resist someone who had a genuine need. 'Draw on me at ten days sight,' is the reluctant refrain too frequent in his correspondence.[10] Annie complained of his not being able to say no, that he was too generous.

The Hill government resigned on 15 October 1878. That day Lieutenant-Governor Archibald asked Simon Holmes to form a government, and a letter from Holmes to Thompson asked that Thompson be present on Monday evening, 21 October, 'in order to give your assistance and advice in forming a Government.'[11] Thompson was sworn in as attorney general on 22 October 1878, the youngest member of cabinet.

His seat in the Assembly forthwith vacated, he had to go to Antigonish to face his third election. There was always to be a certain yeastiness among the village worthies at Antigonish at the prospect of an election. Thompson had got in by acclamation on 17 September, but why he should do it twice running? Archie A. had not given up, nor had others; but their friends and supporters failed to rally round; short shrift was given their overtures, and Thompson was in again by acclamation, confirmed as attorney general of the province.

In the face of the ignominious defeat of the government, Thompson, unlike most Conservatives, was disposed to mercy. The Conservatives were shouting, 'Vae victis!' There was reason for it. In the Post Office for years past correspondence from known Conservatives was never sure of reaching its destination; at some customs houses, Arichat and Sydney especially, goods for Conservatives never had the same luck with customs officials as goods for true Liberals.[12] Some provincial officials would have to be replaced. The Queen's Printer (at the *Acadian Recorder*) would have to change. The deputy provincial secretary, Herbert Crosskill, was an extreme and bitter partisan and would also have to go. But Crosskill refused to go simply on Holmes's curt say-so. Thompson was the one person in the new government whom Crosskill could ask to give him justice – a full year's salary as retiring allowance – and eventually his dismissal was concluded in the proper form.[13]

Premier Simon Holmes, the son of Senator John Holmes, was forty-seven years old, educated at Pictou Academy, and elected for the county in 1871. Among other things, he ran a weekly newspaper, the *Pictou Standard*; he was a country attorney who had had only a modest success at the bar of Pictou. The opinion of the New Glasgow *Eastern Chronicle* that Holmes was 'the stupidest man in public life' has to be discounted, perhaps heavily.[14] Still, his talent was limited and his charm negligible. In the House he was usefully truculent; politics had become for him a route to success, a route made necessary by his weakness as a lawyer. He had experience, but he was apt to be impatient, careless, and dictatorial. He was excessively casual in matters requiring the common action of his colleagues; he disliked cabinet meetings, preferring if possible to do things on his own.

The other important colleague of Thompson's in cabinet was Charles Townshend of Amherst, Thompson's rival for the post of attorney general. Townshend was an excellent lawyer and legal draftsman, but he was not effective in the House. He was a weak, stuttering speaker with little argumentative power, almost wholly without experience in deliberative assemblies.

Two members of cabinet were in the Legislative Council: Samuel Creelman, from Colchester County, the oldest and most experienced member of the cabinet and commissioner of mines and public works; and J.S. McDonald, of Wolfville, minister without portfolio. There were three other members of cabinet from the Assembly, all without portfolio: N.W. White of Shelburne, H.F. McDougall from Grand Narrows, Cape Breton, and W.B. Troop of Annapolis. In the seven-man cabinet, there were thus only three members with portfolio – Holmes, Creelman, and Thompson.

One of Thompson's first tasks as the leading member of the Holmes government was to go with Holmes to Ottawa in January 1879 to press for better terms within confederation. The problems facing the new cabinet were hard ones but the most urgent was money. The settlement of 1867 had been hard on Nova Scotia. Tupper's determination to push confederation through at all hazards meant that the terms were not negotiated with the rigour they might have been. Howe's better deal of 1869 – an extra $82,698 a year for ten years – was an attempt to redress the balance. This subsidy, and the larger debt allowance given to all the provinces in 1873, gave Nova Scotia some breathing room. The Annand and the Hill governments had used this money and mortgaged it into the future in order to build railways. But in 1878 the ten-year subsidy ran out, and the government of Sir John A. Macdonald was not going to prove so easy to deal with as it had in 1869. The Holmes government succeeded to an empty treasury and a large overdraft, in the face of declining local revenues and nothing to look to as a resource save the Dominion subsidy, now down to $370,000 per annum, of which $100,000 had already been spent by the previous government. To many Nova Scotians this was a strong case. But all the Macdonald government had to say was that Nova Scotia would have to live within her means. This it did say, in the bluntest possible fashion, a year and a half later.[15]

Thompson's position was curious. Whatever he thought of the financial settlement of 1867, he believed that since that time the Dominion had been generous. The Intercolonial Railway, the wharves, breakwaters, lighthouses that dotted the coastline, were evidence. Where would Nova Scotia be, he asked the Assembly in 1879, if she were out of confederation? The blame for Nova Scotia's present condition lay at the feet of the Hill government;

it was exceedingly difficult to-day to approach the Dominion government without having to confess with a candur [sic] that was inconvenient, that our position to-day was due to ourselves and to the government of this country during the past eleven years.[16]

In any case, economy at the provincial level was essential. One drastic way of cutting costs was to get the province out from its annual expenditure on local roads and bridges, which consumed 27 per cent of the provincial revenue. Taxing themselves for these local purposes was something Nova Scotians had been notoriously reluctant to do, and not a government of the province had so far had the hardihood to force them.

Other provinces had succeeded: the municipal legislation of Quebec was laid down in 1839–40, though admittedly when that province had no Assembly; Ontario's had been passed in 1849, New Brunswick's in 1877. In Nova Scotia municipalities had to be incorporated by special legislation: Halifax in 1841; Pictou, 1874; Truro and New Glasgow, 1875; Dartmouth, 1877; Windsor, 1878.

There were other reasons why county incorporation was desirable. The counties of Nova Scotia were administered by the quarter sessions, an ancient institution composed of the justices of the peace, and there was some incentive to deprive them of some of their power, for they were mostly Liberal appointees. The sole qualification for the position of justice of the peace, said a stern letter in the Halifax *Morning Herald*, was that of political services rendered. Any one, no matter how ignorant or characterless, could confidently rely on the appointment. Establishing municipal corporations, with a council elected by the county ratepayers, would end the life of an engine of unparalleled mischief.[17]

But outside of the odd letter such as the above, there seemed to be little or no public pressure for such legislation; the bill was the result of the courage, born of necessity perhaps, of the Holmes–Thompson government. It was possible that county incorporation would not have been introduced at all had the Macdonald government in Ottawa been willing to provide financial assistance. In the absence of that, there may have been no alternative.

J. Castell Hopkins has given Thompson the fatherhood of the County Incorporation Act.[18] But he did not draft it; Holmes quite sensibly gave this task to Charles Townshend. Townshend based the Nova Scotia bill mainly on the New Brunswick act of 1877, sending it to Holmes in mid-February 1879.[19] But Townshend was new, ineffective in the House, and ill for much of that session. Once the government decided to bring in county incorporation, the way it was handled, the firm recognition that it was a reform much needed, the way the government went on oblivious of the unpopularity of the measure at the grass roots – all these things suggested the resolution of Thompson. The magistracy of the province was a powerful political machine whose members did not like being deprived of perquisites and power by new-fangled institutions like elected county councils; Thompson went ahead anyway.

The legislature opened on 6 March 1879. The county incorporation bill was announced only obliquely in the speech from the throne. It was late in the session, on 4 April, that Premier Holmes introduced the bill; he liked to take a great deal into his own hands. The attorney general spoke briefly; Thompson said that no money for roads and bridges was going to be available from the province; whatever they were going to do in Antigonish or any other county, they would have to tax themselves for it. The province would give them the authority. The present government, Thompson said, had done what they had to do: tell the people of the province their true position, 'whether popular or unpopular you will have to face the melancholy fact that additional taxation stares you in the face, and you might as well know it now instead of our borrowing thousands and thousands of dollars, and concealing the fact from you for another year.'[20] John Pugh, sea captain, merchant, MLA for Halifax (and married to Annie's aunt), praised the government's courage. Every man in the Assembly, he said, owed the government a debt of gratitude for its moral force. Under an umbrella of impressive party support in the Assembly county incorporation passed second reading by a vote of twenty-nine to seven.[21]

Another method of effecting economies in government was to economize the Legislative Council out of existence. Simon Holmes estimated that would save $15,000 a year. On 19 March he proposed a resolution asking the Legislative Council to negotiate, with the Assembly, an end to its existence. The resolution passed the Assembly unanimously.[22] The Legislative Council was a body criticized by both parties. In theory there was a case for it; but its practice told against it. The Council was worse than useless – it was embarrassing.

In July 1878 there had been eleven Liberals and four Conservatives in the twenty-one member Legislative Council, with six seats vacant.[23] In August the Hill government appointed four new members, a fact kept secret until after the election. Thus the position of the Conservatives, with a majority of fifteen to four against them, was ridiculous. When the address in reply to the speech from the throne had to be moved and seconded, there were not enough Conservatives in the Legislative Council to do it. Two were ill, another, Creelman, was a minister, and the fourth man could not do it by himself. So there the address sat on the table, unmoved, with 'the Council sitting there,' as Thompson told the Assembly, 'like so many mummies, unable to despatch its ordinary business.'[24] The new government filled up the two vacancies left over and one new one with members pledged to support the abolition of the Legislative Council.

The Council declined to accept the Assembly's kind invitation to commit suicide. The Legislative Council committee, chaired of course by a member of the cabinet, reported favourably on the Assembly's bill for abolition; but that was not a feeling shared by the Council. On 15 April it cheerfully gave abolition the three-months' hoist, on a straight party vote of twelve to six.[25] Then the Council passed the County Incorporation Act.

The legislature prorogued on 17 April 1879, after one of the shortest and most productive recent sessions. The state of the province was not something the lieutenant-governor could congratulate the people on, but the legislature had done the best it could to clean up the mess it had found.

Thompson could now turn more actively to being the attorney general of Nova Scotia. By long-established custom an attorney general had the right, really the necessity, of continuing his private practice as a lawyer. It was never understood in the British North American provinces, before confederation or after, that being the crown's law officer compelled one to abandon one's main source of income. Should there be a conflict between the hat he wore as crown officer and the one he wore as a private lawyer, a scrupulous attorney general would be expected to adjust that.[26] The big question in the 1870s was not the right of an attorney general to his private practice, but the right of the Dominion minister of justice to *his*. Was he entitled to the same privilege? When Sir John A. Macdonald was minister of justice he was also prime minister, and had virtually given up private practice. But Edward Blake, Mackenzie's minister of justice, claimed the privilege of keeping his private practice, saying he could not be expected to give up a lucrative income to become merely minister of justice. The Toronto *Globe* supported him. So did the *Halifax Reporter*, assuming that Blake did not neglect public business in pursuit of private.[27]

Thompson solved his problem by taking on a partner, Wallace Graham. When Robert Weatherbe had gone to the bench in September 1878, he had left his partner Graham, an Antigonish Protestant, alone. So the firm of Thompson and Graham was established and a happy relationship it was. Graham was a little like Thompson, hot-tempered and sensitive, and had it less under control; but he was a thoroughly honest man, an able lawyer, and the firm he and Thompson founded soon developed into the most successful one in the Maritime provinces.[28]

Nova Scotia had had some notable attorney generals; Richard Uniacke held the office for thirty-three years until he died in 1830; J.W. Johnston had been attorney general for eleven years between 1841 and 1864. But the post-confederation attorneys general were not very distinguished. Some were notorious. Martin Wilkins, who held the office from 1867 to 1871, had been a good criminal lawyer, adroit, even unscrupulous. He preferred not to know whether his clients were guilty or not; he may have assumed most were. After one trial, where he had successfully got a coloured client acquitted of stealing a cow, Wilkins's curiosity got the better of him. 'Did you, in fact, steal the cow?' he asked. His client said, 'Befo' I heard you, Mistah Wilkins, I thought I did, but after I heard you I's sure I didn't!' But too often in his later years as attorney general, Wilkins presented the picture of an immense old man sitting in his office with a fly-swatter, saying that killing flies was more fun than fishing and a great deal more comfortable.[29]

After Wilkins, there were four attorneys general in the seven years left to the Annand–Hill regime. The *Halifax Reporter* suggested that the office of attorney general did not require practical knowledge of courts acquired from practice at the bar. Most of the criminal prosecutions had for years been turned over to senior QCs. The truth was that the stock of the office had declined sadly. When Alonzo White was appointed in January 1877, it was alleged that the office had been refused 'by nearly every decent lawyer on that side [Liberal] in the province.'[30]

At this low point in its history, Thompson brought to the office energy, probity, intelligence, and courtesy. It was a constellation sufficiently rare anywhere and unique in Nova Scotia. He also brought youth; he was the youngest attorney general in the history of the province.

The work of an attorney general was nowhere defined, the duties were unwritten, embedded in the common law traditions that had grown up in the English societies of North America. The attorney general of a province was the law officer of the crown. It was his duty to oversee the wording of statues and the law they contained, as well as to control the legal appropriateness of the government's administration. He was the official head of the administration of justice in the province, and as such had the duty of acting as prosecutor in criminal cases, and the duty of advising justices of the peace on legal questions.

At the local level, the magistrate – that ubiquitous justice of the peace – was, despite the 1874 creation of county courts, still the workhorse of the Nova Scotian legal system. In Halifax County, for example, there were ninety JPs who had been sworn in since 1848. They were a highly diverse lot. Four were gentlemen, so described. The rest were: twenty-four farmers, fifteen merchants, seven fish merchants, three auctioneers, one butcher, cooper, insurance broker, bootmaker, stipendiary magistrate, and some thirty-two assorted others.[31] Too many magistrates were ignorant of the law they administered. Senator Miller, of Richmond County, Cape Breton, alleged that there was not a single JP in St Peter's who could make out a search warrant to authorize the recovery of stolen goods.[32] Too many other magistrates were weak, producing in certain parts of Nova Scotia a system where the magistrates' ignorance was mitigated only by their pusillanimity. What did an attorney general do with a JP apparently afraid to convict, or to arrange prosecution? Some rocks were thrown through a shop window in Tangier, eastern Halifax County. The shop was owned by the magistrate. 'In common with all the rest here,' wrote an outraged local resident to Attorney General Thompson,

[the magistrate] is afraid to move. The effect of every venture of this kind that is done with impunity, is to lead to greater outrages and I think ... if he is in a position to prosecute, he should be called upon to do so, especially as his position of presiding magistrate here throws upon him a greater responsibility.[33]

Eastern Halifax County was rough country. Mathilda Thorp, of Beaver Harbour, complained to Thompson that a local fisherman, Henry Hawbolt, had abused her and her sister with bad language, and that he had broken a well-established custom, and probably the law,[34] by fishing on Sunday. She said the magistrate was so afraid of Hawbolt that he would not have him arrested. Thompson was sceptical of this, and wrote the magistrate to find out what the truth was. The magistrate's story is a wonderful illustration that there are two sides to everything. One Sunday a school of mackerel made their appearance in the cove where Hawbolt usually fished. Hawbolt and his wife quickly ran a net across the mouth of the cove to hold the fish until Monday. Sunday night some person cut the net and the mackerel got away. Almost certainly this person was Mathilda Thorp, perhaps with the help of her sister or her father. Whatever the facts about that, said the magistrate, it was true that on the Monday, as Hawbolt was returning home past Mathilda Thorp's house, she taunted him from the veranda, lifting up her dress and presenting for his edification her naked bottom, telling him he could kiss that, for all the good his wicked Sunday fishing was likely to do him.[35]

Another example of 'two sides to everything' comes from Antigonish County. The county council of Antigonish passed new jail regulations that the municipal clerk considered barbarous:

... it is provided that debtors as well as prisoners awaiting trial on criminal charges – if they [the debtors] be poor and friendless – are to be fed during the whole period of their confinement on 'a sufficient quantity of wheat bread or biscuit and a sufficient quantity of pure cold water daily.'

A prisoner could be supplied with food at his own expense or the expense of friends, 'if he have any.' Thus prisoners committed to Antigonish jail for petty offences were treated worse than criminals committed to the penitentiary. The Antigonish clerk hoped the government would abrogate such laws. Thompson agreed that such regulations should be changed, but the county council should change them. The council's defence is interesting. The warden of the county, T.M. King, agreed that the regulations would have to be amended, but explained why they were brought in in the first place:

Our [County] Council felt the need of some check being placed in the matter of jail expenditure. This institution had almost become a popular boarding house, and it was found difficult to get some of the inmates to leave. While the Council was in Session in May [1880], the jail contained a man in for neglecting to pay his taxes of $1.00. He remained three weeks at an expense of $6.00 to the County, and had to be turned out ... The regulations were moreover not at all new, but are a transcript of those already in force in the Municipality of Kings County.[36]

The question of imprisonment for debt was a vexed question. Provincial legislatures before confederation, and the Canadian Parliament afterward, wrestled with the problem of insolvency. There is a difficult line between insolvency owing to incompetence or bad luck, and insolvency owing to something like fraud. Imprisonment for debt existed at common law; Dickens's novels are full of it. In British North America, colonial legislatures began to place statutory impediments that had the effect of mitigating the common law rule, something Britain herself did in 1869. This did not end imprisonment for debt. In Nova Scotia it lasted well into the 1880s. There was evidence that it was used spitefully by creditors, sometimes urged on by greedy lawyers. One debtor, Francis Cunningham, writing to Thompson from the debtor's room of the Halifax county jail, thought it should be possible to protect poor debtors, or at least to make a creditor pay something 'for the fun of gratifying his spite.' Attorney General Thompson's bill for doing just what Cunningham asked was reported back in March 1882 by the Assembly committee, but not in time to pass before the end of the session.[37]

There were some problems that no attorney general this side of Heaven could solve. William Currie was a justice of the peace at Maitland, at the mouth of the Shubenacadie River. He wrote Thompson anxiously in September 1879. A young woman in Maitland was delivered of a bastard child, and she applied to Currie for an affidavit to swear out against the father:

This is the third child she has had ... It is not at all probable she knows who is the father ...

Can anything be done with the girl to stop the affair from being repeated[?] she will probably have one every year which the town will have to support as it is doing with the ones she has had ...

The last one before this she had about a year ago. She took [it] to the house of one of the overseers of the poor and threw it in the door and left and threatens to do the same with this one.

An answer to the above will greatly oblige.[38]

One would like to know Thompson's reply to that letter. It would have taxed the wisdom of Solomon. It is hard to know whom to feel the sorriest for – the girl, the magistrate, the taxpayers of Maitland, or the three children.

The attorney general had also the duty of prosecuting for the crown in Supreme Court trials – a task patently beyond the capacity of one man. It had become the custom for the attorney general to prosecute perhaps 10 per cent of the cases in just Halifax County, and some attorneys general did much less than that; the government paid a crown prosecutor to do the rest. It was said to be physically impossible for the attorney general to handle more than a quarter of the criminal business of Halifax County on behalf of the crown; yet Thompson proposed to do all of it if he could without sacrificing his own business.[39] In 1879, out of twenty-one indictments in Halifax County found by the grand jury for the November term, only one case was handled by a paid crown prosecutor, and that was because of a conflict of interest.[40]

When the attorney general could not attend the case – and outside of Halifax this was most of the time – long-standing custom decreed that his responsibility passed to the presiding Supreme Court judge to select the senior QC present in court as crown prosecutor. Were the Nova Scotian QCs chosen for their talents, the seniority rule would not have been so serious. But all too often 'the silk gown in this Province has been known to clothe the grossest ignorance of the law.'[41] The system also meant that no one knew what counsel would conduct the prosecution until the court actually opened.

This was not the case in a famous trial that Attorney General Thompson himself took on, to avoid the miscarriage of justice that might have resulted from the prevailing system. It was a case of murder in Annapolis County, where the evidence was circumstantial and required the utmost care. The story was this. On Wednesday, 1 September 1880, some farmers cutting hay near Milford, on the Clementsport–Liverpool road, noticed smoke rising from a place on some rough land two hundred yards away. They went to put the fire out and noticed a smell as of meat broiling. It came from a hollow in the rock, partly covered with stones, where had been crudely interred the half-charred body of a woman. The subsequent autopsy in Annapolis Royal revealed the body to be of a woman of about thirty-five years of age, six months pregnant, and still alive when she was burnt. She was eventually identified as Charlotte Hill, a pauper from North Range, a little settlement a few miles south of Digby.

The overseer of the poor for the district had indulged in a custom that had grown up there, of farming out the paupers of his district to the lowest bidder. A local farmer, Joseph Nick Thibault (or Tebo as his name was spelt locally) had successfully bid for the privilege and was duly given $300 per annum for boarding an undetermined number of paupers.[42] One of them was Charlotte Hill. Thibault lived with his wife and children at North Range. He was arrested on suspicion not long after the body was found; Charlotte Hill had been last seen in Thibault's presence but three hours later when he was next seen she was not with him. Probably none of this was sufficient to convict. But before the trial started, a man hunting partridge along the same Clementsport–Liverpool road, chased it into the woods and there found a basket containing Charlotte Hill's belongings, a basket last seen in Thibault's wagon.

The crown had four lawyers, including the attorney general; the defence had three. The defence did not try to establish an alibi for Thibault; probably they could not do so. Instead, they tried to show that the witnesses who saw Thibault before and after the disappearance of Charlotte Hill did not know him, that their evidence was unreliable, and that events proved Thibault's involvement only circumstantially.

Thompson's main concern was to marshall the evidence properly. He had his own theories about evidence, based mainly on the ideas of David Hume. How far he had developed them before the Thibault trial is uncertain; they were well articulated by 1883 when he gave his lectures on evidence at the new Dalhousie Law School. He accepted Hume's view that the belief in the existence of an object by a witness 'is neither more nor less than a certain degree of vivacity of the idea introduced by the object in the mind.' It varied enormously from witness to witness but it was the most central part of the whole judicial process.

He disliked reckless cross-examination of witnesses. It had to be done with great care. He used to say, with Jeremy Bentham, that cross-examination fairly and honestly conducted was of the greatest utility. If the witness had concocted a story, it could either be strengthened or broken down, depending upon the skill of cross-examination. A concocted story could not anticipate all questions. A good lawyer could soon discover whether the witness's memory was based upon perceived reality, or upon sources that have rubbed out part of that reality and painted a false one in its place.[43] One witness in this case, Addie Scott, was threatened with contempt of court by Judge Weatherbe for not answering questions. Thompson eschewed such tactics. He did not browbeat witnesses. He was marvellously patient with Addie Scott, coaxing testimony from her about Thibault's house, movements, wagons, horses.

As to Thibault's motive for murder, Thompson could suggest one, but he felt it would not be proper for a crown officer. It was an old common law rule that a man could not, really should not, testify in his own defence. This was to prevent confessions extorted under duress. Thompson as a scrupulous crown prosecutor would not want to sway the jury by alleging motives that could not be proved. He concentrated on the claim of the defence that circumstantial evidence proved nothing. There was not, he said, a single piece of direct evidence that contradicted the circumstantial. The wagon and the horse observed on the road were Thibault's; the driver was Thibault; the basket found had last been seen in Thibault's house. While all this did not mean that Thibault committed the murder, none of it contradicted the assumption that he did. Circumstantial evidence, he continued, could be very strong. Thompson never liked the metaphor of a *chain* of evidence; that suggested something that broke at its weakest link. Evidence was not in his view put together that way; it was like the braids or strands of a rope, weak evidence being interwined with the strong. Thus, strand by strand, Thompson braided together the evidence around Thibault. He succeeded in proving that Thibault had left home with Charlotte Hill about midnight on 31 August, had taken a wagon and horses and driven all through the night, and shortly after dawn, had stopped for breakfast and to feed the horses, after which Charlotte Hill was never seen alive again.[44]

The defence argued that the manner of her death was absurd; no sensible man would commit a crime in so stupid a way. 'Why, in the name of Heaven,' said Motton, attorney for the defence, 'did he start out at night, drive for miles and miles on a public road, continue by daylight with his victim, then murder her?' Why not drop her quietly into a lake at night, conveniently near home, and where the crime would lie hidden for ever? As to motive, that was absurd too; a man does not murder a woman simply because she has become inconveniently pregnant. There were easier ways to solve that kind of problem; 'Fifty or sixty dollars would have made it all right, without resorting to such a horrible crime.'[45]

Thompson's answer on the issue of motive was simple. 'Men are never wise,' he said, 'when they resort to crime. Innocence is the only wisdom.' The defence spoke of charity to Thibault: but where, said Thompson, was charity to the friendless and defenceless Charlotte Hill? The jury found Thompson's argument overwhelming. They were out only an hour and brought in a verdict of guilty.[46]

The attorney general's conduct of this trial was widely praised. He impressed witnesses and public alike with his sense 'of judicial fairness and professional courtesy ... His argument was a model of lucid statement [and] effective massing of evidence.'[47] Thompson was in fact approaching his full powers as a lawyer. Even under stress and excitement he appeared cool and unruffled. J.T. Bulmer told Thompson once that Thompson's apparent sang froid astonished him; he knew he was a man of strong passions and acute sensibilities. Thompson explained that in legal argument 'the least excitement disturbs the measuring power of one's judgement.' He did not claim to be able to dispense with emotion; what he meant was that 'it must be crushed and subdued by the will until it left a lawyer's head as cool and steady as a surgeon's hand.' In this spirit he did much of his legal work. Given his mastery of his material and his lucid mind, he became nearly invincible in court. J.T. Bulmer said he was too powerful:

He carried the court with him far too often, and when a lawyer was making the best presentation possible of his case, there was a certain suspense about the Court, which seemed to say, 'We would admit these common sense propositions at once if it were not that Mr. Thompson is coming after you,' as though Mr. Thompson might disturb the very foundation of this pillered [sic] universe.[48]

The trial at Annapolis concluded on 7 December 1880. Thompson got back to Halifax in time for the birth of a son who was either born dead or who died the same day. Annie was dangerously ill; rumour was that she was not expected to live.[49] The pregnancies of Annie were desperately frequent in these years. After Mary Helena was born in March 1878, Annie had four further pregnancies brought to term in the next five years. Only one of these later children lived, Frances Alice, born in December 1881. In 1883 Annie was only thirty-eight years old, but the effect of nine pregnancies showed in her face and figure. After 1883 there were no more. She and Thompson now had five children living.

Amid Thompson's pressing family responsibilities were those of the government, nearly as pressing. While he was conducting the trial at

Annapolis Royal, Premier Simon Holmes called a cabinet meeting, wanting yet another delegation to Ottawa on his railway projects. It was a meeting that left the cabinet angry and bewildered. C.J. Townshend thought of resigning, and told Thompson the only reason he stayed on was because Thompson was. What was Holmes doing, asked Townshend, with his eternal railways, a preoccupation so overwhelming that it precluded all else? Why did Holmes want 'to shove us all up into a corner leaving everything unsettled?' James McDonald of Wolfville had much the same question. Could Simon Holmes, who could not keep the confidence of his colleagues, keep for long the confidence of the province?[50]

Thompson hated intrigue. He wished people did not always look to him to sort Holmes out. He had his own unease; he felt he was being undermined in Antigonish County by Holmes, his next-door neighbour in Pictou.[51] Nevertheless, he would prefer to let others do the intriguing, and let him get on with his job as attorney general.

Thompson's bent was to understand and to try to make others understand. He did not have Doug Woodworth's penchant for poetry nor his savage humour. He had little taste for the personalities indulged in by Simon Holmes. Nor was he an orator; he eschewed the rotund periods affected by some legislators. Thompson aimed at simplicity and clarity. He had a style that suited both – clear, direct, masculine, forceful, occasionally epigrammatic. Argument and epigram were the springs of Thompson's speeches in the Assembly. 'We have too much law in this country,' said an MLA in exasperation. 'That,' said Attorney General Thompson, 'was a statement which one would rather expect to hear in the Penitentiary rather than in the Legislature.'[52]

The problem that now faced Thompson as the new year, 1881, began was the government of which he had become, with no deliberate intention on his part, the principal strength. Could he prevent the Holmes government from coming apart? Did he even want to?

8

The Fall of the Holmes–Thompson
Government

In January 1881 the Holmes government was two and a half years old. Its accomplishments had not been many. It had been cleaning up problems it had inherited and trying to keep the province financially afloat. It passed the County Incorporation Act, legislation much needed but which won few friends and many enemies. The government had struggled to cut its coat according to the cloth available, but its ruthless economy and its determination to manage the affairs of the province with that consideration in mind gave it little opportunity to endear itself to the public. The premier's abiding passion was railways, their consolidation and organization. Thompson, who always had a partiality for enterprises that tidied up and systematized hitherto ramshackle practices, went along with it. Thompson's immediate preoccupation in January 1881, while the premier was in Ottawa with his railway negotiations, was another inheritance from the Hill regime, the University of Halifax.

The University of Halifax was a well-meaning attempt of the Hill government to mitigate the rivalries and raise the standards of Nova Scotia's six little colleges: King's (Anglican) at Windsor; Acadia (Baptist) at Wolfville; St Francis Xavier (Scotch Roman Catholic) at Antigonish; St Mary's (Irish Roman Catholic) at Halifax; Dalhousie (partly Presbyterian) at Halifax; and Mount Allison (Methodist) at Sackville, six miles inside New Brunswick. The Hill government was influenced by the idea of the University of London, an examining and teaching university set up in 1828; the act of 1876 that established the University of Halifax was hopeful, even idealistic: 'Whereas, it is desirable to establish one University for the whole of Nova Scotia, on the model of the University of London, for the purpose of raising the standard of higher education in the Province ...'[1] The act continued grants to existing colleges, intending that the colleges would use the new provincial university as an examining institution to test, indeed raise, their own standards. But the Hill government was not strong enough, or too wise as D.C. Harvey said,[2] to put real teeth in the act; real teeth meant continuing the grants on condition that the colleges surrender their degree-granting powers. The University of Halifax was left to earn its own standing in the Nova Scotian academic community. It was not easy.

Thompson was familiar with the university. He had been appointed to the embryonic law faculty as examiner in equity and real property in January 1878. The Catholic colleges of St Mary's and St Francis Xavier had not taken much interest in the University of Halifax, neither its inception nor its development. This indifference was not confined to the Catholic colleges. In 1879 the University of Halifax examined some fifty-seven candidates in arts, sciences, law, and medicine. Some seventeen could not pass. In 1880 only twenty applied for the examinations. The university had been set to run until 31 December 1880, when its role would be reconsidered. The colleges also had a deadline; the grants of 1876 would expire at the same time.

There was a good deal of ferment. The Halifax *Herald* and the *Chronicle* published a series of articles on the university question in the autumn of 1880. The colleges were hoping to continue as before. Dalhousie wanted to become the provincial university, to stand in for the moribund University of Halifax. But Dalhousie still had such a strong Presbyterian flavour that the other colleges would not have it at any price as the provincial university.

The position of the Catholics was difficult because Archbishop Hannan of Halifax was by now a broken reed. The administration of his archdiocese had been so much criticized he had had to go to Rome in mid-January 1881. The responsibility for upholding Roman Catholic interests in the university question fell mainly on the shoulders of Bishop Cameron, upon Father Ronald Macdonald, parish priest of Pictou (whom Holmes consulted frequently upon Catholic matters), and upon Thompson, the real mover in the 1881 solution of the college question.[3] There was some danger in Thompson taking a lead, as Bishop Cameron was shrewd enough to recognize. Too much power wielded too obviously by the attorney general might raise the cry of 'papal aggression,' a cry that had so devastated England in 1850.[4] So Thompson was cautious about speaking too much, even in caucus.

Thompson's, and the government's, purpose in the colleges bill was to recognize the inevitable: abandon the University of Halifax, keep the old colleges intact, but use the opportunity to upgrade standards and impose a system of inspection upon the colleges by the superintendent of education as a condition of the government grant. The grant was $1,400 to each college.

In 1881 the Assembly met late, on 3 March, after increasing restiveness in cabinet and caucus owing to Holmes's long absence in Ottawa. Thompson did not himself introduce the colleges bill; he followed the advice of Bishop Cameron, and Holmes did it. The bill got overwhelming approval from the Assembly, by a vote of thirty to one, on 23 March. Not all of this huge majority represented genuine conviction; some Conservatives voted for the bill because they trusted Thompson and wanted to sustain his policies.[5]

In the Legislative Council it was another story. The Anglicans were unhappy: King's College *inspected* by the superintendent of education! The Presbyterians felt Dalhousie was being penalized financially. Behind these motives, there was a genuine desire on the part of some of the 'old fogies' – Bishop Cameron's words – in the Legislative Council to see Nova Scotia's experiment with one university survive, and who were opposed to the government's return to the denominational colleges. James Fraser of Pictou County, a Conservative, seconded a motion in the Legislative Council on 9 April 1881 for the three months' hoist. He cited New Brunswick, which then gave no grants to denominational colleges; nor did Prince Edward Island, nor Ontario. Why should Nova Scotia recommence a practice that had usefully stopped when the grants had run out on 31 December 1880? The way was now clear for a 'central, undenominational teaching university.' Instead of that, the government had bowed to denominational pressures and offered the six colleges $1,400 each.[6] The motion for the three months' hoist took Samuel Creelman, leader of the Legislative Council, by surprise. His desperate attempt to adjourn the debate failed by three votes. The motion for the three months' hoist passed by ten votes to nine, and the colleges bill was in ruins.[7]

This had two effects. It stopped renewal of the college grants and not just for 1881. They were not to be revived for seventy years. The little colleges would learn to live without government money. Their consolation was that they would also live without government inspection. The other effect was that the University of Halifax was still alive. The Assembly then passed a further bill, which the Legislative Council accepted, that prevented the University of Halifax from getting any further funds. Thus though the University of Halifax was not officially dead, it was buried anyway.

The Legislative Council also rejected the Assembly's bridge bill, a means to equalize bridge expenditures made by counties prior to 1879. The bill had passed the Assembly without a division, but it got short shrift from the Council. 'Confound their impudence!' said Councillor T.F. Morrison moving the three months' hoist. So that bill was destroyed too, by a majority of eleven to seven.[8]

With thirty of the thirty-eight seats in the Assembly the government had a strong majority. It was further strengthened through most of the sessions of 1880, 1881, and 1882 by half the Liberals. Holmes and Thompson made a point in 1882 of thanking the Assembly for this bipartisan support.[9] This increased the temptation for the Liberals to use its majority in the Legislative Council to defeat legislation they were powerless to fight in the Assembly.

The Assembly was bitter over the defeat of the colleges bill and the bridge bill, which it had passed with the support of both parties. Thompson felt, with L.S. Ford and others, that the members of the Legislative Council were puppets; men outside the legislature pulled the wires. Through the whole four years of the Holmes–Thompson government, the Legislative Council sabotaged whatever it could. No other Nova Scotian government before or after, down to 1928 when the Council was finally abolished, was as harassed as the Conservative regime of Holmes and Thompson between 1878 and 1882. 'I cannot get over the defeat of these Bills,' L.S. Ford wrote Thompson later that summer. 'So far as I can see we may as well or better stay at home, unless we can in some way control the Council.'[10]

Thompson was the only portfolio minister living in Halifax. In December 1879 a Dartmouth resident was added to the Holmes cabinet – J.F. Stairs, a young thirty-two-year-old industrialist – but he was without portfolio. Of the other executive councillors without portfolio, J.S. McDonald seemed to spend his time in Wolfville, Townshend in Amherst, H.F. McDougall at Grand Narrows in Cape Breton, Troop in Annapolis. This was understandable; they had no salaries and could not be expected to spend time gratuitously in Halifax.[11] Now and then they were called for cabinet meetings, but Holmes increasingly developed an antipathy to having meetings. He preferred to solicit opinions of his colleagues individually, and by mail, a practice Townshend in particular objected to. It was difficult for the 'country members' of the cabinet to find out what was going on, especially since Holmes was careless about replying to letters. Holmes himself spent much time at home in Pictou; inevitably the burden of being the senior member of the government resident in the capital fell upon Thompson.

He worked very hard. He was meticulous at answering letters, in clearing up difficulties. C.A. Smith of Chester thanked him for the 'remarkably lucid manner in which you explain "ways that are dark" to the unprofessionals like myself and the plain satisfactory straightforward answers to letters.' J.S. McDonald of Wolfville prized Thompson's letters as an indication that at least one member of the government was alive.[12] Conservative MLAS and ordinary JPS solicited his opinions on legal questions. L.S. Ford, the MLA for Queens, wrote to ask Thompson's opinion in a complicated case that he believed Thompson could settle promptly.[13] Everyone remarked on Thompson's diligence, clarity, courtesy. But he was overwhelmed with business. Charles Hibbert Tupper, practising law in Halifax a stone's throw away from Thompson's office in Province House, was not able even to get to see Thompson in February 1881. This despite the fact that Thompson was in town, and the House was not in session. Young Tupper had to put his question in a letter.[14] Bishop Cameron wondered why Thompson was unhappy about the state of Catholicism in Halifax, but he did not have the heart to ask such a busy man to elucidate the problem.[15]

Thompson did not mind the hard work; but he was increasingly depressed about political life, which was becoming for him as alien and unrewarding as it was narrow and provincial. There was too little intellectual challenge, and the other political challenges were, for the most part, the kind he scorned. He hated elections; he got little joy from the hustings or from his grass roots contacts in Antigonish. There were too many there like Archibald A. McGillivray. McGillivray had the gall to ask Thompson for $1,000: as Antigonish county treasurer Archie A. had got into trouble and was arrested on malfeasance charges. Thompson loaned him the money. McGillivray then beseeched Thompson to get him out on bail.[16] One has the impression that Thompson disliked going to Antigonish, that his pleasure there came from parish priests, and that this was the compensation for the sordid realities his constituents had in mind whenever their MLA was in town.

Little enough of this appeared on the surface. Perhaps in the long run highly emotional men learn to present a stoic mask to the world. They bruise easily but it is better not to let the bruises show. Cameron would try to buck Thompson up. Don't allow yourself to be depressed, he wrote in March 1881, 'Sursum corda ... remember that He loves the *cheerful giver*. After we have done our best, we are to remember that we are still "unprofitable servants" ... and spurn all feeling of sadness.'[17] Let no one say that Catholicism at its best does not have a strong and healthy asceticism! But by the summer of 1881 Thompson had gradually become aware that politics was not for him. He had little taste for intrigue or the delights of factional infighting. His law practice was growing; he had been made QC in 1879 and his partnership with Wallace Graham was rewarding and agreeable. He might become well off if he kept out of politics and gave his practice a chance.

There was another possibility. Sir Charles Tupper had hinted that there might be in the future a place for Thompson on the Supreme Court of Nova Scotia. At thirty-six Thompson was young for that, but it offered an honourable profession, and a modest but decent salary; he would have time to study, a chance to be a legal scholar, what every good judge ought to be.

In 1881 the Supreme Court of Nova Scotia needed change. Its docket was badly in arrears – in April 1881 there were nearly twenty important cases that awaited decision, all of them involving large amounts of money. The average number of cases, large and small, that could be argued per term was about eighty; at the opening of the Court in December 1881 there were altogether some two hundred cases waiting to be tried. The chief justice of Nova Scotia, Sir William Young, was eighty-two years old. Early in April 1881, he sent for James MacDonald, MP for Pictou and Sir John A. Macdonald's minister of justice, to tell him that illness forced him to give up.[18]

James MacDonald was no political lion. Sir Hector Langevin believed that he was an utter failure in federal politics.[19] The Dominion government now had the opportunity to unload him, one that they could not pass over; he was therefore appointed chief justice of the Supreme Court of Nova Scotia in May 1881. He was to remain there for twenty-three years.

There were two other judges on the Supreme Court bench in Halifax whose tenure was also uncertain: W.F. DesBarres, now eight-one years old, and the able J.W. Ritchie, the elder brother of W.J. Ritchie of the Supreme Court of Canada, seventy-three years old, but not well. Every Halifax lawyer worth anything had his eye on those two places. As soon as rumours got out that someone was ill the letters would start. There was a Halifax conversation about a judge, old and not too well liked:

FIRST LAWYER: 'I hear Judge Smith is ill.'
SECOND LAWYER: 'Nothing trifling, I hope?'

Even at the provincial level of prothonotary the rumour mill worked hard. Martin Wilkins had been appointed prothonotary and court clerk for Halifax County in 1871. In 1881 he was old and unwell. Rumours were rife in July 1881 that Wilkins was dying and private canvassing began. George Johnson, Thompson's old friend from the *Halifax Reporter*, wrote cheerfully on 16 August 1881 that Wilkins was really dead, and would Thompson please include George Johnson in the candidates? Johnson had an offer to go to the Toronto *Mail*, but would prefer to stay in Nova Scotia.[20] It was rumoured that Premier Holmes himself wanted that comfortable berth of prothonotary. Since it was Holmes's appointment to make, giving it to himself would not be a serious problem.

One obvious person for Thompson to see about the Nova Scotia Supreme Court was Sir Charles Tupper. Another was the senior Roman Catholic member of Sir John A. Macdonald's cabinet, Sir Hector Langevin. Bishop Cameron, never one for half-measures, volunteered to go to Ottawa; he did not like, as he said, 'dead-messenger's letters – when a *real* difficulty is to be overcome.'[21] He was as good as his word. He went to Ottawa in October 1881, travelling from Montreal in the train with Sir Charles Tupper, by accident or design. Amiable on other topics, Tupper was snappish about the judgeship of the Supreme Court of Nova Scotia. The bishop wisely let well alone for the moment and in Ottawa called upon Sir Hector Langevin.

Langevin knew of Archbishop Hannan's antipathy to Thompson. Cameron countered by saying that the archbishop had always been a Grit and was angry with Thompson for the Mount St Vincent affair. The pope himself, said Cameron, proved Thompson right, having taken the Sisters of Charity away from Hannan. Langevin urged Cameron to see Sir Charles Tupper. Yes, said the bishop, that will be done; but Thompson's being a Catholic might be used against him, even though the Catholics, with nearly one-third of the population of Nova Scotia, had only one Catholic judge out of the fifteen Supreme Court and county court judges. At this Sir Hector sprang from his chair and exclaimed, 'I will *never* put up with such injustice: his being a Catholic ought to militate in his favour in the circumstances instead of against him.' Then the bishop tackled Tupper. Tupper reluctantly admitted Thompson's qualifications, indeed, that his youth was an advantage, that Thompson's promotion to the Supreme Court was only a question of time; but Thompson was the ablest man in the Conservative government of Nova Scotia and should not so soon be lost to the party. On that note they parted. The bishop remarked, 'We parted on good terms, although possibly not pleased with each other.' The bishop wanted Tupper to go further than he had done; Tupper was disconcerted at having gone further than he wished.[22] Thompson was going to Ottawa later in October for the fall sitting of the Supreme Court of Canada, where he would argue his first cases before that court. He would certainly see Tupper. Bishop Cameron warned that Tupper would try his utmost to get Thompson to waive any claim to the Supreme Court.

Thompson's October visit to Ottawa brings him into light again as a human being. He wrote Annie at length, as she did him. Thursday, 20 October was the Thanksgiving holiday, and Thompson walked around the Parliament buildings, feeling lonesome and cross with himself for not having forced Annie to come with him. 'I suppose if I had given you a good whipping at the outset you would not have refused so obstinately, but you know I never had the heart to do that.'[23] It was a family joke, those beatings. Annie was seven months pregnant – Frances Alice (Frankie) was born on 17 December – and train travel was hardly to be recommended, much less urged, even by as uxorious a husband as Thompson. Looking around Ottawa, Thompson decided that a minister's life there was not for him. 'Please make note of it – I would not live it for $15,000 a year – so that is settled. I can practise law and support the house at that but I *will* have a home whether I make much or little.'[24]

Annie was concerned about Thompson taking the Nova Scotia Supreme Court judgeship. She wanted him to have the recognition that was his due, and if Tupper promised something, even tentatively, then her clever husband ought to have it; still, 'going on the shelf,' as she put it, at the age of thirty-six did not sit well with her. 'I would dearly like to see you a minister with a big house plenty of servants and the best table that money could set for a while and then settle down afterward.' Thompson saw in the role of federal minister only the loneliness and the awful distance from Halifax; Annie saw the career he deserved.[25]

The autumn term of the Supreme Court of Canada opened on Tuesday, 25 October. The Supreme Court was then on Parliament Hill, just west of the West Block. The court was handsome, the room so carpeted that not a footstep was heard. It was impressive: the six judges in scarlet and ermine, the sheriff with cocked hat and sword, enough solemnity to make Thompson nervous. Well he might be: his was the first case on the docket. It was difficult arguing before a strange court where the idiosyncrasies of the judges were unknown. The judges were first rate, he said, and arguing before them was difficult; they were quick, positive, and when they were against you it was hard going. After three days of the most trying labour Thompson believed his success at best indifferent. 'I kept them at bay for two whole days over two of Fairbanks' cases, which will probably be sent back for new trials, a good result in one case, bad in the other.' Thompson had one success, though he may not have known it yet, in *Ross* v. *Hunter*, a property case. Thompson's client, Ross, had lost in the Supreme Court of Nova Scotia, but he won at Ottawa, in a five to one decision.[26]

Annie recognized the symptoms. 'My poor child, I almost think you have a fit of the blues the way you write. Now pet don't get dull and you can be just as stiff as they are stout ... I am only sending you these few lines to bully you into not losing heart.'[27] She always did bully him into not losing heart. He was a tender soul; Annie was a woman of moral strength, resolute and courageous; she was a creature of blood and earth, ready to dare anything for her husband. Between Annie in this world and God in the next, Thompson had found his certainties.

Before leaving Ottawa Thompson had two long interviews with Tupper about the judgeship. Tupper wanted Thompson to help carry the Nova Scotia government through the next provincial election; but in asking that, he agreed that Thompson would have J.W. Ritchie's place on the Nova Scotia Supreme Court when Ritchie resigned. Should Ritchie resign before the election, Thompson would still have the place. Thompson and Graham would also have the agency of the Ministry of Justice in Halifax – that is, represent the ministry in cases arising that required crown action. In return, Thompson and Graham would take into their firm young C.H. Tupper.[28] So was born in 1881 the firm of Thompson, Graham and Tupper.

The session of 1882 came early, its main legislation a long thirty-two-page Act for the Consolidation of Nova Scotia Railways. It was Premier Holmes's *chef d'oeuvre*, that had preoccupied him to the exclusion of nearly everything else. Thompson had been so busy as attorney general that he had been at best Holmes's legal adviser in Halifax and Ottawa. Thompson's interest in railways had mainly been the attempt to straighten out the problems in Eastern Extension. That railway was built and running to the Strait of Canso by the end of 1880, under a private company, owned mostly in Montreal by Sir Hugh Allan and the two Abbotts, Harry and J.J.C. It was heavily in debt to the government of Nova Scotia. Cape Breton was still in 1882 without a railway.

The railway westward from Halifax through the Annapolis valley to Yarmouth was a mess. Over its 250-mile length, the line was in four sections, each with its own peculiar history and problems. Holmes wanted the western railway completed. So did everyone else. There were two ways it could be done. One was for the government to take over all four sections, buy out existing lines, and operate the whole as a government railway. The government was far from being able to afford that. The best it could do was to provide incentives and, with the help of a politically friendly but none too eager Dominion government, get the railways completed and operating under one private company. The company came to be called the Nova Scotia Railway – whose principals were mainly associated with the Western Counties Railway, Yarmouth to Digby, and who wished to rescue their investment by making it into the whole western line. It was by no means a bad idea though the obstacles were formidable. The prospects for traffic – and therefore profits – were not large; effective results depended upon financial considerations, and there was an infinitude of negotiations between the company and government to work these out.[29]

Thus the government's railway consolidation policy looked better at a distance than when closely examined. With the non-railway counties demanding railways of their own, Holmes concluded that the only way to survive was to effect a complete rationalization of all Nova Scotia railways; to knit those already built with new lines that had prospect of success. But Nova Scotia had no money to effect this, and the Dominion government anything but enthusiastic over loaning a nickel. From 1879 to 1882 there were delegations to Ottawa at least every year. Holmes took Thompson with him in January 1879, went alone again Ottawa in February 1880, and in January–February 1881. He was there with Thompson in October 1881. All these visits he devoted to railway business. There is more than a little suspicion that Sir Charles Tupper, federal MP for Cumberland and minister of railways, and Sir John A. Macdonald did not exactly jump with joy when they saw Simon Holmes coming down the corridor with his papers.

His cabinet colleagues in Halifax were also fed up with him. Holmes took so much into his own hands that his colleagues became restive and resentful. Charles Townshend of Amherst summed it up in a bitter letter to Thompson, in January 1881. Holmes is off to Ottawa again, they say:

Now I am quite willing personally that he should go as often as he chooses & I only regret that I was foolish enough to go with him last winter ... What is coming of all these delegations ... & how is it that he is undertaking this without the advice of his Council – Apparently he is taking the whole affair into his own hands & we are to be held accountable for his acts[.] Now I have not, and never had, and if I understand you, you have no confidence in his success in this mad Railway business that he is continually driving at ... There is a growing feeling of dissatisfaction on all sides – I confess to a great deal myself, and to a great unwillingness to remain in the Govt. Indeed I may say conscientiously that for the past year I have stayed more owing to the fact of your being there than anything else – I think you must agree with me that the time has come when other Members of the Govt. ought to interfere & try and redeem ourselves from the obloquy which is everywhere being thrown upon us –[30]

There were suggestions from Townshend and McDonald that Thompson take the lead in bringing Holmes to heel. Bishop Cameron thought it would take Thompson's threat to resign to do it.[31] The government hung together through 1881. Though Thompson had a number of reservations on the proposed contract, the agreement was signed by Creelman on behalf of the government, and E.W. Plunkett of the Nova Scotia Railway Company in September 1881.[32]

The Act for the Consolidation of Nova Scotia Railways was introduced for second reading by Premier Holmes on 25 January 1882. It was a comprehensive piece of legislation and Holmes gave it a long two-day speech, reviewing the history of Nova Scotia's railways from the beginning. The idea behind the Nova Scotia Railway of 1882 was not unlike that of the 1880 Canadian Pacific Railway Company. The CPR gathered up government-built sections of the Pacific railway, agreed to finish the sections in between, and run the railway afterward. It was to be the same with the Nova Scotia Railway. Nova Scotia had acquired certain financial and legal claims over nearly all the existing railways in the province. These rights and claims it would turn over to the Nova Scotia Railway Company on certain terms. As Thompson put it, its great object was 'to sell all rights of, & concessions to the Govt. for a bonus which wd. pay off the debt of our predecessors and give a fund to assist the non-railroad districts, complete the Trunk Line to the extremities of the Prce.'[33]

The scheme was simple in principle, complex in detail. The company was to be incorporated in England and Nova Scotia with a minimum of $10 million capital. It would take over, complete, and operate, the existing railways: the Windsor and Annapolis, the Western Counties, the Halifax and Cape Breton, the Nictaux and Atlantic. It would build three new ones, notably the eighty-mile line from the Strait of Canso to Sydney and Louisburg. It would get running rights over the Intercolonial in order to connect the eastern railways with the western ones. In all it would own and operate 465 miles of Nova Scotian railways.

The Nova Scotia Railway Act caused MLAs difficulty. They took a good deal on faith. One Liberal said he had sat up for two nights and still could not understand the bill, notwithstanding the premier's two days of explanations. Thompson as back-up man came to the rescue; it was rather his role. Dr D.J. Campbell of Inverness congratulated Holmes on having on his left a man who was 'always willing and able to come to his assistance.'[34] Thompson's main argument was that the railway consolidation was essential for Nova Scotian economic growth. Three or four MLAS fought the bill hard, but amendments were voted down by large majorities that included at least one or two Liberals. The bill passed second reading by thirty-two votes to five on 3 February 1882. W.S. Fielding, then editor of the Liberal Morning Chronicle, told Edward Blake that they were having a hard fight in Nova Scotia against the railway scheme. 'We are helpless in the Lower House,' he said, 'but hope to defeat the measure in the [Legislative] Council.' There indeed were attempts to hoist it there, but with minor amendments it squeaked through, by eleven to nine.[35] The legislature was prorogued on 4 March and Holmes was off to Ottawa again. The new act required enabling Dominion legislation.

Behind Holmes's back revolt brewed in caucus and cabinet. He was not a good administrator. He left important papers where they should not be. At prorogation he forgot to arrange for the governor's speech. The governor wanted something laudatory to say about the government's four years of legislation. Holmes passed the job over to Thompson. 'I would draft out something myself without troubling you,' Holmes wrote Thompson, 'but I don't feel exactly in the humour.' That had been thirty-six hours before prorogation was to take place.[36]

Thompson had no ambition to replace Holmes or head a conspiracy against him. He wanted out of politics. No doubt he hoped, as Tupper did, that Justice Ritchie would hang on a little longer. But Ritchie was not well, increasing the backlog in the Supreme Court docket. It was now so serious that special arrangements had to be made that spring session to allow the Court to run double shifts. In April 1882 Ritchie had a slight stroke and decided to resign at once. That was very inconvenient. Sir John A. Macdonald pleaded with him to stay, that even at 75 per cent of capacity Ritchie still did the work of two other judges. Ritchie insisted.[37] Meanwhile Liberal papers were associating Thompson's name with the impending vacancy, much to his embarrassment. The Acadian Recorder satirized him, out of Gilbert and Sullivan's Patience, then playing in Halifax:

> A bright, round and rosy M.P.
> A smiling, bland, legal M.P.
> A demi-poetical, semi-aesthetical
> Going to be a Judge, M.P.[38]

Bishop Cameron, to whom Thompson confided his troubles, saw little alternative but for Thompson to take the government over, not only for the good of the party, but to protect the country against possible encroachment of a powerful company, beyond the existing agreement, on the public treasury.[39] Cameron's sentiments were echoed by a party committee who visited Holmes and urged him to resign to permit reconstruction of the government. Holmes would have none of it.[40] The Holmes government drifted onward, down the river; one could already hear the sounds of electoral rapids in the distance. 'Does any one know where the Premier is or what he is doing?' asked McDonald of Wolfville on 17 April. 'I trust to hear of "Simon" very soon, either dead or alive.' Simon was in Ottawa still; someone saw him there, reported the unfriendly *Acadian Recorder*, 'wandering about alone, apparently without notice and entirely without purpose.'[41]

Thompson was making preparations to resign. It was agreed that when Thompson went to the bench Charles Townshend would be the new attorney general. His resignation was in Holmes's hands by early May. Thompson did not want to take the party through the provincial elections; the hypocrisy of going to elections with the intention of abandoning political life immediately afterward went against the grain. He told Tupper so: 'To say nothing of the waste of labor, the want of honor, in procuring an election to a seat which one does not intend to fill, I should be asked on the hustings to declare my intentions.'[42]

The next two weeks changed this plan. On Friday, 12 May there was a Conservative caucus in Halifax; mounting rumours of mutiny against Holmes circulated in Liberal papers.[43] There was talk of Holmes resigning, Thompson going to the bench, and the Conservative party being led by A.C. Bell of Pictou. None of this helped the morale of the party. While the Liberals had nominated many of their candidates for the provincial election, the Conservatives in most counties were sufficiently demoralized that it was difficult to get nominating conventions together.

In the midst of this, dissolution of the House of Commons in Ottawa was announced, with election day set for 20 June. It was at this point that overwhelming pressure was put on Thompson to stay. Tupper could represent that by Thompson taking the leadership, calling the Nova Scotia election for the same day as the federal, he could save the Nova Scotian government and still have the judgeship.[44]

Thompson did stay on and Holmes resigned. On 23 May Holmes was appointed (or appointed himself) prothonotary of Halifax County. That office with its rich harvest of fees was said to be the best office in the gift of the provincial government, amounting to $5,000 to $6,000 a year. The current holder of the office, J.F.C. Parsons, had been in it only nine months and it was alleged, with some show of truth, that it was a warming-pan arrangement for Holmes. Holmes's appointment whetted knives at the *Morning Chronicle*: 'The Province had lost the eminent abilities of Mr. Holmes, who, seeing that the Government ship of which he was the captain was showing signs of sinking, had sought refuge, as is the wont of a certain rodent in times of peril.'[45]

Thompson fell back on the advice of Bishop Cameron. He would have to lead the party; to do otherwise would be to consign it to certain defeat. On the other hand he owed it to his family and to himself not to waive his claim to the bench. Therefore, said Cameron, 'Accept the leadership, if necessary, but without binding yourself to retain it for a day after a judgeship comes within your reach: go to the country as if a judgeship were not within four years of you: and do your best to strengthen and prepare your Government to be able to shift for itself when the hour of your bidding adieu will have come.'[46] It was counsel sensible enough, but as Thompson well knew, it was impossible to act and work as if the judgeship were four years away. He knew, and the public strongly suspected, otherwise.

The Assembly was dissolved on 23 May and two days later Thompson was asked by the lieutenant-governor to form a government, Holmes's resignation as premier automatically dissolving the cabinet.[47] Thompson's cabinet was a rather meagre one; he wanted room for coalition manoeuvres after the election. A.C. Bell was a strong addition, taking Holmes's portfolio of provincial secretary. Creelman kept his old portfolio of mines and works. But three non-portfolio seats at Council were vacant: J.F. Stairs, the most respected man in the government after Thompson, retired; N.W. White and H.F. McDougall were contesting federal seats in Shelburne and Cape Breton; even Creelman, whose resignation had been predicted, had to sail to England on 27 May to fasten down the details of the railway contract with the Nova Scotia Railway Company. The *Chronicle* was right to sound sarcastic: 'Everything is lovely no doubt when it is found necessary to send this aged member of the Government across the Atlantic.'[48]

The provincial election was called for 20 June 1882, the same day as the federal one. Public issues, federal and provincial, were deliberately confused, to take advantage of the patronage and influence of the Dominion government and whatever strength their superior popularity might bring. Newspapers concentrated their attention on the federal election almost to the exclusion of the provincial one, both in Halifax and in Cape Breton. Macdonald's National Policy overshadowed all other issues. Tupper was confident that the federal Conservatives could repeat, or even improve on, the fourteen seats they had obtained in 1878.

The immediate issue in the provincial election was the railway contract. Creelman was deep in negotiations in London while the election was on, though he promised resolution at any moment. Sir Charles Tupper, never a great enthusiast for Holmes's project, pushed a railway in Cumberland County called the Oxford and Pictou, weakening the Nova Scotia Railway Company's prospective monopoly. The larger issue would be the history and character of the Holmes government.

The role of the premier in Nova Scotian provincial elections seems to have been quite casual. In the provincial elections of 1871 and 1874, Premier William Annand, in the Legislative Council, was not up for election. In 1878 P.C. Hill was defeated in his own constituency, Halifax, where he had concentrated his attention. Thompson's role was similar. He had urgent requests to speak in three counties that were threatened – Lunenburg, Queens, and Annapolis – but his main concern seems to have been Antigonish.

As to election funds, there is little in the Thompson Papers to suggest extensive sources of money were available. The Nova Scotia Railway Company, whose contract was so important both to the company and, presumably, to the government, was an obvious source, but there is no evidence it supplied any. There is a telegram from Sir Charles Tupper to Sir Hugh Allan full of bravado, indicating that the Nova Scotia government would be returned by a large majority, and that 'the hearty support of your road' (the Pictou–Strait of Canso line) would be much appreciated. Sir Hugh Allan said that immediate steps would be taken, whatever that might mean.[49]

Thompson left for Antigonish on 29 May; as usual he was 'full of anxieties and difficulties about nothing.' He was hoping not to be opposed. The other candidate in the two-member constituency was Angus McGillivray, independent-Liberal; Thompson hoped that Conservatives would not rock the boat. That was asking too much. Within three days of his arrival diverse currents of local jealousies and ambitions had been set in motion. To Thompson it was sickening. Everyone, friend and foe, was 'sitting and watching each other like cats on a roof, – ready for a spring.'[50]

Joseph McDonald, Thompson's old opponent from 1877, was in the field. Thompson had to face two more weeks of torment. Within a few days he was anticipating personal defeat. He did not seem to care; all he could think of, writing to Annie, 'nine more days will tell the tale and I will be back to your arms.' How he hated to be away from the double bed in Willow Park! Annie was charmed with all this, but she felt he needed a bit of stiffening. She sent him a letter, apparently artless, really ingenious, delivering both stiffening and cosiness at one and the same time:

My poor old tired Tory

I cannot tell you how glad I was to get your letter this afternoon. I know that you are feeling badly ... I wish I could be with you for one ten minutes to talk square to you. You want to know how I'll feel if you are beaten well child except for you being disappointed and tired to death not one row of pins ... except that we never gave up a fight yet I wouldn't mind if you put on your hat and left them to-morrow[.] it is better to fight as long as you are started and be beaten than not to fight at all. So keep up your courage and I'll go part of the way to meet you coming home win or lose they can't keep you from me much longer. John is very much exercised to know why they should want another man instead of pa ...

So now my old baby you must not be such an awful awful baby until you get home and then I'll see how far you can be indulged.[51]

Thompson won in Antigonish, and at the head of the poll, though not by much: Thompson, 1,166; McGillivray, 1,103; Joseph McDonald, 543. But elsewhere in the province the results were rather a shock to provincial Conservatives They lost ground badly. Charles Townshend and A.C. Bell were returned, but the government did not command a majority of seats. It was close; in twelve seats less than one hundred votes separated the Conservatives from Liberals. Of these, however, nine seats were Liberal; and more substantial victories in Lunenburg, Annapolis, Queens, and Shelburne gave the Liberals a probable majority.

The Nova Scotia Liberals were not a real party. There was no effective leader; the party had fought its battles through the newspapers and the Legislative Council. Its victory in 1882 owed much to the energy of W.S. Fielding, the young and able editor of the *Morning Chronicle*. It was sufficiently inchoate that Thompson tried to undermine it, to re-establish his own government on a broader base. He offered Albert Gayton, Liberal MLA from Yarmouth, a seat in the cabinet. Gayton had been the quondam leader of the Liberals for the past four years; but he was judicious and had latterly supported some Conservative legislation. Thompson represented to him that distinctions of party at the provincial level were meaningless; that in view of Nova Scotia's railway commitments it was of the greatest importance that she have an able government that fast-talking railway entrepreneurs could not get around. Gayton accepted that argument; but his Yarmouth constituents would not allow him to enter a Thompson cabinet. 'You will permit me to say that I should be most happy to have the honor of being associated with gentlemen for whom I have so high a personal regard as I have for yourself and the Honble. Mr. Bell – but in my view present circumstances do not permit it.' Bell went to Cape Breton and sounded out two of the more independent-minded members there, A.J. White of Sydney (former attorney general in the Hill government) and Dr C.J. Campbell of Inverness. Neither refused but both wanted time.[52]

These coalition candidates – for coalition was what Thompson was proposing – believed he would not stay in politics; that as soon as a coalition government was formed, he would take the vacant judgeship. It was a fatal handicap to serious reconstruction. By mid-July it was clear to Thompson that unless he were willing to stay on in politics, he and his cabinet would have to resign. They did, on 18 July 1882. Thompson had been premier for fifty-four days.

The fall of the Holmes–Thompson government was partly due to its tremendous success in 1878. The party had been spoilt by that lush twenty-two-seat majority in the Assembly. In that number were inferior men, picked up by the party in 1878 and persuaded to run, a little in desperation perhaps, and who by the accident of the big 1878 sweep had got into the House. There were at least a dozen men – ship-owners, merchants, small-town manufacturers of ships, shingles or carriages (some embraced all five professions) – men who were worthy in their own spheres but were not legislators, did not pretend to be, and whose childish antics in the House gave the Holmes government the epithet, 'the Holmes opera troupe.' People went to see the Assembly, so alleged Liberal papers, as to a spectacle. One cannot trust the newspapers, but the *Acadian Recorder*'s nasty remarks may have been partly true, that the Conservative MLAS sat in their seats playing like children: 'The brilliant and diverse entertainment of getting the boys who act as pages ... to roll up blue-books, ostensibly for mailing, but really, as it proves, for pelting each other across the floors of Parliament, is an edifying spectacle truly!' And when blue books failed there were always apples![53]

It was alleged that the County Incorporation Act helped defeat the government. That it was resented by many locals of the old roads-and-bridges system was understood; it was also resented by the population at large because of increased taxation. That taxation was levied at the county level did not make it more palatable. N.W. White of Shelburne, John

Morrison of Victoria, Cape Breton, Charles Smith of Lunenburg, all laid the blame on county incorporation.[54] Yarmouth had wanted out of the system in the first year. So did some other counties. They were sternly refused. It was impossible that Liberals would not take advantage of that, though in justice to the Liberals they never promised to repeal county incorporation. After the election, the Liberals fought off motions to do so in 1883 and in 1886.[55]

Thompson was not defeated because he was Nova Scotia's first Roman Catholic premier. J.H. Hearn of Sydney said so, but the sentiment found no echo elsewhere.[56] Seven MLAS were Roman Catholic, including Thompson. All but he were Liberals. This proportion, in a province whose Roman Catholic population was about 27 per cent, was not unreasonable. Strongly Protestant counties returned Thompson supporters: Pictou returned three of three, Colchester two of two.

Nova Scotians voted two different ways in the federal and provincial elections of 1882. The federal Conservatives carried Nova Scotia with the same majority that they had in 1878. Kings County elected a Conservative federally and a Liberal provincially. A Liberal carried Lunenburg federally by the slimmest of margins and was unseated by a Conservative a year later; but local Liberals won Lunenburg by four hundred votes. The gap between federal and provincial voting in Nova Scotia in 1882 was striking, and was uncommon in the rest of the country at the time.

Holmes acquired a reputation for incompetence that was difficult for Thompson to shake. Even as the election was on the railway bargain was still not signed and sealed. It took the Liberals several years of negotiation – an illustration that the railway program was far more difficult than Holmes had assumed. Holmes's preoccupation with railways left the government with little legislation to propose. Admittedly the government was blocked by the ruthless Liberal policy of using the Legislative Council as the official opposition; but, together with the raw, new Assembly, it gave an impression of narrowness and want of vitality. The charge made against the Holmes government in March 1882 by the *Acadian Recorder* sums up the refrain of the opposition:

The Premier [Holmes] is one of the most hopelessly unsuitable men in the country. He has only served to make his position ridiculous. The only man in the administration who is fit for a seat in an Executive is Mr. Thompson, and it is well known that he has given up almost his entire time to his professional duties. The running of the machine has been carried on by the other and inferior members.[57]

The *Recorder* was not quite fair. Thompson himself claimed that his public duties, by which he meant mostly being attorney general, most seriously interfered with his private work and professional advancement. For the honour of being in the cabinet of Simon Holmes, a salary of $1,600 a year had been only 'nominal compensation.'[58] Political life was no compensation at all.

A week after his resignation as premier, Thompson was appointed judge on the Supreme Court of Nova Scotia. After five years of political life, at the age of thirty-six, he was on the shelf, his labours over; his struggle for the franchises of those little people with big appetites, the electors of Antigonish, was at an end.

9

Mr Justice Thompson

The day Thompson received his commission as Supreme Court judge, he told J.T. Bulmer, 'He buried every jealousy, ill-will, and resentment he ever held against any member in the bar.' Bulmer laughed. 'It would take a mountain on some of them to keep them in their graves!'[1] On becoming a judge Thompson gave up, of course, his law practice. There is little evidence of how he did it. His cases and clients were presumably taken over by Wallace Graham or Charles Hibbert Tupper, the two other members of his firm. Young Tupper's election in June 1882 as MP for Pictou meant, however, that Graham desperately needed new talent. Probably after consultation with Thompson, Graham persuaded Robert Borden to leave a country law practice in Kentville and return to Halifax. Thompson knew Borden already; they had been on opposite sides of a case in 1879, when Thompson was attorney general.[2] So the firm of Thompson, Graham and Tupper now became the firm of Graham, Tupper and Borden.

Thompson wound up most of his legal business by early August. As he told Annie, 'I recd. a cheque for my salary as a judge from the 24th of July to the 31st of July and so I thought it was hardly the thing to be doing business as a lawyer any longer.' Annie and her sister Fan were in North Sydney on a visit; Thompson was looking after things at home, taking the children to the North-West Arm to swim to relieve the fierce heat that August. He found it strange not to be at his office in mid-week, to be able to come and go as he pleased, look after the house and children amid a flood of complimentary letters and newspapers.[3] Martin Griffin congratulated him on going to the bench, though he added, 'it will be a financial sacrifice no doubt.' It probably wasn't. Thompson was paid $4,000 a year as a puisne judge: it is doubtful if his law practice gave him that. A few years later, in 1887, Wallace Graham said it was most unlikely that he, Graham, was making $3,600 a year.[4]

Thompson made one resolution at the beginning of his career as judge. He would read law five hours a day. He had experience of judges who had ceased to do their homework, coasting on what they already knew. He had no intention of coasting, and did not; the judgments that he gave, and his 1883 lectures on evidence, sufficiently attest his determination to be a judge learned in the law.

The Supreme Court of Nova Scotia was a provincial court, organized by provincial statutes, given its jurisdiction that way. What the Dominion did was appoint and pay its judges, and enact the criminal law that the Supreme Court administered. The building it occupied, the accoutrements it had, were provincial responsibilities.[5] The building stood on Spring Garden Road, opposite St Mary's Cathedral. It was built in the late 1850s after a competition advertised widely in British North America was won by William Thomas and Sons of Toronto. It opened in 1862.[6] It was a handsome building on the outside, but it rather lacked style within, more the result of its upkeep than its architecture. It had two court-rooms; the one on the east end was more opulent, for the floor had matting, the wood was painted, and the bench itself sufficiently imposing. The west side was terrible, a barn prepared for 'Ethiopian serenaders' as one Halifax paper put it. The acoustics were bad. Witnesses gave their testimony with their backs to the jury.[7] As for the Court's proceedings, they were casual to say the least. At the opening of the November session of 1876, with lawyers, witnesses, all assembled for the opening at 10 a.m., not a single judge showed up. The civil cause docket was started only at 2 p.m., and some of the causes had to stand over until April 1877.[8] The huge backlog of 1881–2 was only partly relieved by the retirement of Sir William Young and W.F. DesBarres, both over eighty years of age, and the appointment of younger judges. It was so bad that Thompson actually changed the law early in 1882 so that the Court, when hearing appeals, could split itself into two divisions of three judges each.

There were seven judges on the Court, a chief justice and six puisne justices. The chief justice was James MacDonald of Pictou, formerly Macdonald's minister of justice. He was, legally speaking, old-fashioned. Thompson's fellow puisne judges were, in order of seniority: Hugh McDonald, a fellow Roman Catholic, from Antigonish; Henry W. Smith, a Liberal appointed in 1875; Robert Weatherbe, able, querulous, another Liberal appointment in 1878; Alexander James, who became judge in equity when Thompson came to the Court; and Samuel Rigby, an old acquaintance of Thompson's whom Tupper had helped put on the bench in December 1881.

Most of these judges were by no means brilliant; some of them were like Mr Justice Darling in England who caused a Birmingham newspaper to remark, 'No newspaper can exist except upon its merits, a condition from which the Bench, happily for Mr Justice Darling, is exempt.'9 There had been comments, muted indeed, about the age of Sir William Young and W.F. DesBarres, prior to their retirement; in England the *Times*'s criticism of Justice Sir James Fitzjames Stephen in 1891 on similar grounds forced his resignation within a month.10 Thompson's own impression of his brother judges, as he came to know them, was anything but flattering. In 1885, after three years on the Court, he pleaded with Charles Hibbert Tupper, 'Do not let us have a lazy judge (I forbear to say *another*), or an inefficient one.'11 There were enough already. Hugh McDonald drank; Wallace Graham reported in 1885 that McDonald, after laying up at the hotel for a few days, appeared in Court in such a tremble that he put off the case before him and went home to Antigonish. Henry Smith was hopelessly dilatory; he did not show up at all for one whole term in 1885 – which may have been a blessing in disguise, given his incompetence when he was there. Alexander James was the worst. J.N. Lyons told Thompson in 1886 that James had got so bad that he would rule half a dozen ways in half an hour and even Dalhousie law students scoffed at his judgments. Finally in 1889 Thompson, as minister of justice, threatened James with an investigating commission if he did not retire within six weeks. That did it. Robert Weatherbe found no one save Rigby who could keep up with him; and Rigby's health was not good. Lyons put the problems with some feeling in 1886, 'Only God knows the evil a bad judge does, as the evil lasts long after the worms have eaten the Judge and his judgments into holes.'12

When Thompson joined the Court in 1882 he could look forward to two main classes of business. In the first class he would be presiding as a single judge at trials; in serious criminal cases with a jury, in important civil cases with or without one. Some of these sittings would be in Halifax, but he would be obliged to take his turn going on circuit, conducting similar trials in the county towns in the province at their semi-annual assizes. In the second class of cases also sitting in Halifax, together with two or more of his fellow judges, he would hear appeals from the decisions of another single judge of the Supreme Court and from the decisions of inferior courts such as a county court or a magistrates court.13

Thompson's first assignment was to go to Liverpool in mid-August on circuit. Liverpool was a pretty town, tucked into a bay where a river and a bar made a convenient harbour, one of the early Yankee settlements on the south shore, dating from 1762. It was not easy to reach; uncertain sea transportation from Halifax he had to avoid as his duty required him to be in Liverpool on Friday the 18th. So he took the train to Annapolis Royal, then by road right across the province a hundred miles to the south shore. He left Annapolis at 3 p.m. by coach and horses, travelled until 11 p.m. without tea or rest, over the roughest road he had ever travelled, making only forty miles for eight hours driving. Then at 3:30 the next morning they were up and off again, for another five hours, this time making the fifty miles or so to Liverpool by 8:30 a.m. Mr Justice Thompson duly opened his first court on time at 10 a.m. that same morning.

It was very strange to him that first day, the more so since the members of the Liverpool bar who appeared before him were so much older than he was. For most of the time the judge was the youngest person in the court-room. But the whole thing ran smoothly and Thompson discovered to his great satisfaction that he was 'as apt for the business as I always thought I should be.' The case was a tedious one, but Monday should see the end of it. The following week, he promised Annie, they would have a holiday, and go to Quebec, Montreal, and Niagara, leaving the children with the girl who worked for the household, and with Fan, Annie's nineteen-year old sister.[14]

Circuit landed one in strange places in Nova Scotia; some Thompson had never seen before. He was in Port Hood in October 1882, the prettiest part of Cape Breton he had yet seen; he had a room with a full parlour and in the bedroom off it he had a 'bed of state five feet high – canopy and all.' He found Lunenburg in 1885 'very dirty, huddled and squalid. Slatternly women and squalling children are leaning out of every door and window and the streets are so narrow that you can hear all that goes in every house over the way as well as across the alleyways which are a popular institution here.'[15]

He met some strange characters. A young lady he met in Sydney, Portia King, had just come from Newfoundland where she had acquired an English accent, in Thompson's words 'officery-speaking as if she had a hot potatoe in her mouth,' presumably acquired around government house, St John's. Portia King had met Lady Whiteway, the wife of Sir William Whiteway, the current premier of Newfoundland, knighted two years before. 'Oh,' Miss King said gushingly to Thompson, 'Lady Whiteway's very much improved. She's not so stout and has *quite a manner* now.' 'So now you see,' Thompson wrote sardonically to Annie, 'how you may improve.'[16] He loved to quote examples of sublime pomposity.

Thompson's first appeal case was in the December term of the Supreme

Court in Halifax, *Lawlor* v. *Mumford*, decided 23 December 1882. It involved the law about the sale of goods, not as yet codified. Lawlor agreed to deliver to Mumford a first-class mowing machine in satisfactory condition. The machine was brought to Mumford's field by Lawlor, who gave it trial run. In the course of the trial a wheel on the machine broke. Lawlor agreed to replace the wheel but had not actually done it when Mumford returned the machine. Lawlor refused to accept it back, claiming the defect was not material to the contract; Mumford refused to pay and the case went to court. Mumford hired young Benjamin Russell of Dartmouth as his lawyer. They lost before the Dartmouth stipendiary magistrate, and again before the Halifax county court. Mumford asked Russell, 'What now? Should we appeal?' Russell said, 'It depends on which three judges hear the case. If Chief Justice MacDonald, Smith and Hugh McDonald hear the case, you will lose; if Weatherbe, Rigby and Thompson hear it, you will win. If you have two of the former and one of the latter, you will lose; if the other way, you will win.' Mumford was a man of considerable tenacity; Russell's advice was enough for him to press on.[17]

The case was actually heard before the chief justice, Rigby, and Thompson, the last of Russell's four options. This looked favourable enough; but Chief Justice MacDonald was noisy and outspoken at the trial, whereas Rigby and Thompson were very quiet. Russell concluded that his prediction was wrong, that his client had lost. As the case finished, Russell handed his gown to the next lawyer saying, 'I hope it brings you more luck than it did me.' But Russell had not lost. Thompson held that Mumford had the right to insist that the machine he had ordered be in satisfactory condition and that the wheel defect *was* material; Rigby gave reasons for concurring with Thompson; thus they overturned the decision of two lower courts. The chief justice dissented but his reasons were not reported.[18]

The bent of Thompson's constitutional views is adumbrated in an 1884 case, *In re Steel Company of Canada*. The facts of the case can be passed by; Thompson recognized a quasi-independent status for Canada, where there was no imperial legislation in the way:

... I presume that, in dealing with the subjects assigned to it, the Canadian Parliament has powers as great as that of the United Kingdom where there is no controlling imperial legislation on the same matter, and where the exclusive powers of the Provincial Parliament are not transgressed ... it is said that because Canada is a colony and has received her power to legislate from the Imperial

Parliament, these powers can only be exercised in relation to persons and rights within her own territory. In this doctrine I am not able to concur.[19]

There would be more to come from that clear-headed position.

Many judges are made intolerant, sometimes spiteful, by the power they are given. Wielding authority tests a man; it can awake every passion and discover every vice, as J.T. Bulmer once said. Not so with Thompson, he added. 'No untried juror or stumbling lawyer ever went from his presence mortified, but at the same time he held his reins with an iron hand, and I have heard him with those who were trifling with the court, pierce with his sword the swollen tissues of insolence and conceit.'[20]

Thompson's judgments in the Supreme Court of Nova Scotia – and there were many – were characterized by one other quality: they were models of lucidity. In the memory of Benjamin Russell, writing in 1921, there never was on the Nova Scotian bench a judge equal to Thompson for orderly, easy, accurate exposition of an argument. Other judges were more widely read, something Thompson would have been the first to acknowledge; but none matched the clarity of his mind. There was something more: Thompson's passion for justice. The other judges on Supreme Court, good or bad, cranky or patient, all probably wished to do justice to the cases that came before them, justice, at least, as they saw it; but with Thompson justice was a fire that burned inside of him. Russell, a Supreme Court judge himself for thirty years, was struck by Thompson's fierceness:

... there is such a thing as a passion for justice, a hot and angry resentment at every appearance of oppression and injustice, and a consuming and cleansing flame that may be kindled in the mind of the judge. If there is one judicial trait that more than any other characterized the late Sir John Thompson it is this.[21]

Thompson's love of justice, his taste for learning, his hatred of both injustice and ignorance, lay behind his support of a great measure to reform the bar of Nova Scotia: the founding of the Dalhousie Law School.

Sir James Stephen once described the bar in the English midlands as 'a robust, hard-headed, and rather hard-handed set of men, with an imperious, audacious, combative turn of mind.'[22] That was true of successful lawyers in Halifax. There were also many who were unsuccessful, ignorant, and badly trained. The old apprenticeship system was ineffective and it was getting worse. Training in law may have cleared a man's perceptions about rights of property, but it was apt to train him narrowly, if it trained at all. 'No moral quality, as such,' once said Arnott Magurn, Ottawa correspondent of the Toronto *Globe*, 'enters into the doctrine of law.'[23] In Nova Scotia less than one lawyer in four had a university degree. Thompson himself always regretted never having gone to university; he was impressed by what he missed.[24] The law student in Nova Scotia was hurried from public school to being lawyer's apprentice, as Thompson had been. If the lawyer to whom the student was apprenticed had a large and busy practice, he would have little time for the student; if the lawyer was blessed with ample leisure, the chances were he was not fit for anything.[25] The examinations for admission to the Nova Scotia bar were ludicrous. There was one two-hour examination covering three or four years' study over the whole range of English jurisprudence. Russell recalled how he was invited to cram for it:

I was confidentially taken into his residence by a friend of mine ... and I was shown a washtub full of manuscripts. I asked him what these were, and I was told they were the accumulated examination questions which had come down from generation to generation of law students, and by the diligent perusal of that washtub full of examination questions ... the candidate would invariably pass, and be very likely indeed to pass with high marks.

Thompson said that with few exceptions legal education in Nova Scotia had been 'no legal education at all.'[26]

In 1874 a group of Halifax lawyers were incorporated under the name Halifax Law School, aiming at a technical law school. It never got off the ground. In 1881, at the time of the failure of the University of Halifax, Thompson arranged to have passed an act to provide for a law faculty at Dalhousie College. It would be the first university law faculty in Canada outside of the province of Quebec. In Quebec there were three university law schools – at McGill (1848), Laval (1848), and at the Montreal branch of Laval (1878). In the traditions of French civil law it was always considered important that the young lawyer should receive his academic training at a university. Laurier, for example, trained at McGill. But in Ontario the training of lawyers was done through the Law Society of Upper Canada as an adjunct of apprenticeship. That version of a law school was opened in 1889 as Osgoode Hall. It was law teaching with the 'hard-nosed practitioner's slant,' rather than the more academic study of law characteristic of Quebec.[27]

Thompson was one of the men who put the Dalhousie Law School together; two others were his close friends, Wallace Graham and Robert

Sedgewick. The financial founder was George Munro, the Nova Scotian who had become a millionaire publisher in New York. Munro was from Pictou and in his earlier days had taught Thompson at the Free Church Academy in Halifax. In 1883 Munro gave $40,000 to endow a chair in constitutional and international law at Dalhousie; to it he nominated Richard Weldon, professor of mathematics and political science at Mount Allison. Weldon, the only full-time teacher, would take on these 'cultural' subjects, but who was to provide the instruction in the down-to-earth subjects that make up a lawyer's life? The answer was a group of unpaid judges and lawyers from Halifax of whom Thompson became one, as lecturer in evidence, at $100 a year.

In April 1883 Thompson, Graham, and Sedgewick went to Boston and New York to see how things were done in law schools there. They had a hot and tiresome journey to Boston but spent their time to advantage. Monday, 16 April they were at Harvard Law School; they took four Nova Scotian students studying there to dinner and to see *Iolanthe*. Tuesday was spent at the more conservative Boston University Law School. That evening they dined with Judge Dwight Foster, formerly of the Massachusetts Supreme Court, Thompson's old colleague from the Halifax arbitration of 1877. Then they went on to New York to look at Columbia.[28]

What impressed Thompson and his colleagues was not the Harvard system of legal education, or Columbia's: Dalhousie Law School's curriculum was *sui generis*. Thompson was impressed with American law libraries. The Halifax bar had the talent to man a law school; but it would gain repute 'far more from the collection of books on legal subjects they were able to bring together than the individual reputation of any man in the Faculty, or for that matter the united reputation of the whole Faculty.'[29] There was a meeting in Halifax in August 1883, to concert donations for a library; if George Munro was putting up $40,000 to endow a chair, the least Halifax judges and lawyers could do was to underwrite the library. Thompson and a dozen others put up $100 each to buy books; donations were solicited with energy, and within a few months twenty-eight hundred law books were garnered, of which one thousand would be exchanged with other libraries. A librarian was appointed, a young Halifax lawyer with a penchant for literature and history and a great friend of Thompson's, John Thomas Bulmer.

Bulmer (pronounced 'Boomer') came from Cumberland County, and was admitted to the bar in 1875. His literary and historical bent was translated into a curious arrangement made by the Holmes government in 1879, by which the Nova Scotia Historical Society, founded in 1878 by Bulmer and others, was given the responsibility for administering the legislative library with Bulmer as librarian. He was a rare character, the antithesis of Thompson – uproarious, grandiloquent, and salty. His conversation was a racy mixture of homely Nova Scotian analogies and literary allusions of considerable diversity. Thompson found Bulmer's company was sheer recreation after a day's regimen on the bench. He enjoyed listening to Bulmer's stories, redolent of rural Nova Scotia – such as the story of Slade's steer. It appears that a friend of Bulmer's in Cumberland County called Slade was leading a young, powerful steer to pasture. Slade had to stop to move the bars of the gate and needed both hands. He foolishly tethered the steer around himself for that half-minute. Just as the gate opened a hen flew up, startled the steer, who took off at full speed into the pasture with Slade tied behind. He was being bounced from hillock to hillock when mercifully the tether broke. Bulmer said to him afterward, 'What did you do a fool trick like that for?' Slade remarked, 'I hadn't been drawed fifty feet afore I seen I'd made a mistake.'[30]

Bulmer was fired in July 1882 when the Liberals came into power and he was thus available to the new law school. He simply moved up Citadel Hill to the school's first rooms in the high school that Thompson had helped to get built four years before. Bulmer was for that first session of 1883–4 an admirable librarian and a promoter of the school's interests. But in 1884 he had to be let go; there was no money to pay him.

The Dalhousie Law School experiment, as Thompson called it, was from the beginning a success. It was badly needed. A Charlottetown lawyer put it to Thompson in August 1884: 'Confederation and the Supreme Court of Canada bring our Maritime Bars in contact with the lawyers of the Upper Provinces, & to hold there [our] own, our young men require better legal training than can be got (picked up) in an attorney's office.' It filled from the beginning a glaring gap in Canadian legal education; as Bora Laskin has written, for more than half a century after its foundation 'it provided intellectual leadership in the critical study of the common law in Canada.'[31]

Thompson's lectures on evidence at the new law school attracted instant attention. They were given on Tuesday and Thursday afternoons, in the first two years of the school's existence, and the school was a handy ten-minute walk up the hill from most lawyers' offices. He made a great impression on the LL.B students; they called him 'silver-tongued;' he had a rich voice that carried easily and pleasantly.[32] But it was his argument that established his reputation.[33]

Thompson's elucidation of law was like an anatomical drawing, rendering clear and comprehensible what was at first appearance confusing. He distrusted general rules; his instinct was to assimilate information, put it through that excellent machine, his own head, and form his own conclusions. For that reason he distrusted Latin maxims, not because they were Latin, or maxims, but because they were conveniences that more often concealed than revealed truth. He was often surprised when talking to even well-read lawyers how often they mistook 'the slipshod maxims of conceited judges' for real rules of law. Take, for example, the maxim 'Falsus in uno, falsus in omnibus;' however true it might be in logic, it ought not to be imported unthinkingly into law, where it could be wholly invalid. Maxims in general, said he, 'have no place in law considered as jurisprudence, at all.'[34]

Thompson's illustrations for his lectures on evidence were taken from his own experience with criminal law. Despite his effective reliance upon, and use of, circumstantial evidence in *The Queen* v. *Thibault* in 1880, he was well aware of the difficulties; circumstantial evidence could be fabricated, as the drinking cup placed in Benjamin's sack by Joseph (Genesis, xliv). More serious, as more frequent, were the inferences drawn incorrectly from evidence: 'There is a natural tendency in the mind of everybody to fabricate coincident circumstances, or draw analogies where they do not exist. This disposition is found most strongly in the most acute minds. The mind,' said he, doubtless influenced by Hume, 'has this property, than it readily supposes a greater order and conformity in things than it [actually] finds.'[35] Edgar Allan Poe's 'The Mystery of Marie Roget' was Thompson's illustration of this problem of misleadingly apparent coincidences. Not only that, but Poe suggested a further problem, unapparent relevance:

... experience has shown, and a true philosophy will always show, that a vast, perhaps the larger, portion of truth arises from the seemingly irrelevant ... The history of human knowledge has so uninterruptedly shown that to collateral, or incidental, or accidental events we are indebted for the most numerous and most valuable discoveries, that it has at length become necessary ... to make not only large, but the largest, allowances for inventions that shall arise by chance, and quite out of the range of ordinary expectation ... We make chance a matter of absolute calculation.[36]

Over the winter of 1883–4 Thompson had another task, assigned him by Alonzo White, the attorney general who succeeded him in August 1882: put the Supreme Court on a modern basis, along the lines of the

British Judicature Act of 1873 and an analogous Ontario act of 1875. These acts could not be adopted en bloc, for some of their provisions were quite unsuited to Nova Scotia. For example, the Ontario Judicature Act gave the Supreme Court judges the power to delegate their work to county court judges; in Ontario county court judges sometimes went on circuit or presided at chambers. C.H. Tupper hoped that Nova Scotia would not be cursed with rules like that. But he need not have feared; Thompson knew that what some Ontario county court judges could do would be nearly impossible for most Nova Scotia ones.[37]

With these broad terms of reference, Thompson drafted an 'Act to improve the administration of justice,' which filled 160 pages of print, one of the longest in the statute book. It stood from 1884 with only slight adjustments until 1950. This act made both major and minor changes in the day-to-day working of the Supreme Court. Minor provisions were, for example, the remodelling, with precision, of the unsystematic and ill-chosen times for the sittings of the Court in country districts. One of the major changes was to replace the sometimes undiscoverable and often highly technical steps that had to be taken to bring a case before the Court with a series of commonsense rules set down in plain English. Thompson's Nova Scotia Judicature Act rescued the machinery of the Supreme Court from a too conservative past and brought it into the daylight of the 1880s.[38]

While Thompson was holding court at Truro in the spring of 1884, the first intimation of broader problems appeared on the horizon. J.J. Stewart, editor of the Halifax *Herald*, wrote on 6 June that he was sending Bulmer to Truro that night with a special message from A.W. McLelan, Macdonald's minister of marine and fisheries, whom he should see on an urgent matter before McLelan returned to Ottawa:

I cannot express in words my sense of the tremendous importance of your decision. The whole destiny of the party hangs in the balance as far as N.S. is concerned, and there is no telling its effects on the Dominion. Please give the matter your very best consideration and remember what issues may hang on it.[39]

The message Bulmer brought with him was nothing less than the offer of a cabinet post in the Macdonald government.

Since confederation Nova Scotia had two representatives in the Dominion cabinet. After 1878 these were Sir Charles Tupper and James MacDonald. When MacDonald went to the Nova Scotia Supreme Court in 1881 he was replaced by A.W. McLelan, MP for Colchester, who became minister of marine. In May 1883 Tupper went to London as Canadian high commissioner, but not being paid for it, he continued to hold his portfolio as minister of railways, as well as being MP for Cumberland. Then in April 1884 there was a quarrel with Macdonald in cabinet: Tupper wanted his way and threatened to resign if he did not get it; Macdonald lost his temper and said Tupper's threat was improper in Council where matters ought to be discussed on their merits. Tupper flung himself out of the meeting. Macdonald adhered to his reasons for losing his temper, but apologized and asked Tupper to return to Council.[40] That quarrel may have been one reason why, after Parliament prorogued and Tupper returned to London, his decision to resign from Canadian parliamentary life was confirmed as of 28 May 1884. This deprived the government of its most energetic minister.

The Macdonald government in 1884 was old and tired, and could not easily afford Tupper's loss. Macdonald himself talked about getting out; he was unwell that summer, his stomach was bothering him, and life was hardly worth living. 'I would leave the Government tomorrow,' he told Tupper at the end of June, 'if it were not that I really think George Stephen [of the CPR] would throw up the sponge if I did.'[41] His colleagues, except for J.H. Pope, Langevin, and Caron, were all sick, lazy, or otherwise ineffective, and Macdonald had to do most of the work.

Tupper's retirement from politics in May 1884 created consternation in the party in Nova Scotia, where Tupper's replacement both in Cumberland and in cabinet were separate problems of some urgency.[42] Any prospective candidate for cabinet was measured against him, and the more one thought about it, the more difficult the options became. One choice – Tupper's – was Senator Miller of Richmond County. A.W. McLelan and Alpin Grant (Tupper's former editor of the Halifax British Colonist) were asked to sound out other possibilities.[43] But there was not much cabinet timber available. It was also obvious that Nova Scotia Conservatives did not want Senator Miller at any price. The best Nova Scotia MP seemed to be Tupper's own son, Charles Hibbert.[44] But at twenty-nine he was very young for a federal minister, without experience, and headstrong in the bargain. Even Simon Holmes was thought of; and he would have accepted for he was already tired of life as prothonotary of Halifax County.[45] Thompson was favoured by J.J. Stewart and others around the Halifax Herald; but Thompson's candidacy was not liked much by Sir Charles Tupper, and for several reasons. He wrote to his son,

Thompson was not a success as a politician and would with all his ability and legal knowledge be disappointing in the House of Commons. I do not like judges coming off the Bench to re-enter politics. It is a matter however in which while I give you my opinion I have no wish to interfere and [would] have you act upon your own judgement.[46]

Thompson might have agreed with old Tupper. After leaving politics in July 1882, Thompson felt strongly that he had deserted friends and colleagues, leaving them to fight on without him, while he settled comfortably on the bench. That feeling had eased; some of his old colleagues had become federal MPs themselves – Stairs in 1883, Townshend in 1884 (taking Tupper's seat in Cumberland). Thompson liked being a judge, the métier suited him. So he turned down Ottawa's June overtures of 1884. Gradually over the next few months, as no satisfactory successor to Tupper emerged, it became clear that the only person the party could agree on was Thompson.

Over the next few months Macdonald's cabinet did not improve. 'We want new blood badly,' he told Tupper in February 1885, when the real strains of a rough session had not even started.[47] McLelan, the other cabinet minister from Nova Scotia, wanted out; other members of the cabinet were unwell, and carried on, at Macdonald's urging, by sheer guts and nerve, like J.H. Pope or Leonard Tilley. When the 1885 session started on 29 January J.F. Stairs sat not too far from Macdonald; Stairs told him that Thompson was the best man, perhaps the only man, but they would have to persuade him to come. C.H. Tupper was pressed into service. Overtures were renewed again.

Thompson hardly knew Sir John Macdonald. There had been brief meetings in 1880 and 1881 when he was in Ottawa with Simon Holmes on Nova Scotia government business and correspondence between the two men in September 1883 when the Halifax bar was exercised over Wallace Graham's membership in a commission for the new edition of the Canadian Revised Statutes. Since that time there had been little communication between Thompson and Macdonald, and it is altogether probable that Macdonald knew Thompson only by face and reputation. In March 1885, to the renewed Ottawa overtures, Thompson said thanks but no thanks.[48]

Sir Alexander Campbell, Macdonald's colleague and former law partner, decided in March 1885 that he would retire after the session was over, though he later put this off until the trials of the North-West Rebellion were completed. Through the 1885 session the Nova Scotia MPs pressed Thompson upon Macdonald, and at the end of May Macdonald again approached Thompson, this time through J.F. Stairs. Thompson was in no hurry to decide. He thought about it for a couple of weeks, especially at Yarmouth in June, waiting for the Court to begin. He had arrived three days early; he visited Yarmouth, its suburbs, read whatever was available, thought over his problems, and so passed one day. His dilemma about going to Ottawa was real and difficult. He was going to write Sir John Macdonald that very night, he told Annie on the 19th.

I have no disposition to go. It may be indolence – and the fear that it is so is a very distressing thought – but I do not feel disposed to make any change. I suppose I should not have made a change before had it not been for your wish and probably I should not do anything like that now unless you feel pretty strongly that I should. There is one thing you have never made me clear about. You have discussed my satisfactions and dissatisfactions but you have never told me whether or not *you* are satisfied with what I have done in the world if it is to end here. You might write me yet on that point and your letter if mailed on Monday will reach me here on Wednesday. The whole truth is that something very loudly seems to say 'don't go' and yet it seems a sacrifice to stay. Then the problem is – Is the voice right or is it only the persuasion of timidity. It does not seem as if I could ask advice outside for no one knows how things are ... so well as you or I. At any rate all the risks are in changing and I suppose that it is something when one has attained an honourable position after an active struggle.[49]

Notwithstanding cool replies from Thompson, Macdonald did not give up. One letter from Thompson to Charles Hibbert Tupper about this time seemed to young Tupper a definite no. He showed it to Sir John who looked at it shrewdly, handed it back, and quoted Byron's *Don Juan*: 'A little while she strove, and much repented, / And whispering, "I will ne'er consent" – consented.'[50] Macdonald was urged on by Stairs and others; and the day the House prorogued, 20 July 1885, he wrote Thompson in his own hand, offering Thompson the reversion of the justice portfolio:

I therefore would press upon you the acceptance of a Cabinet office, with the certainty of being Minister of Justice within a very short period. I look upon that office as the highest in Canada as the Minister performs the political function of the Lord Chancellor in England. Nova Scotia wants a good administrator[?] in the Ministry and you are the man.

Antigonish is open to you so I still hope you will accept. As time is precious I would ask you to wire me your final[?] determination which I trust will be in the affirmative –

Hoping to hail you as a colleague.[51]

Thompson was still torn. He liked his judicial life. His tastes and pursuits, as he put it to Macdonald on 1 August, 'have been altogether within the lines of legal study, and my fitness for active political work – especially campaigning – is probably less on that account than it was when I was in harness in local politics.' He did not want to stand for Antigonish again; he preferred a constituency with at least half of them Protestants. He was unenthusiastic about returning to seek the suffrages of 'village ruffians.'[52]

But Annie was not content with him as a judge. When she walked past the Supreme Court she thought of the 'sere old crows' that sat on the bench with her young and active husband, and wondered why she allowed him to stay there as long as she had done.[53] Thompson consulted Bishop Cameron, whose advice was to stay put. So he had replied again negatively to Macdonald. Macdonald then did what he rarely did, he kept the position open. Thompson was difficult to get but, said Stairs, don't 'be put out with his indecision, because when you once secure his services he will more than repay you for all delay.'[54]

At this point Sir Charles Tupper arrived at Rivière du Loup from London, England. Macdonald told him his troubles with reconstruction, how Thompson refused to leave the bench to join the government. Tupper went to St Andrews, New Brunswick, saw Sir Leonard and Lady Tilley, both of whom told him that Campbell had definitely resigned the justice portfolio. In Halifax Stairs told him that the greatest service Tupper could give the party was to get Thompson into the government.[55] That was what Tupper proceeded to do. He saw Bishop Cameron and persuaded him on certain conditions to urge the appointment on Thompson and, on the supposition that the portfolio was vacant, promised the ministry of justice. The bishop's letter to Thompson showed what a powerful force Cameron was, not only in Thompson's life but in Tupper's:

Yesterday in my interview with Sir Charles Tupper, I told him that I would approve of your resigning your seat on the Bench on condition 1° that you would at once be appointed Minister of Justice, and 2° tht he would reenter the Government before the next General Election. After distinctly and unequivocally pledging himself that both these conditions would be fulfilled, I gave the required approval and authorized him to tell you so ...

I don't believe you should accept any other position – even temporarily – than that of Minister of Justice. A novitiate may suit others, but would damage your prestige. Again, I cannot look upon a reconstruction of the Government as completely satisfactory without Sir Charles. Besides, to have Nova Scotia represented in the Dominion Government by Sir Charles and yourself, would be a matter of pride to every honest man in the Province.[56]

Both of Cameron's conditions were remarkable, the second one surprising. And Tupper did do what he agreed to do.

The bishop's imprimatur was vital to Thompson if he were to count on carrying Antigonish. But the bishop was more than just a political necessity; his support was personal and private. He liked, trusted, admired Thompson. For Thompson, Bishop Cameron was his ecclesiastical mentor, successor to the more ductile (and more worldly) Archbishop Connolly.

But now, at this last stage of Thompson's indecision, it was up to Annie. Thompson would abide by what she wanted. Hector McInnes, a Conservative party stalwart, put it some years later, '... he was not ambitious, but she was. She decided it.' On Wednesday, 2 September Thompson met Sir Charles Tupper in Halifax and agreed to go to Ottawa as minister of justice.[57]

Sir John Macdonald had an awkward time with Sir Alexander Campbell. Notwithstanding Tupper's information, Campbell had decided to stay on as minister of justice, informing Macdonald on 9 September. Campbell had his own piece to say about the weaknesses of Macdonald's government. Let us now try, said Campbell, to get on without 'this eternal yielding to every one, who has, or thinks he has, control of a few votes.' Campbell was blunt:

The country is impoverished by consenting to expenditure which is unnecessary and fruitless ... the constant giving way to truculent demands and our delays and the irritation and mischiefs which they produce are in everybody's mouth, and are evils of which you and I may well take note ...

I hope that we shall take a fresh start, and move with greater vigour than of late we have done.[58]

Macdonald had then to tell him that he wanted Campbell to give up justice and take the post office. Campbell balked. Why should Thompson stipulate what cabinet post he will have? He should take what he was given. Macdonald pleaded with Campbell. The Ontario members of cabinet, Campbell included, had agreed on the necessity of reconstruction last winter and had given Macdonald authority to do it. The whole aim, said Macdonald,

now must be so to reconstruct the Ministry as to have a moral certainty of carrying the Country in 1887. We stand better in the Country than in the House, where we were awfully weak last Session. I would not willingly go through another session like it. Just think! Tilley, sick and away – Macpherson ditto – Chapleau ditto – Pope sick for a good part of the time – Costigan as you know &c. &c. The work all fell upon me and much of it of necessity was ill done, and our friends grumbled ...

If we don't get Thompson I don't know what to do. There are great jealousies among the Nova Scotians as they stand on an equality of unfitness, but they would all yield to the superior abilities of Thompson.[59]

Campbell did not think much of Thompson whom he had met casually once or twice. He grumbled that Thompson might be as able as people say, but he had a nervous air, a subdued manner, as if educated for the priesthood. It was doubtful that Thompson would be any use in the House of Commons. The crisis with Campbell over Thompson was serious enough that Macdonald brought the whole question to Council. Council approved Thompson's appointment on 17 September. But it did not end there; several Conservative MPs came out to Earnscliffe to protest. Macdonald listened to complaints, then answered with that oracular wagging of his head that everyone knew so well, 'Gentlemen, wait until six months have passed before you form your judgement of the new Minister of Justice. Come to me then, if you will, and tell me that I have made a mistake.'[60]

The next move was to open Antigonish. The MP was Angus McIsaac. He was a Liberal, which was awkward, but he was a susceptible Liberal who dearly wanted to be a county court judge. The judge in Antigonish had recently died. Macdonald's was a crude remedy and it had to be managed with care. Thompson knew Antigonish politics. He knew that it was one thing for Angus McIsaac to say he would resign his House of Commons seat if offered the county court judgeship, and another for him actually to do it. Thompson insisted that McIsaac resign his seat and accept the county judgeship before Thompson gave up the Supreme Court.[61] C.H. Tupper was despatched to Antigonish by Macdonald with a special letter to Angus McIsaac offering the county judgeship. Macdonald's instructions were specific: talk it through; having all matters settled, then, and only then, put Macdonald's letter in McIsaac's hand; get his acceptance of the offer in writing; get him to promise to exercise his influence to prevent opposition to Judge Thompson; telegraph what you do to Stairs and to me, Macdonald. Within four days all this was accomplished. On 21 September Macdonald telegraphed Thompson,

Your county vacated – send resignation [as Judge] to Secretary of State – wire despatch of letter – will act on telegram and issue writ [for by-election] – use Stairs cipher.[62]

Thompson wanted to be sworn in as minister of justice before going for election. Macdonald agreed to that too. Thompson arrived in Ottawa on 25 September 1885. Martin Griffin (who had just come to Ottawa as parliamentary librarian from the Toronto *Mail*) and George Johnson met him at the train, cheered him up over lunch at the Russell House. Thompson needed it. He was not happy with his decision. 'I could not stand the depression so long as this,' he wrote to Annie, 'but for the feeling all the time that you wished me to do what I have done.'[63]

A.W. McLelan took him that afternoon to the Privy Council room in the East Block and introduced him to Sir John Macdonald. Macdonald sat down, 'light as a bird,' Thompson said, and wrote out Thompson's resignation which he signed. Then Macdonald took him to meet the cabinet. At noon on Saturday, 26 September he was sworn in as minister of justice and attorney general for Canada.[64]

Ottawa was looking handsome, more so than when he and Annie had last been there in 1882, and that September it began to look even a little friendly; all the cabinet had been cordial, and by the time Thompson left for Halifax on the Monday, he was feeling more cheerful about his Ottawa prospects.

Those in Antigonish began to darken. He returned to Halifax on Wednesday, paused a day, and went on to Antigonish on 1 October. He would now face a hard, indeed desperate, by-election.

PART THREE

THE TRAIN TO OTTAWA: MINISTER OF JUSTICE IN MACDONALD'S CABINET, 1885–1891

10

Minister of Justice

Through a century of Dominion politics, 1867–1968, the federal riding of Antigonish and its 1914 successor, Antigonish–Guysborough, have been Liberal almost continuously. When Thompson came to it in 1885 it had elected Liberal MPs since 1867, a pattern that Thompson would have to break. And since Thompson it has continued to elect Liberal MPs, except for a six-month break in 1926 and support for Diefenbaker in 1957–62.

There were Conservatives in Antigonish. It did not signify that they had not had much success since 1867. In Antigonish, as in Nova Scotia generally, men tended to vote as they had always voted, as their father had done. It was a matter of pride, loyalty, tradition. One elderly Antigonish housewife said in the 1970s, 'Yes, we have been Liberals since before Confederation.'[1] No one wanted to be a turncoat, although the outcome of elections often hinged upon them. Some people in Antigonish talked of 'mixed' marriages, not between Catholic and Protestant but between Liberal and Conservative! Perhaps Fielding was right: the character of Antigonish was simply traditional.[2] It was not a large constituency – about two thousand voters. That was small but not unusual for rural constituencies across the Dominion at the time. Its population in 1881 was eighteen thousand, of whom 82.5 per cent were Roman Catholics. Only one polling district, Lochaber in the southwest corner of the county, had a majority of Protestants. Except for Gloucester County, New Brunswick, Antigonish had the largest Catholic majority of any constituency in the Maritime provinces.

Sir Charles Tupper believed, as did Bishop Cameron, that if the Antigonish by-election were held as soon as possible after Thompson's acceptance of office, he could get in by acclamation. Cameron thought the appointment of Angus McIsaac to the bench 'would undermine Gritism in this County for a long time'[3] With Liberals demoralized, and Conservatives supporting Thompson, there might be no need for a contest at all. The by-election was therefore called at once, for 16 October.

It was inevitable that Thompson would be criticized for what the *Yarmouth Herald* called 'this disgusting shuffling of Judgeships.' His reputation as jurist was, it said, far better than any he had earned as a politician. The whole judiciary of Nova Scotia was disgraced. Goldwin Smith in *The Week* liked it no better.[4] And the Antigonish Conservatives were angry that a plum like a county court judgeship had gone to a Liberal. McIsaac's age – he was only forty-three years old – made it worse. He could hold that judgeship until kingdom come, which in political time might mean forty years.[5] The Liberal papers in Halifax avoided criticizing McIsaac; it was unusual to pursue a lawyer from politics to the bench. It was not the first time judicial appointments had crossed party lines, and in both directions.[6]

With the government fairly counting on an acclamation, the Liberals gave them a nasty surprise. Laurier had been beaten that way in Arthabaska in 1877. The fury of some Tories was such that an independent Conservative candidate appeared, Alexander McIntosh of Antigonish town, the local doctor, who decided to run despite promises to Bishop Cameron.[7] The Liberals sensibly avoided bringing in a candidate of their own and backed McIntosh. Though McIntosh was a Conservative, he was a maverick and that would do. He was even better than a straight Liberal.

By the time Thompson got to Antigonish things were not going well. McIsaac's friends had not helped but were rounding up support for McIntosh, 'whip and spur,' as Thompson put it. Antigonish was intensely local and personal in its politics, and although Thompson was known, a man such as the town doctor had clearly an advantage. The New Glasgow *Eastern Chronicle*, Liberal, believed that Thompson's 'haughty, cold-blooded manner would never win him friends about the warm-hearted Highlanders of Antigonish.'[8]

On the other hand, reports from Ontario helped Thompson. The Toronto *Globe* held Thompson up as a papist, wickedly replacing an Ontario Protestant (Campbell) as minister of justice. It was alleged that Ontario Orangemen were furious; they assumed that the change heralded commutation for Louis Riel.[9] The Nova Scotia Conservative papers made sure that the *Globe*'s sentiments were well ventilated in Antigonish County, and W.S. Fielding, at the *Chronicle* desk in Halifax, winced when he read the *Globe*'s stuff. The last thing he wanted was the injection of religion into the election.

Liberal policy centred on three things. First, avoid abuse of McIsaac, indeed, even any mention of him. Second, say nothing, absolutely nothing, against Bishop Cameron or the clergy. Fielding believed, rightly, that Antigonishers were ready to oppose the bishop, but they would not see him attacked by outsiders. The Halifax *Chronicle* scrupulously refrained from doing so. Third, the Liberals ought not to be too confident publicly of the result, even though Fielding himself was sure that Thompson would be beaten.[10]

Not all the clergy were enthusiasts for Thompson. The bishop certainly was, too much so for some priests. One priest went to Bishop Cameron and begged him, 'for the love of God to have nothing to do with the election. It would injure your usefulness'; Thompson was certain to be defeated. The bishop said, 'Many a better man than myself has been beaten, but no one could say that I will not fight.' He believed he had no option but to back Thompson to the hilt.[11] But the bishop's certainty meant that some clergy were caught between their clerical principles and their political ones.

Thompson was forced to be a hypocrite too. His political persona he had to put on, he said, 'like a dickey.' It felt like that after having been a judge for three years. He was out of practice, and his capacity for hypocrisy in political speeches was limited anyway. J.T. Bulmer said of him once, 'I never knew him to do or say anything to make himself popular.' Exaggerated perhaps, but it gets Thompson about right; honestly austere, reluctant to say what he did not mean, promise what he could not do. He did not even like to ask people to vote for him. All he would say was, 'When you vote on election day, remember me.'[12]

The organizational work of the campaign was managed by Wallace Graham, an Antigonisher himself. As the campaign began to get serious, outside Conservative support was brought in: Senator Poirier and Pierre-Armand Landry, MP for Kent, to nourish the Acadians, who comprised 20 per cent of the Antigonish population; Thompson's former colleague, H.F. McDougall, now MP for Cape Breton, and Charles Hibbert Tupper, MP for Pictou, to help with the Protestants.

On Thursday, 1 October Thompson was met at the Antigonish railway station by the bishop's carriage and taken to the palace for a long talk. His first political meeting was held the same night. All next day he travelled by carriage around the county, to St Andrew's, Heatherton (the former Pomquet Forks), Bayfield, had dinner on board a vessel in Bayfield harbour, and slept at Tracadie. All Saturday he canvassed Tracadie house to house. Sunday morning he addressed the congregation at Pomquet after mass.

That Sunday a circular from the bishop supporting Thompson was read from the pulpit of all the churches. The election law, passed by the Mackenzie government in 1874, declared a federal election void upon proof of 'undue influence.' Aimed at Quebec elections, it could be applied anywhere, so the bishop had to be careful.[13] The bishop's circular was addressed to the parish priests in the county. If Thompson were a Protestant, the circular said, there was not a constituency in Nova Scotia that would not be proud to have him. Antigonish, the most Catholic constituency in the province, if not in all the Maritime provinces, should be no less proud. The bishop trusted that 'if a captious opposition to the triumphant election of the hon. minister of justice is persisted in, both you and your parishioners will inflict merited punishment upon it at the polls. This is the request and earnest entreaty of your and their devoted friend and father.'[14] The bishop was clever; he was not asking his flock to vote *for* Thompson but *against* Thompson's opposition. The *Morning Chronicle* called this being 'careful, while violating the spirit of the law against undue influence, not to infringe the letter.' Bishop Cameron could assert later that no priest had the right to urge Thompson's election in the name of religion.[15] Behind the scenes, however, the bishop was working like a horse, writing letters night and day. He brought nine parish priests into the county from other parts of the diocese, from Pictou, Guysborough, Inverness and Cape Breton, adding to the nine resident ones.

Nomination day was on 9 October. It poured rain but carriages came steadily into Antigonish town from daylight onward. In Antigonish it was always an important day, an indication of how the election was going to go. The streets and the bars were thronged with people. At 2:30 p.m. the speeches started in the drill shed with everyone packed in standing. Thompson had never seen such a crowd. By this time amazing rumours had developed: Thompson's father had been an Orangeman, Thompson was not a real Catholic, he had not been to communion for five years, he had no pew, he had become a Catholic to get his wife's money, Bishop Cameron had imported an Irishman (Thompson) to run out a good Scotchman (McIntosh)!

Thompson's speeches were sometimes better when he had a push from his anger, and he became angry when accused of such things. He had hit at rumours the day before – spread by a ruffian from Halifax he said – and the memory of them continued to fuel his vigour on nomination day.

He led off with an hour's speech; he had three or four drunks in front of him so had to speak with all his force. Opponents interrupted; there was evidence of a conspiracy to stop him speaking. It did not work. The crowd, the excitement, the noise, did not intimidate him, but instead supplied him with adrenalin. So he donned his dickey and spoke like a politician. McIntosh spoke for fifteen minutes in a rather stumbling way, Thompson thought, although McIntosh was no novice at bulldozing meetings and was well encouraged by his supporters. Then Thompson had a rebuttal, dishing out punishment for half an hour; the crowd laughing and cheering at his hits, were clearly on his side. That night drunken Protestants groaned and booed outside Thompson's hotel windows, and cheered loudly in front of McIntosh's house. Thompson assumed this was a good sign, an indication that things had begun to go badly for the Liberals.[16]

There was also a change in the Halifax *Chronicle*. Previously it had been kind; Thompson was, it had said on 25 September, *facile princeps* among the Conservatives elected in 1878. He had, it is true, selfishly deserted his party in 1882; he had infirmities of temper and was narrow in outlook but he had been a good judge. 'He was prompt, energetic, industrious.' Then, two days before the election, the gloves came off. Thompson had to be hit and hit hard. As a legislator, said the *Chronicle* on 14 October, Thompson was terrible, a rank failure. The County Incorporation Act was a huge mess with higher taxes to boot. The railway scheme was a complete bust. Even as a judge Thompson was 'reserved, calculating, distant, intensely dignified, offensively dogmatic, thoroughly self-complacent and selfish.'

There were fears that the clergy were playing a double game. It was alleged, for example, that Father Gillis, of St Ninian's Cathedral, was secretly canvassing for McIntosh under Bishop Cameron's very nose. Some Conservatives went to the bishop and said bluntly that the by-election could well be lost. The result was a second circular, on Sunday, 11 October, in English and Gaelic, explaining how McIntosh had broken his promise to the bishop. It was said on that Sunday McIntosh's children left St Ninian's in tears. That gave Thompson sharp pangs of conscience; he was vulnerable where children were concerned.[17]

A long, cold Sunday of canvassing followed. An early snow fell most of the day, driven by a high wind. At West River Thompson made about thirty calls in the company of young Norman Macdonald, and found the going splendid. Even though three or four said they would vote against him, they were hospitable and thanked him for coming in such bitter weather. The next two days Thompson spent mostly in enemy country, the southeast, St Andrew's, Heatherton, and Lochaber, the last being a Protestant district. By election day, 16 October, he could get up feeling that nothing had been left undone. It had been a hard fight, but whatever the result, there was nothing he and his colleagues need reproach themselves for.

The bishop had set his heart on having Thompson elected. The clergy were asked to support Thompson, and probably many of them did; but their parishioners were a different matter. That the Antigonishers had their own ideas is clear from the returns. Thompson won, but by only 228 votes – 1,020 to 792. He lost Antigonish town, 176 to 178, where the population was 80 per cent Catholic. He narrowly lost in Lochaber, Fraser's Mills, and lost more heavily in St Andrews, Havre Boucher and Heatherton. But in the north and the west, in Arisaig, Cape George and Morristown, Thompson had majorities so substantial that they carried him through the more modest reverses elsewhere.[18] The extent of his (and the bishop's) achievement should not be under-estimated. McIsaac, the Liberal, had been elected in 1882 with a majority of 333; Thompson won in 1885 with 228, a turnaround of 15 per cent of the electorate. Attempts to defeat Thompson in the two provincial elections of 1877 and 1882 had been, as the *Morning Chronicle* admitted when the by-election was over, disastrous failures.[19] Thompson with Bishop Cameron at his back was hard to beat; but without support from the bishop Thompson probably could not have carried Antigonish.

It had been a fight hard and bitter enough that Thompson told Sir John Macdonald he would stop in Halifax and rest for a day or two before going on to Ottawa. Was he even committed to a career in politics? 'It is all over now I hope, earnestly, forever,' he had written Annie from Antigonish just after the election. Annie wanted him to be a minister, well and good; it would bring in almost double the money he had earned as a judge, $7,000 per annum instead of $4,000. But for how long? And if he was lonely after two weeks in Antigonish, how would he be after four months in Ottawa?

Annie did not go with him to Ottawa. Tilley's house had been offered to them, but just at the time Thompson committed himself to going to Ottawa, Annie's doctor advised that she should stay in Halifax and stay quiet. The strains attendant upon Thompson's election had not helped. For at least the next year, except for occasional visits, Annie would have to stay in Willow Park with the children.[20]

Their household was changing. Young John was now thirteen years old, and his further education had to be looked to. One of Thompson's

Catholic friends in Halifax, T.E. Kenny, sent his children to a school he himself had attended, Stonyhurst College in northeastern Lancashire, up against the Yorkshire border. Stonyhurst was run by Jesuits; the school moved to England in 1794 after a series of displacements from northern France and the Austrian Netherlands. To Stonyhurst went J.T.C. Thompson in the summer of 1885 with Kenny as escort. Young Thompson would not find all the boys at the school strangers, knowing the Kenny boys and one or two others from Halifax. He would be there for the next seven years, returning home in the summers. It was not easy for young John or the family.

Why all this? Further education was to be had in Halifax; but Thompson was looking for intellectual challenges for his sons that he never had. A tutor would not solve the problem. That was suggested in 1886 when young John did not want to go back to Stonyhurst. Thompson felt he had to put his foot down. He knew it was hard for a boy to learn alone; he believed it to be impossible. 'I tried it and the result is I have had no education and it is very dispiriting besides.'[21] John's, and later Joseph's, ten-month exile in northern England every year was the price paid for their parents' conviction that sound and comprehensive education was indispensable.

Thompson had another anxiety – the Macdonald government's necessity to have a general election in 1887. He hoped that the price he would have to pay for being minister of justice, that is, largely separated from his family, would not be rewarded by 'being forced and coaxed and brought to go through this slime again.' Some of this was post-election exhaustion. he was bone tired when he returned from Antigonish. But he also wanted to warn Annie that he was not willing to keep at politics indefinitely. Bishop Cameron was confident, however, that in two years there would not be any more fighting. Thompson would get an acclamation next time. The bishop told Annie, 'They see now it is useless to fight against me.'[22]

Certain it was that in Ottawa Thompson would feel the beat of life harder; there would be more challenges and more opportunities. He had not been exactly wasting his talents at the Supreme Court of Nova Scotia; but the Court had come early in life, and Thompson had too much energy to be deployed effectively there. Annie was right in pushing her husband further than he was prepared to go on his own. As she put it to him, 'You will know for the first time what you are capable of.'[23] So Monday, 26 October, a few days after he got home from Antigonish, Annie packed him up, and pushed him out of the house at Willow Park on the long Intercolonial road to Ottawa. Thompson swallowed hard and went.

There had been three other by-elections that autumn, two of them for other new cabinet ministers. Thomas White, the new minister of the interior, was re-elected in Cardwell, Ontario, and George Foster was re-elected for Kings, New Brunswick, as minister of marine and fisheries. All were victories for the Macdonald government, despite its awful weakness that spring and summer and the disaster of the North–West Rebellion. Of the new cabinet ministers, Thompson was the only one who had never been in the House of Commons. Indeed, outside of Sir Francis Hincks, an odd case, Thompson was the only minister brought directly into the government from outside Parliament since 1867. He was a novice in every sense of the word. He knew little of his cabinet colleagues, and less about Parliament's style, customs, traditions. Besides he was, as he told Annie, 'the baby minister,' the youngest in cabinet. He was also the youngest justice minister since confederation, one of the three youngest in Canadian history.[24]

The office of minister of justice and attorney general of Canada was governed by an 1868 statute, repeated almost unchanged in the 1886 Revised Statutes.[25] The duty of the minister of justice was to see that the administration of public business was in accordance with the law. He was to advise the governor general in council, that is, the cabinet, upon legislative acts of the provincial legislatures. As attorney general he had the task of advising all departments of government upon any matter of law connected with their work. He had the superintendence of the prison system of the Dominion. He had the responsibility for the conduct of all litigation for or against the crown in any department of government.

The Department of Justice in 1885 was on the ground floor of the East Block, that large, handsome, neo-Gothic building, one of the three original structures built for Parliament that remains now largely as it was built in the early 1860s. Thompson wrote to Babe, his nine-year-old daughter, and told her if she would look up the picture of the Parliament buildings in her geography book, she would see where he worked.[26] Thompson arrived in Ottawa on Wednesday morning, 28 October; two hours later he was at the East Block. Though it was a working day, he found to his surprise that the first four offices he entered were 'as deserted as the enchanted palace' in *Sleeping Beauty*. Not a soul was to be seen. He found his own office clean and ready for him, 'a beautiful room, with elegant furniture, and wonderful fixings for work.' He found electric bells and dared to press one marked 'Messenger.' A boy actually appeared and performed his first duty for the new minister by bringing him his mail. None of the clerks were on the scene. The deputy minister, G.W.

Burbidge, dropping by on his way to somewhere else, was greatly surprised to find his minister there working. 'We saw you had been given a banquet in Halifax,' he explained, 'and took it for granted that you would not be here for another week.' The department did not seem distinguished by too much punctilio. Thompson wasn't either. Dignified he was, sometimes stiff, but he was averse to ruling his department with an iron hand. Within a week Annie was telling him he would have to learn to make other people do their work. It was ridiculous, for example, for him to bring up the coal for his own fire. But in such matters he followed his instincts. A month later he discovered that fifty legal opinions, requested by other departments, were in arrears awaiting the return of the deputy minister from the West. He told the clerk to bring them and he would do them himself.[27]

The department was modest enough considering its responsibilities, but in this respect it was no different from the rest of the civil service. The department's Ottawa establishment consisted of a deputy minister, two chief clerks, four first class clerks, two second class, three third class. The penitentiary branch consisted of the inspector of penitentiaries plus two clerks. In all there were fifteen men plus three or four messengers. The whole department occupied fifteen rooms in the East Block, numbers 59 to 73. Thompson's office was Number 64; 65 was that of his deputy, 66 that of the inspector of penitentiaries.[28]

The salaries ranged from $3,600 per annum, the salary of the deputy minister, $2,000 to the chief clerk, $1,800 to the first class clerk, down to the messenger, at $400. If there were any annual increments, they could be from $25 to $50; most employees got no annual increment at all.[29] Thompson's brother-in-law, Daniel Sargent, who had been collector of customs at Barrington for fifteen years, had not had an increase since 1873. One of Thompson's earliest letters as minister was to Mackenzie Bowell to try to rectify that; but he apologized for writing, saying that the fact that Sargent was his brother-in-law was reason why what he had to say 'should be received with some qualification.'[30]

A new minister is always a shock to a civil service department. He comes, as Lady Bracknell alleged a fiancé should come to a young lady, as a surprise, 'pleasant or unpleasant as the case may be.' It was alleged by outsiders, *The Week* for one, that a new cabinet minister was almost helpless in the hands of his department, struggle as he might. The civil service machine, well oiled and almost frictionless, would always control him. The moment he tried to make changes he would be 'gripped by the Machine, bought tight with red tape, paralysed by party interests. His subordinates are his masters.'[31] Like many observations about the civil service, it depended upon what department and what minister. No one should under-estimate institutional resistance to change. Of the dozen deputy ministers in 1886, at least one had been in place since confederation. T. Trudeau, in Railways and Canals. The next oldest were J.L. McDougall, auditor general, appointed in July 1878, and J.M. Courtney, finance, appointed about the same time. The others had mostly been appointed since 1882.[32] Thompson's deputy ministers were exceptionally able, but he was to have three of them: G.W. Burbidge (1882–8); Robert Sedgewick (1888–93) and E.L. Newcombe (1893–1924). All three ended as Supreme Court judges, two of them put there by Thompson. All three were Nova Scotians either by birth or adoption. Burbidge had been a lawyer in Saint John, New Brunswick, though he was born in Nova Scotia.[33]

Ottawa when Parliament was not sitting was said to be a terrible place; 'almost like a city of the Dead' was Hugh John Macdonald's opinion in 1871. Those less youthful than Hugh John, or who knew Ottawa better, had found, at least by the mid-eighties, that it was not so bad. Ottawa was by that time nearly as large as Halifax – twenty-seven thousand inhabitants – and it was not quite the same raw lumber town of twenty years earlier. It had ugliness certainly, not helped when Eddy's began to make pulp paper in the 1890s. Upon Thompson, anyway, Ottawa made a favourable impression. The houses were of stone and brick (unlike the wooden reality of Halifax), the streets were clean, well paved, and furnished with wooden sidewalks.[34] Ottawa's residents had a civilized interest in life that came from the absence of large commercial ventures and from a fixed amount of leisure. There was also, for most, a fixed amount of income, so patent that most people knew each other's income down to the last dollar. Some important people lived beyond their incomes; according to C.H. Tupper, all the justices of the Supreme Court of Canada, save the chief justice, had discounted their $7,000 per annum salary cheques nine months in advance. The bank manager said that there was less danger in giving such loans than in refusing them![35] There was some ostentation; Lady Macdonald thought people lived beyond their means. Ottawa people discovered that they had resources denied to others; they had the Parliamentary Library, the Archives and, of course, the National Art Gallery and Fisheries Exhibit – a curiously Canadian juxtaposition, that – at the corner of Queen and O'Connor.

Thompson was soon taken up by friends and colleagues. One of his first invitations was to dinner with Sir John and Lady Macdonald at Earnscliffe. The house was dark and a little sombre, but full of handsome things and, unlike many Victorian houses, uncluttered. Lady Macdonald he found on first acquaintance pleasant enough but 'ugly as sin.' Lady Tilley, who was staying there at the time, 'tried to be very pleasant and did not need to try to be ugly.' Thompson would not have minded a few sirens, as he wrote to Annie, but so far they had let him alone. Annie did not worry about the sirens; she was concerned about other importunities. She worried about money anyway, but especially since Thompson found it hard to resist a woman who pleaded poverty or necessity. Annie laid a positive injunction upon him that he was 'not to lend any money without telling me.' If Thompson had had his eye on ladies, it was not a very lecherous one. At dinner a month later he commented that there were two miraculously ugly ladies, one of whom he had to escort; she had a heavy beard and was otherwise in keeping. The other was a young woman, 'all bustle and bosom with just a slight scarf between.'[36]

Macdonald's dinner was not untypical of those in Ottawa at the time; with oysters, consommé, fish, lamb cutlets, and cabinet pudding, Charlotte Russe, lemon ice, and fruit for dessert. Sherry and claret would be assumed. Men were frequently judged on the quality of their claret. Griffin told Thompson, 'Of *course* go to dinner with Sir Alex. [Campbell]. That is an *event* – he gives very perfect dinners; and his claret, you will notice is in perfect order.'[37]

In due course Thompson would repay Lady Macdonald's invitation by calling. This was a ritual, now almost extinct, but universal in the nineteenth century, and it would last for a long time. It was still the custom in Fredericton as late as 1939. It was *de rigueur* if someone called and left their card that you did the same, unless you really wished to cut them. If you returned the call but preferred not to speak to the person you tried discreetly to do it when you knew they were not officially 'at home.' The bishop of Ottawa came to see Thompson at his boarding house; Thompson would have to return that call. On 7 November, five days after his dinner at Macdonald's, Thompson visited Lady Macdonald to thank her. He left cards at the bishop's, the chief justice's, and a dozen 'small fry,' as he put it, who had called on him. He also left his name – apparently one did not leave a card? – at Rideau Hall.[38]

He had been introduced to Lord Lansdowne a few days before by Sir John Macdonald and took to the governor general at once. Thompson found agreeable Lansdowne's lack of pomposity, his quiet competence, his intelligence. Lansdowne had been governor general since 1883 and was well liked. 'He is very quiet – takes a great interest in all that one can tell him about the country and not only has no airs but not even any manner. Sir John says he has had to do with seven Governors and that Lansdowne is the best of them.'39

Thompson lived unpretentiously, ten minutes from Parliament Hill, in the same boarding house as Griffin and George Johnson. All the boarders, Thompson included, ate together at the same fly-blown dining-room table. Thompson's only luxury was having two rooms, a bedroom and a sitting-room. But the bed was so hard that some nights he could not sleep. Thompson told Annie, on learning Wallace Graham was ill, to tell him that he had no right to feel miserable until he had been a judge and been turned out into 'the cold water again.' One night Thompson half wakened, struggled to remember what part of Antigonish County he was in, then came the delicious thought that he was at home. Then the truth came: he was in an Ottawa boarding house. The realization was, he said, 'simply horrible.'40

He would get to the office every morning just after nine. The Nova Scotia mail arrived about one o'clock – he always looked anxiously for that – and at three in the afternoon there was, at least in these days of early November 1885, a cabinet meeting that lasted until six. It was held in the handsome Privy Council room, lit by windows that opened out on views to the east and north. The ministers began to improve on acquaintance, and it was remarkable to Thompson how much more smoothly and punctually work went forward in the Macdonald cabinet than it had with the Holmes cabinet in Halifax.41

There were thirteen cabinet ministers besides himself. Sir John sat at the head of the table, nearly seventy-one years old, handling cabinet meetings with the aplomb and experience of his years, though still losing his Highland temper once in a while. Two recorded instances were with the Tuppers, Tupper Sr in 1884, and Tupper Jr in 1890, both deserved.42 Macdonald had considerable patience, great perspicuity, both served by a ripe and well-stocked mind. His useful attribute as chairman was that he usually knew the point he wished to arrive at. He was the oldest man in a cabinet whose average age, not including Thompson, was fifty-seven. The cabinet had the customary profile: five ministers from Ontario (not including Macdonald), four from Quebec, and two each from New Brunswick and Nova Scotia. There was no minister from Prince Edward Island, and there was none from the West until Edgar Dewdney arrived in 1888. Of the thirteen ministers, six were Roman Catholics. Two of the Ontario ministers were senators – Sir Alexander Campbell, now postmaster general, and Frank Smith, a Catholic from London, Ontario, without portfolio, and by that time president of the Toronto Street Railway

Company. Thomas White, Macdonald's new and able minister of the interior, though from Montreal, sat for an Ontario constituency, and that made him an Ontario minister. Mackenzie Bowell was minister of customs, an expert on patronage, vain, with little parliamentary panache, but faithful, hard-working, and scrupulous.[43] John Carling, minister of agriculture, was a successful brewer from London, Ontario, had style and good looks but not much else. A.W. McLelan, Thompson's fellow minister from Nova Scotia, was the new minister of finance (after Tilley's retirement to New Brunswick as lieutenant-governor). McLelan was one of those quiet men to lean on when there was difficulty, but he was not popular either in Parliament or in Nova Scotia. John Costigan, of Edmunston, New Brunswick, the minister of inland revenue, was an uncertain quantity, with a taste for drink. The Quebec ministers were a mixed group. The feud between Hector Langevin of Quebec City and Adolphe Chapleau of Montreal was in the potential rather than actual stage. Thompson never developed any intimacy with Langevin, minister of public works, but he liked Chapleau from the start and the feeling was mutual. Caron was another minister whom Thompson saw socially, and when Annie came to Ottawa for a visit in February 1886, she and Alice Baby Caron saw much of each other. The other Quebec minister was J.H. Pope, minister of railway and canals, from the Eastern Townships, a rough, abrasive character whose capacity Macdonald depended upon; but Thompson never liked him.

The October and November cabinet meetings were difficult and tense, but Thompson remarked that however difficult they were, 'everybody keeps the most exquisite courtesy.' The issues were of course the North-West trials and Louis Riel. There was enormous public pressure, on both sides. Macdonald's old friend and colleague, Senator James Gowan of Barrie, Ontario, said that nothing was talked of there but 'Riel – Riel!! I never knew public opinion so set and determined.'[44] Even Annie had written Thompson about Riel. She was on the other side from Gowan; she did not want Riel hanged. 'Let Riel go to prison,' she told her husband, 'if you hang him you make a patriot of him. If you send him to prison he is only an insane man.' It was sensible advice. Thompson was in no position to do much about it. The reports and recommendations on most of the North-West capital cases, including Riel's, had been made by Thompson's predecessor, Sir Alexander Campbell. Thompson had nothing to do with the Riel case other than giving his vote as a member of Council.[45] But he could and did revise the sentences passed upon some of the Indians, and one or two cases he had to decide on his own.

Several of the capital case files arrived on Thompson's desk for consideration, or reconsideration. One was Pa-pa-mah-cha-kwayo, 'Wandering Spirit,' who, with Big Bear's son, Imasees, was responsible for the Frog Lake massacre on 2 April. The Indian agent, two priests, and six others including a Métis, were shot down in cold blood. Wandering Spirit was tried before Judge Rouleau at Battleford. Thompson let the verdict of guilty stand, and Wandering Spirit was hanged on 27 November. The case of Eungana, or Fast Runner, was different. He had been convicted of murder before Richardson at Regina, but the jury, as in the case of Riel, had put in a recommendation for mercy. Due to be hanged on 13 November, Fast Runner's sentence, on Thompson's recommendation, was commuted by cabinet on 31 October to life imprisonment. Thompson approved his release from Stony Mountain three years later.[46] Two other Indians were recommended for commutation in the same way. One of these, Louison Mongrain, had been convicted before Judge Rouleau at Battleford for the murder of David Cowan at Fort Pitt. But Thompson noted the sworn statements of two of the white prisoners at Fort Pitt, Anne and William McLean, as to the humanity displayed toward them and other prisoners by Mongrain during their captivity, and his continued efforts to save the prisoners from ill-treatment by other Indians. Consequently Thompson recommended to cabinet, in view of Mongrain's 'courage and humanity, that his death sentence be commuted to life imprisonment.'[47]

In the light of the Riel case another of Thompson's commutations is interesting. John Esterbee was in Welland Gaol under sentence of death for murder, due to be hanged on 30 November. The evidence fully justified the sentence, but the prisoner's conduct was so odd that Mr Justice Rose reported it. Thompson asked that the judge be authorized to have a specialist examine Easterbee. Dr Wallace reported, 'the prisoner's congenital mental deficiency, extremely low moral stature, and his dense ignorance, no attempts ever having been made to teach his anything ... he is not responsible.' The sentence was commuted to life imprisonment.[48]

On Sunday evening, 8 November 1885, Thompson was put out of action for a fortnight. All day he had kidney pain. After tea it got worse. By the small hours of Monday morning it was so bad that Thompson got George Johnson to go for a doctor. It was not easy to get a doctor; he was rushed off his feet with smallpox cases and vaccinations. By the time he arrived about five in the morning, Thompson was in such pain he had to have something to knock him out. The doctor said it was the passage of gravel through the kidney to the bladder and gave him a hypodermic. That day the Ottawa *Free Press* called to interview Thompson about Riel. Griffin and Johnson would not let Thompson be visited by anyone, whereupon a story about Thompson's illness appeared in the Ottawa paper, that he was so ill that not even his mail was being sent to him. Thompson without his mail! Sensational stories get copied, so Griffin and Johnson, unknown to Thompson who was almost insensible from pain and hypodermics, decided that if the Halifax papers came out with such news Annie would collapse. So Griffin wired her twice, once in Thompson's name and once in his own, telling her that Thompson was ill but that everything was all right. Everything was *not* all right, but none of the men, including Thompson when he knew what was going on, wanted to reveal the nature of the illness, it being one that women were not supposed to know anything about.

Annie was bewildered, as if the world was slipping from beneath her feet. The Halifax papers did not carry the Ottawa story. She got Wallace Graham to wire that she was coming to Ottawa at once. Thompson did not want Annie's first social appearance in Ottawa in such circumstances; Graham received a wire back, 'Please prevent wife leaving am all right again;' Annie got one, 'Do not think of coming, am quite recovered and will be very much distressed if you leave Halifax.'[49] Annie did not come; after that, she said, no woman would. But she was furious. She wrote him a cross letter which he received in one of the periods of intense pain when the doctor could not come. She began to realize that he was probably going to get better, even without her, but in her more sympathetic letter of 18 November she was right. It is a letter that says much about them both:

You poor child,
  ... I think I was right. You tell me how weak you are and how much you have suffered and all the time you are trying to deceive me with four airy telegrams and breezy notes. Of course I was not blindfolded a bit. All the time you were suffering not knowing what moment inflimation [*sic*] might set in and I was left to suffer at home without being able to do anything for you[.] As to that trash about women not knowing anything about that complaint I did not suppose you would make such a childish excuse and you can leave the case to Sir John or any right minded lawyer and if they dont say I was right I'll give in. And if you want to test the case in another way put it to yourself and think of my being as sick as you were and not letting you come to see me. You could not say a crueler thing to a woman than to tell that she could be done without ... let me know the truth. Did the stone pass down without the Dr having to crush it; Is he sure that it all passed away. Is it likely to leave you weak long ... Now dear do tell me the truth and never try your dodging again because what is the good of bogus news? You know how fond I am of you and if I were able how much I would do to push you to the first and mind, remember I never at any time pretended to have wings.

Thompson's excuse was that the doctor anticipated a crisis of short duration, instead of which it lasted a week. As to the hard things she had said, Annie was clear her case stood on its merits. When Thompson mailed her his photograph but sent Griffin's by mistake, Annie's humour was restored. She told him she was so disappointed in getting the wrong picture that in revenge she was going around Willow Park showing Griffin as Thompson's new nurse!

Thompson was teased about having the cabinet's disease; Macdonald, who had had the same thing, only worse, in 1870, sent a solicitous letter. In Thompson's case the treatment was almost as bad as the disease: 'Hypodermical injections every night, until last night, injections for bowels, morphine pills every 4 hours, evervescing mixture every 4 hours, milk and soda every few minutes, bethesda water every four hours night and day, hot baths, sometimes two a day, and hot linseed poultices renewed every 4 hours night and day.' Small wonder Thompson's bed was wet with perspiration. He had to watch his diet; he was allowed only poultry and game as meat. He was to avoid soup and turnips and eat only baked potatoes and celery as vegetables; he was to take lots of milk, oatmeal, tea. Oysters were strongly recommended. He was allowed no wine or beer, but whisky was fine.[50] Improbable as all that sounds, it worked. Within two weeks he was virtually feeling himself again, in time to experience the full force of the Riel agitation.

Riel had been hanged on Monday, 16 November. In Ottawa the excitement was considerable, and in Quebec more so. It was, said Thompson, 'far worse than our papers make it appear.'[51] Sir John A. Macdonald seems to have had few doubts that Riel was guilty, that he was legally sane, and that there were no circumstances, legal or political, that could permit Riel to be got off. Senator Gowan, a considerable legal authority himself, wrote Macdonald on 18 November:

From what you wrote me I did not doubt the result but I felt most uneasy to the last knowing how public men are often obliged to take a course they do not individually approve. The fact may affect you prejudicially with Lower Canada but looking at the subject with all anxiety to see the wisest course for you to take I felt it would have been an act of political insanity to yield, simply because the man was of French blood.[52]

It has been sometimes averred that Macdonald sacrificed Riel to Ontario opinion. Ontario opinion undoubtedly would have been furious at Riel's being pardoned; but fundamentally Riel was sacrificed not to Ontario but to the law. French Canadians, however, had expected a reprieve, and when Riel was hanged they were outraged. The French, said Thompson, have gone mad over him. 'There is nothing spoken of here except *Riel*.'[53] Sir John A. Macdonald and the three French-Canadian ministers, Caron, Chapleau, and Langevin, were burnt in effigy day and night in Montreal and Quebec City. The governor general, Sir John, and the French ministers were all threatened with the direst consequences, including death. Macdonald told Thompson that in his lifetime he had been threatened at least a hundred times with death. Thompson opined privately that politicians found their life so unpleasant that the threat of death was the last thing to terrify them.

Thompson was unsympathetic to Riel. The excitement was much more than there need be about 'such a paltry hero who struggled so long and so hard for the privilege of hanging.'[54] Nevertheless, the departure of Sir John for England, and the consequent delay of the opening of Parliament in 1886 Thompson greeted with relief. It would leave him time to be better prepared – there would be a heavy load on his shoulders – and he believed by that time the 'French madness' would have died down. By the end of November he began to feel the tide turning. Bishop Cameron came to Montreal and Ottawa to speak out on the Riel issue and the government was grateful.[55] Other bishops could follow where Cameron had been bold enough to begin. The cabinet waited, hoping the storm would blow over.

One cabinet colleague whom Thompson had not liked was J.H. Pope, minister of railways and canals. Pope's talent was delivered to cabinet colleagues and public alike by means of fairly primitive manners. He was a rough customer; he said no with undiplomatic force and disconcerting frequency. His deputy minister, Collingwood Schreiber, was nearly as bad as he was. The two of them ran the railway department like the captain and first mate of a Nova Scotian square-rigger, tough, abrupt, unforgiving, but carrying tremendous sail with a great deal of capacity. Thompson and Pope crossed swords when one of Pope's subordinates, Douglas Stewart, decided that he would like to become Thompson's private secretary.

There were pressures for that position. Bishop Duhamel of Ottawa asked Bishop Cameron to write Thompson about appointing a friend as Thompson's secretary. Cameron was astonished; Bishop Duhamel should not have asked him to intervene on behalf of someone whom Cameron knew not at all. He told Thompson that he would remind Bishop Duhamel that 'the choice of a private secretary, like that of a wife, ought to be left to whom it most concerns.' The bishop also had good advice to Thompson. Don't work so hard. '"Hasten slowly" ought to be your motto (and mine, though it is not).' Take exercise. But as to a private secretary, choose your own.[56] Thompson did.

Douglas Stewart was the younger brother of J.J. Stewart, editor of the Halifax *Herald*. They had first met in October 1881, when Thompson was in Ottawa for his first Supreme Court cases; he had lent young Stewart his room to write up reports of the Court for the *Herald*. Douglas Stewart was then a young but rising clerk in the Department of Railways and Canals who already knew his way around the civil service. He was, according to Thompson, 'intelligent, hardworking, discreet, a Protestant, and a Nova Scotian and it [the appointment] would gratify J.J.' Douglas knew all the Nova Scotian members and many of their failings and strengths. Within a few days, having had approval from Bishop Cameron and from Annie, the left and right bowers of Thompson's life,[57] Thompson decided to take Stewart on as of 1 December. Stewart was delighted, but came the next day broken-hearted. J.H. Pope, 'that licentious, ignorant old brute,' would not allow it; Stewart was too valuable in Railways and Canals.[58] Stewart was left to see what he could effect on his own. He had a knack, found also in Sir Charles Tupper, of using what he called 'brass and bluff' to get what he wanted. He was pertinacious, finally arranging an exchange with another clerk.[59] Stewart was thus able to break through the barriers Pope put up. As of 7 February 1886, he became Thompson's private secretary and would remain with him from then on. It took a little time before he was really useful. Stewart had to start by learning Thompson's shorthand and there were some special tricks to it.[60] Thompson frequently drafted letters in shorthand.

A civil service custom Thompson found peculiar was the habit of eating lunch at one's desk. Even the deputy minister ate a cold lunch that way. Old hands who liked a drink kept themselves well enough reinforced with alcohol during the day so that they did not get hungry. Narrow and severe in some ways, the civil service was generous with sick leave: if a man were away a year, he was still paid.[61] Thompson kept breaking civil service customs. For example, when the deputy minister came to discuss business, usually an hour at a time, it was so awkward to see him standing that Thompson, several days running, told him to sit down. Burbidge never did, letting on he had not heard the request. Thompson only found out in mid-January that it was standard procedure for the deputy minister to stand, not so much from deference, but to distinguish him from other callers in the minister's office.

Protocol and Thompson were a curious mixture. In some ways he was intensely dignified; but his stiff manner was mostly the essential protection his shyness needed. Canon O'Donnell, who had met Thompson just before Christmas 1885, wrote about him to Bishop Cameron:

I was a little awed at the precision of his conversation at first. The feeling didn't last, and I soon felt at home. Everything about him has an air of candor, sincerity, modesty as winning as it is meek and gentle. He is a person one could easily confide in without fear that either judgment, discretion or fidelity would be wanting.[62]

Thompson had been counting the days until Christmas. He had to try hard, especially on Sundays, not to yield to ineradicable pain of loneliness and grab the train home to Halifax. He would lie awake thinking of all the times he had been ugly or cross, and resolve never to be like that again. One Sunday ruminating about Annie and their double bed in a letter, he asked her, in shorthand, if her December menstruation would be over when he came home. 'I suppose you will think this is pretty bold but you are used to my being bold are you not?' Annie answered obliquely, 'I will answer *your pert question as to December in a day or two.*'[63]

Whenever he was feeling lonely and bereft, Annie would try to cheer him up. It was true, she said, 'that we have taken the world hard and therefore we are not just as kitten-like' as some others. But, she said, don't mope in that fashion on Sundays. Go out to dinner with the men. Above all don't act like 'such a poor old child out in the cold with such a nobody-to-care-for-you-tone.' When Thompson talked about giving it all up and coming home for good, Annie wouldn't have it. 'No, you shall not, you are there and the world must see what you are made of – so now no more coaxing.' That was the way things were often decided, by him getting alongside her, then Annie would announce her decision beginning with, 'Listen!'[64]

Thompson also felt strongly the loss of his métier as judge that had suited him and was 'free from anxiety.'[65] But Annie would demonstrate they would soon be more comfortable financially; she would try to find $100 so he could join the Rideau Club, though no miser ever held onto a bank book more tightly than she did. That had been the rub of their old life. Sometimes it made Annie angry to recall how her husband had walked the mile and a half home, all the way out to Willow Park at two o'clock in the morning after working nights downtown at the office. After fifteen years of married life how little materially they had to show for their work![66] Thompson, in his turn, would console her for that; there were years ahead of them where they would accomplish much more than they could 'when we were struggling at the foot of the ladder.' Annie wanted little or nothing for herself; she wanted a great deal for her husband and her children. She hated having to begin 1886 with a debt of $500 on her back, but they were both confident that a few more months would see them in the clear.

She was passionate about her mail. She would walk the mile and a half into town to the Halifax post office just for her letters – something that Thompson sternly insisted was too much for her – and if she couldn't go for them, she would send someone, even twice a day. The greasy clerk at the post office who gave out letters became annoyed one day with Annie's importunity, and threw letters and a book at the wicket. Then Annie *was* angry; she was a sea captain's daughter and she was just not having *that*. She raised up Wallace Graham, and the postmaster, and put them furiously into action. Postmaster Blackadar under her anger was like a ship running before a gale, scudding downwind 'under bare poles,' as Annie put it graphically to Thompson. Out of the storm came a nice post office box for Annie with a key, so that she could go to the post office as often as she pleased. Her sister Fan wrote Thompson that Annie had simply become 'an immense sheet of paper, bottle of ink and bad pen' since Thompson had left. At the least provocation Annie would take up her pen and pour her joys and woes, 'real and imaginary' – Fan put it with a sister's irreverence – in letters to Thompson. Why, said Fan on 20 November, Annie is at it now and will be until the wee hours.[67] On 4 December Annie wrote three letters to Thompson, a cross one in the morning (the result of a querulous one from Thompson over which she cried), a forgiving note midday, and a long twelve-page letter in the evening, which she signed, 'Goodby kitten such I am the torment of your life, Annie.'

To this torment Thompson happily returned on 20 December, ready to rest for a week. Annie wished that Thompson's cousin, David Pottinger, would ask them all to Moncton for Christmas; she was sure the relaxation would be taken out of Thompson's holiday by people coming to see him. But Annie was also sure that David Pottinger wouldn't ask them, so she and Thompson would ask him. She was ready to hire someone to help her in getting Christmas dinner for her own family of six, plus Fan, her mother, David Pottinger, and perhaps the Armstrong children thrown in for good measure. The Armstrong children had lived over the way, but were now boarding at the Mount. R.F. Armstrong, the father, had lost his job, had been thrown 'in the lee scuppers' as Annie put it. She had plenty of nautical metaphors at her command![68]

Thompson was on his way back to Ottawa by 4 January, stopping in Truro to talk politics with A.C. Bell, the leader of the Conservative opposition in the Nova Scotia House, seeing David Pottinger at Moncton, and where G.E. Foster, the new minister from New Brunswick got aboard. 'Very intelligent and acute without being conceited' was Thompson's initial impression of Foster, the former classics teacher from the University of New Brunswick, newly become minister of marine.

Thompson did not return to the boarding house in Ottawa. Annie would come to Ottawa in February and he was certain the boarding house was unsuitable. He moved into the Russell House, where he had a handsome corner room with a view. It cost him $2.50 a day, room and board – most Canadian hotels were on American plan – which Thompson found ferocious. He was not uncheerful, but his weekends were a trial. He would work Saturday until six o'clock, have dinner, sometimes with Johnson and Griffin, and then play whist, a game he had to learn since everyone in Ottawa played it.[69] Sunday he would go to eight o'clock mass. But after dinner on Sunday evening, as he sat down to write to Annie, the sense of loss would come in at him through the very walls of the Russell House. How could they live like this? Annie could not commute between Halifax and Ottawa; she would be as lonesome in Ottawa without the children as they would in Halifax without her. He wrote ruefully, 'Transplanting a man like me is very hard work. He withers all the time.' An illustration of how she was needed in Halifax had already come. Annie was busy the week before getting the children ready to start school again. Helena needed her almost as much as Thompson did; Annie was busy, Helena waited patiently on the sofa, quiet as usual, and at last she broke out, much as Thompson might do, 'I am waiting patiently until I can have you all to myself!' Thompson's unhappy Sunday letter hit Annie between wind and water. She wrote:

Oh my Pet my Pet,
    Can't you bully things out when I am trying to do so ... Baby you break my heart, if you don't try to be more of a boss, and look this thing in the face and make the best of it for a little while until I can be with you ... On Sunday too, as it rained and stormed I thought if only I could be with you long enough just to kiss and hug you and run my hands through your hair, that I would be satisfied; and tonight at Truro, as we met the Quebec Express going through I wanted so much just to get

on board and run up to see you, that I looked quite wistfully after the train as it passed out of sight.[70]

His Sunday walks in Ottawa grew a little shorter; he grew resentful when he passed other people's houses of their luxury of home and family when he had none. How dare his friends and colleagues, and legions of others, have wives when he was so far from his! He could endure the hardship of living alone if only others would do the same.[71] Thompson consoled himself with reading as much as possible. He and Annie exchanged comments on books, and Thompson sent parcels of them down from Ottawa, to be duly returned to the Parliamentary Library. He recommended Stevenson's *Treasure Island*, and sent Annie *Kidnapped* when it came out in the summer of 1886. Novels were light relief from the piles of papers at the Justice Department. Thompson read Rider Haggard's *King Solomon's Mines*, just out, but he objected that it made too impudent demands on his credulity. Jules Verne, he told Annie, was child's play compared to Rider Haggard. Thompson did not like Tolstoy either. *Anna Karenina* he read later that summer, and it seemed to him the most unhealthy book he had ever read. Every one of Tolstoy's characters was peculiar, and he himself had all their idiosyncrasies put together except, of course, he insisted to Annie, Anna Karenina's jealousy.[72] Thompson much preferred Balzac to all of them. Perhaps Balzac's realism, his profound understanding of the difficulty of a woman's role, fascinated Thompson.

For all Thompson's tenderness toward women, especially those in distress, his humour had a sardonic, almost savage quality, evident in his descriptions of ladies he met at dinner parties. They were not often flattering. Hattie Griffin, Martin Griffin's wife, 'had a low white dress on and ten warts showing above the low water mark. Others were not counted.'[73] Where did that sarcasm come from? Some atavistic fear of women, or was it simply telling Annie that no woman he met came close to her in his appreciation? Thompson's humour had a mordant bite to it, as his impression of a sleigh ride one cold February evening from Ottawa to Aylmer and back. A group of twenty engineered it, at the invitation of the Costigans. It was a bitter, moonless night, the temperature twenty below. When they got to Aylmer there was dancing for the young, cards for the old, with 'just enough of cards to spoil the dancing and of dancing to spoil the cards.' They got back to Ottawa at one in the morning, covered with frost and snow, the horses so much so that they looked as if they had been dredged in icing sugar. And Ottawa people called that, said Thompson, pleasure![74] Thompson never did quite adapt to these queer central Canadian customs, disguised as he would say under the name of social amenities.

Other parliamentary customs he would have to take more seriously, if ever he was going to master procedure and the order paper of the House of Commons. It was a place he did not know. It had its own style, its own *ambiance*; what would it make of a new man from the provinces, wholly unacquainted with it, and a minister at that?

11

Defending the Macdonald Government

The old House of Commons, before the great fire of 3 February 1916, had a different shape; the Speaker did not sit, as now, at the end of the long axis of the House, but at the end of the short one. The old House of Commons was spread deeply on either side of the Speaker, seven rows of desks, forty-four feet on each side. The House had been originally designed for the 130 members of the Legislative Assembly of the Province of Canada. Now, in 1885, it had 211 seats, upholstered in dark green leather and the walls to match. It was apt to be hot and stuffy, for gas lighting tended to exhaust oxygen; members had been complaining since 1867. Various remedies were tried; the introduction of electric light after 1887 eased the problem without curing it.

There was, and was not, a House of Commons bar. It had been officially closed in 1874, but it had been unofficially open since. MPs had to have a restaurant; by custom the privilege was farmed to a restaurateur who would not take it unless the profits of a bar were attached. When Laurier first entered the House of Commons in 1874, it was not uncommon for half the MPs to be under the weather when the House adjourned at midnight. In 1885 Parliament had not changed much. The Senate had a bar which had a reputation for port; the specialty of the Commons bar was an amiable decoction of rum which, as one newspaper correspondent observed, 'was very comforting to the wounded heart.'[1]

Commons debates could be rambunctious, although most received only cursory attention. MPs tended in a big debate to speak for Hansard or the press gallery. During Guillaume Amyot's speech in the Riel debate, the *Montreal Star* made a census of the forty-four Liberal members present in the House: six were asleep, nine were reading papers, four were writing, six were talking, and nineteen were paying attention to the debate.

Perhaps 45 per cent attention was all one had the right to expect. The *Star* seemed to expect better.[2]

Lord Lansdowne opened Parliament on 25 February 1886, and Thompson was introduced to the Commons by Sir John A. Macdonald and A.W. McLelan the same afternoon. For most MPs it was their first look at him. Barely middle height, a little portly, his composure patently a mask for his timidity, Thompson made no profound impression. He was unknown; his provincial reputation was no recommendation to the members of the House of Commons. But for the first time in five years, the minister of justice would be in their chamber rather than the Senate. They would be able to get at him directly. Many were looking forward to that. Thompson seemed to the opposition like an innocent Christian in a chamber full of lions.

For his part Thompson could survey the Liberal front bench fifteen feet away. The leader of the opposition since 1880 was Edward Blake, now fifty-three years of age and at the height of his career at the bar. Tall, broad-shouldered, Blake was not only a physical presence but an intellectual one. An MA in classics besides being a lawyer, Blake had a powerful, wide-ranging intelligence; like many intellectuals, Blake believed there were no easy simplicities, and decisions for him were like the unravelling of a legal issue, tortuous and difficult. Blake's mind required a powerful will to move it into action, and that Blake did not have. He was cartooned as Hamlet agonizing over questions major and minor. He was also difficult to work with. He thought little about others; sensitive himself to slights, he was extraordinarily blind to the effects of his actions upon others. He was a formidable figure in the House of Commons because he knew so much; but he wore about him a quality of pusillanimity that was disconcerting.[3]

Next to Blake was Laurier. Tall, slim, pale, *soigné*, Laurier looked like an elegant poet from a literary salon. That was close to the truth; Laurier loved literature more than law or politics. If you wanted the best new books from the Parliamentary Library you would find that Laurier had got there first. Laurier may have looked weak and willowy: in fact he had hidden toughness. While he was never to enjoy robust health, nor the income commanded by Blake, he was better capable of ruling himself, and still more of commanding the devotion and loyalty of others. Laurier was also an actor, born and bred to the parliamentary stage, and he performed superbly. His speeches were pure theatre: they had a marvellous ring to them, some people suspected, because they had been rehearsed beforehand. Laurier was not remarkable for his quickness and readiness in debate, but given a little time he could bring off splendid effects.[4]

Others on the Liberal front bench had powerful idiosyncrasies that the House knew well. Sir Richard Cartwright was the lion of the Liberals, versatile, well-read, hard-hitting, using literature with skill, even with savagery. He had a stentorian voice, at its most powerful in denunciation. He was a renegade Conservative who had never forgiven Macdonald for the Pacific Scandal of 1873, nor the Canadian people for being so crass as to re-elect Macdonald in 1878.

On 3 March, a week after Parliament opened, Thompson introduced Bill No. 9, the Revised Statutes of Canada, 1886 edition, politely and carefully turning away offhand jabs from Blake. It was the same with Bill No. 10, a new system of land transfer in the North-West Territories. He answered questions on the Riel trial, and ordered papers to be brought down. (Incidentally those requests for Riel papers were carefully gone through by Sir John A. Macdonald, even from his sickbed.)[5] Then on 11 March, 1886, just as the session was getting its breath, A.G.P.R. Landry, MP for Montmagny (and president of the Quebec Conservative Association), moved 'that this House feels it is duty to express its deep grief that the sentence of death passed upon Louis Riel, convicted of high treason, was allowed to be carried into execution.'[6] Landry said that his motion was to express his own abhorrence at Riel's execution. That may have been so, but every Conservative knew the Liberal party was badly divided; the Landry motion was, if not concocted, at least very convenient for the government. It allowed French-Canadian Conservatives unhappy with the Macdonald government's execution of Riel to have their say against it. The best trick was blocking Liberal amendments to the Landry motion by moving the previous question directly Landry sat down.

At the beginning it was thought that it would be mainly a French-Canadian debate, but it quickly gathered momentum. To everyone's surprise, Clarke Wallace, an influential member of the Orange Order, spoke on 12 March and other English-speaking MPs followed. As the debate went into the following week, it was clear that it was going to be long and passionate, with tempers under control but with feelings deeply stirred. The galleries were packed. Archbishop Taché of St Bonface watched the debate from the senators' gallery, Lady Macdonald, Mrs Thomas White and Annie from the Speaker's gallery.

Despite the government's efforts the Landry debate did not go well. Chapleau was ill; Macdonald, ill at home with the flu and sciatica, had not been in the House five minutes since the debate started; Sir Hector

Langevin, Joseph Royal, Clarke Wallace on the government side were no match for opposition speakers like Guillaume Amyot and G.-A. Gigault, both of whom spoke in English and more effectively than English-speakers on the government side. Amyot was a firebrand, but Gigault's speech was the more effective because he was moderate. And then on the Tuesday night of the second week came Laurier.

The circumstances were odd. J.C. Rykert, Conservative, and François Béchard, Liberal, had spoken and half-emptied the House. It was 10:30 p.m. No one got up. The government did not want to use its big guns until Laurier and Blake had spoken. Neither had. The Speaker was considering calling the question when, after a couple of minutes' silence, Laurier rose. Laurier spoke but two hours; it was so quiet during parts of his speech that the ticking of the parliamentary clocks could be heard. The government, Laurier said, had caused the North-West Rebellion. No one else. When trouble came, then and only then the government moved. But it was too late. Had the government taken as much pains to do right as they had to punish wrong, history would have been vastly different, for the law would never have been violated at all.

It was going to be hard to follow Laurier. Thomas White, the new minister of the interior, tried; he defended the government's record the next day, a skilful defence of a bad position, and it was the only decent speech so far from the government benches. In fact, the Liberals up to that point had pretty much, as the *Montreal Star* said, wiped the floor with the Tories.[7]

Then came Blake on Friday, 19 March. It had taken him three months to master the subject. The mountain of books and papers on his desk impressed – and dismayed – those who knew what Blake was capable of. He ploughed through it all, book by book, point by point, for five mortal hours, part of the afternoon and all of the evening. Blake lost the interest of the House before he was half-way through; down that long road with Blake, especially after supper, most of his followers were asleep. Cartwright despatched one of the whips to wake them up, for if Blake saw them asleep he was capable of flinging down his voluminous papers and leaving the House forthwith.[8] Blake went on until one in the morning. The debate was then adjourned until Monday, 22 March, at which time the government's major defence would fall squarely upon Thompson.

Thompson wanted his young son Joe in Halifax to go to church and pray for blessing on his speech. By the time Thompson knew he had to speak, it was too late to send a letter to Joe; to telegraph such a delicate request was impossible. On Monday noon when the Nova Scotia mail came in, there was a letter from Joe, saying he had seen by Saturday's paper in Halifax that the time for his father's speech had come and on his own had gone to church to ask blessing for his father. Nothing helped more than that note, Thompson said, to give him confidence that day.[9]

The galleries were full that afternoon, Monday, 22 March. Lady Lansdowne was there with the governor general's ADC; so were Bishop Taché and Annie. Others crowded in for Thompson's performance. He knew it had to be one. About four o'clock he rose. He was not without advantages; his solidity was imposing; he had a resonant voice, pitched a little low but almost musical in its cadences; he had a natural, easy felicity of expression that, like a clear brook, carried his ideas. There was no mass of books and papers, no tortured metaphors, no finely drawn arguments, nor even attempts at eloquence. He appealed to neither sympathies nor passions. He set himself to address the reason and common sense of the House, allowing these to carry his argument by their own proper force.[10] He did not attempt to justify the government's administration of the North-West. For one thing the debate did not turn on it; for another that was the responsibility of the minister of the interior. Thompson concentrated his four-hour speech upon the issue central to the Landry motion: that Riel ought, or ought not, to have been executed.

It was extraordinary, said Thompson, that the House of Commons was considering such a subject at all. For the past twenty-five years no papers connected with a criminal case had been laid before the British Parliament or the Canadian one. Was the House of Commons the place to retry a criminal case, an appeal in effect from the legal system of Canada? For all the opposition criticism of the North-West trials, it was a system established under Edward Blake, minister of justice in 1875 and approved by Parliament. Hugh Richardson, the stipendiary magistrate who tried Riel, was appointed by Blake in 1876 and was the senior magistrate in the North-West Territories.[11] Thompson quoted the Winnipeg *Free Press*, that 'Riel was fairly tried, honestly convicted, laudably condemned and justly executed.' (Laurier privately agreed that there was 'no fair ground for imputing partiality to anybody connected with the trial.')[12]

Great issues exercise a kind of hydraulic pressure under which even well-settled judgments will bend. The Riel question is an example. Riel was not always sensible but he was not a fool. He was an intelligent and in some ways capable man. He had delusions, almost adolescent dreams of glory. He lacked tough-mindedness, a capacity for dogged persistence, so that difficulty or frustration made him unstable. He could lose his temper, and storm and rail at those whom he believed were in his way. Perhaps the most dangerous aspect of Riel was that he had learned in 1869–70 Machiavelli's dictum that it is useful to be feared. He used his temper almost deliberately to intimidate those who resisted him. With this went a massive, unwholesome vanity. Father André who knew him well wrote F.-X. Lemieux, Riel's lawyer, after the trial was over, an opinion Thompson studied:

Riel est un veritable phenomène à étudier, il est remarquable sous bien des points. Il faut le connaître et surtout l'étudier de près pour voir qu'il est en proie à une illusion invincible, qui le prive de cette faculté qu'on appelle *bon sens* ... Riel n'a pas assurément de bon sens qui lui montre la portée de ses actes et principalement quand il s'agit de religion et de politique.[13]

Riel was not insane in the nineteenth-century legal meaning of the word, but as one juror put it, he was 'a very decided crank.'[14]

Thompson's main point was that the Indian massacre at Frog Lake and other murders were set in motion by Riel. How could Wandering Spirit, the author of the Frog Lake massacre, be executed when the man who had set the Indians aflame, who had started the 'war of extermination,' be let off? 'You don't know what we are after,' Riel had shouted at Thomas McKay, a Scottish half-breed, just before Duck Lake, 'It is blood! we want blood! It is a war of extermination! Everybody that is against us is to be driven out of the country.'[15] At this point in his speech, Thompson turned toward the Speaker and said with a powerful voice,

Sir, I say that the man who undertakes, in the North-West ... to incite these Indians to rise and to commit war and depredation ... takes his life in his hand, and when he appeals to me for mercy, *he will get justice!*

At this, cheers broke from the government side – the first cheers the government had had the whole session.[16]

Gigault had cited the case of Lord George Gordon, the alleged inciter of the London riots in 1780, declaring that clemency had been extended to Gordon and denied to Riel. Thompson stopped a moment, looked across at Gigault, and said quietly, '... there was, at least, a slight difference between the two cases, as even the member for Rouville will admit when his attention is called to it. Louis Riel was convicted. Lord George Gordon was not. He was acquitted.'[17]

Blake had discredited Dr Lavell's opinion that Riel was sane. Blake alleged that at a trial in Napanee Dr Lavell had given incorrect evidence and could not be depended upon. Thompson replied that he had checked the Napanee trial: Dr Lavell had not been on the witness stand at all. Blake then denied he had made the original allegations. Thompson quoted Blake's own words out of Hansard. 'Caught again,' Rykert jeered across the House at Blake.[18]

Thompson did not believe in Riel's insanity. The evidence he had seen suggested strongly the wisdom of the serpent, that Riel could always control his conduct when he felt like it. As Thompson put it, Riel had always the capacity 'of getting possession of his senses when he wanted them.' Asylum was no answer. What would have been the security for life and property in the North-West? In 1885 Riel said the rebellion of 1869–70 was not a patch upon what the new one would be; if he escaped justice in 1885 he would have said that both rebellions together would not be a patch upon the next one. Thompson concluded;

I am not disposed to be inhumane or unmerciful ... but in relation to men of this class ... I would give the answer to appeals for mercy which was given those who proposed to abolish capital punishment in France: 'Very well, but let the assassins begin.'[19]

Thompson took his seat amid resounding cheers from his party. He probably knew, and they certainly did, that his speech would rally not just Conservatives but Liberals whom Blake had not convinced. Thompson struck through the fine-spun web of Blake's long argument. His iron logic was all but irresistible; he had hit Blake's Liberal party with the strongly felt, but unspoken, arguments of Blake's own followers. It was, said the *Montreal Star*, 'by long odds the most powerful argument yet made for the Government.' It was so recognized by everyone. Or nearly everyone. The Halifax *Chronicle* called it weak and disappointing. Bishop Cameron, on pins and needles in Antigonish the next morning, threw the *Chronicle* down in disgust and refused to believe it. As he did, a knock came and a telegram was delivered from A.W. McLelan:

I congratulate Antigonish on her representative here. His reply to Blake on Riel question was magnificent and overwhelming. Our party delighted, and Nova Scotians proud and jubilant. A.W. McLelan. I join in the above with great pleasure. Hector Langevin.[20]

Sir Alexander Campbell made amends for his earlier scepticism. 'Every-one says you made an admirable and most convincing speech – full of argument and that "Blake was smashed." Hurrah!!' Liberals reluctantly admitted the same. John Charlton admitted that night in his diary that Thompson had 'badly upset most of the positions taken by [D.M.] Cameron and Blake.'[21] The greatest praise of all came from J.S. Willison, the Toronto *Globe*'s parliamentary correspondent. Liberal though he was, Willison watched Thompson with respectful amazement:

When he [Thompson] sat down after his first [major] speech in the House of Commons it was realized that a great figure had emerged from a curious obscurity. Parliament is seldom deceived. There are first speeches that dazzle with metaphor or rhetoric, but these reach the ear only ... Soon the benches empty and the sounding phrases become the jest of the smoking-room. The House of Commons distrusts eloquence. It is seldom that a great platform orator catches its atmosphere. A long training in Provincial politics constitutes a positive disqualification for the Federal Parliament. But from the first ... John Thompson had the manner of Parliament. From the first he commanded its interest and confidence. He was simple, lucid, persuasive and convincing. He seemed to be interested only in the logical structure of his argument. He was not so anxious to achieve a personal triumph as that he should be understood and that the cause for which he pleaded should suffer nothing by imperfect statement or intemperate advocacy. In short, he gave an impression of simplicity, sincerity and integrity, and in Parliament these are the qualities that prevail.

There were rumours in Ottawa that the successor to Sir John Macdonald had at last been found.[22]

The members of the press gallery had a bet what the government majority would be. The *Globe*'s correspondent estimated seventy-five votes, the *Gazette*'s sixty-one, the Toronto *World*'s forty-six, the others in between. They were all wrong: the government majority that night was a surprising ninety-four, 146 votes to 52.[23] The extent of the Liberal vote against the Landry motion was wholly unexpected. In that great debate Blake failed to grasp that the country as whole, outside of Quebec, whatever might be the government's management of North-West affairs, was satisfied that Riel had been justly executed. That was the main point. On this vote, virtually open, the House of Commons confirmed the opinion of English Canada.[24] Not since the days of the Pacific Scandal of 1873 had the Liberals had such an opportunity to beat the government; they could do nothing with it. The stick had been broken in their hand.

Annie could not help but be pleased; her belief in her husband's talent had been amply proved, and in a forum and in circumstances of some risk. But now that the test was over, she was ready to return to Willow Park and the children. Thompson was jocular, writing to Joe, 'I think she is longing to do some housecleaning and as she would not be allowed to clean the hotel she wants to go to Willow Park.'

So at the end of April Annie left Thompson to toil in the 80-degree heat already taking hold in Ottawa; Thompson's consolation was that Joe, Babe, Helena, and Frankie would have their mother again. The ladies at the Russell House inquired anxiously after Annie, wanted to know how Thompson was getting on without his wife; he said, 'I keep my door locked at night and am quite safe so far.'[25] In truth he did not get on very well at all. Sundays were always the worst; not even mass in the morning, vespers in the evening, and six hours' work at the office in between seemed to help much. He wrote long letters home. He had instructions about getting the strawberries planted, about keeping the back field for pasture, and worries about the children. He worried about Annie's walks to the post office and back – three miles altogether – and was going 'to put that down *"with a strong hand"*.' He would admit to getting no real rest 'unless I get my head on your shoulder. So am I not a great fool and very childish?'[26]

By mid-May MPs on both sides of the House were getting restless, not to say sulky. They too wanted to get home. Blake was disgusted with both heat and Parliament, and the rest of his party not far behind. The Liberals were much disappointed with the session of 1886. The Riel business had failed them; the Canadian Pacific Railway was finished and the 1885 loan already repaid; there seemed to be little to get a handle on.

In his first session at the House of Commons, Thompson had been of immense service to the government. Macdonald's illness – serious enough to require hypodermic injections to relieve the pain in his hip – lasted over seven weeks. He had been out of the House for over half the 1886 session and without Thompson, McLelan confessed to Tupper, the government would have fared badly. Macdonald's long absence also set people thinking about the future. The best part of Thompson's success was that Ontario Conservatives accepted him on his own terms.[27] Ontario MPs sometimes heaved a weary sigh when an ineffective Maritime or Quebec minister was the unhappy consequence of Ontario's being in confederation. But with Thompson one need make no apologies; he could stand on his merits.

Parliament was mercifully released on 2 June, and Thompson headed off for three weeks in Nova Scotia, to Annie, to cool winds, and the sea. He was also going to try to help Nova Scotia Conservatives in the 'repeal' election of 1886.

The Liberal premier of Nova Scotia, W.S. Fielding, had to have an election in June 1886. It had been four years since the Liberal victory of 1882; the times were not good, 1886 being a bad year both in the United States and Canada. The Nova Scotian government still needed money, under Fielding as under Holmes and Thompson. Claiming better terms from Ottawa, and objecting vigorously when better terms were refused, made excellent sense. It was easy for Nova Scotians to argue, as the Liberal *Morning Chronicle* did, that Nova Scotia 'thrived before we endured the exactions of Canada, [and] we shall thrive when we are once again free from these exactions.'[28]

Thompson was asked by Sir John A. Macdonald to go down to Nova Scotia and do what he could to defeat Fielding and repeal.[29] So was McLelan, the other member of cabinet from Nova Scotia, and several Nova Scotian Conservative MPs. It was not the first or the last time that federal cabinet ministers and MPs would be asked to help rescue provincial brethren in distress. Thompson did what he could; he made speeches in Halifax, went to Antigonish, promised that a Conservative government at Ottawa would subsidize extension of the railway into Cape Breton from the Strait of Canso to Sydney. Cape Breton was good territory for Conservatives, for it liked and supported the National Policy. Indeed, a resolution was passed at a public meeting in Sydney on 15 May calling for separation of Cape Breton from Nova Scotia should repeal succeed.[30]

Despite Thompson's best efforts and those of Nova Scotian Conservatives federal and provincial, repeal carried the election for Fielding and carried it handsomely. It increased the Liberal majority in the Nova Scotia Assembly; Liberals would now have twenty-nine MLAs in a house of thirty-eight. The results surprised the Liberals themselves. One sensible constituent in Antigonish wrote Thompson, ... 'in reality the success was neither Grit nor Tory. It was the embers of the great fire of '67 that still smouldered and blazed anew with the Repeal cry.'[31]

Repeal was a peculiarly Nova Scotian cocktail: a few teaspoons of pure extract of secession, two or three generous cups of better terms, with other well-tried ingredients, such as Maritime union and reciprocity, thrown in. But the will that created it came from the frustrations of an economy in transition, the slow decline from the great shipping and commercial life of the 1860s and 1870s, from a conviction that that world was now passing, and that only the National Policy and railways had been put in its place. For all the ills attending these changes confederation was to blame.

Conservative strength held in the northeastern counties where the

National Policy was already having important consequences; but in the export-oriented counties in the west and the south, repeal was very effective. Thompson was dismayed at the Liberal success. He considered repeal a shibboleth and found it demeaning that Nova Scotians went for it. The success of Fielding posed questions of his own political strength in Antigonish (where two provincial Liberals were elected), to say nothing of the Conservative party's strength in the province as a whole. He was so disgusted he was ready to resign. Stairs warned Macdonald that Thompson must not be allowed to consider that.[32] On 18 June Macdonald asked him to return to Ottawa because of questions arising from Canada's arrest of the American schooner *David Adams.* Thompson went off taking his gloom with him. McLelan had arrived back already, unable to give Macdonald any intelligent account of the Nova Scotian disaster; he had a wash and shave and arrived at council with his hair slicked down. Macdonald looked at him with a derisive smile and said, 'Why, McLelan, you look as if you had had a good *licking!*'[33]

Macdonald was thinking now of the need to have Sir Charles Tupper back in Canada. McLelan and Thompson both offered to give up their cabinet posts for Tupper, Thompson the more willingly since he did not relish being in harness with Sir Charles. Macdonald answered that immediately. He came over at cabinet on Saturday, 26 June, put his hand on Thompson's shoulder, and said, 'I got your letter, but it's no go. You've got to stay here and work as long as I am here.' Thus within nine months Macdonald had discovered how right John Stairs had been in urging Thompson with such persistence. Thompson was worth all the trouble it had taken to get him and more. Thompson seemed almost pleased to tell Annie in long Saturday and Sunday letters that Sir John Macdonald would not let him go.[34]

By June, the political picnic season had started. Thompson and Foster were told by Macdonald he wanted them to come to a Catholic picnic. They were all the rage but Thompson did not like them. The public expected politicians to perform as if they were trained bears, showing their tricks; all he got from political picnics was sunburn and biliousness. He felt his cabinet colleagues were too free in promising his attendance, but of course he added to Annie, 'when Sir John says so we must go.'[35]

The cabinet meetings were long and some of them were so hard and strenuous that Thompson went back to the Russell disgusted with things he did not even write to Annie. Perhaps it was discussion over the North-West amnesty that Thompson proposed early in July. He asked that a proclamation be issued 'granting a general amnesty to all persons who were guilty of crimes or offences of a political nature during the late rebellion in the North West Territories excepting such persons as are now undergoing sentences.' This was followed by his recommendation for an amnesty for Ambrose Lépine. Lépine, convicted in 1874 of the murder of Thomas Scott, had had his sentence of death commuted to two years in prison and permanent loss of civil rights. Thompson recommended that 'an unconditional pardon be now granted.' Both recommendations were accepted by cabinet, though not, perhaps, without difficulty.[36] It is curious that Gabriel Dumont, then in New York, reacted to Thompson's Lépine amnesty much as Riel might have done – by looking to the Canadian government for compensation for personal losses and expenses.[37]

It was now full summer and Ottawa had been sizzling. Thompson's consolations were cold baths, strawberries, and work. It was 95 degrees in the shade on Sunday, 4 July, while he was working at the East Block, and did not cool off until dawn on Monday. The only way he could sleep was to sit in his nightshirt near an open window until he succeeded in dozing off. He thought of the cool veranda and deep shade at Willow Park, the long swims in the North-West Arm. When he would actually get to Halifax was not clear. The cabinet quorum was four, and junior members of the cabinet, especially if they had an important portfolio, were fairly stuck. The best hope was late July. In the meantime his deputy minister, Burbidge, was off on holidays, and on at least one day his assistant deputy minister, Power, was off drunk, and the other clerks were 'out'; they all seemed to think that a little work for the minister in the hot weather would be good for him![38]

On Friday, 9 July, at the last cabinet meeting before Macdonald's departure for the west coast via the new CPR, Macdonald broke it up by saying, 'Well! Tomorrow I am going to do what the devil never did – leave you.'[39]

Thompson got away from Ottawa eventually on 20 July, stopping in Montreal to see his officials at St Vincent de Paul Penitentiary, and thence to the installation of Cardinal Taschereau at Quebec. In the harbour Chapleau had arranged to have the steam yacht of some friend, so Thompson went on to Rivière du Loup by river. He stopped at Bathurst, New Brunswick, for a day or two's fishing; he was in Antigonish for a few days of electoral tending and mending, and then settled in at last on 11 August for a blissful week of *dolce far niente* on the big veranda at Willow Park.

He came back to Ottawa, via Quebec, bringing John and Joe and his sister-in-law Fan for a visit to the old city. John was fourteen years old now, bright and sensible, but did not relish going back to Stonyhurst. He would have preferred a job in Halifax as lawyer's apprentice. Thompson would not accept that. It would not be good for John's character to leave Stonyhurst after only one year there. John would have to stick it out. Joe, who was just twelve, Thompson felt more tender about; Joe was so loving, so sweet-natured that Thompson shrank from forcing him to Stonyhurst, such a hard bump into the world. Thompson tried to cheer him up. He would get over feeling lonesome; real loneliness he would feel when grown up, with a family of his own and be forced by circumstances to leave them. That was Thompson's greatest strain, 'losing my home,' as he put it. Whenever he returned to Halifax it was like bringing a half-drowned man to life again. These absences made him peevish and cross and he had driven poor Annie distracted more than once since that awful change in his life of September 1885.[40] Thompson left the decision about Joe squarely up to Annie, who had made up her mind. However Thompson might flinch, Joe was going to go. But in the end he did not, not that September 1886. He badly injured his arm; it would not be strong for months, and so he would stay in Halifax. Thompson was amused. 'The little scamp is such a hand at his prayers that I am sure it has all been arranged for him.'[41]

With the autumn of 1886 came a spate of electioneering. Tupper arrived from England in late August; from the West, Macdonald instructed Thompson to initiate discussions with C.H. Tupper and McLelan about Nova Scotia. If, as a result, Nova Scotia looked promising enough for the autumn, 'I still think it would be well to try a General Election.'[42]

The Nova Scotian election had sharpened the sense of danger in the Macdonald government. The last Dominion election had been in June 1882, and there had to be another within a few months. The Prince Edward Island Conservatives under W.W. Sullivan had been re-elected in late June, but that was thin consolation against forthcoming provincial elections in Quebec and Ontario, where the Conservatives could lose both. An early indication would be the federal by-election in Haldimand, called for 8 September. The seat had been Liberal since 1841; Conservatives did not really expect to take it, but they wanted to make a good fist of trying. Thompson went down and made speeches in the stifling heat of the Grand River valley in early September. The Liberals won, but by a margin close enough to give energy to the Conservatives (they were in fact to take the seat in 1887).

Macdonald was also anxious to announce the appointment of a royal commission on the relations of capital and labour at an Ottawa meeting of the Conservative Workingmen's Association. It was almost his first consideration on returning from the west coast at the end of August. 'I want to issue a Comn. on the labour question,' he wrote Thompson on 1 September, 'and specifically as to the organization of a Labour bureau ... Will you try your hand at a draft? ... The Labour Comn is most pressing.' A few days later he told Thompson to contrive a few sentences about the relations of labour and capital, how best those relations could be arranged to advance the trade and commerce of Canada. The last was deliberately designed to bring the commission within the orbit of Dominion power. Thompson's background for drawing the commission came from familiarity with Connecticut, New Jersey, and Kansas labour legislation. The resulting commission repeated the preamble of the Connecticut statute of 1885 almost to the letter, adding the essential legal point that it would advance the trade and commerce of Canada.[43]

Macdonald then put on his war paint and by mid-September they were off once more to the battlefields of Ontario. London, Ontario, John Carling's constituency, turned out in force. The streets were crowded as far as the eye could see, Thompson said, the houses covered with flags and inscriptions. At the fair grounds before a crowd of three thousand, Thompson was suddenly asked to lead off. He thought he did pretty well for someone with nothing prepared. Macdonald's address was cut short by a pelting rain that drove everyone to shelter.

Thompson followed this by a two-week foray into Nova Scotia in October, trying with Tupper to carry the burden since A.W. McLelan was regarded a little unfairly as harbinger of ill-luck. Thompson was sceptical about political meetings, but young Charles Hibbert Tupper (and his redoubtable father) was not. Both Tuppers felt that Nova Scotia needed political attention. The program should begin with a Conservative rally in Halifax, followed by others in Truro, New Glasgow, Antigonish, Sydney, then the Annapolis valley towns, and so finally to Amherst whence Thompson and McLelan could return to Ottawa. As young Tupper put it, 'We want a stirring up of dry bones here badly.'[44]

The failure of the Quebec Conservatives to win the Quebec provincial election on 14 October 1886 was ominous and the Cabinet decided on 30 October that there should be a general election before the next session of Parliament. That seemed better than attempting to fight legislation through against an enlivened opposition. Rumours got out; the volume of requests across Thompson's desk mounted. 'Rumours of an election are bringing hordes of wolves down on us wanting plunder before we take the plunge,' Thompson wrote to Annie. He was pleased with one thing: the general election would determine finally where he would make his home, Halifax or Ottawa.

In mid-November Oliver Mowat, the Liberal premier of Ontario, called the Ontario provincial election for late December. For the Conservatives there were two strong reasons for having a strong push at Ontario – first, to help the struggling provincial leader, W.R. Meredith, defeat Mowat, and second, to help themselves. The main burden of the strong Conservative campaign waged in Ontario fell upon Macdonald, Thomas White, Thompson, and Meredith. Thompson estimated that in his thirteen months in federal politics he had addressed forty-three meetings, besides those connected with his own by-election. For someone who began political life with a horror of public meetings, Thompson found the shoe pinching at its sorest point.[45]

Macdonald had no such horrors. He seemed to revel in meetings; they charged some battery within him. The two men spent 11 November at Renfrew, a full six hours of it before a big, rough crowd packed in standing. Buildings that accommodated that many people were not usually heated; they were cold, draughty, and after three to four hours of speeches, one was chilled to the bone. Thompson was not dissatisfied with his performance, but was hungry and cold at the end of the day. Macdonald continued to surprise him; 'He goes through all these hardships quite gaily while his daily life at home is of itself tormenting enough without all these extras.'[46] Little is known about Macdonald's daily life at home, but Macdonald's seventeen-year-old retarded daughter Mary, and his home presided over by a devoted but waspish wife, may justify Thompson's comment.

Campaigning with Macdonald in Ontario, Thompson continued to be struck by Macdonald's resilience and his love for the life. They rattled around southwest Ontario like minstrels for two weeks and, owing to the Ontario Assembly being dissolved, spoke to enormous crowds. It was so crowded at Stratford that it was planned to get onto the stage via a trap-door; but Thompson's guide tried to press through the crowd in the hall. The crush was so bad that Thompson could not move and he began to feel claustrophobic; he yelled and cursed and finally they caught him by his clothes and hoisted him up – 185 pounds of him – and passed him over their heads to the platform amid deafening cheers and laughter. At Port Hope the students from Victoria College formed a line on the station platform; one called out, 'What's the matter with Sir John?' and all the others answered in unison at the top of their lungs, 'He's all right! Oh yes! Oh yes! He's all right!' At the meeting that followed, Thompson said that after the next election when the question went out, 'How is Sir John Macdonald?' the answer would come back, just as it had at the Port Hope station. At this the Victoria College boys in the audience caught up the refrain again. The effect, Thompson said, was splendid and he was able to escape in the uproar. There were banquets; at Peterborough one was held after the meeting, when two hundred sat down to dinner at 11 p.m., and the toasts *began* at 1 a.m. No wonder Thompson arrived back in Ottawa on 5 December thoroughly done in. And they were back at it a week later at St Thomas, with huge processions and meetings, and one banquet, so-called, that began at one o'clock consisting of oyster soup, apples, and green tea! Toasts were drunk in tea cups, 'the folly,' as Thompson called it, 'lasting until half past two.'[47]

Folly or not, Macdonald believed the tours had gone well in Ontario and thought that in the Dominion election they would be all right. The problem was more difficult in Nova Scotia. As Macdonald wrote Tupper, the only hope of Conservatives holding their own in Nova Scotia was 'your immediate return and vigorous action. It may even be necessary that you should for a time return to the Cabinet, McLelan I know would readily make way for you. Now the responsibility on you is very great.'[48]

Tupper had strengths and weaknesses. He was impulsive and exigent, a dangerous combination when joined to his tremendous energy. He was adept at promoting Tupperdom – that is, his family relations – and he did so in a barefaced fashion that made others blush for him. Neither Macdonald nor Thompson liked that side of Tupper. For example, in 1886 the British government was considering a commission on the Canadian-Alaskan boundary. Tupper knew this and cabled Macdonald asking that Canada recommend as Dominion representative Colonel D.R. Cameron of the Royal Artillery. Macdonald did not doubt Cameron was a good man, but felt it was indelicate of Tupper to take advantage of confidential knowledge to push the appointment of his son-in-law.[49]

Unlike Macdonald, Thompson did not believe that Tupper's coming would do the party much good, and it made Thompson irritated at the Old Man, as he was called. Macdonald was used to getting his own way in cabinet; Thompson, one of the new boys of 1885, more independent than Foster or Thomas White, was less inclined to take it when he felt Macdonald was in the wrong. In January 1887 Macdonald had been throwing his weight around, so Thompson ignored Macdonald's view of a legal question and talked to other members of cabinet over his head; as

Thompson told Annie, Macdonald could go to hell and get over his sulks there.[50]

Tupper arrived on 24 January and was sworn in as minister of finance. There were other cabinet difficulties; Chapleau resigned on 21 January but was talked out of it. Dissolution had been announced on 15 January 1887, the election to be held on 22 February. The winter campaign got under way slowly. Thompson thought he had Antigonish County in fairly good order. The county lived mainly by its Dominion public works, especially its breakwaters, at Arisaig and other small ports along Antigonish County's sixty or seventy miles of coastline. Thompson had got several new post offices installed and had succeeded in getting down the railway rates on the Eastern Extension Railway, to say nothing of considerable attention to other patronage.

Thompson's constituents in Antigonish County ate and drank patronage; the long winters and halcyon summers seemed to nourish it. Thompson was not proud of this side of being the member for Antigonish; his constituents seemed greedy, impatient, unforgiving, with alarmingly tenacious memories that kept past wrongs firmly in the world of the present. Sometimes Thompson could not stomach it. 'I revolt against Antigonish the more I think of it,' he grumbled to Annie later. One day in October 1886 Archie A. McGillivray, then in Cape Breton, noticed in the paper that the Antigonish stationmaster had died. 'May his soul rest in peace,' said Archie piously, 'I hereby apply for the situation ... and finding that this situation would suit me, I demand it. All I want from you is a decided answer.' Thompson said no in a letter written as usual, Archie claimed, 'in that cool faraway tone.' It made him furious. He railed against Thompson's rank ingratitude after all that Archie had done for him in Antigonish County; Thompson's 'dark, ungrateful heart' would rue the day that he had refused, once again, the modest exigencies of Archie A. McGillivray.[51]

B.F. Power, another constituent with more brains and clout, preferred telegrams. The same day the stationmaster died B.F. Power thoughtfully reminded Thompson that his brother Henry was available. When the new stationmaster was appointed it was neither Archie nor Power's brother, but D.H. McDonald, the stationmaster from Tracadie, eighteen miles farther along the line. B.F. Power kept a watchful eye on things. Two months later he sent a telegram: 'If stationmaster here be dismissed for drunkenness you have a right to confer that office on me. I pay all telegrams answer before sixteenth as I will be away state salary.' That was brash enough. Thompson did not ignore it, however; he telegraphed his cousin, David Pottinger, the chief superintendent of the Intercolonial Railway at Moncton for information. The pay, said Pottinger, was forty dollars a month; but he added that McDonald was not in any trouble so far as he knew.[52] But McDonald was.

The Intercolonial Railway rules about drinking by employees were strict. Only men of known sober habits were to be employed in the movement of trains. Rule No. 60 was specific: any employee drunk on duty *or* off duty will not be kept on the Intercolonial Railway service.[53] What had actually happened to D.H. McDonald is not clear – it seldom is on such occasions. On the nights of 6 and 7 December McDonald and some friends had a party; McDonald got pitched out of a sleigh into an adjacent snowbank; this was followed by good-natured but very drunken wrestling with the baggage master in the snowdrifts in front of the Central House, Antigonish's main hotel. This was not drunkenness, McDonald told Thompson, but animal spirits; all he had to drink was whisky and milk taken for strictly medicinal purposes. Whatever McDonald's explanations, he was dismissed and Power was given the position. It was a clear patronage appointment and Pottinger did not relish it. 'The usual and proper course,' he wrote to his cousin, 'would be to promote some experienced person to a station like this, but I suppose we can't.'[54]

The general election of 1887 was now at hand. Thompson set aside $350 for his campaign expenses, and in due course his card was sent out from Antigonish town modestly soliciting support. One enterprising voter from Hallowell Grant, William Dunn, replied; he would love to vote for Thompson, but sadly he owed twenty-five dollars to the Liberals and they seemed to want his vote. 'If you wish to make that good for me before election day,' said Dunn delicately, 'I would be very happy to support you.'[55]

The Liberals nominated Angus McGillivray, a formidable opponent. He had been a candidate at the time of Thompson's first provincial election in 1877, but had withdrawn under strong pressure from Bishop Cameron. Elected in 1878, McGillivray had been MLA for Antigonish ever since. He was a 'pet native Scotchman, having a host of relatives' and commanding what Power called 'the ledger influence of all the merchants in Antigonish except four.'[56]

Thompson installed himself at the Central House on 5 February and braced himself for the next seventeen days. He felt his prospects were fair but he did not worry about defeat. His committees were organized by J.A. Chisholm, a young Conservative lawyer who had opened a practice in Antigonish the year before. These committees were confident, too confident in Thompson's opinion; McGillivray was less unfit for Parliament than Dr McIntosh in 1885. Thompson did not anticipate any easy victory. Despite his ten-year association with the county, he could not know it as a native like McGillivray. Thompson found at West River that he had lost ground over the week past because McGillivray had been working night and day, house to house, something that Thompson, much more an outsider, could not do easily. Besides, the Liberals had spread the rumour that the Macdonald government was certain to be defeated anyway, whether Thompson won or not; consequently it would be better to have McGillivray on the government side in the new House of Commons than Thompson on the opposition.[57]

Bishop Cameron did not intend that Thompson be defeated. He sent out a strong letter alleging that 'designing politicians' proposed to mount a factious opposition to the re-election of Thompson. Some even said, the bishop noted with a certain grim emphasis, that Bishop Cameron no longer supported Thompson![58]

Thompson's prognosis gave him a thin majority of 100 votes in a total of about 2,500. It was closer than that: his majority was just 46. He lost Antigonish town, as in 1885; then it was by 2 votes, now by 38. He kept his traditional strength in the north and west, lost in the south and east. The count was 1,253 to 1,207. It was as Thompson's private secretary said, 'a close shave.' Stewart attributed it to French-Acadian votes – about 400 – going almost solidly against Thompson. The 1885 Franchise Act, bringing in new electors, may also explain some of the results, for the total vote increased some 35 per cent over that in 1885.[59]

Overall Nova Scotia was, however, a considerable success for the Conservatives; they completely reversed the verdict given by the electorate in the provincial election of 1886. The federal election of 1887 in Nova Scotia repeated the results of 1882: of twenty-one seats, fourteen were Conservative and seven were Liberal. The Conservatives won Annapolis, Digby, and Queens from the Liberals, and held Antigonish that Thompson had won for them in 1885; the Liberals gained Kings, Lunenburg, Richmond, and one seat in Halifax.

Such a result could not but seriously compromise the repeal movement. A.G. Jones, the winning Liberal in Halifax, said before the election, 'Should you now return candidates hostile to repeal you will render almost worthless the great victory of last spring.'[60] There was a huge Conservative rally in Halifax to celebrate just such a rendering, with addresses from the three Nova Scotian cabinet ministers – Thompson,

Tupper, and McLelan. Thompson tended to exaggerate before large political crowds, and his Halifax victory speech showed him, as in the fall campaign in Ontario, giving his best and his worst:

In the Northwest every rebel, in Nova Scotia every secessionist, in Quebec every enemy of law and order and throughout the Dominion every traitor and annexationist was found actively arrayed against the government. (Loud cheers.) It was against this disgraceful and disloyal combination that the government of Sir John Macdonald had contended and over which they had triumphed. (Renewed cheering.)

Nova Scotia could now hold up its head again. No longer could people turn to him with a sneer and ask, 'What's the matter with you Blue-noses?'[61] Best of all, there would be no elections in Antigonish for a while.

12

Administering the Department of Justice

In 1887 Annie and Thompson began to talk of moving to Ottawa. Joe would go to Stonyhurst in September; two of the girls could board at Mount St Vincent; Frankie would come to Ottawa with her parents. The big question was to find a house in Ottawa that they could afford. Sir Alexander Campbell would part with his Ottawa house for $14,000 but Thompson had nowhere near that kind of money. Sir Charles Tupper, newly arrived back in Ottawa, asked Danny O'Connor, an Ottawa lawyer, to buy a house for him, a good large stone one for $4,000. O'Connor smiled grimly. Thompson added that while O'Connor was about it, he might just as well get two like that at the same time![1] The humour says much about house problems in Ottawa. Nothing turned up until the autumn of 1887. John Carling had been renting a furnished house from Mrs J.S. Dennis at 277 Cooper Street, just west of Metcalfe. Carling was buying Campbell's house (at $10,000) and moving as of 1 November. Thompson had a look at the Dennis house. It would need only a few renovations. Thompson took the house for a year, at a rent of $75 a month.[2] Not cheap, but possible; at $900 a year the rent was 13 per cent of his $7,000 salary. Tupper did not buy a place either.

Tupper was not always friendly; you never knew quite where you were with the Tuppers, senior and junior. The rule for dealing with them was to remember the alleged derivation of their name, from the French 'Tu perds,' you lose. Thompson could get irritated with both of them and their hustling ways. In April 1887, he told Annie, he was so cross with Tupper Jr he would like to spank him so that he couldn't have sat down for a week.[3] As for old Sir Charles, during the whole session of 1887 he seemed to be looking for a quarrel.

His manner was almost unbearable but I was too cute for him. I strengthened myself with my colleagues and avoided him and pretended not to notice his antagonism. Of course there was always a danger of my bad temper exploding but when such was the case I often kept out of the way – sometimes not going to Council until it would be nearly over.[4]

It made Thompson feel good to know that his own narrow victory in Antigonish was not petitioned against, whereas Tupper's and McLelan's were, much to their annoyance. It was intended that McLelan would go to Government House, Halifax, as lieutenant-governor, but it would never do for him to go there following an upset in an election petition.[5]

Annie came up to Ottawa for a fortnight in March 1887 but this year Thompson was alone when Parliament opened on 13 April. Almost at once the House was plunged into a long and passionate debate on Irish home rule brought on by J.J. Curran, Conservative MP for Montreal Centre. This was hopelessly quixotic and Macdonald believed that it would achieve exactly nothing; but feelings both inside and outside Parliament were strong. It did not need Irishmen in Canada to persuade Canadians about the virtue of home rule. Home rule was another expression for something Canadians cared very much about: self-government. Macdonald determined to have the matter out, to air as quickly as possible this festering question. The government did not, perhaps could not, take a stand and the debate would be on the basis of a free vote.

Thompson's position on British domestic questions was that of a Gladstonian Liberal. He had never been to Ireland but his sympathies for her problems came naturally, and he had unbounded admiration, so Lady Aberdeen reported a few years later, for Gladstone and Gladstone's courageous Irish policies.[6] By no means all informed Canadians shared Thompson's views; Goldwin Smith in Toronto had a dyspeptic opinion worth quoting: 'Gladstone's moral tone is very high, but his sense of responsibility is very low[;] self-worship is at the core of his character and there are no tricks which his casuistry cannot play with his conscience.'[7]

The Irish debate in Canada had been brought on, perhaps aggravated, by a stormy year and a half in Britain. Gladstone was defeated in the House of Commons on the second reading of the Irish home rule bill in June 1886; he plunged the country into its second general election in nine months, an election that he made a plebiscite on home rule. Gladstone and the Liberal party were decisively defeated. With relief Queen Victoria confided the government once more to Lord Salisbury and the Conservatives.

Ireland's problems were exacerbated in 1886–7 by a steep fall in the price of agricultural produce; some Irish landlords used the opportunity to evict tenants who were in arrears of rent. This in turn led Irish peasants to set the law at defiance. The government of Lord Salisbury then brought in the Coercion Act of April 1887.

By this time the Irish in Canada were thoroughly aroused. On 26 April 1887 the Canadian Parliament supported Irish home rule by an overwhelming 125 to 47. Since the fate of the government by no means hinged on the result, there were some curious bedfellows: Laurier and Sir Hector Langevin, for example, were side by side; most French Canadians sympathized with Irish home rule. So did Thompson. On the other side were some members of the cabinet – Tupper, McLelan, Bowell, Foster – as well as the MPs of the Orange contingent from Ontario and New Brunswick and some from Quebec.

That division said nothing at all about the power of the 1887 Macdonald government. The first real test came on the Queen's County, New Brunswick, election case. The public are puzzled sometimes at the intensity that surrounds the franchise, electoral boundaries, returning officers' powers, disputed elections, what could be regarded as the legal minutiae of politics. To most MPs they were life and death issues; and political parties were bound to take them seriously. The Queen's County election was in Thompson's charge not only as minister of justice, but also because, increasingly now, Macdonald began to rely on Thompson to take charge of awkward and difficult questions. Thompson, besides being scrupulously polite to opponents, was judiciously firm, imperturbable, and was already familiar with working rules of the House, as well as its daily order paper.

The Queen's County election had been close: B.G. King (Liberal), 1,191 votes; G.F. Baird (Conservative), 1,130 votes. The returning officer, J.R. Dunn, claiming King's nomination papers were invalid, put Baird's name on the writ returned to Ottawa. There was a storm of protest from Liberals. B.F. Skinner, Liberal MP for Saint John, moved in Parliament that the House of Commons overturn the decision. Thompson replied that in 1874 the Canadian Parliament had deliberately given to the courts most of the jurisdiction in disputed elections; there was no point in returning such questions to the cockpit of the House of Commons. In Thompson's view it was a question of real justice versus party justice:

I perfectly agree with the argument the hon. gentleman made, not only as to the importance of this case, but as to the right of the majority to have their candidate returned. In this case, however, whichever way the majority of votes were cast, the rights of other parties are concerned, and let not this House, in its zeal and haste to do justice to the majority, violate the rights of any other persons whomsoever.

The proper disposition of the case was a hearing in the Committee on Privileges and Elections, a committee which the leader of the opposition himself had praised for its fairness.[8]

With bets all around that the government's majority would be less than 25, it won the first party vote of the session by 109 to 77. The excitement, Thompson told Annie, was as great as on the Landry motion of 1886; he won golden opinions from Macdonald, and even from Tupper. Of course in the Committee on Privileges and Elections the government won. As Thompson wrote with his usual ironic humour, 'It is a great comfort when you have the law and justice of the case on your side to have the jury packed.'[9] Indeed! The case ultimately ended in the Supreme Court of New Brunswick – a much better place than the House of Commons – and where Baird, the Conservative, was declared elected.

Thompson's position was more ambiguous in divorce cases that came down to the House from the Senate. The working rule in the House was that in clearly proved cases such as would justify divorce in England, divorce bills were allowed to pass. Where proof was not substantially clear the divorce bill was carried on a purely denominational vote, the Catholics all voting against it, regardless of its legal merits, and the Protestants all voting for it.[10] As a Roman Catholic Thompson was compelled, as were the other Catholics in the House, to vote against some divorces on principle as a private member. As minister of justice, however, he was compelled to explain the law as to why the divorce should be granted. The case of Susan Ash Manton is an interesting example of the juxtaposition. At the age of sixteen, her mother dead, Susan Ash married in 1868, at Kingston, John Manton, a man much her senior. She lived with him for five or six weeks, found him drunken and shiftless, and she left him against his will to go back to live with her father. Manton then went to Boston, got a Massachusetts divorce on the grounds of his wife's desertion and married Mary Hatch of Stirling, Ontario. They moved to Boston and had a family.

Thompson sorted out the legal questions for the House. Manton's Boston divorce from his first wife was illegal by Canadian law, on two grounds: he was not domiciled in Massachusetts though he said he was; and Canadian courts would not recognize such a divorce, even if he had been properly domiciled. On these grounds Susan Ash Manton was not entitled to a Canadian divorce, whatever the unhappy circumstances of her marriage. The fact that Manton then proceeded to contract a bigamous second marriage and have children gave Susan Ash Manton her entitlement. Having detailed all that, Thompson still voted against the divorce petition. It passed 50 to 42.[11]

Despite his position on this question, which everyone understood, discussions began in July with Senator J.R. Gowan of Barrie who wanted a statute on divorce and a code of rules about evidence to be used in the Senate. J.R. Gowan, nephew of Ogle Gowan, the grand master of the Orange Order of the 1830s and 1840s, had been a county court judge in Simcoe County from 1843 to 1883, and then went to the Senate. Thompson's position was that he did not want divorce more easily granted than at present, but he agreed that it would be useful to make more regular the procedures in Parliament for dealing with it. 'Mr. Thompson will no doubt tell me what he thinks of the scheme,' Gowan wrote to Macdonald, 'and I shall be glad to do anything that is desired. He is perhaps impassive in manner, but I feel he is genuine – Of course he knows very little of me and is naturally cautious.' Gowan concluded, 'The more I know of Mr. Thompson, the better I like him.' Thompson in the meantime drafted an elegant little memorandum for his deputy minister, indicating where Burbidge should seek the divorce rules that prevailed in England.[12]

Thompson liked to run his own department. When he had to be away from Ottawa for more than a week, it was usual to arrange for an acting minister, at first Sir Alexander Campbell. Campbell had to go to England for his health in May 1886 and when Thompson went to Nova Scotia for the repeal election, Sir Hector Langevin acted. Burbidge asked Thompson if the arrangement was to be a general one. No, said Thompson, he did not think so. The truth was he arranged for acting ministers with reluctance; he did not like anyone else running the department and kept it under his own hand, even when he was away from Ottawa. This had many advantages; Thompson and his deputy minister could keep in touch by telegram and letter (the letter service between Halifax and Ottawa being usually a day and a half); but it had some inconveniences. Burbidge on one occasion had to ask Sir John Macdonald personally whom he ought to go to in case there was something requiring immediate action.[13]

By 1887 Thompson's hold on the Department of Justice was secure. It was his métier, the only portfolio in the government he had ever wanted and the one he kept to the end. The department came to regard him with respect, admiration, loyalty, and perhaps, in the case of the lazy or the incompetent, fear. One could not trifle with Thompson. He was intolerant of slackness, waste, corruption, stupidity, indeed of intolerance itself; what chiefly aroused his anger was injustice, petty or gross, some official throwing his weight around, especially someone whose pretensions exceeded his capacity. Thompson would not stand for bullying by officials or judges. Conspicuously fairminded himself, he wanted to see it in his subordinates. Justice! An abstraction to many people, no doubt; a hard word to some others; but to Thompson justice was rich with meaning. Justice was possible.

His sense of justice was based upon knowledge. Thompson took immense trouble to master his facts. He wrote and argued with unusual conviction and trenchancy, with an almost uncanny surefootedness. Thompson brought to the Department of Justice a mind not widely cultivated but of exceptional cogency and determination. He had dignity without pomposity, and a command of his own competence that was the more remarkable, perhaps the more intimidating, because it was unobtrusive.

Thompson's passion for fairness and justice would not let him rest when there was a question of power abused by superior officers, either by wardens or by the inspector of penitentiaries. He himself was generous with subordinates, giving them full credit for good work. It was usual that departmental publications went out under the minister's name; W.E. Hodgins, a first class clerk, under Thompson's direction had been responsible for compiling a voluminous work on allowance and disallowance of provincial statutes. By Thompson's insistence, young Hodgins's name appeared on the title page. The father wrote Thompson a private letter of thanks;

I understand that by your kind permission his [my son's] name appears on the title page.

As an old civil servant – being 'chief of the staff' in the Educational Department of Ontario for 42 years, I can appreciate the value of such an act of kindness. To me it is particularly grateful ...

My son has not the slightest idea that I write this note to you; but I do so to express my personal sense of your courtesy and kindness.[14]

Some subordinates, such as G.W. Burbidge, his deputy minister until 1887, did not relish hard legal responsibilities, and liked a minister who had the legal brains and moral courage to take hard decisions. 'I "funk" very much,' Burbidge confessed, 'in taking such serious responsibility in such cases.'[15]

In 1887 on Thompson's initiative Parliament abolished appeals to the Privy Council in London in criminal cases. The Canadian government had found it more than a little inconvenient when Riel's lawyers moved for leave to appeal to the Privy Council. (The leave to appeal was denied.) The Privy Council was not enthusiastic about appeals in criminal cases; Lord Kingsdown in *Falkland Islands Co.* v. *The Queen* said such a right was extremely awkward.[16]

More important was a major departure in the structure of the Supreme Court of Canada – the establishment of the Exchequer Court. (It was renamed Federal Court in 1970.) The Exchequer Court was designed to adjudicate claims of ordinary citizens, contractors, and companies against the crown. The old system, the Dominion Board of Arbitrators, was clumsy; it took three times as much evidence as needed, much of it inadmissable in a court of law. Appeals were allowed from the board to the Supreme Court of Canada; but the Court, too, was handicapped, having little special knowledge of such business. Three of the Supreme Court judges, S.H. Strong, T. Fournier, and W.A. Henry, were the original judges appointed in 1875 by the Liberal government of Alexander Mackenzie; of the other three, H.-E. Taschereau was appointed in October 1878, and J.W. Gwynne and the chief justice, Sir W.J. Ritchie, in January 1879.[17] Indeed, the Exchequer Court had to be created to protect the crown against Supreme Court decisions.[18] A series of judgments against the crown over several years produced awards much in excess of what the government thought was fair. These cases involved mainly the departments of Public Works, and Railways and Canals. Thus the Exchequer Court was not really intended to enlarge the remedies available to the subject against the crown; it served rather to deal with the relations of the Dominion to companies and contractors of all kinds. That was where the majority of suits against the crown arose.

The Exchequer Court bill had been before Parliament since 1885. It was let go and in 1886 Macdonald was still uneasy. In April 1886 he told Thompson that he had grave doubts about it and wished it to lie over for another year.[19] But in 1887 Thompson got his way. All existing Exchequer jurisdiction of the Supreme Court of Canada was transferred to the new Exchequer Court although appeals were still allowed out of the

Exchequer Court to the Supreme Court. The existing system was changed; the four Dominion arbitrators would now be converted into referees of the new court. The Exchequer Court would have only one judge, who would travel to different parts of Canada to hear his cases. That in itself would be a great saving of time and money; bringing a full set of witnesses and lawyers to Ottawa for the Supreme Court had been supremely expensive.[20]

The appointment of the Exchequer judge was an awkward choice, resting between George Burbidge and Thompson's old Halifax colleague, Wallace Graham, now the senior partner of Graham, Tupper and Borden. Graham was a better lawyer than Burbidge; it was also probable that Annie Lyons Graham had put it to her husband that he should be offered the position of Exchequer Court judge.[21] The two families were close. It would suit Thompson to appoint Graham, his old partner, who had had a distinguished career. Graham was that summer in London arguing a case before the Privy Council; his vivid impressions of London and the Privy Council gave Thompson a good deal of amusement. None of the Canadian lawyers, Graham observed, had the address or deliberation required to argue well before the Privy Council. Canadians were too vulgarly oratorical in their tone and gestures.[22] But Graham's health rendered him incapable of handling rapid or fatiguing work; a long, arduous Exchequer suit would have killed him. Burbidge was healthy and he had had five years as deputy minister, excellent experience in helping to resist claims against the government.[23] Burbidge was appointed in September 1887. It was, Thompson wrote to Annie, 'best for the country beyond comparison.'[24]

Thompson had a principle of organization for the department. The deputy minister should be a lawyer from the bar of the English-speaking provinces. Of the two chief clerks, the senior should be from the Quebec bar, the other from English Canada. By 1893 the department had a deputy minister and a staff of twelve, plus the penitentiary branch with a director and two clerks. This was no larger than when Thompson came in 1885, but the structure had been altered. After the deputy minister, there were the two chief clerks, Augustus Power, an Irish Catholic from the Quebec bar, and G.L.B. Fraser, a Presbyterian from Kingston; four first class clerks, from Montreal, Nova Scotia, Newfoundland, and Toronto, all Protestants; two second class clerks, among them P.M. Côté, the only French Canadian in the department; and three third class clerks, of whom one was Roman Catholic. In the penitentiary branch, J.G. Moylan, the director, was Catholic, and his two clerks were both Maritime Protestants.

Of the fourteen men in Thompson's department below the deputy minister, four were Roman Catholic. None of the deputy ministers who served under him were.[25]

Have I a free choice as to my new deputy? Thompson asked Macdonald in September 1887. Assuming so, Thompson went on, the Department of Justice would get a much better man in Nova Scotia for the money than anywhere else. Besides, Nova Scotia's share of the civil service positions in Ottawa, according to Thompson's estimate, should be seventy, but she had only twenty-six. She had no deputy minister, no chief clerk. Nor had Nova Scotia shared in the legal appointments in the North-West.[26] Thompson offered the deputy ministership to Wallace Graham, but gave him the choice of that or the next vacancy on the Supreme Court of Nova Scotia. Graham opted for the latter.[27]

Thompson's next preference was for Graham's junior partner, Robert Borden. Borden was tempted; $4,000 was more than he was getting from the law firm in Halifax. Graham agreed to release him, but made it clear how important Borden was to the firm. 'If he left my firm as it is at present constituted I would be obliged to leave the country!'[28] Graham would have been glad to part company with C.H. Tupper, the middle partner, but of course, Thompson told Annie, young Charlie Tupper as deputy minister of justice was 'out of the question.'[29] In January 1888 the offer was made to Robert Sedgewick of Halifax and accepted.[30]

About this time Macdonald began to think again of retiring. He came to Thompson in June 1887 and told him that Sir Charles Tupper wanted to return to England as high commissioner; further, that Tupper 'does not see how I can retire just now.' Thompson pretended not to notice the part about Macdonald's retirement and concentrated his talk upon Tupper; but Macdonald's oblique question to Thompson was repeated more than once.[31] Macdonald was probably serious. J.H. Pope told Stephen that Macdonald wanted out in 1888. Who was the successor to be? Sir George Stephen suggested to C.A. Dansereau during a leisurely train ride between Ottawa and Montreal that Sir Hector Langevin had long had his mind set on succeeding Macdonald, and that perhaps such an arrangement would be pleasing to French-Canadian Conservatives. Dansereau, a close friend of Chapleau's, replied with some heat that nothing could be further from the truth.[32] With rivalries among the French Canadians Macdonald was thinking of Thompson as successor. Thompson did not know, no one did, but he tried to pretend to Macdonald that he was ignoring the subject.

The session of 1887 ended on 23 June; everyone who could left. Ottawa was stifling. There was no mail, no clerks, everyone was on holiday, and yet the office was awash in work. 'How I envy you the cool evenings in Halifax,' he groaned to Annie.[33] Suddenly on 2 July he was on his way to Nova Scotia with David Pottinger. He had word that his mother, ill for some time, had taken a turn for the worse. Thompson seems to have gone to see his mother as a duty he could not avoid. 'I suppose if Mother lives until after the Session,' he had written in mid-June, 'I should go to see her as it will be the last time I shall have the chance.'[34] It was said with some sang froid. Charlotte Pottinger Thompson died at Barrington on 9 July, with Thompson, his two sisters and David Pottinger there. Not a word exists about how Thompson felt about his mother's death. It is right to suggest dispassionateness; Annie had long since become his mistress, wife, mother figure.

When Thompson returned to Ottawa after his mother's funeral, Macdonald put him in temporary charge of the government. Macdonald wanted to go to Dalhousie, New Brunswick, to escape the heat; in mid-July he turned to the cabinet and told them Thompson was in charge until August. He added, only half in jest, 'I can't trust you, but I can trust Thompson, though nobody *could* be as honest as he looks!'[35] This meant also going to political meetings. One at Renfrew on 26 July lasted for six mortal hours, with the temperature 93 in the shade. That kind of punishment justified what he next did. He and Burbidge wanted to make a tour of the two largest Canadian penitentiaries, Kingston and St Vincent de Paul; they would do it via an excursion on the St Lawrence. They took the train to Brockville, where they boarded a private yacht, and made their way up-river to Kingston over a couple of days. Monday, 1 August they visited Kingston penitentiary, then came down river by moonlight, stopping at Thousand Island House on the American shore. They reached Montral by regular St Lawrence steamer in order to visit St Vincent de Paul.[36]

The penitentiaries branch of the Department of Justice administered the five federal penitentiaries, their officials, and their inmates. The director, J.G. Moylan, had been a newspaper editor in the 1860s (the Irish-Canadian weekly, the *Canadian Freeman*, of Toronto) whom Sir John A. Macdonald had appointed when he was minister of justice after confederation. Moylan was apt to be officious and arbitrary, used to getting his own way.[37] A serious issue arose with Moylan in 1888 over complaints from Dr Bourke, the surgeon and overseer of the hospital at Stony Mountain penitentiary, appointed by Thompson some months before. Thompson was convinced that Bourke's complaints were unjustified, but the more he looked the more reasonable they were. Bourke may have exaggerated – as Moylan believed – but the impression left with Thompson was that 'there was a set purpose to make the place too hot for Mr. Bourke on account of his having been appointed by me.' Bourke asked leave to appeal the warden's rulings to which the warden replied, 'Certainly not.' Thompson noted that not only was such refusal illegal but 'harsh and impolitic' besides. There was a list of issues; the point was to see that such complaints as Bourke's were dealt with firmly. 'If not,' Thompson warned Moylan,

we shall have acts of insubordination on the one hand and oppression on the other which will lead to incalculable confusion and finally prevent our determining who is right and who is wrong ... It will be necessary that the view which I take of this matter shall be communicated to the Warden and surgeon, and I should like to see the draft of the letters in which my views are conveyed.[38]

The number of inmates in federal prisons was not high, about one for every 4,000 of the population. (In the 1980s the figures are about one for every 3,000.) As of 30 June 1886 it was 1,195, of whom about 4 per cent were women. Kingston had 500 prisoners; St Vincent de Paul, 325; Dorchester, New Brunswick, 155; Stony Mountain, Manitoba, 100; New Westminister, British Columbia, 115. Of the 207 new prisoners admitted to Kingston over the year 1885–6, most were under forty years of age; 85 per cent were labourers, the rest farmers, carpenters, or other trades. Their offences were mostly stealing and burglary.[39]

At St Vincent de Paul the proportions were much the same, save that for some reason Quebec enjoyed a higher proportion of felonious shoemakers. There had recently been trouble at St Vincent de Paul, culminating in a riot on Easter Sunday, 1886, which Thompson had investigated. The warden, Godefroi Laviolette, was taken hostage by a group of prisoners and ordered to open the gates of the prison. Laviolette refused and told the guards to fire on the prisoners who held him. The guards hesitated, then fired. One convict was killed and Laviolette was shot three times from behind. He was permanently disabled. On investigation, Thompson concluded that Laviolette was guilty only of laxness of discipline, due to an easy-going disposition. He therefore proposed full salary as Laviolette's pension in the 1887 estimates. Laurier did not oppose this increase in Laviolette's pension, but he claimed that St Vincent de Paul was staffed too much by 'creatures of the Government.' Thompson disagreed. The warden of a prison, he said, 'has the absolute appointment' of all guards, indeed of nearly every official in his institution.[40]

Nevertheless, wardens themselves had often been chosen politically; Thompson was determined that the next one would not be if he could help it. Warden Botsford of Dorchester Penitentiary, the brother of Senator Botsford, died in April 1887. Within twenty-four hours Thompson received fifteen telegrams about four possible candidates plus a letter from Sir Charles Tupper. Moreover Senator Botsford had his own idea about who should replace his dead brother. Thompson cut out all that. He promoted the deputy warden, J.B. Forster. He argued politely but firmly to an irate Conservative in Dorchester that promotion of good men to the highest positions was the very stuff of a good service. 'If these officers find the higher positions disposed of according to political claims, some political advantage may result but the service will soon be in a useless condition.'[41]

Thompson also tackled the matter of the perquisites of penitentiary officers. The principal officers of each prison had a house, together with the right to keep horses, cows, and other stock, on prison land, and the right to the use of prison fuel and light. The warden of Kingston got a salary of $2,600, but there were perquisites of at least another $400, plus $500 for the house. It was even found that in computing pensions these perquisites were calculated as salary. Thompson cleared this up by establishing new salary scales, different for each of the five penitentiaries, and making it clear the the only perquisite prison officers were entitled to was that of a house.

Thompson's views of prisoners and their lives was judicious rather than generous. He was sympathetic to prison reform; indeed, by 1892 he had become convinced that substantial changes would have to be made. But he could see no alternative to prisons as such. The bent of his mind was to remedy real injustices, points where the legal system worked badly, where a case were doubtful, inadequately proved, or where plain vindictiveness were involved. He was sensitive about young offenders. It sometimes happened that parents, tired of supporting a refractory child, would have the child convicted by the magistrate for some trifling offence and sentenced to a term in a reformatory. By an Ontario law passed in 1880 a parent or guardian of any boy between the age of ten and thirteen could arrange that he be sent to a reformatory for up to five years, if the judge deemed that the boy was beyond control, by reason of incorrigible or vicious conduct.[42] Thompson was convinced that there was no justification for such action, either in provincial reformatories or federal penitentiaries. Sir Oliver Mowat on this issue was much tougher than Thompson; he was a generation older. Thompson was angry, writing about it to Mr Justice Rose of the Ontario Court of Common Pleas:

I remember one case in which a youth was sentenced to five years in the *Penitentiary* for wearing some article of clothing belonging to the convict's father – on a trumped-up charge of larceny. In another case a youth was sent for a long term to St. Vincent de Paul Penitentiary for taking a few cents from the trousers' pocket of his brother.

These cases are not uncommon as to boys sent to the Reformatory, many parents seeming to think that the Reformatory is a place for supporting and training their children. In such circumstances I look upon the parent as guilty of a heinous crime ... and the magistrate is often their accessory, and under such circumstances I would not hesitate to order a release, no matter what the warden thinks of the boy's condition and progress.

Sir Oliver's opinion seems on the other hand to be, when I last discussed the matter with him, that these circumstances should have no weight, and that a boy should be imprisoned at the will of the Warden. If we come to that in this country, it will be better that such penal institutions be abolished by the legislature or even destroyed as being instruments of evil.[43]

Not only was Thompson concerned with boys sent to prison on trumped-up charges or inadequate evidence. This concern applied to all prisoners, especially to those convicted of murder. As a matter of course all capital cases came to him as minister of justice, and he reviewed them with great care. Whatever judge and jury might have decided, where Thompson suspected the evidence he acted.

One case of inadequate evidence, as Thompson saw it, was that of Alexander Gillies, convicted of murder in January 1886 and sentenced to be hanged. Thompson reported to cabinet that the evidence on which Gillies was convicted was circumstantial and rather thin. Gillies had some of the personal effects of the murdered man, had bloodstains on his clothes, and had made some effort to conceal his identity. While this may have been sufficient to warrant conviction, Thompson said, 'it is not such conclusive proof of the convict having committed the murder as to make it safe, in the interests of justice, that the prisoner should be executed.' Thompson's recommendation of life imprisonment was accepted. It is curious that later ministers of justice, and some deputy ministers, took a different view of this case. Augustus Power represented in 1901 that the evidence was believed by judge and jury to be ample, that the verdict of guilty of murder was wholly justified, as execution would have been. Gillies was lucky that Thompson had such a tender conscience. Gillies was released from prison in 1907.[44]

Thompson's tender conscience was only given rein where evidence allowed. One of Thompson's old Halifax friends, G.G. Dustan, a loquacious sugar manufacturer, wrote him about clemency in the Buck case. 'Buck,' or Robert Osler, had murdered a constable and was to be hanged at Dorchester on 1 December 1892. Thompson told Dustan that the evidence at the trial and the confession of Buck's accomplice showed 'a deliberate murder by a desperado of a brave and faithful officer who was fearlessly performing a perilous duty for the protection of society; and while the Minister cannot but appreciate and highly honour the philanthropic motive which prompted your letter, he also feels under the grave responsibility towards society which devolves on him.'[45] Thompson's views were well brought out in Parliament in 1887. T.S. Sproule, Liberal MP for Grey East, moved that Parliament celebrate Queen Victoria's golden jubilee by reducing all life sentences currently in force to a reasonable term of years; further, that all those who had already served ten years of a sentence short of life, be set free. Sproule's sentiments, Thompson replied, did him great credit; they were admirable, generous, and, Thompson believed, shared by three-quarters of the MPs in the House of Commons. Unfortunately they were wrong: most MPs were under the impression that the twelve hundred or so men and women in Dominion penitentiaries were there either through judicial mistakes or sheer misfortune. Too many MPs, Sproule among them, seemed to believe that the unfortunates in Canadian federal prisons were really victims, caught in the toils of the law of Canada. Thompson could not accept that. He believed it would be a poor way to celebrate the jubilee by letting loose 'upon the community a class of people who have shown themselves able, by long experience, to inflict the greatest injury.' His opinion was that there was no country that gave criminals such consideration as did Canada. Criminal procedure from the first moment of a man's arrest to the last moment of his departure from prison devised 'means for his escape.' Thompson detailed the ways it worked:

1 The justice of the peace warns him not to say anything that might help his conviction.
2 He cannot be put on trial without a clear majority in the grand jury, 'a tribunal devised in his interest, the most ingenious tribunal the wisdom of man has ever devised to enable criminals to escape.'

3 Before conviction he had to have the unanimous concurrence of the petit jury, 'a jury which is susceptible to all the sentiments of compassion or sympathy.'
4 Appeal of every kind, not just for executive clemency, but through the judge himself.

Thompson was convinced that at least in Ontario and Quebec justice was reasonably efficient, that the judges were mainly actuated by motives of clemency. Certainly, he said, in the majority of cases that came to him in which executive clemency was asked for, had he the power he would have increased sentences rather than diminished them. Good intentions were a poor guide in such matters. Four or five months ago, Thompson said, he was induced to let a prisoner go who had served twelve years for a 'very shocking offence.' The prison authorities believed that clemency was right. The freed prisoner was back before the courts within two weeks. Thompson said, 'I am a real accessory to the second offence!'[46]

Thompson had confidence in justice in Ontario and Quebec, but he kept a watch on Nova Scotia; he knew from experience the nature of legal administration there. There was, for example, the case of J.R. Power. He was a customs detective in Baddeck, Cape Breton. In September 1886 he was charged with rape and convicted of indecent assault before the magistrate in Baddeck. It was quite possible, Thompson told Mackenzie Bowell, minister of customs, that Power was wholly innocent. One could be convicted in Nova Scotia on some trumped-up charge without having committed any crime, unless one defined as crime that of incurring the displeasure of a venal magistrate. What happened in Power's case, Thompson thought, was that Power was about to expose some conspiracy to which the magistrate was himself a party, and the magistrate prevented that by fixing upon Power a false charge. There were disreputable magistrates like that in Nova Scotia, Thompson said, 'appointed in obedience to local political influences.' Would the customs department initiate a review of Power's case? Power had not the means to launch a Supreme Court appeal.[47]

Not all law enforcement in Nova Scotia was bad, and some of it showed an instinctive adaptation to local attitudes. Justice Meagher told Thompson of a curious case in Truro in 1891 on the Supreme Court circuit. A sixty-nine-year old postmaster at Wittenburg, a hamlet in the Stewiacke valley, was charged with having unnatural relations with a young heifer. The magistrate who committed him had the evidence of two sworn witnesses. The old man was asked if he had anything to say. He replied,

'What was wrong with having relations with a heifer?' At the Supreme Court trial the witnesses would not come forward, the jury disagreed, and so the postmaster was released, to go back to his job of tending to letters for the hamlet of Wittenburg and, perhaps, to heifers.[48]

Even in Ontario and Quebec the judges were not perfect, though every effort was made to keep them up to the mark. For example, the county court judge of Wentworth County, Ontario, absented himself from judicial duties to earn extra money. Thompson ordered that a sharply worded letter be written asking why time was taken up by matters outside his judicial responsibilities.[49] Judge Miller of Guelph, county court judge for Wellington, was deaf but would not retire. 'Let me suggest,' wrote Macdonald to Thompson, 'your writing to Judge Miller that you will be obliged to make inquiry into the charge of deafness and consequent incapacity and suggesting his applying for a pension. We must get rid of this old fellow in some way.'[50]

It was not easy. Thompson strongly disliked interfering with judges, who, in his view, were 'completely independent of the Government and of Parliament in everything except malfeasance of office.' Their private life was their business even if they got into debt.[51] The case of Jeremiah Travis is instructive and curious. Travis was raised and educated in New Brunswick; he was about fifty years old and living in Winnipeg when in July 1885 he was appointed by Sir Alexander Campbell, Thompson's predecessor, as stipendiary magistrate at Calgary at $3,000 per annum, perhaps on the recommendation of Sir Charles Tupper.[52] Travis was in trouble in four months. Administrators sooner or later encounter a man like Travis, agreeable and pleasant on the surface but underneath vindictive, unreasonable, inexhaustible, and treacherous as a snake. Travis ordered the imprisonment of H. St Q. Cayley, the young editor of the *Calgary Herald*, for contempt of court. Cayley had been hardy enough to criticize Travis's decisions.

Governor Dewdney of the North-West Territories warned Thompson that Travis ought to be stopped. Thompson, four months into being minister of justice, was disposed to leave Travis alone:

The cases in which a Minister interferes with proceedings before a Judge are very rare indeed, if any can be said to exist. I think I ought to assume that Mr. Travis is qualified for his office, and if he is he should know, as well as I, what his authority is, and what circumstances call for its exercise.

The Editor referred to will of course have redress if the proceedings are not within Mr. Travis' jurisdiction. If I on behalf of any alleged offender interfered with any proceedings I might be defeating Justice, and I should certainly be weakening the authority of the Magistrate ...

These are my impressions about the matter, and they are so strong that I feel bound to act on them until further advised. I, however, wrote to Judge Travis on Saturday expressing very strongly a desire that he would exercise with prudence and moderation, in all matters, the authority which has been conferred on him ...[53]

But prudence and moderation were not given to Jeremiah Travis. He refused to allow a lawyer to practice in his court because the lawyer had been unwise enough to attend an indignation meeting against him. Indeed, his behaviour was such to suggest that Travis's usefulness (if he ever had any) was finished in Calgary.[54]

Thompson looked into Cayley's case; he discovered he had no option but to order Cayley's release. He asked Travis to issue the order himself in order to help Travis recover some of the popularity he had lost. Travis, in his paranoic way, assumed Thompson was asking him to do Thompson's dirty work.[55] Thompson named Justice Taylor of the Supreme Court of Manitoba as commissioner under the Public Enquiries Act to hear charges against Travis. Justice Taylor in due course reported that most of the charges against Travis were true.[56] Travis came east, and only succeeded in proving how right everyone had been. He was incapable of objective assessment of facts. Words in Travis's mind became invested with a diabolical life of their own. He was like Humpty Dumpty in *Through the Looking Glass*: 'When I use a word it means just what I choose it to mean, neither more nor less.'

Travis was not dismissed, although he could have been. By the North-West Territories Act his appointment, like all stipendiary magistrates, was at pleasure. Thompson neither wanted nor needed that route; the office of stipendiary magistrate simply expired. When the new 1886 Act for the Administration of Justice in the Territories was proclaimed, Travis's tenure expired with it. The other stipendiary magistrates, plus two other judges, were appointed to the new Supreme Court of the Territories; Travis was not.[57] He ended back in Winnipeg, where he freely damned Thompson and all his works in the *Manitoba Free Press*; Thompson had been elected in Antigonish in February 1887 by shameless bribery, and this for a minister 'who passes,' said Travis, 'where he is not better known, as an apostle of purity.'[58]

Provincial attorneys general were also a preoccupation of the minister of justice. The question of disallowance was vast and formidable but there were a host of other matters occasioned by the functioning of the Canadian federal system. The division of powers in the British North America Act was in its practical application neither simple nor neat. Perhaps the most interesting were Thompson's relations with Sir Oliver Mowat. These had begun when Thompson was attorney general of Nova Scotia, over whether the provinces or the Dominion should have the right to give the title of Queen's Counsel. Thompson, on legal and practical grounds, urged that it be the Dominion government, and the leading case on the subject, *Lenoir* v. *Ritchie*, in which he was counsel, went that way. Ontario indeed argued that the Supreme Court of Canada decision (it was five to three) lacked the advantage of argument from Ontario counsel before the Court. Ontario was not ready to accept it, and continued to insist on having its own QCs. Thompson said in a report to cabinet, 12 May 1886, that neither the Dominion nor the province should intervene officially.

It must happen that the validity of Acts of Parliament and of the Legislatures of the Provinces will constantly be in question in the ordinary litigation between private persons, and it is ... neither convenient nor necessary for the Governments of Canada and of the Provinces to intervene ... in all cases in which such questions arise.

One result of Thompson's judiciousness and Mowat's aggressiveness on this issue was that it was still being discussed in the law journals in the 1890s.[59]

After Thompson became minister of justice, Mowat began with an adroit move. The Ontario legislature, he said, had in 1884 passed an act for protecting workmen in factories. It was not proclaimed owing to doubts about Ontario's jurisdiction. A bill similar to Ontario's had been brought in the House of Commons in 1885 but it too was withdrawn. 'We ought to be able to devise a way,' said Mowat smoothly, 'in which questions of jurisdiction could be dealt with without exposing private individuals to injury and litigation. I had some correspondence with your predecessor on the subject, but he did not see his way to acquiescing.' Would Thompson like to arrange to have an act passed confirming Ontario's jurisdiction?

Thompson was polite but firm. 'I think such a course would be open to much objection. If the provincial act is within its legislative authority an act of the Parliament of Canada purporting to confirm the provincial act would of course have no validity.' Thompson added, in Mowat's own style,

'Why do you doubt the authority of the Ontario legislature to act?' Mowat replied that he did not have doubts, but the Dominion government had hitherto questioned Ontario's right to pass such legislation. 'I shall be glad to learn,' Mowat said, 'that you take a different view, and do not regard the validity of the Ontario Act as open to any doubt.'[60] Thompson replied in August 1886 that the real test appeared to be between Ontario and private interests opposed to such an act. 'I should suppose that the resolution of the Dominion Government to leave the Ontario Act to its operation, and to decline to contest its validity by litigation, would be all that could reasonably be asked by your Government.' There may be, indeed, aspects to factory legislation that the Dominion Parliament should deal with, Thompson suggested. 'In this respect, the Act seems to me to be like any other Act, on a subject which may, in certain respects fall within both Federal and provincial jurisdiction, and on which the Provincial Legislature has chosen to pass.' Mowat then had his deputy attorney general jump the gun by asking Burbidge to accept the service of a writ. The Department of Justice still said no.[61] One month after this came the appointment of the Dominion Royal Commission on the Relations of Labour and Capital.

Thompson's relations with Mowat did not end there. Despite the opening gambit over factory legislation, their cordiality grew. By 1888 there were private letters between them on a variety of subjects. Mowat, for example, in November 1888 sent a draft of an official letter on the rights of the Dominion and Ontario in harbours and rivers. Thompson said he would look at it as soon as he could. 'Allow me to say,' he added, 'that I fully appreciate your willingness to discuss and dispose of constitutional questions which necessarily arise between the two governments, in the most friendly spirit and I propose to avail myself of your disposition.' By 1890 there seems to have been almost an agenda of items discussed between them, usually in Toronto.[62]

More startling than constitutional pourparlers was Mowat's urgent request in 1891 for an official public executioner. The administration of justice was a provincial responsibility but the Dominion had a duty to review for the possibility of the Queen's clemency all capital sentences that were recommended by cabinet to the governor general on the initiative of the minister of justice. The responsibility for carrying out death sentences rested with the province, through the sheriff of the county. It is not clear what prompted Mowat to raise the question of a public executioner; one suspects some grisly bungle at the gallows in Ontario. But raise the question Mowat did, and urgently, with Thompson in 1891. Thompson recommended in January 1892 an order-in-council,

at the urgent solicitation of the Attorney General of Ontario he representing in effect that it was highly desirable in order for the due and proper execution of capital sentences that some one individual specially experienced and qualified should be designated as a permanent officer for that purpose ... holding himself available for all capital cases that might occur in any part of Canada.

The appointment of an official hangman was subject to conditions: that he hold office during pleasure, that he be paid only so long as Parliament voted the money ($700 per annum), that he report his residence to each provincial attorney general, and finally,

He is at all times to hold himself in readiness to do such duties in connection with the execution of capital sentences as he may be required to do by any Attorney-General or Sheriff in Canada ... on the understanding that he is to be paid by the local authorities only his reasonable travelling expenses from his residence to and from the place of execution ...

The undersigned further recommends that he be authorized ... to communicate by secret despatch the contents [of this report] to each Provincial Attorney-General ...[63]

Thus began, in January 1892, the regime of J.R. Radclive.[64] He had been a British sailor on the China station and had often been detailed to hang Chinese pirates from the ship's yard arm. Radclive felt sorry for the poor blighters, murderers or not, so he worked out the quickest and most merciful way. He had become subsequently the steward for a rowing club in Toronto.[65] In 1890 Radclive heard about a criminal that hung for fourteen minutes before he died. Radclive turned to his wife and said, 'I will offer to hang the next man and put a stop to that sort of torture.' Radclive always dressed in a plain black suit and was not masked. When he hanged Buck at Dorchester on 1 December 1892, it took just thirty seconds from putting the noose around Buck's neck until he was unconscious.[66]

The ambiguity of legal issues between the Dominion and the provinces is reflected in Indian treaty rights. Here Thompson seems to have taken a clear line. An act in 1886 gave the superintendent general of Indian affairs – Sir John Macdonald – power to grant licences to cut trees on

Ojibway land on Lake Huron. There was conflict between this act and an Indian treaty. In Thompson's view if the crown gave timber licences in such circumstances,

it would be a breach of trust against the Indians, because the Treaty is the instrument which declares the trust ... The fact that the Indians might have no legal redress is, I imagine a strong reason why [the matter?] should be more carefully dealt with. They should not be at any greater disadvantage by having the Crown for a trustee than by having a private individual.[67]

This high-minded view of Indian rights became academic a year and a half later. In December 1888 the Privy Council decided that the right to cut timber on Indian land in Ontario belonged neither to the Indians nor to the Dominion government but to the province of Ontario.[68]

Dominion-provincial relations were not confined to the Ministry of Justice. Thompson as MP for Antigonish encountered some curious problems. There was a small Dominion public building in Antigonish town housing the customs office and the post office, but it had room for more. It happened that the postmaster of Antigonish was the caretaker of the building. He was also sheriff of Antigonish County. The county found the office space convenient; it was also cheap since it cost nothing. Thus were accommodated the registrar of deeds, registrar of probate and other county officials. The registrar of probate was a magistrate and did his magistrate's business there, rather to the discomfiture of other occupants. Since the municipality of Antigonish County contributed nothing to cost or upkeep, should not the situation be regularized in some way? It seemed so to Thompson. There was surely no objection, he suggested to Sir Hector Langevin, minister of public works, to housing municipal officers in Dominion public buildings, but there ought to be some regular system.

There was an odd consequence to this. The town of Antigonish discovered that the best place to hang the town's fire bell was on that building, on the northeast corner. Thompson thought that would do no harm. But the postmaster-caretaker-sheriff objected: hanging the firebell on that northeast corner would ruin, quite ruin, his flower garden! It took the bishop and a peremptory telegram from Thompson to get the bell placed where the town wanted it.[69]

Such was the infinitude of questions, little and big, that filled so much of the life and time of Thompson the administrator. Trips away from the office only made it more certain that the correspondence would be piled higher and deeper upon his return. And whenever it was known

Thompson was going to be away, his outer office would fill up with MPs and other callers who had the belief, usually mistaken, that it was essential to give their 'matter' a small shove ere the minister get away.

Thompson's first real holiday since 1885 was his first trip west in 1887. It had been planned that the Thompsons, the McLelans, and the O'Connors (an Ottawa lawyer whom Thompson liked) would go westward together in August 1887. It was originally to have been in connection with a CPR arbitration, but the timetable changed. The Thompsons decided to go anyway. Annie and the children came to Ottawa, and on 11 August they embarked on the CPR car 'Matapedia' for the long journey west. They did what Macdonald had done the summer before. Though inevitably the business of the Justice Department kept crowding in from time to time, the trip was for them all a great delight. That is about all one knows. Information about Thompson's trip is confined to a few thin newspaper comments. When Thompson, Annie and their family are together, their life disappears behind a veil of silence as thick as the berth curtains on the 'Matapedia.' They were in Vancouver on 16 August, went on to Victoria, and installed themselves for ten days or so at the Driard House.

On their return journey an official address to Thompson was presented by the bar of Calgary, headed by James Lougheed, who would become senator in 1889.

In no Department of the Government has such radical and judicious reform, in the administration of Northwest affairs, been accomplished as in the Department of which you, Sir, are the head.

The judicial system which, thanks to your efforts, now obtains in this country, is one that, for the first time, places the Northwest on some degree of equal footing with the Provinces of Canada.[70]

Lougheed meant the establishment of the new Supreme Court of the North-West Territories in 1886, to which the judges were appointed in February 1887. He also meant the rules under which it operated, mainly the circuit court system. The new circuit courts in the North-West in the late 1880s imposed hardships on the judges. Justice T.B. Maguire had to go from Prince Albert to Battleford in March 1888, a trip of 140 miles:

Nearly 100 miles of that was through *unbroken* snow where the horses were half of their time up to their bellies in snow and where they scarcely ever went past a walk. We had to travel in what are called 'flat sleighs' which are simply a *strong toboggan* with canvas sides, drawn by one horse. We were 6 days coming and all that time, with the exception of one night, were under Canvass [sic] with the thermometer at about 25 or 30° below zero.[71]

Thompson had extended the jury system to cover more types of trial; by the new act the use of a jury would no longer be controlled by the amount of money in dispute or the crime charged. Thompson also wanted to enlarge the jury to the regular twelve, instead of six as it was by the old act of 1875. It would bring the North-West in line with the rest of Canada. Macdonald, reading Thompson's proposed act from his sick bed in 1886, demurred. Your act looks fine, he said, 'but I think it would not be well this Session to make a Jury of twelve necessary – It would at once be said in Quebec that after *murdering* Riel with 6 we found the thing indefensible, and so altered the law to make it like all other English Courts.[72] So six-man juries stayed for the time being. Thompson had also given the lieutenant-governor in council the right to make ordinances about the administration of justice in the North-West territories, 'in as full and ample a manner as the Legislature in any Province of Canada could.'[73] All of this was appreciated in the North-West and in Calgary; no doubt, too, the removal of Travis helped the feelings of the Calgary bar.

The Thompsons came back to Ottawa on 9 September refreshed, relaxed, and, like many people in such condition, were by no means ready to shoulder the burdens of duty. Annie went on to Halifax to get her boys off to Stonyhurst. She celebrated her return by having a party, the kind that made Thompson tremble with nervousness. Annie gathered such a queer crowd of people together and expected them to be happy and amused more or less spontaneously. But her party came off with style.

Annie and Thompson were to have set up housekeeping in Ottawa that autumn, beginning in November when Thompson took possession of the Dennis house. But by late October it was clear his family would have to stay in Halifax a few months more. Sir John Macdonald asked Thompson to go with Sir Charles Tupper as senior legal adviser to meet the Americans in Washington.[74] In the dangerous work of opening up the Convention of 1818, Macdonald needed Thompson's good law and strong mind.

13

Adventures in Washington

Old John Allison Bell, in 1888 at the age of seventy-one still Halifax's city auditor, said that there had always been a fisheries question. 'I cannot remember a time when there was not some sort of trouble about the Yankees and the Fish.'[1] There were several kinds of fish, but the one the Americans pursued most avidly was *scomber scombrus*, the mackerel of the northwest Atlantic. It is not a large fish – about fifteen inches long and a pound or so in weight – but good for eating and for bait. It winters in deep water; in March or April large schools move north to the coasts of Maine and the Atlantic provinces, and appear off Nova Scotia and in the Gulf of St Lawrence in May and June.

The Canadian three-mile limit was the main American problem. But another was ice to keep the mackerel until they could be got to market or until used as bait for the cod on Banquereau, Georges or the Grand Banks. What therefore came to be increasingly important to the Americans was commercial freedom in Canadian ports – the privilege of buying ice and bait, of shipping their catches by rail to the Boston market from Canso, Halifax, Pictou, Yarmouth, or Saint John.

But the Americans had no right to do any of these things. In 1818 they had given up all such commercial facilities in British North American ports and the right to fish within the three-mile limit, mainly because the British had given them extensive fishing and drying rights on some six hundred miles of the west coast of Newfoundland and the southern coasts of Labrador. The terms agreed upon in 1818 were quite specific: in return for that 'American shore,' as it was called, American fishing boats could enter British North American ports for only four purposes, all of an emergency character – shelter, repairs, wood, and water, and 'for no other purpose whatever.' They were barred from fishing inside the three-mile limit in all other parts of British North America. Thus Canadian fishing vessels in American ports had regular commercial privileges; American fishing vessels in Canadian ports did not. The Americans had that six hundred miles of Canadian, mostly Newfoundland, shoreline to use; Canadians had nothing on the American coast.[2] (Unlike fishing vessels, ordinary American shipping in Canadian ports had the usual commercial privileges.)

That would seem to be reasonably clear. But it was not. The Americans found the restriction 'for no other purpose whatever' impossible to accept. They tried to get around it, through it, underneath it; but it was terribly comprehensive. It was the real nub of the Canadian case. As A.A. Adee, American second assistant secretary of state, told T.F. Bayard, President Cleveland's secretary of state, in May 1886, 'The more I think of it, the more I am convinced that the dispute turns on the meaning to be attached to the words "and for no other purpose whatever".' The way the Canadians interpret it, Adee said, would make it impossible for an American fisherman to buy a newspaper or even post a letter in a Canadian port.[3] Was it possible that that could be meant? Thompson thought so. The Convention of 1818 might as well be repealed if it were allowed to be breached like that.[4] Adee and other Americans took the view that the 1818 Convention did not apply to deep-sea fishing vessels at all. It was as good standing ground as they could find.

Then there were the problems of definition. Where did the three-mile limit run? Did it run from headland to headland, as the Canadians contended, or did it follow the sinuosities of the coast, as the Americans argued? There were several large bays where this mattered. The Bay of Fundy, some forty miles wide, was impossible to close. But there were many others that could be: Miramichi Bay in New Brunswick, Egmont Bay in Prince Edward Island, Fortune Bay, Placentia Bay, Sir Charles Hamilton Sound in Newfoundland; in Nova Scotia, St Ann's Bay, Chedabucto Bay, Harrington Bay, St Mary's Bay, all of which were to be subsequently singled out in the treaty.[5] Canada contended that bays under ten miles in width were wholly under Canadian jurisdiction.

The 1818 rules were enforced until 1854 – how well it is difficult to know[6] – and in that year the Reciprocity Treaty, in effect from 1855 to 1866, restored the inshore fisheries and commercial privileges to American fishermen. They were again given to the Americans by the fisheries clauses of the Treaty of Washington of 1871, in effect from 1873 to 1 July 1885. Congress recklessly abrogated the articles in consequence of what Americans thought, rightly, was the outrageously high award of the Halifax arbitration of 1877. Canada allowed the Americans to use the fisheries for the 1885 fishing season as an act of grace, in return for the promise of the appointment of a joint high commission. But the Senate refused to have the commission; Canada was thus bound to enforce the old 1818 rules, as she had from 1866 to 1872, if her rights meant anything at all.[7] Perhaps the question might have been avoided altogether if the Americans had offered to give back to Canada and Newfoundland the 'American shore'; they claimed it was not much use to them, but they were not willing to give it up. Indeed, Thompson believed that the American shore was of great value to the Americans, whatever they might say.[8]

How to enforce Canadian rights thus engaged the serious attention of the government in the spring of 1886. Macdonald reviewed G.E. Foster's instructions to his fisheries officers and had Thompson check them over. Unless the Americans came through with their promised joint high commission, which seemed unlikely, seizures were going to be made on the first clear violation of Canadian law. It was important to avoid any ambiguity, as Macdonald pointed out to Thompson in March 1886:

While the right to draw the line from Headland to Headland should be asserted, it would be well *at present at least* to confine our forcible interference to points where the Headlands question does not arise.

It would be a great misfortune if in our first seizures that question would be raised and there will certainly soon arise a sufficient number of trespasses on the open coast to insure several convictions where the u s Gov't must assent to the legality of our acts –

Bye & bye we may give more stringent instructions ... whether the right to get wood and *water* includes ice –

My own opinion is that it is not worth while seizing or objecting to the shipment of ice.[9]

Fishing captains are an independent lot, not easily amenable to rules made by distant diplomats. American fishermen had never accepted the Canadian view of the 1818 Convention and were not disposed to do so in 1886.[10] Thompson, who had had some experience, said that they had no compunction about getting around fishery regulations whenever it suited them. Fish were real; the three-mile limit was an imaginary line in the sea.[11] One is tempted to apply to fishing captains a jingle from the 1860s:

> I am monarch of all I survey,
> There is none to dispute what I wish,
> We goes where I say to go,
> And we fish when I say to fish.[12]

Many of the skippers and crew of American fishing schooners were originally Newfoundlanders or Canadians from Nova Scotia and New Brunswick, who liked to come back and visit friends and relations. They naturally knew the coast and the good places to fish, where and how one might avoid patrol vessels.

The mackerel were independent too. One could not predict where they were going to be. The Americans had managed quite nicely in their own territorial waters until 1886, when, for unknown reasons, the mackerel largely disappeared off the New England coast.[13] This forced the Americans to find their bait in the waters off the Maritime provinces of Canada.

One day early in May 1886, Alden Kinney, the twenty-five-year-old skipper of the schooner *David J. Adams* of Gloucester, Massachusetts, took his vessel through Digby Gut into Annapolis Basin. He avoided Digby town where he might have reported to customs (indeed, *should* have); he covered up the port of registry of his ship and went up the basin towards Clementsport. Kinney was a New Brunswicker, had relatives on Annapolis Basin, and knew the territory well. He bought two tons of ice and one and a half barrels of fresh bait. On his way back he was boarded by officers from the fisheries patrol vessel *Lansdowne*; he said he had no fresh bait aboard and was allowed to proceed. But he hung around the basin and the officers of the *Lansdowne*, hearing from local gossip that things aboard the *Adams* were not what Kinney said they were, went aboard her a second time, found the fresh bait and arrested the vessel on two grounds; failing to report to Canadian customs, and buying bait contrary to the Convention of 1818.[14]

The Americans protested sharply against this 'arbitrary, unlawful, unwarranted and unfriendly action on the part of the Canadian Government.'[15] Newspapers on both sides of the border had a busy time with it. Wallace Graham, the Department of Justice's legal agent in Halifax, was appalled at what the papers in Halifax said, and was also not pleased with some actions of Canadian customs. At Souris, PEI, an American schooner had been caught with illegally bought potatoes; customs seized the potatoes and allegedly sought to nullify the purchase completely by administering an emetic to the captain and the mate.[16] But there was no doubt in Graham's mind that the *Adams*, that 'stinking little schooner,' had been stealing 'Digby chickens.'[17] The *Adams* case was sufficiently flagrant that cabinet and Parliament insisted that the law be tightened up. 'In the Commons,' Macdonald told Lord Lansdowne, 'a violent assertion of Canadian rights was imminent, which would have done more harm in the

U.S. then our legislation.'[18] This was Bill 136, passed in May 1886, after the arrest of the *Adams*. The American government protested against that too.

It would take more than Canada's eleven patrol vessels to deal effectively with illegal fishing. Between East Point, Prince Edward Island, and St Peter's, thirty miles to the west, some 150 American vessels were fishing in the summer of 1886. When the *Critic*, the patrol vessel, went west, the Americans came inshore on the east, the home ports of the vessels shrouded in canvas. The arrest and detention of the *Adams* was followed by the arrest of the *Ella M. Doughty* in Sydney for the same offence as the *Adams*. After that, however, the patrol vessels were told to seize no more vessels for buying bait; the *Adams* and the *Doughty* would function as deterrents.[19] Altogether, in the 1886 season some seven hundred vessels were boarded, of which fifteen were arrested: twelve were released on payment of a fine of about $400.[20]

The case against the *Adams* was to have been heard in August 1886, with both Americans and Canadians making it a test case. Thompson's view was that there was no reason to hurry on adjudication – the longer it was put off the better. The Americans abetted this policy by asking for an adjournment; Alden Kinney had already gone off for the summer's fishing on another vessel. The Canadian case looked strong: the *Adams* had clearly violated the 1818 Convention, to say nothing of the Customs Act of 1883 that required the *Adams* to report at Digby. Thompson wrote an elegant memorandum that went through to London (pending the writing of a proper despatch) as a rough text for Lord Granville to preach to Mr Edward Phelps, the American minister in London.[21]

Behind the actions of the Canadian government there was impressive unanimity of political support; indeed, Liberal papers were more belligerent than Conservative. In the United States the Republican papers heaped obloquy upon the allegedly supine position taken by the American secretary of state, T.F. Bayard. 'If the Canadians go much further in the warfare on American fishermen,' said the *New York Tribune*, 'Mr. Bayard will actually be obliged to take notice of it.'[22] In the paper's view, Americans ever since independence have been outdone by the diabolical cleverness of Anglo-Canadian diplomacy; it was 'a lottery in which the Canadians have always drawn the prizes and the Americans the blanks.'[23] Congress, in a mood of punitiveness in the spring of 1887, passed a non-intercourse resolution giving President Cleveland the power to cut off all trade with Canada if satisfaction were not given for the seizures of the *Adams* and the *Doughty*.

T.F. Bayard, civilized, intelligent, and reasonable, thought negotiations were better. He got Sir Charles Tupper to visit him in Washington in April 1887, meeting him with the frank declaration, 'Well, Sir Charles, the confederation of Canada and the construction of the Canadian Pacific Railway have brought us face to face with a nation and we may as well discuss public questions from that point of view.' Bayard admitted that there was some awkwardness in dealing with the questions owing to Canada's 'imperfectly developed sovereignty.'[24] Americans could not help but wonder what would happen to international treaties if a dependency or colony – as Americans regarded Canada – could render null and void treaty obligations under the plea of making police regulations.[25]

Canada's own rueful perspective about this imperfect sovereignty is suggested in a satirical conversation in *Grip* in 1877, between John Bull, Yankee Jonathan, and a small boy named Canada whose rights were evidently of no particular account:

MR. BULL. – Rights be blowed! ... Small boys has no rights. Who's 'e? ... My boy Canada will be 'happy to surrender hanythink for his parent. You can have 'em hall, cheap.[26]

This well represents Canadian fears; but in 1887 it does less than justice to British diplomacy.

From the discussions between Tupper and Bayard came the proposal for a joint high commission to meet in Washington in November 1887 to deal with the whole range of Canadian-American relations – fisheries, reciprocity, even the burgeoning Bering Sea question. Macdonald was supposed to be the Canadian plenipotentiary, but he did not want to go. At the age of seventy-two he could say that once (in 1871) was enough. He was uneasy about American designs; he suspected a trap baited with Anglo-American friendship to induce the British to reopen the Convention of 1818. That process, Macdonald felt (as did Thompson) would be much to Canada's disadvantage unless great care were taken.[27]

The Canadian–British commissioners consisted of Sir Charles Tupper, Sir Lionel Sackville-West, the British minister at Washington, and Joseph Chamberlain as senior plenipotentiary. Chamberlain was brilliant, talented, just fifty years old, a Liberal Unionist who had broken with Gladstone over home rule in April 1886. Chamberlain wanted his staff kept small and so were added two Foreign Office officials – Thompson called them flunkies – Henry Bergne, who had been in Halifax in 1877, and

Willoughby Maycock, who had got himself attached because he was private secretary for the parliamentary under-secretary for foreign affairs.[28] The British government had apparently intended that Bergne and Maycock would act as counsel to take charge of the British–Canadian case; that was blocked by Canada in no uncertain terms, according to Thompson:

There was nearly another fuss like that which happened at the Halifax Commission – by the English Gov't sending out counsel to take charge of the case but I have stopped that. They may send counsel to advise Mr. Chamberlain if they please but the case is to be in my hands.[29]

In this determination Thompson was supported by Macdonald. Macdonald did not trust Chamberlain, thought the British side too weak, and remembered the clever Americans who had so effectively directed the American side at the Treaty of Washington in 1871. He told Lansdowne, 'Thompson knows the legal bearings on the questions which will affect Canada – better than any English counsel.'[30]

Sir Charles Tupper needed expert assistance; he was a doctor not a lawyer. Nevertheless, by long experience he had acquired expertise on fisheries questions, and he had some knack for negotiation, confined mostly to a native shrewdness of wanting to get value for concessions. He had also bulldog tenacity and considerable energy. His great asset was a prodigious memory that he put readily to the service of his causes. Formidable as this combination was, Tupper was unreliable, apt to say too much. As Macdonald told Lord Lansdowne, 'all his colleagues fear his impulsiveness, if acting alone at Washington.'[31] Tupper pretended that it was he who insisted upon Thompson's coming to Washington as legal adviser. That was Tupper's way, to claim influence he did not possess for purposes he may not have wanted. It was Macdonald, perhaps also the cabinet, who insisted upon Thompson's going.[32]

Thompson's knowledge and experience offered Canada unusual advantages. The American side of the fisheries question was almost an open book to him; after all, a decade earlier he had helped prepare the American brief to the Halifax commission. He had already recognized from American despatches glaring holes in their case.[33] Thompson asked Wallace Graham to come to Ottawa (and Washington) to help him get up the Canadian case, and the two of them set to work around 23 October. For three weeks they went at it together until 10:30 most evenings, and then walked the autumn streets of Ottawa to shake loose the cobwebs.[34]

There was very little time to prepare their case. Further, Thompson no longer had his deputy and he had to do Burbidge's work. His cabinet colleagues had interminable matters to discuss before he went away. Some days all he had time for was to eat and say his rosary, and not half enough time for rest. He wanted Annie to come to Washington with him – Mrs Tupper was going – but all Annie could manage was to come to Ottawa with Annie Graham for a week before their husbands set off.[35]

They left for New York on 15 November 1887, Tupper with Colonel Cameron and C.C. Chipman as his staff, Thompson with Wallace Graham as legal support, George Johnson as statistician, and Douglas Stewart as his private secretary. They arrived the following morning and spent that day with Joseph Chamberlain. Thompson was pleased with Chamberlain, 'very keen and shrewd, both in perception and expression,' was his initial verdict to Macdonald, 'we have much the better team on the British side.'

Some who professed to be near Bayard had told Chamberlain that American interest in the conference was not with trade questions of any kind, only the relaxation of the Convention of 1818. Chamberlain was not going to accept that. He told Bayard's friends – intending that it should get back – that surely that could not be, otherwise 'why should he have put us to all the trouble of coming here?'

They reached Washington Thursday night, 17 November and were installed in the Arlington Hotel near the White House. They dined in state with Chamberlain that night, full dress, 'lots of etiquette' as Thompson put it, so much so that the next day he and Wallace Graham went out to buy ties and other necessaries for the stiff round of formal life ahead of them. It was going to be formal dinners every evening.[36]

They met Bayard on Saturday. Bayard, tall, well groomed, impressed Thompson as 'the best looking American I ever saw'[37] but he was puzzled why such an intelligent and pleasant man could have approved such poor despatches. Bayard took them to meet President Cleveland. Cleveland was not thin in photographs Thompson had seen but he was a good deal thicker in real life, 'older and far more corpulent ... when he tries to stand up his head falls back and his stomach protrudes.' A description unattractive enough; Thompson reported it to Martin Griffin, parliamentary librarian in Ottawa. Griffin said that he had heard the same and hoped that 'the pretty girl who had married this hog must have made some conditions.'[38] Frances Folsom was indeed pretty, and young. She had married Cleveland in 1886 when he was forty-nine and she was twenty-two.

Thompson went to mass on Sunday but liked neither church nor service. The singing, said Thompson, was 'what Mark Twain would have called the delerium tremens of music.'[39] He was uncomfortable anyway, for he had developed a pronounced rheumatism in his right arm, and though it was ministered to by Tupper, it remained extremely painful for another fortnight. Thompson punished his writing arm unmercifully. That did not prevent him from going to social events, though he hated pomp and fuss. The British legation offered dinner that Sunday night in honour of Joseph Chamberlain. Sir Lionel Sackville-West, the minister, was sixty years old, tired, and costive. Bayard attributed part of the difficulty between Canada and the United States to Sackville-West's indolence. (When it was known in 1885, for example, that Sackville-West was going to visit Ottawa, Bayard specifically asked him to mention several issues to Sir John Macdonald. Sackville-West quite forgot. During the thirty meetings of the 1887–8 conference, Sackville-West opened his mouth once, to ask that a window be closed.[40]) His eldest daughter, Victoria, presided as hostess at a dinner for twelve that included Thompson, Tupper, Bayard, and the other two American plenipotentiaries, W.B. Putnam of Portland, Maine, and Dr J.B. Angell, president of the University of Michigan. Thompson admired Victoria Sackville-West; he said she was the only beautiful woman he saw in Washington.* Thompson was evidently more discriminating than Willoughby Maycock, who seemed to find dozens of pretty women, including Mary Endicott, the daughter of W.C. Endicott, the secretary for war in Cleveland's cabinet, whom Chamberlain met that night. Chamberlain married her a year later, his third wife. Thompson's preferences leaned to aristocratic women who had style and intelligence to go with their good looks. Thompson found in the Corcoran Art Gallery a Venus and a statue of a female Greek slave; the resemblances to Annie stirred his blood more than the Washington women.[41]

The conference opened in earnest on Tuesday, 22 November, in the large reception room adjacent to Bayard's office in the State, War and Navy building, just across the little park from the White House.[42] It was a vast apartment, forty feet long, with windows that looked south to the Potomac and the glistening white shaft of the Washington monument. Various American secretaries of state brooded from the wall: over

* Victoria Sackville-West (1862–1939) was the toast of Washington. She married in 1890 her cousin (same name as her father) and was the mother of Vita Sackville-West (1892–1962). See Nigel Nicolson, *Portrait of a Marriage* (London 1973), 63–6.

Chamberlain's head were the blazing eyes of James G. Blaine and facing him was Daniel Webster. This first meeting was stormy. To their surprise, the Canadian—British delegation got a long printed argument from the Americans which omitted everything tentatively agreed on as agenda between Tupper and Bayard. All the Americans concentrated on was the iniquity of the Canadian seizures. So much did this American opening create consternation that Putnam and Angell called on Chamberlain afterward to explain privately the difficulty the Americans were under, owing to pressure from the Senate. The American submission would have to be answered of course, and the conference immediately adjourned for a week for the purpose.[43]

That was Thompson's responsibility mainly, and the Canadian reply took him the next three days, after which he had to start on another brief. The Canadians were, said Thompson, 'busy as nailers' on a roof; breakfast at 8:30, work until dark, except for lunch at 1:30, preparing documents, copying documents, discussing them with Chamberlain and Sackville-West. From the book Maycock later wrote the reader gets an impression of leisurely life at Washington, and small wonder: he and Bergne went off to play tennis every morning, dressed in white flannels crowned with lawn tennis hats and were not seen again until dinner. Then they appeared, Thompson remarked, in 'sea-green plush.'[44]

For the Canadians, even on Sunday the work went on; after mass at 9 a.m. it was work until midnight, except for Tupper dragging Thompson off to vespers in the Catholic Church. Tupper did not usually go to Catholic services, and Thompson suspected that evening that Tupper was up to something. He was. Tupper intended Thompson as a gooseberry, to provide the third party to cover a flirtation. En route to church, Tupper called for a young lady. Thompson wasn't having that role. 'I paid him off by taking her entirely under my charge. She is a Catholic and very nice and sensible. He had met her travelling in England with her father who is since dead.' The story so amused Annie that Thompson gave her another of the same. The next evening at dinner, Tupper remarked a rather pretty woman who sat near them regularly. Thompson pointed out a good-looking young man who was interested in her too. On the way upstairs out of the dining-room, Tupper asked to have the young man pointed out. Thompson did so and then suggested, 'Should we not challenge him?'

TUPPER: 'Ah, I'm afraid there would be no use in my taking part in an affair of that kind.'

THOMPSON: 'Why not?'
TUPPER: 'You have youth on your side.'
THOMPSON: 'Vigour counts for everything.'
TUPPER: 'Oh, I should only be pulling chestnuts out of the fire for you.'

So, said Thompson, he did not expect that Tupper would discuss such subjects with him again.[45] In the Thompson Papers there turns up another Tupper adventure. Occasionally Tupper and his secretary, C.C. Chipman, employed for confidential typing a Miss (or Mrs) Josephine Bailey. She had good references, and Tupper and Chipman used to go to her house to give her papers. According to her story, she became pregant as a result of Tupper's visits, whereupon he asked her to have an operation, which she did. She subsequently came to Ottawa to see him and asked for a position in the Canadian civil service. Tupper said no. The result was a summons served on Tupper in New York in 1891, in circumstances that looked like blackmail. Tupper denied her story, except that Mrs Bailey had done confidential typing. The suit appears to have been dropped or settled out of court. Why this correspondence should be in the Thompson Papers is a curious and unanswered question. But the incident could not have endeared Tupper to Thompson.[46]

The Canadian reply to the opening American argument, covering some three hundred pages of foolscap, was handed in on 28 November. The Americans would probably need an adjournment to digest *that*. While Thompson was in the ante-room he wrote Annie and Macdonald, and from these letters comes the only account of the conference outside of official minutes, the odd letter from Tupper, and the social froth offered by Willoughby Maycock. Thompson could not understand why the Americans had chosen to open the argument with a recitation of their fishermen's woes and with demands for compensation for the arrest of the *Adams* and the *Doughty*. So much correspondence had already taken place on this subject that the British–Canadian plenipotentiaries had no reason to expect the Americans would have bothered. Thompson began to think they did it to get it on the record, perhaps from fear of Congress; perhaps they may have believed that Canadians did not have materials at hand for a full reply. 'If this was their game,' wrote Thompson to Macdonald with a certain grim cheerfulness, 'they have been mistaken. The preparations we had in getting up the brief before leaving Ottawa made us armed at all points. Chamberlain and his English assistants have left the preparation of the Replies implicitly to us.'[47]

American complaints about Canadian legislation being expansions of the 1818 Convention were unjustified, Thompson said. None of that legislation changed the 1818 terms. All it did was to prevent and punish infractions. 'What was the true and proper interpretation when the Treaty [of 1818] was made,' Thompson insisted, 'must be its true and proper interpretation now.' It was true that seventy years had elapsed, and no doubt a more modern treaty should be made; but when such modernizations were made, in 1855–66, 1873–85, they were rescinded in both instances by the United States. The American colonies prior to 1783 had not been co-owners with Great Britain of the fisheries. They enjoyed the use of the fisheries by virtue of being British subjects.

When the Colonies became independent they renounced the benefits as well as the burdens of British subjects ... There was surely no reason why the Colonies which had remained loyal to the crown should be divested of valuable territorial rights for the benefit of those who had renounced their allegiance.[48]

Negotiations were moving very slowly, if at all. There were hints from Bayard that if the causes of American irritation at Canada were removed, Congress might be amenable to putting fish and possibly other items on the free list. This meant that American fishermen could make Canadian ports their base for supplies, and from which they would be able to transship their catches, in return for a possibility that some items might be admitted free into the United States. It was sufficiently blatant for Chamberlain to express surprise at a proposal asking so much and offering so little; they were terms as 'would be exacted from a country defeated after a great war.'[49] All this time Thompson and Graham were hard at work, briefs going to the Canadian–British group on every imaginable point; but for Thompson this busyness, combined with a lack of real progress, was irksome. It was clear, however, that far from investigation showing the Canadian case weaker, 'our case seems to grow stronger every day.' For example, the Americans contended that by the law of nations a vessel entering port for shelter was implicitly free from harbour dues and pilotage. The Canadians found, on investigation, that in every treaty the United States made, this matter was expressly stipulated for. Not only that, but Americans had seized Spanish vessels on the Florida coast for not reporting to customs, even though the Spanish vessels had come in just for emergency. The Americans did not seem to know their own ground and they disliked very much finding it out from Thompson's briefs.

The balmy December weather in Washington made Thompson reluctant to do anything else than fisheries; he disliked having to tackle the shoals of letters from Antigonish County correspondents that came to him even in Washington. The theatre was undistinguished; he saw two second-rate farces, one of them played as badly as possible, the other a 'wretched play, abominably played, and the audience in ecstasies.' He couldn't understand it.[50]

At this point, early in December, Chamberlain privately proposed to Bayard that, under licence, American fishermen be allowed to buy bait and supplies, and transship fish, on condition that the United States admit Canadian fish free and abandon all rights to the American shore. This was by far the most sensible and constructive proposal made by either side, and one on which Thompson, Foster, and all the British–Canadian plenipotentiaries agreed. Bayard replied that Congress could not be brought to renounce the American shore, but he would agree to propose that Americans renounce all fishing in Canadian waters, and that Canadian fish would be given free admission into the United States. Chamberlain agreed to take these suggestions to Ottawa over Christmas.[51]

Thus they broke up on 11 December. A pilgrimage was made by warship down to Mount Vernon, and then the Canadians went north to New York. Thompson tried to do some shopping; he was never good at it, always getting cheated, and he admitted that in a shop he was a perfect fool. Graham, lucky man, was going to Halifax via Boston; Thompson had to go to Ottawa and whether he would get to Halifax for Christmas was doubtful. 'I fancy I shall have to sneak away from Ottawa like a thief in the night if I am to get home for Xmas.' He was homesick; despite the lavish entertainments in Washington that so rejoiced the heart of Willoughby Maycock, all Thompson could do was write letters. On the last Sunday in Washington, 'My darling, how I wish you were with me and that we could always be together. If I had known how hard it is to be away from you, the negotiations of 1885 would have had a different result.'[52]

He arrived in Ottawa on 15 December, bringing Sir John Macdonald a Christmas present of Annand's *Speeches and Public Letters of Joseph Howe* (1858) that he picked up in Washington. Macdonald joked about Thompson's wanting to go to Halifax all the time, that the climate in Ottawa was clearly not wet enough for him! Off Thompson went anyway on 22 December. He had only just arrived in Halifax when, on Christmas Eve, he was recalled to Ottawa by Macdonald, 'Chamberlain leaves Ottawa Thursday morning [28 December] important you should confer with him before leaving G.G. [governor general] desires this much please answer.'

So poor Thompson was off to Ottawa again on Boxing Day. It was by no means clear when he got there that Chamberlain needed him, but the governor general did.[53]

The governor general had a New Year's reception on 2 January 1888, but Thompson found it shabby. After that he went round Ottawa with Foster and paid twenty-two visits. He hated calling. It was bad enough in Halifax, but when one had called on the lieutenant-governor, the admiral, the general, the archbishop and one or two friends one had covered the ground. In Ottawa it was far worse. The next day Thompson's office was crowded with people; when it was known that a minister was going away for any length of time, scores of gentry remembered that there were things that needed pushing alone; they flocked to Thompson's office to remind him, mostly, in Thompson's opinion, of mere nothings.

That evening he shared a light family supper with the Lansdownes, so light that Thompson found his good appetite a mixed blessing; he spent the rest of the evening closeted in Lord Lansdowne's study.[54] In this long negotiation Lansdowne was increasingly aware of the difficult nature of British–Canadian relations. Britain had no other problem like Canada. Lord Salisbury, the British prime minister, was succinct: 'The position of England towards Canada is so unexampled – so anomalous – so eccentric – that any larger measure ... may open for us wholly unexpected embarrassments.'[55]

By the time they returned to Washington, American conditions had shifted again. Bayard was caught between the treaty demands of the British and Canadians on the one hand, and the ferocity of the American Senate on the other. He could not afford what might be thought of from an American perspective as a weak treaty. The Americans had hitherto said that the Canadian inshore fisheries did not matter to them; now, in January 1888, they said that they would like the inshore fisheries too. This sudden departure produced a stormy reaction from the Canadians and the British. Chamberlain was 'wildly indignant with the whole lot of them and has come to the conclusion that they are a lot of dishonest tricksters.'[56] He was thinking of breaking up the whole conference and returning to England. The Americans were asking for the surrender of Canada's commercial rights *and* the inshore fisheries in return for almost nothing. They did not even concede that Canada had any commercial rights, as such. Thompson concluded, 'These Yankee politicians are the lowest race of thieves in existence.'[57]

The Canadians also were uneasy with Chamberlain. He had introduced, *ab initio*, the question of the Alaskan boundary. The saving grace was that, as Thompson told Macdonald, 'even a Plenipotentiary cannot alienate territory without special instructions and ... he has written home on the subject.' Cracks in the British–Canadian delegation were beginning to appear. Chamberlain found the Canadian position difficult, especially their resolute refusal to grant right of transshipment without a strong quid pro quo. Chamberlain believed that this right, which had been given to Americans in the Treaty of Washington, was permanent. Thompson said it was not, that it had been abrogated when the fishery articles had been abrogated. Thompson had made this point before in briefs to the conference. Chamberlain undertook to refute Thompson with citations from Henry Bergne, of all people. Bergne's ideas on the subject of transshipment in Thompson's opinion were silly.[58] A cable went to England asking for the opinion of the law officers of the crown. Thompson's brief on this subject was already in England; the attorney general of England read it and pronounced Thompson's position entirely correct. Chamberlain had wanted to get an opinion that would shut Thompson up, but, said Thompson, 'he got shut up himself.' That night Tupper explained to the dinner table how *he* and Chamberlain had differed as to the right of transshipment and the English law officers had sustained *Tupper*! Thompson was cheerful and sarcastic writing to Annie the next day, 'We should be humble in the presence of such gifts![59]

The question still remained, however. Should Canada give the point up? Thompson did not want to; Foster, who was now in Washington, agreed with Thompson that the right of transshipment was all-important. Thompson was not content with even the idea of reference to a tribunal of this question; if the firm Canadian line were broken, it would leave Canada with nothing and might allow the Americans to set up claims for damages for the seizures Canada had made. Chamberlain believed that the American claims for damages might have to be submitted to outside arbitration; unless that were done, how could Canadians get redress for American seizures of Canadian vessels in the Bering Sea in 1886 and 1887? Chamberlain was wrong again, Thompson contended. There was no comparison between the two issues. The Canadians were right in their seizures of American vessels, and the Americans were dead wrong in their seizures of Canadian ones in the Bering Sea. (Indeed, Bayard was privately very uneasy over the legality of the Bering Sea seizures.)[60] To allow American claims to the Atlantic fisheries, or even to submit them to the adjudication of the German government – Chamberlain favoured this – would open up all the questions that had arisen around the 1818 Convention for the last seventy years. If Canada was clearly in the right, as the law officers of the crown said, there was no reason at all why Canada should consent to a reference. 'One of the advantages of having a good title,' Thompson wrote to Macdonald with some urgency, 'is that one can avoid litigation ...' But even Tupper was wavering under Chamberlain's pressure; Thompson wired Macdonald to wire Tupper whether Canada should or should not yield the point. Cabinet proved to be as opposed to giving it up as Thompson and Foster were.[61]

Washington's social life continued unabated. Thompson's letters were full of ironic comments about it. Lady Tupper went the rounds every day, eternally calling. Wives of Washington judges received one day, wives of cabinet ministers another, and so on the livelong week. 'They feel,' Thompson grumbled, 'simply insulted if you do not call and Tupper is quite indignant because I do not go ... Rushing in and out of strange houses may be grand fun, but I will leave it for lunatics and Yankees.'[62] Thompson liked the Washington countryside, half-green like early autumn in Canada, but the climate struck him as treacherous. He thought Ottawa at 22 below or Halifax's blinding winter snowstorms were preferable to 'this sneaking bleak weather.'[63]

It was the eternal receptions that he hated the most. Bayard had a reception on 23 January so crowded that it was simply impudent to consider it entertainment. It took half an hour just to get from the hall to the living-room. You shook hands with your elbows wedged in at your sides. The women might or might not have had anything on; so great was the press of people, Thompson could only see the bare shoulders, leaving dresses to be imagined. 'The clack was dreadful.' *That* was Washington society! The tomfoolery ended, happily for Thompson, the next day – the Portuguese minister died. It was idiotic that receptions stopped on that account, but stop they did. Thompson had bought a five dollar ticket to some charity ball but, he said cheerfully, 'my grief for the Portuguese Minister was such that I could not go.' He went to see *Romeo and Juliet* with the Tuppers and noted for Annie's benefit that all the Washington ladies had their dresses made without sleeves, just a strap over the shoulders. 'I have a lot of directions for you about dressing – some of them will surprise you,' he warned.[64]

By early February, Macdonald was uncomfortable with key ministers so long away. Things were tense in Washington partly because of anxiety to bring matters to a conclusion. Thompson thought all three British plenipotentiaries were not careful enough. None were lawyers, all wanted a treaty, and all wanted to go home. Thompson knew how much litigation turned upon wording, upon one comma! Macdonald and Thompson were lawyers, Foster, Tupper, and Chamberlain were not, nor was anyone on the British side, except Thompson, Wallace Graham, and C.C. Chipman. Lawyers tended to look at the world outside lawyerdom as a world, as Trollope once put it, 'of pretty, laughing, ignorant children; and lawyers were the parents, guardians, pastors, masters, by whom the children should be protected from the evils incident to their childishness.'[65] Thompson worried about his colleagues inside that room at the State Department, trying to come to terms with 'weak, shuffling and disingenuous negotiators.' The work done by his own side was anything but satisfactory to himself as a professional lawyer. They listened to what he said and simply replied that on this or that clause, they had done the best they could. But there was some very necessary cleaning up to be done, especially in the language of some of the clauses where it was so inexact that two or three different interpretations could exist.

Chamberlain had been against Canada from the beginning on Canadian liability for American claims for damages. Thompson was convinced that Chamberlain had misunderstood Lord Salisbury; it would have been incredible if Salisbury had been willing to give Canada away, to allow her rights to be savaged by a foreign tribunal. Thompson prepared a remonstrance for Tupper to read to Chamberlain on this point, drawing, once more, 'a very plain distinction between the character of the claims against us, which are for the acts of responsible officers in our own country ... and the character of the Behring Sea claims which relate to injuries [?] done to our citizens on the high seas where they could not have expected to be made amenable to the laws of the U. States.' Chamberlain put Thompson's paper to the conference on 6 February, even though it was a remonstrance against his own views. That was one of the likable things about Chamberlain: he was frank and he was fearless. As Thompson's argument was supported with about twenty quotations from American secretaries of state – the strongest being from Bayard himself – the Americans were naturally at a disadvantage. The claim for damages Bayard finally withdrew.

A further point to be watched was in preparation of the protocols for publication. The record as it stood looked good for the Canadian case. The Americans, Thompson feared, would try to pare it down, and he added, 'our English friends are so complaisant and want to be so agreeable that I fear they will acquiesce.' Thompson warned Tupper to be on his guard. He added to Macdonald, 'I hope to leave Washington soon – and forever.'[66]

The treaty was signed on the evening of 15 February 1888. Back in

Ottawa at last, Thompson had word from W.L. Putnam in Portland that he for one was satisfied with the treaty. Even if never ratified, as in the United States now seemed likely, 'the principles acted on by the Plenipotentiaries in framing it will direct the relations of the two countries in the future.'[67] It came to the Canadian Parliament in April. Tupper made a long speech in its favour; the Liberals made speeches against it, and Thompson took occasion to label most Liberal arguments as mere party polemics. The only advantage of Liberal criticism of the treaty was that it might help it pass in the American Senate. The Liberals did not press their criticism and the treaty passed the House of Commons without a division. Newspaper support was general; the more die-hard Liberal papers protested against the treaty, but moderate ones, such as the Saint John *Telegraph*, believed the treaty would be supported by moderate Canadian public opinion.[68]

For the 1888 treaty was fair and sensible. The Americans gave up the claim to the Canadian inshore fisheries, and conceded Canadian bays. The Canadians gave the Americans full commercial privileges and got free admission of Canadian fish into the United States. As Chamberlain observed in a private letter to Lord Salisbury, it gave Canada all her essential rights whilst avoiding having to construe these in a hostile spirit.[69]

In the United States, however, the treaty got a vicious partisan battle. There had been war between presidents and the Senate since the end of the Civil War in 1865. In 1888 it was, if anything, worse, since Cleveland was the first Democratic president since 1856. As for the treaty, one is reminded of J.W. Davis's remark, 'A treaty entering the Senate is like a bull going into the arena; no one can tell just how or when the final blow will fall – but one thing is certain, it will never leave the arena alive.'[70] Senator G.F. Hoar of Massachusetts, one of the leading Republican opponents of the treaty, bitterly condemned the exclusion of American fishermen from important mackerel bays, especially Baie des Chaleurs, Egmont Bay in PEI, and St Ann's Bay in Cape Breton.

In August 1888 the Senate rejected the treaty by a vote of thirty to twenty-seven. Canada then fell back upon the modus vivendi that had been sensibly inscribed as a protocol to the treaty, and which had already been in force for the 1888 season: a licence fee of $1.50 per ton for the vessel, with American vessels having full commercial privileges in Canadian ports. If the United States should remove the duty on Canadian fish, the licence would be free. There would be no forfeitures except for fishing within Canadian territorial waters.

Dr J.B. Angell of Michigan, the third American plenipotentiary with Bayard and Putnam, wrote Thompson afterward, asking for a copy of his House of Commons speech; could he also recommend a book or two on Canadian history? (Thompson had to confess that there wasn't one.) Thompson was bitter over the the treatment the Americans had given the treaty, after those months of work. Canadians were hoping that things between Canada and the United States would be settled quietly,

but we feel that we can hardly open negotiations on our side after the summary way in which the Senate and President Cleveland dealt with the subject last year, the former in having rejected the Treaty and the latter for having insisted that as punishment for the action of the United States Senate, Canada should be done all possible harm with as little harm to the American interests as possible. Of course after the Retaliation message we could not look on President Cleveland as anything but an infamous imposter and demagogue, but I have often regretted the ill luck of Mr. Bayard, whose good intentions certainly deserved a better fate ...[71]

Thompson's had a fate rather more curious. On 27 August 1888 a cable came from Lord Salisbury in London, 'The Queen has been pleased to confer on you a Knight Commandership of St. Michael and St. George in recognition of your services at the Conference at Washington.' It quite took his breath away. The source was Joseph Chamberlain. Early in April 1888, Chamberlain wrote to Tupper telling him that Lord Salisbury had recommended a baronetcy for Tupper and a KCMG for Thompson. It was to be kept secret until after the treaty was disposed of in the American Senate.[72]

The news surprised Thompson; he had assumed that the rejection of the treaty by the Senate would prevent any conferring of honours. Should he accept? Macdonald knew about it through the new governor general, Lord Stanley, and was not very comfortable, though he said nothing to Thompson. It was proper for Chamberlain to urge Tupper's recognition; Tupper had been appointed directly by the imperial government, but it was another matter for him to recommend Thompson, who had been appointed by the Canadian government as Tupper's legal adviser. Not only that, but Thompson was, after Foster (born in 1847), the youngest member of cabinet. Knighthoods created jealousy; no one knew it better than Macdonald. Only four members of cabinet were knighted – Macdonald, Tupper, Langevin, and Caron. That left the other senior members, J.H. Pope, Bowell, Chapleau, Carling, Abbott, and Frank

Smith all unknighted. When Thompson wired Macdonald whether he should accept, Macdonald had thought it through. 'Accept by all means,' he wired back.[73] Thompson did. It says much about the frankness of their relations that when Macdonald returned to Ottawa he told Thompson of his earlier uneasiness with the knighthood, and how he had 'remonstrated against it' with Lord Lansdowne.

The day the news came out, Thompson had to speak at a political picnic in Haldimand with Sir Hector Langevin and Adolphe Chapleau, among others. Chapleau cancelled at the last minute, perhaps at vexation over Thompson's new title. As to that, it took some getting used to. At the picnic Thompson found it strange to be addressed as 'Sir John,' especially by children. Senator Gowan wrote from Barrie that he was not at all surprised at the news; he happened to know how much Thompson's work had been appreciated in London. Thompson's knighthood was accepted in Canada as an honour well bestowed and well deserved. The *Halifax Herald, parti pris* of course, put it simply, 'Sir John Thompson! Well, no worthier man ever bore the title.'[74] John Allison Bell in Halifax was more sceptical. Tupper a baronet! 'Now we shall have Sir Charleses until the stock is run out.' As for Thompson, Bell, like many old men, found it difficult to judge the achievements of men whom he had known in their childhood. 'And John D. Thompson is knighted. Surely nothing need surprise after that. What would his good old father think, or what does he think of all this if watching from the loopholes of the other world he takes any interest in mundane affairs[?]'[75] Young Frankie was saucy. She said to her mother, 'If you had a friend who was used to calling you Mrs. Thompson, and she had to call you Lady Thompson, wouldn't it make her throat tickle?'[76]

14

Overseer of Provincial Law:
Thompson and Disallowance

In 1888 the Thompsons finally moved to Ottawa. The fifty-year-old house at Willow Park was given up; Annie wanted to rent it but Thompson thought it needed too many repairs. The floors had cracks in them so big that when the wind blew the draught was strong enough, Thompson said, to lift the roof off. The house was open 'as a basket.' Even if it were repaired, it would, if let, still have to be refurbished when the Thompsons wanted it again. 'I should feel like a vagabond if I had not the right to go there. We will sell it when we can but will keep it till then.' Thompson never did sell it.[1] So Willow Park was left untenanted, and Mrs Dennis's house at the northwest corner of Metcalfe and Cooper streets became their new home. They would rent three other Ottawa houses, all in that same area, where Lisgar, Cooper or Somerset streets crossed Metcalfe.[2] The family came in March 1888: Annie, Frankie, Annie's sister Fan, her cousin Minnie Pugh, plus Bob the dog who, the moment he saw Thompson on the station platform in Montreal, decided Thompson needed a good licking.

Their arrival marked the first real go at Ottawa entertaining. This was a formidable responsibility for cabinet ministers. Sir Adolphe and Lady Caron claimed to entertain four hundred people during the session of Parliament, at luncheon and dinner parties, and in one year the number reached seven hundred and fifty! Caron gave Thompson hints about buying wine; most of their colleagues bought claret by the barrel, a hogshead of fifty gallons, from which one could draw about twenty dozen bottles. Earnscliffe, Macdonald's house, was the centre of parliamentary entertaining. Every Saturday afternoon during the session Lady Macdonald had tea at five in the big old-fashioned drawing-room that looked out through pines and birches to the river. Occasionally Macdonald himself would drop in to chat in the jocund way he had. He held forth to more purpose at their Saturday night dinner parties. Not many Liberals came to either teas or dinners at the Macdonalds; Liberal entertainment Saturday evenings was at the Grand Union Hotel (at the corner of Elgin and Queen, now torn down), where Mme Laurier and Mrs Alexander Mackenzie presided.[3]

During the session Thompson and Annie gave dinner parties every Monday and Tuesday nights for MPs and their wives, about twenty each time. On Wednesday Annie received visitors, so for the first three days of the week she was busy. She had help; she brought a cook from Halifax, Annie Cullen, who was paid twenty-five dollars a month and board. Frankie, going on seven years old, clever and energetic, went about Ottawa visiting with Annie (presumably in the second half of the week), and praised all the babies she found. She would also go into the gallery of the House of Commons with her mother and throw kisses at her father down below.[4]

The session of 1888 was distinguished by only two major issues and a House of Commons in unusually good temper. In early February, with Parliament opening on the 23rd of the month, Macdonald still did not know what he was going to put in the speech from the throne, and he was still ruminating about it on 21 February. He missed his key colleagues, since Tupper, Thompson, and Foster were still in Washington. In October Thompson had been asked to get legislation ready,[5] but Washington pre-empted nearly six months of his time. The treaty was obviously one question for Parliament. *Faute de mieux* the Liberals offered their own suggestion a couple of weeks after Parliament opened: commercial union with the United States.

This movement had been started in the summer of 1887 by Laurier, who was looking for a policy and risking the consequences. He did not know much about trade or tariffs, but he liked a clear-cut policy, and did not much care what it was, as long as it was intelligible, likely to appeal to voters, and offer the party a workable common goal. By the time commercial union got to Parliament in 1888 it had changed its name (and perhaps its meaning) and become unrestricted reciprocity. The Liberals served it up as their offering to the thin bill of fare offered by the Conservatives.[6] Neither Macdonald nor Thompson said a word in the long debate on this subject, from 14 March till 6 April, when the Liberal motion was defeated by 67 votes to 124. The Fisheries Treaty was then presented and passed, and Parliament was left with supply, and some odds and ends.

One of these was the government's bill to control fraudulent use of trademarks. The bill rendered null and void any contract where goods were labelled with a false trademark. David Mills objected that this interfered with provincial civil rights, namely the right of contract. Thompson's reply to Mills is instructive. When the Dominion was dealing with questions over which it had constitutional power, such as trade and commerce, it had the right, insofar as it was essential to legislate fully, to take possession of any subject relegated to the local legislature, civil rights included. All kinds of federal legislation impinged upon, sometimes infringed, civil rights.

We are given power to legislate with respect to these subjects, and the giving of that power implies the power to legislate so fully that it may be necessary for us to take up other subjects which are not given to us at all. Everytime we legislate with respect to rivers, harbours or the public domain, with respect to the erection of public buildings, lighthouses and so on, we take power to expropriate private property, and invade in that way, and necessarily, in the fulfilment of our functions, the domain of civil rights in its very citadel, the rights with respect to real estate in the Provinces.[7]

The government found life that session of 1888 easy. The worst blow came from their own ranks. Thomas White, the minister of the interior, who had joined the cabinet in 1885 with Thompson, was taken ill in mid-April. He had worked hard and won golden opinions in the West. But a cold became pneumonia; his secretary wrote to Joseph Pope on 20 April, 'It may be some days before Mr. White is able to look at any letters.' It was worse than that. White died the following evening. He was only fifty-seven. Thompson, who liked him, was shocked; Macdonald, who loved him, was devastated. When the House of Commons met on Monday, it was struck silent. Poor Macdonald could not even move the adjournment of the House.[8] There was blank silence about White's successor. Macdonald asked Thompson to be acting minister of the interior, and Thompson, ungrudging, added it to his other burdens until a new man could be found.

As this happened another lay dying whose fate affected Thompson more directly. Justice W.A. Henry of the Supreme Court of Canada died on 4 May. Thompson began to think that the Supreme Court of Canada was a good place to be. But, according to the Ottawa *Free Press*, the Conservative party was unhappy about Thompson going to the Supreme Court.[9] Thompson's departure from cabinet would seriously weaken it.

Liberals, especially those in Antigonish, crowed that Thompson would at last get the easy berth he had always 'hankered after.' Thompson was well aware of party pressures. His friends told him the party should not be so exacting. He had taken office in September 1885 when the fortunes of the party were singularly unpromising, and a year before a general election; he had fully earned the right to retire.[10] As for Antigonish, his friends there told him it was an ungrateful and faithless constituency:

... Antigonish is not worthy of you. If the wealth of Golconda was scattered amongst them, and all the favors which the Gov't could bestow were given them it would not avail. They would cry for more. They cannot be kept bought, deception is too much in their nature, unless it is one of themselves cradled in broom and browsed upon thistles, there is no safety nor are they to be depended upon. ... I never include our dear Bishop Cameron. He even expressed himself that he was sorry that it is his native county.[11]

There was talk about converting the vacant puisne judgeship into the chief justiceship, by persuading Chief Justice Sir William Ritchie to retire. Thompson could then be chief justice of the Supreme Court of Canada. That was easier said than done. Ritchie was no friend of the government; just the intimation that they would like him to retire would be enough to persuade him to hang on. Altogether, the party needed Thompson; he had become not only Macdonald's legal adviser but his right-hand man. Thompson's administration of the Department of Justice won him approval on both sides of politics. That June, on the way from Montreal to Antigonish, Bishop Cameron travelled with A.G. Jones, the leading Nova Scotian Liberal in the House of Commons. To the bishop's surprise, Jones turned to him and said, 'Mr. Thompson is the best Minister of Justice we ever have had.' The bishop smiled, wondering if Jones were being sarcastic. Jones saw the smile, but reiterated: 'There's no doubt about it. No one *ever* kept the office of Minister of Justice so well as Mr. Thompson.' But, said Cameron in his letter to Thompson, 'your elevation to the Bench would have the blessed effect of getting me clean out of politics.'[12]

Thompson hesitated. He certainly had never liked politics, or the uncertainty and turmoil. Thompson's craving for the bench was known and made it more difficult to retreat. John Stairs in Halifax felt he should definitely not step into the first good office that came along.[13] In the end, notwithstanding Bishop Cameron, Macdonald and senior members of the party persuaded Thompson to stay on. This decision was made toward the end of July 1888.

Thompson was now asked by Macdonald who the successor to Justice Henry should be. Replacing a Nova Scotian on the Supreme Court bench suggested the appointment of another Nova Scotian, and there were two possibilities, Thompson said. One was Wallace Graham, the ablest lawyer in the Maritimes, but without any experience of the bench. This experience, Thompson believed, was a *sine qua non* for the Supreme Court of Canada. The other possibility was the chief justice of Nova Scotia, James MacDonald, 'vastly better than Henry ever was – but that is saying nothing.' MacDonald never had what every good judge must have, patience and care for detail. As for New Brunswick, it had no one at the bar equal to Graham; on the bench, G.E. King of the New Brunswick Supreme Court was better than MacDonald of Nova Scotia, but not that much better; A.L. Palmer of the same court was impossible; he would ruin the reputation of any minister of justice who had the hardihood to recommend him. To sum up, added Thompson, if the government wish to find a good reason for departing from the practice of appointing a new Supreme Court of Canada judge from the province whence came the old one, now is the time. In that case, look to Ontario. There were many judges in Ontario who were not as good as Graham, MacDonald, or King; but there were also some first-class ones. The problem will be whether any of the best would accept.[14] In the end the appointment went to C.S. Patterson, judge of the Ontario Court of Appeal. Justice Palmer in Saint John did not like it. He assumed his appointment had been blocked by some ancient enmity of Sir William Ritchie.[15]

Thompson was so busy – it was August, at the time of Cleveland's message to Congress – that he could not even go to Rimouski to see his boys off to Stonyhurst. He was sad at this because they did not relish going. They had both done well in their year there, but they hated leaving home. It was hard for parents too. Thompson tried to console Annie; his letter reads almost as if he were talking to himself. The children 'are leaving us little by little every day.' He wrote elegiacally;

The little boy [John] we sent on the steamer in August 1885 never came back and the 'poor Joe' who was on the car with us for a month last summer we shall never see again. They will never be in little cots again in our room as they were in Victoria last summer. So we must make the most of the pleasure of having them and of being as we are. The steamer will bring back to us ... two fellows who will have enough resemblance to our two little boys to keep up the traditions and the little girls do not grow up out of our sight.[16]

But two of the little girls did. Babe (Aloysia) and Helena in September 1888 were sent to the Sacred Heart Convent at Sault aux Récollets, on Rivière des Prairies, ten miles north of Montreal. It was a calculated move. Thompson believed it was churlish not to be able to speak French, and at Sault the girls would hear only French. It was not altogether unknown at the time. The sisters at the Sacred Heart were from France; the accent English-Canadian young ladies would acquire in French was generally approved of, even in French Canada. Thompson urged French upon the boys in England as well. It will, he said, 'be very important in Canada.'[17] Thompson hated to be separated from four of his five children. The only justification was that politics had so unsettled his home that it was the only way for them to get a good education. But if they found life too hard, he told the boys at Stonyhurst, he and their mother would not ask them to go again. 'But all these trials,' he told Joe, 'have to be endured to enable people to make their way in the world. We all have to separate – eventually we separate for good, and you have to be able to make your way alone.' It was perhaps what he had learnt from Bishop Cameron; Cameron used to quote from St Cyprian (c. 200–58), 'Poenae sunt pennae.'[18] Afflictions were wings by which man learnt to rise above the ills of the world.

These were the philosophical notes that Thompson could introduce to his children growing up. Now in the autumn of 1888 the tangible proof of their family life, their furniture, including the family piano, came up to Ottawa from Willow Park. Their new Ottawa house, unfurnished, was on the east side of Metcalfe, near Cooper Street, on a large corner lot. It was centrally heated with hot water – a great change from Halifax – and was sunny and bright with light from the south and west. The south windows were full of plants and the house was full of clocks. It had two of its own and Annie brought two of hers. The hours passed noisily in the Thompson household! Young Frankie had her canary and she was also given a St Bernard puppy – this in addition to Bob – that would eventually be huge. She had a slate and a primer and was so bright that she would learn to read in no time. She was also full of fun; 'mischief brimming over' was Annie's description.[19] She saw all the visitors to the house and became fond of Sir Adolphe Caron. One day in December 1888, when she was briefly ill in bed, she heard Sir Adolphe talking to her father in the hall downstairs. She immediately sent down for him. Up he came to flirt with her. The next day she received a huge bouquet of flowers from her new lover; she said that since she was so fond of him, she thought she would marry him! Frankie was remarkably good-tempered, never fussed, and was a great comfort to Thompson and Annie in the absence of two brothers and two sisters.[20]

Thompson liked to keep his family life private. At the time of Thompson's knighthood in August 1888 G.E. Desbarats of the *Dominion Illustrated News* asked him to have a new photograph taken by Topley of Ottawa at their expense in order to have a full-page engraving made. Thompson agreed with reluctance. In 1889, asked for interviews about himself and his family, he replied that he would prefer that there be no mention of his family, and Annie through him specifically refused to be interviewed for an article on the wives of cabinet ministers.[21] Lady Macdonald's teas at Earnscliffe might be in *The Week*, but not Annie's.

Close as Macdonald and Thompson were, they had differences; sometimes it was a little bad temper over minor matters; but they differed politically as well. Macdonald was apt to take a harder line with the provinces than Thompson. Macdonald seems sometimes to have thought that Thompson was too much a federalist, as opposed to Macdonald's being a centralist. Thompson may have imbided something of Joseph Howe's Liberalism: that was the way he had started, as he admitted to Parliament in 1887.[22] Thompson saw the Canadian political system as a federation, working within a reasonable construction of existing law. He was not prepared to put down the provinces, right or wrong, as Macdonald was. Macdonald's grounds had been frequently personal or political, less often legal. In Thompson's mind such questions were matters of law. He would put down provinces too, if they tried end runs around what he believed was a Dominion prerogative. But federal issues were complex, and in Thompson's mind the balance did not always tip in the Dominion's direction.

Macdonald had been under constant pressure from the CPR to control an obstreperous Manitoba, illustrated by the celebrated battle of Fort Whyte in October 1888.[23] Fort Whyte was a CPR engine ditched at the crossing of a branch of the Red River Valley Railway. It was a quarrel between a Dominion chartered railway and a Manitoba government one. It ended at the Supreme Court of Manitoba, where argument was heard in November 1888. Macdonald wanted the Dominion government to appear at the hearing, since Dominion railway legislation was being implicitly challenged. Thompson believed otherwise. Dominion legislation was not being attacked, not yet at least. 'It seems to me,' Thompson wrote Macdonald, 'that in this case we should carefully abstain from any appearance at the argument ... We are not suitors in this case but our Railway Committee [of Cabinet] is really a quasi-judicial tribunal and ought to keep the *appearance* of impartiality as well as the reality.'[24]

The broader question suggested by this incident was what had first embroiled Manitoba with the Dominion government – disallowance. Macdonald had used disallowance with a frequency disconcerting to the provinces, as in June 1868 he said he would.[25] So had Mackenzie. In practice disallowance was more allowing than disallowing. It meant an annual review of every province's legislation, act by act, clause by clause, conducted by the Department of Justice, and in Thompson's case, with substantial input from the minister. It was Thompson who commissioned the fifteen-hundred-page review of the whole disallowance correspondence with every province and the North-West Territories, from confederation to 1895.[26] From this vast correspondence, it is clear that some ministers of justice left the framing and argument of this intricate subject to their deputy ministers, simply adding concurrence. Some ministers undoubtedly made sure their own views were substantially embedded in those reports. All went through cabinet and became cabinet documents. The most searching and determined ministers of justice were Macdonald, Edward Blake, and Thompson.

Before Thompson's arrival in September 1885, the Canadian government under Macdonald and Mackenzie had disallowed some forty-three provincial statutes since confederation. That says nothing of many others in which changes, some of them substantial, were urged. In Thompson's nine years as minister he recommended disallowance for twenty-one provincial statutes. That was no significant change. What was significant was the argument, often at some length, with ample legal authorities. Still more important was the fact that after Macdonald's death in June 1891, Thompson never used disallowance again. Review, comment, suggestion, expostulation, private correspondence, yes: disallowance, no.

Thompson could not change cabinet policy overnight. When he came there was war with Manitoba, war with Ontario, skirmishes with Quebec, over the use of disallowance. Of Thompson's twenty-one disallowance recommendations, thirteen affected statutes from Manitoba, nine of which had to do with railway legislation; British Columbia had four acts disallowed. What is noticeable across Thompson's years as minister of justice, especially after 1891, is the steep diminution in the volume and acerbity of the correspondence. In part this was due to his avoiding arbitrary or vindictive interference with provincial legislation, in part also to smoothing out relations with Ontario.[27] This was a result of Thompson's informal talks with Oliver Mowat, the great champion of provincial causes. These began in 1886, and their general effect was to render unnecessary, as far as Ontario was concerned, the formal apparatus of disallowance. The tone of this correspondence was one of mutual respect, even friendliness.[28]

Thompson's politeness was velvet glove over an iron hand. Accommodating, generous where the law was ambiguous or uncertain, he was markedly less so when he believed he was right. 'Please remember however,' he told Macdonald in 1889, 'that I am not sensitive about my work being corrected.'[29] Thompson was willing to be proved wrong. He even corrected his own mistakes, and in front of cabinet, one, for example, reducing a prison sentence he had himself imposed in 1884 when a judge.[30]

Although nearly half of Thompson's disallowances concerned Manitoba railway legislation, this drew to an end with the CPR's surrender of the monopoly clause in its charter in 1888. Thompson's disallowances for other provinces arose mainly from conflicts with existing Dominion legislation, such as a Nova Scotian act of 1886 that affected shipping, a British Columbia act of 1887 affecting criminal procedure, a Manitoba act of 1890 on quarantine for animals.[31]

Where a provincial legislature attempted to by-pass the courts, Thompson's response was firm. The British Columbia Land Act of 1885 was disallowed in 1886 because it attempted to confirm land sales already in question before the courts. Provincial governments could also put up controversial questions in innocent-looking parcels. Titles and preambles were not always good indications of what the acts contained. The J.-J. Ross government of Quebec passed a statute in 1886 to authorize certain corporations to lend or invest money in Quebec. The preamble was all sweet reason. But two sections of the act required any bank chartered either in Great Britain, or in Canada outside Quebec, to take out a licence before it could do business in Quebec. Thompson insisted that Quebec should delete the application of the act to banks chartered in Canada; if so, the act would be allowed to stand. By the time the Quebec government replied to this, the time for disallowance had passed.[32] This delay may have been deliberate; by that time the Privy Council had allowed, in *Bank of Toronto* v. *Lambe*, the right of the provinces to tax by direct tax or licence a Dominion-chartered bank.

The history of allowance and disallowance is strewn with references to a question still more difficult: the right of a province to punish for infractions of its own acts. A province could not make such infractions crimes or misdemeanours. Macdonald, dealing in 1873 with the new province of British Columbia, was specific: 'a local legislature can enforce laws, by fine, penalty or imprisonment, without declaring any breach of those laws to be a crime.'[33] Usually it was not necessary to disallow; a dispatch that a certain section of a statute trenched upon Dominion power was usually sufficient to procure repeal of the offending section. But the distinction between what was a crime or misdemeanour on the one hand, and a breach of provincial statutes on the other, was clearly difficult. Division of law into federal and provincial aspects was not so much division of facts as division of the rules governing their management. For example, chapter 5 of the Ontario Acts of 1888 was an attempt by Mowat to establish the pardoning power of the lieutenant-governor in respect of penalties imposed by the province for violation of provincial acts. Thompson's letter of 4 February 1889 was clear, polite, but firm. 'I desire to call your attention in an informal way, if you will permit me to do so, to chapter 5 ... about the constitutionality of which I have been unable to satisfy myself.' Thompson admitted the question was difficult. 'The division of powers, in relation to crimes and offences, between the provincial and federal parliaments is, I think you will admit, very difficult to trace in very many places.'[34] Mowat did not accept Thompson's basic position that the pardoning power of the governor general was indivisible, but it was agreed between them that a reference case should be started. Thompson's argument lost in the Ontario Court of Appeal, and when it came to the Supreme Court in the autumn of 1893, it was faced with an 1892 decision of the Privy Council in a collateral question, *Maritime Bank of Canada* v. *Receiver General of New Brunswick*. In the end the pardoning power of the crown took the form of the aspect doctrine.[35]

Usually provincial legislation conflicted with Dominion power over criminal law only by inadvertence. But sometimes the conflict was deliberate. Macdonald was exercised on this subject writing to Thompson in July 1888 with the Quebec Magistrates Act in mind:

It seems to me that the time has arrived when we must resist the continual encroachment of the Provincial Legislatures. Under the clause of the B.N.A. Act which enables them to punish by fine or imprisonment breaches of statutes, the Local Legislatures are steadily usurping the control of misdemeanors and this must be stopped. I shall be glad to hear from you on this subject and when we meet we must lay down some system with respect to checking such encroachments.

Thompson, then in Halifax, thought the Quebec Magistrates Act should be disallowed from what he had gleaned of it. Macdonald agreed.

By all means disallow this act respecting Stipendiary Magistrates. It is an impudent usurpation – but we are not blameless. The shilly-shally course of our colleagues from Quebec as to the app't of Judges is the cause of this legislation, and it really holds us up to ridicule –[36]

Neither Thompson nor Macdonald disputed the right of Quebec, or any other province, to reorganize its judicial system; what they did object to was Quebec appointing judges, and regulating their salaries and tenure by calling them district magistrates. Thompson hastened to disallow the act to avoid confusion and private injury in the administration of justice in Quebec. Premier Mercier did not like it. He swore he would not issue the proclamation of disallowance in the *Royal Gazette* (without which it could not take effect). A.R. Angers, the lieutenant-governor of Quebec, succeeded in persuading him.[37] Thompson did not like to impute motives; rather, he worked the other way round, giving Mercier the credit of wanting to set up new legal tribunals to meet Quebec's needs. Nevertheless, one principal misconception in Quebec's reply to the September disallowance was that

the allowance of provincial legislation is, in all cases, an admission of the validity of such legislation ... No such inference can properly be drawn ... many provincial statutes which have been left to their operation contained provisions beyond the powers of the provincial legislatures ...

The most remarkable instance in which provincial legislation has over-run the limits of provincial competence, has been legislation in reference to the administration of justice ...

Quebec could not assume, because a series of enactments had gone on across several years without disallowance, that the District Magistrates Act was *intra vires*. If that were allowed, the Executive Council of Quebec would be able to obtain control of every court in the province by using the word 'magistrate' to conceal their intentions.[38]

Mercier, undeterred, introduced early in January 1889 the same bill a second time, with only minor changes. Thompson urged Macdonald to have Angers reserve the bill. Reservation was a technique that interested Thompson. After a bill was duly passed in the legislature, a lieutenant-governor had three choices: he could give assent, he could refuse assent, or he could reserve it for the signification of the governor general's pleasure. This last had advantages; the bill so reserved did not become law; it was dead, having no validity whatever. The governor general had a year to decide whether he would accept it. If he did not, nothing happened.[39]

Thompson seems to have felt reservation was a useful instrument of policy, especially for a bill already disallowed once. The practice of reservation had fallen into desuetude, however, and Angers was reluctant to provoke trouble with Mercier; Angers pointed to the disallowance, not the reservation, of Ontario's Rivers and Streams acts. Thompson dissented; reservation was a tool which, had it been used in Ontario, would have lost Ontario none of its rights, 'while a good deal of ill feeling would have been spared.'[40] In the end Angers got his way and it was left to Ottawa to disallow, a second time, what *La Minerve* irreverently called Mercier's 'basse-cour.'[41]

This was more awkward because Mercier brought his act into effect the day of royal assent, 21 March 1889, appointed his judges, and within a short time some one thousand judgments had been rendered by the new courts. Disallowance was published 6 July 1889. Thompson was less tender; he argued forcibly that Mercier was taking away the jurisdiction of federal courts and transferring it to judges appointed by the provincial executive. A problem arose; the Quebec *Royal Gazette* had to publish the notice of disallowance. Mercier squirmed, hated publishing it a second time, sought Alphonse Desjardins's opinion about what he should do. 'Talk to Thompson,' Desjardins said, from the editorial desk of *Le Nouveau Monde*. Mercier preferred Desjardins's intervention, adding that he was anxious to bring about a peaceful solution.[42]

Thompson was tougher than the year before. To Desjardins privately Thompson had hard words to say about Mercier:

I can hardly help thinking that he willfully defied the power of the Federal executive in setting up the District Magistrates Court, and with him must rest the responsibility for the inconvenience to suitors and litigants which must result from the promulgation of an Act which he was distinctly warned would be disallowed. Perhaps some means may be devised for rendering valid the judgements which have been delivered by the District Magistrates Courts.[43]

There were other problems. What of enforcement of Dominion and provincial law by ordinary magistrates? For example, the Post Office complained that Ontario justices of the peace were not giving due weight and assistance in trials of post office robberties. C.H. Tupper, as minister of fisheries, found New Brunswick JPS less than enthusiastic about enforcing federal fishery law. The opinion of the deputy minister of justice, Robert Sedgewick, was that JPS must enforce all law equally, whether federal or provincial.[44]

Did the provinces have the right to appoint magistrates at all? They had exercised that right since confederation, but in Thompson's view because they exercised it was no reason to suppose that they had it. There had been judicial decisions both ways, but no court of appeal had yet finally pronounced upon it. Thompson's view was:

No legislative body can, by legislation, increase or diminish the authority conferred upon it by the constitution; nor can any expression of opinion or course of legislative action by either, afford any conclusive or even satisfactory guide to its interpretation.[45]

Given the difficulties of getting questions of jurisdiction right, Thompson showed an increasing willingness to let the courts, not the cabinet, decide. The boundary between Dominion and provincial power was usually unclear and when there was no serious inconvenience to the public in letting legislation stand, it was better so. Let the courts decide law. That was what they were for.

Into this context came, in the summer of 1888, the Jesuits' Estates Act. It stirred up a hornet's nest in Ontario, made trouble in Manitoba; but it affected the Maritimes, the North-West Territories, and British Columbia hardly at all. The act itself was simple. It was solely an adjudication, at the urging of the province of Quebec; the pope was the guarantor that the settlement was satisfactory to the several elements in the church that were quarrelling over the estates, especially the Jesuits and the Archbishop of Quebec. It was a Quebec provincial problem, interesting, awkward, with a deliciously complicated past. Mercier was trying to cut through it.[46] That he did, and with very little opposition from Quebec Protestants. He had the good sense to offer them a solatium of $60,000, a direct quid pro quo on a per capita basis, for the $400,000 going to various elements in the Catholic church. The vast majority in Quebec, Catholic and Protestant, were glad to see the end of it. It was also wholly within the constitutional competence of the province.

The torch that lit the fire was the *Toronto Daily Mail*. The *Mail* was looking for something to do that summer of 1888; the commercial union agitation had gone stale, and something new was needed. It was found in the Jesuits; the *Mail* editorials were written by a renegade Catholic, Edward Farrer, educated at Stonyhurst, who hated the church and all its works, especially the Jesuit order. Gone were the memories of Jesuit heroism at Fort Ste Marie and the other Jesuit missions in darkest Ontario in the seventeenth century. Perhaps in ordinary times the editorials might have passed as an exercise in Protestant spleen; but the late 1880s were not ordinary.[47] Embedded in religious prejudices were powerful racial ones. Unruly foreigners lacked Anglo-Saxon self-discipline. If Anglo-Saxons did not defend themselves against the swarming thousands of Irish, Italians, Poles, and other races, if 'the master race of this continent' were subordinated to foreigners, the result would be disaster. The problem was put biologically: 'the strong, fine strain' of the Anglo-Saxon must be saved from degeneration.[48] Joseph Chamberlain hymned the glory of the Anglo-Saxon at the Toronto Board of Trade dinner on 30 December 1887, in one of the most dramatic speeches of his life.[49]

Anglo-Saxon prejudices were defended, perhaps made into offensive weapons, by what Ruskin called 'masked words,' words that everyone used and few analysed: liberty, freedom, race, separation of church and state, equal rights.[50] The cartoons in *Grip* reveal far more than words, masked or unmasked, about Ontario attitudes, a sometimes poisonous mixture of primitive and Protestant. Bengough's Roman Catholic clergy were fat, greedy, and powerful, with no vestige of Christ or charity, wearing their clerical garb with the swagger that in the secular world was affected by aristocrats and millionaires. In *Grip* mere politicians bowed low before bishops and priests:

MACDONALD. 'Black yer boots, sir? Let *me* do it, sir, and I'll get right down on my knees to the job!'
LAURIER. 'Don't have *him*; let *me* shine 'em for you, mister. I'll lick 'em with my tongue, 'thout extra charge!'[51]

The core of this anti-Catholic feeling in Ontario was fear, the belief that the Catholic church was an engine of conspiracy, operating tirelessly, silently, ruthlessly, to extinguish Protestantism. The Jesuit order was its most effective instrument. The reality of such prejudices could hardly be denied, and there was some substance to them, however grossly distorted. The French-Canadian clergy had powers in Quebec that few clergy, in other Catholic or Protestant countries of mixed religion, had. The church's tithes were protected by law, and the church's ministers had a good deal of freedom. One must not, however, overstate this clerical freedom, for it was changing. In the 1877 Charlevoix election case that ultimately went to the Supreme Court of Canada, judgment was given by Justice H.-E. Taschereau that 'sermons and threats by certain Parish priests of the constituency of Charlevoix amounted in this case to undue influence.'[52] That case was not alone. By the beginning of the 1880s it was clear that in certain circumstances priests were actionable for slander, and words uttered from Catholic pulpits were not wholly privileged.[53]

Unreal Ontario prejudices and fears created their own reaction in French Canada. French Canadians were afraid of having everything they lived for – language, religion, society – swept away in an Anglo-Saxon flood, a bitter sea of hate and immigration. French Canadians were divided, said Mercier on St Jean Baptiste Day, 1889, and they could not afford to be. Let us, he said, swear to end French-Canadian party struggles and unite to face the common threat of the Anglo-Saxon world.[54]

That threat was something English Canadians were hardly aware of. Most of them did not want to force French Canadians to change; if asked, they would have turned the question the other way: they did not wish French Canadians forced into survival. They meant by that the institutional propping up of ancient ways, 'anachronistic' traditions, against a 'natural' evolution into English. In two or three generations, by this argument, the French-Canadian problem would be largely at an end. The Jesuits' Estates Act, said John Charlton in June 1889, was bad for several reasons, but basically because it retarded this natural assimilation to English.[55]

With none of this could Thompson have agreed. For one thing he was Nova Scotian and Nova Scotians saw the French-Canadian relation to Canada in a cooler perspective. That was the result of distance, the thousand miles of forest, from those hard Ontario prejudices; it was also the result of Nova Scotia's fairly easy accommodation to Irish and Scotch Catholicism. Thompson seemed content with the idea of a dual nationality, finding it the only sensible way to conduct political relations within Canada. He and Annie worked on French; their children were brought up to appreciate it. To Ontarians a dual nationality seemed a temporary anomaly, a political accommodation hopefully evanescent, that for the moment could not be avoided. D'Alton McCarthy called this accommodation a 'bastard nationality,' an anachronism, another version of the feuds of the old world so out of place in the new.[56] When was this cossetting of French Canadians to end, McCarthy asked, as end it must? Is the French Canadian in 1889 less French than he was in 1760 or 1867? Not at all. 'To my certain knowledge,' McCarthy told an Ottawa audience in December 1889, 'the Frenchman is more French ... more French is spoken in the House of Commons than when I first came here in 1876, and it is still growing ... if we are to go on in this way, what is to be the end of it?'[57]

McCarthy was civilized and intelligent. He was not an Orangeman; educated in Dublin and in Barrie, Ontario, he had risen above the back-country Protestantism of Simcoe County. He was for that reason the more dangerous. He reasoned from political theory, English in character but continental in origin, that nationalism in the modern world of the 1890s was based upon language and the sense of community that only a common language and a common literature give.[58]

McCarthy was a power in the Conservative party. He had been a major force in founding the Toronto *Empire* in 1887 when the Toronto *Mail* had broken with the party. He had fought numerous legal battles for the Dominion at the Privy Council, indeed in the summer of 1888, at the time of the passing of the Jesuit Estates' Act, he was fighting the Dominion's case in *St. Catherines Milling and Lumber Company* v. *the Queen* and had been given carte blanche by Thompson to use the best London help he could get. McCarthy's relations with Thompson had been correct. Thompson was even invited to stay with McCarthy in Toronto in December 1888.[59] But by this time McCarthy was estranged from Macdonald and began to make mischief. His guns were first brought to bear in the debate for disallowance of the Jesuits' Estates Act in March 1889: his intellectual integrity, his fierce conviction that he was right, his passionate English-Canadian nationalism. For he was a nationalist, like Thompson. His premises were different. He was also unwise enough to boast that he had many pledges of support from Conservative MPs of Ontario. Macdonald made a personal appeal to every MP McCarthy mentioned, and to caucus.[60]

The debate had a large following. The galleries were crowded when Colonel W.E. O'Brien introduced the motion for disallowance on the House going into supply, on Tuesday, 26 March 1889. It was not a great debate except toward the end. Not a single member of cabinet spoke the first day. When McCarthy rose on the afternoon of the second, he was clearly annoyed by the government's coolness. He allowed his annoyance growing room, and his speech became provocative, even bitter. He was astonished, he said, at the supine indifference of the Quebec Protestants; how could they be so blind? The Jesuits' Estates Act violated Henry VIII's Act of Supremacy of 1534, hence Queen Victoria's supremacy, and it trailed her name 'in the dust' behind the pope's.[61]

The main weight of the government's defence fell upon the minister of justice. Thompson had spent some time getting ready, reading Canadian, British, and ecclesiastical history. He spent the weekend prior to the debate shut up with his books.

His reply to McCarthy was unsparing. Naturally O'Brien and McCarthy, being Conservatives, would have to be handled with some respect – in the party they were and would remain for some years. Thompson referred to McCarthy's speech as 'admirable' but that was as far as he could go. It was too much to expect him to be dispassionate; he could not abide McCarthy's pernicious distortions. The Jesuits' Estates Act involved no part of the Queen's domains. The distribution of that property affected neither her spiritual nor temporal powers. The whole arrangement was a business transaction relating to land mainly in Quebec City. The land the Quebec government had long had control of; what it wanted, and what it got in the act, was clear and undisputed title. How else was the title to be cleared except by an act of the Quebec legislature? The act arranged to get the two parties in the dispute, the Catholic church represented by the archbishop of Quebec, and the Jesuits, to agree to an arbitrator. The pope was the only arbitrator that the two parties would recognize. What was so terrible about that? When the facts about the property were brought into the daylight surely 'it is impossible to misunderstand, and almost impossible for ingenuity to misrepresent, the preamble of this Act.' Besides, how could the government of Canada disallow an act simply because of a preamble? Not a single act of any British North American colony had ever been so disallowed by Great Britain.[62]

The problem was, said Thompson, that the language and the correspondence used to justify the act to the Cardinal Archbishop was too easy to misrepresent. It was easy to invent sinister meanings that were simply fabrications. The honourable member for Simcoe, with all his great qualities, should not have found emotional satisfaction in doing it. Canada simply could not wallow in emotions that way. Canada could not work if McCarthy dragged out ancient skeletons like the three-hundred-year old Act of Supremacy of Henry VIII which, under the spirit of a more tolerant age, had been left happily in the grave. If all the legislation still on the statute books were enforced, said Thompson, one-third of Ottawa would be in prison: for heresy, non-conformity, failure to take the sacraments, or being a Unitarian. Besides, Canada had created ecclesiastical corporations, and Catholic ones at that. The bishops of Upper Canada were incorporated in 1850, those of New Brunswick in 1862. College Ste

Marie in Montreal, a Jesuit College, was incorporated by the Province of Canada in 1852, with only seven votes against it. Canada lived by its tolerance. Thompson concluded:

I think that whenever we touch these delicate and difficult questions which are in any way connected with the sentiments of religion or of race or of education, there are two principles which it is absolutely necessary to maintain for the sake of the living together of the different members of this Confederation, for the sake of the prospects of making a nation ... that as regards theological questions the State must have nothing to do with them, and that as regards the control which the federal power can exercise over Provincial Legislatures in matters touching the freedom of its people, the appropriations of its people or the sentiments of its people, no section of this country, whether it be the great Province of Quebec or the humblest and smallest Province of this country, can be governed on the fashion of 300 years ago.[63]

It was a great speech. Parliament rose to it. Edward Blake at once walked across the floor of the Commons and shook Thompson's hand. To the Ottawa correspondent of the *Toronto Daily Mail*, it was the greatest speech he had heard in the Commons since confederation. Martin Griffin, not exactly an impartial witness, was enthusiastic. It was better than Thompson's 1886 speech on Riel. 'You have dished McCarthy – that is the general opinion. It serves him right. He is inexcusable.'[64] Sir John Macdonald agreed. It was a magnificent effort, he told McLelan in Nova Scotia. 'In fact, it was too good.' There was too much ginger in it. Thompson, upset at McCarthy's tone, the sheer impolicy of McCarthy's argument in a country 40 per cent Roman Catholic, hit McCarthy hard. McCarthy, thin-skinned at the best of times, was 'greatly incensed,' Macdonald said. Macdonald wanted to keep the party together despite such unfortunate departures, but found the prospect of controlling McCarthy diminished by Thompson's speech. The secret of the government's success was also not only Thompson's speech, but the fact that French Canadians in the party were told firmly to leave the issue alone. It was a debate where a single word could have done a great deal of harm.[65] David Mills from the opposition said what Thompson could not have said; 'We have in this motion [of Colonel O'Brien's] in the name of toleration, a demand for intoleration.' It was a motion laden with mischief. As Laurier said, it was always in some sacred name or other that 'the most savage passions of mankind have been excited.'[66]

The House of Commons disliked, and it resisted, the hard, intransigeant tone of the supporters of disallowance. O'Brien's motion went down to defeat, 13 to 188. Even old Alexander Mackenzie came to record his vote against disallowance, at 1:45 a.m. on 29 March. Credit for this victory the ultramontane daily, *L'Etendard*, of Montreal, gave squarely to Thompson.

Et d'abord, il parait évident qu'à Sir John Thompson, surtout, revient le mérite principal de la victoire; c'est à sa science de notre droit public et à sa connaissance du droit des gens, que l'on doit avant tout que la désaveu ait été rejeté.

Il ne s'agissait pas seulement de se montrer éloquent et habile ... il avait fallu auparavant justifier le refus du désaveu auprès de collègues dont les bonnes dispositions de quelques-uns étaient pour le moins douteuses.[67]

But that was not the end of the agitation. The end of the session early in May brought only a little relief. Thompson wrote John and Joe at Stonyhurst,

... there is at last a little quiet and a chance to get to bed before 3 in the morning although there is no rest but more work each day than can be done ... the preachers have been making a great uproar through the country ever since [March 29th] and holding public meetings to condemn us. They have not found anything bad enough to say about me ... In a few months, it will be forgotten. Sir John Macdonald called the 13 'the Devil's Dozen,' but the parsons call them 'the Lord's Dozen!'[68]

It is not certain if Thompson saw the following anti-McCarthy doggerel, but he would have been amused by it:

> But Dalton McCarthy condemned all the rules
> And Jesuit maxims as taught in their schools;
> They teach black is white, and right wrong, I ween
> 'You must be our chief,' said the Devil's Thirteen.[69]

The Protestants had the devil in them all right and were off at full gallop. Senator Gowan wrote that the agitation in Ontario could not be quelled by the House of Commons vote. If anything, it was increasing. His own view was that Canada had been too long ruled by the influence of the French-Canadian vote. There was certainly a spirit of unrest in Ontario that would have to culminate, sooner or later, in action. While the government might be safe for a session or two yet, new combinations were bound to arise that would threaten it.

Thompson agreed that the 1889 session had ended with no sign of improvement, and with many signs of ebullient bigotry on both sides. English Canadians were not much less English than fifty years ago, and the French Canadians were more French. Thompson was frank and a bit rueful, writing to Gowan; he saw the ancient quarrel that had once racked the old Province of Canada breaking out again, thirty years later. But he did not accept the idea of an Ontario victory:

... I agree with you that there is a strong repugnance of races at the bottom of all the exasperation evinced ... To my mind it is clear that this repugnance must cease or the country will go to pieces. It cannot be made to cease by the mastery of either race – because the other is too strong to be mastered quietly and because the Lower Provinces will walk out rather than take either side of the quarrel. We knew when we came into the Union that Ontario and Quebec were a couple that – under other names – had had many a domestic broil, but we never doubted that you had all made up your minds to live together and forget the past ... Time may work a cure – but if not the country will be in a bad way and British North America will have become Yankee while trying in vain to settle whether it should be English or French.[70]

In June 1889 Hugh Graham, the founder and editor of the *Montreal Star*, probably the most popular daily in Canada, presented a petition to the governor general asking for disallowance; failing that, for reference cases on both the incorporation of the Jesuits in 1887, and the Jesuits' Estates Act. He enclosed a cheque of $5,000 to expedite the process. Thompson drew up a long and decisive answer. Reference cases should not be used for such purposes as Graham had in mind, Thompson said. For the guidance of cabinet the system was valuable no doubt, but as a means of solving legal problems that did not directly concern the government of Canada, they were not only inappropriate but dangerous. To use reference cases as a means of compelling adjudication of private rights and interests would pervert reference 'into an arbitrary and inquisitorial power, anticipating, and interfering with the ordinary course of justice.' The Supreme Court of Canada was never intended to function that way, nor was it desirable that it should.

Graham's request for disallowance of the Jesuits' Estates Act was impossible. 'No doubt existed then, or exists now ... that the enactment is within the power of the legislature of Quebec.' The decision of cabinet had already been made, and the lieutenant-governor of Quebec notified, that the act would be allowed. Of the hundreds of acts passed every year by the Canadian provinces, there were many of doubtful validity. This course was nearly always followed 'unless some interference with the powers of the federal government would result, or where serious confusion or public injury was likely to ensue ...' Besides, the House of Commons had declared by an overwhelming majority that the Jesuits' Estates Act should be left to its operation.[71]

The Jesuits' Estates quarrel was not simply between Quebec and Ontario. It was an internal quarrel in Quebec as well, within the church. The act might not have been accepted so readily in Quebec had not the Protestants in Ontario made so much fuss and put Roman Catholics on the defensive.[72] There were bitter words from Israel Tarte's *Le Canadien* about the Jesuit 'foreigners' getting good Quebec money when Quebec's honest 'clergé national' deserved it more. *La Patrie* was furious with the Jesuits and their supporters:

Nous tenons les Jésuites responsables de la plupart des querelles religeuses ou semi-religieuses qui sont venus périodiquement bouleverser nos diocèses d'abord et le Canada tout entier ... Vous êtes du parti des Jesuits et nous, nous sommes du côté du clergé national, avec des évêques que vous voulez régenter et que nous voulons suivre.[73]

Thus the furore out of Ontario obscured issues in Quebec. It was as if the Ontario papers never read a line published in French.

The Equal Rights Association was formed in Toronto in June 1889. Thompson caught up with them, literally, early in August. He was travelling by boat from Montreal to Quebec (to meet his sons at Rimouski) and found himself with a great crowd of Equal Rights delegates from Ontario. They were carrying with them enormous petitions for disallowance (one of them 160 yards long) that they were going to lay before Lord Stanley at Quebec. E.D. Armour, the founding editor of the *Canadian Law Times*, was with them and invited Thompson to join the group. 'Too late,' Thompson replied. 'The whole thing is too late,' Armour said. One more cheerful delegate told Thompson, 'It's a wild goose chase, but a d———d fine trip.'[74]

The governor general's reply to this delegation was quite different from what Thompson expected. He anticipated something merely formal, instead of which Lord Stanley ignored the huge petitions and lectured delegates on the need for tolerance. Some disgruntled Equal Righters seemed to think that Thompson wrote the speech for him. In fact Lord Stanley wrote it himself while in Gaspé at Stanley House. He stopped at Rivière du Loup station on his way to Quebec to see Macdonald and check the draft with him. Macdonald hinted that he and the cabinet would be quite willing to take over the responsibility for what the governor general would say – as they were paid to do it! – but Stanley stuck to his draft, and except for one or two verbal changes, his address to the Equal Rights Association was his own.[75]

Thompson himself thought it was manly of the governor general to come out as he had, and it would give Protestants some good reasons for cooling off. Of course, he added, writing Macdonald from Halifax, there was not 'the slightest interest in the question here.'[76]

Equal rights began slowly to die as the autumn of 1889 came. There was a large meeting in Toronto on 10 October, but there was little enthusiasm and even McCarthy was unable to prevail against an audience ready to go home. He lasted only twenty minutes.[77] In effect the Equal Rights agitation was being changed into other forms. Like the broom in the 'Sorcerer's Apprentice,' two forms appeared where there had been but one before: the anti-Catholic agitation in the Ontario provincial election, where the campaign started in December 1889; and the more serious and distracting questions of language and education in Manitoba and territories to the west. The Protestant key to containing the Catholics was public education. It was the principal organ, one might say, of democratic digestion. In the Protestant conscience of Ontario and Manitoba, there was the strong, unequivocal perception that, as an American put it, 'the Bible and Common Schools were the two stones of the mill that would grind the Catholicity out of Catholics.'[78]

15

Dragon's Teeth

That summer of 1889 Macdonald had gone down to Rivière du Loup at the end of June, settling himself into the comfortable house at St Patrice where he had gone so many summers before. He teased Thompson from amid the cool winds of the lower St Lawrence. 'The weather is delightful here,' he wrote cheerfully, 'and it is all the more enjoyable when we know that there is only a sheet of brown paper between you Ottawaites & Hell.'[1] That was consolation when one was sweltering in Ottawa! Macdonald had one big grumble that he confided to Thompson: he could never get his colleagues to express opinions on the overall policies of the government. Diligent they no doubt were in their several departments, but whenever Macdonald proposed anything comprehensive all he got was general acquiescence. That would not do. He needed frankness.

Macdonald was getting used to confiding in Thompson. There were a number of changes that strengthened Thompson's role. White died in 1888, J.H. Pope in 1889; old Sir Charles Tupper went back to being high commissioner in London in 1888, his place as finance minister being taken by George Foster. Foster's post of Marine and Fisheries went now to the thirty-four-year-old son of Sir Charles, Charles Hibbert Tupper, perhaps with some encouragement from Thompson. Sir Charles was pleased and told his son how proud he was that Charles Hibbert's elevation to cabinet came upon his own merits.[2] A.W. McLelan went to Government House, Halifax, as lieutenant-governor in July 1888, leaving Thompson and young Tupper as the two cabinet ministers from Nova Scotia. At that point Macdonald urged Thompson to assume the management of Nova Scotian affairs. 'Charly,' said Macdonald, 'has got the bumptiousness of his father, and should be kept in his place from the start.'[3]

It was good advice. Young Tupper entered office with the utmost energy and seriousness. An enthusiastic conservationist, within a year he succeeded in alienating two powerful interests over his determination to enforce fishery regulations: the lumbermen, because Tupper claimed their sawdust was polluting salmon and trout rivers and ruining fishing; and the east coast fishermen, because Tupper insisted that all lobsters be over the regulation minimum of nine and a half inches. Macdonald tended to be more upset with Tupper than with lumbermen or fishermen. By and by, he said, when the timber is exhausted, the sawdust menace will end, and Canadian generations in the future can restock the rivers with salmon fry. He did not like young Tupper's violent enthusiasms. Perhaps he saw his own youth as a departmental reformer. Thompson, to whom Macdonald confided most of this, said he knew nothing about the sawdust question but would get posted on it when he got to Nova Scotia in August 1889. But Tupper would be all right, Thompson assured Macdonald. He had the failing of the young in taking things hard and earnestly, but, added Thompson, 'he is of good metal and is the best of his name.' An ironic comment on old Sir Charles in London.[4]

What shall we do, Macdonald asked Thompson, about the Yankees? It was clear that Lord Salisbury would stay put until motion came from the United States, and Americans would not move. 'Now,' said Macdonald, 'shall we? and if Yes, in what mode or direction? The Modus Vivendi will expire next February and our troubles will recommence. We must not like so many foolish virgins set [sic] with our lamps untrimmed. "I pause for reply".'[5]

Thompson suggested both issues and answers. 'Yes,' he said, 'we should move.' Those big questions required action. It was all very well for countries the size of the United States or the United Kingdom to allow the lapse of a decade in what to them were small external difficulties. They did not have to be in a hurry. But with Canada, such issues were large and important:

... the country is young and eager and poor, though thriving. We have a good chance to open the negotiations which we so much desire, without sacrifice of dignity, or danger of a snubbing, because, in one particular – the Behring Sea question, we are demanding redress, and in another, the Atlantic Fishery question, we are near the end of an amicable arrangement which can only be extended by our own action.

The seizure of Canadian sealing vessels in the open ocean – the Bering Sea – by the United States, and the American threat to continue doing it, required action. That would mean the imperial government's moving for an arbitration commission. On that issue Thompson was confident. Americans could continue to save their prestige by refusing to pay for the vessels they seized, but sooner or later Canada would win. 'I believe,' he told Macdonald, 'we cannot lose, but if we should we will be no worse off than we are now – practically shut out of Behring Sea, because our vessels only go there by stealth, and armed then, a semi-piratical condition.'

As for the modus vivendi: if it continue as a fixed arrangement, it was clearly no longer a modus vivendi. Does it do to allow the Americans to assume that the cost of a licence was in effect the value of the concessions? Was a $3,000 or $4,000 harvest of licence fees all that was left? Every dollar Canada spent on railways increased the value of American access to the right of transshipment of their fish, increased the value of those five precious words in the 1818 Convention, 'for no other purpose whatever.'

It might also be a good time to discuss reciprocity, perhaps quietly by only discussing lumber. The functioning of the bonding privilege on both sides was uncertain; Thompson thought there might no longer be a legal basis for it, and Cleveland had made noises about it before leaving office in March 1889. Canadians used the privilege for access to New York, Boston, and Portland; Americans used it across southern Ontario. It was not an issue in the United States; therefore, said Thompson, 'Let us try to get a renewal of it.'[6]

These were the immediate questions with the Americans. There was also a serious problem with Great Britain: copyright. Macdonald thought some ministers should go to England in September 1889, to discuss both American and British issues with the Colonial Office and Foreign Office. Macdonald had Thompson in mind, and himself; the trouble with that happy idea, said Macdonald, was 'if you or I went, ... Council might make some mistake on the Jesuit question and commit us on other matters. There would be great pressure from Quebec and the Maritimes in our absence. All this entre nous. What think you?'[7]

Thompson thought Macdonald should go to England and that he, Thompson, would stay home. He had no wish to go; he believed he could do nothing there worth his going, and Council could agree not to take up anything doubtful in Macdonald's absence. Thompson ended that letter with the hope that Sir Hector Langevin would soon be in Ottawa, so he could get away; the Ottawa heat had put him out of condition, and he was longing for a swim.[8]

A few days later, early in August, Thompson and Annie left Ottawa on the train, headed for Grand Narrows in Cape Breton. The three girls, Babe, Helena, and Frankie, were already there with Annie's sister Fan, staying at a comfortable old hotel at Christmas Island, run by Thompson's friend and colleague from Nova Scotian cabinet days, H.F. McDougall, now MP for Cape Breton. McDougall had been born there, in a charming part of the Bras d'Or Lakes, where Great Bras d'Or narrows at its western end toward Barra Strait. The new railway from Antigonish and the Strait of Canso went past on its way to Sydney.

At Rimouski, as Thompson and Annie awaited the steamer from England, they had news that Frankie was seriously ill with whooping cough. Annie knew what that meant. She went to Cape Breton at once to bring Frankie to Halifax, and Thompson went out to the ship alone to greet the boys returning from Stonyhurst. Four children stayed at Christmas Island; Thompson and Annie ended in Halifax looking after Frankie, taking turns day and night. In the 1880s and after, whooping cough was one of the most dangerous diseases of childhood; the yearly death rate was greater from it than from scarlet fever and typhoid combined. Anyone who has nursed a child through it knows how frightening it is, especially at night. But after a fortnight Frankie was over the worst, and Thompson and Annie accepted an invitation from Charles Gregory, a railway contractor from the old days of the Eastern Extension, to stay for a few days in Antigonish, close to the warm sea bathing of Northumberland Strait.[9]

Altogether, it was not much of a holiday. S.E. Dawson of Montreal was going to wish him a good summer holiday when he remembered Thompson never really took any.[10] Thompson and Annie returned to Ottawa with Frankie early in September, when the boys left for Stonyhurst and the girls for Sault aux Récollets. Thompson and Annie got the Ottawa house (181 Lisgar Street) in order, carpets down and pictures up. With his inveterate concern for manners and good form Thompson wrote the girls at Sault that they must write to Wallace Graham, to congratulate him. He had been appointed to the Supreme Court of Nova Scotia, that September.

Graham was sorry and pleased at the appointment. He would be making financial sacrifices, now that his firm was doing so well from the mighty work of Robert Borden. But he hoped to make the Supreme Court of Nova Scotia more civilized, less distasteful to the Nova Scotian bar and public than it had been for years past. Thompson's, and Graham's, old firm would now be Borden, Ritchie, Parker, with J.A. Chisholm of Antigonish added. Chisholm was one of Thompson's young protegés and supporters in Antigonish; he would now come to Halifax to work. Chisholm had also met Annie's sister Fan, and would soon see a great deal more of her.

Thompson and C.H. Tupper planned a short political trip in western Nova Scotia. There would be a provincial election in 1890, and the Nova Scotia Conservatives had strong hopes of upsetting W.S. Fielding. The central Conservative committee in Nova Scotia was run out of the *Herald* office in Halifax, its directing genius one of the editors, Charles Hazlitt Cahan. Cahan came from Yarmouth County and had taken law at Dalhousie; instead of practising, he had gone to the *Herald* in 1886. Cahan was clever, vigorous, opinionated and young, and was neither the first nor the last bright young man sitting in Halifax who tended to see the province from Citadel Hill outwards.

The Halifax that Thompson had come to in August 1889 and returned to that October was the old town he had known, but slowly, almost insensibly, he was growing away from it. It looked much the same; Archibald MacMechan, the new professor of English at Dalhousie (out of Berlin, Ontario, via Johns Hopkins), was reckless enough to fall in love with it. MacMechan was charmed by the old place, the way the sea closed the vista of the short hilly streets, became the horizon above the dun brown or grey houses, with their dormer windows and chimney pots.[11] But for Thompson, Halifax seemed less like home. His Halifax political friends he sometimes found querulous or exacting. Willow Park was gradually being stripped of furniture for the home in Ottawa; when Annie came down a year later to get the last of it, she confessed that Willow Park did not look much like their old home and Halifax did not feel like it either.[12] Thompson was already half out of Nova Scotia, halfway to becoming a Canadian in the broader sense of the word; as if to mark this he was invited in 1889 to become a member of the Ontario bar, an offer he accepted.

It was arranged that Thompson and Tupper would speak in Annapolis, Digby, and Yarmouth, but it was to be set going by a big political reception for local Halifax Conservatives at the Halifax Hotel. It was the usual noisy and crowded affair; Thompson was wise enough to arrange to sleep at another hotel. His speeches in the southwest concentrated on the wickedness of the Liberal policy of commercial union. Liberals had begun as free traders, said Thompson; now they were wanting to disrupt confederation. Only Edward Blake had the good sense to accept the idea of the National Policy, but then he had resigned as Liberal leader. By contrast, the Conservative government had achieved three great objectives: protection for Canadian industry; the development of the physical capacity of the country through railways and public works; and the beginning of a vast foreign trade. The last was à propos in the Annapolis valley, where trade in apples to the United Kingdom was getting under way. And Nova Scotian industrial output in the 1880s rose faster than Ontario and Quebec.[13]

The Halifax Chronicle poured scorn on Thompson's speeches. It was party journalism. In the Liberal Chronicle nothing but corruption came out of a Conservative government: in the Conservative Herald the Grits were cheerfully consigned to picking their teeth with a knife, or bathing, reluctantly, once a month.[14] Thompson indulged in those gibes himself on the hustings every so often. On the other hand, in a party newspaper it was nearly impossible to discuss political questions with a degree of fairness. No sooner did an editorial writer have the temerity to make a concession, however unimportant, to the argument of the other side, than it was 'caught up, torn from its context, made to imply something quite different or of vastly more consequences than its real meaning, and triumphantly heralded before those who, as a rule, read only one side.'[15] And personalities were thrown in as salt and pepper. The Chronicle writer did that with Thompson and, curiously, got a rocket from the owner, Charles Annand.

Annand had laid down specific instructions that Thompson was never to be attacked personally; only his political views were to be contradicted. Annand wrote Thompson and apologized: 'I would not have you feel that my gratitude for past favors was so short lived, and I hope that hereafter, no matter how you and the Chronicle may differ in political issues, no one will be able to point to anything personally offensive to you in the Columns.'[16]

On Thompson's return to Ottawa he was given an honorary LL.D from the University of Ottawa. He did not care much for these honours, nor was he an enthusiast for Bishop Roger Duhamel, but the doctorate might give him some additional political strength in Quebec and Ontario, and it would have been churlish to refuse. Martin Griffin teased him that he could now address D'Alton McCarthy in Latin, using Cicero's famous speech against Cataline in 63 BC, 'Quo usque tandem abutere, Cataline, patientia nostra!'[17]

It was more apt than Griffin could have known. The moment Parliament met, on 16 January 1890, D'Alton McCarthy brought forward a private member's bill for amending the language clauses of the North-West Territories Act.

There was a history to this, turning around Archbishop Alexandre-Antonin Taché, one of the early Oblate missionaries to the North-West. In 1869 Taché had feared confederation, but was brought reluctantly to accept it upon categorical assurances from Sir George Cartier that the rights of French Canadians, Métis, and Roman Catholics in the West would be respected. Cartier embodied these guarantees in the Manitoba Act of 1870. Twenty years later, Taché was no longer the strong, vigorous young prelate of the 1860s; his broad, kindly face masked deep unhappiness with the new and uncomfortable conditions that confederation had brought to him and his flock by 1890.

Taché's archdiocese included part of northwest Ontario, part of Keewatin, all of Manitoba, and most of the Territory of Assiniboia. Regina was within his archdiocese. Taché's troubles of his later years began there.

Until 1887 the Catholics of the North-West Territories had been quite successful in keeping their separate school system, laid down by the Dominion North-West Territories Act of 1875, intact. It was 'a mixture of dualism and uniformity,'[18] not bad for a Roman Catholic minority that represented barely 20 per cent of the North-West population. Of that minority, only one-quarter or less were French-speaking.

The North-West Territories had been given in 1887 the right to have a new Territorial Assembly, and its first meeting was held in October 1888. There were twenty-two elected members and three legal advisers, with executive authority remaining with the lieutenant-governor, who also controlled the parliamentary grant from Ottawa, some 83 per cent of the revenue.

Within the orbit of federal law, the North-West Territories Assembly could flesh out its own school system, but of course the Dominion was bound to protect the main lines of the separate school system as laid down in 1875, as it was required to protect the use of French, laid down in 1877. The first meeting of the North-West Assembly threatened the separate school system. And some newspapers were already urging 'one nation, one language' as an appropriate territorial motto.[19]

In September 1888 Thompson spoke in Montreal on the French language question in the North-West. There was a Dominion by-election in Montreal East where the Conservatives had nominated a working-class candidate, A.-T. Lépine. Caron, Chapleau, and Thompson all went to drum up votes. Thompson apologized for speaking in English but assured his east-end audience that should he have started in French they would soon have insisted upon English! French in the North-West, Thompson said, was part of the North-West Territories Act and would remain there as long as the act itself.[20] In St Boniface the old archbishop was much heartened to read this in *La Minerve*. Thompson privately promised Taché that while in many North-West matters it was vital to defer to North-West opinions, 'in all matters affecting their religious interests Your Grace will find that we will not defer.' But, Thompson went on, the government need to know when you think 'an effort is to be made to resist that which would be injurious and when religious interests are in jeopardy.' Thompson suggested that the North-West Council's school ordinance of 1887 should really have been amended, but on the assurance that the Catholic clergy were satisfied, it was dropped.[21] Taché for his part had told Sir John Macdonald that the 1887 ordinance had not satisfied him; but not receiving a reply from Macdonald, Taché had inferred it was useless to pursue the matter further.[22]

When, in November 1888, the new North-West Assembly talked of banishing religious instruction from the schools and other measures, and, in effect, French-language instruction, Taché was confident that Sir John Thompson would be the church's strong right arm.[23] He warned Thompson that trouble could be expected from the North-West, that Thompson's fair words at Montreal might now have to be translated into action. 'You easily understand,' Taché wrote, 'that the Catholic hierarchy will not remain silent in such an emergency and it is easy to forsee also what commotion would be the unavoidable result of our appeal to the Catholics of all the provinces.' Taché was convinced that the Dominion government, with the strong support of Thompson, would not fail to discover 'how to quench this disastrous conflagration prepared by the inexperience of the new legislators sitting at Regina.'[24]

There was not much Thompson could do. In his report to cabinet on the 1888 legislation he did point out that the North-West school ordinance did not conform to section 14 of the North-West Territories Act. By the latter, a Protestant or a Roman Catholic minority could establish separate schools in any school district: the ordinance gave that right to the minority only after the majority saw fit to organize a public school. Thompson could not recommend disallowance of the 1888 school ordinance: it was merely a re-enactment of what had already been passed in 1887 and had been allowed to go into force mainly by the failure of the Catholics to pay any attention to it.[25] Thompson, who did notice it, thought if the church accepted it, why should he make an issue of it?

The public of the North-West seemed not much preoccupied with the North-West school question, but newspapers were, and both newspapers and D'Alton McCarthy inflamed the issue so that in October 1889, the North-West Assembly decided to ask the Dominion to delete the French-language clause from the North-West Territories Act, as well as deleting the clause permitting separate schools. The former carried seventeen to two, the latter unanimously.[26] The language issue was raised in Parliament in 1890 by D'Alton McCarthy.

It created an intense debate, much sharper than the Jesuits' Estates debate of 1889, indeed one of the great debates in the history of the Canadian Parliament. It was the kind of debate the Commons preferred to avoid – emotional, intense, stripping away the Commons' instinctive shyness about confronting and discussing what Canada was and what it should be. The *Montreal Star* got off the aphorism that the difference between Liberals and Conservatives on this issue was that 'the one is afraid to say what it thinks and the other dare not.' Like many aphorisms, it was a gross distortion: the debate was only too full of sincerity. If anything, the debate proved the adage that hell is paved with sincerity. By the end of a wrenching week most MPs realized that 'using race prejudices for party purposes is like playing with fire.'[27]

McCarthy's bill might not have created such a furore had he not put a preamble to it. It was the preamble that did the business, and it is fair to say it was intended to: 'Whereas it is expedient in the interest of national unity in the Dominion that there should be community of language among the people of Canada ...' To that the Commons rose, like the pack of cards around Alice, and denounced McCarthy. Chapleau asked, Why not expunge 'Dieu et mon droit' from the royal arms? Or, while they were at it, 'Honi soit qui mal y pense?'[28] To all this, and much more, McCarthy remained remarkably controlled; he was subjected to all the abuse the House rules permitted, if not more. He was alone, or almost alone, in doing what he regarded as an unpleasant but necessary duty. He got small thanks for it. One man's duty is another's poison. Surely, said Parliament in effect, McCarthy could not inflict upon Canada his patent machine for squeezing Frenchness out of French Canadians?

In the end Parliament accepted a compromise proposed by Thompson near the end of the debate. Thompson believed that courtesy required that every province allow an MLA to speak in the language that best suited him. Even in Nova Scotia, he said, where there was no official policy, an Acadian could speak French if he chose. 'We can safely leave that subject to the Assembly,' Thompson said with a fair dose of official optimism; the local Assembly was the best place to decide how it would conduct its debates, record its proceedings. But, said Thompson, the language of the courts was a different matter. The responsibility of the Parliament of Canada was to see that the language of the courts of the North-West Territories could be English or French:

It is not mere fancy, but I am repeating what has been said to me, that in some distant sections of that country, if that provision be obliterated, we may have the misfortune of seeing men brought to the bar of justice in our own courts, tried before our own judges, convicted, condemmed and sentenced in a language not one word of which they understand, and unable to offer a plea for justice and mercy.

This, in Thompson's mind, was a more serious matter than the mere language of the Assembly.[29]

It was a crowded House. The galleries glittered under the new electric lights, the seats crowded with spectators. The Speaker's gallery had along one row an indiscriminate mixture of Conservative and Liberal wives – Lady Macdonald, Lady Thompson, Mme Laurier, Mrs Charlton. While the whips were rounding up the members for the vote, MPs sang songs; P.-A. Choquette, Liberal, sang 'Alouette,' Colonel Prior from British Columbia rendered a navy song, while J.J. Curran, the Commons primo in singing, rendered 'Old King Cole,' with Macdonald and George Foster (of all people), joining in the chorus. Macdonald was the first to vote; he and Thompson watched contentedly as the Conservative majority climbed into the nineties. Thompson's amendment carried by 149 to 50.[30] The 50 did not all represent support for McCarthy either; some few French Canadians were opposed even to Thompson's compromise. Liberal J.D. Edgar said he was proud that day to be an MP, 'to have listened to a great debate like this. The questions which are before us ... are those which underlie our national existence, and upon the peaceful settlement of these questions depends our hope for the future of Canada.'[31]

Edgar, Thompson, and Parliament were right. McCarthy's ostensible aim was one thing, his real aim was another. It was one thing to admit that there was no sufficient reason to print official documents in French in the North-West Territories where only 5 per cent still used French; it was quite another to say to Canadians, whose constitutions, Dominion and provincial, sometimes compelled the use of two languages, that such usage ought in the long run to end. French could not be abolished. McCarthy would find, *The Week* suggested, that the logical consequence of what he proposed was not national unity but a fatal obstacle to it, namely, a bitter sense of injustice that could last for generations.[32]

From this same western context arose a still more intractable issue, the Manitoba school question. The Manitoba school system was based upon the dual structure used in Quebec; it catered to 13 per cent of the Manitoba population, in a community where assimilation of German, Icelandic, as well as of French-speaking peoples, was regarded as reasonable and natural. Prescriptive rights of the kind enjoyed by the Manitoba Roman Catholics seemed anachronistic in the face of modern ideas about the unity of language and equality of schools.

Macdonald feared these questions of language and schools. He told

Judge Gowan, 'McCarthy has sown the Dragon's teeth – I fear they may grow up to be armed men. Canada, as just punishment for her ingratitude for her blessings, is about to undergo a time of trouble. The demon of religious animosity which I had hoped had been buried in the grave of George Brown has been revived. God only knows what the results may be.'[33] J.C. Aikens, lieutenant-governor of Manitoba from 1882 to 1888, told Macdonald that the French in Manitoba had brought it on themselves, for their political treachery to the D.H. Harrison Conservative government in January 1888.[34]

Whatever the origins, the agitation was well illustrated in Brandon newspapers, both the Liberal *Brandon Sun* and the Conservative *Brandon Mail*. The latter concluded that in the name of national equality, special privileges would have to go:

It has come to this, all distinctions as to class, creed and nationality have got to be wiped out – the dual languages in the Local Legislature must be discontinued, separate schools must be abolished, tax exemptions on churches, schools, etc. must be suspended and all must be brought to the eternal principle of national equality for the sake of building up the country.[35]

Not all Manitoba papers followed the inflammatory opinions in Brandon – the *Manitoba Free Press* did not – but the Greenway government found, in the autumn of 1889, that it had a tiger by the tail, impossible to let go.

Dr John Schultz, the lieutenant-governor, kept Macdonald informed and was anxious that the Dominion cabinet authorize reservation of the bills, soon in train, for abolishing official use of French and for abolition of Catholic schools. Macdonald seems to have been willing to give Schultz authority to reserve such bills; Thompson, who liked reservation when a provincial bill was clearly both unconstitutional and inconvenient, as with Mercier's District Magistrates Act, 1888 and 1889, was cautious when it came to Manitoba school legislation. Schultz himself was bold enough; he even talked of dismissing Joseph Martin, the *deus ex machina*. Thompson certainly did not like that. He believed that Martin would eventually be the author of his own doom. Martin was attorney general in the Greenway government, 1888 to 1891, a Protestant maverick out of western Ontario, with a style and manner that belied his University of Toronto education. In any case, Thompson believed that reservation was too crude an instrument for a question so constitutionally intricate.[36] Thus Macdonald and Thompson accepted *in toto* a resolution proposed by Blake in April 1890 in the Commons, leaving such questions of constitutional law up to the courts.[37]

Other Manitoba acts that year that clearly controverted existing Dominion legislation could be, and were, disallowed. Two of Manitoba's 1890 acts fell under Thompson's axe in 1891.[38]

Despite hopes for an end to Joseph Martin,[39] it was clear by March 1890 that the school legislation would pass and that it would create serious problems. Premier Greenway felt sure the Education Acts would be disallowed or that the courts would declare them unconstitutional and, according to Schultz, mightily regretted that he had ever been persuaded to bring them in.[40] Still, there they were, and with an increasingly stubborn, not to say boisterous, public opinion supporting them. Father Cherrier of the Catholic Board of School Trustees in Winnipeg reported to Macdonald that Archbishop Taché wanted disallowance; he did not trust the courts. Taché seems to have suspected that, at least in Manitoba, public opinion would exercise a kind of hydraulic pressure under which principles of the law would bend, as Justice Holmes was to put it a decade later in the Northern Securities case.[41] Cherrier told Macdonald and Thompson that if they did not want the awkward question of disallowance pressed by the Roman Catholics,

no time should be lost now to prepare a case to test the validity of the Act, so as to commence action immediately after this new Act comes into force. A contest of that kind will cost a large amount, but upon the other hand, if it comes upon the floor of the House at Ottawa, it may cost the country a larger amount, besides pleasing these radicals and giving them food and agitation for their general elections.

Sir John, I have given you the facts and there is *not one day to lose* ... I can assure you they [the radicals in Manitoba] are not slow, and they will never stop until we stop them by the courts.

You remember what it cost the Government in the St. Catherines [Milling and Lumber] Co. case.[42]

Two days later, on 12 March, Cherrier was more urgent:

There is no hiding the fact that as soon as the new School law comes into force, the greatest confusion and wildest excitement will prevail, all over the province. The minority will appeal to and clamor for your interference immediately, by way of disallowance, they are already anxiously looking towards it. You will see by this new act that the separate schools must hand over, on the 1st of May, all monies and assets to the local Government, and a few months later will begin the collection of taxes, which will be resisted to the bitter end, and result in bloodshed.

Macdonald endorsed this letter over to Sir John Thompson with the comment, 'I have told Cherrier that I adhere to the opinion that recourse must be had to the Courts. I suppose we had better offer to pay expenses.'[43] By late April Father Cherrier announced that he would have a test case ready from the first week of May; that way it might be possible to avoid an acrid discussion in the House of Commons before prorogation in mid-May 1890.[44]

Archbishop Taché had done his best to hold down the excitement but his instinct was to go to Ottawa and make a personal appeal to every Roman Catholic MP. That would have shaken the government. It explains the vigour with which the Dominion acted in getting the school case before the Manitoba courts. Taché did not come to Ottawa; he refrained out of personal regard for Thompson and his colleagues. Instead two emissaries came, A.A. Larivière and J.P. Prendergast, who saw Thompson in mid-April. The reports they brought back from Ottawa deeply chagrined Taché. Perhaps Prendergast was no friend of the Conservative party, as Cherrier alleged; perhaps he misrepresented Macdonald's and Thompson's position; but Taché was disturbed by what he heard; as he put it to Thompson, he was 'sadly disappointed and but poorly regarded.' The Dominion government, represented by Macdonald and Thompson, appeared to lack will; its reliance upon the courts was to Taché a sign of weakness, not strength. He had once nourished the hope that there was will and vigour enough in Ottawa 'to guard the constitution,' but both seemed to him wanting.[45]

Thompson's reply to this deeply felt letter was not very soothing. He had few soft words for his aggrieved client. He did not like juxtapositions between words and thoughts. He did not always reveal what he thought, but he thought out, and believed, what he said. The archbishop's words about guarding the constitution became Thompson's text for reply. Whatever the rights of Catholics in Manitoba, they were not, Thompson believed, rights that had existed by law prior to 1870. If Manitoba's constitution had been the same as that of other provinces, there would be no question whatever that Martin's abolition of separate schools would be valid. The one word that Manitoba Roman Catholics had to protect them was the addition of 'practice' in section 22 of the Manitoba Act.[46] That safeguard was important, said Thompson, but what did it mean?

What the rights were which existed by practice, and how far at that time the practice can be held to have secured the system of separate schools, which was afterwards established, from legislative abolition, as being within the saving provisions of the Manitoba Act, are mixed questions of fact and law which can only be determined satisfactorily by legal tribunals, and cannot fairly be disposed of by mere executive action ...

A decision of the [Dominion] executive based on an *ex parte* statement of facts, as regards the practice existing at the formation of the province would be open to be challenged by any person disagreeing with our decision, as based on controvertible facts ... Such a decision would be regarded, very widely, in Canada as an interference with legislation of a purely domestic character probably within the legislative powers, and as influenced very largely by the fact that the legislation was distasteful to Roman Catholics; and the public would remember that we had just refused, in the case of the Jesuits Estates' Act of Quebec, to interfere with legislation of that purely domestic character because it was within the powers of the Provincial Legislature, although it was distasteful to a great number of Protestants.

To do otherwise, Thompson asserted, would be to raise religious excitement, not calm it. Far from disallowance ending the struggle, it 'would only be a challenge to a fiercer and wider conflict.' A court decision would be accepted by Canadians. What legislatures have power to do were 'peculiarly questions which require to be sifted by process of law.'[47]

Thus began the case of *Barrett* v. *Winnipeg*. The government had breathing room, but it established nevertheless a special cabinet committee on the Manitoba school question.[48]

Parliament did have constructive moments in the 1890 session. For a year or more Thompson had in hand a systematic review of the common law governing bills of exchange – cheques, notes, drafts. He always liked to get his legislation down upon fundamental principles. The Bills of Exchange Act had been introduced in 1889, and copies had been sent to the chartered banks for their opinions; but the act was withdrawn and further suggestions were incorporated. It was a comprehensive statement, and in some cases an improvement on existing common law. There were some conflicts between French Canadian civil law and the English common law, but François Langelier and other French-Canadian lawyers accepted the working principles of Thompson's bill, 'because our business relations are much more extensive' with England and the United States than with continental Europe. Quebec's rules about protesting a dishonoured draft or cheque were still retained; in fact, insofar as 'protest' was concerned, Quebec was left to deal with that as by the Code Civil. But on other issues, Thompson was apt to stick to the principles established by the bill.[49]

It was this same systematic mind behind the 1890 Criminal Law Amendment bill. There were several issues. Section 2 was put in with the agreement of the Knights of Labour to protect factory girls against exploitation by foremen. Dr D. Bergin, MP for Cornwall, was afraid of blackmail. Thompson conceded this point, but argued that protection for a foreman, unjustly accused by a factory girl, lay in the fact that he was allowed by the bill to give evidence on his own behalf. Peter Mitchell, the one-man Independent party in the House, wanted the right given to factory girls extended to all female labour, to shop girls, stenographers, girls who worked in telegraph and telephone offices. Parliament was not quite ready to accept that.[50]

The most serious party issue in 1890 was the Rykert scandal. J.C. Rykert, MP for Lincoln since 1878, had succeeded in getting a very large – four hundred square mile – timber limit in the Cypress Hills, Alberta Territory, for one of his friends, John Adams of Winnipeg. Eventually it was sold to a Michigan lumberman, Louis Sands, for $200,000, this sum being divided between John Adams and Rykert's wife. Probably Nannie Rykert had received about $50,000 before the transaction was broken off. Rumours of the deal got out in 1883, in 1886 and 1887 that Rykert flatly denied.[51]

In 1889 John Adams, Rykert's former associate, died; the Adams family became convinced that the expenses Rykert incurred to get the original licence issued were faked. Rykert's correspondence was still extant and on Saturday, 8 February 1890 the Toronto *Globe* published a whole fat page of it. It made interesting reading. Sir John Macdonald recognized at once that there would have to be investigation.[52] The question was, ought it to be investigated as if the House were a judicial body? There were no precedents for a member accused, as was Rykert by Sir Richard Cartwright, of conduct 'discreditable, corrupt and scandalous,'[53] or for the impassioned way Cartwright had brought it before the House. On 11 March Thompson moved the adjournment of debate until appropriate measures could be considered; this passed on a party vote of 94 to 72. Macdonald was ill, so the Rykert affair and the conduct of it by the government fell upon Thompson.

Rykert himself wanted a committee.[54] A week later, after Martin Griffin hunted the Parliamentary Library for British precedents, Thompson conceded that although Rykert did not appear to be entitled to a committee hearing as of right, perhaps justice might be better served that way than in the full House.[55] Macdonald, who was back in the House again, sensibly let the minister of justice handle the question. Macdonald had been minister of the interior from 1878 to 1883 when Rykert got Adams his timber licence, and the issuing of that licence was one of the many shadows in the Rykert scandal.

The defence that Mackenzie Bowell used in 1887 when he defended the government's system of patronage – 'you consult your friends when anything is to be done –'[56] was not used by Sir John Thompson in 1890. Rykert had not just consulted his friends: he had abused their confidence and suborned a civil servant or two in the bargain. Thompson believed that the letters published in the *Globe* were authentic, that it was 'a most shocking correspondence ... without a parallel in the history of any Parliament.' Nevertheless, the purity of Parliament was best preserved by a scrupulous regard for justice. In his speeches in the Commons, Rykert had not succeeded in convincing Thompson or many others of his innocence. As far as Thompson could see, the charges of Sir Richard Cartweight stood. But charges so grave, one that almost amounted to a sentence of death as an MP, required that Rykert should have every chance to clear himself. So Thompson recommended that the affair go to the Committee on Privileges and Elections. But let no one think, said Thompson, that the government was conniving to save Rykert from his just deserts. Thompson pledged his word and that of his colleagues that 'every influence the Government can bring to bear will be brought in order to have this matter speedily brought to an issue, so that the result may be recorded before the prorogation of the session.' Laurier accepted Thompson's argument and asked his colleagues to accept Thompson's motion. On 17 March the Rykert affair went to committee without division.[57]

The Committee of Privileges and Elections was large, forty-four members, chaired by Désiré Girouard. Rykert seemed very sure of himself.[58] By 1 April reporters were speculating that the committee might exonerate Rykert as well as the Department of the Interior. Désiré Girouard seriously doubted that the House of Commons had any jurisdiction whatever in Rykert's affair. Not a single precedent existed for trying a member whose offence took place under a previous parliament. Once the electorate had pronounced upon the alleged misconduct of an MP – as Lincoln allegedly had in the 1887 general election – then the House of Commons' jurisdiction was at an end. Girouard made his anguish clear to Thompson: 'That is my trouble and the only one I see; but I cannot get over it. Perhaps you can ... If not, no matter how reprehensible the language used by Mr. Rykert may be, and disgusted and indignant we may feel, it seems to me we ought to hesitate before we establish a dangerous precedent.' This was the point that Rykert's defence lawyer, William McDougall, made; no House of Commons had any power whatever to deal with any private acts of an MP. That was the MP's business, not Parliament's.[59]

However, the testimony of William Laidlaw, a Barrie lawyer connected with the firm that had applied for almost the same timber limit that Rykert had secured, damaged Rykert further. Laidlaw privately explained to Thompson that both Rykert and a Department of Interior employee, Ryley, had deliberately deceived McCarthy and Laidlaw who had a prior claim to the limit, that Ryley had failed to discover on three 'searches.' Laidlaw was quite uncompromising: 'if the Conservative Party can decide that it is consistent with its honor and dignity to pass over such an offence, I venture the opinion that the public ... will pass a very different verdict – The opposition are waiting in hope that the Government will not – and of course the stump speakers will say – dare not [act against Rykert].'[60]

A report drafted by Blake was prepared by a subcommittee consisting of Girouard, Blake, Davies, and Thompson. Thompson, anxious to secure unanimity, made a few modifications. The Department of the Interior was not directly charged – the Conservative party might not have been able to stomach that – but by implication it was shown to be incompetent, if not worse.[61] The correspondence showed Rykert intended either to bribe ministers and their relations, or to persuade Adams that he had done so. There was even evidence that Rykert had planned to go on to bigger and better developments in the same line. The subcommittee recognized that Rykert's course had been, as Cartwright alleged, 'discreditable, corrupt and scandalous.' Its report went to the full committee, for Monday, 5 May 1890, certain to be accepted.

On 2 May Rykert rose in the House on motion of privilege. He was resigning. He walked to the Speaker, handed him a letter, and left the House by the door behind the Speaker's chair. There was dead silence. Not a word was said, not a friendly hand extended, not a sign of sympathy. On both sides of the House the silence was the silence of the gallows. 'Rykert is dead,' said a prominent MP to a neighbour.[62] Almost, but not quite. Rykert ran again in Lincoln in a by-election in late May, and won; but he never sat in the House again. The 1891 general election finally laid him low.

As if the session of 1890 were not yet full enough, Canada had developed a formidable agenda of external problems, with Newfoundland, the United States, and Great Britain. Newfoundland's Bait Act was bothersome and awkward to deal with. The aggressive seizures of

Canadian sealers on the high seas by the American navy in 1889, and threatened for 1890, were heightening tensions only recently allayed by the 1888 modus vivendi on the fisheries. The British would have to be persuaded of the rightness of the Canadian case, and this meant, among other endeavours, pushing the British minister in Washington further and faster than he wanted to go.

Charles Hibbert Tupper spent six weeks in Washington on that subject in March and April 1890, technically as Sir Julian Pauncefote's assistant. Blaine refused to accept a Canadian representative unless disguised! Tupper was outspoken and too headstrong; within three weeks Blaine refused to see him further. Nor was Pauncefote much happier with Sir Charles Tupper's aggressive son. But young Tupper was confident; he wrote Thompson that the American case was so bad that Canadians would be able to drive a coach and horses through it. And he was right.[63]

Probably the Bait Act and the Bering Sea seizures could be solved by diplomatic pressures and precedents. The most serious issue for the long run seemed to be a developing domestic quarrel between Britain and Canada, one where both sides were convinced they were right, and where both had powerful lobbies behind them. It was a nasty mother-daughter quarrel, where Britain wanted to exercise a function that her daughter thought had long since lapsed. Thompson was never more dangerous or more ruthless than when he was convinced he was right. Somewhere near the centre of Thompson's character lay a fundamental disinclination to bend to the opinions of others. He was his own man: the person who could change him was a woman, not a man. Women indeed could bend him, and Annie continually had to keep him on his guard against that. Thompson came to his conclusions slowly, patiently, taking the time to master his material as he went; in the end he was extremely difficult to shake. This imperturbable, almost frightening, self-confidence he had established out of necessity. That sensitive nature could not survive being continually buffeted by uncertainties caused by gaps in his own knowledge, failures of his own logic. The ferocity that made him lay siege to work was his protection against failure.

Thompson was a nationalist; he was born in Canada and proud of it. The Parliament at Westminster did not make him feel inferior but confident: Ottawa's was no worse. Canada was his country: after the Bering Sea arbitration in 1893 he wrote Lord Ripon, the colonial secretary, 'I shall be forever grateful to him [Lord Hannen] for the earnest sympathy which he felt and showed for my country – as regards her claim for justice and fair treatment.'[64] Canada's claim for justice and fair treatment: precisely what Thompson was to insist upon in 1890. The case looked to him so clear, Britain so definitely wrong, her ministers so obstinate, that it roused his nationalism, engaged his energy. And he was never to give it up. As long as he lived, it was in the forefront of his discussions in Britain. That issue was copyright.

Copyright does not sound like an important issue; it was not a popular one in the usual meaning of the word; but it was on the issue of copyright, more than perhaps any other, that Thompson and Canada discovered a widening breach with the British government. It was an issue deeply felt in the publishing business, in Parliament, in cabinet, especially so by Sir John Thompson; over it the Canadian government were to fight a series of skirmishes, and occasional pitched battles, from 1889 onward. Indeed Thompson and others, notably John Ross Robertson of the Toronto *Telegram*, ended almost savage at the recalcitrance of the British. By 1894, Robertson told Thompson (and be believed) that he would not trust himself in the presence of F.R. Daldy, the spokesman for the British authors and publishers. Robertson found it increasingly difficult to bear the sneers of the Englishman who said, 'When the day comes that Canada has a right to ride roughshod over the Imperial act, the connecting link between England and Canada will be severed.'[65] Thompson, though more patient and judicious, was as unrelenting as Robertson, and as time went on became more, not less, determined to try matters to their conclusion. S.E. Dawson, head of Dawson Bros., publishers, of Montreal, and Queen's Printer, 1891–1909, put it dramatically: the Canadian Copyright Act of 1889 raised 'a profound political question upon a very insignificant issue. It is nothing more or less than a Declaration of Independence.'[66]

Copyright was a tangled question, impossible to make popular. One British secretary of state listened for an hour to a deputation about copyright, and said, 'Gentlemen, before you commenced I thought I knew a little about Copyright; now I know I never did know anything about it; and what is more, I never shall.'[67] The copyright question was created by three forces, Great Britain, the United States, and Canada, each pulling in a different direction. British copyright was based upon a British statute of 1842, an imperial copyright for an imperial domain. It protected British authors in the colonies, and it protected colonial authors in Britain. After 1867, Canada developed a Dominion registration of copyright for books published in Canada and extended to the rest of the empire. This was, in effect, a reciprocal arrangement of British and Canadian copyright rules. It looked more reasonable than it was. The problem was, as Thompson put it, 'For a country that produces so many working men and so few authors it may be open to great question whether the reciprocity is not theoretical merely.' Canadian publishers could never have made a living publishing Canadian authors: there were far too few of them. Canadian publishers, like the American, depended upon reprinting works by foreign authors produced abroad.

Canadian publishers could reprint British books legally only by arrangement with British publishers. But there was a rub: British publishers frequently refused to allow Canadian publication, even though offered a fair return for the privilege. The reason was the United States. The United States had copyright only for its own residents. Every author copyrighted in the United States had to be American. No Canadian or Britisher could get American copyright for anything. Charles Dickens made his American lecture tours in the 1840s and 1860s simply in order to capitalize on his books. In no other way could he have got a nickel; every book he published was neatly pirated in Boston, New York, or Chicago. As time went on, the better American publishing houses in the East developed the practice of giving, voluntarily, compensation to British authors whom they published, by way of moral right. Although that was a good deal less than the British author would have got from the United States by an Anglo-American reciprocal copyright, it was a great deal better than nothing at all.

As that practice developed, so also did the American practice of saying to the British author or publisher, 'You will get no compensation whatever from us, if you permit any Canadian house to publish your work. We want the Canadian market ourselves.' The English author literally farmed out Canada as publishing ground to American publishers.[68] American copyright law was a one-way valve.

Cheap American reprints caused the difficulties. British books were expensive: the American version was frequently one-quarter of the British price. Canadians bought the American edition by preference, paying only the Canadian customs duty which included a drawback for the British author.

All of this left the Canadian publishers nowhere. They had a further grievance, Thompson reported. It was too easy to obtain British copyright. Some American authors could, by a short temporary residence in Britain, or in Canada, and publication of a small edition (often already printed) in England, obtain British copyright. By this means they would have control of the markets of Great Britain, Canada, and, being Americans with American copyright, of the United States. And all of this without complying with any Canadian law whatever. Mark Twain, with what Canadians believed characteristic American ingenuity, fastened upon this. He was able to live in Montreal for a short time, send a book ready-printed to London, and get a British copyright that prevented any re-publication in Canada. To top it off he did not sell in Canada his British edition; he sold his American one, and chuckled as dutiful Canadian customs officers collected a drawback at the Canadian border for that well-known 'British' author, Mark Twain![69]

British authors by the 1880s were aware of these niceties. Rider Haggard, after the astonishing success of *King Solomon's Mines* in 1886, published his next novel in 1888 simultaneously in London, New York, and Toronto. The date of the issue of *Allan Quartermain* was known to everyone in the trade. Harpers in New York guarded their printers and proofs carefully, but Hunter, Rose in Toronto were more permeable. A week or two before *Allan Quartermain* was due to appear a Chicago pirating firm sent a clever emissary to Toronto. A printer was bribed to lift a set of proofs; the agent brought them to Chicago (they were too precious to be entrusted to the mail), where a large printing staff had been assembled. *Allan Quartermain* was set, printed, bound, and on the market a few days before the more honest edition.[70] Harpers at least offered Rider Haggard compensation by arrangement; from Chicago he got, of course, nothing.

In return for American pirating of British authors, the British, when they could, pirated American ones. Hence Mark Twain's actions. As Thompson put it, the British in that respect professed to stand on the Mosaic law, saying to American (and Canadian) publishers, 'Thou shalt not steal (unless the American publishers steal), in which case thou mayest steal from American authors.'[71]

Canada's position in the tug-of-war between Britain and the United States was to get the worst of both worlds. What brought it finally to the boiling point was the Berne Convention. First established in 1885, ramified further in 1887, it was accepted by Great Britain in 1886 with further orders-in-council pursuant in November 1887. Given the 1887 state of Canadian copyright law, Canadian publishers (and the printing unions) were alarmed by the implications of the Berne Convention. If applied to Canada, the inhabitants of any country that subscribed to the convention would, by virtue of British copyright, have full and automatic copyright in Canada, without the necessity of the book being made in Canada or Canada having any say in it whatever. The Toronto *Telegram* attributed it, quite bluntly, to the British. 'The effort to bring Canada in under this [Berne] convention is really an effort of the English publisher to control the trade and kill the book, printing, and publishing business in Canada.'[72]

The grievances of the book trade were put forcibly to cabinet on 22 January 1889 by a delegation from the Copyright Association of Canada headed by its president, John Ross Robertson. A memorial signed by two thousand, including three hundred publishers, three hundred book-sellers, the printing unions and others called for a National Policy in the book trade – that is, copyright in Canada, established by Canadian law, the basic condition of which would be publication in Canada.

The cabinet took these representations seriously; an act was put together and came before Parliament that 1889 session. It bore the marks of its origin, but there was input also from John Lowe, the deputy minister of agriculture (the department that supervised Canadian copyright), and from Thompson, who soon made the subject of copyright his own. It was piloted through Parliament not by John Carling, minister of agriculture, but by Thompson.

It did not need much piloting; there was no opposition to it. The questions in Committee of the Whole tended toward making the act even more nationalistic, more strict, than Thompson proposed. As the act stood, a United Kingdom author would have to obtain a Canadian copyright for his work within a month of its publication in Great Britain; if after a month, no copyright had been taken out, the minister of agriculture would have the power to grant a licence for any Canadian to publish the book. When that licence was given, it required that an excise duty be collected internally in Canada on the sales of all books published under that licence. The amount so collected would be remitted to the British author or publisher by the Department of Inland Revenue. The Canadian act was in principle what the British Royal Commission on Copyright, 1875–8, recommended but had never been acted on.

To some of the lawyers in Parliament the new Canadian Copyright Act conflicted with British legislation of 1886 that implemented the Berne Convention. Davies of Prince Edward Island asked, 'How do you propose to repeal the Imperial Act by an Act of this Parliament?' Thompson replied that, under the British North America Act, Canada had the right to legislate, even if it contradicted British statutes.[73] The two most important British statutes on this question were the British Copyright Act of 1842, and the Colonial Laws Validity Act of 1865. The latter declared colonial statutes invalid if repugnant to British ones. Thompson argued, however, that neither of these statutes inhibited Canada's right to legislate its own copyright. His view was that ample powers had been given to Canada in 1867 by the British North America Act; this amplitude nullified the Colonial Laws Validity Act of 1865. Since 1867 Canada had 'repealed, sometimes by implication, and sometimes directly, scores of Imperial enactments, in addition to volumes of the Common Law of the United Kingdom.' If the objection urged against Canadian copyright – that is, that it conflicted with imperial law – was generally applicable to other Canadian acts, it would strike out, according to Thompson, half the Revised Statutes of Canada. Thompson insisted that Canada could legislate on subjects given to its control by the British North America Act, 'irrespective of anterior legislation by the British Parliament.'

Thompson buttressed this position by three recent decisions of the Privy Council. In his view these decisions established clearly the right of the Canadian Parliament to repeal in effect an imperial statute. All three cases came in 1885.

The first was a New South Wales case, argued in London in February 1885, *Apollo Candle Co.* v. *Powell.* The judgment in the Supreme Court of New South Wales sounded like a trumpet call of British imperialism:

There is no Legislature within the wide bounds of the British Empire which is not in subordination to, and under the control of, that Imperial Parliament, and which does not derive its jurisdiction from that source. It follows that every such subordinate Legislature, of which ours is one, is limited by the authority which created it.[74]

The Privy Council put that down. Sir Robert Collier, citing an Indian case and a Canadian one (*Hodge* v. *the Queen*), said that a colonial legislature, within the area of its powers whatever those were, was unrestricted; it was not an agent or a delegate but was in effect sovereign.[75] This was followed a week later by another New South Wales case, that turned upon the right of New South Wales to repeal a British act from the time of James I. Sir Barnes Peacock said that 'the colonial legislature had the power to repeal the statute of James I if they thought fit.'[76]

The case that Thompson put the most weight upon was *Riel* v. *Regina,* an appeal by Riel's lawyers asking that the Regina decision against Riel be set aside on the ground that its procedure violated a British statute of William III of 1697. The Privy Council denied leave to appeal. They said, through Lord Hailsbury, that the Dominion of Canada, once given the North-West Territories by Great Britain in 1870, had the right to establish whatever criminal procedures in the Territories the Parliament of

Canada deemed appropriate. The 'peace, order, and good government' clause of the British North America Act could 'authorize the utmost discretion of enactment ...'[77]

Notwithstanding these powerful utterances from the Privy Council on the nature of the sovereignty of self-governing colonies, Thompson anticipated, accurately as it turned out, that Canada would have a difficult constitutional question to settle with the Colonial Office. Given the law decided by the Privy Council, the Colonial Office might in ordinary circumstances have given way; but the circumstances were not ordinary. On this issue of copyright those who held a strong imperial position would be backed by a powerful and popular lobby, the Copyright Association of Great Britain. Thompson did not blink at the difficulty: he just thought that he was right. And Thompson, when he thought he was right, was apt to be unrelenting.

The Canadian act passed Commons and Senate without a division. And with a clause in the act that brought it into force only by special proclamation, Lord Stanley acquiesced.

It ran into difficulties at once. The Colonial Office was of two minds. Sir Robert Herbert, the permanent under-secretary, interpreted the powers of the British North America Act much as the Privy Council and Thompson did. Herbert, KCB, Eton, Balliol, fellow of All Souls, was the first premier of Queensland, Australia; he had been permanent under-secretary since 1871, and perhaps because of his colonial experience was sympathetic to Canadian arguments. He was unwilling to recognize any imperfection in the powers granted to Canada in 1867.[78]

The colonial secretary, Henry Holland, Baron Knutsford, thought otherwise. He had been assistant under-secretary at the Colonial Office in the 1870s and was something of an expert himself on copyright; by 1890 his views were less liberal then they had been a decade before. Lord Knutsford had been appointed colonial secretary by Lord Salisbury and held the office until 1892. He found the theme of the British Copyright Association appealing: a British author's right running clean around Britain's big red empire. This position seemed to contradict legal views at the Privy Council. But those law cases were, it must be said, decided on narrow, perhaps obscure, points of law. Knutsford's views, and those of the British Copyright Association, represented feelings widely held in England by the end of the 1880s.

The British were upset and annoyed at the Canadian copyright act. S.E. Dawson predicted correctly that they would fight on the issue. It was not that they cared so much for the Canadian market; Canada's proximity to cheap American editions could not really be got around. British authors and publishers were looking rather at the danger to the markets in South Africa, Australia, and New Zealand where, while protected from American pirates by distance, a Canadian copyright precedent, once legally established and confirmed by the Privy Council, would seriously hurt the British publisher.[79] Thompson's Copyright Act thus encountered formidable obstacles; it would require some mighty pushing to get the British government to move on a question opposed by so powerful a lobby, an articulate and outspoken section of the British public.

Thompson and Macdonald and the cabinet were ready enough to push. 'We must make a determined stand,' Macdonald wrote to Tupper, 'as to our exclusive right to deal with it.' Behind those words lay Thompson's resolve. But where else in the cabinet lay the same strong will? No doubt in C.H. Tupper, in George Foster, perhaps in Mackenzie Bowell, who was however showing signs of age. The cabinet was old, Macdonald wrote Sir Charles Tupper; Langevin, Macdonald's French-Canadian lieutenant, whom in 1888 he had still thought of as possible successor, had now aged and become 'inert and useless except in office'; worse, Langevin had no real following in Quebec, and his quarrels with Chapleau and Caron had allowed Mercier to win the Quebec provincial election of 1890. Colby of Quebec and Costigan of New Brunswick had great frailties (mainly alcoholic). Thompson, upon whose shoulders so much had been placed, was wearing himself out. 'I fear for Thompson's health,' Macdonald said, '[he] has been so fagged and run down by the Session.'[80]

Thompson was tired. It had been a particularly hard session for him; the dragon's teeth had tested and exploited his resources, and he was now troubled by headaches and insomnia. Macdonald hoped that a trip across the ocean would relax and strengthen him, something it had always succeeded in doing for Macdonald. Thus with the blessing of Macdonald and cabinet Thompson took passage in the *Parisian*, leaving Montreal on 25 June 1890, bound for Liverpool. Annie would go with him. The girls with Fan would stay at the Carons' summer place, near Macdonald at Rivière du Loup; the boys he and Annie would see in England. It was Thompson's first trip overseas.

16

Thompson's Canadian Diplomacy

The *Parisian* was an Allan Line vessel, carrying 750 passengers in three classes; she was the usual late-nineteenth-century conglomerate of steam and sail. Two large and imposing funnels were set amidships; forward were two square-rigged masts, aft two fore-and-aft rigged ones. She was graceful, the *Parisian*, too much so; slim in the beam, she liked to roll, as Thompson discovered during a day of lying to on the Grand Banks, where a heavy ground swell over forty fathoms of water produced disconcerting results. Then the weather dried up, the sun came out, the sea calmed down, and as Thompson put it, it was like living in a seaside hotel with four meals a day and music every evening. They arrived at Liverpool Sunday evening, 6 July, eleven days out of Montreal.[1]

The two hundred miles from Liverpool to London could be managed by fast train in between five and seven hours. Thompson and Annie got to London Monday evening and installed themselves in the large, comfortable Westminster Palace Hotel. It was a hotel with a long history of Canadian associations; Macdonald had frequently stayed there, and it had been the site of the London Conference of 1866–7 on confederation. If walls could speak it had much to tell. It stood at the corner of Victoria and Tothill streets, about a hundred yards west of Westminister Abbey. Victoria Street, lying between the Abbey and Victoria Station, was really colonial row, with most of the offices of the colonial governments there: Queensland at Number 1, New South Wales at Number 9, New Zealand at Number 13, Victoria and West Australia at Number 15, and the Canadian high commissioner at Number 17. The United States embassy was at that time there too, at Number 123. The British Colonial Office was in Downing Street, opposite Number 10, perhaps a quarter of a mile away.

The London Thompson encountered in 1890 had a population of something over four million, and had already its first underground railway around what is called the Inner Circle. The original power was steam, which must have been unusually dirty underground even with the tall tunnels; that very year was opened the first real 'tube,' from South London to the City, run by electricity. Above ground the usual conveyance was by bus – that is, a large horse-drawn vehicle, pulled by a team. London had some thirty thousand horses for that purpose, plus another twenty thousand for the eleven thousand cabs. Thus the streets of London were inescapably equine in appearance and smell.

Thompson arranged to meet Lord Knutsford for a 'preliminary canter,' as Knutsford put it, over the subjects on the Canadian-British agenda. In the meantime Thompson spent five hours in the visitor's gallery at the House of Commons, not without a certain 'child's pleasure at the first play,' as he put it to Hibbert Tupper in Ottawa.[2] He was not that impressed with the British House of Commons. He heard Arthur Balfour, then secretary of state for Ireland in Salisbury's Conservative government, under fire on the Irish estimates. The Liberal opposition at Westminister were just as irascible as at Ottawa; Thompson thought the British Liberals were infringing the patent on recalcitrant opposition held in Ottawa by William Mulock and James McMullen! Certainly, he told Macdonald, 'I shall never again be ashamed when I see strangers listening to our discussions in Supply.'[3] On that subject at least the British House of Commons was no better.

Lord Knutsford was sixty-five years old, a handsome man with considerable charm. But his forensic skills were few and he delighted not in the rough and tumble of parliamentary debate. He had not been Salisbury's first choice for the portfolio. He was the sort of person American newspapers would satirize as 'Sir Forcible Feeble,' a *grand timide*, who defended his opinions not by argument so much as by stubbornness, and when this failed, persuaded himself that difficulties could be smoothed over with forms of words.[4]

On 14 July Thompson went to copyright at once. He found Knutsford well posted by those who opposed Canada but ill informed about her side of the question. Knutsford seemed 'uninformed and obstinate in equal degrees.' When Knutsford was discussing a matter he did not understand he was apt to become peevish, which made it hard to set him right when he was going all wrong. For Thompson it was especially hard to do this without becoming irritated himself, ('Which,' added Thompson archly in a letter to Mackenzie Bowell, 'you know I never am!') Nor did it help Thompson's state of mind that Knutsford immediately sent for Sir Henry Bergne, the Colonial Office adviser; Thompson remembered him from Washington in 1887–8, spending his days playing tennis, his evenings at parties, and being generally useless. According to Thompson, Bergne had had a hand in much of the mischief done to Canada in recent years; Bergne believed that 'pigeon holes were made for complaints from the Colonies.'[5]

While waiting for this paragon, Thompson discussed the constitutional question, the powers Thompson believed Canada possessed by virtue of the British North America Act of 1867. Thompson opposed the British claim that the Colonial Laws Validity Act of 1865 had any overriding power. He claimed that the copyright issue had been put so strongly by British publishers that it had taken possession of the British mind. Knutsford would not admit this; he fell back upon the views of the law officers of the crown – as distinct from the Judicial Committee – and held out no hope of persuading them to change their mind. Thompson replied that the consequence of British denial of Canadian power to legislate 'were so great and so far reaching as to affect nearly every branch of legislation in Canada – Dominion and Provincial.' It was so serious, Thompson went on:

... the publication of his despatch denying our power to interfere with the British legislation of 50 years ago on the subject of copyright would lead to many other Statutes being challenged and proposed that he should have an Act passed declaring the Colonial Laws Validity Act of 1865 did not restrict the provisions of the BNA Act. I reminded him that the opinion of the Law Officers was that the BNA Act was merely a distribution of existing legislative powers between the Federal and Provincial Parliaments[,] while the interpretation of the Judicial Committee was that that Act was a new gift of powers ...

Prior to leaving Canada Thompson had had the impression that Knutsford was willing to concede Canada's point if he could do it without legislating directly on the copyright question, simply using a general act to clear out of the way the obstruction created in the minds of the law officers by the Colonial Laws Validity Act. Thompson was surprised and pained to discover in London that he had been mistaken; Knutsford seemed unable to grasp Canada's difficulty, one that Thompson insisted 'menaced' Canada. Thompson's dialogue with Knutsford went something like this, and fascinating it is:

KNUTSFORD (irritated): I should have expected that instead of general propositions you would be putting pressure on us to have specific power conferred on Canada to deal with the copyright question.

THOMPSON: That indeed is one of the objects of my visit to London. But I beg you to consider the general constitutional question as well.

KNUTSFORD: There have never been questions raised about Canadian powers in other branches of legislation.

THOMPSON: Precisely. That is why we have so much confidence in our powers to legislate Canadian copyright. Not only that but there are the recent cases in our favour decided by Judicial Committee of the Privy Council.

[Here Thompson cited the cases mentioned already in chapter 15.]

KNUTSFORD: There are only two British statutes extending to the self-governing colonies, the Copyright Act and the Merchant Shipping Act.

THOMPSON (quiet but seething): I have a list of 200 such Acts and I am not confident my list is complete.

KNUTSFORD: What sort of acts are they?

THOMPSON: The Supremacy Act and other religious acts extending to all the colonies. They had been infringed by at least 20 colonial statutes and by the recent Jesuits' Estates Act of Quebec.

KNUTSFORD: I was not aware that any of those acts related to the colonies.

THOMPSON: The question had been raised and bitterly fought. Had the Law Officers' opinion been otherwise on the Jesuits' Estates Act nothing could have avoided a civil war but change in the constitution.

KNUTSFORD: But if the current of discussion is thus altogether in your favour, what more do you want?

THOMPSON: We do not want our powers to be denied when we touch the subject of copyright; or if they are denied on high authority, we would want them confirmed.

By this time Sir Henry Bergne had arrived, and Thompson and Knutsford left the constitutional branch of the subject on the understanding that Thompson would prepare a memorandum. But Knutsford warned that he did not necessarily accept Thompson's view.[6]

With Bergne and Knutsford Thompson rehearsed specific Canadian copyright grievances, beginning with the imperial act of 1842 that still mainly controlled the law. Knutsford admitted that the British royal commission of 1878 had recommended that colonial publishers should be allowed to reprint under licence. Why not, Knutsford suggested, keep up the pressure to have the Canadian act recognized?

That looked promising. As Thompson told Macdonald, 'He would surely not ask us to press for what he did not want us to obtain.' Thompson thought that Knutsford was set on giving Canada her liberty and that his hesitations were owing to considerations of the interests that he would have to fight. The interview was to be resumed in ten days. Thompson came away convinced that Canada would get her way if she were firm and persistent. But she ought not to ease the pressure. 'We must worry them as if we were Irishmen,' Thompson told Bowell. To do otherwise would be to leave Canadian problems in Colonial Office and other Whitehall pigeon holes. Canada, said Thompson tersely, 'had been pigeon-holed now for twenty years and had got too big for the place.'[7]

Thompson did not like London. The Whitehall working day was only about four hours and it took an enormous commitment of time and effort just to get appointments arranged and questions discussed. Langevin, in London a decade earlier, was outspoken. 'Si tu savais combien je suis fatigué et harassé de cette vie-ci! Et cependant il faut y aller *doucement*. C'est le principe anglais.' You complain, Langevin told his brother, about the slowness of our civil service in Canada: I can tell you we are electricity compared to these people.[8] Thompson complained to Caron that everything had taken so long it would be impossible to get over to Paris. It rained constantly. Even in full summer London seemed to be dark, dank, and dirty. Thompson much preferred New York. It was, as he had seen it in 1887 and 1888, brighter and cleaner than London and the climate better.[9] Nor did London's male world – clubs, leather armchairs, ceremony, uniforms, and haberdashery – have much charm for him. Everything he had seen in London was smaller and meaner than the photographs; only the Atlantic Ocean was more magnificent than he had imagined! 'Canada,' he told Helena, 'is the place to live in after all.'[10]

At the weekend Thompson and Annie took the long train journey northward to see the boys at Stonyhurst. It took two days: one travelled five or six hours to Manchester, then took local trains northeastward across Lancashire through Blackburn to a little hamlet called Whalley. There one got a horse and carriage and drove across a pretty countryside, the great fells of western Yorkshire looming up to the north; then you came upon Stonyhurst, a mile or two from the Yorkshire border.

Thompson was well pleased with what he found. The size of Stonyhurst, its handsome buildings, pictures, its library, were really surprising.[11] They spent the weekend together and the boys accompanied them part way back on the Monday. Thompson and Annie were back in London Tuesday evening, 22 July.

By the next interview with Thompson on 24 July, Knutsford's position had hardened. He refused to give Thompson the opinion the law officers used against Canada; the rules did not permit it. All that he would do was explain the law officers' opinion; that the 'powers of legislation conferred upon the Dominion Parliament by the BNA Act of 1867 do not authorize that Parliament to amend or repeal an Imperial Act conferring privileges within Canada.'[12] Thompson thought this was far too perfunctory, taking no account of the distinction between statutes passed before 1867 and those afterward. It was clear that there were two main obstacles to Canadian copyright: the Colonial Laws Validity Act of 1865 that Knutsford refused to touch; and the British interpretation of existing imperial copyright legislation. If either were amended it would do. All that was needed in the case of the Colonial Laws Validity Act was a brief amendment or a declaratory act. In Thompson's view the 1865 act had been intended to remove doubts as to earlier powers of colonial legislatures, powers that had developed and expanded under imperial despatches and commissions. Its effect on British North America had never been thought worth bothering about. Suddenly, Thompson found, it was being applied to the 1867 BNA Act, and to protect British publications. The specific remedy, altering imperial copyright, or giving power to Canada to do so, was more direct but, according to Knutsford, more difficult. All this came as a disagreeable surprise to Thompson after what had been said ten days before.

Canadian representation on the Judicial Committee of the Privy Council was another item on Thompson's agenda. The 1890 death of Sir Barnes Peacock had raised it. There was a school of thought in Canada, Thompson affirmed, that urged the judicial independence of Canada, the complete ending of appeals to the Privy Council. This sentiment would gather strength as Canada grew in population and power. That was not, Thompson insisted, the policy of the Macdonald government, who regarded it as one of the ties of Canada to Great Britain. Lord Knutsford interjected, 'It is *the* tie, and I should be very sorry to see it cut off.' The problem was, said Thompson, that the Judicial Committee 'had failed to do justice in several remarkable cases, for want of knowledge of language and geography.' One obvious remedy was to appoint a Canadian to the Judicial Committee. Knutsford had objections here – expense, the Australian colonies would each want a representative – but it was agreed that Canada should open up the subject formally by order-in-council. In the end it was concluded by the law officers that no person could sit on the Judicial Committee unless he had been a judge of a superior court in the United Kingdom or a practising barrister. In other words, 'no *colonial* Barrister or judge is eligible.'[13]

The following day Thompson presented himself to Cardinal Manning, now an austere old man of eighty-two, with new laurels from having helped settle the big London dock strike of 1889. Thompson presented a letter from Macdonald, whom Manning well remembered; indeed Manning knew something of Canada and the colonies, having worked for two years in the Colonial Office in the 1830s under Lord Goderich. Thompson was charmed by Manning's simplicity and at parting received a blessing which, Thompson said, 'ought to carry us half way through the next general election.'[14]

By now Thompson and Annie had had enough of the elegant quarters of the great Westminister Palace, and after seeing their boys off to Canada from Liverpool on 31 July moved into an apartment in Half Moon Street, off Piccadilly, with Louisa Carling; the three would share a sitting-room, a dining-room, which, with two bedrooms, they had for £3 a week.

Thompson had a long and profitable interview on copyright with W.H. Smith, the son of the founder of W.H. Smith and Son. Smith had come into the House of Commons in 1868 as MP for Westminster (defeating John Stuart Mill); by 1890 he was first lord of the treasury in Salisbury's government and the leader of the House of Commons. He was not brilliant; but he earned respect for patience and zeal and was more powerful than Lord Knutsford. For Thompson, Smith was a refreshing change especially since he was entirely in favour of letting Canada manage its own copyright. When and if Canadian copyright came before the British cabinet there would be, Thompson assured Macdonald, a friendly voice heard in its support.

Thompson and Sir Charles Tupper went back to Knutsford again early in August about arbitration of Canadian claims against the United States for Bering Sea seizures. Macdonald was uneasy over having the United States' claim to the Bering Sea as *mare clausum* mixed up with the Canadian claims for compensation. Macdonald wanted to concentrate upon the latter. Thompson did not share Macdonald's fear of a wider base for a Bering Sea arbitration: he was confident that the Canadian–British case, even on the wider front, was too strong to fail.[15]

The Bering Sea question went back to 1884, when British Columbia sealers first took seals in the Bering Sea. By 1886 there were thirteen Canadian schooners there. The United States seized three that summer in Bering Strait, seventy miles from the nearest land. Four more were seized in 1887, probably both sets in consequence of the *David Adams* seizure by Canada in 1886. The Canadian schooners were technically British ships on the high seas and it was really a matter for Washington and London to settle; but it was unavoidable that Canada would be concerned about it. Sir Julian Pauncefote, the British ambassador in Washington, was anxious to have the question settled.[16] The American view was that everyone was minding their own business peacefully and profitably when out of the blue in 1884 came Canadian sealers wickedly asserting their right to kill seals on the high seas.[17] Thompson and C.H. Tupper contended that the seals could be well protected by following the usual international rule, the three-mile limit around the Pribiloff Islands, the main sealing ground. Blaine was angry with Canada; she was forcing Lord Salisbury to take a hard line. Canada had no more right to interfere with the British than California with the United States.[18]

The last of the long interviews with Lord Knutsford was held on 3 August, with Newfoundland delegates present at Knutsford's request. The issue under discussion was the Newfoundland Bait Act. Thompson knew its long history. The immediate question was four years old and the problem much older. The origin of it was the French Shore, first established by the Treaty of Utrecht in 1713, as a shore where French fishermen could land and cure their fish. It was very extensive, almost one-third of the whole northeast and the west coast of Newfoundland. It excluded permanent establishments by either French or English. By the 1880s, Newfoundland governments became exasperated with the French presence on that coast, the more so since the French competed with Newfoundland in south European markets. The French government had, since the eighteenth century, subsidized her own fishermen, and bounty-fed cod, as the Newfoundlanders called it, seriously affected Newfoundland's own exports.

This might have passed as friction inevitable with all anachronistic treaties, but there now intruded into diplomacy the hitherto despised lobster. Even before 1867 Nova Scotians were canning west-coast Newfoundland lobster, usually at the end of the salmon season; by the 1880s lobster-canning was an important industry, owned mostly by Nova Scotians and Prince Edward Islanders, employing some one thousand Newfoundlanders in two dozen factories. It had become the mainstay of Newfoundland's west coast. This was against the treaty. A modus vivendi was negotiated between Britain and France in 1884 that was not unreasonable, but imperial complications with France in the south Pacific, and the fall of Sir William Whiteway's government in 1885 in Newfoundland upset confirmation. Newfoundland's paucity of bargaining power drove her to the Bait Act of 1886, an attempt to force the French to bend. Bait was essential to the whole fishery, and Newfoundland had it in profusion. Britain refused the first Bait Act, but accepted another in 1887 that came into force in 1888. French fishermen needed bait; so did

Canadian and American. But it was difficult to prevent Newfoundland fishermen from making money selling it, and the act still did not prevent the decline of Newfoundland's export markets, which had as much to do with the poor quality of the Newfoundland cure as with the competition from France. The Bait Act, as one author remarked, was like an ancient cannon, a menace to friend and foe alike.[19]

Two separate Newfoundland delegations went to London in the summer of 1890 to press the Newfoundland case. The Canadians were unhappy about the application of the Bait Act to Canadian fishermen. Sir William Whiteway, the premier since 1889, was disposed to be reasonable, but he would be reluctant to do much, and certainly would not repeal the act without a quid pro quo from the French. So it was left for the moment. There was a further sidelight to all this; delegates from the west coast of Newfoundland were opposed to legislative rule from St John's and were in favour of confederation with Canada. Thompson believed that Canada was interested, though on what terms, and whether acceptable to Newfoundland was another matter. Confederation was indeed a complication of all the other issues between Canada and Newfoundland.

At last Thompson and Annie sailed from Liverpool on 14 August, glad to be away. Their company on the voyage out was the Earl and Countess of Aberdeen, who were to take the CPR to the west coast for a holiday. Other fellow passengers were Sir Alexander Campbell, Thompson's predecessor as minister of justice and now lieutenant-governor of Ontario, as well as the ubiquitous Sandford Fleming.

Thompson and Annie were both anxious to be reunited with their family at Rivière du Loup. But Thompson was afraid that his cabinet colleagues would think he had been away long enough and would insist on his returning at once to Ottawa.[20] He spent the weekend at Rivière du Loup with his children and with Macdonald, and was off to Ottawa on Monday, 25 August.[21] It was so hot on the train coming to Quebec that Thompson had to stop over in Quebec with Caron. By the time he reached Ottawa, young Tupper had flung himself off to the Pictou County beaches for a holiday, Langevin had left for Quebec City, and Mackenzie Bowell was in the West. Thompson faced Ottawa, without Annie, in the dog days of August. His Ottawa home was so uninviting that he accepted an invitation to stay with his deputy minister, Robert Sedgewick.

In September came bad news. Little Frankie had disease of the hip and the Montreal doctor, Dr Thomas Roddick, professor of clinical surgery at McGill, said that traction, for at least three months, was the only answer.

Annie's heart went down to her shoes at the news; for Thompson it was almost a relief to have a long-standing problem diagnosed and treatment started. On 22 September Frankie began her stay in bed with six-pound weights on her bad leg, the weights getting heavier as the weeks went by.[22] The doctor had said three months but probably not even he knew. Frankie was sharp. One day when Dr H.P. Wright, the Ottawa physician, called on her, she said to him, 'How much longer must I stay in bed?' Dr Wright hesitated. 'I think, Frankie,' he said, 'the Court will keep that to itself.' Frankie looked at him intently. 'Yes, but does the Court know itself?' Thompson nicknamed her 'the dizzle-dazzle.'[23] Even Lady Aberdeen called, on her way back from the West. Frankie kept bright and cheerful, but wanted to be constantly amused; as time went on she developed quite a levée each afternoon.[24]

At the end of September Thompson, Macdonald, and young Tupper left for Nova Scotia for a series of meetings that were an examination of what happened in the provincial elections of May, and plan for reorganization and revival for the future. The Conservatives had been confident of winning the May elections. They lost; among their excuses was Tupper's diligence, in particular his allegedly disastrous enforcement of salmon regulations against Nova Scotian sawmill owners, and his insistence on fishermen taking lobsters of the right size. Mainly at Tupper's insistence, there was a reorganization of the party, for Tupper found the Halifax Conservatives both apathetic and greedy.[25] The central executive of the Nova Scotia Conservatives was composed of six members from Halifax plus three from each county, including Halifax County.[26] Macdonald came down and made a fighting speech at a huge Conservative picnic at Rockingham, on Bedford Basin, on 1 October. Thompson did the same. The Liberals, he said, throw at you the old weather-beaten story about vast American markets, the natural markets for Canada. What is the point of that, he asked, 'if they are so closed that we cannot sell our products there?' Let us sell our products elsewhere.[27] It was good talk, in Halifax or in Nova Scotia. Halifax had factories: two sugar refineries, the Dartmouth Rope Works, the Dominion Paint Company, and Starr's nationally known skates. And the first big shipments of Annapolis valley apples were going that year to England; by 1891 apple exports from Nova Scotia were double that of potatoes.

Thompson went on to Antigonish County, visiting faithfully his big constituency. But it needed more attention, Thompson said; he told Annie they would simply have to spend the summer of 1891 there. While in one of the Antigonish houses, the owner congratulated Thompson on his son's first in the Oxford and Cambridge entrance examinations. This was news to Thompson. The owner produced the London *Tablet* to prove it.[28]

Thompson was back in Ottawa by mid-October in time to organize a Rideau Club lunch for Lord Aberdeen on his way back to England from British Columbia. Thompson had taken to Aberdeen.[29] He was intelligent, judicious, fair, a little gentle for this rough world; his gentleness was, however, made up for by Lady Ishbel Aberdeen, strong-minded, brisk, capable, with a heart big enough, as a woman friend remarked, for any fate.[30] Lady Aberdeen liked Thompson very much. 'I never met,' she said later, 'a high official with less red tape about him. He will talk about political matters as one human being to another.'[31]

The same autumn of 1890 James Blaine had a delightful opportunity to get at Canada. The Newfoundland government had sent Robert Bond to Washington to discuss a fishery reciprocity arrangement between Newfoundland and the United States. Bond may have had authority to negotiate such an arrangement; the British minister in Washington, Sir Julian Pauncefote, was sure he did not. Blaine saw his chance and took it. Rather to Bond's surprise, and certainly to Sir Julian's, the matter prospered exceedingly; and the Bond–Blaine Convention of October 1890 was the result.[32] It left Thompson and the cabinet breathless. A cable went at once to Sir Charles Tupper in London:

Can scarcely believe Newfoundland has received authority from Imperial government to make separate arrangements respecting fisheries ...

Please represent urgently how fishery and commercial interests of Canada might be injured by such an arrangement as Bond is currently reported as making and how disastrous from a national point of view it would be for a separate colony to effect an arrangement with the United States more favourable than would be given to the Confederated provinces.[33]

The imperial government was not seized of the importance of nullifying the Bond–Blaine Convention, nor was Lord Stanley. Thompson could not believe that London was serious: letting Newfoundland work out a convention with Washington that would so compromise Canadian interests! London was serious and pressed the point. Macdonald's cabinet was resolute, more perhaps than he was himself. 'I consulted Thompson yesterday on the cable about Newfoundland affairs,' he wrote Stanley on 17 November, 'and have called Council together for this morning at 11. I fear it is a bad business.'[34]

Thompson had strong reasons, some of them given by A.B. Morine, a Nova Scotian lawyer resident in Newfoundland. Morine was former editor of the St John's *Evening Mercury*, who had been elected to the Newfoundland Assembly in 1889. He was a confederation agent in the Newfoundland camp. If Newfoundland got free entry of fish into the United States, he said, the fishermen of the Maritime provinces would be discontented and blame confederation; it would encourage Maritime annexationism and much hinder the cause of confederation in Newfoundland.[35] Canada was fairly caught. If she opposed the Bond–Blaine Convention, Newfoundland would be furious; if she did not oppose it, there was a possibility of Newfoundland going adrift, and beginning to pull Nova Scotia, Prince Edward Island, and New Brunswick with her. Blaine was aware of this and deliberately aimed to create tension between Canada and Newfoundland.[36]

Thompson was not so concerned about confederation in Newfoundland as was Morine. Thompson felt that the advantage in Newfoundland's joining confederation were mostly on the Newfoundland side, in Canadian development of public works and in free trade with Canada. The main advantage of having Newfoundland in confederation would be 'the frustration of American diplomacy ... and the counteracting of the effect of that diplomacy in Canada.' All other alleged advantages, Thompson said, 'are merely sentimental and could as well be obtained by a union a hundred years hence.'[37] Thompson was more worried about the effect of Blaine's actions upon Canada than upon Newfoundland. If, as Morine believed, Lord Knutsford was afraid of offending Newfoundland, he should be impressed with the view that it was better to annoy little Newfoundland than big Canada.[38] Morine also asked for personal financial help and there is evidence that he may have got it.[39]

In early December Blaine intimated that discussion about a reciprocity treaty with Canada might be possible. Canadian attempts to get such a treaty had been so often rejected in the past that Canada would no longer raise it. Now, however, as Macdonald pointed out to Thompson, 'this suggestion of Blaine's gives us the opportunity.'[40] Thompson's draft paper of December 1890 on Newfoundland thus incorporated the possibility of Canadian reciprocity with the United States. Negotiations went forward on three fronts: Blaine who wanted to string Canada along dangling the hope of a reciprocity treaty; Newfoundland who desperately wanted the Bond–Blaine Convention; and Canada who wanted a treaty but was too proud to beg for it. The British government was in between, wanting to placate Newfoundland for French Shore grievances yet not wishing to go against Canada. Thompson was unwilling to let the British government off the hook; to give Newfoundland the Bond–Blaine Convention would be to co-operate with the United States in destroying the allegiance of Canada. He said so bluntly to London.

The British government were unhappy with the Canadian attitude. Macdonald began to feel that with Blaine's apparent willingness to negotiate Canada might be content and let the Newfoundland convention proceed. Canada had made her protest and might now try a little accommodation. Thompson was still adamant. Well, said Macdonald to Thompson late in January 1891, as he cabled the British government that he was about to dissolve Parliament, 'You can fight this out with Lord Stanley. I'm going to Toronto.' With cabinet backing, Thompson did fight it out. The *Globe* alleged later that Thompson told the governor general that if Britain ratified the Bond–Blaine Treaty, he and C.H. Tupper would resign from the government. Thompson denied that it had ever got to that point.[41]

The Bond–Blaine Treaty was a device positively devilish, that worked in several directions at once: not just Newfoundland–American relations, but British–Canadian, to say nothing of the not-so-hidden workings between Blaine and members of the Liberal party.[42]

The tensions around all of it were increased by the McKinley tariff, going into effect 6 October 1890. It would put a higher tariff on all Canadian farm produce going to the United States. The Ontario farmers dreaded it and the Macdonald government were extremely uneasy, despite their bold words in Halifax; for there were substantial Canadian exports of barley, eggs, cattle and other agricultural products to the United States that could be hurt by the ban proposed by McKinley.[43] There was something to be said for the idea of having a dissolution of Parliament before the full effects of the McKinley tariff be felt.

Blaine for his part was mightily annoyed with Canada for blocking the Bond–Blaine Convention. He promised, in reply to British representations, to negotiate with Canada but he was in no hurry to start and he was not bound to conclude a treaty even if he did begin.[44] He insisted that any negotiations be private not public. He was thus in a position to say publicly whatever he wanted to Canadian Liberals about their project of unrestricted reciprocity, while denying publicly that there were any negotiations with the Canadian Conservative government. The sheer effrontery of this two-faced policy surprised neither Thompson nor Macdonald. Blaine had always taken the position that if Canada really wanted the advantages of the American market she could become American; he did not intend that Canada would have the best of both worlds.[45] There was no doubt that his purpose was to kick or kiss Canada into the American union.[46]

This was the background to Macdonald's dissolution of January 1891 and the main reason why he took the rather desperate step of fighting it on the issue of loyalty to Canada and to Great Britain. There was really no other way. Still it was a bold move to dissolve the House before the session, and especially before the redistribution consequent upon the 1891 census; certain advantages could well be lost, such as estimates slanted for an election, or a little ingenious footwork with constituency boundaries!

Newfoundland kept Thompson in Ottawa until his departure for Nova Scotia early in February. On 28 January Thompson wired Macdonald in Toronto that cabinet would decide the following day on the actual text of the Newfoundland minute.[47] Stanley cabled Knutsford that same day with the hope that the Newfoundland treaty would not be sanctioned until Canadian negotiations with the Americans were well in hand.[48]

One last duty before leaving Ottawa for the front in Nova Scotia was Macdonald's request that Thompson write the eight Catholic bishops of Ontario soliciting their support.[49] His letter was probably like one he sent the six Maritime bishops, a model of judicious hesitation:

I make no claim with regard to matters in which religion has been in any degree concerned except that the Government has done its duty, sometimes at the risk of loss of support and with some degree of odium.

In the present campaign almost every interest which affects the security and the stability of the country seems to be more or less at stake, and I cannot refuse, even at the risk of appearing to intrude myself, thus to solicit respectfully as much favour as your Lordship can, consistently with your duty and position, accord to our candidates in the coming election.[50]

The bishops were willing enough but none too sanguine. Bishop N.J. Lorraine of Pembroke said he could not openly support the Conservative candidate, Peter White, who had made himself disagreeable to Roman Catholics; he would therefore be ostensibly neutral. He thought that the campaign would be a hard one, the hardest 'we have had for many years.'[51] Bishop Macdonell from Alexandria said he would do what he could in a quiet way, but he was not without fears of defeat.[52] No one seemed sanguine, not even Bishop Cameron in Antigonish. Liberal proposals of unrestricted reciprocity were seductive, and the promises were supported by American money that J.W. Longley and Ernest Pacaud had brought back from Washington. Both Nova Scotian bishops, Archbishop O'Brien of Halifax, and Cameron, supported the Conservative party; but it was support too obviously Catholic to suit C.H. Cahan at the Halifax *Herald*. He felt it would not do, not any more, to allow the impression that Thompson owed his election solely to the support of Catholic bishops. Thompson seemed willing to risk that. Bishop Cameron thought Thompson would take Antigonish, provided that every inch of the ground be fought for.[53] The Liberals were anxious to defeat Thompson; they had been only forty-two votes from victory in 1887, and they were hopeful for 1891. Angus McGillivray, MLA for Antigonish, resigned his seat in order to fight Thompson.

Thompson spent the early part of the campaign outside his own county. Thompson's speeches on the stump were always exaggerated from his normal mode, but in the 1891 campaign they had a ring of sincerity. Distrust with the Liberals' repeated visits to Washington, he said, had grown into disgust. Sir Richard Cartwright's visit to Washington in 1890 was followed by the introduction of the McKinley tariff imposing American duty on Canadian eggs, poultry, and other farm products, no doubt suggested by Cartwright; Blaine's outspoken comment was that Canada could not have the British flag and American markets at one and the same time.[54]

It was hard campaigning. Some leading centres were not accessible by rail, only by sea or horse and carriage. The thirty miles from Bridgewater to Liverpool took Thompson three and a half hours, and that with a good team of horses. Finally on 16 February he telegraphed Macdonald from Kentville that it was essential he and C.H. Tupper now go to their own counties, where Thompson arrived late on 19 February.[55]

Then began the regime of two meetings a day, from one schoolhouse to another for the next twelve days. Friends were sanguine, for the meetings in other counties had gone well, but Thompson was not. In Ottawa they were profoundly worried; Annie, despite frequent recourse to saints and prayers, had worried herself into illness.[56] Antigonish had lost none of its greediness; one voter suggested delicately that since his vote helped Thompson to be minister of justice at $7,000 a year, that vote could be bought, 'strictly below board,' at $400.[57] Thompson was sure his opponents had plenty of money; some $20,000 in road money from the Fielding government of Nova Scotia had already been spent and more promised, he told Annie. This had made Liberal ranks solid and made inroads on Conservative. Thompson said he had lost ground in districts where he had been strong in 1887 and had now to try to make inroads where his opponent's strength was. On 24 February nine days before polling day, it looked to him as if he might win by twenty votes or be defeated by one hundred. Thompson tried not to worry about it; he and Annie would make their plans for life afterward. He had no wish at all for another campaign, not unless there was no other way to make a living. To Thompson's relief, Annie agreed that he would not have to go through another election.[58]

Thompson's Ottawa secretary, Douglas Stewart, had seen John Haggart, the postmaster general, and was on his way east by 25 February with ammunition for the Nova Scotia campaign. Thompson seems not to have wanted it himself; he told S.H. Holmes that he did not need any money. Holmes sent Thompson $250 anyway, a gesture of goodwill no doubt for the Stewiacke and Lansdowne Railway that Thompson had helped to forward.[59] But there were others in need. Chipman in Kentville, trying to help W.C. Bill defeat F.W. Borden in Kings County, wrote anxiously that they had raised $1,500 in the valley, had got $1,000 more (presumably from Ottawa), and wanted a further $2,000. Chipman promised to raise this extra $2,000 himself, provided he were promised the vacant Nova Scotia seat in the Senate. Thompson's response was not helpful. F.W. Borden won by 161 votes; Chipman claimed afterward that had Thompson come through with the promise of the Senate seat, W.C. Bill would have won by 50 to 100 votes. Chipman never did get a seat in the Senate.[60] Joseph Pope telegraphed Thompson from Kingston that if more ammunition were needed in Nova Scotia, Thompson could draw up to $2,500 from W.A. Allan of Ottawa. Sir John Macdonald suggested leaving Cumberland to its own devices (where Dickey, Sir Charles Tupper's successor, seemed a certainty), and sending $500 to John McDonald in Victoria, Cape Breton (who won), and $500 to J.N. Freeman in Queens (who didn't).[61]

The result of the federal election in 1891 in Nova Scotia surprised everyone, Liberals and Conservatives alike. Thompson won Antigonish by 227 votes, a much bigger majority than in either 1885 or 1887. In the province as a whole the Conservatives took sixteen of twenty-one seats and 53 per cent of the popular vote, compared to fourteen seats and 50 per cent in 1887. It looked good, perhaps some of it owing to Thompson and young Tupper.

The Conservative vote tended to follow the Dominion railway lines. Railways made good politics; Macdonald had to tell one anxious Nova Scotian MP that the railway he was proposing would not carry enough traffic to justify construction. The MP replied with some heat, 'Traffic be damned! I wanted the road to carry me back to Parliament.'[62] Nearly all the government railways were in eastern Nova Scotia. If a line were drawn across the map from Moncton to Halifax, east of the line would be found all but one of Nova Scotia's ten senators; the two members of the federal cabinet; and all the railways east of that line were owned and operated by the Domion and had lower rates. Railways west of that line were company railways. So complained W.C. Bill, the Conservative candidate who had just lost Kings to F.W. Borden.[63]

In the opinion of Thompson's Halifax friends much of the Conservative success in 1891 was owing to the execrable generalship of the Liberals in raising unrestricted reciprocity again; the Conservatives won in Nova Scotia in 1891 not on their merits but because of Liberal mistakes. Within a fortnight of the election a Liberal round robin went to W.S. Fielding urging the muzzling of the annexationists in the party. A.G. Jones, defeated in Halifax by J.F. Stairs, blamed Sir Richard Cartweight and 'that d—— f—— Longley' for his misfortunes.[64] The Halifax *Herald* was partisan but right: the election of 1891 in Nova Scotia was not a contest between Canadian political parties on domestic questions, it was between the Canadian people on the one side and a faction of the Liberals and their American allies on the other.[65] Cartwright's Boston speech was quoted and requoted, that unrestricted reciprocity would mean for the Americans 'the addition of half a continent for commercial purpose, and the ... creation of a new tier of northern states.'[66]

The three Nova Scotia champions, the two Tuppers and Thompson, embarked on the Intercolonial after Declaration Day (Monday, 10 March) and were fêted all along the route. Their train got into Montreal well after midnight, and their darkened car deterred not at all an ebullient band and a hundred followers who woke Thompson up and got him to make an impromptu speech *en déshabille.*[67]

In the rest of Canada the Macdonald government polled a higher popular vote than in 1887, but won less seats. It picked up two seats in Nova Scotia, two in Prince Edward Island, and three in New Brunswick; but in Quebec the government lost five seats to Laurier and in Ontario seven. Only twenty-seven seats separated the Liberals from power. Rural Ontario seemed to have gone against Macdonald; they had really wanted unrestricted reciprocity. Sir Richard Cartwright, with that awful facility with words that so characterized him, was indignant that the Conservative party should have won; its power was but 'a thing of shreds and patches, made up of the ragged remnants of half a dozen minor provinces ... held together by the cohesive power of plunder.'[68] Thompson reacted joyfully to this. The Conservative party must not do anything to discourage Sir

Richard, he wrote Judge Johnstone in Sault Ste Marie, 'he is a great treasure to us. I do not know what we should have done ... without his foolish speeches in the u.s. and elsewhere, and his recent references to the Maritime provinces will place us under renewed obligation to him.'[69]

Edward Blake's West Durham letter the day after the election, criticizing his own party, came as a shattering blow to the Liberals. Some in the Conservative party and cabinet felt that it surely was an opportunity, heaven-sent, to detach Blake from the Liberal party. Thompson did not share this view. Thompson never really liked or trusted Blake. Though Blake could on occasion be open, frank, generous, his West Durham letter seemed to Thompson to illustrate every weakness of his character – his vanity, spite, and inconsistencies. Thompson told an Annapolis valley correspondent,

A man who possesses all these peculiarities in so exaggerated a degree can never be a useful friend or ally to anybody, as Mr. Blake has shown his own party so severely on two or three occasions, and therefore, in regard to that point I am unable to concur with you. I hope we shall never be so unfortunate as to 'win him by kindness' or by any other means.[70]

The Liberals did not take their losses in Nova Scotia or elsewhere lying down. Petitions were filed on 20 April against Conservatives in Shelburne, Kings, Pictou, and against Thompson in Antigonish. In Thompson's case it was the usual charges of bribery by agents, of clerical intimidation. Robert Borden and his Halifax firm would act for Thompson and the other protested elections in Nova Scotia.

The Liberal protests were generated by two things: the closeness of the election, and the gathering scandal against Thomas McGreevy and Sir Hector Langevin. That matter was making all Conservatives uneasy. Israel Tarte and some French-Canadian Conservatives had gone repeatedly to Macdonald in 1890 with strong evidence that McGreevy had been manipulating contracts given out by the Department of Public Works, and that Sir Hector Langevin was also implicated. Macdonald went to both Langevin and McGreevy; both denied that there was anything in Tarte's accusations but spite.

Macdonald preferred to let tried and true ministers run their own departments. Thompson remarked that he had never known in all his six years under Macdonald Sir John to make a promise about anything connected with the Department of Justice without consultation.[71] The obverse was that Macdonald could be caught in a Laocoön entanglement brought on by too great trust. He was devoted to Langevin, who had stood by him through a many a dark day; and now, by Heaven, Macdonald would stand by Langevin and accept his word that all was well. To delegations that alleged wrong-doing, to Tarte, Caron, and others, Macdonald threw up his hands. 'You may be right,' he told them, 'but what can I do? The Province of Quebec has its leader and I cannot do anything else than let things go.'[72] He was not quite that helpless. He wrote A.R. Angers, the lieutenant-governor of Quebec, who did not believe that Langevin could be guilty of anything other than the great imprudence of his long Ottawa co-habitation with Thomas McGreevy. McGreevy had had a room in Langevin's house ever since 1878, and lived there whenever he was in Ottawa. Angers thought McGreevy should resign his seat so that a parliamentary committee could not get at him. In January 1891 Macdonald was thinking of sending Langevin to Spencer Wood as lieutenant-governor of Quebec, and bringing Angers to Ottawa; Angers did not like that much. If Langevin had to be got rid of, he should make a decent show of it by going abroad for a year. Langevin's health was not good anyway; he had been advised in October 1890 to take a complete rest for six months. As Angers reasoned, Langevin could then on his return be rewarded for his past services.[73] By this time elections were on and the matter was dropped. But Macdonald lived in daily anxiety that sometime in the future the 'searchlight' would be applied.[74]

Langevin seems to have convinced himself that the whole matter would be disposed of by his answering no to a couple of questions in committee. Thompson believed, however, that Langevin was going to need a lawyer and a good one. He did not know how to broach the subject and asked Sir John Macdonald to drop a hint. In the end it was a chance remark of J.J. Curran's that brought Sir Hector around to Thompson's office in the East Block.[75] Thompson thought Langevin's position dangerous enough that he telegraphed B.B. Osler, in British Columbia on the government–CPR arbitration, if he could come. 'Can act if prior request to act for McGreevy is not in way ...' was Osler's answer.[76] McGreevy saw more clearly than Langevin the need for a good lawyer, but he was in more serious trouble. Osler would take some time to arrive; he did not in fact get to Ottawa until 23 June. Thompson thought it essential for Langevin to have counsel even in the interim and brought up Hugh Henry, QC, from Halifax.

Parliament opened at the end of April, and on 11 May Tarte moved, as he said he would, for an investigation of the scandals alleged against Thomas McGreevy, MP for Quebec East, and, by implication, Sir Hector Langevin, minister of public works. The issue went, without division, to the Committee on Privileges and Elections, which held its first meeting on 15 May.

On 12 May Thompson introduced Bill 32, his and his department's codification of the criminal law. Thompson did not intend that the Criminal Code pass that session, but he wanted it printed, circulated, and discussed. After second reading the bill would be deferred until 1892. Senator Gowan believed that a measure like the Criminal Code could not be pressed too hard or too soon. 'If you, as I suppose you will, invite fair criticism and promise ... to give effect to all that commends itself to you next session,' that is all that could be expected for such a large and important measure.[77]

The day that Thompson brought in his Criminal Code, Macdonald became unwell. A slight stroke occurred in an interview with the governor general. At the House that afternoon as he left to meet the governor general again, Macdonald called Thompson to follow him. They went to his ante-room beside the Commons, where Macdonald sank into a chair. He told Thompson something was the matter with his throat. He could not speak very clearly. Thompson saw his condition all too plainly, but tried to cheer him up, speaking of Macdonald's need for rest, that he should spare himself as much of the hard toil of the session as possible. Macdonald, ashen-faced, turned to Thompson and said, 'That is no use. The machine is worn out.'[78] Neither Lord Stanley nor Thompson, nor indeed the cabinet, liked the look of it. 'Sir John's condition is such,' Thompson wrote Annie, 'to make us all uneasy.'[79]

Thompson was also uneasy about his own family. Frankie was operated on in Montreal by Dr Roddick on 5 May for the problem of her hip. Thompson was so busy he could not leave Ottawa even to visit her. All he had was letters. Senator John Boyd reported the operation had gone well, that he had been in to see Frankie, who was as happy and smiling as if in full health, 'so I sat on one side of the bed, and her mother on the other; she just enjoying our talk ... Lady Thompson is *so anxious* to see you, that I thought I would write and urge you [to come] for she says, you think more of you[r] dear little daughter than all the Govt, and I believe her!'[80]

Macdonald rallied around too, and Thompson could report on 22 May that Macdonald was well and bright again. He was back in harness at the Railway Department and the House, though nursing his strength against late-night sittings.[81] Some of the other ministers were not so fully in harness. Chapleau had a dinner party on Thursday night, 21 May; so did Edgar Dewdney. The result of two ministerial dinners was that the government was actually defeated, on motion to adjourn, by 65 to 74. It was the first time that had happened in its thirteen years of office. Macdonald was upset by it; he had to come in from Earnscliffe to help bolster the Commons, while the juniors were out feasting. The government redeemed the defeat later that same evening, by winning – as it had to – the adjournment motion, 98 to 80, but the defeat put new vigour into the opposition. It was already vigorous enough. The House of Commons on 19 May Thompson reported as having been more disorderly than he had ever seen it.[82]

The burden of running the government fell squarely upon Thompson. Macdonald was nursing his strength. Langevin, the senior minister, was unwell. The following week Macdonald was in bed with a cold. Thompson would go over to see him every day, as also to see the governor general on business about the Bering Sea, Newfoundland, and cables from the Colonial Office. The opposition in the House grew still more noisy, 'like a lot of pirates prepared to make a rush,' Thompson reported. The prospect was anything but pleasant. Macdonald did not seem to be getting much better. Macdonald was afraid of another stroke, not a stroke that would kill him but one that would not. 'I hope to God,' he told Sir James Grant, 'I won't hang on like Mackenzie.' Mackenzie, afflicted with creeping paralysis, had sat in the House of Commons year after year, perpetually shaking and almost never speaking. The chances are, Thompson wrote gloomily to Annie on Friday, 29 May, that Macdonald 'will not be in the House again this Session – if ever.'[83]

Macdonald's last words to Thompson that morning had been about the succession. A few days before, at the end of a cabinet meeting, Macdonald put his around Thompson's shoulders, looked at him seriously and said, 'Thompson, when I am gone, you will have to rally around Abbott; he is your only man.' Now on that last Friday Macdonald had clearly changed his mind. Abbott, he told Thompson that morning, 'is too damned selfish.'[84] In mid-afternoon, a few hours after Thompson's visit, Macdonald sustained the massive stroke that deprived him of all speech.

In the House of Commons they were at it hot and heavy over the conduct of Sir Charles Tupper in the late elections. There was a Laurier amendment, on motion to go into Supply, that Sir Charles Tupper's conduct was a breach of his duties as Canadian high commissioner to Britain. Then at 9:50 p.m. Langevin announced the sudden, terrible stroke of Macdonald's. The House grew suddenly quiet, and with Laurier's agreement debate adjourned until Monday, 1 June.

Jane and Edgar Dewdney became Thompson's liaison with Earnscliffe. Jane Dewdney reported on 31 May that Macdonald was living on champagne and Apollinaris; she was not unhopeful, but Dr Powell's report to Thompson that day was that Macdonald was slowly dying.[85]

Thompson had intended to go to Montreal that weekend but that was now impossible. There were a dozen issues needing his attention. What happened constitutionally when a prime minister died in office? It was certain that the cabinet was automatically dissolved, and that a complete new government would have to be formed. What was not certain was whether the members of such a new government had to go to their constituents for re-election. This was a serious problem, since all the money votes from 1890 for salaries expired on 30 June. Macdonald had been concerned with this in his last interview with Thompson.

That weekend, too, Thompson was trying to bring about an arrangement by which J.J.C. Abbott would succeed as prime minister. This was discussed at Thompson's on Monday night, 1 June over supper and until the wee hours of the morning. Opposition to Abbott came principally from French Canadians who did not much like him, and from those in the party who feared that his prime ministership, inevitably temporary, would be simply a warming pan – as the *Globe* put it – for Sir Charles Tupper.[86] There was a great deal of talk of himself, Thompson ruefully admitted, but his intention was to refuse any such suggestions 'peremptorily.' Meanwhile, the Liberals could 'hardly keep their feet on the ground for joy.' The House of Commons continued to sit, with Conservatives busy cabinet-making in the lobbies. Conservative gossip was amusing to watch, Thompson wrote Annie detachedly, 'their new Premier will have the devil of a time and yet they fancy it is a vast honour.'[87] It was not an honour he wanted.

Macdonald died Saturday evening, 6 June. The following Monday Thompson and the cabinet went out to Earnscliffe to see him in the big room by the river, and the following day at the Senate where he lay in state for the public who, despite crushing heat, crowded in.

Time, events, and responsibilities had brought Thompson and Macdonald close together. Their relations were warm, cordial, built upon that slow accumulation of trust and even affection that Macdonald inspired. Macdonald admired much that Thompson did, especially his state papers, so cogent, spare and clear-headed; he valued his advice; he relied upon Thompson in the House. 'The best thing I ever invented,' he once told T.C. Patteson, 'is Thompson.'[88] Thompson's law was more coherent, compact, perhaps tougher than Macdonald's: the old man was better read in literature, biography, history. They complemented each other. One might even say that Thompson's abilities ended about where Macdonald's started. In the Commons their styles were different. Thompson's speeches were fluent, clear, precise; Macdonald's were rather slow and hesitating. Macdonald tended to choose his words as he went, like a man picking his way, stone by stone, across a brook. His speeches usually read better than they sounded. Nor would Thompson emulate Macdonald's practice, when the House was in Committee of the Whole, of leaving his front row seat and moving to the back benches to gossip. The House was much deeper set than now, and back in the sixth or seventh row Macdonald would gather half a dozen MPs and entertain them with his fund of experience and rollicking stories.[89] Rarely has Thompson opened up more than in his recollection of Macdonald. 'He was the father and founder of his country,' Thompson told the *Montreal Daily Star* reporter in Ottawa,

There is not one of us who ... had not lost his heart to him ... His wonderful tenderness, sympathy and patience gave him that attractiveness which has been called magnetism ... No one ever regarded him with fear, and yet no greater master of men appears in modern [Canadian] history. Few know how toilsome in detail and routine was the life which seemed full of great projects and great achievements. And fewer still can realize the gentleness and kindness of his disposition. History will have little to say of this probably, but our love follows him to the grave.[90]

The two men had in common their love of children, enjoying their company, listening to their ideas. The old man saw much of Thompson's family at Rivière du Loup in the summer of 1890 while Thompson and Annie were in England, and spoke affectionately and a little enviously of Thompson's 'little flock,' how they were all thriving in the summer sun and cool winds at St Patrice that Macdonald would see no more.

PART FOUR

BECOMING PRIME MINISTER, 1891–1894

17

The Wages of the Macdonald Era

Wednesday, 10 June 1891 was a scorching summer afternoon, so hot it drew 'the very soul out of one' as Thompson reported.[1] Macdonald's funeral cortège came slowly back from St Albans' Church toward the station at Sapper's Bridge for the journey to Kingston; the sunlight turned into a yellow sultry haze and an immense thunderstorm gathered to the west. As Macdonald's coffin was passing Parliament a sudden, fierce clap of thunder cracked out over the buildings and rain came down in torrents.

The inheritance of Macdonald began at his funeral. There was much that he had left undone, a whole range of loose ends, from the Crow's Nest Pass to patronage; many of the strands were crossed or seemed to lead nowhere. Of recent years Macdonald had drawn much into his own hands. His taking up the strenuous Railways and Canals portfolio in 1889 after J.H. Pope's death was symbolic of much more. There were few close colleagues who could advise him; Thompson and Langevin were about the only ones, and Langevin had since the late 1880s carried less and less weight in Quebec politics. Lord Stanley wrote that outside of those two none of the cabinet were any use outside their own departments. 'I think they all depended on him too much,' was Lady Macdonald's view, a month later.[2]

It was anything but easy after Macdonald's death. The party was in disarray, the session on, Supply not yet through, the Langevin scandal getting warm, the opposition hungry, eager, and ready to take power. Lord Stanley was virtually certain the government would go to pieces under the strain. The best that could be expected was a few months. Parliament adjourned for only a few days for Macdonald's funeral and the government found difficulty getting its breath. Strictly speaking, there was no government, for it was dissolved by Macdonald's death. Lord Stanley refused to consider having a new government until after Macdonald's funeral. Thompson was cross at 'the child in Rideau Hall' for this delay.[3] When Lord Palmerston had died in office in 1865, the Queen called Lord Russell the next day to form a government and that when Parliament was not even sitting.[4] The longer delayed the worse the problem got. The governor general's course, said the *Montreal Daily Star* severely, 'is not justified by precedent, not called for by sentiment.' The truth was that Lord Stanley wanted to know whom Macdonald wished as successor. Macdonald never said but it was rumoured that he had written it down or that the secret was in his will. Stanley told Laurier that the position of affairs was unprecedented.[5]

The members of the old government returned to Ottawa from Kingston by special train late Thursday night, 11 June, and the next day cabinet-making started in earnest. Reports from the graveside were that Thompson should have no hesitation in becoming prime minister.[6] Thompson himself had many. 'Few even in Ottawa,' he wrote to Bishop Cameron on 8 June, 'realize the difficulty of the situation which now presents itself ... it will be a very difficult task to reorganize the Government as we have a great number of conflicting interests and ambitions. My only personal desire is to avoid assuming further responsibilities myself. In this I believe I shall be successful.'[7] It was perhaps in part selfishness; mostly it was Thompson's reluctance to make the party follow the difficult path he had to walk. Being a convert was thorny enough without forcing himself upon the party.

Thompson was Stanley's first choice and the governor general pressed his point in ways that made Thompson's position both awkward and unpleasant. Thompson would try. He would need a Protestant lieutenant from Ontario, first and foremost. D'Alton McCarthy was frank enough; he said he would not serve under Thompson.[8] McCarthy's following in Parliament was not large, but that in Ontario was a more uncertain quantity. Another Protestant possibility was William Ralph Meredith, who was thought to be willing, and who believed that no one should be prevented from being prime minister simply because of being Roman Catholic.[9] That was fair enough, and it was widely held. Despite what French-Canadian papers said, it was not so much that Thompson was a Catholic as the fact that he had been converted to it that rankled. Protestants found that hard to abide. Rev. Dr George Douglas, principal of Wesleyan Theological College, Montreal, told the Niagara Conference of the Methodists that he 'must protest as well as pray against the appointment of Sir John Thompson to the premiership.' For Thompson was, according to Dr Douglas, not just a Roman Catholic but an extreme one, sending his sons to Stonyhurst; 'the Jesuitism of Stonyhurst,' Dr. Douglas elaborated later, 'from Pampeluna to Paraguay, and back again to the Vatican and Stonyhurst, has been, with disastrous finesse, the troubler of nations, as it is this hour a troubler of Canada, protected by the aegis of men like Sir John Thompson ... He is a clerical creation. He owes his political existence to the dictum of the Bishop of Antigonish.' Dr Douglas seemed to the *Gazette* like a Methodist Torquemada. According to *La Presse*, his main effect was to produce an intense pro-Thompson reaction.[10] J.J. Curran's advice from Montreal was that Thompson should have nothing to do with either McCarthy or Meredith. 'Such a coalition will destroy you and not save the party. I know some people [who] imagine they can do what they please with the French Canadian vote in this province – They are mistaken.'[11]

Still, the McCarthy contingent were worrisome. If the Liberal, J.D. Edgar, is correct – he often had access to accurate information – things became tense that Friday 12 June at the Rideau Club. 'I never saw,' Edgar wrote his wife that evening, 'such flushed and excited men as were at the Club just now – Abbott, McCarthy, Haggart, &c. &c. I think Thompson will fail, and I doubt if Abbott will try. Langevin *I know* is very sore today – as no one had spoken to him at all up to 5 o'clock.' Caron had not yet been invited to join any government; W.B. Ives (MP for Sherbrooke) was bitterly disappointed at not being asked to take C.C. Colby's place, who retired as president of council. C.H. Mackintosh was in trouble for his outspoken editorial in favour of Sir Charles Tupper that very morning.[12]

Tupper was the clear preference of a number of Conservatives, including Lady Macdonald. An attempt to boost Tupper began before Macdonald's funeral. C.H. Tupper encouraged it – family loyalty was one of the more agreeable traits of the Tuppers, father and son – but the idea of Tupper Sr was not strongly supported, and young Tupper was, according to Thompson, 'as mad as he can be at the cold shoulder which the old tramp has got in many quarters.'[13] Ontario Protestants, like Sam Hughes of the Lindsay *Warder*, wanted Tupper. He suggested that Thompson and Tupper should just change places. 'Quietly hold the boys together on those lines,' was his advice to Clarke Wallace.[14] Some elements in the party were so anti-Tupper that they promised to take the party into opposition rather than have him. Then old Sir Charles said he would not come anyway; he would be risking his health and his pocket to no good purpose.[15] Chapleau and French-Canadian MPs were for

Thompson with unequivocal enthusiasm. *La Presse*, a paper Chapleau had influenced since 1888, was embarrassingly fulsome on 4 June:

La voix publique très forte, très accentuée, a nommé Sir John Thompson. Il a plus que tout autre dans le groupe anglais, des méthods sociales de Sir John, sur lequel il l'emporte par l'éloquence parlementaire et la science constitutionelle. Son caractère est au-dessus du moindre reproche. Il est comme pétri d'integrité, d'honorabilité, son sens énorme de la rectitude dans les voies politiques, son amour du vrai, de la justice adéquate, ses vues larges dans les grands questions nationales, son intelligence étudiée avec précision, avec recherche même des besoins multiples d'une société cosmopolite comme la nôtre, si diverse dans son origine, dans ses exigences, l'habitude inveterée du respect pour les croyances religieuses de tous, sa tolérance inaltérable même des préjugés de ses compatriotes, toutes ces qualités portées au plus haut de degré font de Sir John Thompson un homme à part, appelé, s'il le veut, à faire face aux pénibles circonstances que nous traversons.

Chapleau and his friends were pushing too hard, Thompson told Annie.[16]

La Presse suggested that it was a case of 'No Catholic needs apply,' its English a little awry. French-Canadian Liberal papers assumed that if Thompson failed to form a government, it was clear evidence of strong Protestant prejudice in Conservatives. 'Ce que nous ne voulons pas voir consacré dans notre jeune pays, c'est que le poste de premier ministre du Dominion n'est pas accessible au plus méritant. Si celui-ci appartient à une religion qu'à une autre ...'[17]

Langevin's situation was sadder than anyone's. His son-in-law, Thomas Chapais, editor of the Quebec *Courrier du Canada*, expected that Langevin would be called to form a government, but suggested that it might be better to work under Thompson as prime minister rather than risk being stabbed in the back.[18] In the meantime, Langevin had an interview with the governor general that could not have been very welcome.

From a personal point of view, what could have been more agreeable to me than to have turned to Sir John's old friend and colleague, the 'doyen' of the Cabinet, and to have asked him to carry on the Government ...? But chance has decreed that, at this very moment, the Department, over which you have so long and so ably presided, has been placed (as it seems to me) in a regrettable position ... I have therefore applied to one of your colleagues to form a new Ministry. If you have been caused pain in this connection as I fear you must have been, let me hasten to say that personally a fully equal share of that pain has been felt by myself.[19]

Stanley, as consolation, promised Langevin a GCMG if all went well – that is if he and his department emerged immaculate from the inquiry.

That interview took place on Saturday, 13 June. It was on that day, or the day before, that Thompson gave up trying to form a government. He recommended J.J.C. Abbott, the senator from Montreal. On the Sunday morning, Abbott walked as usual to the Rideau Club for breakfast. His companion was J.D. Edgar of Toronto. They talked frankly. Abbott told him what a distasteful job he had now in hand. Both men had a high opinion of Thompson; Abbott was worried about Langevin. He would like to have known what the evidence against Langevin was, and hinted broadly to Edgar to that effect.[20]

Abbott took on the job of prime minister with great reluctance. The office came to Abbott, as Lawrence Power said in the Senate, like Diana's kiss, 'unasked, unsought.'[21] The party might have held under Thompson – there were many who believed McCarthy's pressure had little weight in it – but the party could not risk even a small defection of Ontario supporters and Thompson preferred the self-denying principle. Abbott was a stop-gap and called himself one. He was seventy years of age, had a comfortable home at Ste Anne de Bellevue on the western end of the Montreal Island and a substantial legal practice as a railway and corporation lawyer. Politics had for many years been for him something apart; it had never been the métier it had been for Macdonald. Abbott may have been selfish, but with his health uncertain, with no real aptitude or style for politics, he took the prime ministership mostly from a sense of public duty.

It was an awkward and thankless task, pulling together a government out of the conflicting elements in the party. Macdonald's strong hand removed, the party tended to revert to its several primitive origins: French Canadians with their internal divisions, Langevin versus Chapleau, with Caron as wild card; English Canadians from Quebec with their divisions; Irish from New Brunswick, Protestants from Ontario. It was Bleu, Green, Orange, and several shades in between. Some in the party believed that Abbott was not sufficiently a fighting man to be able to rouse the Conservatives. Donald MacMaster of Montreal thought he was too quiet, too tired, too much of an unknown to do good to the party.[22] Within a fortnight of his assumption of office, Abbott was regretting it. He found, for example, that Sir John Macdonald had taught everyone who wanted anything, 'situations and plunder ... fishery license or a railway,' to come to him. So deputations came. Abbott hated them; and, as with Sir John Thompson, deputations were apt to be counter-productive. Abbott told Hugh John Macdonald that anyone who thought he, Abbott, 'could be influenced by a deputation was a damned fool.' Abbott had soon decided that his term of office as prime minister would be as short as possible.[23]

There is a curious footnote to all this. That Sunday evening, 14 June, an elderly gentleman of unpretentious appearance called at Joseph Pope's house in Sandy Hill asking for him. Pope was not home, whereupon the visitor asked to see Pope's wife, Minette. The reply to this was not very satisfactory either, but the visitor persisted a little. Could he come in and sit down? The evening was hot and he was tired. Minette Pope, coming downstairs at this point, was surprised to find the prime minister of Canada waiting modestly in the hall. He had walked over, he said, to ask Pope if he would act as his secretary for a few months until Abbott got the lay of the land.[24]

Abbott took more to himself than just Macdonald's private secretary: Abbott rented Earnscliffe. Lady Macdonald became Baroness Macdonald of Earnscliffe in July 1891, but despite that she did not live there. She and Mary went first to a house on Gloucester Street, then west to Banff and Victoria. Abbott moved in to Earnscliffe in early July. It was very strange, Thompson reported. Abbott began giving dinners, of course, and guests came to them; but they looked silently about them in a strange kind of reverie, from which Abbott found it sometimes difficult to rouse them.

Abbott offered Thompson Macdonald's old rooms just outside the Commons on the way to the Library. 'Sir John, take them,' said Abbott when Thompson demurred, 'and do not disturb yourself. They belong to the Premier.'[25] Thompson refused as gracefully as he could. Eventually in the fall, pressed by Abbott again, he relented.

One condition Abbott made was that Thompson lead in the House of Commons when and if Langevin the senior minister, stepped down. This Thompson accepted; but another request of Abbott's, that Thompson occupy Macdonald's old seat, he refused. Thompson had for some years sat with Chapleau in the second row, behind Langevin and Macdonald. Thompson preferred to stay where he was and Macdonald's seat remained, for the time being, empty, a mute tribute to his death. Only in February 1892, at the beginning of that session of Parliament, was the change finally made.[26]

Parliament resumed on 16 June where it had left off ten days before. The government was not reconstructed. In fact nothing happened. Each member of cabinet was reappointed to his old portfolio, Sir Hector Langevin among them. The government was worried but resolute. The censure of Sir Charles Tupper was not to be a motion of want-of-confidence. This meant that upon C.H. Tupper would fall the main burden of defending his father, not upon the government. Consequently the debate ended relatively soon; the government won by twenty-one votes. Supply would be brought on, as the McGreevy–Langevin inquiry continued in the Committee on Privileges and Elections.

The Parliament that Thompson faced in May and after Macdonald's death was new in several respects from those he had faced before. Many faces had changed. John Carling, minister of agriculture, was now in the Senate; an easy-going, avuncular brewer from London, Ontario, Carling had been defeated in the election. He was still minister of agriculture, but had not much influence in cabinet; the *Globe* put it irreverently, as much as 'a babe in a riot.'[27] Edward Blake, the melancholy Dane of Canadian politics, was no longer in the House; the familiar sight of Blake's tired head resting on outstretched arms, partly hidden under his slouch hat – that was gone. The words that 'Blake is up' would no more run through the lobbies.[28] Peter White, MP for Renfrew North, had been the new Speaker Macdonald had chosen; he would remain Speaker for the next five years. His bald head and Arthur Bourinot's, Clerk of the Commons since 1880, made a curious combination.

On Peter White's right were the government front 'benches' – more properly desks, two by two. There were no benches, then or now. Most MPs did not have offices or secretaries; they sat in the House, listened to debate, did their correspondence as best they could. In the front row was Macdonald's empty seat, with Langevin beside it. According to parliamentary precedent, Sir Hector Langevin as senior minister led the House in Macdonald's absence. But beginning about 1889, more and more Thompson had taken over the work.[29] Even now, however, Langevin was still officially leader in the House of Commons, though his efforts became increasingly perfunctory. He carried in his manner his failure to be called to form a government. As one French-Canadian paper noted, his cheeks were still burning from the shock of it. In the House his bad humour was visible; when Thompson found himself a little uncertain about quite how to defer to Langevin, what role to assume, one correspondent said that Langevin did not even turn around from his desk, just ahead of Thompson's.[30] To Langevin's right were Bowell and McCarthy, to his left Caron and Foster. Foster's appearance – long, lean, and cadaverous – was eminently suited to his lugubrious personality. The minister of finance liked to sit sideways with one long leg over the arm of his chair, arms folded, and a tall white hat pulled down over his eyes. Caron, his desk mate, was the exquisite of the House; he frequently affected yellowish tweed, carried a rose in his buttonhole, and always sported a monocle.

Behind Langevin, and Macdonald's chair, were Chapleau and Thompson. Chapleau was in striking contrast to Thompson – Thompson compact, heavy-set, his smooth, bland appearance belying power and force: Chapleau, a long pale face, almost ravaged, his black eyes, sunk deep in their sockets, flashing out in anger under heavy grey eyebrows and an enormous mane of long grey hair. Chapleau looked stern, sad, saturnine; his was a tragic face, suggestive, as the Hamilton *Spectator* correspondent observed, of 'great power, inflexible purpose, terrible experiences'[31] – like Robespierre's. Macdonald thought Chapleau the most dangerous man of his acquaintance, capable of anything.[32]

Thinness was not a common attribute in the Commons. The biggest man in the House was the Liberal MP for Guysborough, Nova Scotia, D.C. Fraser, a giant in height and width, weighing in at 289 pounds. In August 1891, the members of the press gallery irreverently made a bet about which side of the House could produce the twenty heaviest men. The Conservatives won easily. John McLennan, MP for Glengarry was the Conservative champion at 278 pounds, followed closely by La Rivière of Manitoba and Earle of British Columbia. There were a dozen others, including Thompson, over 200 pounds.[33]

To Thompson's right in the same row were John Costigan and Edgar Dewdney. Costigan, minister of inland revenue, was a burly, lazy, Irish Roman Catholic from New Brunswick, with a pronounced taste for liquor and rarely seen without a cigar. He was described by an unfriendly critic as 'born tired.'[34] Edgar Dewdney, minister of the interior, a particular friend of Thompson's, was tall, good-looking, with a wealth of iron-grey hair. Neither Costigan nor Dewdney intervened much in debate except when their own departments were concerned. Nor was John Haggart, the postmaster general, much different. Haggart had married a bad-tempered and demanding woman, Caroline Douglas of Perth; and he seemed to have an eye for plump and accessible lady typists. It was hard to prove much against Haggart, but he enjoyed a raffish reputation that Thompson tended to believe was unjustified. Brusque, unpolished, able, he looked like a well-to-do shopkeeper, his light-grey coat thrown comfortably open, his knee against his desk, his thumbs stuck in the armholes of his white vest. The other important cabinet member was C.H. Tupper, minister of marine and fisheries. Tupper affected a huge brown felt hat and seemed to be always in motion. His actions were very like him: he was given to hurrying in and out of the House, plumping himself down into his seat, opening his desk briskly, looking at a few papers, then banging the desk closed again. He had much of his father's force and eloquence, but he had a touch of humour too often lacking in old Sir Charles.

One new member in 1891 was old Sir John's son, Hugh John Macdonald. He was a smaller Macdonald in every sense, shorter, narrower in mind, with something of the look of his mother Isabella Macdonald, the shrewd, alert expression of a fox.

Laurier was for the opposition what Caron was for the government – sleek, debonair, and polished. Laurier's grey coat and trousers were perfect – that is without a crease (formal creases in trousers became fashionable only in the early decades of the twentieth century) – his waistcoat white as snow, and like Caron, he always wore a flower. Laurier was much admired by the ladies in the gallery and looked as if he were ready to break into a smile. Indeed, it went further than that: Laurier left the dirty work of opposition to others, to Edgar, Charlton, Mulock, Davies, and especially to Cartwright. Laurier hated to hurt people. 'We have just come,' he wrote on 7 August to Emilie Lavergne, 'to what must prove the most unpleasant part of my task. To accuse, to recriminate, to hurt, to wound is not congenial to my nature.'[35] Laurier had a natural fastidiousness: he did not like dirt of any kind. He was content to leave disagreeable and nasty details to others in the party with less distaste for them.

Sir Richard Cartwright kept the opposition primed, with whispers, instructions, notes. In Blake's time he would even keep an avuncular eye on the party in case too many of them fell asleep in a Blake speech after supper; Blake was apt to take that amiss. Cartwright was one of the most incisive speakers in the House, and a master of saying vitriolic remarks in parliamentary language. He had a high, rasping voice; he reminded one of a bluejay, vigorous, noisy, and brilliant. He had a fierce face, grey side-whiskers, and looked the parliamentary fighter that he was. He had a decided habit of pronouncing blue-ruin speeches that despaired of Canada's past, present, and future. In June 1891 he had a boisterous *Schadenfreude* at the toils the government was in. In general Cartwright approved of Thompson, and said so in his backhanded way. Thompson, he said, deserved the respect of the House; his conduct was greatly to his credit, especially seeing the company that he had, unfortunately, so long kept.[36]

This seemed to be the general opposition view of Thompson in June 1891, to which were added a variety of metaphors to describe his power in the government. D.C. Fraser, the Guysborough giant, used a Japanese analogy: Abbott was the Mikado, the ruler *de jure*, but Thompson was the

Taikun, the leader *de facto*. He was, as Edgar put it, 'the brains of the combination. I believe the Minister of Justice will shape the policy ... Perhaps it was the stupid wing of the party that prevented his assuming that responsibility. All I can say is that he will have his revenge on that stupid wing before he gets through with them, and he knows it. He will dominate them as Disraeli dominated the country squires in England without their knowing it.'[37] At the Conservative caucus of 18 June the assembled senators and MPs welcomed Thompson as one who, having endured the slings and arrows of Dr Douglas and D'Alton McCarthy, had emerged stronger and better than before. For several minutes the cheers made it impossible for him to speak.[38]

Thompson and Abbott were determined to clean up the McGreevy-Langevin scandal. Abbott's big practice in Montreal was based on his legal expertise – he had not been dean of law at McGill for nothing; the two able lawyers who led the government in the Commons and in the Senate were going to scrub the government clean. Senator Gowan, Macdonald's old friend, said to Thompson, 'Mr. Abbott and you must succeed for you are both animated by pure motives, pure and patriotic motives, and your manner of life will make the work of purification less arduous to you both.'[39]

For there was no denying, not by the more discerning and honest of Macdonald's old admirers, that much was wrong with his methods. Not all the party accepted that, but some did, Thompson among them. Macdonald thought more of the ends than he worried about the appropriateness of the means.[40] Lady Macdonald thought the civil service had got into bad habits from what she called 'social nonsense' of Ottawa, that seemed to oblige civil servants of all classes and incomes to keep up what they called their 'position.'[41] That was only part of the problem. The government would of course have to be preserved; neither Abbott nor Thompson had any doubt of that. *Salus concilii suprema lex* was a rule Abbott and Thompson both accepted; but it would have to be scrubbed down, overhauled, and perhaps one or two doubtful timbers replaced.

That was clearly the question with Sir Hector Langevin. Owen Murphy on 26 June was the first to implicate Langevin directly. He said he gave Sir Hector $10,000 in $100 bills. There was no documentary proof of this; B.B. Osler's cross-examination of Murphy brought out adventures in escaping the American police and made doubtful his evidence.[42] Even the *Globe* admitted that one could not convict Langevin on the evidence of Owen Murphy. Still, as the Toronto *Telegram* put it, 'If Sir Hector Langevin knew what was going on in the Public Works Department and profited by wrong-doing he is a rogue. If all this crookedness existed and Sir Hector did not know of it, he is a fool. In either case he is unfit to be chief of one of the two great spending departments of our Government.'[43]

As much as possible Thompson wanted to get facts into the open. The Committee on Privileges and Elections had some one hundred sittings across that steamy summer, plus an additional thirty more of the sub-committee (which included Thompson) that was to draft the report. Thompson attended nearly every meeting of that big, forty-two member committee which met at 10:30 a.m. every parliamentary morning.

Thompson was still living alone in the house at 187 Lisgar Street. Mercifully the scorching June weather cooled briefly and for a time early in July it was so cold and wet that Thompson had a fire in the grate all one Sunday. Annie had taken the girls to a comfortable old hotel on the shores of Bedford Basin near Halifax, and where for the moment it was colder and wetter than in Ottawa; but they had as consolation what Thompson called, nostalgically, a view of 'that lovely sheet of water.' His own compensation for Frankie's absence was that every time he walked home from Parliament to Lisgar Street the little girls round about his house would come running to ask him how Frankie was. In his letter to her he hoped that 'my little razzle-dazzle must soon be running to meet me as she used to do.'[44] Thompson celebrated his twenty-first wedding anniversary on Sunday, 5 July by having Charley Tupper and Edward Kenny in to dinner. When they left at five o'clock the blues descended. The only way to ward them off was to work fourteen hours a day.

Thompson's weekday regimen began with the Langevin committee at half past ten. That lasted until one o'clock. He lunched usually with Charley Tupper, which was followed by Council from two to three. Then the House of Commons began and lasted until midnight or later. He was so busy during the week he could hardly find time to write Annie and could not get to the Department of Justice at all. By mid-July the weather had become blistering hot again. On the night of 16 July it was 82 degrees at ten o'clock in the Parliament buildings and the air was terrible.[45] With his style of dressing, it was doubly uncomfortable; not for Thompson the flamboyance of Caron or Laurier. In summer he wore a black frock coat, buttoned tightly across the chest.[46] 'It must be a great trial to you,' his old friend J.T. Bulmer wrote from Halifax, 'to be in a crowded room, at a temperature of 100°, with your temper at 1000°, hunting clever and unscrupulous thieves in the service and out of the service, knowing all the while that this is creating in the public mind ... a fear of the future and a distrust of men ... We look to you to defend the country from corruption, peculation and fraud and to probe right down to the bone.'[47]

The work of the committee proceeded *diem de die* under an impressive reign of harmony from both parties, simply because it was clear from the start where Thompson and the government stood. They would indeed go right to the bone. In fact the Committee on Privileges and Elections took up so much time that there were complaints from other committees that they could not get any of their own work done.[48] Israel Tarte was given a great deal of latitude in proving his charges, and was given legal assistance by the government defence lawyers, Osler and Henry. Tarte's own lawyer was paid by the government. Altogether some $15,000 had to go into the supplementary estimates to pay counsel for what the Department of Justice called, 'the Tarte–McGreevy matter.'[49]

It was generally admitted that the engineering work carried out by Larkin Connolly – the engineering firm with which McGreevy and Langevin were allegedly connected – was well done. If the profits were large, they were not much larger than normal, perhaps the difference between 20 and 24 per cent. Still, 4 per cent on contracts of $3 million over a dozen years was a tidy sum. There was also another inquiry instituted, through the Public Accounts Committee, on the costs attending the building of the Langevin Block. It was built between 1883 and 1888. Again, the efficiency of Langevin's department was brought under scrutiny.

There was a striking contrast between the way Thompson acted in the Privileges and Elections Committee and other ministers in the Public Accounts Committee. In the latter the old habits of ministerial reticence were strong. Mackenzie Bowell and John Haggart had a tendency to squirm at frank testimony and obstruct when the going got awkward. In the Langevin–McGreevy committee, Thompson was detached, dispassionate, like a judge; on questions about production of documents, procedure, or admissability of evidence, he was just as likely to side with Liberals as Conservatives.[50]

The civil servants were being hit by the Langevin inquiry. The chief engineer of public works, Henry Perley, was one. He had been with the department since 1871. Perley's grey hair, worn face, wasted frame, made one pity him; cross-examiners turned the shafts of questions this way and that, dropped them, picked them up again, as Perley wearily struggled to dodge the worst.

'Poor Perley,' Thompson wrote Annie, 'has rec'd his death blow. It was proved by one of these rascally contractors yesterday that they made his wife a present of some silver and jewelry to the amount of about $1900 about 4 years ago. He confessed to it all today ... He will probably be dismissed today and his grave will not be far off.'[51]

Sir Hector Langevin in the midst of this remained surprisingly calm and bright. Thompson was not ready to abandon Langevin; it would not be just or generous to throw Langevin to the wolves at the first cry of the pack.[52] Nevertheless, carrying him was a strain. Thompson admitted to Annie on 23 July, 'his scandals are dragging us under every hour.' The hours got worse. A few days later Laforce Langevin, his son, 'gave himself and his father away pitiably,' Thompson said.[53] The Liberals were confident in late July of forcing the resignation of the government over the Langevin–McGreevy and other scandals, reckoning on the sensitivities – Thompson used the word 'treachery' – of some Conservatives.

By this time the interest had long since gone out of the Commons. Thompson complained how dull it was.[54] The galleries were empty, and the House was barely maintaining a quorum; the sport was in the Committee of Privileges and Elections. The Liberals had built their hopes on the budget debate and it was dragged along day after day in the anticipation that something would be elicited from the McGreevy scandal that could be turned to advantage. The debate had been going on since June and their opportunities for confidence motions were numerous – whenever the House went into Committee of Supply. These were to continue through until the end of August; Laurier, Amyot, and especially Cartwright were active. Most evenings were debates on various attempts to unseat the government. One of the Liberal front-benchers told Thompson that they would be quite willing when they formed a government to have him as *their* minister of justice! Thompson replied, 'It will be so long before you form one that it would not be worth my while to wait on this planet for that!' Nevertheless, Thompson was anxious, half dreading, half hoping for Langevin's examination before the committee: perhaps the air would be a bit cleaner after that.[55]

Abbott and Thompson had concluded by now that charges of Langevin's receiving public money as presents or kickbacks could not be sustained, and they hoped Langevin's evidence would fully deny it. On the other hand, said Abbott to Langevin, 'the wholesale spoliation of the government by Charlebois – and other similar disclosures [in the two investigating committees] created a strong feeling against the efficiency of your department – which reacts to a considerable extent on yourself.' The danger was omnipresent: a motion of censure against the department, or the Commons refusing to vote Supply. Abbott's view, and Thompson's, was that such a motion might be supported by some Conservatives, and the result could be disastrous.[56] Something had to be done: what Langevin had to do was to submit privately his resignation, pending the decision of the committee. Sir Hector did not like that; but when he came before the committee on 11 August he had handed in his resignation as minister, though it had not yet been accepted. Laurier asked a question about it in the House of Commons that very afternoon.[57] Thompson admitted they were appointing an acting minister for the Department of Public Works in the meantime.

Langevin denied much; he denied too much. He seemed astonishingly ignorant of what was going on in his own department. He strained credibility too far. He said, for example, he had no McGreevy letters: the committee might well have suspected the truth of that remark.[58] When the evidence of others incriminated Langevin, he simply denied the truth of it.[59] In private letters to friends, he asserted, as in the committee, his complete innocence. He told L.-O. Taillon, leader of the Quebec Conservatives. 'J'ai toujours fait mon devoir consciencieusement, tâchant de faire autant de bien que possible et d'éviter de faire du mal ou du tort aux autres. J'ai servi mon parti, mon pays, et ma souveraine de mon mieux ...'[60] It was the same in committee; he seemed determined 'to sacrifice everything and everybody rather than admit the least trifle affecting himself,' as *The Week* remarked.[61]

At about this point the Baie des Chaleurs railway scandal, launched by the Conservatives in the Senate on 4 August, started to take hold. 'The Grits are in the soup now,' Thompson wrote Annie, 'over the revelations about Mercier and are quarrelling among themselves.'[62] The scandal pointed directly at the Mercier government and the Liberal party in Quebec, and it was plainly intended by Abbott as an antidote to the McGreevy–Langevin inquiry. Laurier admitted ruefully on 17 August there was not much hope any more of making any serious breaches in the government majority.[63] Israel Tarte on 26 August told the Committee on Privileges and Elections he would take no further action. He would not even address the committee. The Liberals on it stared at each other in dismay.[64]

The government grew a little more confident. Narrow though it was, the majority seemed to be holding, and Thompson carefully avoided opposing what looked dangerous to oppose. They held when they knew they had to. Cartwright on 13 August took the government to task for allowing testimonial gifts to ministers. He said it tended to corrupt not only the minister but departmental officers. His motion that such gifts be banned was accepted *in toto* by Thompson, much to Cartwright's surprise. It was a great satisfaction to the party to see the wind taken so completely from Cartwright's sails.[65] Amyot's motion about the Kingston graving dock was defeated by eighteen votes on 20 August; a week later the government weathered another Cartwright motion by fifteen votes. There was a cheerful Conservative caucus with the party in better fettle than it had been for some time, though, Thompson added, everyone is 'dying to get away.' Parliament was not over yet. McCarthy was still very sour on the front benches; he had been away much of the session, deliberately it had seemed to Thompson, but now he was back, cross that the government had fared so well in his absence.[66]

Thompson gave a big dinner on Monday, 31 August for Bishop Cameron and two clerical friends, Father Quinan from Antigonish, and Canon O'Donnell from St Denis, all of whom were heading west on the CPR the following evening. He had thirty guests at Lisgar Street; he had to hire a table that was big enough. It all looked handsome with asters and gladioli. The menu he was very proud of, sending it to Annie with comments:

> Little Neck clams
> Clear soup (splendid)
> Broiled mackerel (delicious)
> Mushrooms on toast
> A cold chicken entrée (very nice)
> Filet of beef or boiled turkey
> Snipe on toast
> Cheese soufflé
> Iced pudding
> Fruit cigarettes coffee etc.[67]

It is small wonder with dinners like those that the press gallery would place bets on parliamentary avoirdupois!

It was temporary relief only. Thompson was now saddled with drafting the report of the McGreevy–Langevin committee. McCarthy looked as he were now going over to the Liberals on the Langevin vote and Thompson feared unease among Ontario supporters. McCarthy was confident, he told Dewdney, that Thompson would 'bite the dust' from sheer exhaustion ere the session was over.[68] Thompson was sure that he would not. He wondered how many supporters McCarthy might pull with him? It was of the utmost importance to have the party fully behind the report of the

Langevin committee, but was it possible to do so and still save Langevin from condemnation?

For his resignation was, in reality, still pending. Although he no longer attended cabinet, and although there was an acting minister of public works, there was not yet a full minister. Langevin was still expecting to have his resignation refused. The Conservative majority on the Committee on Privileges and Elections were ready to whitewash Langevin if their conscience could take it, but they were not going to do it and have Langevin slide back into office. It was suspected this was what Langevin wanted to do. That was one reason why Thompson had great difficulty in getting the sub-committee drafting the report to agree; if the report did not condemn Langevin severely enough, he might resume charge of the Department of Public Works. Abbott put the matter squarely to Langevin on 5 September:

You will have noticed that questions have been put in the House lately as to whether or not your resignation had been accepted ... you might prefer to have the resignation accepted now, rather than allow the motive prolonged which they now have for embittering the feeling. – As of course we all know that the question of the finality of the resignation is now only one of a couple of weeks [i.e., to the end of the Session] ... It would be easy to write me a note stating that you perceive there is some misunderstanding about your position, and that in order to put an end to it, you ask me to accept your resignation.[69]

Langevin replied two days later in virtually these terms. There were questions in both Commons and Senate about his position; the reply was the government's chance to announce officially that Langevin's resignation was accepted 'as final.' Thompson presented it on 7 September to the Commons with the gloss that a resignation was a resignation the day it was received unless specifically refused.[70]

Thompson's report, signed by all three Conservative members of the sub-committee with Liberals Davies and Mills dissenting, was adopted by the main committee by majority vote on 16 September. The report said that Larkin, Connolly and Company had conspired to defraud the Dominion government and the Quebec Harbours Commission, in which they had been materially aided by Thomas McGreevy. 'This conspiracy,' wrote Thompson, 'has been all the more powerful and effective by reason of the confidence which the late Minister of Public Works had in the integrity and efficiency of his officers and [of] Thomas McGreevy.' The evidence, however – this was where the whitewash came in – did not justify the committee in concluding that Langevin knew of the conspiracy or 'that he willingly lent himself to its objects.'[71]

This came to Parliament with a minority report attached that went further, alleging that the money acquired illegally by Larkin, Connolly went into McGreevy's pocket, into Langevin's Montreal paper, *Le Monde*, and into party funds in Quebec managed by McGreevy in Langevin's interest. This cut closer to Langevin, but it still did not condemn Langevin directly enough to suit D'Alton McCarthy. He told Thompson some days before that he would not accept the majority report about Sir Hector's innocence;[72] it was clear he would not accept the Liberal minority report that merely implied Sir Hector's lack of innocence. McCarthy's motion censured Langevin directly. It was mowed down by both Thompson's forces and Laurier's by a vote of 184 to 2. The only person that voted with McCarthy was a Conservative, William O'Brien, MP for Muskoka.[73]

McCarthy was not moving close to Laurier. Just at that point, indeed, they were furious with each other. McCarthy went at Laurier in the House over Laurier's misquoting one of Sir John Macdonald's old speeches. Laurier took McCarthy's remarks much amiss. According to one source (admittedly Conservative), 'Laurier, white with rage, jumped to his feet, pounded his desk, and indulged in an exhibition such as was never before witnessed.'[74] McCarthy, discontented and restless, unhappy about the French, not at all comfortable about Thompson, was nevertheless a Conservative still, and still on the Conservative front benches. It is a curious sidelight on this that when young John T.C. Thompson started articling in Toronto in 1892, he went with the firm of McCarthy and Osler.

In Parliament the debate turned upon which version from the committee the House accepted. Israel Tarte refused to vote either way; he would not say what he believed. McCarthy and O'Brien continued to vote against the government. Notwithstanding, the government won, by 101 to 86, at 2:30 in the morning of 26 September. Some Conservatives stayed resolutely loyal to Langevin. 'Who can look at the faces of the men who confederated these provinces and not feel pained at the present fate of Sir Hector Langevin?' was E.M. Saunders's comment in the Halifax *Herald*, 'A fate he does not deserve ... Had the late Sir John A. Macdonald and Sir Charles Tupper been in the cabinet Sir Hector Langevin would not have been put aside, dishonored ... treated cruelly by his friends.'[75] The opinion in Montreal among Sir Hector's friends at *Le Monde* was, however, that it could have been much worse.[76]

That was not the end of it. Merely to uncover the wrong-doing was not enough. According to advice around Thompson, there would have to be prosecutions. Larkin, Connolly would have to disgorge what they had defrauded the country of. On that a civil case would go forward; Thompson hired B.B. Osler and Christopher Robinson for the government and eventually it was settled out of court. The more agonizing question was criminal prosecutions of the McGreevys and Nicholas Connolly for fraud. McGreevy was expelled from the House that September. Langevin believed that expulsion from the House was punishment sufficient of itself for McGreevy, but that view was by no means widely shared. There were suggestions that Uncle Thomas McGreevy knew too much to be prosecuted without danger to the government. *Grip*, on 16 January 1892, had a cartoon of Uncle Thomas threatening Thompson with a little black bag (resembling the one that Tarte carried) labelled, 'What I know of the inside operations of the Dominion government.' Said Uncle Thomas, 'Now then, Mr. Justice, you let up on this prosecution foolishness or I'll let this satchel drop!'

Nevertheless prosecutions went ahead. Robert McGreevy, Thomas's brother, whose machinations had brought on the scandal and who was just as guilty, went to prison in May 1892. His daughter wrote to Thompson that her father was innocent. Thompson was solicitous, but replied that there were no reasons for Robert McGreevy's release that could be brought to cabinet; it was unfortunate but impossible to take into account 'the distress occasioned to relatives ... The circumstances of your father's case have been a matter of very deep regret to me ...'[77] Robert McGreevy was released in the autumn. The trial of his brother Thomas and Nicholas Connolly, who eventually returned from the United States, came a year later. With the help of Robert McGreevy as crown witness,[78] they were convicted in November 1893 and sentenced to a year in prison. There were soon petitions for their release. It was said that McGreevy had avoided the 1891 committee to save his political friends, not himself. His wife and daughter, according to Martin Griffin, were penniless.[79] McGreevy was then sixty-six years old and Connolly only a few years younger. Imprisoned in Carleton County jail, they each became ill and Thompson was advised by the prison doctor that they ought to be released. McGreevy had inflammation of the middle ear, Connolly kidney disease; both had insomnia. Désiré Girouard, who had been chairman of the McGreevy–Langevin committee, visited them in prison in January 1894 and said he would never want to go through such an experience again. Both men were in pain, wretched, in tears, at their wit's end. Thompson recommended their release to cabinet late in February 1894.

There was a delay. It was rumoured that the governor general had, contrary to constitutional usage, refused the recommendation of cabinet. What had really happened was that the governor general suggested the government get a second medical opinion. The rule in such cases in Britain was that the recommendation of the prison doctor alone was not sufficient. Thompson accepted the suggestion at once, saying that it would be a useful precedent. The second doctor corroborated the first and the governor general signed immediately the order for the prisoners' release.[80]

As for the Liberals, they toyed with the idea of getting Sam Blake, the great Edward's brother, to talk to Thomas McGreevy, but McGreevy had only one aim, to get out of prison. According to Laurier, if the government commuted his sentence McGreevy would say nothing; if not, he would tell everything.[81] McGreevy lived to run for, and win, Quebec West once more, in April 1895, but died a few months later.

At the end of the 1891 session much of this was in the future. Thompson and the party breathed a vast sigh of relief on 30 September as Parliament prorogued at last, ending perhaps the most arduous session in the history of Parliament up to that time. But Thompson was at once plunged into a new crisis, sadder than any in Parliament. Already the Charlottetown *Examiner* had noted in its Ottawa report, 'Sir John Thompson's daughter is dying.'[82]

18

Steadying the Helm

Frankie had had a hip problem for some years, perhaps owing to an attack of infantile paralysis. Heroic efforts with traction in 1890 had no specific result. In late April and early May 1891 two operations to remove abscesses on Frankie's hip were performed in Montreal by Dr T.G. Roddick of McGill; during Frankie's convalescence Thompson worried and Frankie seems to have amused herself. J.J. Curran reported that the uproarious laughter going on inside Frankie's room at St Lawrence Hall – a long-established old place on St James Street – suggested that Frankie and her friends were 'having a high old time.'[1] Late in June 1891, Annie and all three girls went to Nova Scotia to the Bellevue Hotel on Bedford Basin nine miles from Halifax, a haunt of Haligonians who wanted to escape from town but still be able to keep an eye on it! Frankie did not improve much at Bedford and her condition continued to discourage Thompson and Annie.

In August the boys, John and Joe, arrived in Ottawa from Stonyhurst. Thompson saw that they got to *HMS Pinafore*, then playing in Ottawa (a curious accompaniment to the Langevin inquiry); he hoped to take them fishing up the Ottawa River but found it impossible to get away. They did not go by themselves, for which Thompson was grateful; he feared they would meet 'a fast set of young fellows.'[2] Still, John and Joe were after all, nineteen and seventeen respectively. They left Ottawa on 17 August for Bedford. Dr Parker, Thompson and Annie's Halifax doctor from older days, saw them all at Bedford and was not sanguine about Frankie. 'Her case is likely to be tedious,' he warned Thompson, 'and will require a continuation of her good mother's care and nursing ...' And, he added sternly, look after yourself; 'The brain like other organic structures of the human economy has a limit to its powers of endurance.'[3] F.J. Tremaine, another old Halifax friend, saw much of the family at Bedford that summer and was charmed by them. Frankie he got to love as one of his own, and the devotion of her mother and daughters and the way that the boys 'seconded themselves in everything to her' showed their character.[4] During all this the boys thought they would divert themselves by learning Thompson's shorthand; Annie asked Thompson to send down the requisite information, notably the four systems of joining characters that the shorthand required. Thompson said it would not be easy to learn. Some words were difficult and required a special technique; since there were no vowel sounds represented, words like 'deed,' 'roar,' 'favoured,' had tricks to them.

It was pale consolation to Thompson to explain all that by mail. The two older girls went back to Sault aux Récollects in September, and the boys set out for Stonyhurst. It was to be John's last year; he would be captain of the Stonyhurst soccer team over that winter, but it made Thompson 'exasperated beyond bounds at the idea of my not seeing the girls or boys any more for another year,' he wrote bitterly. 'What a year it has been!'[5] On top of that came news that Frankie was unwell again; something was very wrong with not only her hip but her throat and perhaps her lungs. It was all 'very, very discouraging. I was in hopes that that trouble was over and that the only question for the future was about her lameness.' He was left, as he put it with sardonic emphasis, 'worried and hurried.'[6] He could not even get down to Montreal to help Annie and Frankie off the train when they came to visit Dr Roddick once more. 'I could not keep my temper yesterday,' he wrote on 22 September, 'when I reflected after all we have gone through this year I could not even leave to help you ... I cannot help thinking of you and poor Frank every moment.'

The news from Montreal was much worse than they expected. Frankie was brought painfully to Ottawa to be nursed for the next three months, Thompson never sure what week would be her last. Almost as hard to bear were the too solicitous letters. J.A. Chisholm, Fan's fiancé, said how sorry he was 'to learn of the hopeless condition of Frank's health ... She is the brightest and best child I ever knew.'[7] Thompson's clerical friends were more experienced and would write about something else or tell a clerical story.[8] In the midst of this Fan Affleck was married to Joseph Chisholm on 4 November 1891 in a quiet ceremony at St Patrick's on Kent Street. There were no festivities beyond a wedding breakfast at Thompson's Lisgar Street house, after which the couple left for a honeymoon in Toronto and the eastern states before going back to Halifax. The first of six children was born in Halifax ten months later.

By mid-November Thompson thought each hour would be Frankie's last. Father Whelan was sure she was at death's door and said prayers for the dying. But, said Thompson with a palpable rush of cheerfulness early in December, 'the little pet would not hear of it and after being nearly into heaven she fought her way back and demands something to eat!' Frankie did not eat much, suffered a good deal, but managed to drink a quart of champagne every day. Thompson began to believe she would live. He wrote the boys that they were not to allow themselves to worry about her. They were doing the best they could with studies and with prayers and that was a great deal. 'Your progress,' Thompson wrote, 'is a constant source of comfort and pride to us.'9

Frankie recovered slowly, though never completely. Her hip would always be a problem and she remained lame. In May 1892 J.R. Gowan wept at the suffering he saw in her eyes.10 After canvassing New England possibilities, Dr Roddick suggested they all go to St Andrews, New Brunswick, for the summer of 1892.

Thompson's deepening sadness over Frankie in October and November 1891 was noticed by those close to him, strive how he might to carry on as if nothing were the matter. It turned up in negotiations with Christopher Bunting of the *Toronto Mail*. Bunting and the *Mail* had broken with the party in 1887 over commercial union, and the Jesuits' Estates question the following year added fuel to the bitterness. The Conservative party founded the Toronto *Empire* to be the standard bearer of the party in Toronto, though it never did have the bite or vigour of the *Mail*. Bunting claimed his ties with the Liberals had largely dissolved with Edward Blake's separation in March 1891. Bunting was, it appeared, ready to consider supporting Abbott and Thompson; he did not want to crawl back to the party but was ready for negotiations. At a meeting in Ottawa in September 1891, he found Thompson fighting shy of him and was displeased. This came to Thompson through a mutual friend.

Thompson took up the opportunity. 'I value the influence of the *Mail* very highly indeed,' he wrote. 'On more than one occasion his [Bunting's] paper has acted toward myself in a manly independent way which made me very grateful.' He cited the way the *Mail* had defended him when Travis tried to make a scandal. As for being shy with Bunting, Thompson admitted that was true, but not for the reasons that Bunting thought. Several times Thompson reflected how he must have dampened the feelings of the company that day. The cause was Frankie, who that day had been found to be much more seriously ill than he had supposed. 'We cannot always control our appearances when these things happen,' Thompson confessed.11

For the moment nothing came of these negotiations. Bunting's jealousy of the *Empire*, possibly Thompson's and Abbott's refusal to give a senatorship to Charles Riordan, the owner of the *Mail*, helped to keep the *Mail* at arm's length from the party; in any case the annexationist tone of the paper, Bunting's protestations notwithstanding, alienated Ontario Conservatives. By 1893 Thompson, while willing to try again, was no longer sanguine.[12] The end of the story was, however, that in 1895 Riordan bought out the *Empire* and the official Conservative paper in Toronto thus became the *Mail and Empire*.

Abbott embarked on a reconstruction of the government once the Langevin scandal was out of the way. This had been urged from the beginning, but seeing himself as interim chieftain, he made few serious efforts at first. His hand was forced by Chapleau.

Chapleau was restless after nearly ten years as secretary of state. There had been rumours that he insisted on the railways and canals portfolio when Macdonald died,[13] and to block that, Mackenzie Bowell was made acting minister. It was said in Ontario that Chapleau was after a department that had some blood in it; his alleged vampire-like qualities were frequent topics in the newspapers. A cartoon in *Grip* early in 1892 showed Abbott in his shop, 'Offices and Perquisities,' with Chapleau:

MR. ABBOTT (obliging shopman) – 'Er – um – Great Spending Department, sir? Sorry to say, I'm just out of 'em, sir! Last one I had in stock gone just before you came in, sir!'
CUSTOMER – '!!?**!!??' (expurgated translation from the French).

On the counter is a small but important-looking parcel, marked 'Mr. J. Haggart, the portfolio of Railways and Canals.'[14]

Thompson seems not to have shared this view of Chapleau, but like Abbott had to reckon on the antipathy to Chapleau and his style in Ontario. Ontario's antipathy was resented in Quebec. Israel Tarte warned that not all French Canadians could follow Chapleau's example of 'false moderation' in continuing to defer to Ontario pressures.[15] Chapleau on the other hand admitted there had been differences with his colleagues. He had threatened resignation more than once rather than yield. But in all of that he asked nothing for himself, he said. Whatever he asked was for his province. Why was there, he asked, 'a disinclination to recognize my liberality, an attempt to deprive me of an influence which I exercised only for the benefit of the party?' Ontario Conservatives should not judge Quebec by Mercier.[16] Chapleau even gave a speech at the Commercial Union Club of Providence, Rhode Island, to prove he was a loyal

Canadian, emphasizing the determination of Canadians to work out, at all hazard, their own national destiny.[17]

Early in November it was decided in cabinet that everyone should resign their portfolios, and let Abbott start with a *tabula rasa*.[18] This took time; most of the changes were not gazetted until January 1892. In a number of portfolios no change whatever was made: Thompson in justice (since 1885); Tupper in marine and fisheries (since 1888); Foster in finance (since 1888); Costigan in inland revenue (since 1882); Dewdney in interior (since 1888). These were the two Nova Scotian, two New Brunswick, and the Western portfolios. All others changed.

J.-A. Ouimet took over Langevin's public works portfolio. A conscientious and fair-minded administrator, Ouimet was the only French Canadian in public life to have graduated from Victoria College in Cobourg and he had a distinguished record as commander of the 65th Battalion in the North-West Rebellion. Haggart gave up the post office to Caron, so it went from being an Ontario portfolio to a Quebec one. Mackenzie Bowell, who had been minister of customs since 1878, now took over militia and defence. Customs also went from Ontario to Quebec. That was Chapleau's new role, minister of customs. The big railways portfolio that Chapleau had wanted went to John Haggart, the MP for South Lanark, able, businesslike, tough, and practical.

There was one more portfolio to be settled. Who would replace Macdonald as cabinet minister from Ontario? This was a major problem, to bring into the government a powerful, able, Ontario Conservative who would help consolidate the government's hold on Ontario Protestants. The principal candidate was William Ralph Meredith.

Meredith was a native of Middlesex County, five years older than Thompson, who had an exceptional career at the bar. He had become leader of the Conservative opposition in the Ontario legislature in 1878, and for thirteen years had laboured in that hard, ungrateful vineyard, trying to wrest control of Ontario from Oliver Mowat. In the recent election campaigns of 1886 and 1890, becoming a little desperate, Meredith had ridden hard the Protestant horse, arguing forcibly that Mowat's control of Ontario was owing to underhanded skill at keeping the Roman Catholic vote. Meredith made much of this in the 1890 campaign; but in his struggle with Roman Catholics he never secured Protestant support equivalent to what he lost.[19]

Abbott wrote Meredith on 23 June 1891 with overtures. Meredith had no great wish to enter federal politics; he told Clarke Wallace he would join the Ottawa government only under the whip of party necessity.[20] Senator Gowan thought Meredith decent, well-educated, with a capacity for work much needed in the government; Goldwin Smith found Meredith intellectually flabby and thought he would be too pliable to represent Ontario properly.[21] That was not, however, the opinion of the Catholic church, who had found Meredith their main enemy in assaults on their separate school system over the past years.

Meredith felt that a Catholic prime minister in Canada was quite possible; it would be a calamity if party policy ever got to the point of excluding a Catholic. At the same time he was opposed to bargaining with the church for political support. On language, Meredith considered that outside of Quebec English should be the language of the country. On these last two positions Meredith considered compromise impossible.[22]

The missing element in Meredith's confession of faith was separate schools, their present and their future status. Thompson was uneasy about Meredith, however great a respect he had for his abilities. Abbott gave Thompson the correspondence. Thompson was ready to accept Meredith if they could agree, but the letter in front of him did not ease his suspicions. The ideal Christian state could never be realized; that could be conceded from the start. 'For my part,' said Thompson, 'I am satisfied to take our constitution as it is and to work within[?] it while I am in public life.'

But Meredith's position on separate schools troubled Thompson. The conscience of the Catholic citizen was to Meredith the dictation of the Catholic church. He seemed not to understand the claim for separate education which was, for Thompson, 'that the state ought not to impose a system of education on any of its people whose conscience it oppresses – ought not to enforce taxation for such a system on the property of those who cannot avail themselves of that system without a violation of conscience.' Meredith's position on French language also seemed to Thompson impossible, likely to lead only to 'disturbance and irritation.'

If Meredith were apologizing for the past, Thompson concluded, all well and good. As apology it was not very adequate, 'but the past is of little consequence.' If, however, Meredith were adumbrating a program for the future, then no good could come of alliance with him. The Conservative party had lost Catholic supporters in Ontario because of Meredith's bitter comments in the 1890 election. Indeed, said Thompson, 'I should certainly have voted against his candidate, at the last general election in Ontario, if I had voted at all. Sir John Macdonald made the same declaration openly.' Before Meredith could join the Abbott government, the party would need to be sure that the acrimony of the 1890 Ontario campaign were a thing of the past.

Abbott's gloss on this softened Thompson's firmness. Abbott stated as simply as he could his government's policy on Manitoba schools and dual languages in the North-West. 'We hold to the legal construction of the B.N.A. Act,' he said. 'As respects Manitoba we expect these questions to be settled by the Courts before which they now are.' In the North-West, education and language will be left to be determined by the people of the North-West. Perhaps the idea that Meredith was against Roman Catholics and the French language, Abbott went on smoothly, 'might be removed by the exercise of a little tact without any sacrifice of principle whatever.'[23]

The proposal for Meredith to join the cabinet did not stop because of Thompson's serious reservations, nor did Thompson intend that it should. But the Catholic vote in Ontario was sufficiently important that precautions would have to be taken to ensure that Meredith was acceptable to the Catholic hierarchy. Upon Bishop Cameron's return from British Columbia in September 1891, he was asked by Thompson (and presumably Abbott) to visit the most recalcitrant of the Ontario Catholic bishops, Archbishop James Vincent Cleary of Kingston, and in such a way as to avoid suggesting he was an emissary from Ottawa. Bishop Cameron was welcomed in Kingston, but he failed to budge Archbishop Cleary from resolute opposition to Meredith. Cleary said he would be labelled a traitor by his own people if he countenanced Meredith's entrance into the Dominion cabinet. Furthermore, Archbishop John Walsh of Toronto felt exactly the same. 'Does Your Grace have anyone to suggest?' asked Cameron. Cleary suggested McCarthy! When Cameron remarked that McCarthy seemed a man of poor judgment and a party maverick in the bargain, Cleary then suggested Kirkpatrick (MP for Frontenac). This to Cameron's considerable surprise, for Kirkpatrick was by no means obvious cabinet material.[24]

This failure in September was not considered final. Bishop Cameron reported in November 1891 that Archbishop Cleary was still on the warpath against Meredith, animated by a vindictiveness unworthy of a Catholic prelate. In his time Martin Griffin had hit an archbishop harder than Meredith, to say nothing of Mercier's cuts at Cardinal Taschereau. All of this Cameron told Cleary: but he was impervious to reason.[25] Another attempt was made in December to sound out the archbishop in case his views had changed. They had not; if anything he was more convinced than ever that Meredith was impossible. So were his two suffragan bishops, Peterborough and Alexandria. Cleary's language was colourful. The 'bigoted fag end' of the Conservative party, represented by Protestant extremists, did not need Meredith in the government to keep them quiet. They would support the government because they had nowhere else to go. 'Why will the Government,' Cleary asked, 'cast aside the 400,000 Catholics of Ontario on account of Mr. Meredith and his handful of bigots?' And if the Conservative party was silly enough to alienate the Catholics, then the Liberals would 'take the Catholics to their bosom and hug them and pamper them to their hearts' content, and, then, good bye for many a long year, to any further alliance with the Conservative party.'[26]

There, at the end of 1891, was where hopes for Meredith joining the Abbott government ended. Although he was the darling of a section of the Conservative press, and although several of Thompson's correspondents suggested his name from time to time, Meredith remained leader of the opposition in Ontario until August 1894, when Thompson appointed him chief justice of common pleas in the Ontario High Court. The new Ontario representative in the cabinet was not Meredith but J.C. Patterson of Windsor, MP for Essex since 1878 but defeated in 1891. He became secretary of state in January 1892 and the following month would wrest Huron West from the Liberals.

Huron West was one of an extraordinary series of by-elections in 1891–2, Liberal legal protests on various grounds against Conservative seats won in the 1891 election, and, as offsets, Conservatives contesting Liberal ones. The Liberals hoped to use shock waves from the McGreevy–Langevin scandal to upset enough Conservatives to bring down the government. Between 31 December 1891 and November 1892 fifty by-elections were held, forty-four of them in the six months prior to June 1892, and most before April 1892.

Besides the by-elections there were some fifty-four other elections questioned on one ground or another before the courts. Of Nova Scotia's twenty-one seats, for example, seventeen were under protest, including Thompson's in Antigonish. Of these seventeen, twelve were against Conservative MPs, and five against Liberal ones. Thompson's old Halifax firm, now Borden, Ritchie, Parker, and Chisholm, handled most of these cases and did exceptionally well. Borden succeeded in saving seven Conservatives, including Thompson, from having to fight new elections, often on narrow, tricky technical grounds. It helped that in the midst of these struggles a New Brunswick judgment, *Emmerson* v. *Wood*, gave a victory to Wood in Westmorland very much upon the same grounds as those taken by Thompson and Borden. According to Thompson's friends in Antigonish, it was just as well that he was saved from having to run in a by-election just then.[27] So Borden's work was all the more appreciated. Borden even put up deposit money when Halifax friends were short. It confirmed something Thompson thought characteristic of Halifax, everyone 'wanting the earth and grumbling at everything and everybody,' and not willing to put up hard cash to back their talk.[28] Thompson considered it was not cricket to fall back upon Borden's good will and generosity, but he was grateful to Borden and said so;

I cannot express to you how grateful we are for your successful conduct of all these cases, including even those which resulted in the unseating of our members [3 of the 12 seats] ...

At the present stage of political affairs the Government cannot afford to have the slightest suspicion falling on ministers and even the unseating of Mr. Tupper and myself (should the petitions have had that result,) would have caused exultation among our enemies and depression among our friends which in ordinary times would not be realized.

We are conscious likewise that these cases have consumed a great amount of the time of yourself and your firm and that you are probably yet without any compensation. Will you at once make arrangements for calling on all those interested, including ourselves, to pay ...?

That letter says much about why people close to Thompson liked and respected him: his scrupulousness, his transparent honesty, his straight-forward bourgeois concern about other people's money, his gratitude for services well done. Thompson trusted Borden's legal acumen and judgment, indeed he gave Borden his 'most implicit confidence;' and it is clear from their long correspondence on this issue that they saw legal problems very much as one mind.[29]

The first of the by-elections was North Lanark, on 31 December 1891. Thompson went to Perth with John Haggart (whose constituency was South Lanark) to show support for Bennett Rosamond, the Conservative candidate, and to back up Haggart. Thompson had rather resented criticism of Haggart. The attacks against him came, Thompson felt, from Haggart's obvious usefulness; it was wrong to desert a man merely because of nasty insinuations. The MP mainly responsible for the attack on Haggart was one who, Thompson said, had been recently caught by a husband in the wrong Ottawa bed. It was not Haggart's fault, either, that a quarter of a century ago he had married a 'wild virago.' George Grant of Queen's University, Archbishop Cleary of Kingston, both of whom wanted Haggart out of public life, were too sensitive, especially Grant; 'sensitive politicians of the Grant class,' said Thompson, registering a native dislike of hypocrisy, 'are able to swallow a camel any time and make their reputation on gnats.'[30]

North Lanark had been opened by the appointment of the incumbent Conservative to the bench and had been Conservative since 1882. It was the first by-election since Abbott and Thompson had taken over the government. Of course they would not begin a long series of by-elections with a doubtful constituency, but the size of the majority surprised even the government, going from 301 at the general election of 1891 to 428. The trade question, the main issue between Conservatives and Liberals, did not decide the issue in Lanark. Rather it was decided by the results of the 1891 parliamentary session in Ottawa. If North Lanark was any indication, the Liberals had nothing to hope for from the McGreevy–Langevin scandal. That was the opinion of *The Week* on 8 January 1892.

In mid-January 1892, Thompson and young Tupper took the road for Nova Scotia, where there were seven by-elections (eight seats, since Halifax was a dual constituency) to be held between 21 January and 13 February. Reaching Halifax, they were plunged at once into the fray of political meetings, interviews, telegrams, demands. Both were taken ill. Tupper got a massive cold, said he was no use, and flung himself back to Ottawa.[31] But a huge political meeting had been arranged for Saturday, 16 January; the committee thought it should be postponed. Thompson, ill himself with something gastro-intestinal, said postponing was no use, got out of bed, went to the meeting, and earned a splendid reception. Even the *Morning Chronicle* was complimentary.[32] The next week he had to go to Antigonish, in the process investigating such delights as what was the matter with repairs to the Cape George lighthouse to occasion a long correspondence in the Department of Marine and Fisheries. He visited Richmond County and found the results there – the first of the Nova Scotia elections – decidedly cheering. On the train back to Montreal on 26 February he had the good news from Victoria in Cape Breton, a victory that even Cahan had thought improbable.[33]

The work continued after his return to Ottawa. Young Tupper went back to Nova Scotia to help fight Queens, Kings, Digby, and Halifax. Tupper was sure they could win the first two with money, probably about $2,000 for Queens, $1,000 for Kings. Indeed, he said, 'ammunition [was] indispensable.'[34] A.B. Morine, the Nova Scotian who doubled improbably as a Canadian spy in Newfoundland (and who had a seat in the Newfoundland Assembly), was running as the Conservative standard-bearer in Queens County. Morine left Thompson with the feeling he had a tiger by the tail. Eager, enterprising, erratic, energetic, and exacting, Morine insisted in repeated telegrams (collect) that he would have to have more money or else retire from the contest. The following is a fair sample, sent from Halifax, 9:11 p.m., Saturday, 6 February 1892:

Came here tonight for extra funds [.Have] only seventeen fifty[.] With three thousand can win[.] with less will certainly lose[.] can get cash for remaining twelve fifty if payment assured[.] must have that assurance tonight so can go to county tomorrow or all lost[.] will that assurance be given[?] rush reply tonight as I await it and delay [will] destroy me.[35]

Other telegrams to the same effect pursued Thompson across Ontario. Henry Cargill, trying to recapture East Bruce, was furious because no one important from Ottawa was coming to *his* constituency. Curran was then asked to go and Thompson got to Walkerton in East Bruce somehow. Carling wanted him in London. Carling was attempting to recapture London for the government after nine months as a senator.[36]

Morine did not succeed in Queens, however much the sum that finally went to him.[37] He reduced the Liberal majority but the result, 242 to 171, does not suggest that more money would have made a substantial difference, though Queens County was said to be thoroughly venal. 'I see,' wrote Thompson to Annie, 'that Morine was defeated in Queens by a small majority. There is a good deal of consolation in that.'[38] Morine would not be in the Canadian Parliament, to Thompson's considerable relief; Newfoundland was the place for him.

Thursday, 11 February 1892 was a great day for the Conservatives. Six by-elections were held that day, three Conservative seats and three Liberal. The Conservatives won their three, including the two-member Halifax riding; but the Liberals held only one, Peel County. Bruce East and Victoria North, in both of which Thompson had made speeches, went Conservative. (Victoria North brought Sam Hughes into the House for the first time.) The Liberal Montreal *Herald* called the day a Waterloo as it tried to salve party wounds.[39]

By the time the returns of the next few weeks were in, the Liberal party was fairly staggered. The Conservatives retained twenty-two seats, Liberals eight; but the body blow was the Conservatives taking eighteen Liberal seats. Liberals took only one from Conservatives and that was an extra seat Langevin had won. The Government majority in the Commons, from being twenty-seven in 1891, was now over sixty.

Goldwin Smith claimed that the Conservatives had won the by-elections on the strength of the public belief that they, not the Liberals, could bring reciprocity from the United States.[40] Laurier believed the same thing, convinced that Liberal weakness came from voters' belief that the Liberals could not deliver what they were advocating. Laurier told John Charlton in March 1892 that American endorsement of the Liberal party's unrestricted reciprocity was vital. So much was this the case that Charlton was sent in great secrecy to Washington late in March to secure it.[41] *Grip*, on 26 March 1892, was sceptical. 'What a toothache the Reform party has! Government majority over sixty and more to come!' The answer was to get rid of some of the bad teeth in the Liberal jaw. The Liberal party would have no comfort until some pulling was done. That unrestricted reciprocity incisor ought to come out and the Cartwright molar as well.

One redoubtable Conservative who had been largely absent from the by-elections was Chapleau. He had left for Savannah, Georgia, for his health. There were hints in February that he might like to join Canadian ministers on negotiations in Washington. Abbott took an instant dislike to that. Either Chapleau was sick or he was not. If he was too ill to work in the by-elections, he was too ill to appear in Washington. Moreover, Abbott told Thompson, he knows nothing about the subjects under discussion.[42]

There was always a considerable agenda of American business in these years between 1886 and 1892. The British minister in Washington did his best with the long-standing and often prickly tangle of Canadian-American relations. Usually it meant an awkward three-cornered correspondence with London and Ottawa. Sir Julian Pauncefote complained of this method and began to write to Lord Stanley directly. There were three main items of business: the Bering Sea fur seals, reciprocity, and the Alaskan boundary.

The North Pacific fur seal was valuable for a thick inner fur, like that of beaver. It was pelagic, like most seals and sea-lions (it resembled more the latter), swimming north along the one-hundred-fathom line of North America and Asia in May, to reach the Pribiloff Islands in Alaska and the Kommandorski Islands in Russia. The bulls arrived first, and as the females arrived they were incorporated into various harems of about fifty or so each. The pups were born on the islands, for the cows were usually pregnant. Hence the danger of pelagic sealing to the American herds and why the United States tried to stop it. It could be argued that the land-based lessee, the Alaska Commercial Company, could at least choose seals for slaughter better than could the pelagic sealers. The three-year-old bachelor seals were superfluous, for example. The Americans decided that they had a moral and commercial duty to protect the seals on the high seas while at the same time killing them on land. In order to do this they had to strike some new and hitherto unsustained arguments in international law; so far they had done so on a wholly unilateral basis.[43]

In 1890 the British government, driven by Lord Salisbury, had ordered the British navy to protect Canadian sealers in the Bering Sea. The United States could not be allowed to act as if the Bering Sea were their private lake.[44] Following that, Pauncefote and Blaine reached agreement on a modus vivendi that would prohibit sealing until May 1892; in the meantime each country would send an investigator to the Pribiloff Islands and proposals for arbitration could be discussed. The Canadian government were uneasy about these discussions; they feared arbitration of the Bering Sea question; they were certain Americans would back out of compensation, still pending, for the Canadian vessels seized by the Americans in 1886, 1887, and after. Lord Stanley could not see why the issue of specific damages need be mixed up with the overall arbitration, but Thompson and Tupper had been insistent. The Canadians, Stanley told Lord Salisbury, 'are firmly convinced that the United States will wriggle out of the payment of damages (should the case be given against them) after they have once secured the arbitration.'[45] Salisbury continued to exercise pressure on the Canadians through Stanley. He had taken up the practice of telegraphing Stanley behind the backs of Lord Knutsford and the Colonial Office. The issue was fought all that August and September 1891, the Canadian cabinet led by Abbott and Thompson kicking hard and the governor general trying to make peace. By early October a slight opening occurred. If Salisbury were willing to back the Canadian claims for damages, the cabinet might concede the general point on arbitration.

Thompson's reluctance was based upon fears, going back to 1871, that the British would not stand by Canada if it were in British interest to do otherwise. In this respect Salisbury's action in readying British ships in 1890 to back Canadian sealers had helped to some extent. Still, said Lord Stanley, in a reflective mood,

Canada is just at the stage when she cannot walk alone, and yet rather resents being led. Another quarter of a century will see her either an independent State in defensive alliance with the mother country, or else annexed to the United States. Personal loyalty to the Queen is a stronger feeling than it appears to be at home, but it is personal to her, and the Presbyterians and Methodists who are the backbone of the Dominion, have been grievously exersised [sic] over the doings of the Queen's immediate descendants ... I do not think that the co takes a sufficiently broad view of questions such as Copyright, Loadline legislation, etc. A little latitude about such matters is a cheap price for the alternative route to India and Japan, and I fear that this is what our departmental friends in the co are apt to forget.[46]

Pauncefote signed the agreement to arbitrate and the procedure for it on 18 December 1891. The February 1892 meeting would then deal with reciprocity and the Alaskan boundary.

Stanley briefed Pauncefote. Three men were coming to Washington – Thompson, Bowell, and Foster. Thompson, whom Pauncefote knew already, was more at home in law than in business; Bowell, former minister of customs, knew details but don't expect, Stanley said, broad views. Bowell was straightforward and honest. G.E. Foster was straight but narrow. Before leaving Ottawa the three came to see Stanley. He warned them not to be touchy if they did not see as much of Blaine as they felt they should. They ought not to mind being handed over to Blaine's assistant, General J.W. Foster, unless it was meant as a deliberate slight. Stanley thought that the sensitivities of the Canadian ministers were not so much on their own account, but they did not want to do anything that 'might be supposed to be *infra dig.* by Parlt. here where every little detail will be criticized by a very bitter opposition.' Canada did not want favours: only fair dealing.[47]

They left Ottawa on 8 February, the snow heaped up as high as the roof of the railway car, and arrived in Washington the next afternoon, the grass six inches high, flowers for sale in the streets, the sun hot and their heavy coats impossible. As for their fur hats, Thompson said, they did not dare let those even be seen![48] They were installed in a fine suite at the Arlington on Vermont Avenue north of the White House. The British embassy was near Dupont Circle, just off Connecticut Avenue, a half-mile distant. They met Pauncefote there at 10 a.m. on Wednesday, 10 February, and went on to the State Department for conference with Blaine.

These meetings continued for the next two mornings, and they were not handed over to J.W. Foster, although he was there. Blaine was unusually affable and forthcoming, really on his best behaviour. There was much good will on both sides, the British minister noted. Despite that, there were no commercial concessions. Thompson telegraphed Abbott, 'Blaine favoured unlimited reciprocity. Declined again to agree to arrangement which would not include manufactures. He intimated that it would be indispensable that Canada should make her tariff uniform with the States and discriminate against all other countries – especially Britain.' Abbott kept trying to keep the door open: 'Pray consider if we should not show a disposition to go beyond strict limit of natural products but guardedly.' To this Thompson replied, with a certain terseness, 'Can you suggest any manufactures to be admitted with discrimination?' Abbott could not.[49] At one point toward the end, Blaine burst forth, 'Gentlemen, there is only one satisfactory solution of this question – *it is to let down the bars.*' He then proceeded with all the force and verve of which he was capable to lay down a program for complete commercial union.[50]

Thompson, Foster, and Bowell could only point out that Canada's relation to Great Britain, as well as her own financial needs (70 per cent of her revenue coming from the tariff) stood in the way. The United States would not give reciprocity on natural products alone. Canada could not give the United States preference in manufactures over Great Britain. Blaine simply asked more than Canada could give.[51]

Thompson also put to Blaine, more informally, a proposal to refer the Alaskan boundary question to some impartial authority to decide what the true boundary was. Blaine countered with the idea of a joint survey, which would report in two years. Although Thompson recognized that the key was the interpretation of the Anglo-Russian Treaty of 1825, Blaine's proposal was accepted and the survey begun in 1893.[52]

On the Saturday morning they were invited to meet President Harrison. Thompson, who had not much admired Cleveland, found Harrison no better, 'a contemptible no-body with all the airs of an emperor.'[53] Blaine continued to be gracious, walking back to the Arlington with them, chatting all the way. They dined with General Foster that night, with Blaine Sunday night. One of Blaine's last remarks was a complaint about alleged discrimination by Canada in tolls on the Welland Canal, about the only jarring note.

Blaine had had prolonged bouts of illness, hence the presence of General Foster at the president's request. Pauncefote had found Blaine difficult to deal with, dilatory, erratic, and while gifted, now afflicted with painful lapses of memory.[54] Nor were Blaine's relations with President Harrison good. Blaine had hopes of winning the Republican nomination in 1892, and would resign as secretary of state in June in order to run for it. He did not get it, his health continued to deteriorate, and he died in January 1893.

In the long and complicated history of Canadian-American relations the February 1892 negotiations marked a distinct stage. The Canadian government finally turned away from prospects of reciprocity with the United States, and within a year and a half even the Liberals altered their position.

Blaine's complaints about discrimination on the Welland Canal were not without cause. Canada had offered in 1891, by order-in-council, a 90 per cent rebate of Welland Canal tolls for all wheat of whatever country being sent on to Montreal. Discrimination between the vessels of the two countries in tolls on the Canadian canals was forbidden by the Treaty of Washington in 1871. Technically, indeed, there was none; but usually only Canadian vessels sent wheat to Montreal. To Blaine's objections the

Canadians said there was no discrimination; if the Americans wanted the order-in-council eliminated there would have to be a quid pro quo, such as free navigation of the New York State canals. The Americans said no, and then imposed a blatantly discriminatory toll on Canadian vessels using the American canal at Sault Ste Marie.[55] The problem for Canadians was that although the American action violated the spirit of the Treaty of Washington, the Sault Ste Marie canal was not specifically mentioned in that treaty.

Abbott had a badly divided cabinet on what to do. In early August when the Sault Ste Marie question arose, the cabinet was a mere rump, only Bowell and Dewdney. Young Tupper was in England, Thompson was at St Andrews with his family, and the others spread all over. In the three-man cabinet, Bowell was inclined to be tough, Dewdney peaceful. Abbott, and Thompson too by letter, disliked very much the humiliation of being compelled to back down from doing what they believed Canada had a right to do. But to Abbott peace seemed better than entering upon a squabble with no discernible end. There was a whole host of uncomfortable possibilities if the Americans chose to get nasty. In August 1892, with a presidential election campaign already beginning, Americans could hardly be expected to be solicitous. Dewdney felt that Canada had to give way or show fight, and in the latter case Canadian shipping interests in Lake Superior would suffer.[56]

As the cabinet gathered in mid-August, the division ramified. Haggart, Bowell, and Foster were all for resistance; Abbott, Dewdney, and Chapleau were for peace. Chapleau was vehement that the Yankees were right. He had apparently been in correspondence with President Harrison's son, and was in any case ready to needle his colleagues for excluding him from the Washington negotiations in February. The positions of Ouimet, Carling, and Smith were unknown. Young Tupper in England would almost certainly have been for fighting. Thompson, as usual, was for the position he believed was right, cost what it would. He backed the resisters. The Montreal *Gazette* supported Abbott. The fact was, it said, that 'the Americans propose simply to apply our own methods to ourselves.'[57] Thompson would not have agreed with that, but at the meeting on 13 August the doves had their way, and Canada backed down. As face-saver for the hawks, the question was to be reconsidered over the autumn and winter. Abbott proposed to cancel the offending order-in-council and compensate those who had made contracts on the assumption of its continuance.[58]

But it was humiliating to have to knuckle under to inflammatory editorials such as that in the *New York Sun*, 'Put the Screws to the Canadian Tories!' urging the same retaliatory Sault Ste Marie technique be used against the Grand Trunk and the Canadian Pacific railways, to bring Canada to her knees and to give a strong push for 'the political fusion of Canada and the United States.' It was equally humiliating to have independent friends, such as the Toronto *Telegram* come out with:

Canada is disgraced, betrayed and humiliated by a Government that takes a position which it cannot maintain with honour and from which it must retreat with infamy ...

If a back-down is to be the climax of the Government's canal policy, then that Government's true function is mirth-making in a comic opera.[59]

Afterwards Bowell still remained tough-minded, urging Thompson to get Haggart to set up three relays of men every twenty-four hours in order to finish the Canadian Sault Ste Marie canal.[60] The Canadian canal was ready in 1895, and in 1896 the Americans opened a vast enlargement of theirs. Traffic in both canals was by that time enormous. In 1905 the traffic in both was double that of Suez.

It was fortunate that Parliament was not in session. When it had opened late in February 1892 it wore a different appearance from the previous session. Langevin had been moved across the House to the front row of a group of seventeen Conservatives that sat on the Speaker's far left, near the sergeant-at-arms. This group included Amyot, Davin, La Rivière, and a dozen others. Langevin looked worn, old, and ill, and was probably suffering from jaundice. The Liberals looked ill too, from other causes; they were gloomy, and their gloominess would get worse.[61]

The government had come unabashedly to Parliament and reported that on reciprocity the Americans said no, and as far as Canada was concerned, that was the end of it. In a few crisp sentences Foster laid before the Parliament the main results. Thompson did not hesitate to ascribe the aggressiveness of American intentions to the Canadian Liberals, whose machinations were highly suspect, and whose banner of 'war, pestilence and famine' would never rally Canadians, young or old.[62] The fact was that the Canadian wheat crop of 1891 – so heavy that Dewdney reported the CPR could not handle it all – and bad European crops, had produced a marvellous escape from the effects of the McKinley tariff.[63] It was very difficult, said young Tupper, needling Sir Richard Cartwright, 'to howl very loudly into the mouth of a cornucopia...' The best Sir Richard could do, said Tupper, was to hope that good crops would stop; but he would have to be patient, awaiting the arrival of bad crops, weevils, and potato bugs.[64]

Then, on 16 April J.D. Edgar launched his ten charges against Sir Adolphe Caron. The charges were sweeping: from government subsidies to railways in the Lac St Jean region, Sir Adolphe, as MP and minister, had creamed off substantial amounts into Conservative election funds between 1882 and 1891. If successfully prosecuted, Edgar's charges might stem ebbing Liberal support and prove that Thompson's and Abbott's claim of pure government was a myth.

Sir Adolphe Caron was about Thompson's age. He had been a gay blade in Ottawa in the 1870s, a young, gregarious MP for Quebec County, who had won his knighthood for his administrative performance in the Saskatchewan Rebellion. He was connected through his sister Corinne with the Liberals; she had married Charles Fitzpatrick, who was now professor of criminal law at Laval University and MLA for Quebec County. Fitzpatrick was sometimes thought of by the Liberals as a Conservative spy in their camp; and indeed there was some truth in this. In a private letter to Caron, Fitzpatrick warned him that Edgar had framed his charges, especially the tenth, to compel production of Macdonald's correspondence with McGreevy, and it was doubtless in Caron's interest, as well as the government's, that this be prevented.[65]

Caron denied the Edgar charges absolutely. Thompson, who for many years had been a close associate of both Caron and Alice Baby Caron, took on Caron's defence. Whatever Caron's guilt might or might not be, said Thompson, there were different places for different accusations. For a start, no one in the House of Commons had been an MP from 1882 to 1891. There were only MPs from 1882 to 1887, 1887 to 1891, and 1891 to the present. What Edgar was really after, Thompson said, was what Caron had been doing in the elections of 1882, 1887, and 1891. The place for claims about corrupt elections was the courts not the Commons. The place for claims against the government for making improper subsidies to railways was, indeed, the House of Commons; but there was neither duty nor right on the part of the House to deal with the private character of any MP. That was for the constituencies. What the House of Commons could do was judge whether an MP had betrayed his trust as MP. Even that the House did not do well, for those were 'judicial functions,' said Thompson, 'which we so rarely like to exercise, and which we so rarely exercise well.'[66]

Edgar wanted his charges tried by the Select Committee on Privileges and Elections, but for several reasons the government resisted that. Its experience in 1891 with McGreevy–Langevin had made it wary. The committee was very large for one thing; its rules of evidence were such that the committee required constant and vigilant watching by the government. Consequently the government moved that all the charges – save the tenth that Thompson deemed simply an enormous election trial – be referred to a royal commission to examine the evidence. This would take the Edgar charges out of committee, and for the time being even out of Parliament. Committees end when Parliament prorogues; a royal commission can marshall its evidence and witnesses at leisure. When the royal commission reported to Parliament, its freight being mainly evidence, would be the time when Parliament would be able to consider how serious (or not) the charges were.[67] The Liberals opposed this tactic, but they lost by 63 to 125, a majority that made very clear the new strength of the government.

As Thompson suspected, the Edgar charges were contrived to arouse Conservative fears, on the principle 'where there's smoke there's fire.' Newspapers and politicians were always making accusations. In 1885 the Winnipeg *Free Press* made charges against Caron saying, 'We are not making these charges at random ... We know that they are true; we can prove that they are true.' That sounded decisive; it was not. Asked about the charges subsequently the *Free Press* editor blithely said, 'Of course newspapers cannot wait ... when they honestly believe a thing, they treat it as a fact.'[68] Still, Conservatives were uneasy. One supporter from Quebec wrote Thompson, 'I *never* heard a public man spoken of as well of as you ... Good God, is there no way of that name being retained ... the general opinion is that Caron ought to resign and relieve you – because you are the one that suffers.' Thompson replied that the government's conduct in ordering a royal commission investigation ought to 'remove from your mind any impression that we were unwilling to submit one of our colleagues to have his conduct investigated.' Every charge was there, said Thompson, but the last one, and every charge would be investigated.[69]

It was a stand Thompson had made several times the past winter; real evidence of wrong-doing by any official, MP or minister, would be fully investigated. *Grip* portrayed Thompson outside a pawnshop, turning his pockets inside out, looking for the pawnticket to redeem those pledges. In another, *Grip* showed McGreevy and Langevin in a bog marked 'boodle,' trying to drag Caron in, with Caron clutching determinedly at Thompson's legs to save himself.[70] Conservative reaction to the royal commission was expressed in a note to Thompson:

God knows I could not well tell you what my 'impressions' were. I know well enough what my *fears* were. I was afraid some Bob McGreevy might be in the cupboard who could be got to swear any thing desired – and then where would you ... be? God knows we were a long time waiting for men like you to turn up, and now that we have you there we don't want to see you go under![71]

After the session Thompson appointed A.B. Routhier and M.M. Tait, Superior Court judges in Quebec, as royal commissioners to review the evidence and report back to Parliament in 1893. Edgar refused to appear. When Laurier urged in the autumn that it would look bad if Edgar did not go to the inquiry that he himself had launched, Edgar still said no. 'As things stand,' he wrote Laurier, 'if I appear before them [the Commissioners] I simply do so to court certain failure. The public, I fear, would then accept the view that I had tried to prove my charges and had failed.'[72] It was better to send off letters from Toronto implying more than you could prove. Not even suggestions that the Department of Justice might pay Edgar's expenses helped.[73] In the end the Edgar charges amounted simply to a long report of evidence in the Sessional Papers of 1893. Caron remained postmaster general until 1896.

Thompson had also determined, early in 1892, that there would be a redistribution of parliamentary seats consequent upon the 1891 census.[74] Quebec and Ontario stayed as they were, with sixty-five and ninety-two seats respectively; New Brunswick lost two seats, Nova Scotia and Prince Edward Island one each; Manitoba gained two; British Columbia and the North-West Territories stayed the same. Even in provinces where the representation remained the same there were a number of internal adjustments. The opposition alleged chicanery, petty or gross depending upon the newspaper or MP. The Montreal *Herald* believed that hiving Liberals was going to be done in Quebec with emphasis upon Chambly, Chateauguay, Napierville, and Rouville. There were indeed changes there, though not necessarily to Conservative advantage.[75] McCarthy went so far as to regret having supported Macdonald's 1882 gerrymander of Ontario, saying he would not repeat his sin in 1892.[76] The *Herald* suggested, in view of the very cold wet June, that Sir John Thompson had engineered a gerrymander of the signs of the zodiac! Thompson believed that the only fault that would be found with the 1892 redistribution was that it had not gone far enough. The opposition press had made a great deal of noise about not very much. An attempt by the *Globe* to cartoon Rouville as a gerrymander was simply false.[77] Reasonable men by and large accepted as sensible the 1892 redistribution that took the House down two seats to 213 members.[78]

The most startling event of the session was Thompson's attack on Cartwright. Usually Thompson was mild as milk in the House of

Commons. For years Cartwright's command of language, his forensic skill in his use of English literature, his high, rasping voice, his doom-and-gloom speeches about Canada, his patent and long-standing hatred of Sir John Macdonald and all his works, had irritated Conservatives. Young Tupper liked to shiver a lance now and then, but Thompson used only the measured criticism of ordinary debate. But Cartwright's speech of 28 June 1892 was too much. He teased Thompson with being like the lady immortalized by Alexander Pope,

> A very heathen in the carnal part
> But still a sad, good Christian at her heart.

Yes, said Cartwright warming to his work, there really was a Jekyll and Hyde in Sir John Thompson, and it looked as if Thompson the sinner has entirely got the better of Thompson the saint.[79] Thompson might have passed that, though the quotation from Pope was peculiar; he might even have passed Cartwright's gross distortion, that in 1885 the Liberal MP for Antigonish, McIsaac, was induced to 'sell his seat' to Thompson. When Thompson was under stress, racked between intense emotion and a powerful will, he would clutch his fingers so tightly that the knuckles showed white, as if he were in pain. Afterwards, when he rose, from his bland courtesy and reasonableness few could guess at the strain he was under. But this time something in the last few minutes of Cartwright's 'ruffianly speech,' perhaps Cartwright's comment that Thompson had been 'an expert defender of dangerous criminals.' (nothing in Thompson's career warranted that), or Cartwright's gloomy prediction that Canada could not exist much longer, took Thompson away from his moorings. Now was the time, he thought, to remember Polonius's advice:

> Beware
> Of entrance to a quarrel; but being in
> Bear't that the opposed may beware of thee.

Thompson confessed he had never spoken so brutally in his life; he was not familiar with the weapons he now unsheathed.[80] But use them he did:

SIR JOHN THOMPSON ... I am much obliged to the hon. gentleman, further, for not allowing Parliament to separate, after a session of nearly five months, without his giving us another of those war, famine and pestilence speeches which have so often carried constituencies for the Government ... Sir, I decline the hon. gentleman's brief.

SIR RICHARD CARTWRIGHT ... You must have the fee first.

SIR JOHN THOMPSON ... I have some experience, both in defending criminals and in prosecuting them; I have never shrunk in my calling as a member of the bar, from taking any man's case ... but I have sometimes spurned the fee of a blatent [sic] scoundrel who denounced everybody else in the world, and was himself the truculent savage of them all ... Why, Sir, the hon. gentleman would rather abuse his country and defame it, than eat his breakfast any day ... I have only to say this, that speaking as the hon. gentleman has done with regard to being ashamed of his country, he has laid himself open to the very obvious answer that the history of the past twelve months has proved that his country is desperately ashamed of him.[81]

The House enjoyed that fight, none more than some Liberals, who had had all of Cartwright they could stand. Thompson felt a little ashamed, as if he had fought a chimney sweep and used the sweep's own soot-bag against him.[82] It says much about the justice of Thompson's rebuke that Cartwright was silent. Thompson never used such chastisement again.

That session Thompson reintroduced his Criminal Code. It owed much to Sir James Fitzjames Stephen's original of 1879 in England, but its Canadian form was due to the work of three Nova Scotians: Thompson, who conceived the undertaking and took on the responsibility for carrying it; G.W. Burbidge, his former deputy minister and now justice of the Exchequer Court; and Robert Sedgewick, his current deputy. Burbidge and Sedgewick did the leg work preparing the code, adapting the English version for Canadian use. The Canadian Criminal Code was thus a product of Thompson's genius for systematic law and his courage in assuming the intimidating responsibility in shouldering such a measure through the House of Commons; but Thompson was lucky in finding two able jurists who could give the Criminal Code expression and form.[83] Thompson had proposed it to them in 1890 and from the first they took it up with alacrity. Thompson was always one to close up anomalies, make clear what was unclear. Canada did not have a criminal code; she had a series of enactments by various parliaments, going back to confederation, consolidated every so often. The whole criminal law needed coherence, system. It needed, in fact, what it got, a code.

The Stephen draft code which the Canadians used as their base was no model of moral clarification. Stephen, and Thompson, were not radicals in the school of Jeremy Bentham. Crime was a wrong that should be punished and be seen to be punished. The Canadian code was a plain distillation of seven hundred years of common law. The Canadians had also before them some American examples; Virginia, New York, and

California had all acquired some form of law code in the later years of the nineteenth century.

The Canadian origins of the Criminal Code were more diverse. There were many articles about a code in the legal journals from the 1870s on; until Thompson came on the scene J.R. Gowan was its principal advocate. Gowan, an old friend of Macdonald's, had gone to him in 1871 and made an urgent appeal for a code, offering to do the work himself. 'Well, Judex,' said Macdonald, 'have we not been laying the foundations and if I live and prosper I meant to build on them.' Then came the Pacific scandal of 1873 and Gowan's hopes died out.[84] Now in 1892, old Gowan warmed at the thought: 'just think of it,' he wrote Thompson, 'Canada in the van – The first to enact a complete codification ... It is far and away the best measure of the kind ever submitted to any legislature.' Gowan told Abbott very much the same, that the code was 'most skilful and *eminently conservative.*' Only a great lawyer, one of large grasp and constructive ability, could have put it together so well. Gowan would have gone further than Thompson, and would have made the code complete in itself, dispensing with 'external means of construction.'[85] Canadians were never really to use the Criminal Code as a code, but treated it rather as a compilation from the common law. Thompson's instinct about what would happen was right.[86]

The changes Thompson effected were considerable, though he did not emphasize them. He proposed to abandon the distinction between principals and accessories; he would discontinue the use of 'malice aforethought' which, aggravating the guilt of murder, could be positively misleading; more important still, Thompson proposed the complete abolition of the distinction between felonies and misdemeanours. The distinction had ceased to be of any use or sense, but it was such a radical change that it required revision of the whole criminal law.[87] It meant that all offences had to be reclassified according to their seriousness. This mattered; the right to jury trial depended upon it. Thompson's code was thus in advance of both Stephen's of 1879 and that of New York. Stephen's code left out summary offences, New York's left out procedure; Thompson's included both.[88] Not all the parliamentarians knew law well enough to be able to discern the changes. In the Commons William Mulock noted some; he was not necessarily opposed, but he thought they might have been noted more plainly. 'Up to the present time,' Mulock said on 19 May, 'I have assumed that there has been no change whatever, that we have been simply declaring the law as it exists.' Thompson interjected, 'I do not want the hon. gentleman to assume that, – I never said it.' In general Thompson had tried to point out significant departures in the Criminal Code from common law or statute law, but there was a natural tendency to underplay them. Mulock argued that there was too much understatement, and that Parliament had to know what the real changes were. 'Otherwise,' he said, 'we are not codifying but legislating by wholesale.' Thompson admitted that in the code they were trying to strike a medium between old law and new, in order to allow the courts working room for discretionary judgments.[89]

Thompson claimed little credit for authorship of the Criminal Code. He was happy and lucky to find willing and able help from Burbidge and especially from Sedgewick, for to many people such arduous work would have been singularly uninviting. Gowan urged Thompson on with such long letters, he said it was lucky no stenographer was available in Barrie! It reminded Gowan of a story. A Scotsman was attacked by highwaymen and after a hard fight the highwaymen succeeded in subduing him, to find only two copper halfpennies on him. The leader of the gang exclaimed, 'The Lord be thanked he had na mair – had he possessed six pence he would have murdered us all!!'[90]

Thompson did not have a difficult time with the Criminal Code in the Commons but it was a long and tedious process. The two-year program for its dissemination, the extensive comments that it had received from bench and bar between 1891 and 1892, all helped to make the Commons tractable. The most revolutionary change, the abolition of the grand jury, Thompson seems to have given up with reluctance. One excellent scholar makes an interesting argument that abolition was a red herring, to draw off opposition to the code. That would be unlike Thompson's usual style. Although Thompson was convinced that the grand jury was cumbersome and useless, he let it stand in deference to public opinion. Laurier for one opposed abandoning the grand jury. In such matters, Laurier said, 'I am a conservative to the hilt.'[91] Laurier and many other MPs on both sides of the House subscribed to the view that abolition of the grand jury would throw too much power into the hands of the JPs, 'an ignorant and prejudiced class, such as nine-tenths of our Justices of the Peace are ... would legalize oppression and tyranny.'[92]

The code went to a joint committee of House and Senate for detailed discussion, and Thompson had to shepherd it through both that stage and the Committee of the Whole stage in the House. Gowan had sensible suggestions. Get the code through in some form; it could be polished up afterward. Accept little amendments that fully commend themselves rather than handicap the code by arousing antagonism. Gowan believed that the code would have an easy time in the House if it passed the joint committee. Not many people knew enough to make comments; and those who wanted to would not have the advantage of the ammunition gathered together against the 1879 English Code. Gowan had got the essential book from the Parliamentary Library and had taken it home to Barrie! Do be careful, he told Thompson, on the question of letting a prisoner testify on his own behalf. Don't take the ground 'that or nothing!' The best lawyers differ on the question.[93] Thompson had however always been persuaded that prisoners should be able to testify in their own defence; that was part of the code he wanted very much to keep, and keep it he did.

For all Thompson's flexibility, he needed also toughness and persistence. There were four or five lawyers on the opposition front benches who made progress heavy and ponderous. In two full afternoons' work during the week of 15 May, the House passed only one hundred of over nine hundred sections. The trouble was, according to Thompson, that even those front bench lawyers knew little about criminal law, and were too lazy to read the code thoroughly. They insisted that the House chairman read each section, and as it was read, they would try to determine what it meant. They would then dispute whether the common law had changed and asked volleys of questions about this or that effect. It was, confessed Thompson ruefully, 'very trying to the temper but I will worry along as best I can.' Gowan, nursing a sick wife in Barrie, was disturbed that well-read lawyers like Laurier, Mills, and Davies would oppose as they did. Thompson dispelled such illusions. 'Mills is well read,' he wrote Gowan, 'Laurier far from it, and Davies a mere gabbler of phrases which he has picked up in a very inferior practice.'[94]

There were a number of attempts to lobby for the inclusion of new moral standards, one of them, at least, successful. D.A. Watt of Montreal, the moving spirit behind the Society for the Protection of Women and Young Girls, was an energetic and able publicist, and with the sympathy of Thompson and the Department of Justice, got into the Criminal Code a comprehensive system for the protection of young women and girls from male predators. The old age of consent (it went back to 1869) was twelve years of age. The Criminal Code raised it to fourteen. Watt even wanted it raised to twenty-one, but he did not get that![95] Another lobbyist, from Manitoba, urged that adultery be made a criminal offence. He complained that in his town, a married man (with a wife and family in Quebec) was keeping house with a young unmarried woman. 'Unmarried persons should not be allowed to cohabitate,' J.K. McLennan insisted, 'Such a thing in a community is to say the least terribly demoralizing to its moral well-being.' Thompson's reply to this was unusually circumspect even for him, saying only it would be taken into consideration.[96] One delightful suggestion (rejected) was that no child 'actually or apparently under sixteen years of age shall smoke' in any public place![97]

At last on 28 June the Criminal Code cleared the Commons and went up to the Senate. There it ran into a hard fight. The senators had somehow found the comments against the English draft code of 1879. The Liberal senators were unhappy: the government that had survived McGreevy, that seemed to be weathering Caron, that succeeded in destroying Mercier from the committee rooms of that very Senate chamber not ten months before,[98] would now get the credit for passing the Criminal Code.[99] A dead set was made at it; there was an unprecedented debate on first reading. Abbott could hardly believe it. Senator R.W. Scott of Ottawa objected not only to the code but having to take up such a vast piece of legislation so late in the session. No matter that it had been before Parliament for over a year, such a code did not exist anywhere else in the world; no matter that R.W. Scott had never attended a single meeting of the Joint Committee of Commons and Senate; he was opposed root and branch to any code whatever, and no committee was going to be allowed to get near changing his mind. Senator Read (Quinte), closer to the point, said that nearly one-third of the clauses defined new offences and laid down new penalties.[100] Abbott – since 1 July 1892 Sir John Abbott and sometimes called Sir John the Second – at one point feared he would have to give the code up altogether. He appealed to the Senate. 'Let us begin,' he said, 'and go on with it as long as time allows us to do it, carefully and promptly. The moment that time fails us we can stop. But let us do what we can to save the necessity of the great labour of passing that Bill again through the House of Commons.'[101] The Senate did what he asked, though the opposition grumbled. Nor did it harm the code; according to Thompson it emerged improved, purged of several minor errors. On 9 July, the next day, Parliament prorogued.

The Criminal Code was widely accepted. It earned praise in England: Gowan was insistent that copies go immediately to proper quarters there. There was, however, one public protest from Justice H.-E. Taschereau, on the Supreme Court of Canada since 1878. Taschereau had himself published extensively on the criminal law and his published comments were used in law schools. He hoped to have the Department of Justice purchase four hundred copies for appropriate distribution, which the department denied the necessity for. He also offered himself in the preparation of the new Criminal Code, an offer that was turned down.

Taschereau's public letter of January 1893 had something of sour grapes in it, the more so since there had been a full year and a half (and more) in which to make private criticism.[102] Taschereau received little support. Sedgewick said Taschereau's criticism boiled down to the amendment of eleven sections, only two or three of which were really necessary.[103]

Behind Sedgewick's position, and perhaps behind Thompson's too, lay the proposition that the common law would have a continuing relevance, notwithstanding the Criminal Code. There was no way to get rid of the making of case law. The habit was too ingrained, and it would grow up again even after a comprehensive consolidation like the code. Perhaps consolidation was all that could have been expected.

Senator Gowan, less critical and more enthusiastic, wrote from Barrie how splendid it all was, this triumph of Thompson's and Abbott's.[104] 'No one can deny,' said Gowan, 'we are a progressive people, and our public men have not the advantages they enjoy at home, in the many ... experts to aid in every mortal thing.' Sir John Macdonald, he added, felt this lack at confederation. There were no experts on anything. 'I must do it alone,' Macdonald then complained to Gowan, 'there is not one person connected with the government ... who has the slightest knowledge of the nature of the work, not one person in the Conference (except Galt on finance) has the slightest idea of constitution making.' The more reason why in 1892, as in 1867, credit was well deserved.[105]

Nor was Macdonald forgotten either. When the House met on 6 June 1892, the first anniversary of Macdonald's death, there was a huge bouquet of roses on the Clerk's table, and all the ministers and most Conservative MPs wore in their lapels a rose and a maple leaf. The House of Commons still seemed strange without him.[106]

The session over at long last, Thompson heaved a huge sigh of relief. It had been long and tedious, he told Hugh Henry, who had come from Halifax in 1891 to help Langevin; still, the worry and anxiety in 1892 were trifling compared to the 'ordeal in which you found us in '91.'[107] In truth Thompson was not fond of parliamentary sessions of whatever kind. 'At last the dreary Session is a week into the past,' he wrote to C.H. Tupper in England, 'and I wish Parliament would never sit again.' Jane Dewdney, who saw him at about this time, said that Thompson was like a boy out of school now the House was over. Frequent cabinet meetings and Treasury Board sessions could be tolerated, now that there was some breathing time in between.[108] Désiré Girouard offered Thompson a day or two at Lac St Louis; Senator Sanford offered him his island in Muskoka for a few days; Caron suggested Thompson join them at Rivière du Loup; but to no avail.[109] Immediately after the session, Thompson took Annie and Frankie down to the new Algonquin Hotel at St Andrews, returning at once to Ottawa. He was looked after by Thomas, the handyman who presided in a casual fashion over 181 Lisgar Street. Thomas had to phone Jane Dewdney for some help on how to prepare things for Thompson, and added that, since Thompson had made no complaints, he guessed 'things are right.' Jane Dewdney advised Annie to get Thompson down to St Andrews for a rest as soon as possible, for he seemed 'to have to spin out his brains for all the others!'[110] Thompson finally got away to St Andrews at the end of July.

He had been there all of three days when word came from Ottawa that Sir John Abbott had been taken ill. Abbott had been in the WC in the East Block when he was seized with dizziness so severe that he would have fallen had not a wall nearby saved him. He managed to call a messenger and was helped to a sofa in the big East Block office that Macdonald used to have. Abbott was tired, anxious, and frightened. The Sault Ste Marie canal question and the news, just received, of the amazing decision of the Privy Council in *Winnipeg* v. *Barrett* were worrying him very much.[111] Abbott needed rest; all morning that 6 August he received visitors in his office lying on the old sofa.[112] He managed a few days later to get down to his home at Ste Anne de Bellevue, hoping to be able to conceal the real state of affairs. That state was, the doctors told him, weakened heart and bad circulation; the remedy was to stop responsibilities and start rest. Dr Powell threatened serious and immediate consequences if Abbott disregarded the advice. 'I shall have to give in, I suppose,' Abbott told Thompson, 'but, I am not saying so, and shall try to keep things running somehow, till we can make other arrangements, and in the meantime will shirk all I can.' That was not difficult: Abbott was so weak he could scarce walk around the lawn at his home.[113] In mid-August, after the hard cabinet meeting in Montreal on Sault Ste Marie, Abbott took off down the St Lawrence for a sea voyage; Mackenzie Bowell, the senior minister, presided temporarily at Ottawa; Thompson went back to St Andrew's to rejoin his family for whatever holiday he could still extract from the concatenation of crises. From the beaches and docks of the sunny, summery village he watched the sweep of New Brunswick tides, hoping that Sir John Abbott, three hundred miles or so distant on the Gulf of St Lawrence, was regaining strength and health.

19

The New Prime Minister

Dear Sir Abbott, we implore you, do not leave us in the lurch,
In the face of rising clamor o'er the influence of the Church,
Mere suggestion of Sir Thompson for Premiership appears
Sure to raise the very devil of a storm about our ears.

You are sick, we know, and weary of the toil of party strife,
And you well may seek retirement from the cares of public life;
Gladly would we aid your purpose, but we dare not yet instal
Thompson as the actual Premier – that, we fear, would ruin all.

We will give you leave of absence, and however long you're gone
We will do the business for you and your stipend will run on;
Let no public cares annoy you – heed not shouts of praise or blame,
We don't want your able counsel – all we ask for is your name.

Sir John Thompson will relieve you when you go away from home,
Leave him power of attorney to effect a deal with Rome,
And to hoodwink Orange bigots who his machinations dread,
If you cannot be our captain please remain our figure-head.[1]

Thompson could certainly have agreed with that! It was essential that
Abbott stay on. There were now problems that Thompson should not be
expected to solve. It would be impossible for a Catholic prime minister –
and he would be the first – to take on the Manitoba school question, laid
squarely at the government's feet by the Privy Council. No Protestant
would find it easy to believe that Thompson would be able, even if willing,
to act judiciously, fairly, upon a matter that lay so close to the Roman
Catholic conscience. Much the best way was to let Sir John Abbott or
someone else assume that role. It was rumoured that Thompson

canvassed his cabinet colleagues telling them he was willing to serve under any one of them except Sir Charles Tupper.[2]

For Thompson it was time to get out of politics. He had had seven long years of it, and taken on the hardest tasks. Thompson had never shirked responsibilities, nor was he given to complaining; but there was justice in his rueful reflection in a letter to Gowan in December 1892, 'It seems to me that since I came here [to Ottawa] I have had to take the full weight and personal responsibility for all the difficulties which have arisen.'[3] One can almost hear the sigh behind that sentence. Thompson had lived through, and in the process mastered, a formidable agenda of problems: he had arrived in Ottawa in September 1885 in time to have to take on the defence of the government in the Riel agitation; in 1887–8 there was the fisheries question with the Americans at Washington; in 1888–9 the Jesuits' Estates issue; in 1890 the North-West language question and the Manitoba schools; in 1891 the Langevin scandal; in 1892, the Criminal Code; in between all the rest copyright and the questions between Canada and Newfoundland. What more? Was it only to be work and worry? As early as 1889 Bishop Cameron observed that Thompson was 'so over-whelmed with business that he is to be pitied.'[4]

In August 1891 Thompson wrote Frankie a curious little note, contrasting his healthy appearance with his gloom over not seeing his family. 'I am as well and fat as ever ... It is too bad that I had so little chance to see you and all the others this summer, but it is my usual luck.' And 'too bad' with Thompson was an expression not of mild but bitter regret. A year or so later he wrote Helena a note from his East Block office desk where, he said, the letters were piled as high as his head.[5] It was getting worse, not better, as time went on. When some of his old friends complained of delays in correspondence with him, he replied that there were two courses of action open to him. One was to get some secretary to send a formal acknowledgment – which would relieve Thompson, as it seemed to relieve others, of consideration of the letter's contents. Some of Thompson's colleagues boasted that every letter was answered within twenty-four hours. To Thompson that was humbug. He for one would not do it. He would take the only other course possible. 'I work as rapidly as I can and as long as I can and those who expect more from me than I can do will be disappointed.'[6]

It was getting time to stop. Abbott could probably continue on as prime minister into 1893, and Thompson could quietly step out of politics. There would soon be a vacancy on the Supreme Court. The chief justice, Sir William Ritchie, was not well, and the chief justiceship would allow

Thompson to bow gracefully out, his duty to the party amply fulfilled. He could go honourably to a sphere where he was needed and where serious improvements could be made. On 25 September 1892 the chief justice died rather suddenly, leaving this option very much available.

Thompson's instinct to get out of politics was probably sensible. Men do best what they like doing. Thompson had always loved law and the bench; at heart he was an academic. Politics was to him a form of service, not to say servitude; he did not enjoy it as Macdonald had, a game played for itself. Like Robert Baldwin or Robert Borden, Thompson seems to have believed that his political life was his duty as citizen.

With Thompson's dislike of the *tracasseries* of political life went his conscientiousness at discharging its obligations. At the heart of Thompson's Catholicism was a dedication to service, righteousness, and integrity that other ages might have called jansenist – substitutes for asceticism that mercifully he never had to endure. What was missing in this continual testing of himself in politics, in fortitude and hard work, was any delight in it. Macdonald too had worked hard both as politician and administrator, but there was not much doubt of Macdonald's fundamental fascination with it. With Thompson it was otherwise. Perhaps Thompson had no seismograph that registered power. He tended to register the person rather than the power he or she had. Beauty, money, reputation, all are forms of power; Thompson tended to be not so much indifferent to them as contemptuous of what they represented. One could even say, as one former Halifax colleague and political opponent did, that Thompson lacked political gifts; it would be useless to expect him to construct a brilliant cabinet because he did not have that kind of ability in him.[7]

Annie was important to Thompson for many reasons, not least that he was in love with her from the start; but she had also important qualities that he had not. He was apt to be naïve, giving people the benefit of the doubt, charitable not just from principle but from instinct. Annie was always warning him to look out for ladies with a sob story; and he admitted his weakness. In shops he would always get humbugged. His absentmindedness only made it worse. He could never keep a pair of gloves going for more than a day or two without losing one or both of them. That kind of artlessness was easy to take advantage of. Annie had a harder, more cynical view of the world. She was less disposed to judge well of others, readier to think of politics as a game of chess in which one could calculate, watch, and weigh the power of each piece on the board.

There is some reason to doubt that Annie wanted her husband to go to the Supreme Court yet. She may well have believed that the full summit of his achievements had not been realized; with the prime ministership now so close, her ambition for him was tempted. When Abbott's illness threatened in August and Thompson pointed out the opposition in Ontario to him as possible prime minister, Annie said that was no reason why he should get out of politics and go to the Supreme Court. 'Bide your time,' she told him, 'there will come a time soon when they *cannot* do without you.'[8] Thompson was not sure that he was looking forward to that. But Annie was right: the party could not get along with Thompson. The prospect of Abbott giving up *and* Thompson going to the Supreme Court was too awful for the party to contemplate. Had Abbott thoroughly reconstructed the party in October 1891 as he had been urged, the position might have been different. As it was, the great majority of the cabinet could not in October 1892 consent to Thompson taking the chief justiceship. It was Gowan's opinion that 'no new govrnt could be formed just now at all events, without Sir John [Thompson] whatever parties I could name, may assert or think. I know full well what was the opinion of poor Sir John A. [Macdonald] about the best of them.'[9] It was no disparagement of Abbott's cabinet, as *The Week* argued, that it contained no man whose calibre could suggest passing by Sir John Thompson. Indeed, it added, 'there is scarcely an alternative.'[10]

If Thompson did not take the Court, he faced the prospect that down the road in two years or so there would be elections and possible defeat. What would that mean for Thompson? He had no income but his ministerial salary. A law practice in Toronto? Martin Griffin raised it with James Gowan. 'Your dismal picture of Sir John Thompson opening a law office in Toronto rather amuses me,' he wrote back to Griffin, 'all honor I hope is not dead in the Conservative party. I know one member of it at all events who would strain every nerve to prevent ingratitude and injustice.'[11]

Abbott left for England early in October to see the London doctors, bearing with him the hopes of colleagues, especially Thompson, that he would get a clean bill of health. Abbott was only seventy-one years of age; perhaps his indisposition of August was temporary. His health was surely better than he himself believed; older men do develop hypochondria. The Ontario wing of the party was especially anxious to keep Abbott, since some of them believed that Thompson may have promised too much to the bishops.[12] Sir Oliver Mowat – knighted partly upon Thompson's recommendation that summer – wrote a kind letter, hoping that Thompson would take the vacant chief justiceship. 'Though we differ about constitutional questions ...' Mowat said, 'I should be more than content to submit all such questions, as well as every other, to you as judge, Tory as unfortunately you are.'[13] That was fair praise, fairly meant. Liberals were puzzled by the resistance to Thompson as prime minister. 'I could never understand,' Louis Davies wrote to Laurier, 'where the opposition to Thompson came from ... But it would seem that there must have been kicking in some influential quarters or the present compromise of keeping a poor sick man in office would not have been resorted to.'[14]

The first news from London was good and Thompson entertained hopes that all might go as planned. That was shattered on 22 November when a letter arrived from Abbott, written on 10 November. Sir Andrew Clark confirmed the diagnosis of the Canadian doctors. While Abbott's general health was not bad, the problem with the circulation of blood in his brain required that he give up work. Abbott decided he would have to resign and enclosed a formal letter to that effect to be dated at Thompson's convenience. Abbott did not accept Thompson's suggestion about a successor. Thompson had suggested someone other than himself, perhaps Mackenzie Bowell. Thompson told Senator W.D. Perley in October that there was no rivalry about being prime minister. Mackenzie Bowell had the respect of everyone, and 'any of us would willingly follow him while we could agree with his policy.'[15] Whoever it was that Thompson preferred, Abbott did not believe he would be to the advantage of cabinet or country. Abbott talked it over with Foster, in England on Canadian financial business; Foster shared Abbott's opinion. There was no doubt, Abbott went on, that 'the feeling of the party points directly and unmistakedly to yourself.' No other person could hold the party together. All you need, said Abbott, is a strong Ontario Protestant; he hinted that, even now, Meredith might be the best choice.[16]

Thompson was now left to decide the future, and on his own. Abbott did not intend to return to Canada immediately; he preferred to spend some time in Europe, in Genoa, Rome, and Naples, out of the way of Canadian politics, trying to get his health back. That did not work, either; Abbott's health and strength continued slowly to deteriorate.[17]

Thompson met the governor general at the East Block on the afternoon of Wednesday, 23 November 1892. He was asked to form a new government, and invited so to inform his cabinet colleagues.[18] The news was out by Saturday morning, 26 November.

By this time Thompson and Annie had talked through the hard choice that lay ahead of them. The choice was barely his at all. As Ouimet told a Montreal dinner in December, 'c'est la position qui s'est imposée à lui ... il a sacrifié l'hermine de la Cour Suprême pour accepter une position beaucoup moins stable ... dans un moment difficile, plus difficile qu'on ne le croit généralement, au moment de la crise la plus sérieuse peut-être que nous ayions eue dans notre existence nationale.'[19]

In the circumstances of his elevation to power, Thompson might be excused from having any clear-cut ideas of what he proposed to do with it. He had to face big problems for which there were no easy answers. Manitoba schools looked difficult and intractable, with little room for manoeuvre. An election should be held in 1894 or 1895, so Thompson would have two years lead time. And once engaged on politics there could be no turning back. Thompson still smarted whenever there was a gibe about his going to the Supreme Court of Nova Scotia in July 1882, leaving his party, as it seemed at the time, in the lurch. Thompson would not lay himself open to the same charge, however distorted, again. Whatever hesitations Thompson may have had, when the call came he had already made up his mind where lay his duty. And the party made no bones about its own needs. The *Montreal Daily Star*, hitherto apt to be independent, was sympathetic to Thompson now that Abbott had gone.[20] 'If there be such times as great national crises,' it said on 28 November, 'Canada stands face to face with one during the opening days of this week; and Sir John Thompson holds the keys of the future.' Whatever corruption there may have been in the past, there was no need any longer to allow the baser elements in Parliament their head. 'Sir John Thompson comes not only into office but into power ... He has a smashing majority in Parliament, which with all its strength needs him more than he needs it.'

There was no one else. Mackenzie Bowell was decent and hard-working but lacked force, intelligence, and the modesty that ought to have been the concomitant of their absence. Young Tupper was too brash and headlong, Foster too waspish, Chapleau too dangerous, Caron too light, Haggart too bohemian; Daly was too new, as were Ouimet and Patterson; the best that could be said of old stand-bys like Costigan, Carling, and Frank Smith was that they represented their regions and their religions. Just the month before Dewdney had gone out to Victoria as lieutenant-governor of British Columbia, and with him in the person of Jane Dewdney went Annie's only close friend in Ottawa. The Conservative cabinet was old and shop-worn and could stand some young and vigorous stock.

That was easy enough to say. For a party long in power, with ancient rivalries in cabinet and caucus, with the rather thin selection of good men made available by the electorate, it was a moot point how much newness was possible. Thompson may have lacked the ability to recruit good men; he had already acquired something of an ice-wagon reputation. He would not say yes merely to please, and he could say no decisively when it might have been more expedient to give a hypocritical yes. He told one correspondent in Port Colborne, 'You begin your letter by asking the question, "Why do you refuse to give me a position?" In reply I beg to suggest a still more pertinent question – why do you persist in demanding from me a position that is in no way connected with my department and which is not in my gift?'[21] He was going to be a good deal tougher in this respect than his predecessors, certainly than Macdonald. J.D. Edgar observed, 'He will rule the party with a rod of iron. He did that before he became premier.'[22]

The impression in Ottawa was of an exceptionally smooth changeover. Arnott Magurn, the Ottawa correspondent of the *Globe*, reported on Sunday, 27 November:

No political change was ever accomplished so quietly as the succession of Sir John Thompson to the premiership. It created no stir in Ottawa, whatever may be said of it on the outside. There was no scurrying about of ministers in cabs, no visits to government house, no hasty consultations, no Waterloo alarm with hurrying to and fro or mounting in hot haste. Everything was cut and dried, and the new premier slept that night [Friday, 25 November] with a list of the new cabinet under his pillow.[23]

It was in reality less simple, as the developments of the following ten days were to show. There was the question of the missing fortnight. Abbott's resignation was received on 22 November and Thompson was asked to form a government the next day. But no government was sworn in until 7 December. The governor general, probably on Thompson's instructions, did not officially accept Abbott's resignation until 4 December. The reason for this proceeding was that the government could not be dissolved, as normally it would be, upon the resignation of the prime minister. The cabinet had to continue to meet, for there had to be a hearing of the cabinet sub-committee on the Manitoba appeal, set for 25 and 26 November. Only when that was done, and the new government ready, was the old one officially dissolved.[24]

While keeping the best, and most indispensable, of Abbott's cabinet (by no means the same thing), Thompson's main aim was to make the government more vigorous. While he retained nine of Abbott's fourteen-member cabinet, he brought in some new men.

Thompson consulted not just his colleagues but Conservative newspaper men. W.F. Maclean, owner and editor of the Toronto *World*, and the new MP for York East, dined with Thompson Sunday night, 27 November; David Creighton of the Toronto *Empire* arrived in Ottawa early Monday morning for the same purpose. R.S. White, editor of the Montreal *Gazette*, had spent much of the previous Friday and Saturday in consultation with Thompson. His advice concerned both Quebec and Ontario, Maclean's and Creighton's mostly Ontario. Those were the only two provinces that seemed seriously to trouble Thompson's reconstruction. Nova Scotia and New Brunswick would stay as they were, Nova Scotia represented by Thompson in justice and Tupper in fisheries, New Brunswick by Foster in finance and Costigan as secretary of state; the West was now represented by T.M. Daly in interior, who had joined the cabinet early in November consequent upon Dewdney's move to British Columbia as lieutenant-governor.

Daly's appointment was well received, except at the *Regina Leader* where N.F. Davin, who had expected the post himself, was shocked into a long drinking spree.[25] That left the other nine members of the cabinet to be sorted out between Ontario and Quebec.

In Abbott's cabinet Ontario had been represented by five members, Quebec (including Abbott himself) by four. Thompson proposed to amend that. His element of flexibility was the act of 1887, left unproclaimed until 3 December 1892. The 1887 act abolished the ministries of Customs and of Inland Revenue and replaced the ministers with controllers; another act of that same year, also left unproclaimed, set up the office of solicitor general to assist the minister of justice. None of these three was a cabinet portfolio; they were, however, part of the government and the heads of their departments; like members of cabinet, they had to resign their House of Commons seats on appointment to office and go for re-election. Their knowledge of ministerial business they acquired through the relevant cabinet minister, the new minister of trade and commerce, or the minister of finance, or, in the case of the solicitor general, the minister of justice.[26]

After a week of speculation the new minister of trade and commerce was announced. Mackenzie Bowell's long experience – fourteen years as minister of customs – and his considerable capacity for detail gave him solid qualifications. Bowell was a worker, whose information and common sense made him a useful if uninspiring colleague. There was no brilliance or debating power in him. As his private secretary said after Bowell's death in 1917, 'mediocrity must toil or fail.'[27] Perhaps the *Globe*, critic though it was, was not far wrong in saying that the new office did 'not use the talents he has and asks for talents that he has not.'[28] Bowell, at the age of sixty-nine, was quite ready to leave the Commons and go to the Senate, which he did. J.R. Gowan thought he would have to make some adjustments in his parliamentary style if he hoped to keep out of hot water in the Senate. That Bowell managed to do. He had a temper but he struggled to keep it under control. His native stubbornness was beyond remedy.

Thompson originally proposed to have equal numbers from Quebec as from Ontario: four ministers and one controller from Quebec, three ministers and two controllers from Ontario. He tried this idea out on David Creighton, who at first found it unexceptionable, but on his way back to Toronto realized it would never wash.

I am afraid the effect would be to immediately raise an outcry that this Province, the largest and most populous in the Dominion, was having its voice in the councils of the country reduced to 3, while a Province much less populous was getting 4. This would be the cry by the people generally, but our own friends would add to it that a delegation of 55 members was being put off with 3, while the 30 from Quebec were getting 4.[29]

In the end Ontario would get five plus two and Quebec four plus one, perhaps a sensible decision in view of the number of Conservatives from Ontario.

Thompson had not planned it that way. One Ontario minister refused to go gracefully. Edgar Dewdney suggested to Thompson that Caron and Carling be dropped from cabinet and Thompson agreed that at least Carling should go. There was talk that George Moncrieff, MP for Lambton East, might succeed Carling. That was sat upon by young Sam Hughes who said, in his pugnacious fashion, that the party barely tolerated Imperial Oil out of the cabinet and would certainly not want it in.[30]

It was not going to be easy, however, to get rid of Carling. The *Montreal Star* thought it would take the power of Niagara.[31] Carling was not popular – it was said he had scarcely a friend in caucus – but he had been in office a long time; he was rich, sensitive, and held a key constituency. Thompson approached him with infinite tact. The most disagreeable part of cabinet-making, Thompson wrote, was that of asking colleagues to step down. 'I believe you will give me the credit for sincerely desiring to avoid this horrible responsibility.' There were difficulties; though Carling's administration of the Department of Agriculture had been wise and beneficial, some changes were now essential. One of them was that Carling resign his portfolio and retire from cabinet.[32] Carling was furious. Not even hints at a Senate seat assuaged his wrath. He flung himself back to London, Ontario. A delegation came from London including the editor of the *London Free Press*. Thompson was forced to temporize and think of Carling as a minister without portfolio. Carling would have none of that either. He was sixty-four, had had the agriculture portfolio since 1885, and had been MP for London since 1878. Defeated in 1891, he had gone briefly to the Senate, then had resigned his Senate seat in order to rescue London for the party in the 1892 by-election. He had been offered the lieutenant-governorship of Ontario upon the death of Sir Alexander Campbell in May 1892 but it had been agreed between himself and Sir John Abbott that it was unwise to open up London again. Thus Carling had stayed on; and though there was criticism of his age and his ineffectiveness in Parliament, he had done his duty to the party. So Carling took demotion, even to minister without portfolio, badly. He said he was disgraced, maligned, traduced. Then Governor General Stanley talked to him, telling him what a compliment it was to be asked to stay on in cabinet after giving up a portfolio. Carling weakened a little; at last Lord Stanley hinted at a KCMG. 'I think,' said Lord Stanley to Thompson, 'this told.' It did. Carling stayed on as minister without portfolio through Thompson's administration and was duly knighted in June 1893.[33]

Keeping Carling made some sense. Around his London constituency were the four Middlesex county seats. Three were Conservative, one Liberal. To open London, either by Carling resigning in a fury or by his going to the Senate (which he did not want) might result in Liberal recapture of the centre seat; to leave him out of cabinet would, according to local opinion, demoralize a dozen other Conservative seats in southwest Ontario.[34]

There had to be a well-known and strong Protestant from Ontario in the cabinet. Meredith's candidacy had run upon rocks; Archbishop Cleary had preferred Clarke Wallace or even McCarthy. But McCarthy disliked Thompson and was ready to wreak havoc pursuing that.[35] He was now impossible; Wallace, however, was both strong and popular among Ontario Conservatives. Ontario also liked Hugh John Macdonald; he seems to have been solicited to consider being in cabinet as an Ontario MP but turned it down.[36]

Clarke Wallace was Thompson's age. His father had come from County Sligo in 1834 and had settled in Woodbridge, northwest of Toronto, where Clarke Wallace was born in 1844. Wallace married Belinda Gilmour of Ottawa and notwithstanding 'some little storms,' they had a happy marriage and four sons and three daughters.[37] Since 1887 Wallace had been the Most Worshipful Grand Master of the Grand Orange Lodge of British America. He was a solid back-country merchant, who had built up a successful milling business and had been elected for York West since 1878. He was also one of the thirteen who had voted in 1889 for disallowance of the Jesuits' Estates Act. Wallace was not much liked by Catholics such as Martin Griffin nor by high-minded Protestants such as Gowan; but with a handsome presence, a thick shock of silvery hair and an agreeable voice, and some intellectual vigour, he would be at least potentially, one of the stronger Ontario men in the cabinet.[38] He was also to earn the enmity of McCarthy whose replacement he largely became. Wallace told Thompson some weeks before he joined the cabinet that he was not in favour of remedial legislation for Manitoba schools. Such action would be certain, he thought, to rend the party. The best standing ground would be simply 'to accept the decision of the Judicial Committee [in *Winnipeg* v. *Barrett*].' *Saturday Night* of Toronto referred to Wallace a few months later as 'a square man and a valuable official'; and so within his own limits Wallace became. But he did not carry the cachet that Meredith would have done. Ontario was served only by good second-raters. It was not really Thompson's fault that the Ontario electorate did not furnish the party with better materials for cabinet-making. That was Gowan's opinion.[39]

Quebec created difficulties too. There was first the mighty Chapleau. Montreal *La Presse* had been saying all summer and autumn how jealous they were in Ottawa of Chapleau and how badly they were treating him. (Chapleau liked to use *La Presse* to tell his colleagues home truths.) 'He is a poor "hostage for himself" just now,' Thompson wrote to Charles Hibbert Tupper in London, 'His usefulness in that line is gone.' It was an open secret that Thompson forced Chapleau's retirement from politics. From the day he joined the Macdonald government in 1882 Chapleau had the sense that his hands were tied. He grew to resent being manipulated, as he saw it, by Langevin and McGreevy. But he had carried on, according to *La Presse*, from his sense of duty. But by 1892, Chapleau's enthusiasm for politics had largely gone. 'La corde vivante etait brisée ...' was *La Presse*'s eloquent description.[40] Rather than remain muzzled and impotent in Ottawa, Chapleau preferred to be muzzled and impotent at Spencer Wood as lieutenant-governor of Quebec. In some ways Chapleau was his own worst enemy; he would sulk, he would threaten, he would storm; he was, as the French consul at Quebec, Comte de Turenne, warned Paris, 'un esprit sans consistance et un caractère mobile.' Chapleau claimed frequently that his bad health required the *soulagements* of Paris. It was a French-Canadian euphemism for a luxurious fling at the gay life! The French consul at Quebec had to tell his minister in March 1893 to look out – Chapleau was coming again.[41]

Chapleau's translation to Spencer Wood was not easy. Chapleau as usual imposed conditions: L.-O. Taillon should get his long-deferred judgeship on the Superior Court of Quebec; Chapleau's brother should become collector of customs, Montreal. None of these would wash.[42] Taillon would become premier of Quebec, part of another complication. The existing premier, Charles Boucher de Boucherville, content with the incumbent lieutenant-governor, A.R. Angers, would have nothing to do with Chapleau as Angers' replacement. De Boucherville, austere, old, and self-righteously ultramontane, disliked Chapleau and all his works. He would *not*, repeat *not*, stay on as premier with Chapleau as lieutenant-governor. Thompson appealed to de Boucherville more than once, arguing that history would judge him ill for resigning simply because of a change of lieutenant-governors. Thompson appealed to Angers to get de Boucherville to change his mind. It was all to no avail.[43]

There was also talk in Quebec that Chapleau's coming to Spencer Wood would cause no end of trouble among Quebec Conservatives. G.-A. Nantel, de Boucherville's minister of public works, told Thompson not to worry, that Chapleau would be received at Quebec with a generous spirit. He hoped the same would be true of politics at Ottawa – a generous spirit *and* a firm hand. In the past, 'trop de laisser-aller et de bonhomie a laissé vaciller au gré des passions et des préjugés.'[44]

At the last, as de Boucherville was resigning, he became cordial to Chapleau. Chapleau even dared to suggest to de Boucherville that his decision had in it too much pride and too little duty. They parted on good terms, gossiping about horses and cattle in two interviews on 13 and 14 December.[45] Probably de Boucherville's retirement and his replacement by L.-O. Taillon was a relief to Chapleau. Chapleau was thus installed at Spencer Wood and Angers came to the Senate to be the new minister of agriculture. It gave the Quebec wing of the cabinet at least one man of rugged integrity.

The Anglo-Protestant from Quebec to replace Abbott was nearly as much trouble. Thompson wanted W.B. Ives, MP for Sherbrooke. Ives had married the only daughter of J.H. Pope, the old 'brute' whom Thompson had disliked, who had played an active role in business and railway affairs in the Eastern Townships. Ives's range of interests extended much further. In 1882 and 1883 there was a cattle-ranching scheme in Texas that he and Rufus Pope had been instrumental in pursuing; it was the cause of sharp debate. Senator A.W. Ogilvie, Sir Charles Tupper, and others had put money into the scheme and lost much of it. They believed it was a swindle. The *Montreal Star* had been full of it – Hugh Graham had suffered too – and both Sir John A. Macdonald and Sir John Abbott believed the allegations of the *Star*. Sir Charles Tupper even wanted to prosecute Ives, but J.H. Pope, so it was said, protected him.[46] Hugh Graham strongly opposed Ives's appointment to the cabinet. Thompson, however, accepted Ives's explanations that there had been no wrong-doing; so did R.S. White of the Montreal *Gazette*, G.E. Foster, and Senator Drummond. Hugh Graham liked Thompson – the *Star* had a friendly editorial on 26 November – but it was essential that Graham be persuaded to accept Ives. C.H. Mackintosh of the Ottawa *Citizen* went down to Montreal as peacemaker and got an earful from Hugh Graham and Senator Ogilvie; Mackintosh thought it providential that Ives was bald, for Graham was really after his scalp.[47] Hugh Graham sent off affadavits to Thompson showing losses of $150,000 in the ranch scheme, including $33,000 of Senator Ogilvie's and $10,000 of his own. Mackintosh believed that there were two sides to the Texas ranch deal and that both belonged in the courts, not the Privy Council chambers. In the end there was a personal meeting beteen Thompson and Graham, Thompson got his way, and Ives joined the cabinet as president of the council.[48]

On Wednesday, 7 December 1892 the new cabinet was sworn into office in the presence of the governor general. It was a cabinet not greatly different from other federal cabinets before and since, old and new patched up together. But it was strong enough to give senior Liberals pause. Laurier was sure the government of Sir John Thompson was solidly in place and the only hope of upsetting them was if they made some monumental blunder. Senator Lawrence Power of Halifax, Laurier's correspondent in this gloomy appraisal of Liberal chances, could only agree that Laurier was right.[49] Even the Montreal *Herald*, Liberal though it was and claiming that Thompson was cloaking the Conservative party in 'a shining mist of seeming morality,' was forced to admit that 'he has rendered the Conservative party more valuable service since Sir John Macdonald's death than perhaps any other living man could have done. It is a question if the old chieftain himself could have brought the party safely through these cruel embarrassments.'[50]

This kind of bipartisan support allowed Thompson to shrug off another attack from the redoubtable Dr George Douglas, principal of the Wesleyan Theological College in Montreal. Douglas was a sixty-seven-year-old Scotch Methodist theologian, a mixture sufficiently intractable. The Montreal *Witness* on Christmas eve published an interview with Dr Douglas. Thompson, he said, could only have risen so dramatically with the help of the Roman Catholic bishops. How else was it possible for a young lawyer aged thirty-seven to have become a judge on the Nova Scotia Supreme Court? Thompson's main achievement was 'to consolidate the Jesuit influence in this Dominion.' Like most converts Thompson espoused the most extreme side of Catholicism – the Jesuits – evidenced by his sending his sons to that Jesuit-run school, Stonyhurst. Thompson was nothing but 'a clerical creation.' Antigonish was as much a pocket borough as any Old Sarum in England. Mr Justice Rose of Toronto told Thompson to pay no attention. He had information from his brother, Dr S.P. Rose who taught at the same college, that Dr Douglas was sick, old, and prejudiced, and was not listened to except by a few extreme Methodist groups in Ontario.[51] The *Toronto World*, the most popular Conservative paper there, said Dr Douglas's stuff was loathsome. Thompson was prime minister because he was the best man in the party and for no other reason.[52]

It was easy to be cheerful that December 1892; all four of Thompson's new ministers were returned by acclamation. The *Empire*'s women's page had a sketch of the new prime minister written from a young woman's summer memory of Rivière du Loup in 1890. She had been travelling by carriage with a New Brunswick MP over the hilly roads of Témiscouata County on a beautiful August morning, the roadsides glowing with buttercups. Faith Fenton and the MP were greeted by Sir John Macdonald at his rambling summer home at St Patrice, his grey hair blowing a little in the morning breeze. The two were brought into the big drawing-room and introduced to Thompson, newly arrived from England. Macdonald carried off the MP for a chat, and Thompson put his book down and began to talk with Faith Fenton, who had just come from Newfoundland. As they were leaving, the MP asked,

'How did you get on with Sir John Thompson?'

'He is very quiet,' I answer with a sudden sense of delinquency.

'Quiet?' echoed the Member, 'Yes, perhaps he is. But,' turning to me with forefinger raised impressively, 'Sir John Thompson will remember every word you have spoken long after you have forgotten them. He never forgets.'

'Oh, dear,' I say dolefully, 'and I talked so much, and Sir John just listened.'

'Yes, he listens and remembers. That's his way always,' repeated the Member, confidently.

It is only a summer memory; yet, vivid as an etching it returned to me ... I saw again the blue water, the great golden buttercups, the hilly roadways, the quiet, earnest face that somehow won my confidence in the shaded drawing room ...[53]

Thompson's first public occasion as prime minister was the Board of Trade dinner in Toronto on 5 January 1893. It was an immense affair held in the Pavilion, a vast emporium at Carlton and Jarvis streets, sometimes used for flower shows, sometimes for political banquets. A driving snow storm failed to deter some three hundred guests; street-cars (Toronto had its first electric ones in 1892) and carriages always did handle snow storms more effectively than automobiles could. On the platform inside the Pavilion were the governor general, the lieutenant-governor of Ontario, Thompson, Foster, Sir Frank Smith, Sir Oliver Mowat, Laurier, and some newspaper men, Creighton, Willison, and Bunting representing the *Empire*, the *Globe* and the *Mail* respectively. The guests tucked into a robust dinner: oyster soup; turkey, ham, and beef; roast suckling pig; jellies made of rum and champagne; charlotte russe and angel cake. Wines of course. And toasts. The speeches started around half past nine and went on till after midnight. Toasts to the Queen, the governor general, lieutenant-governor, were drunk and acknowledged; Thompson's duty was to reply to the toast to her majesty's ministers, using Tennyson's theme, 'That man's the true Conservative who lops the moulder'd branch away.' As Thompson rose to speak, he was greeted by the audience standing up and singing 'He's a daisy.' Audiences with all that food and wine aboard liked to let off a little steam!

Thompson categorically denied any resemblance to a daisy. Indeed, thirteen of her majesty's ministers, himself included, were anything but daisies, averaging forty-seven years of age; their girths suggested the relevance of Caesar's remark when eyeing the too-lean Cassius,

> Let me have men about me that are fat;
> Sleek-headed men, and such as sleep o' nights.

'I could make you tonight a little boast,' Thompson went on, 'about the girth and weight of my colleagues, if it were not that my friend Cassius here – (great laughter) – my friend the finance minister, breaks the record and utterly destroys the average!' No doubt Foster smiled down the length of his long face and long beard, for he was lean enough.

The most difficult problem facing Canada, said Thompson, was the religious feelings of its people. Some weeks ago Thompson pleaded for toleration, and one newspaper implied he meant it for himself. He did not mean it that way. He was prime minister only because others believed he could serve the state. He was a public servant and serving the state was his only proper ambition. And there were many others who could serve Canada equally well in the same position, and from both parties. Did Thompson glance at Laurier perhaps? As to Canada herself, 'this country ought to be a nation, will be a nation, and please God we will and shall make it a nation.' This did not mean independence, Thompson added. No realistic Canadian could believe that independence, as currently conceived, was other than a stepping-stone to annexation. Canada still needed the protection of the British Empire, which had given Canada, 'every facility which a self-governing, independent people desire to have.'[54]

This theme Thompson took up at more length a week later on 13 January, again at Toronto, in a major speech to the Young Men's Liberal-Conservative Association. A vast crowd of some three thousand people assembled, the hall jammed to the doors an hour before Thompson was to begin. As to independence, he said, 'let no one mistake my meaning ... no nationality, no set of people, no race living in any one country fail to keep before them as an object of worthy ambition that they should become a great and independent people.' Canada was independent now, in the sense of being able to determine most of her own business while under the protection of the most powerful parent in the world. No doubt in future Canada would become wholly independent, but that could only happen when Canada's population was closer to fifty million than to five million. With the United States so 'immensely powerful even in peace, and intensively aggressive in pursuit of every interest that belongs to them,' to talk in 1893 of independence from Great Britain 'is to talk absurdity, if not treason.'[55] And with the *New York Sun* saying just a month earlier that Canada could be bought for $300 million cash and was cheap at the price, there was reason to emphasize Canada's nationalist pride, even if developed under British protection. A few weeks after the Toronto speeches he told L.H. Taché, of the Montreal *L'Opinion Publique*, that 'any withdrawal of Imperial protection would place us entirely at the mercy of our Southern neighbor.'[56]

That did not prevent the Canadian government from pressing for a Canadian attaché at the British legation in Washington. Both sides of the House of Commons supported this and a resolution to that effect had been passed in May 1892. Both Abbott and Foster pressed the point in London in October.[57] The Colonial Office officials, notably John Anderson, the exceptionally able clerk who had become private secretary to the new permanent under-secretary, Robert Meade, were not unsympathetic to Canada's case. They recognized that there were stresses and strains; there had been something close to a major row between Sir Julian Pauncefote and C.H. Tupper in 1890. 'Every question,' minuted Anderson, 'that can arise between the u.s. and Canada is a Canadian domestic matter with which the people naturally feel they ought to be allowed to deal in their own way ... the position of Canada is unique.' Much the greater part of the business of Britain's Washington legation was Canadian. The problem was how to satisfy the Canadian demand without involving the imperial government in responsibility for communications over which they had no control. A Canadian attaché having access to all the documents at the British legation could produce embarrassing breaches of security. It was well known in London that once anything got to Ottawa, it appeared in the newspapers the next day. Robert Meade argued that the longer the present system could continue the better. And no Canadian attaché in Washington, under whatever name, would readily be accepted by the Foreign Office.[58]

The Foreign Office would soon have another reason for complaint. There was the question of Hawaii. The Hawaiian state flag is the only American one to carry the Union Jack; Captain Cook had after all landed on the Islands, and died there, in 1779. A century later, in January 1893, Queen Liliuokalani was deposed by an American-inspired coup d'état. This raised numerous questions. President Cleveland, who assumed office on 4 March 1893, immediately disavowed this bare-faced attempt to make Hawaii an American colony. Everyone was uneasy: questions were raised in the Canadian House of Commons; Thompson was sure the British government would have the most delicate, difficult, operation possible, if they wished to upset the designs of the Americans on Hawaii. Thompson believed that the only hope of keeping Americans from seizing Hawaii was to play it very coolly. Then opposition to the annexation in the American Senate might prevail. But active British interference would put an end to opposition in the United States.[59]

It was good sense. Not everyone so acted. In September 1893, when Mackenzie Bowell was in Honolulu on his way to Australia, he and Sandford Fleming had had brought to their attention a small, unoccupied rocky island 240 miles to the west. Bowell wrote Thompson that it would make an excellent site for a cable station, and the British should annex it.

The matter ended in London. The British, sensibly, decided it might be better to negotiate with Hawaii. But the British GOC North America, Sir Alexander Montgomery Moore, thought it would be more enterprising to simply take it and put up the British flag. This wild enterprise was brought to the attention of the British government through Fleming. The Foreign Office were angry and Lord Ripon, the colonial secretary, agreed. He told Campbell-Bannerman, secretary for war, that General Moore should be closed down at once, if spared being shot! As Ripon put it, 'It is impossible to allow ourselves to be driven into annexations by every filibuster[er] in the Colonies, even if he be a General Officer. I beg you to give Gen. Moore a trouncing which he will not forget in a hurry.'[60]

Hawaii threw into relief problems with Esquimalt, the Royal Navy's only dockyard on the Pacific coast from Arctic to Antarctic. In 1878, in response to British pressure, Canada had put up a makeshift earthwork battery at Macaulay's Point. The British offered in 1889 to provide a garrison of marines, armament for the forts, and supervision of construction, if Canada would pay for troops and works. Macdonald and the Canadian cabinet decided that building the 1878 battery and putting a company of gunners there in 1887 was enough. In January 1892 very little had been done, but the files had got longer and the British more pressing. When Mackenzie Bowell became minister of militia, with the encouragement of Abbott and Thompson he took hold of the problem vigorously. Bowell went to the west coast in the summer of 1892 (with 'two of the most appalling females I have ever encountered,' according to the unhappy British GOC Militia who accompanied them, Major-General I.J.C. Herbert) and worked out an arrangement for splitting the costs of Esquimalt between Canada and Britain. Bowell became minister of trade and commerce in December 1892, but his grasp of the problem was not lost; Thompson was anxious that the whole matter be settled, and the new minister of militia, J.C. Patterson, was instructed to go on with it. That he did, though in his own lazy fashion. However, by the spring of 1893 the arrangement was in place, and Lord Ripon and Lord Stanley breathed a sigh of relief. 'Sir John Thompson,' Ripon wrote to Stanley, 'deserves great credit for the manner in which he has dealt with it.' Even Patterson got some kudos. Lord Stanley told Thompson that Patterson was difficult to get into harness but was excellent 'once he has been roped and brought up from the pasture! I like him much and am sure he will be useful to you.' The legislation went through Parliament in late March, under Patterson's supervision. In August 1893 British marines arrived at Esquimalt and the Canadian battery left for Quebec City. The defence of Esquimalt would remain in British hands until November 1905.[61] By that time it was clear what some officers in Canada suspected all along, that Esquimalt was not really defensible.

Patterson did not do so well with the next episode. Under circumstances that are obscure, Patterson was persuaded by Major-General I.J.C. Herbert to make a unilateral offer of Canadian troops to help bolster the defences of Hong Kong. This pronouncement created embarrassment all round. It happened on Wednesday, 10 October 1894. The governor general was in the west somewhere between Regina and Calgary and in his absence the country was administered by the chief justice. Thompson seems to have been on his way to Toronto, to give a speech at the unveiling of the Queen's Park monument to Sir John Macdonald. In their absence, perhaps because of it, Patterson was persuaded that a Canadian offer would be welcome to the British and, though it would probably be refused, would give Canada good notices in London. It did not go through cabinet; it went to the chief justice who, as usual with him, signed it without looking at it. Off it went to London, not even in cipher. The British were nonplussed, as well they might be. The Colonial Office were ready to take up the Canadian offer; Campbell-Bannerman at the War Office knew something of the provenance and saved the day by preventing it from becoming public. In Canada, Thompson was furious, and the Canadian embarrassment was covered up by explaining that the offer was meant to refer to defences at Halifax, not Hong Kong.[62] It would not be the first or the last time that Thompson had reason to distrust the actions, or even the ordinary common sense, of his colleagues.

Thompson also found relations with some of the Catholic bishops difficult. He had had experience with Archbishop Cleary's passionate dislike of Meredith. But none of them, least of all Archbishop Taché, were very tractable. They expected more of a Conservative government and a Catholic minister of justice than either government or Thompson was capable of producing. Thompson's relations with Archbishop Taché over Manitoba and the North-West were a sad story; disappointments on both sides, misunderstandings, plain bad luck, to say nothing of remarkable casualness in the handling of Canadian government business by their London lawyers. On Taché's side, there was a strong disposition to colour reality, to discern persecution where none was intended, to find plots where there were none. It was not surprising that an old man of over seventy, who had lived through so much, who had had to cope with the Manitoba government driven by Joseph Martin in full determination of its goal to making Manitoba schools non-denominational, was by now slightly paranoic. Thompson's letters to him showed remarkable patience; but by 1892 Thompson's private comments were apt to be less patient.

Just when Thompson became prime minister in November 1892, the Manitoba schools question had reached an awkward, not to say critical, stage. That had been the result of the almost incomprehensible decision of the Privy Council in *Winnipeg* v. *Barrett*. In Manitoba the city of Winnipeg, backed by the Manitoba government, was successful in its contention that the Manitoba Act did not guarantee to Dr J.K. Barrett his right to Catholic schools. On February 2 1891 the Manitoba Supreme Court concurred. Within a few months the case was argued on appeal before the Supreme Court of Canada; there, on October 28 1891 five judges agreed in throwing out the City of Winnipeg's (and Manitoba's) contention. Dr J.K. Barrett and the Catholic separate school system were vindicated by the highest court in Canada. Unfortunately for Thompson, for Taché, and for everyone perhaps, it could not stop there. Manitoba appealed immediately to the Privy Council in London.

It was in London where things began to go awry. Archbishop Taché and his Winnipeg lawyer, J.S. Ewart, the local powers behind Barrett, naturally wanted the best counsel they could get. The Canadian government was footing the bill, but Taché pointed out that money was 'a mere trifle compared to the magnitude of the consequences.' He and J.S. Ewart wanted Edward Blake. Thompson did not trust Blake, was not at all sure of his disposition toward Manitoba Catholic schools, and despite pressure from Bishop Taché, refused.[63] Then there was the question of the senior counsel, who had to be British. The most brilliant advocate at the British bar was Sir Horace Davey. Canada's London lawyers, Bompas, Bischoff, were ordered to put Sir Horace on retainer. Thompson could not believe the rumours circulating in December 1891 that Davey had been retained by Manitoba. He reassured Archbishop Taché on Christmas eve that there should be no difficulty.[64]

But to the chagrin of Archbishop Taché, the surprise and vexation of Thompson, it was discovered that Sir Horace Davey had, indeed, been secured by the government of Manitoba! How had such an astonishing event occurred? The Canadian government was not named in *Winnipeg* v. *Barrett*; Sedgewick had instructed Bompas, Bischoff by cable to retain Sir Horace Davey in the 'Manitoba Separate School case' on appeal to the Privy Council. The parties were not named and Bompas assumed, since the Dominion government was involved, that the Queen's name would appear in the case. When at last they actually asked for more information and got it, they delivered a copy of the whole argument to Sir Horace Davey and his colleague D'Alton McCarthy, both retained by Manitoba! Thompson was angry with Bompas, Bischoff for two reasons; their being too casual by half in not following up Sedgewick's cable; and in delivering the whole Roman Catholic case to the counsel for Manitoba.[65]

That was bad enough. Bompas, Bischoff then retained the attorney general of the Salisbury government, Sir Richard Webster, later Lord Alverstone. British attorneys general were allowed, up to 1895, their own private practice. Webster had an enormous one. He had also to conduct the legal business for the crown, and as MP for the Isle of Wight, was suddenly in June 1892 – a month before *Winnipeg* v. *Barrett* was due for argument – plunged into a general election called by his own government. Moreover, Webster was neither clever nor learned. He had made his way up by luck, persistence, industry, and a flamboyant personality. He was not very sympathetic personally to the position of Manitoba separate schools, and he believed the words 'by practice' in the crucial section 22 of the Manitoba Act meant nothing. In fact, Webster blundered from start to finish, so badly that Samuel Blake, the great Edward's brother, could say little or nothing without contradicting his own senior counsel.[66] Samuel Blake was not altogether helpful himself. At one point during the argument of the case – 12–14 July 1892 – Lord Shand interjected that if Barrett won his case, would that not continue denominational education for all time to come? Sam Blake replied, 'I dare say that that may be the result of it ... I, for one, deplore it in my own province of Ontario. I had a great deal rather it was not so [*sic*]. I was one of those who struggled against it.' So much for frankness in advocates! Even Lord Shand felt constrained to reply to Blake, 'I do not say that it is not right, if the statute does it, but I want to see the result.' The Privy Council decision was handed down on 30 July 1892. It threw out the Roman Catholic contention, with costs.[67]

Far from ending the question, the Privy Council decision in *Winnipeg* v. *Barrett* made it worse. Protestants were quite willing to accept the ruling from the highest tribunal in the empire that Roman Catholic separate schools in Manitoba had no legal validity. Even the Toronto *Empire* said it was now impossible to do anything for the Roman Catholic minority in Manitoba.[68] Many in Ontario heaved a sigh of relief and cheerfully consigned the Manitoba school question to the limbo of forgotten transactions. J.R. Gowan was under this impression. Thompson corrected him:

From the tone of your observations about the school question it seems to me that the details of the case have not been before you. The judgement of the P Council – instead of settling the question has closed our only avenue of escape and has thrown it upon us to settle – by virtue of the clauses of the Constitutional [BNA] Act about an appeal.[69]

Roman Catholics who looked hard at the Manitoba Act and the BNA Act discerned grounds for action by the federal cabinet and even by the federal Parliament. It was made abundantly clear by St Boniface that it would insist on an appeal to cabinet. In Thompson's view a hearing on the merits of such an appeal was justified. A Conservative MP called on Thompson at his house in December 1892 urging that no action be taken. Thompson said to him, 'What would you do if you were in my place, and these people, believing they had a right of appeal, came to you for a hearing?' 'Well,' replied the MP after a pause, 'I think I would hear what they had to say, but —' 'That,' interrupted Sir John, 'is precisely what we intend to do, and that is all we have so far determined to do.'[70] There would have to be preliminary questions heard first, namely, procedures for an appeal and whether there were legal grounds for it.

Procedure was not difficult to arrange; but the ground for an appeal was a more substantial legal question. The Manitoba Act and the BNA Act differed, and whether there was an appeal to the Dominion cabinet depended upon one's interpretation of both in the light of *Winnipeg* v. *Barrett*. Did section 93 of the BNA Act apply to Manitoba at all? Was it not overridden by a specific, and later (1870), enactment on the question of education? The Roman Catholics said no. The Protestants said yes. The Protestants claimed that the differences between the BNA Act and the Manitoba Act represented a deliberate attempt to give the province of Manitoba more complete control of its own education.[71]

It was arranged in October 1892 that a committee of cabinet should be struck to consider these matters, to hear J.S. Ewart, counsel for the Catholics, argue the justification for the cabinet hearing such an appeal. The committee consisted of Thompson, Bowell, Chapleau, and Daly, and it first met on 25 and 26 November. It was a public occasion and so intended. It was in fact the first meeting of a judicial committee of the Canadian Privy Council. It was made public because it purported to deal with a question judicially, not politically.[72] Newspapermen were invited to the Privy Council room in the East Block, where in the ante-room a large crowd were welcomed by Sir John Thompson in person and invited in to hear the case. If the committee recommended favourably, the appeal would be heard by the full Council, with both the province of Manitoba and the Roman Catholics given the right to appear. Thompson continued to envision a judicial, not a political role, for the cabinet in this appeal; Chapleau was unhappy over the abandonment of cabinet's political function.[73] In his Toronto speech to the young Conservatives on 13 January Thompson had been forced to make clear, as a result of questions from the floor, what exactly the policy of his government was. That there were warm feelings in Canada on both sides of the Manitoba school question Thompson admitted. But there was only one solution for it, as far as his government was concerned. That was 'to stand strictly by what the constitution provides.' No member of his government had any wish to interfere with the legitimate rights of the provinces; but neither 'will we desert any duty which is imposed upon us by the constitution, no matter how painful it might be to our feelings or obnoxious to others (cheers).'

I want simply to impress upon you this one thing, that candidly and honestly we intend to be guided ... by the constitution, and the constitution as it will be expounded by the highest authorities that can be got to expound it, and not by the private opinion of any member of the Government. (Great cheering.) When I tell you, therefore, that we intend to be guided by the constitution, I am not equivocating and I am not concealing.[74]

That was clear-headed and sensible enough, and as good standing ground as could be found amid the waves, currents, and gales that were sweeping around the question. Whether the rock of the constitution was as firm or solid beneath the government as Thompson would have liked was another matter.

The rights of Roman Catholics in Manitoba before 1870, so the Privy Council had said, were not affected by the 1890 school acts. That really meant that they had no rights to be deprived of. The questions now facing Thompson were basically three: Was a separate school system set up in Manitoba between 1870 and 1890? If so, and if abolished, is there a remedy? And where is the power to give the remedy – in the BNA Act, section 93, subsection 3, or in the Manitoba Act, section 22, subsection 2? These three issues broke legally into six questions, and the report of the cabinet on 29 December 1892 was the basis of *Brophy* v. *Attorney General of Manitoba*, the case that was launched after the further hearing of January 1893, at which Manitoba declined to be represented. In February 1894, judgment was given in the Supreme Court of Canada. It decided all six questions in the negative, by a narrow three to two majority. The Supreme Court of Canada, following the principle of *stare decisis*, felt bound to construe the Brophy case in the light of *Barrett.*

At this point, the Thompson government were in the clear. The Roman Catholics in Manitoba had no rights left. To escape completely from the clutches of the Manitoba school question all the government had to do, as Caron pointed out, was 'se croiser les bras à laisser faire.' Some Conservative papers in Ontario assumed that. The *Toronto World,* on 21 February 1894, with visible relief rejoiced that 'the Manitoba school question has received its final quietus.' Even J.J. Curran, Catholic though he was, rejoiced at the news.

That was not Thompson's view. There would have to be an appeal to London, an appeal that, he was sure, would vindicate the rights of Manitoba Roman Catholics. Thompson did not breathe a sigh of relief in February 1894: he was resolved that there would be a constitutional remedy. If there were not, if the Privy Council failed the Catholics, he would then do what he could to obtain a constitutional amendment.[75] Archbishop Taché was by now so sceptical that he thought the appeal was a waste of time; a legal opinion in the Brophy case was only an opinion, and if the government did not like it they could ignore it. The old archbishop was by now tired to death with the legal subtleties surrounding legislation that he had, after all, helped sponsor years earlier. Poor Taché! The last letter he wrote to Thompson, three weeks before his death in June 1894, on the North-West school question, was full of well-meaning but real errors of fact or argument. Thompson wearily and with some asperity scribbled corrections in the margins, page after page, some as to facts, some as to glosses on the facts.[76] And as late as October 1894, Thompson refused to interfere with amendments Manitoba had passed in 1894 to its school acts, changes that allegedly affected Catholic control of their school property. Thompson told Senator T.-A. Bernier, the mayor of St Boniface, '... we cannot undertake, by the power of disallowance, to correct all the improprieties and unfairness in provincial legislation ... they, not we, are the judges of what is according to "public order" and propriety.'[77]

So it was that from January 1893 for the next two years legal questions surrounding the Manitoba school question were relegated to the courts, and in the courts they stayed. One member of the opposition, Israel Tarte, thought this was too clever by half. It was 'the tactics of the tomorrows,' he said. The government dared not risk the displeasure of the Roman Catholics, for no government in Canada could stay in power against the wishes of the Catholics. Tarte said the government had grossly deceived the Manitoba Catholics; Chapleau had promised Taché in 1890 that all would be well, even if the government did not disallow the Manitoba acts. Tarte's view was that the government had taken refuge behind a screen of legalisms. His motion, made on going into Supply, on 6 March 1893, a month after Parliament opened, was that the government had now assumed judicial functions in the place of its normal political ones, and that these judicial functions were 'wholly unknown to the law,' and were subversive of the government's proper political responsibilities.[78]

Thompson went over the history for the House. Not a single member of the government in 1890 had wanted to use disallowance against Manitoba school legislation, certainly not after the precedents from the New Brunswick school question, 1872–5, and the Prince Edward Island one after 1877. Thompson shared that reluctance. 'If the [Manitoba] Acts were *ultra vires* they do not need to be disallowed; if they are *intra vires* they should not be disallowed.' That became government policy.[79]

Some Protestant MPs suspected that the government was trying to get around the Privy Council decision in *Winnipeg* v. *Barrett.* That was D'Alton McCarthy's view. McCarthy's drift to leeward, away from the close-hauled tack taken by the government, was already observable. Late in December 1892 the Toronto *Empire* warned its readers that McCarthy was ready to make a break with the party. It concluded that McCarthy was jealous that his strictures were having no effect; public affairs and the Conservative party seemed to be going on just as if he did not exist.[80] Whatever instrument he used to get at Thompson seemed not to function.

Not everyone in the party thought the *Empire* was right in going after McCarthy. A Conservative family quarrel need not have been brought into the open; one result was to give joy to the Liberals who badly needed it. Griffin thought McCarthy would do well to remember the fate of other politicians such as William McDougall, Howe, Brown, who had sought power from sectional prejudices. David Creighton pointed out to Thompson that only two of the Ontario Conservative papers had spoken in McCarthy's favour. Out of fifty that was a good record.[81]

Thompson recognized that some MPs were bound to suspect the government of wanting to bury *Winnipeg* v. *Barrett.* Equally, he knew that others thought the government was playing for time, teasing out litigation, leading the Roman Catholics 'a dance through the courts.' But, he told the House, the government was doing neither. It could not act, not because it was unwilling, but because the law was unclear. It would have put Canada in a most anomalous position if, in dealing with such a delicate and sensitive question, the government proceeded to make remedial orders, or asked the House to pass remedial legislation, and then discovered that 'we have simply bungled our work. The province [of Manitoba] would laugh at us and defy us and disregard our authority.' No; that would not do. Thompson was forced to admit, however, that the Roman Catholics were not enthusiastic about returning to the Privy Council in London with the Brophy case. The Catholics feared that unfriendly Privy Council. It had ruled against them already.[82]

The debate on Tarte's motion went on for three days. On the Wednesday afternoon, the third day, there was a great gathering of Conservative MPs in Room 16 of the Centre Block to wish Thompson God speed and good luck on his forthcoming trip to Paris. Thompson was forced to climb up on a chair – 'to attain the height of our stalwarts,' he said – and thanked them for their wishes and hopes that he would be able to approach the Bering Sea Tribunal in a judicial spirit. 'Well,' said he with a smile, 'I shall not quite know until the conclusion of the present debate in parliament whether one is even at liberty to approach a subject in a judicial spirit (cheers and laughter).'[83] Despite Thompson's sally, aimed at the wording of Tarte's amendment, the debate in the Commons was more dispassionate and judicious than might have been expected. The vote came at 5:50 a.m. on 9 March. McCarthy, O'Brien, and three French Canadians voted with the opposition; but the government still won by a clear fifty votes, 121 to 71.

While Thompson would be gone, Mackenzie Bowell, senior member of cabinet, was acting prime minister, with Foster as leader of the House of Commons. Thompson's acting minister of justice was not Caron, but Ouimet, for which Thompson apologized gracefully in a private note to Caron.[84] There was also a change at the Department of Justice. Thompson burnt his bridge of retreat from politics and filled the appointment at the Supreme Court of Canada. The new pusine judge would be Thompson's own deputy minister, Robert Sedgewick, one of the ablest candidates. Thompson liked to encourage talent within the civil service by promoting good men to positions all too often filled by political patronage. Sedgewick was the second deputy minister he had sacrificed that way.

Sedgewick's successor was a third Nova Scotian in that role, E.L. Newcombe, of the Halifax firm of Meagher, Drysdale, and Newcombe. Newcombe was only thirty-four years old, born in the Cornwallis River valley, his great-grandfather having come from Connecticut in 1760.

Newcombe graduated from Dalhousie in 1878, had been called to the Nova Scotian bar just before the formation of the Dalhousie Law School, and was soon attached to the school as lecturer in marine insurance. Newcombe was not as brilliant or as quick as Robert Sedgewick, but made up for it in being painstaking and industrious. J.A. Chisholm of Halifax was pleased that Thompson and the Department of Justice would be served by so methodical a deputy minister.[85] Newcombe arrived in Ottawa the weekend before Thompson's departure for Paris, and was to stay as deputy minister of justice for over thirty years.

Ottawa, that March 1893, was piled so high with snow that the sleigh taking Thompson, Annie, and Frankie to the station in the afternoon of Friday, 9 March was broken before they got there. New York was not much better. *La Bretagne*, a fine, big French Line steamer, left for Le Havre on the Monday with Thompson and family aboard. Even the Toronto *Globe* wished them bon voyage;[86] whatever may have been the *Globe*'s confidence in Thompson's politics, it had ample faith in his law and diplomacy.

20

The Paris Interlude, 1893

La Bretagne ploughed eastward, the weather getting milder by the day. It was delightful, like summer, a fine ship and not many passengers. There were Thompson, Annie, Frankie; Babe and Helena came with them to be installed in the Sacred Heart Convent in Paris. Only Thompson and Babe were seasick, and that only for a day or so. Most mornings Thompson was on deck at seven taking a tramp, usually with Lady Alice Caron, who was an excellent sailor. They landed at Le Havre in the same summer weather, the cows already out in fields and plants burgeoning everywhere. They arrived in Paris via the boat train from Le Havre on Monday afternoon, 22 March, to be met at Gare St Lazare by Charles Hibbert and Janet Tupper as well as Joseph and Minette Pope. The Thompsons were installed in the same hotel as the Americans (and the Empress Eugénie), the Continental, a vast palace, facing the Tuileries Gardens. But, said Thompson, 'our rooms were too *high* in more sense that one.' They moved down rue Castiglione to the Hotel Dominici, to rooms that were cooler, more accessible, and cheaper, in a quiet hotel between the rue Honoré and Place Vendôme.[1]

Paris was looking glorious. Grass already up, fresh produce coming in from the south, day after day the city was radiant with sunshine and spring. Not a drop of rain fell until 7 May. Thompson could walk to the arbitration sittings held at the Foreign Ministry, across the Tuileries Gardens, across the Seine by the Pont Solferino to the Quai d'Orsay. The Foreign Ministry, built in 1846, lay a few hundred yards westward along the Quai. It was a Paris opulent with flowers and blue skies and Thompson fell head over heels in love with her from the start. 'He is wild about Paris,' was Griffin's description after Thompson had had four solid months of it – four months of the arbitration, four months of the heat, and still adored the place. He was an avid and indefatigable sightseer, and armed with Baedeker learnt its history in that most agreeable fashion, by walking it and looking at it. 'I have been so much impressed by Paris,' he wrote Griffin in mid-April, 'that I look on it as rather a hardship that I shall have to spend a few days in filthy, brutal London before going home.' Notre Dame was far superior to Westminister Abbey; it was in perfect order, whereas Westminster Abbey was crumbling owing to the British being too niggardly to repair the roof properly. Thompson could have echoed the *cri de coeur* of Henry James, 'Oh, the grimness of London!' James added, 'And, oh! the cookery of London!' Thompson, unlike James, rather relished the London grill, chops, steaks, and other dishes cooked on the grid-iron. For Thompson the London grill-rooms were all that made the idea of going to London endurable.[2]

Those grill-rooms! Thompson liked to eat and it was showing; he was heavy and getting heavier. His coat stretched tight across his chest, he looked to the public a little stern – buttoned up, as modern jargon has it; but when he laughed his whole frame laughed with him, as a sunny summer portrait of 1894 shows and numerous correspondents testify. He was, as his new 1893 Canadian passport had it, five feet, seven inches and stout, his brown hair greying.[3]

That he had needed his passport that year at all had been uncertain. Questions arose after Thompson became prime minister. When appointed to the Bering Sea Tribunal by the British government, Thompson was minister of justice; the other British arbitrator was a judge. Of the two American arbitrators, one was a Supreme Court judge, the other a hard-line anglophobe southern senator. The British Foreign Office came to the view, late in November 1892, that it would be improper for Prime Minister Thompson to sit as arbitrator on a matter in which his government was the plaintiff. The Foreign Office cabled through Sir Charles Tupper asking whom Thompson would recommend as arbitrator in case he felt unable to attend. The purport of the cable was that Thompson should believe himself disqualified. There was a more specific reason also. The Bering Sea Tribunal was to meet in Paris on 23 February 1893 for the exchange of protocols and documents, and would then adjourn for a fortnight while documents were studied. Thompson assumed that his presence was unnecessary at this first, pro forma, meeting; certainly the Canadian Parliament made his presence in Paris at that time impossible. The struggle behind the scenes comprehended, thus, two points: in Sir Charles Tupper's mind was the awkwardness of the timing; what most concerned the Foreign Office was the impropriety of Thompson's going at all.

Thompson for his part was determined to carry on if possible, and he believed it was his problem whether he could make Paris or not. He did not deign to reply to the first cable. To a second, late in December, he sent a sharp rejoinder. 'The c.o. need not try to oust me from the Arbitration.'[4] Thompson felt that he were deliberately being shunted, perhaps by the Colonial Office, perhaps by the Foreign Office, and that both might have been abetted by old Sir Charles Tupper. In fact both telegrams were sent on the initiative of Lord Rosebery, the foreign minister in Gladstone's government. Thompson asked Lord Stanley to write Lord Ripon and Lord Rosebery that he was anxious not to give up being arbitrator.[5]

At the Foreign Office the permanent under-secretary, Sir Thomas Sanderson, seemed to think that neither the United States nor Canada had any sense of decency, an opinion that Sir Robert Meade at the Colonial Office was inclined to share. He was however ready to give way to Canadian insistence:

On the whole I am clearly of op^n that it is not desirable to quarrel with Canada over a point of diplomatic etiquette. We have clearly learned that Canada wishes to keep her Arbitrator.

If we insist and drive out Thompson and the arbitration in its result is displeasing to Canada, which is quite on the cards, she will say that her case was given away by our refusing on (what she considers) a point of pedantry to let her have the one arbitrator who knows best her case.[6]

That was sensible enough. Ripon said the same to Lord Rosebery. That was not the end of it, however. The Foreign Office cabled the British minister in Washington for his opinion on the continuation of Thompson's appointment. That possibly meant ascertaining from J.W. Foster, now American secretary of state, what *his* view of Thompson's appointment would be! The Colonial Office bridled; Meade wrote Ripon that 'the F.O. are making a hideous mess of this Arbitration business.' Ripon urged Rosebery to have Pauncefote reined in. 'At present I share the objections felt by Meade and think if it got out, as it almost certainly would do, that we had consulted the u.s. Sec'y of State on the matter, the effect in Canada would be bad – But you may be able to convince me this is a mistake.'[7] Ripon made no mistake. Pauncefote was reined in. Moreover, the 23 February meeting of the tribunal was also inconvenient for the Italian and the Norwegian arbitrators, and it became purely formal, as Thompson expected.

The Bering Sea Tribunal was organized by international treaty and protocol. Great Britain and the United States each appointed an agent, to lead the research for his side. The British government appointed C.H. Tupper, minister of marine and fisheries, and the Americans appointed J.W. Foster, sometime before he became American secretary of state in succession to Blaine. The treaty between Britain and the United States laid down that each should appoint two arbitrators of the total of seven; the other three were 'neutrals;' from Italy, Marquis Visconti Venosta, a nephew of Cavour's; a Norwegian Supreme Court judge, Gregers Gram of Christiania (Oslo), later prime minister of Norway and Sweden; and Baron de Courcelle of France, recently French ambassador to Germany. An unusual provision in the treaty was that Italy, Norway–Sweden, and France were requested to choose jurists who were acquainted with English. The French foreign minister took exception to this unusual – he used the word bizarre – stipulation, when Paris was the place of meeting and French the normal diplomatic language of the world.[8] Having made this point, the French then accepted English and behaved like the civilized hosts they were. The British appointed as arbitrators Baron Hannen, member of the Judicial Committee of the Privy Council and one of the ablest jurists in England, and Thompson. The Americans appointed Justice John Harlan of the Supreme Court of the United States and, much less to their credit, the senior Democrat on the Senate Foreign Relations Committee, a notorious anglophobe, Senator J.T. Morgan. In the United States it was felt that President Harrison, a Republican, deserved credit for appointing a Democrat![9]

There was a battery of lawyers on each side charged with arguing the case before the tribunal. For the British the senior counsel was the Attorney General Sir Charles Russell, appointed by the Gladstone government, a much abler man than his predecessor from the Salisbury government, Sir Richard Webster, who, with a nice touch of courtesy by Lord Rosebery and Gladstone, was included as counsel on the British team, with Christopher Robinson of Canada. The American legal group were headed by E.J. Phelps, who had been minister to Great Britain during Cleveland's first administration when the sealing question had first arisen; J.C. Carter of New York; Judge H.M. Blodgett of the US District Court in Chicago; and F.R. Coudert of New York, the only member from the United States who was fluent in French.

The British–Canadian case was not a sure thing. Lord Hannen's and Thompson's stay in Paris was made continually uneasy by well-justified fears of the result. The treaty conferred no power on the arbitrators to touch the privileges of the Alaska Commercial Company, and in consequence Canada stood to lose everything and gain little or nothing. It was not Canada's or the arbitrators' fault that Lord Salisbury had agreed to a treaty stacked the wrong way. Thompson said privately that Lord Salisbury's acceptance of the Arbitration Treaty 'was one of the worst acts of what I regard as a very stupid and worthless life.'[10] Thompson would have agreed doubtless with Bismarck's famous description of Salisbury, 'lath painted to look like iron.'

The real business of the tribunal opened on Tuesday, 23 March at the Foreign Ministry on the Quai d'Orsay, at 12 noon. The pace was leisurely; meetings four days a week, Tuesday through Friday; four hours a day, from 11:30 am until after 5 pm, but with a substantial break at 1:30 pm for lunch. It was not exactly lunch! It was a sumptuous meal set out in the Foreign Ministry dining-room, and was served up, said Thompson, as if they were kings: six or seven courses, four or five wines, choice fresh fruit, cigars. 'No feasts are more insidiously unwholesome,' wrote the correspondent of the London *Daily News*, 'than those prepared by great French cooks.' Thompson complained, and Annie more often than he did, of this serious change in their regimen.[11] The private entertainment was as lavish as the official. Within three weeks Thompson and Annie had been to the notable theatres, and with the Carons and the Grams had occupied Madame Carnot's box at the opera. They lunched with President Carnot himself, then at the height of his popularity, on Saturday, 15 April.

It was very easy-going. The utensils at the Foreign Ministry were designed for an age more stately than the late nineteenth century. Joseph Pope recalled the entire absence of blotting paper – they still used sand for blotting ink at the Quai d'Orsay – and the exclusive use of quill pens. Not for the French Foreign Office such new-fangled gadgets as steel nibs![12] This kind of pace suited the Americans. They were not in a hurry; they received a handsome per diem, so they and their families were hoping for a long arbitration, whereas the English lawyers got only the modest overall fee fixed by law. Thompson and Lord Hannen were each paid £1,000 as were the three foreign arbitrators.[13] 'There will be no unseemly precipitation,' Thompson wrote Lord Stanley, 'no House of Commons hours. Lord Hannen sighs deeply when he reflects on these un-English arrangements ... diplomatic usage is followed and no idea of business seems to trouble the foreigners or the Americans – the latter being nearly all men who have no particular duty at home and have brought – each one – his family with him for the summer.'[14]

The seven arbitrators were seated behind a long table that stood on a dais stretched across the end of a spacious room in the Foreign Ministry. Baron de Courcelle – elected president of the tribunal that first day, a courtesy to France – sat in the middle. De Courcelle was a short little man, anything but a passive participant, always asking questions, to the annoyance of the lawyers. To de Courcelle's left sat Justice Harlan, the tallest man there, well over six feet and all of it straight up. The Italian marquis was next on the president's left, with a square white beard, a huge shock of white hair, and a look in his face that suggested he was not being wildly amused. At the far end was Senator Morgan who intervened – perhaps the word is interfered – frequently in the proceedings, some-times belligerently, and looked like an old-fashioned southern statesman from Civil War times. Both American arbitrators were flanked by huge spittoons, not there for ornament. Joseph Pope used to watch in amusement the trepidation of the stately old Italian on hearing warning signals from either side of him of impending use of those spittoons; the marquis never seemed willing to rely upon the accuracy of the Americans' aim. To de Courcelle's right was, first, Lord Hannen, erect, handsome, intelligent, apt to be quiet. Next, Gregers Gram, the Norwegian, was equally reserved, and had the habit of holding his round-bearded face in both hands as if he were concentrating on taking in the English and not finding it easy. Thompson sat on the president's far right, and seemed to reporters now and then to succumb to a disposition to nod. Justice Harlan used to shake himself up by pacing behind the seven chairs and long table, and it seemed to have the same effect on Thompson, shaking him up too.[15]

For the first two weeks they heard motions and argument about admission of different kinds of evidence. E.J. Phelps, the senior American counsel, arguing against the admissibility of certain evidence, seemed to be attacking not only the existence of the tribunal but the Republican president who had the hardihood to agree to it.[16] Phelps was a New England lawyer, tall, stoop-shouldered, with a cold, thin, reedy voice. His principal colleague, J.C. Carter of New York, was ruddy, full-faced, and double-chinned, and took to wearing a little skull cap to conceal his baldness. All the Americans were inclined to address the arbitrators as if they were a jury not judges. This did not sit well with the four European arbitrators or with Thompson.

From the beginning the lawyers on the British side resolved to argue only what could be sustained judicially. This moderation told. The British–Canadian contention was that the waters of the Bering Sea were like those of any other sea, that the territorial waters of the Pribiloff Islands were the three-mile limit. Outside of that seals could be taken by anyone. The problem for the Americans was to argue on the basis of what they believed the Russian position had been prior to 1867.

The Americans were not helped by weakness in Russian. There were numerous Russian documents in the State Department from which, it was believed, ample justification for the American position would be found. In 1892 J.W. Foster, after some difficulty, found someone who would translate documents for him. The translator, anxious to please, cooked the translation to suit the taste of his masters. The Americans published both the Russian and the English texts. The British Foreign Office read some of the documents in Russian and discovered, as did some American officials, that the American translation and the original Russian by no means agreed, indeed differed materially on the very points the Americans were anxious to rely on. Foster was acutely embarrassed, as well he might be.[17] The American contention that Russia had treated the whole of the Bering Sea as her territorial waters, that the seals were her property duly acquired by the Americans, was suspect. Russia had not treated the Bering Sea as a *mare clausum*, nor had she enforced rules against sealing on the high seas. These contentions, originally made by lawyers for the Alaska Commercial Company, would be difficult to sustain.

The lawyers' arguments began on 11 April with J.C. Carter's opening speech for the American side, which lasted for three mortal weeks! Carter's arguments were as impassioned as if he were addressing a jury. Thompson wrote to Griffin as Carter launched into his second week, 'Here we are still at the beginning of the beginning. Brother Carter has orated and narrated and having done so for a week is engaged today – at the beginning of another week, in showing that the u.s. Gov't have been consistent. We hope that by next week he will start at his argument.' It was not until 2 May that Carter 'delighted us by concluding.'[18] He was followed for the rest of the week by his fellow New York lawyer, F.R. Coudert. Then on 9 May Sir Charles Russell launched the British–Canadian case.

Tall, graceful, white-haired, Russell had a commanding presence. He was a lawyer armed at all points, cool, disdainful, ironic by turns; he could also be aggressive and impatient to the point of rudeness. He took snuff and not just a little; Thompson marvelled at the way Sir Charles seemed to move through 'billows of snuff which keep him waving a red silk handkerchief and blowing fog horns all the time.'[19] The stories about Sir Charles Russell in Paris were legion. When he first arrived, he ordered an English breakfast. Of course nothing was right. 'What is that?' Russell disdainfully asked, turning over an omelette in disgust, 'It looks like a geological formation!' Russell was the French caricature of the Englishman abroad, insular and argumentative. It was said that the only person who could teach him manners was Minette Pope. This he did not seem to mind, especially when Minette was mixed with whist or poker. All in all, Thompson wrote his Halifax brother-in-law, J.A. Chisholm, it was interesting to see the array of famous counsel; none of them lived up to their reputation. Sir Richard Webster was very ordinary; Sir Charles Russell was much better, vigorous and quick, but ill-mannered and undignified. J.C. Carter was always speaking with a quid of tobacco rolling around in his mouth.[20]

Newspaper correspondents found the long opening arguments wearisome, but to the initiated the proceedings had their own drama, not always peaceful or dignified. On 11 May Russell was arguing that the American assertion of property rights in the seals was impossible to sustain, that even the American secretary of state, T.F. Bayard, had never tried to justify the American seizures of Canadian vessels on that shaky ground. At this, Russell was interrupted by Senator Morgan, the American arbitrator, and by E.J. Phelps, the American lawyer. Russell became angry at interruptions; Morgan and Phelps expostulated that they were not going to guarantee payment of damages to Canada even *if* the tribunal found against the American case. At this Lord Hannen, the English arbitrator, exclaimed, 'Then our whole arbitration is useless and the whole question will have to be re-opened!' That was patched up. The following day Russell and Morgan clashed again, over the American seizures of Canadian vessels:

MORGAN – If the seizures can be justified on other principles than those advanced at the hearing of a case, is it not open to the United States to raise them?

RUSSELL – No. The United States seized ships on certain grounds. The judge punished the men in accordance therewith. A great nation cannot shift and change her position. Moreover, the reasons now advanced, even if admitted, do not justify the fining and imprisoning of sailors.[21]

Of course Russell ridiculed Carter's contention that the seals visited the Pribiloff Islands voluntarily to submit themselves to human control![22]

Thompson's interventions from the dais were aimed mainly at keeping the discussion on track. The question of malice in the prosecution by Americans came up; Thompson simply asked, to what branch of the questions before the tribunal was the issue of malice relevant? Thompson hardly ever spoke, but when he did, as on this occasion, he settled the point. What impressed Russell was Thompson's extraordinary mastery of detail; 'he really seemed to know the correspondence and the evidence by heart.'[23]

Annie and Frankie, with Alice Caron and her daughter, went off to Lourdes. It was in southwestern France, in the shoulders of the Pyrenees, and had been a shrine only since 1858. By Thompson's time the pilgrims averaged half a million a year. Thompson hoped it would secure some treasury of blessings for himself and Caron that they could draw on. 'I fear,' he wrote Caron, 'that my account at the Bank of Heaven is terribly overdrawn.' Thompson did not expect any miracles at Lourdes for Frankie; he laughed at contemporary reports of miracles.[24]

Chapleau, also in Paris, did not go to Lourdes for cures; he was, said Thompson, 'to try conclusions' with his surgeon in a few days. In the meantime, Chapleau, Masson, and Fabre (the Canadian agent in Paris), invited Thompson to join them for 'breakfast' at 12:30. Clearly Sir Charles Russell's kind of breakfast was not intended![25]

Despite these manifold diversions, Thompson could not escape problems from across the Atlantic. He had a sharp reminder the moment he got off the train in Paris on 22 March. Young Tupper urgently pressed an envelope into his hand. It was old Sir Charles Tupper's resignation as Canadian high commissioner. The commercial treaty with France negotiated by Tupper under the aegis of Lord Dufferin, the British ambassador in Paris, had been, so it appeared, repudiated by the Canadian government in Ottawa. Sir Charles was furious, to put it mildly; his son added that the British government was annoyed, the French government upset, and matters of great pith and moment between Britain and France put at hazard by the dangerous and unreliable Canadians in Ottawa![26]

Canada had wanted a trade treaty with France for some years. She had been specifically excluded in 1873 when Britain renewed a commercial agreement with France: Canadian products went into France at maximum rates, British at minimum. Sir Alexander Galt had tried and failed in 1878 to get that changed. Sir Charles Tupper took it up late in 1892. After some difficulties, a treaty was negotiated, signed, and sent to Canada for ratification. The Canadian government wanted more information, Parliament was about to prorogue, and there were questions about the terms.[27] The contretemps that developed in March 1893 between Paris, Ottawa, and London arose from Tupper exceeding his instructions and, not least, from bad communications, a Reuters despatch giving the opposite of what had been said in Ottawa adding fuel to the flame. But the whole question was grossly blown out of proportion by Tupper Sr in London and, it has to be added, Tupper Jr in Paris. Thompson, who was abruptly presented with it all, thought he was fortunate even to be able to get to his hotel!

Thompson blamed the incident mainly on Sir Charles. He had worked on the fears of the British so successfully that Canada might have been compelled to swallow the treaty without knowing fully what it meant had Thompson not been on the spot in Paris to see things for himself. Thompson then cabled Ottawa, and Ottawa cabled London, that they had the prime minister's authorization for saying the excitement was largely imaginary, that there was no reason to depart from the principle of delay established by the Canadian cabinet before Thompson left Canada.[28]

Thompson dished out soothing syrup to old Sir Charles: Tupper should wait to see the official reports from Canada about what had really transpired in Ottawa; nothing the Canadian government had done was to be construed as a reflection on Tupper, Lord Rosebery in London, or Lord Dufferin in Paris. After ten days of diligent inquiry, Thompson concluded that the great indignation alleged in London and Paris was 'confined to the members of one family represented just now in the two cities.' The Paris representative had been at work at Lord Dufferin, and the London one with Lords Rosebery and Ripon. Thompson concluded that Ripon's far-fetched allusion to the arbitration itself being threatened by irresponsible Canadian delays in the French treaty was so absurd that it was 'statement of which no British minister would have been capable without a malignant suggestion from outside.'[29]

Finally Sir Charles Tupper came to Paris to see Thompson, and Thompson expected a battle; but Tupper was mild, quiet, and, according to Thompson, very conscious of his breach of duty. The more one looked at the episode the worse Tupper's breach seemed to be. After receiving a cable from Bowell indicating that the Canadian government could not make out what the cabled provisions were and had not yet received the draft treaty itself, Tupper had actually executed the treaty with Lord Dufferin and the French, telling both that Canada was perfectly satisfied! In Ottawa, George Foster was resolute and angry. Sir Charles Tupper was becoming unbearable, with leaked cables to the *Montreal Star*, recklessly bulldozing his way:

There is a very strong feeling here – unanimous in fact, against his course, and I do not see how a gov't can fail to take notice of it. He rushed into the press, tried to inflame the feelings of the Home authorities & the susceptibilities of the French, and practically assumed to dictate the course of the Gov't and force its hand. Our colleagues all feel strongly on this matter.[30]

The Colonial Office, not knowing the extent of Tupper's departures from Canadian instructions, were convinced that Canada had a lot to learn about diplomacy. 'It is curious,' wrote Sir Robert Meade to Ripon, 'how ignorant these eager Treaty makers are. Even Sir John Thompson was ignorant enough to suppose that his gov't could, if they thought proper, refuse to ratify a treaty which had been negotiated under their instructions. It was a revelation to him to learn that Parliament might refuse, but unless their negotiators had exceeded their instructions, the Government could not repudiate the Treaty.'[31] That Tupper exceeded his instructions was precisely the opening Thompson took.

Lord Dufferin completely accepted Thompson's explanation. The alarm of the British government was owing to serious difficulties with France over Newfoundland and Egypt, but that was no reason why Canada should be hustled – Thompson's verb – into acceptance of a treaty the terms of which were such that Canada was not sure she wanted it. Thompson felt that any British insinuation of bad faith by Canada ought to receive a sharp rejoinder; however, since Canada had got her own way after all, 'we ought perhaps to be satisfied without seeking a triumph of words.' Altogether it was, said Thompson after ten days of rattling around with it, 'much ado about nothing.'[32] After some other delays, the French treaty was ratified by Parliament in July 1894 and officially brought into force in 1895.[33]

The French treaty affair was not the only case of much ado about not much. Thompson's cabinet, like Macdonald's, was a balance, sometimes precarious, of potentially discordant elements, held together by loyalty, patronage, tradition, and power. *Saturday Night* observed waspishly, 'The exponent of whisky, prohibition, religion, Romanism, Protestantism, and everything else except pure patriotism can be found in that Cabinet.'[34] Such a cabinet resisted instinctively issues that would upset its balance, but there were some to which it was vulnerable. The most notorious was Ireland: home rule and an Irish Parliament again in Dublin was meat and drink to Irish Catholics, anathema to Irish Orangemen. Sagacious direction could have provided a safety valve for this Irish steam, but in Thompson's absence the only two men in the cabinet who possessed the requisite tact and sagacity, Angers and Bowell, were both in the Senate; the incident happened in the House of Commons.

At 4 p.m. on 21 March, G.E. Casey urged censure of Clarke Wallace as a member of the government for a recent speech he had made in Kingston against home rule. The Liberals mixed up in the motion expressions of loyalty to England and condemnation of the seditious tendencies of Wallace's utterance. Wallace had been indiscreet; he said that the Ulster Protestants could expect help from Ontario in opposing home rule. The subsequent motion of censure placed Irish Catholics on the Conservative side of the House in an awkward position. It was John Costigan who caused the trouble. G.E. Foster, leader in the Commons, pleaded with him. If the motion of censure against Wallace passed, Wallace would resign and he would be followed by the three Ontario members of cabinet. Costigan should simply deny Wallace's sentiments while denouncing the Liberal motion as party clap-trap. Costigan did not follow that sensible advice. He said he would vote for the Liberal motion. Roman Catholic Conservatives, who had held ranks up to that point, were unhinged; French-Canadian Conservatives began to follow and confusion reigned supreme.

At the supper adjournment the cabinet met in Thompson's room and Foster laid down the law: the Liberal motion as it stood might carry and if it did the most serious consequences would follow. Caron and Ouimet, together with Angers, went to work on the French Canadians; the ranks steadied and at midnight the government survived by thirty-one votes.[35] J.J. Curran thought that the Catholics had taken enough.

Swallowing a shovel full every morning before breakfast will make even a political stomach revolt. We feel that if a large section have accepted your premiership it is not for love but because the party could not stand an hour without you. The events of the past few weeks, and the utter inability of any one in the party here to guide the ship ought to satisfy our *ultra* friends that they can only get along only under your leadership. Perhaps good may come out of ill, but I consider the protestant element are making no sacrifice in tolerating an indispensable Catholic premier.[36]

Even the *Toronto World*, Conservative and Protestant though it was, thought the Wallace incident had hurt the government. 'It is high time that Conservatives of all classes and creeds deprecated the introduction of the feuds of Ireland into our political life. We have plenty of troublesome questions of our own.'[37] A year later, 14 July 1894, there was a cartoon in *Le Canard*, a Montreal comic weekly, showing Thompson riding a bicycle, with Catholicism as the front wheel (slightly damaged) and Orangeism as the back one (intact). Laurier saw him.

LAURIER: Tu ferais bien descendre de ce bicycle. Il est endommagé une croûte. Tu vas te casser le col.
THOMPSON: Ça ne fait rien. J'irai moins vite. Mon bicycle est encore bon pour un an malgré ses avaries.
LAURIER: Un an! Je pense que tu débarqueras avant ça.

Sir Adolphe Caron also survived, and nicely, the Edgar charges. The government got a fifty-vote majority in his support, partly indeed because of Caron's yeoman work in helping to defend Wallace. Caron had been indiscreet in accumulating party funds in 1882, 1887, and 1891; suspicion was that some might have come from government subsidies. Caron was much relieved by the vote and embarked on a week of rejoicing. Some of that time he could hardly keep perpendicular. Langevin and Langevin's supporters were bitter over the contrast between the fate of Caron and of Langevin.[38] But Caron garnered and spent the money for election purposes; Langevin had mixed party purposes up with personal ones.

Parliament prorogued 4 April 1893. 'All's well hallelujah!' cabled Mackenzie Bowell.[39] Parliament *was* prorogued, and all *was*, more or less, well, but there was one more adventure the government had to face up to – the Lachine Canal question that surfaced in mid-May. Bridges were built across the Lachine Canal at Wellington Street, Montreal, a work that was to cost at the outside $190,000. It was supposed to be completed in March and April and be ready for traffic by 1 May. Both money and timing went awry. The payrolls for one month's wages alone came to $130,000. Every ragged denizen of Curran's Montreal ward was, according to Foster, on the payroll. A day-labour contractor named St Louis was given the cost of the payroll plus 5 per cent, and he had not stinted, while the local superintending engineer, Parent, certified the accounts. Parent was instantly suspended and Collingwood Schreiber, chief engineer of railways and canals, was ordered by Foster and Haggart to investigate. Thompson thought the whole business appalling, but was not surprised. It was, he believed, a remnant of the regime of John Page, the deputy minister of public works who had died in December 1890. In those days, Thompson said, 'we were accustomed to throw away millions every year without any supervision whatever.' Eventually the contractors whose payment had been suspended entered action against the crown in the Exchequer Court of Canada. When the contractor's chief clerk admitted that all the time-books had been destroyed, the case was abruptly non-suited.[40]

Another question Thompson had to deal with, though at not so long a distance, came from the financial problems of the province of Quebec. J.S. Hall, treasurer of Quebec in Taillon's Conservative administration, was in Europe in May and June 1893, seeking to renegotiate a loan of 20 million francs ($4 million) that Mercier had made in July 1891 and due in July 1893. Hall showed some lack of business capacity in Paris and London, but 1893 was not a good time for the renewal of any colonial loan, let alone for Quebec, whose credit the Mercier scandals had damaged. The 1891 loan had been negotiated in Paris through La Banque de Paris et des Pays Bas, which, according to Thompson, was run by 'Jews of the original type.' When Hall came for the renewal, 4 per cent was changed to $7\frac{1}{2}$ per cent; the bankers busied themselves in every part of Europe to prevent anyone taking the loan for less than $7\frac{1}{2}$ per cent. Thompson was concerned not only with Quebec but with Canadian credit. It was known by late June that Hall had not been able to raise a dollar though he had gone to London and had 'been in the hands of every huckster in England.'[41]

Hall pleaded for help from Ottawa. Thompson was willing to arrange something, such as hypothecating the federal subsidy, but this, it was discovered, was impossible except through imperial legislation, and Thompson's willingness was based upon the belief that Quebec had monies owing to it from the complex debt distribution, post-1867, between Quebec and Ontario.[42] Hall found little help in London. He cabled Thompson in Paris that Quebec's position was critical, and that unless Foster came through, default was imminent.[43] In the end the Paris financiers came around, though at a price Hall did not enjoy bringing to Quebec. Thompson was spared having to loan Quebec money. He was well out of it. As Thompson put it, 'our own credit would be gone the moment we began.'[44]

At this point came change of governors general. Lord Stanley had to resign. His brother, the 15th Earl of Derby, died in April 1893 and Lord Stanley now became the 16th earl. Stanley sent a warm note to Thompson; 'I shall always remain deeply indebted to you for your valuable assistance, at all times so freely and willingly rendered, during the stormy times which during the past five years, we have successfully weathered together.'[45]

Lord Ripon, the colonial secretary, at once wrote to Lord Aberdeen, then in Chicago at the 1893 world's fair: would he accept the governor generalship of Canada, the front rank of colonial governorships? Ripon warned that Aberdeen's brief experience as secretary for Ireland in 1886 would be misleading. Aberdeen was a serious Liberal dedicated to home rule for Ireland; he might not find the going easy among Canadian Orangemen, the great proportion of whom were ardent Conservatives and opposed to home rule. It was said that Lady Aberdeen was even more outspoken than her husband, that every room in her house had a picture of Gladstone in it.[46] None of that bothered Thompson. He had long been an admirer of Gladstone; Gladstone's integration of politics and morals appealed to him.[47] He wrote the new governor general (not yet sworn in) on 1 July that he did not expect to be finished in Paris even by 1 August. 'I have ceased to grumble,' said Thompson resignedly, 'having gone up with the balloon I must simply wait until it comes down.'[48]

The Bering Sea Tribunal went on and on. Gladstone was so impatient to have his attorney general back in the House of Commons that he telegraphed *en clair* to Lord Rosebery, 'Russell's continued absence is an outrage. Cannot that extraordinary Tribunal sit on Mondays? Such a display of childish indolence as they exhibit was never witnessed in this world before.'[49] Phelps had been giving the American argument in reply to the British, day after day for nearly three weeks. Thompson was appalled by Phelps; he was laying down as legal propositions that which had no legal authority whatever. 'He was equally heroic in falsifying the facts.' Thompson reported to Griffin, 'He is the greatest liar on land.'[50] Phelps's eloquence, however passionate, could not but weary a tribunal that had been going since late March.

At last on 8 July the argument of counsel ended and the seven arbitrators could come to a decision. That began on 10 July, a day so hot that two of them were prostrate from heat. But there were more impediments than heat; the disagreements between Thompson and Senator Morgan alone were going to make things difficult. Pope reported that in the hot debates of the next five weeks over the decision, and over the framing of regulations consequent upon the decision, Thompson in a moment of passion pulled Senator Morgan halfway across a table! On another there was so much noise coming from the room where the tribunal were arguing that the French foreign minister, who was discussing with Lord Dufferin some sticky points about Siam, sent a polite message asking them if they could contrive to make a little less row![51]

In the meantime Thompson made the best he could of life in Paris and ceased to worry about getting home. C.H. Tupper was not so tranquil, had become fed up with Paris, and longed to get back to 'dear old Canada ... the happiest country I have yet been in.' Thompson's words were about 'sweet France.'[52] On 22 July, the feast of St Mary Magdalen, he entertained some forty or so French-Canadian students in Paris to dinner at a celebrated restaurant on the Boulevard Bonne Nouvelle – the Café Marguéry – with Joseph and Minette Pope and others, where they had sole à la Marguéry and disported themselves in the warm evening.[53]

The Canadian party kept steadily dwindling all through the latter part of July, joining the French in the exodus that follows Bastille Day. Thompson met and sat to a well-reputed French-Canadian sculptor, Louis-Phillippe Hébert then in Paris, who wanted to do a bust; the sittings went on through May and June whenever Thompson could get away for the odd evening. The two struck up an acquaintance over 'petits diners' in Paris cafés. That was not the end of their acquaintance, either. Thompson gave a major commission to Hébert in January 1894: the Macdonald statue now standing in the grounds of the Parliament buildings in Ottawa. In September 1893 the white marble bust of Thompson was shipped to Canada by Hébert. It is in the Archives of Nova Scotia in Halifax, the only such likeness of Thompson in existence.[54]

Thompson's own family left Paris on 27 July. The three girls – Babe, seventeen years old, Helena, fifteen, and Frankie, twelve – were all in Paris by mid-July, and Joe, now nineteen, came from Stonyhurst on 26 July to join them on their travels southward. Thompson put Joe in command of the little group. The guide, philosopher, friend, was Abbé LeClère, a French-Canadian priest from Montreal whom Thompson knew, who had been in France for the past two years and knew the country well. To Joe's worries about lack of French, Thompson was reassuring. 'You cannot have less than your Mother had and she got along by pointing to her watch, and the wheels and all natural objects and waving her arms.' Annie was an excellent traveller, the good abbé reported from Rocomondour early in August, 'qui prend toujours en riant les choses imprévues de voyage.' The children were trudging, teasing, laughing behind them. They would go to the Gorges du Tarn, then to Cahors, where Thompson was to write them poste restante. A few days later Thompson wrote to Joe, in a fashion sufficiently mysterious, probably about money.

Something you said in your letter alarmed me. Do not mind the mere matter of money, and, above all, do not let it be observed that you have discovered anything and keep the strictest care of your mother and the children. You are a fine big fellow now and well able to take my place. When I saw you in Paris I was quite glad to see what a man you had become.

Joe and the two older girls would remain in Europe at school; Annie and Frankie would return to Canada early in October.[55]

At last, on Tuesday, 15 August 1893 the award was announced officially from the French Foreign Ministry, in English and French. All the questions put to the tribunal by article 6 of the treaty went in Canada's favour, though not all of them were decided unanimously. Question 1, that Russia had never exercised more than a cannon shot's distance of jurisdiction from the shores of the Pribiloff Islands was accepted, six out seven (Senator Morgan dissenting). Question 2, that Britain had never recognized any other distance even after the Americans had bought Alaska, was accepted by the same vote. Question 3, that the Bering Sea was included in the Pacific Ocean in the 1825 British-Russian treaty, was accepted by everyone, as was the case with Question 4, whether all rights of Russia had passed to the United States. Question 5, whether the United States had any right of protection over, or property in, the fur seals outside of the three-mile limit – the critical question – went against the United States, by five votes to two, the two Americans dissenting. Canada won every point.[56]

The tribunal had also the task of establishing working regulations for the functioning of the seal hunt in the future, and in this respect it was hampered by not having any power to touch the privileges of the Alaska Commercial Company, the American lessee in the Pribiloff Islands. The regulations that the tribunal laid down (and accepted by only four of the seven arbitrators) were for Canadians stiff and unpleasant. There were imposed two practical restrictions on the seal hunt: first, a protected zone sixty miles in radius was established around the islands within which no sealing whatever (other than that of the resident company) was allowed; second, a closed season was established in the North Pacific and Bering Sea, that is north of latitude 35°N and east of 180°W, from 1 May to 31 July, during which no pelagic sealing was allowed.

The London papers announced a great British victory. Thompson and Charles Hibbert Tupper set sail from Liverpool on Thursday, 17 August in the *Parisian* with the plaudits of the English papers ringing behind them. But in Canada the reaction was cool. What Canada had won in principle seemed defeated in practice. There was amazement in Canada at the length of the closed season and at the depth of the prohibited zone around the Pribiloff Islands. Canadians had talked of a possible twenty-five-mile limit: sixty miles was appalling. Thompson's and Lord Hannen's worst fears had been realized.

That was reason why Thompson's arrival in Canada ought not to be much celebrated. It was also entirely inappropriate for Thompson, who had been an arbitrator, though suitable enough for C.H. Tupper. Young Tupper got his reward, announced as the *Parisian* docked in Montreal on 26 August – a KCMG. He would now be Sir Charles *Hibbert* Tupper, to distinguish him from his father. Thompson was given his welcome at Alexandria, Ontario, later that same morning, where Bowell, Angers, and Caron came to meet him; later that afternoon in Ottawa the mayor and two hundred citizens greeted him as he came off the train at the Canada and Atlantic Railway depot at Sapper's bridge. But generally he was not disposed to make of it a triumph.[57]

There were some ironies in all this. The Americans did not like the award, however much they may consoled themselves with the regulations.

They were now liable for something like half a million dollars in damages for the seventeen Canadian vessels (and their crews) that the United States had recklessly seized between 1886 and 1890. The ships now lay rotting on Alaskan beaches and harbours and there would be damages for unlawful imprisonment. In August 1894 Canada made so bold as to refuse an American offer of $400,000 as inadequate. There would be negotiations over that. Another arbitration in 1896 gave Canada $473,151.26, paid by the United States in 1898.[58]

Canada's, and Thompson's, unhappiness over the 1893 regulations turned out to be unjustified in the working out of the seal hunt. The truth was that a twenty-five-mile or a sixty-mile zone around the Pribiloffs did not make much difference. Female seals went far out to sea for food, up to two hundred miles. Nor was the closed season that restrictive. The sealing catches were substantial between 1894 and 1896. It was the Japanese seal hunters – Japan had no treaty with the United States – after 1896 that began to seriously weaken the Pribiloff herd.[59] Even in 1984 Canada still takes seals from around the Pribiloff Islands. Canada did not do badly in 1893; it can be said, as Thompson did to the mayor and citizens of Ottawa that August day in 1893, that 'the best indication of the justice of the decision is that it is not entirely satisfactory to anybody.'[60]

21

The Weight of Responsibility

On the same day that Thompson came home to Ottawa so too did his eldest son. With young Marty Griffin, John had come down the Ottawa River from North Bay by canoe. Thompson took them to the Rideau Club where the boys, bronzed and fit after a month in the open, created as much sensation as the newly arrived prime minister.[1] Thompson was proud of them and showed it. One of his worries in Paris had been that canoe trip. Like many Nova Scotians of his day, he feared canoes; they were treacherous things. Nova Scotians liked their boats solid and sturdy. Thompson had told John he could go, provided he remembered that a canoe was 'an abominable trap except for an Indian,' and that Ontarians think they know something about watercraft and really know nothing. 'To see the way the Ontario people hover about the brink of hell in their skimming dishes on the Great Lakes is to see that they know absolutely nothing of marine matters.' Griffin reassured him; Griffin's lack of such experience made him reluctant to deny it to the boys; so he saw them off on the train to North Bay on 24 July with a staunch canoe and enough food for a month.[2] The boys canoed down the Ottawa for four weeks, shot some rapids, portaged more, occasionally lived by their guns, and came to Ottawa healthy and hard as nails.

In September the Aberdeens arrived at Quebec aboard the *Sardinian*. Thompson, Caron, Ouimet, Angers, and Costigan went on board to meet them, on a wet, rainy Sunday, 17 September; the Aberdeens were duly installed in the Citadel and sworn in the next day. Thompson knew them already, having come out to Canada with them in the *Parisian* in August 1890. Sir Charles Tupper told both Lady Aberdeen and his son (in 1895 when there was no fear of contradiction) that Thompson believed the Aberdeens came out intending to turn out the Conservative government and install a Liberal one if they could manage it.[3] That Thompson believed it seems hardly conceivable. If Aberdeen brought his home rule and Liberal sympathies with him, there is no evidence that he brought them to bear on Canadian affairs. The fact that Thompson had an Irish father and some home rule sympathies undoubtedly helped; but the friendship between Thompson and both the Aberdeens would never have flourished had Aberdeen in mind bringing in the Liberal party by the back door. The Aberdeens were delighted with Thompson; he suited them – modest, intelligent, patient, hard-working, and thoughtful. 'Mind you remember to say exactly what you want,' he told Lady Aberdeen that first evening at Quebec, 'Do not scruple about this. You are to have just what you like.'[4]

They were a remarkable pair, the Aberdeens. He was John Hamilton Gordon, the 7th earl, two years younger than Thompson, well educated, with two great passions in life – iron horses and real ones. He dumbfounded the House of Lords in his maiden speech with an erudite discourse on signals and shunting. It was said he was the only person in the House of Lords who could drive a train from Edinburgh to London. Aberdeen was also a sportsman, not only excellent on horseback but the best skater and curler ever to grace Rideau Hall before Canadian governors general came along. It might be inferred that Aberdeen was bluff, vigorous, and out-going. He was not. He was gentle, retiring; he lacked what the Germans call *Sitzfleisch*, capacity for grubby hard work. He succeeded to the title at the age of twenty-three; when in 1877 Ishbel Marjoribanks made no secret of her feelings for him, her mother, Lady Tweedmouth, pressed the young (and reluctant) earl into marrying her daughter.

Quiet, self-effacing men do sometimes marry aggressive women, seeking perhaps a complement, instinctively, to weaknesses in their own nature. Ishbel Marjoribanks was vigorous, intense, confident, and with a temper to go with all of it. She would help fight battles her 'gentle Johnny' could not or would not. They were both intelligent; as J.T. Saywell points out in his elegant introduction to her journal, hers was 'the most critical; his the more tolerant and understanding.' They were both dedicated to Liberalism and public service; both subscribed to Gladstone's high principle that the true worship of a Christian is his service to man.[5]

The Aberdeens struck up a friendship with the Thompsons from the start. They became fond of Thompson's children as they came to meet them; and those relationships would last many years. The Thompson children, the girls especially, came to think of Lady Aberdeen as their foster mother.[6] Lady Aberdeen admired Thompson and perhaps found in him qualities wanting in her husband – resolution, toughness, endurance, and a tremendous capacity for work. In public Lady Aberdeen admired Thompson's 'strong, elevated, trained character'; to her diary she confided, 'my dear Sir John.'[7]

Few things were more characteristic of the attitudes of both Lady Aberdeen and Thompson than their work for the National Council of Women. It started in the United States in 1888; the establishment of the Canadian branch had been first mooted at Chicago in May 1893. At that time it was mainly representative of Ontario and of Ontario organizations such as the Women's Christian Temperance Union and the Young Women's Christian Association. The Canadian beginning was at the Horticultural Pavilion in Toronto, in October 1893, where Lady Aberdeen gave an address showing how, using local councils, a federation of women's societies could be put together. She agreed to be the first president.[8]

The first major national meeting of the National Council of Women was in Ottawa, at the Normal School buildings on Lisgar Street, on 11 April 1894. The opening prayer was silent, since the council comprehended both Jews and Catholics. This annoyed Protestant women, who were wont to claim that silent prayer meant shirking it. Lady Aberdeen fought hard to control such refractory elements and largely succeeded. The WCTU wanted to use the National Council to advance the cause of temperance; that too Lady Aberdeen got into line. The National Council was also non-political; the first two vice-presidents at large appointed in April 1894 were Lady Thompson and Mme Laurier.

Support for the National Council of Women among men was uneven. There was a male suspicion that the council meant only two things, women's suffrage and prohibition, neither of which boded good for Canadian maledom; most women's meetings dealt heavily in those topics.[9] The National Council raised other pressing issues: conditions of working women, factory problems, sweated labour, home nursing, in effect representing the weak social conscience of both political parties, the Liberal party as much as the Conservative. The council went cautiously, feeling its way. Women, said the Hamilton *Spectator*, were 'exploring new worlds with cautious steps. They are subjects of a revolution none the less great because it is silent.' Women were not throwing off chains so much as assuming them. 'They are asserting their right to stand beside their husbands and their brothers – not with any desire to do what men alone can do, but to do what women can do.'[10]

Thompson entered into the ideas and problems of the National Council of Women from the beginning. He always seems to have admired women's courage and endurance; perhaps Annie and Frankie had taught him that. He found it difficult to say no to women. Here, however, an important exception struck Lady Aberdeen. Thompson could not stand cruelty; influence was brought to bear for remission of sentence of a woman who had been cruel to her two-year-old child. As minister of justice Thompson tried to see prisoners personally, and on this occasion the woman presented to Thompson her petition for release. Thompson was as grim as death. 'Do you expect to get out[?] I tell you, if you lived for a hundred years and I was still Minister of Justice, you would never get out with my consent.'[11] It was part of his love for children: his passionate hatred of those who abused them.

Lady Aberdeen asked him to speak at the closing of the meeting of the National Council of Women at the Normal School on 12 April 1894. Thompson agreed to come and to share the platform with Laurier (who backed out at the last minute). Up to that point there was a disposition on the part of Ottawa men to laugh at the council. Thompson faced that down. He gave an excellent talk which was received with delight and satisfaction. For he believed in the usefulness of the council; he did not patronize women as politicians were wont to do. Not many men, reflected Lady Aberdeen, would have left the House of Commons when an important division was to take place – Cartwright's amendment on Foster's budget speech – walk down the hill to the Normal School to give an address to a roomful of women, and stay there until the meeting ended. Then, and only then, did Thompson return to the House.

Thompson was playful in little things, graceful in many, and serious in the big ones.[12] He was the first prime minister in whose time the 'National Parliament of Women' had been assembled, and so far as he had been able to observe, their proceedings were an example to other bodies, notably the one up on Parliament Hill from which he had just come. These women, he said, had dealt expeditiously with a couple of dozen subjects in two days, whereas the other parliament had taken a week to do one. Thompson had more reason than courtesy to emphasize the contrast: the debate on Cartwright's amendment to the budget had been long and breathtakingly arid. 'Within the walls of the brother Parliament,' he concluded, 'there were no critics of this movement, nor was there any division of opinion as between Liberal and Tory in the admiration with which it was there viewed.'[13] A graceful touch of official optimism!

Thompson believed that women were good for political life and did not like discrimination against them. It was owing to Thompson that the Aberdeens opened Government House to Mrs Addie Foster, wife of the finance minister. It was an odd story, not untypical of the way late Victorian Canada struggled with moral questions. After G.E. Foster came to Ottawa in 1885, he fell in love with his Ottawa landlady, Mrs Addie Chisholm, whose husband had deserted her some years before. She could have obtained a Canadian divorce via the Senate but that was expensive; after two years' legal residence in Chicago she got an Illinois divorce and married Foster there. They came back to Ottawa in September 1889 as man and wife. But according to the usual interpretations of the time, they were not legally married. She was open to a criminal charge of bigamy, so Macdonald believed, and Foster to a civil suit of what the common law calls delightfully, 'criminal conversation.' Ottawa tongues wagged; Sir John Macdonald shook his head dubiously – he was certain that Mrs Foster would be shut out of Ottawa society and her life in Ottawa made miserable. Certainly as far as Lady Macdonald's writ would run it was, and Lady Macdonald ruled Ottawa society with a rod of iron. The Stanleys did not receive Mrs Foster. But the Aberdeens were disinclined to continue this and at a birthday party at Thompson's for Frankie's twelfth birthday, in 1893, Thompson had opportunity to put to the Aberdeens the case of Addie Foster. He considered her Illinois divorce legitimate (or so he told Lady Aberdeen), and although it could not be recognized by the Catholic church, the Thompsons had always called on her and received her. He was very decided that the Ottawa exclusion of the wife of an important cabinet minister ought to end. End it did the following week when the Aberdeens held their first major public entertainment, a concert to which they invited everyone who was anyone in Ottawa. Before the concert they had a private interview with the Fosters to explain their decision. 'They are so thankful,' Lady Aberdeen wrote, 'and Sir John Thompson is delighted.'[14]

Thompson that autumn made a political swing around western Ontario that began late in September 1893. Not all the press were encouraging. Before the tour started, *Saturday Night* likened Thompson to Edward Blake, 'lacking in magnetism, and nobody could be quite sure that he would not be more loved "sight unseen" than as a political iceberg at a banquet.'[15] Such comments tended to die out after Thompson began his tour. It was through territory that he had visited with Macdonald in the fall of 1886: Mount Forest, Arthur, in Wellington County, Mitchell in

Perth, Lucan in Middlesex, Owen Sound in Grey, and then down to Dunnville in Haldimand, where the 'maidens' of Dunnville greeted Thompson with the 'Maple Leaf Forever,' the ministers and all present joining in the chorus. Thompson's theme in these talks was the impossibility of free trade;[16] Laurier talked glowingly about free trade, but if Laurier were in power tomorrow he would not be able to implement it. The policy of the Conservative party would be the protection incidental to revenue. Canada had to have revenue: therefore it must have a tariff. 'We think the best way is to put it on those articles coming from foreign countries which we can produce in our own country. Now so far as that means protection we are for protection. In so far as it means a revenue tariff we are for a revenue tariff.'[17]

Thompson talked so much about tariff reform that Martin Griffin, whose long editorial experience on newspapers made him more politically sensitive, thought it would be well to flag down the Thompson express. 'You have been talking a good deal about "Tariff Reform",' Griffin wrote in December, 'It is ... "a whoreson phrase" ... Reforms are generally the instigation of the devil.' Don't frighten the manufacturers, Griffin argued. 'You must have an election in a couple of years. If you make every contractor in Canada secretly your enemy [a reference to Thompson's purges in the Lachine bridge affair] and if you put the Manufacturers in terror of their lives, where is your fund to come from? Do you think the "Tariff Reformers" will help you? Go slow.'

Thompson would not have it. He wanted tariff reform and he was out to get the 'till-tapping contractors.' Griffin, at home in Sandy Hill with the 'flu, replied with asperity that contractors followed where politicians led. McGreevy's money had gone to French-Canadian MPs and newspapers. McGreevy had told Griffin that himself. He ran away to save not himself but his friends. Why, said Griffin, 'when you take this very high tone, does Brother Haggart look you square in the eye? does Brother Patterson ejaculate amen?' Who keeps pious Sir Oliver Mowat in power? Every saloon-keeper in Ontario. Griffin had no doubt that Thompson had effected an enormous change for the better in political morality, but how much could be done when surrounded continually with men and examples like those? Don't be so vindictive.[18]

In that autumn swing around Ontario Thompson dealt with another vexing question, one that would require a great deal of patience from everyone: prohibition. On 24 June 1891, three weeks after Macdonald's death, the House of Commons agreed there should be a royal commission on the liquor traffic in Canada. *Grip* was in favour of prohibition, but could not resist making sport:

> ... But don't you see, this clever scheme
> Of a solemn Royal Commission
> Will give the Government a rest
> From troublous Prohibition![19]

There were delays in getting the commission appointed because of the government's preoccupation with the Langevin inquiry. The commission was issued in March 1892 to Sir Joseph Hickson and four others, to obtain information on the effect of the liquor traffic, to recommend measures that would regulate it, and ascertain the social and other effects of prohibition. The government did not exactly stack the commission, but prohibition enthusiasts claimed that four of the five commissioners were bitterly opposed to it. That may overstate it. Temperance advocates were some of the most intemperate people in Canada. But it was true that the government found it convenient to get the question out of the way. There was a cartoon in *Grip* showing Foster as a woman (Thompson, the man, in the distance) furtively handing over a baby (prohibition) to a mysterious lady (the Hickson Royal Commission) saying, 'Here, take it away, and don't let me see or hear of it for years!!'[20]

No doubt prohibition was one solution to a difficult social problem. Canadians drank, and drunkenness was only lightly condemned. Lady Aberdeen, no prude in such matters, was disconcerted at how much champagne disappeared at the levée at Government House on New Year's Day, 1894 – some ten dozen bottles in the first hour.[21] Thompson felt about prohibition much the same way as about school questions in Manitoba and the North-West: get it out of the realm of rhetoric, propaganda, and partisan utterance into a framework of facts where it can be dealt with in some rational way. There were evils in intemperance, no one denied that; the royal commission would find out the facts and make recommendations thereon. The Dominion Parliament, Thompson believed, had the requisite power to make legislation to that purpose.[22]

That was the reason why, when Oliver Mowat raised the matter of a reference case on the powers that belonged to each government, Dominion and provincial, Thompson agreed to it, without waiting for the result of the Hickson Royal Commission, which did not in fact report until 1895. The two questions, the legal basis for legislation, and the royal commission report that would provide the factual basis could proceed *pari passu*. While Thompson was in Paris, Mowat raised the question of jurisdiction with Mackenzie Bowell, the acting premier. It was most important, Mowat urged, to have it settled and by the highest authority: do the provinces have the power to prohibit the sale of liquor? Bowell did nothing about it in Thompson's absence, and Mowat put his own reference case to the Ontario Court of Appeal. On Thompson's return he was willing to accept Thompson's wording of the reference if a Dominion one could be set up in time to take over Mowat's Ontario one. (Mowat did not want abandonment of his reference misconstrued in Ontario.) Thompson acted at once, and the cabinet approved Thompson's report of 21 October 1893, where he recommended that the several questions comprehended should go as a reference case to the Supreme Court of Canada.

As Thompson expected, the Supreme Court found largely for the Dominion, but on appeal to the Privy Council it came out in a peculiar way, giving Dominion local option legislation priority over provincial acts, but only in cases where there was a conflict. The Privy Council also laid down that manufacture and importing could not be controlled by the province. But with these restrictions a province could prohibit the sale of liquor within its borders.[23]

Mowat and Thompson joined together publicly in Hamilton on 1 November 1893 to unveil a handsome statue to Sir John Macdonald, commissioned by the city, and carved from New Brunswick granite. Thompson almost never prepared a text for a speech but he did one for that occasion. It was full of sentiment for the old man, and Thompson liked to keep sentiment in public under firm control. Macdonald often warned him, Thompson remembered, that the life of a politician was not to be thought of if you wanted domestic happiness and peace of mind. The task of a public officer was unending, grinding labour with no thanks from anyone. Thompson's remarks might well have been about himself:

We who knew him well know that for years before the end came, he longed for rest and retirement ... Day after day was filled by unceasing toil, unwearying watchfulness and painful labour at details. Night after night, when men in all other occupations were enjoying rest in their homes, he was at his work in the House of Commons, seldom leaving his place until early morning – often the last to leave and often beginning a long and arduous effort after midnight ... It was not mere love of power ... It was devotion to duty which became more pressing and unavoidable as years rolled by. He could be replaced when he was no more, but while his services could be had no man could replace him.

No doubt Macdonald had love of fame, that 'sovereign passion of public men,' but the price was heavy; yet, to the worries of office, the greed and selfishness of others, Macdonald turned, said Thompson, only kindness, forbearance, and humour.[24]

That evening there was just time to board the train to Montreal for the funeral of Sir John Abbott, who died on 30 October. Abbott's death occasioned surprisingly little comment; there was hardly a ripple in the newspapers.[25] A year later, the Aberdeens moved into Abbott's house at 919 Sherbrooke Street West for a two-month stay in Montreal; by then it seemed as if the seventy-two years of the life of Sir John the second had passed almost unnoticed, annexationism of 1849 and all.

The annexationism of 1891–4 was of more immediate concern to Thompson. He exhibited much caution in his public statements, but he was uncomfortable at tendencies he observed in the Liberal party. He was a Canadian nationalist, but in 1893–4, with American expansionist energies so manifest, to talk of Canadian independence from Great Britain was closer to treason than nationalism.[26] There were those in Canadian political life who might be bribed or twisted into annexation. Some may have believed in it out of conviction. David Creighton of the Toronto *Empire* thought it would be useful to send a Canadian agent to New York to keep an eye on the activities of American annexationists and their Canadian confreres. For once Thompson agreed and a secret file was prepared at the Department of Justice.[27]

In 1893 there was formed in New York an association of which Charles Dana of the *New York Sun* was the moving spirit, that included Andrew Carnegie, Chauncey Depew (president of the New York Central Railroad), John Jacob Astor, Henry Cabot Lodge, Theodore Roosevelt, and others. It was called the National Continental Union League, and it put together a substantial fund to promote Canadian independence, which it conceived as the stepping-stone to annexation. Its working headquarters was in Brooklyn, and its working head Francis Glen.[28]

The Canadian wing was called the Continental Union Association and it had some Liberals in it. The emphasis of the two groups, American and Canadian, came to be more upon French-Canadian than English-Canadian Liberals, for French-Canadian Liberal arguments were more directly useful. French-Canadian Liberals sympathetic to the movement were Charles Langelier, F.-X. Lemieux, Amédée Papineau (the son of Louis Joseph, and the uncle of Henri Bourassa), and not least, Mercier. Mercier had been driven from office by the Baie des Chaleurs scandal. Dismissed as premier by Lieutenant-Governor Angers in December 1891, he and his Liberal party were defeated in the 1892 provincial election. Leader of the opposition, Mercier now leaned to independence from Great Britain. In Montreal on 4 April 1893, speaking on the future of Canada, Mercier argued that Canada owed nothing to England, that Canada should separate. Mercier was by now really an annexationist, the last great card he had to play. He was also short of money and Americans were ready to provide it. Not all French-Canadian Liberals agreed with Mercier's position; as Louis Jetté put it, 'Pour rester français nous n'avons qu'une chose à faire: rester anglais.' Jules Tardivel, too, was sure annexation would be bad for Quebec; English-Canadian annexationists were looking to drown French Canadians in the great English sea of Anglo-America.[29]

In Toronto the *Mail* had leanings toward annexation, but articles in 1890–2 had interfered seriously with its subscription list; annexation was given up in favour of an aggressive anti-Catholicism and municipal reform. L.V. Ellis, the proprietor and editor of the *St. John Globe*, was accounted an annexationist, as was Elgin Myers of the Toronto *Telegram*. Goldwin Smith was well known. In Parliament John Charlton and Israel Tarte were reputed sympathizers, and Tarte's letters appeared from time to time in the *New York Sun*.[30]

On 1 December 1893, at Andrew Carnegie's house in New York, it was agreed between Goldwin Smith, Dana, and Carnegie that no money would go to help Laurier. Funding would go to help Mercier obtain control of the Quebec legislature at the next election, on a platform of independence. It would be the first step to continental union; Liberal tariff policy was now too mild to be of any use.[31]

Some Canadian papers, like the Winnipeg *Free Press*, pitched into the movement, and were used by Glen to get more sympathy and support in the United States. This, said the Canadian spy in New York, T.B. Grant, was wrong tactics; Glen had to be ridiculed in Canada as a crank, 'a lonely bittern standing on a rock and screaming in the middle of a lake ... a man fooling good and respectable Americans.' That way Glen and his movement might be harmed.[32]

All of this came to Thompson, partly through private correspondence but mostly through the Department of Justice. By January 1894 he concluded that the continental union movement would not amount to anything, though he raised it with Lord Aberdeen for possible discussion by secret dispatch with London.[33] Thompson's scepticism inhibited Lord Aberdeen from raising an alarm with imperial authorities. Thompson met the undercover movement in a curious way, as if he were playing a hand of poker, by suggesting in an Ottawa speech on 14 February 1894 that he knew a great deal more than he was willing to disclose.

The speech to the Ottawa Macdonald Club was frankly political. He urged supporters of the Conservative party to look to voters' lists, to increasing party membership, to making their weight felt through the press. The time had gone, Thompson said, when legislation was settled in Parliament alone. Laws were discussed on platforms and in the news-papers long before they got to Parliament. Parliament 'only recorded what the public feeling had already decided.' Canada had escaped the 1893 depression better than any other country; even so, there were demagogues and agitators who were not satisfied, who wanted to change the country's constitution. There were even some who wanted to change Canada's flag. Thompson averred he could give the names of the men paid by Americans for propagating annexation; but he would leave them in the contempt reserved for those who would sell their country.[34] This oblique reference was all that Thompson would say. In the end it came to what Thompson believed it would, a fizzle. Laurier had been wise in keeping the movement at arm's length since 1892.

Keeping the Americans at bay was easy compared to trying to cool Roman Catholic hopes, allay Roman Catholic fears. Thompson was Canada's first Roman Catholic prime minister. As he said in January 1893, the greatest problem facing Canada was the religious susceptibili-ties of its people. If only Canadians could live and let live! If only they were not finding plots and conspiracies behind every move made by Protestants, or, *mutatis mutandis*, Roman Catholics. Some Catholic bishops were no better than Protestants in this respect, and they looked to Thompson to defend the church, preferably on ground that the bishops themselves chose. The ground they picked was not usually what Thomp-son either needed or wanted. They did not always get their facts right or their legal argument secure; they seemed to Thompson, the western bishops especially, unreasonable, even uncompromising. In 1892 Taché might have been able to make a suitable compromise with the Manitoba government. He would not. He intended to hold the Dominion govern-ment to full restoration of Roman Catholic schools. On the other hand, the Manitoba Protestants were a hard and ungenerous majority. Thomp-son rightly got impatient when he learned that German-speaking

Mennonites had more language privileges than Franco-Manitobans, doubtless because Mennonites were Protestants. In 1894 Manitoba amendments designed to redress that disparity ended by making things worse. So Lieutenant-Governor Schultz reported. What kind of government was Manitoba's, Thompson wondered, ready 'to tear this country to pieces?' When he read the text of the amendments, however, they seemed innocent of evil intent, mere administrative tidying up.[35]

As if Manitoba was not enough, there were serious questions about Catholic schooling in the North-West Territories. The Dominion government could escape those even less because it had the duty to oversee North-West Territories legislation. Such legislation affected every aspect of schools – school board elections, when and how a separate school could be established, licensing of teachers, normal schools, textbooks, what kind of history, even what kind of poetry should be taught. Catholics complained that one school text had a poem that actually sanctioned elopement! Davin quoted it in the House of Commons in 1894, Scott's *Marmion*:

> O young Lochinvar is come out of the west,
> Through all the wild Border his steed was the best

to rescue Ellen from an unworthy bridegroom. As everyone knows, Lochinvar did just that in a great gallop of a poem that schoolboys would learn into the 1930s. Such were the minutiae that concerned Canada's legislators in 1894![36]

The Catholic church had once been strong in the west; in the 1870s it was virtually the established church. As Anglo-Protestant settlement developed this control was undermined. In 1892 the North-West Territorial Assembly, no doubt infected by events in Manitoba, asserted the right to establish full territorial control over education, within the separate school system prescribed by the Dominion Act of 1875.

The North West School Ordinance of January 1892 was the most important school legislation in some years. The North-West Council would appoint the Board of Education and inspectors and examiners. The Catholic section would continue to manage its own schools, select additional textbooks in history and science, while the Board of Education kept control of inspections and had partial control of examinations.

Bishop Grandin of St Albert saw this 1892 ordinance as a devilish device by Protestants to secularize underhandedly separate schools that they could not legally abolish.[37] The Catholic church really wanted a wholly divided school system with a prominent role for the clergy, analogous to the system in the province of Quebec; what the North-West Council sought was a separate school system analogous to Ontario, from which province three-quarters of the territorial legislature came. Thompson was asked by Grandin whether Protestant inspectors could be imposed upon Catholic schools; Thompson replied that if the church thought rights were being infringed, they could petition. They did not do so. In December 1892 in a further ordinance the Board of Education was replaced by a body called the Council of Public Instruction, with separate school rights, though slightly qualified, largely intact. Any minority, Protestant or Catholic, could establish a separate school in any organized public school district. The support of a minority school was voluntary: Frank Oliver came up with the argument that minority rights 'would be violated if the majority of any minority were allowed to coerce the minority of a minority.'[38] The sweet delights of sectarian controversy!

The December 1892 ordinance reached Ottawa early in 1893. It seemed to Thompson reasonable. The church was mute. Aging and ailing, Bishop Grandin had gone to Europe for his health. Archbishop Taché had other worries, not least of which was chronic inflammation of the bladder, the same illness Grandin had. The issue of that 1892 ordinance only developed momentum late in 1893. The new Council of Public Instruction made rules about teaching licences, about readers. That convinced Father Hippolyte Leduc at St Albert that godless schools were in train, that a war against the convents and the teaching orders of the church had already started.[39] Leduc appealed to Thompson in November 1893 to have the 1892 ordinance disallowed. By then there was very little time to find out facts that might justify disallowance. Further, as Thompson was to assert time and again, there was misapprehension of the facts by Roman Catholics, including bishops. They created problems where they did not exist.[40]

The ordinance would become law on 7 February 1894. The Catholic bishops pressed; Archbishop Taschereau of Quebec had his coadjutor write to Caron insisting upon disallowance.[41] After 7 February passed and the ordinance still stood, Caron was given the job of soothing ruffled feathers.[42] Archbishop Taché prepared a memorandum for all the Canadian bishops; Bishop Emard of Valleyfield arrived in St Boniface in April, as liaison between the Quebec bishops and the western ones. A petition was signed by the Ontario and Quebec bishops and was then taken to the Maritimes, especially to Bishop Cameron of Antigonish. This mission, in April 1894, was undertaken by Paul Larocque, the new bishop of Sherbrooke, with Father Lacombe. The petition stated that the Catholics of Manitoba and the North-West Territories had grievances and the governor general in council should try to redress them. Bishop Cameron was willing to listen, but insisted that Bishop Larocque and Father Lacombe must be under some misapprehension about Sir John Thompson. 'The facts seem to be,' lectured Cameron sternly, 'that they [the French-Canadian bishops] are under the impression that an honest Christian statesman is a mere creature of the imagination ... Of all the provinces, you, French Canadians, ought to be the last to raise your voice against the Government for not vetoing the Martin bill [the 1890 Manitoba School Act] and thus encroaching on the autonomy [of the provinces] ... You now act like bullies.' But the wording of the petition was mild enough to allow Bishop Cameron to sign it. He had barely time to put down his pen before Father Lacombe covered Cameron's pen hand with kisses. Father Lacombe was not allowed to leave without further expostulation. How could you believe, Cameron asked, that Sir John Thompson was capable of being corrupted by party necessity? He was incorruptible; he acted from Christian motives and his Manitoba and North-West policies have to be read that way.[43]

Thompson's difficulties were not made easier by accidental or wilful blindness as to facts. In a long and wearisomely patient speech to the House of Commons, 26 April 1894 Thompson said, 'in almost every step of the inquiry, we are met by a controversy as to what the facts are.' One thing was certain: the heart of separate schools in any province, at any time, was 'the domestic control of the trustees of the [school] section.' The separate school supporters in the North-West were controlling their own schools, they were receiving official money for their schools, they elected their own trustees, and 'no teacher can cross the threshold of a school-house, unless under engagement with the trustees of the district.'[44] What more can one reasonably expect in a mixed society?

Thompson's speech, the litany of his complaints against both sides but especially the Roman Catholics, did not go down well in St Boniface or St Albert. Father Leduc, the high-strung administrator at St Albert, thought Thompson's performance pitiful.[45] Archbishop Taché addressed a long and bitter letter to Thompson on 30 May 1894. The House of Commons was advised by its prime minister to believe, said Taché, 'as overzealous and misled, the Catholic Bishops, Judges, priests, lawyers, members of the Legislative Assembly, school trustees ... in fact all those closely connected with the management of Catholic schools, and to rely only on the word of men who take no interest in the same schools, from a Catholic point of view.'

Thompson read Taché's long missive grimly. Beside the above statement he scribbled in the margin, 'Because their [the Catholic bishops' and others'] statements were found to be contrary to fact.' Again and again, as Thompson read over what Taché was saying – his letter was in English – he was struck by how far apart they were. There was anger and bitterness in Thompson over the old archbishop's misrepresentations and it spilled out into his pen: 'false and evasive'; a 'trick of expression'; 'a wicked piece of garbling'; that last on Taché's misapplication of something from Frank Oliver's *Edmonton Bulletin*. Thompson began a draft reply, meeting Taché point by point. The main thrust of his argument was in the final paragraph:

I have reason to hope that the appeal which has been made by the Government to the wisdom and moderation of the North-West Assembly will not be in vain; but it will certainly be in vain if the subject is not approached with calmness and prudence by the [Catholic] minority throughout Canada. If it should be approached in a spirit of antagonism, defiance or menace by those who are of our race and belief, we shall have less to expect in the future than we have enjoyed in the past.[46]

By the time Thompson drafted this the old archbishop was dead; Thompson's letter counselling prudence and calm never reached him. Instead Thompson sent J.J. Curran to represent the Dominion government at his funeral.

Trouble over Taché's successor at St Boniface was already brewing. Father Adélard Langevin, the administrator of the archdiocese during Taché's last illness, was an Oblate like Taché; the secular clergy were looking for someone from their ranks, arguing that no Oblate could do the position justice. The story in St Boniface was that Father Langevin, a couple of days before Taché's death, pointedly asked Taché if he had any instructions to give him. Taché, with equal point, replied, 'None whatever my dear child.'[47] Despite these portents, the secular clergy lost. Adélard Langevin, the Oblate, was consecrated archbishop in 1895.

In Parliament the North-West school question was almost at an end, save for a last kick at it from D'Alton McCarthy. McCarthy had been holding back until the last days of a long session. It was said he had done that deliberately so that there would be a small House, anxious to prorogue, when his motion might pass. On third reading of the North-West Territories Amendment Act, McCarthy moved that all education in the North-West Territories Act of 1875 be now transferred to the control of the territorial legislature.

Thompson, who had endured much that long session, was still patient. He said nothing about McCarthy's motives in raising the matter three days before the end of the session and on third reading. He simply said that as long as the Territories were under the guardianship of the Dominion government, then the toleration stipulated by the act of 1875 would be the rule. Toleration was more expensive – a point McCarthy made – but it made sense in the growing section of the country. What kind of education the Territories might get in the future when they were to become provinces was not for Thompson or Parliament to say. The guarantees in section 93, subsection 1 of the BNA Act that perpetuated separate schools if established prior to union applied, Thompson said, only to the original four provinces of confederation. It did not apply to new provinces. 'What the constitution of the future provinces shall be ... will be for Parliament to decide when it decides to create those Provinces.' Until that time Thompson trusted that Parliament would leave the 1875 arrangements stand. They were as useful in 1894 as they had been since 1875.[48]

McCarthy's motion was defeated, 21 to 114. All that remained was for Thompson and the cabinet to reply to the bishops' petition. On 26 July 1894, three days after Parliament prorogued, an order-in-council, drafted probably by Thompson, recalled the hard work and sacrifices of Catholic missionaries in the North-West which gave the church a strong claim for generous recognition by all the legislative bodies of western Canada. The North-West Assembly was asked to redress 'any well-founded complaint or grievance.'[49]

With that, the North-West Territories school question disappeared from the Dominion Parliament for a decade. The passion and heat of debate had not created this settlement.[50] It was Thompson's patience, coolness, and determination in holding the Commons to toleration in the Territories. And the House trusted Thompson's good sense.

There was more to the session of 1894 than the North-West school question despite its enormous drain on Thompson's patience and energy. He had expected that it would be a hard session, at least four months, and the opposition, expecting it to be the last session before a general election, would be bumptious and noisy. He was confident that the government had nothing to fear from religious and educational questions unless from 'malice or caprice,' as he put it to Joe.[51] He tried to smooth the path a little; he began the session with a gracious compliment to Laurier and the opposition, thanking them for having so helped to conduct Parliament in 1893 that Thompson found it possible to get away to Paris. In that, Thompson said, they showed 'a high sense of patriotism and public duty.'[52]

Thompson's own sense of public duty covered a great deal of ground, not least his belief in entertaining members of his party at home. It is difficult to get a sense of this, for Thompson hated social descriptions in the papers, that Sir So-and-so and Lady 'were entertained at the Prime Minister's gracious residence on Saturday night last.' That stuff was not for Thompson or Annie. They liked their entertaining generous but unobtrusive. 'It is my private hospitality,' he said, 'and I don't like to have it blazoned.'[53]

Early in 1894 they moved into another house, rented from Justice Burbidge, at 276 Somerset Street. Burbidge wanted to sell, asking $11,000; Thompson had to say no; he could not afford it. There was a rumour some months later in the *Regina Leader*, Nicholas Davin's paper, that party supporters were willing to put up $14,000 to buy a house for the prime minister, but that Thompson would have nothing to do with it. The house still stands, at the southeast corner of Metcalfe and Somerset streets, a generous, rambling brick house built in the 1880s in a style common in Ontario, with deep verandas, large bay windows, with a comfortable air of solid commodiousness.[54]

It was a busy place. On Saturday night, 21 April Thompson and Annie had their fourth dinner of the session that had been opened only five weeks. Annie was having twenty wives of MPs. The following Tuesday, she had thirty of the men, with herself the only woman present. Annie wrote young John a little breathlessly, for she was in the middle of cleaning out the living-room, getting ready for Tuesday. Before the men arrived for dinner, Annie had to receive all afternoon, after which she was to go to a tea dance. It was a fierce regime. On Thursday night there was to be a state dinner at Rideau Hall; on Friday night a ball at the Russell House; on Saturday night another function at Rideau Hall. No wonder Annie felt that things were rather in 'a whirlwind!'[55]

Annie's recipe for entertaining Ottawa society was succinct: 'feed them, feed them, feed them – nothing else will satisfy them.'[56] And feed them she did, often doing the cooking herself. In 1892, short of money and nursing Frankie, Annie took to the kitchen and personally cooked the dinners for all the 250 guests who dined that session at their house. Even in 1894 they had only two servants to help.[57] Thompson was not extravagant himself, but entertaining was something they both liked to do nicely. Probably he was too generous. He was hard up. In April 1894 he wrote to a friend in Halifax to whom he had loaned money, asking if a remittance could be sent, as 'I am somewhat short of money.' It was worse than that. 'I am abominably hard up just now, and will be so for a few weeks,' he wrote J.A. Chisholm in Halifax. Could Thompson postpone a payment until one of his Halifax properties could be sold?[58]

Old Sir Charles Tupper thought Thompson's conduct of his own finances little short of criminal, that Thompson's family suffered from his determination not to take any money from anyone for anything. Tupper told his son that Thompson had ruined his own family by that kind of conduct, and that he, young Tupper, should look out that he did not do the same. Tupper took the position that 'he who does not provide for his own household is worse than an infidel.'[59]

That was never Thompson's view. He explained his failure to accumulate money for himself and his family. It was quite simple, he said, 'I detest the idea of being beastly rich.' Macdonald had been amused by millionaires; he looked upon them as an adult did a child with a new toy. Thompson was more discriminating and critical. He believed that it was impossible for a man with right instincts to derive satisfaction out of wealth. The late nineteenth century race for wealth was a delusion. To him the pursuit called up metaphors like the hog wallowing in a golden trough.[60] Thompson did not exactly scorn millionaires; the 105 men of the St James Club who tendered him a dinner in November 1893 to counteract the ravings of Dr Douglas were, Thompson said, the best people of Montreal;[61] he simply did not share their views about money, or, indeed, what one did with money if one had it.

Parliament's main work in 1894 had been the extensive tariff revisions. C.H. Mackintosh, former editor of the Ottawa *Citizen* and now lieutenant-governor of the North-West Territories, told Thompson to have no mercy on the implement manufacturers. Instead of putting the best materials into their binders, reapers, and wagons, holding the market against foreign competition, they sheltered behind the tariff. This, Mackintosh said, caused the western agitation against the tariff. 'I found many in Alberta district who purchase American waggons because they last six times as long as the Canadian article. The same story is told me by men in this District [Assiniboia], and from Manitoba.'[62] When the changes were announced in Foster's budget speech on 27 March, they gave much satisfaction, according to Clarke Wallace, who was inundated with congratulatory telegrams.[63] However, Hart Massey did not like the reduction Thompson's government had made to the tariff on agricultural machinery, from 37 to 20 per cent. Someone in the Massey firm had assured Canadians that Massey's did not need the tariff, that their success had been achieved in spite of it. Thompson and his colleagues made due allowance for rhodomontade when they reconstructed the tariff. 'Had I not made these allowances,' he told Hart Massey, 'manufacturing implements would have been placed on the free list.'[64]

There were some 665 revisions in the tariff, most of them downward, or conversions from specific to *ad valorem* duties that had the same effect. Foster did not fail to note for the benefit of Liberals who harboured thoughts of being Americans that from 1879 to 1893 the u.s. tariff on dutiable goods was never below 43 per cent, and indeed had been over 50 per cent. The Canadian average was 28 per cent. If dutiable and free goods were combined, the American was $27\frac{1}{2}$ per cent, the Canadian 19 per cent.[65]

Thompson came to the House in the evening of 12 April to help the Conservatives defeat the Cartwright amendment on the budget. The debate had gone on for two full weeks and the vote was to be taken that night. It was, traditionally, reserved for celebration. The Commons had to approve individual items of the budget in Committee of the Whole, but when the overall principles were to be voted on, the House always made a night of it. Annie, Lady Caron, Mme Laurier, and others came up to see the fun. There was coffee for them in the Speaker's apartment. At midnight the debate was still going on, and Laurier stepped across the floor to consult Sir John Thompson. They whispered together, laughed, and finally at 1 a.m. came calls of 'Question! question!' The press gallery filled up, the Speaker ordered members called in, the whips (half a dozen for each side) sallied forth. The mps in the House threw paper wads at each other, and there was a call for Colonel E.G. Prior, the Yorkshireman from Victoria, bc. He knew what to do. He began his song, an Irish ditty about the sticks that went whacking and the skulls that went cracking 'when McCarty took the floor at Euniscarty.' Then there were calls for François Béchard, Liberal mp for Iberville, who sang 'La Marseillaise.' The House caught up the chorus, and sent it swelling up to the high ceiling,

> Aux armes, citoyens!
> Formez vos bataillons!
> Marchons, marchons!
> Qu'un sang impur abreuve nos sillons!

So budget night 1894 ended. The members streamed out into the soft April darkness flooded with moonlight. Faith Fenton of the Toronto *Empire* said to her male companion,

> 'Well, now that the vote is taken what comes next?'
> 'Oh, now the House will settle down to passing the various items!'
> 'Items of what?' I queried.
> 'Items of the Budget, of course!' answered the man of knowledge in a tone of much enduring patience.
> I wheeled about and faced him in the middle of the pavement.
> 'Do you mean that after debating for two weeks over the budget as a whole they are now going to begin and fight over every detail for another two weeks?'
> He nodded.
> 'But what – what was this first fight for; just to obtain the right to begin again?' I asked.[66]

The reductions in the tariff meant reductions in revenue, and it put Foster as minister of finance in the position of having to tightly control the Estimates. The current year's revenue was $36 million and current Estimates were over $37 million. If the demands for the next year were met, the deficit would be an additional $3 million. Foster's complaint to Thompson was that no minister would give up anything. Foster found it difficult to keep his patience. He flung himself out of one cabinet meeting mad as a hatter, and still had not quite cooled off some hours later when he wrote Thompson. He was still right, he said. 'I hate to add to your troubles which are now quite enough but that last vote added to all the other circumstances of our Finances quite overcame me.'[67]

He would get over it and cabinet would go on, somehow. Petulance was not unexpected in one's own party and could be fully anticipated from the opposition. Tarte and Martin were perhaps the worst. Thompson anticipated them in a famous speech in Antigonish in December 1893, commenting on the Winnipeg by-election that brought Joseph Martin, the Protestant champion, into the House of Commons. It was the first the Liberals had won in a long time. With a parliamentary majority of sixty-three, Thompson said, the Conservatives could afford to be generous. Besides, getting Martin was no gain to the Liberals. Another victory like the one that gave them Martin and the Liberals would be ruined; Martin was author of the Manitoba trouble. The Liberals also had Tarte, the Roman Catholic champion. Thompson went on, 'I like to see the color on both sides of the clothes we wear. I don't wear yellow on one side and black on the other. Mr. Laurier is perfectly welcome to his black Tarte and yellow Martin.'[68] That jibe – yellow means Orangeism – followed both Tarte and Martin around Canada. It did not make them more tractable in the House of Commons!

On 26 June 1894 Thompson proposed a resolution that Supreme Court justices after fifteen years of service should be given their full salary as pension. Senator Angers was in the gallery; seeing him, P.-A. Choquette, Liberal MP for Montmagny, opened fire, saying up there was the next judge heading for the bench. Then Israel Tarte jumped in, saying that judges that had been used in public inquiries became accomplices in the iniquities they were supposed to investigate, and Belley, MP for Chicoutimi-Saguenay, accused Tarte of throwing out half-baked accusations. Thompson intervened; 'les bouledogues étaient empoignés,' as *La Presse* put it and peace was patched up. Both Thompson and Laurier hated that kind of nastiness, hated to see Parliament made into a cockpit. To do Thompson and Laurier real justice, added *La Presse*, you had to be there and see 'les âmes deplorées de Sir John et Laurier, désespérées de voir cette bataille.'[69]

By late June the House of Commons could become insufferable from heat, and that last fortnight of June 1894 it had been murderous. Cartwright asked Ouimet, minister of public works, if some fans could be installed. Even the air that circulated in the corridors outside the Commons came from sources all too heterogenous – the kitchens below and, as one newspaper added, 'les closets en haut.' The heat affected Thompson and he found it difficult to sleep at night.[70] His patience was tried with the inordinate length of the tariff debate; Supply was worse. Almost every time the House had to go into Committee of Supply there would be a motion about something or other, usually not very much. It was as bad *in* Supply as *going* into it. Thompson complained on 25 June that the House had gone into Supply at four o'clock, and at ten o'clock at night they had passed only one resolution. One whole hour was taken up with the conduct of the lieutenant-governor of the North-West Territories, in connection with the vote for NWT schools. That was Joseph Martin's doing.[71] Perhaps the Speaker had not been firm enough. Thompson was entirely for a strong Speaker, and thought that the current one, Peter White, MP for Renfrew, who was Speaker through all these years, was entitled to respect from Parliament, press, and public. 'Nothing can possibly prevent the lapsing of a House, such as this, into disorder ... unless the authority of the Chair is implicitly obeyed and implicitly respected.'[72]

Thompson also believed that the Ontario provincial election campaign, in May and June of 1894, had something to do with the prolixity of the House in Supply. If so, said he, why not come out with it and the House could go onto something else? The election was on 26 June 1894 and the Mowat government came as close as ever it did come to being overturned: forty-nine Liberals, twenty-seven Conservatives, sixteen Patrons of Industry, and two independents.[73] This thin Liberal majority held for Ontario elections in 1899 and 1902, but the Conservatives came in in 1905 for the next fourteen years. The children of the 1880s and 1890s ended by supporting Conservative governments in Ontario.

That session the children of Ontario, and other provinces, had some reason to be grateful to Thompson. The Criminal Code of 1892 had established the principle that child offenders under the age of sixteen could be tried separately and without publicity. This procedure was optional and few magistrates or judges liked it. In 1894 Senator G.W. Allan of Toronto, and to some degree the Ontario government, persuaded Thompson to sponsor a bill that provided for the mandatory application of the closed door principle for the trial of child offenders. Thompson took an interest in the legislation and owing to his personal intervention it passed.[74] Rev. J.E. Starr, the Methodist minister who had done so much for the Children's Aid Society, wrote Thompson warmly,

Though I knew it must come sometime, yet I scarcely dared to hope that the present Session would see the enactment of the crude outline furnished by me to Senator Allan for the Law Officers of the Crown, and little did I think that so much of the Memorial which I addressed to you about two years ago, would so soon be crystallized into not only Provincial, but also Dominion legislation.[75]

It was only part of Thompson's disposition about prison reform. One of his first anxieties had been to separate the younger from the older, and Thompson's assumption was more hardened, criminals. In the 1894 session $10,000 was appropriated for the purchase of a site and the preparation of plans for what was to be called a Reformatory, meant to be what its name suggested. It was the beginning of a process that can be called differential treatment of offenders, based upon perceived degrees of criminality.[76] There were suggestions that a Dominion-provincial split could be arranged whereby the provinces would deal with the young offenders and the Dominion with the more experienced ones. Thompson did not think that would benefit anyone. He failed to discover any class of offender that could not be dealt with as well by federal as provincial authority; and since the constitution, as Thompson called the BNA Act, gave penitentiaries to the Dominion, and the pardoning power to the governor general in council, Thompson could not support asking Parliament to transfer that authority, even in part, to the provinces.

A more promising initiative was the idea of parole: the principle of cutting a prisoner's time in prison, in effect serving the rest of his sentence outside of prison.[77] That Thompson was ready to discuss with the provinces. He was however opposed to indeterminate sentences, that is, a sentence from three to ten years depending on behaviour. It sounded fine; but as Thompson saw it, it put the prisoner at the mercy of his jailors, and became in effect a system of personal slavery. Indeterminate sentences might have good results when, Thompson said, 'the Jailors are wise, humane and firm.' But for ordinary jailors and ordinary criminals, whatever support the idea might have among philanthropists, it would be 'a very bold and dangerous measure.'[78]

These pressures, some undoubtedly useful and most well-meaning, were part of a general shift in opinion about rehabilitation of criminals, to make the prison a place not so much of punishment as of reformation.[79] Prison as punishment can be seen from the size of the cells at Kingston Penitentiary, constructed in the 1840s. It was superior for its time, being dry and well ventilated, but the cells were very small and only alterable at enormous expense: length, 8'3"; height, 6'6"; width, 2'5". J.G. Moylan, the inspector of penitentiaries, said he had complained several times since 1872 in annual reports, but nothing had been done by any minister of justice until Thompson came along.[80] Thompson ordered work to be begun on remodelling the prison wings at Kingston.

Remodelling Kingston was uphill work; but any changes in prisons and prison systems were difficult. Thompson was at the centre of a three-way pull of disparate forces: the general public represented by Parliament and newspapers; the prison staff and the system they knew and lived with; and the reformers, the Children's Aid Society, the Prisoners' Aid Society, the National Council of Women, and other groups created to bring pressure for change. While Kingston and New Westminister were the penitentiaries that gave Thompson the most trouble, he was badly handicapped by the unreliableness of too many officials. The evidence he received often presented glaring contradictions. Whatever he wanted to do had to be defended in the House of Commons against criticism; but how could that be done if his defence had to be based upon contradictory evidence from his own officials? Thompson seemed genuinely perplexed by the tangle.[81] One constant complaint in newspapers and Parliament was that penitentiary life was too soft. One MP argued vigorously that convicts should not have tobacco, a luxury that many a poor man had to deny himself.[82] It was commonly alleged that Kingston was not too hard but too easy. The *Kingston Whig* complained that convicts got plum pudding and cake at Christmas.[83]

Thompson had another piece of social legislation up his sleeve. Ever since the Report of the Royal Commission on Capital and Labour had appeared in 1889 he had tried to find ways to implement at least some of its recommendations. Nearly all of them fell within the purview of the provinces. The provinces had begun in their several ways to embark upon factory legislation, workmen's compensation, hours of labour. Some municipalities had already begun to set aside one day a year as a holiday in honour of labour. That at least could be done without conflicting with provincial laws. Thompson put the legislation to Parliament in May 1894. Someone asked if there were any application for such a holiday. Thompson replied that the government had hundreds of petitions.[84] Labour Day was established for the first Monday in September, beginning in 1894.

Thompson seemed to be growing steadily in the country's appreciation, friend and foe alike. Even the critical *Saturday Night* was disposed to admit that much, a few months later. Liberals were ready to concede something to his capacity and honesty. One told Faith Fenton, 'I'm not a Conservative but if I had spent many more nights in the [Commons] gallery I'd have come mighty near conversion ... Sir John Thompson is rising in the esteem of the people on both sides every day.'[85]

There was an imperial fillip to all this. Canada sponsored in late June 1894 the first intercolonial conference held outside Great Britain. It had been Mackenzie Bowell's idea. Thompson and the cabinet had sent him, as minister of trade and commerce, to Australia in September 1893 by the new Vancouver-Sydney steamship line. Bowell returned enthusiastic about the possibilities of Australian trade, since the Australian and Canadian growing seasons were at opposite ends of the calendar. Bowell persuaded Thompson and the cabinet, with active encouragement from the governor general, to hold a colonial conference at Ottawa in the summer of 1894. Six of the seven Australian colonies sent delegates, as did Fiji, Cape Colony, and also Hawaii, still independent of the United States. The British government was not certain it liked such goings-on but was not disposed to prevent it. The British Treasury balked at subsidizing delegates from Fiji, but Lord Ripon was ready to fight that through cabinet. The British sent a representative, the Earl of Jersey, though he came as observer.[86] Ripon kept an avuncular eye on the agenda: he did not, for example, like the Australian colonies discussing Samoa, a sore point between Britain and France. He was not sure he would succeed in stopping discussion. 'If the Colonies interpret Imperial Federation to mean that they are to manage our Foreign relations,' he wrote Rosebery, 'we shall have some curious results.' Lord Kimberley at the Foreign Office was more severe than that. It was better not to stimulate the colonists by even letting them look at such matters. 'We have quite enough pressure from them already. Talk at Ottawa will only irritate them and render the Samoan question more acute.'[87]

The conference opened in the Senate, on Thursday, 28 June 1894, the Senate having conveniently adjourned for the purpose. After an address by the governor general, Thompson welcomed the delegates on behalf of Canada. He did not indulge in speculation about imperial federation as did some newspapers. However, customs union among the self-governing colonies was desirable; if Britain could not join it because she had no tariffs to lower, that was too bad, but colonies could go ahead and get obstacles to trade removed.[88] This was incorporated into the resolutions of the conference. Bowell, Foster, and Caron, and Sandford Fleming, Canada's delegates at the conference, urged on such questions, while Thompson looked after the House of Commons.

By the end of that long session of 1894 Thompson was starting to feel as if he had had more than enough. He always believed that a strong constitution measured a man's responsibility to his work; blessed with good health, he had never hesitated to push his own capacity to the limit. But in a perceptive letter to Lady Aberdeen in the fall of 1894, Thompson warned her not to work so hard:

I cannot help reflecting ... that there is an end to the burdens which the greatest energy and the strongest constitution can bear. I did not think this a few months ago but I found it out before last Session was over and I see it now. Sometimes the warning to stop and rest comes very suddenly and sternly.[89]

It was Thompson more than Lady Aberdeen whose problem was writ in that letter. His colleagues noticed Thompson's sudden pulling up. T.M. Daly wrote in early August, 'All I hope is old man that you feel better & better every day & that you are really resting & getting [enough?] of sleep, you played nigger long enough & should be able at least for a few weeks to exist like a white man.'[90]

Thompson did take a holiday. On 30 July, he and his family arrived at

Muskoka Wharf and Port Carling. They had rented a cottage at Senator Sanford's summer retreat in Lake Rousseau; Thompson would settle in there for three weeks, his family until late September. Senator Sanford gave it out that Thompson and family were his guests, but Thompson insisted on renting the cottage. Daly was indignant that Sanford intimated otherwise.[91] It was a holiday intruded into; various deputations came to call. One of them had come all the way from England.

A.D. Provand was promoter of the Chignecto Ship Railway, a project designed to transport small vessels by rail across the Isthmus of Chignecto, from Baie Verte on the east to Chignecto Bay on the west, a distance of fifteen miles. It would save five hundred miles. The company needed another $3 million from the government and were willing to put up a further million of their own. Foster, minister of finance, though from New Brunswick, was not happy with it. 'There is no trade[,] there will be not trade of any account.'[92] Despite Provand's visit to see Thompson in Muskoka, and despite the strong support of old Sir Charles Tupper, the Chignecto Ship Railway was turned down in September 1894. It was perhaps owing to caution of this kind, and to Thompson's reputation in England, that in October 1894 Foster placed a £2,250,000 loan in London exceptionally well.[93]

Thompson broke off his Muskoka holiday for a few days, coming to Toronto from Queenston via T.G. Blackstock's yacht *Cleopatra*; Toronto city council entertained him to luncheon on Toronto Island. Thompson's speech, like many of his speeches now, was strongly nationalistic. Though most of his audience were old enough to remember when sectionalism prevailed, Thompson said, that time had gone by. No longer did Nova Scotia say that Ontario was getting the best of confederation.

The time has come for the young men, born in the days of Confederation, to take their place in the field of public life in Canada, and these men realize that the first principle of national life, national obligations and national hope is that they are Canadians, above and beyond everything else.[94]

Thompson went to Ottawa to a cabinet, on Tuesday, 21 August with Bowell, Costigan, Haggart, and J.C. Patterson, to decide what Canada was willing to settle for from the Americans for the seizure of Canadian sealing vessels.[95] He spent a working evening at the Justice Department, scribbled furiously for another day, then retreated into Muskoka for a final week.

It was a good place. Joe, and Thompson's two young Parisiennes, as he called them, had arrived from overseas the week before. Thompson and all his family were on an island in Lake Rosseau, the most beautiful of the three Muskoka lakes, Thompson thought, the air balmy and the water warm as milk.[96] Who cared if the fishing were only fair? Sanford's place, Sans Souci, was the centre island of a dozen, two miles north of Port Carling, and housed Sanford, his family, and some Great Danes, on an island of pines and Precambrian rock. Across three hundred yards of water was a smaller island and a smaller cottage, Lorelei, close down by the lake. That was where you would have found Sir John Thompson had you arrived there, as one correspondent did, one morning that week. Thompson was on the veranda – called piazza then – but got up from his papers and came down to greet the canoe. On that particular morning the young people were out in the boats, Annie was swimming; an Indian deputation had come that day before Thompson was up.

The interior of Lorelei was oiled ash and oak, with a vast stone fireplace in the living-room. A tent up the hill accommodated John and Joe. Few in Canada knew anything of the home life of Sir John Thompson; he did not choose to make it public and the long description by Faith Fenton owed more to Thompson's respect for her than for newspapers. Thompson's family life impressed whoever discovered it. 'It is rarely given,' said Miss Fenton, 'to see affection so strong, tenderness so great, sincerity and reverence so evident.' All that the world could give would be as nothing in that family.

Thompson's communication with Ottawa was the occasional telegram at Port Carling; once in a while Douglas Stewart, Thompson's private secretary since 1886, would arrive with news and a mailbag. Otherwise Sans Souci lived up to its name. Mackenzie Bowell joined them, made jokes, told fish stories, even as they made plans for fishing the next morning. Among Thompson's fish stories was one he heard from J.C. Mackintosh. There were five MPs on a fishing trip up the Ottawa. On their arrival at camp the host said with hidden irony, 'Who's going fishing?' Mackintosh promptly allowed that he was. A look of horror passed over the faces of the MPs, one of them exclaiming, 'That beats the devil! I never yet started out with the boys on a fishing excursion, than some idiot brought fishing tackle with him! Ives – did you bring the chips?' There was no fishing done that day, or the next.[97]

Some such story as that in the middle of a picture-taking session on Lorelei Island produced a curious photograph. By the mid-1890s, George Eastman's new Kodak, that used roll film and was faster than plates, made photography available to anyone who could press a shutter.

Thus the new meaning of the word 'snapshot,' that dates from the 1890s. There are two snapshots of the Lorelei crowd taken in succession. Thompson and Annie sat in Darby-and-Joan chairs with Frankie, the little brown maiden with sparkling eyes, between, while the others, including Bowell and Sanford, disported themselves lazily on the ground. A second snapshot caught the whole group laughing. Faith Fenton recalled, 'Once we were snap-shotted in the middle of a hearty laugh ...'[98]

There was frequently an afternoon cruise in Sanford's *Naiad*, a steam yacht. She would leave Sans Souci at two in the afternoon. A few minutes before, the Thompson family would come across in two skiffs from their little island. Annie would bring bread, baking powder to make tea biscuits, and the *Naiad* was ready to sail. Thompson was the admiral and sat in the bow, as he used to do sailing with his father years ago in Halifax. He wore a gold braided cap to denote his high rank but graciously relinquished the duties of navigation to the commodore, Senator Sanborn. In this fashion they sailed over the three lakes, Rousseau, Muskoka, and Joseph. The shores were already lined with cottages and camps, occupied now with summer visitors from Toronto and Hamilton; as 'Admiral' Thompson and *Naiad* passed, there would be cheering from the shore. On that particular day they set off through the narrows at Port Sandfield into Lake Joseph, and went up the lake to Port Cockburn and back, a cruise of some forty miles. Annie had Frankie next to her, and the whole tribe of five children were lively and full of laughter. Thompson sat in the bow and beamed with quiet content upon them all.

So passed the nearly halcyon summer days of August 1894.

22

The End of Things

Thompson spent Canada's first Labour Day Monday, 3 September, labouring in Ottawa. It was very quiet and lonesome; the whole city seemed, as he put it, 'out of town.' He went to Toronto to open the Canadian National Exhibition on 5 September, meeting Annie and John there. Annie was downhearted and John grave. Thompson tried to cheer them up; it was not so bad, he said, the swelling in his legs had gone down. He insisted they try to make the best of their Muskoka holiday.[1]

His problem began late in the session, feeling unwell with swelling in his legs he could not seem to get rid of. He said little but wondered about Bright's disease. Cartier had died of it. While on Blackstock's yacht in August he had met Dr J.F.W. Ross of Toronto, and liking him, arranged to have an examination in Toronto on 4 September. Ross found evidence of Bright's disease but also that Thompson was suffering from valvular disease of the heart. Ross recommended that he be examined carefully. Thompson replied he could arrange to go to London that autumn; at some point he should be sworn in as member of the Imperial Privy Council. The best time was that quiet season of parliamentary life, November. Ross recommended that Thompson consult Sir Russell Reynolds of London.[2]

It was impossible to keep this from Annie or John and it was not news they had taken well. He promised to see Dr T.G. Roddick of McGill. On his return to Ottawa Thompson saw Sir James Grant, the chief physician to the governor general. Grant took a more cheerful view. Thompson's heart was sound; a moderate reduction of weight, a careful diet, and no whisky (Thompson had developed a taste for Canadian rye) should put things right. On Sunday, 9 September, after mass in Montreal, Thompson saw Roddick, who sided with Grant's optimistic diagnosis. Nothing was seriously wrong with Thompson; confirmation would have to await the result of urinalysis, but Roddick predicted that there was nothing to prevent Thompson from living another thirty years.[3] Thompson and his family could breathe more easily. His letters took on a jauntier tone. By the end of another ten days, he reported the swelling in his right foot had almost entirely gone, and was only slight in his left. He was not quite to be believed; according to his brother-in-law, J.A. Chisholm, who saw him in Halifax, he was still far from well.[4]

Thompson was in Halifax for meetings, politics, personal business, and to open a monument at Springhill to 125 coal miners who had died in the explosion of 21 February 1891. Springhill had been created by the Intercolonial Railway; there had hardly been a house in Springhill before 1872; now it was a town of five thousand, of whom a quarter were employed by the mines. Thompson's speech was an appeal to toughness and courage. No one, he said, faced daily danger with a braver face than the coal miners of Nova Scotia and Cape Breton. The monument thus unveiled was to remember Springhill's dead, but it was also to remind ourselves that we are a people ready again to face difficulties, 'as we have done successfully since the tragedy of 1891.'[5]

Thompson's life in Halifax was hurried and interrupted. He was cheered by his agent, partner, and friend in real estate, R.F. Armstrong, having sold some lots that had been on Thompson's hands for years in Willow Park and along the Kempt Road. Thompson also succeeded in selling a house and property on North Park Street for $1,700. He seems to have hoped for $2,000 but needed the money.[6] The full Privy Council uniform, if needed for the investiture at Windsor Castle, was expensive; Ede's in Chancery Lane were asking 170 guineas.[7] That would be over half what he received for the North Park Street property! Young Joe would not be able to return to England to do law, but would work on it in Toronto as his elder brother was doing. The only child of Thompson's now going overseas was Helena, who would leave at the end of September to finish her year at the Sacred Heart in Paris.

He went up to Antigonish to direct the revision of electoral lists already under way – that pointed to an election ere long – and to look after his constituency.[8] He saw Bishop Cameron just back from Newfoundland. Cameron had for years been urging Thompson to slow down and in no uncertain terms. In February 1894 Cameron had threatened to set Annie, Canon O'Donnell, and 'other terrible people' upon Thompson, to conspire against his obstinacy and bring him to heel. 'It is not when you will have undermined your health that I wish you to follow my prescription, but *now* ...' Bishop Cameron was uneasy and said mass for Thompson on the feast of St Michael, 29 September. That may have been the result of a report he had received from Thompson, who returned to Montreal and Ottawa on 23 September.[9] Thompson found himself in a major going-over by three doctors, Grant, Wright, and Roddick. They were not so optimistic this time. According to Lady Aberdeen (who had it from Annie) they recommended that Thompson should give up work for a year. There was no problem with his heart, but there were symptoms of kidney trouble they did not like. Here at last Annie urged him to resign. Thompson would not; he could not in conscience resign until he had taken the party safely through the next election in 1895. If they won, he would resign. In the meantime he would carry on.[10]

In October Thompson came to Toronto for the unveiling of the bronze statue of Macdonald. It still stands facing down University Avenue from the southern end of Queen's Park. Saturday, 13 October was a handsome blue, autumn day, a large crowd was in attendance and none looked in better health and spirits than Thompson. His portly figure, his jolly, smiling face, his alert appearance, his whole ensemble, as the *Mail* said, from his well-brushed hat to his boots, a rose in his buttonhole and all: he looked like a man in the vigorous prime of life. One of the speakers following Thompson suggested that Ontarians would cheerfully honour the prime minister who stood before them with a similar statue. The idea of commemorating a dead-and-gone Sir John Thompson when there he was very much alive was so ridiculous that Thompson and everyone else burst out laughing. Thus the ceremony ended with that very human touch.[11]

The crowd that day was estimated by an enthusiastic Toronto *Empire* at thirty thousand. The *Empire* was another of Thompson's burdens. He did not like the paper much; he did not read it more than once a week.[12] The *Toronto World*, a fellow Conservative paper, in a moment of exasperation with the *Empire*, called it a disgrace to Canadian journalism.[13] There had been discussion among Toronto Conservatives for two or three years about amalgamation of the *Toronto Mail*, the Conservative maverick, and the *Empire*, the paper created to replace the *Mail*. The *Empire* had never taken hold of the party; perhaps it had been too much a party hack, using too little of its own gumption and ideas; perhaps it was owing to the editor, David Creighton; whatever it was, by 1894 it was holding neither party nor public. It was in debt to the tune of $25,000 and needed another $25,000. Creighton would not resign voluntarily and would have to be hived off probably with a postmastership. Sir Frank Smith suggested

Owen Sound at $2,000 a year. The *Mail* would then be brought into line and a joint paper could be run by the *Mail* people. The plant of the *Empire*, according to Smith, was not worth 25 cents on the dollar.[14]

Thompson hesitated. He did not altogether trust Bunting and Riordan of the *Mail*. He did not like the party again dependent in Toronto on the friendship of those who had not hesitated to betray Sir John Macdonald in his hour of need in 1885; he wanted sufficient control over a *Mail and Empire* to prevent it from being turned against the government. Owing to Senator Gowan's efforts, the *Empire* was kept going for another few months; amalgamation would come in 1895.[15] Thompson's last words to Gowan before leaving for England were on that subject. Thompson hoped to see his Irish cousins whom he had never met and through whom he was distantly related to Gowan. Thompson signed off cheerfully, 'Farewell! for a little time my dear Senator.'[16]

Caron, Frankie, and Annie came with Thompson to New York. Annie would not go overseas this time; their long trip in 1893 had been so expensive that she feared the financial burden that her coming would entail.[17] Thompson anticipated being away only four or five weeks. New York was drenched in a cold October rain the day that Thompson boarded RMS *Majestic* on 31 October. It was so wet that Annie, who had apparently broken her wrist a few days before, stayed at the hotel. Caron escorted them back to Ottawa.

A week later Thompson arrived in London apparently in good health, having passed Foster on the high seas. He arrived in time to catch the editorial in *The Times* of 5 November, a tribute to Canada's standing in the British financial community. The new Canadian £2,250,000 loan had been a triumph. Its success owed something to the receptiveness of the money market; still it was significant that the price of the tenders was much higher than for the Canadian loan of 1888 or 1892, averaging £97.9s.2d., against the £92.0s.11d. of 1892, and the £95.1s.0d. of 1888. 'The Government of Sir John Thompson,' said *The Times*, 'will be able to meet its critics with increased assurance ... but the confidence which has really been expressed is not so much in one party or one policy ... as in the essential soundness of Canadian finance, and the prosperous future that lies before the colony.'[18] The *Toronto World* celebrated Canada's success, a cartoon showing Cartwright saying to Laurier, 'You know, that's the sort of thing that makes a man weary of life.'[19]

Thompson saw Lord Ripon at the Colonial Office on 8 November, the first time they had met, and the following day set out a considerable agenda for discussion. There were eight points, not all of them minor, though some appeared so to the Colonial Office. One was the table of precedence for Canada, which Thompson had found difficult and delicate. The Colonial Office minute suggested it was time Canada had a Lord Chamberlain to deal with 'this heart-breaking question!' But four other questions were heart-breakers on either side of the Atlantic:

V. Cable and steam communication, in accordance with views expressed at the Colonial Conference in Canada.
VI. Modification of the Australasian [colonial] constitution[s] so as to give effect to tariff arrangements between colonies.
VII. Better representation of Canadian interests at foreign capitals.
VIII. Subject of copyright in Canada 'as that matter has now reached what I consider a critical stage.'[20]

On Canadian representation at foreign capitals, mainly Washington, the Colonial Office was not hopeful. The United States would not be disposed to facilitate British-Canadian relations; the Republican party would take 'a fiendish pleasure in playing off any Canadian Agent against H.M.'s Ambassador; that any Canadian Agent would have to act in strict subordination to the British Ambassador, and that any independent action would have to be rigorously forbidden and punished by immediate recall.' To which John Bramston, assistant under-secretary, added, 'It will be necessary that Sir J. Thompson should explain more fully what exactly they want.'[21] Foreign Office reaction would be much stiffer than that.

As to copyright, extensive papers were again circulating at the Colonial Office. A timely but offensive letter by F.R. Daldy in *The Times* asked, 'Is Canada part of the British Empire or is she not?' If Canada was British, Canada must not be allowed 'nefariously to seek her own aggrandizement by seizing the copyright property of others.' Such was the gloss the British Authors' Association put on Canadian copyright law![22] A deputation arranged to meet Lord Ripon on 26 November, a few days before Thompson was due to return from the continent.[23]

Sir Russell Reynolds, the London specialist, gave Thompson much the same diagnosis as the Montreal and Ottawa doctors; if anything he was more hopeful. Thompson needed rest; there were some symptoms of kidney disease but his heart was peculiarly strong.[24] Thompson was much cheered by this and so were his family in Ottawa. He resolved to go to the continent for a short holiday, accompanied by Senator Sanford, and his daughter Muriel; Thompson would be joined by Helena at Paris. Thompson was in good spirits and ready for a holiday. Perhaps his strength and energy would be restored; he could return to Canada for the work of the 1895 session and the next general election. The little party went to Nice and Monte Carlo, thence to Genoa and on to Rome. Thompson was proud of Helena: how well-mannered and poised she was, with her fluent and elegant French and even by now some Italian. Little is known about those three weeks. There was one spectacular piece of unwisdom in Rome: Thompson climbed all the way to the top of St Peter's dome, some 404 feet above the pavement. One could climb 150 feet to the gallery that circles the bottom of the dome; the ascent to the top is 250 feet higher still. According to Helena, from that time on her father suffered from breathlessness, and in Naples had to stay in bed for a day or two. Thompson left Rome on 25 November for Florence, thence to Venice, and so to Paris and London via Milan. They arrived in London early in the morning of Saturday, 1 December.[25]

They took up quarters at the Royal Palace Hotel in Kensington High Street, overlooking the Gardens. Sir Charles Tupper went over to the hotel that morning around ten o'clock and found to his surprise that Thompson was at work down at the Canadian High Commission at 17 Victoria Street, near Westminster Abbey. Since Thompson had arrived at six that morning from the continent, Tupper remonstrated that he ought to have gone immediately to bed. They were to have lunch together, but Thompson was so troubled with breathlessness that it was thought better that he go back to his hotel. There, on Tupper's recommendation, he consulted Dr Travers.[26] Travers told him he had strained his heart; its action was not satisfactory and he would have to be careful. Thompson managed to stay in his hotel for two or three days, then felt so well he resolved to go about his business.[27] Thursday, 6 December he lunched with the Tuppers at their home in Cromwell Road, then had dinner with the Huddarts (Huddart of the Pacific Steamship line and other interests). Thompson was in very good spirits.

There were shoals of invitations. Lord Ripon had gone 'down' to Yorkshire (as they say in England) to Studley near Ripon, and would see Thompson after his return. James Bryce, with the portfolio of the Duchy of Lancaster, wanted him for lunch on Sunday, 9 December. It is not known whether he went; he saw, however, Sir Charles Russell (now Lord Russell of Killowen) on that Sunday and spoke of his health as being somewhat impaired, that doctors had advised him to rest, and he proposed to try to follow that.[28] Sir Richard Webster offered dinner for Tuesday, 11 December or Friday, 14 December; Thompson agreed to the latter. Robert Meade, the permanent under-secretary at the Colonial

Office, offered the weekend of 15 and 16 December for a country visit, an opportunity to meet the lord chancellor, Lord Herschell, and Cecil Rhodes, premier of Cape of Good Hope, both very anxious to meet Thompson.[29] Not least of the invitations was from William Ewart Gladstone to lunch at Hawarden (pronounced 'Hardin') in Cheshire, 'even though my age, close upon 85, is now withdrawing me from all general society.'[30]

Gladstone was put up to that by Lady Aberdeen. She wrote him from Government House, Victoria, that Thompson had unbounded admiration for Gladstone and his Irish policy, and could she ask that Thompson be invited to look in at Hawarden? 'We have of course hinted at no such possibility to him, but he has expressed to us his very great desire to see you and share a conversation. Forgive me for suggesting this, but I know that such an opportunity would be an inspiration for Sir John and he is working so hard and so honestly for his country that I cannot help putting the possibility before you.' Thompson replied to Gladstone that he would be delighted to take up the opportunity; he hoped there would be time to finish his business in London and still get to Hawarden en route to Liverpool. His boat was due to leave for Canada on 19 December.[31]

If Thompson had an agenda for the Colonial Office, they also had one for him. One of the most immediate items concerned Sir Charles Tupper. In October 1892 the British scheduled Canadian cattle – that is, they refused to admit Canadian live cattle, on the ground of disease. Canada protested that her cattle were free of it, but the permanent officials at the Board of Agriculture, all very strong protectionists, dearly wanted to exclude Canadian live cattle and they succeeded. Lord Ripon was certain the main effect on his Liberal party was to lose them votes, especially in Scotland. This effect was abetted by Sir Charles Tupper in a by-election late in 1894 in Forfarshire. Tupper allowed himself to speak against British exclusion of Canadian cattle with, no doubt, the aim of influencing the vote. Lord Rosebery, the British prime minister, from Scotland himself, was nettled, and with reason. What was there to prevent Sir Charles Tupper from stumping the whole of northeast Scotland at the next general election? 'Could you not,' suggested Rosebery to Ripon, 'talk to Sir John Thompson and point out that Tupper's action is an actual impediment to our doing anything [about Canadian cattle], besides its gross indecorum?'[32]

More serious and more permanent were Colonial Office hopes, fears, long-suffering patience, and periodic bouts of impatience, with Newfoundland. Abbott's policies and Thompson's were at one about Newfoundland: end the Bait Act squabble, but not at the price of assenting to the Bond–Blaine Treaty of 1890. The stiff Canadian opposition to that treaty had created strong anti-Canadian feeling in Newfoundland, to which was added anti-British feeling for Britain's refusal to override Canada.[33] The Colonial Office was not of one mind about it. In February 1892, when the United States refused to give Canada the same treatment as Newfoundland, John Anderson favoured putting an end to the wrangle by sanctioning Newfoundland's treaty with the Americans.[34] This was not done. Thompson and Abbott were anxious to adjust their quarrel with Newfoundland, but not at that price. There was talk in May 1892 that the Newfoundland Bait Act and the Canadian riposte to it (duties on fish and fish products from Newfoundland) could be mutually rescinded; it came to nothing. Perhaps Canadian help sent to Newfoundland after the terrible St John's fire of 8–9 July 1892 may have eased feelings. The fire devastated three-quarters of the city and left nearly eleven thousand people homeless.[35] In response to a suggestion from the Canadian cabinet, Newfoundland agreed to discuss the issues between them at Halifax, in November 1892.

Among these was an unstated but real question, confederation. Both Abbott and Thompson felt that the benefits from confederation were more to the advantage of Newfoundland than Canada. These Thompson took to be the development of Newfoundland's public works, notably the Newfoundland railway and the relief of the indebtedness that the railway had created; free trade with Canada, the immediate result of which would be a substantial reduction in the cost of living for Newfoundlanders. Moreover, Thompson believed, Canada could better defend Newfoundland's fishing rights than Newfoundland could herself. There would be expenditures by Canada on lighthouse service, wharves, militia, post office. Thompson was convinced that the smaller provinces of confederation, far from having been victimized by central Canada, had obtained a 'far larger share of consideration (including expenditure) than the larger [provinces], and have more influence than could be claimed on account either of territory or population. The fact that they have always been more troublesome than the larger ones is perhaps one of the reasons.'[36] The only benefit that Canada would get was the frustration of American diplomacy in Newfoundland. Other than that, the only gain to Canada was the sentimental one of having Newfoundland in. Thompson felt sentiment could wait a while, if need be another fifty or a hundred years. Sentiments did not make unions necessary, though they might help to effect them when other conditions were ripe.[37]

Canada was ready to have Newfoundland in confederation if the terms were not too onerous, and on that point the 1869 terms, satisfactory to Canada, did not appear to be so to Newfoundland in 1892. Thompson and Abbott also believed it essential that the French Shore problem be solved first; Canada did not want to import a quarrel with France with a confederated Newfoundland. Thus, in 1892, if peace could be patched up between Canada and Newfoundland it would be up to Newfoundlanders to decide upon what terms they wanted to enter confederation and put them to Canada accordingly.

By the early 1890s the Conservative 'party' in Newfoundland were mainly pro-confederation, and the Liberal 'party' under Sir William Whiteway were neither yes nor no. The Whiteway government was bitterly divided internally and sought to capitalize on whatever popularity could be got by espousing, or opposing, confederation. The Newfoundland delegates that came to Halifax in November 1892 – Sir William Whiteway, the premier; Robert Bond, the colonial secretary, author of the great convention with Blaine; and A.W. Harvey, anti-Canadian and alleged annexationist – were on the *qui vive*. Thompson, Chapleau, and Bowell, the Canadian delegates, tried to iron out differences over the Bait Act. It was also expected that confederation would be discussed. In Newfoundland, A.B. Morine was frantic, urging Thompson not to negotiate confederation with treacherous Liberals like Whiteway, Bond, and Harvey.[38] Morine need not have been alarmed. The delegates from Newfoundland refused to do any business unless Canada withdrew opposition to the Bond–Blaine Convention. Harvey was exceptionally recalcitrant about that. Confederation was only touched upon. The Halifax conference failed to achieve anything. It confirmed Thompson in the intransigeance of Harvey, the slipperyness of Whiteway, and the vigour, power, and conceit of Robert Bond, Newfoundland's 'incorruptible commoner.'[39]

Thompson did not mince words. The Newfoundland delegates, he cabled C.H. Tupper in London, only came to get Canadian consent to the Bond–Blaine Convention and while they were at it insist on their right to fish in Canadian waters. Cabinet in Ottawa would review, but it might be useful to put the result to the Colonial Office.[40] Newfoundland in 1893–4 bears out the ancient Chinese curse: 'May you have an interesting history.' The best that Sir Terence O'Brien, the long suffering, sixty-year-old soldier-governor could recommend was confederation or a British royal commission.[41] Newfoundland drove into a violent storm, ferocious economic gales with high political seas, and the frail Whiteway vessel with her mutinous crew were in no condition to meet any of it. On 11 December 1894 two Newfoundland banks, the Union and the Commercial, failed. There were telegrams to Lord Ripon the day before prophesying it.[42] Ripon may have broached the question of Newfoundland with Thompson in their interview that Tuesday, 11 December.

Thompson's immediate concern – that day was to be the start of several days' discussion – was not so much Newfoundland. Newfoundland would have to be solved in due course, at more length. It was essential that the all-party agreement on Canadian copyright in Ottawa be pushed through to a conclusion. Let Canadian copyright be conceded. That festering thorn could be drawn. Even the London *Times* that day, in a leading editorial, admitted some justice in the Canadian case.'[43]

That evening, Thompson saw Helena off to Paris on her way back to school, accompanied by Senator Sanford; Helena was pleased at how well her father looked. He then dined with Tupper at the Colonial Institute, stayed for a meeting afterward, laughed at jokes, spoke himself to turn back criticism of the Ottawa conference, and seemed in good spirits. Thompson and Tupper went home together, Tupper leaving Thompson at his hotel at eleven o'clock.[44]

Wednesday, 12 December was a bright day, characteristic of the lingering generosity of late autumn in England, the temperature a mild, equable 50 degrees or so; primulas still bloomed, and in sheltered gardens even a few roses. It was the day of Thompson's official swearing in as a member of Her Majesty's Privy Council. The only other Canadian admitted had been Sir John A. Macdonald, the result of his work for the Treaty of Washington in 1871. Thompson's had been for the Bering Sea arbitration. Thompson dressed with care; the invitation said 'plain morning dress'; that meant black knee-breeches and black silk stockings. That expensive Windsor uniform could wait for a while![45] A special train of the Great Western Railway would leave Paddington at twelve noon for Windsor. Paddington station was just north of Kensington Gardens; Thompson was there half an hour before train time, the first of the party to arrive. He seemed in good health; he told Mrs Sanford the previous morning that he felt better than he had for months.[46] If Thompson had read *The Times* that morning, he would have reflected about the financial crisis in Newfoundland. He had doubtless already read the sensible and judicious review of the copyright question the day before.

The train journey to Windsor took under an hour. The ceremony of the Privy Council was set for 1:15 p.m., under the superintendence of the Lord Steward of Windsor, the Marquis of Breadalbane, six years younger than Thompson. Attending Council – Council *pro forma* – were the Marquis of Ripon representing the prime minister, Lord Rosebery; H.H. Fowler, the secretary of state for India; Arnold Morley, the postmaster general, and the usual gentlemen and ladies of the court. Despite later rumours to the contrary, it was not a long ceremony, which was fortunate, for the Marquis of Ripon was sixty-six years old and Queen Victoria was not fond of allowing any of the company to sit down. The whole affair took not much more than twenty minutes.[47] Notwithstanding, Thompson seemed rather crushed by the strain. It then appeared that he had not slept well the previous night but had made little mention of it. The company adjourned to the Octagon Room for lunch; after Thompson was seated, but before he had touched any food, he fainted. Lord Breadalbane and a servant helped him to a writing room nearby. There he sat down, his head in his hands, was given some water and the marquis sent for brandy. Thompson revived somewhat but was distressed at having made a scene, remarking to Lord Breadalbane, 'It seems too weak and foolish to faint like this.' Breadalbane replied sensibly, 'One does not faint on purpose. Pray don't distress yourself...' Thompson wanted him to return to the Octagon Room, but Breadalbane waited until Thompson felt better then accompanied him back. Breadalbane offered his arm but Thompson walked in unaided, saying cheerfully, 'I'm all right now, thank you.'[48] It was about 1:45 p.m. In the meantime the queen's doctor, Dr Reid, had been sent for and arrived as Thompson again sat to lunch, and took a place beside him. Thompson mentioned that he had had pain in his chest. Suddenly, without a sound he collapsed, half against the doctor. The luncheon stopped abruptly; Dr Reid administered brandy and felt for Thompson's pulse. There was none. Thompson was dead.

In Montreal, Ottawa, and Toronto it was 8:45 a.m.[49] Scarcely anyone believed the first flashes of news that began circulating in Montreal around mid-morning, emanating from the press and telegraph companies. There had been a false alarm the year before when Thompson was in Paris and this too was thought to be a hoax. The messenger at the Department of Trade and Commerce brought the news to Bowell in a telegram from C.R. Hosmer of the CPR in Montreal: '11:36 A.M., Dec. 12, 1894. Reported from Windsor Castle that Sir John Thompson expired after meeting of privy council...' Bowell refused to believe it. 'It is mere newspaper rumour,' he said. Sandford Fleming, there at the time, volunteered to wire for confirmation. Within half an hour Hosmer reported that Thompson's death was confirmed. And a message now came from Sir Charles Tupper. All hope was at an end. Bowell put the telegrams on the desk and burst into tears. Foster and Costigan were with him by this time.

'Poor Lady Thompson!' Bowell muttered, 'who can we get to take the news to her?'
'It is your duty, Mr. Bowell,' Foster suggested.
'My God, I cannot do that!' Bowell seemed wholly overcome.
'But it is clearly the duty of some member of the Ministry to tell her,' was Foster's unrelenting answer.

At this point Douglas Stewart came in, white and shaken, and it was agreed that three of them would go to tell Annie.[50]
Perhaps Annie Thompson knew. A reporter, having heard the rumours in town, telephoned the house of the prime minister and asked Annie if news had been received of Sir John Thompson's death. Having had no intimation of any news, Annie's reaction can only be imagined. Whether she believed it or not, one could not envy Bowell, Foster, and Stewart making their way to 276 Somerset Street that wet afternoon, an afternoon of grey hopelessness, and, as it wore on, of wind-beaten rain tearing at the half-masted flags. Over the wind came the sound of tolling bells.[51]
Lady Aberdeen went to Annie from Montreal. By the next day Annie was brave, strong, almost natural, but utterly overwhelmed at the aloneness that loomed ahead of her. Thompson had been everything to her; society, other people, were almost matters of indifference unless through them she could in some way help him; it had been that way ever since she had first fallen in love with him:

never to hear his voice again, never to hear him come in at the door, never to hear him come up the stairs again – never, never – oh! I am afraid of the nights & I am afraid of the days & I am afraid of the years & if it were not for the children I should long to creep away in some corner & die.[52]

Old Gowan would not have known what to say to Annie if he had met her face to face. To set down on paper what he felt was nearly as impossible. His words came out as icicles. 'Poor Thompson!' Chapleau telegraphed, 'the cup of his life was filled with mighty work, manfully done ...'[53] Many Canadians felt so. The Montreal Stock Exchange simply dried up. The city had not been so struck since the assassination of McGee in 1868.[54]

Laurier in Arthabaskaville was strangely moved; Thompson was a gentleman and an opponent with whom a contest was a positive pleasure. Who was there now, Laurier wondered, to hold the Conservative party up to the level that Thompson had brought it to? 'The loss of so able a man,' Laurier wrote to J.D. Edgar in Toronto, 'is irreparable to the Conservative party. Whatever they do, there is a gap which cannot be filled.'[55]

The sense of loss filled Ottawa. It was almost like 'un cri de coeur,' one Ottawa paper said. Thompson had taken on everything, he had earned everything. His success had been amazing. 'Les honneurs ont plus sur sa tête. Tous les postes, toutes les missions lui ont été confiés. Il semblait indispensable.' D'Alton McCarthy, in Ottawa that day on a law case, made amends for years of bitterness. Thompson was, he said, a statesman of the highest order; but as a lawyer he was unexcelled: 'he stood amidst all the members of the bar of the Dominion of Canada unsurpassed.'[56] L.-O. Taillon, in the Assembly of Quebec, got the news and adjourned the Assembly with a eulogy to Thompson. Taillon was generous then and six months before, when he had thanked Thompson for some kindness – 'c'est votre coeur qui l'a dictée.'[57] W.S. Fielding, premier of Nova Scotia, campaigning that day in Port Hood, Cape Breton, was handed a telegram. He stopped his political speech. 'I don't want to remember Sir John as a politician. I remember him only as an old Halifax school mate, a true friend, and one of the best men the country has ever produced.'[58]

In London that afternoon Tupper had been galvanized into action by peremptory telegrams from the queen's equerry at Windsor. Thompson's body was laid out in Clarence Tower at Windsor Castle, where, on the queen's instructions, a requiem mass was held just before midnight. Thompson's body thereafter lay in state in the Marble Hall. The following day, Thursday, it was taken from the castle in a plumed hearse and brought to London, where it was embalmed by a French specialist, Dr Charles Bayle. On Friday it was placed in the Chapel of St James, Spanish Place, Manchester Square. By this time poor Helena Thompson had been brought back from Paris and was received by the queen at Windsor with the Sanfords. The memorial requiem mass was held on 14 December, with a large group of colonial and British statesmen in attendance: Cecil Rhodes, Dr Jameson (a year away from his famous raid in South Africa), Lord Tennyson, Lord Mount Stephen, Sir Charles Tupper, the Marquis of Ripon.[59]

Ripon was inexpressibly shocked by Thompson's death and determined that it would be marked in every way fitting Thompson's standing.

That determination may have been aided by the fact that Ripon too was a convert to Catholicism. Ripon and his colleagues acted with speed and decision; Ripon wrote Sir William Harcourt, chancellor of the exchequer, that Thompson had no money and his widow and family would be left very badly off. Would it not be proper, and gracious, to offer to pay the expenses of the removal of Thompson's body to Canada? No precedent could be established; it would be a long time before another important colonial minister died in the queen's palace. Harcourt agreed and went one better. When the American philanthropist, George Peabody (who had put money into London slum clearance) died in 1869 in London, his body was sent to the United States in a British man-of-war.[60] Harcourt felt they could do no less for Thompson; it would be employment for the navy besides giving great satisfaction to Canada.[61] A cable went to Lord Aberdeen: 'Admiralty offer HMS Blenheim to take Sir John Thompson's body to Canada. Please ascertain Lady Thompson's wishes.' She agreed; the Admiralty then cabled Gibraltar where *Blenheim* was lying and ordered her home. She left Gibraltar on the afternoon of Friday, 14 December.[62] It was all done in forty-eight hours. HMS *Blenheim* was one of the newest and fastest cruisers in the British navy. She was only three years old, and could cross the Atlantic with as much speed as a regular liner.

Lord Ripon was anxious that everything be done to make the ceremonies at Portsmouth, and especially at Halifax 'as becoming and imposing as the circumstances admit.'[63] HMS *Blenheim* would re-provision, re-coal, and leave for Halifax on Saturday, 22 December. The intention was that Sir Charles Tupper and Senator Sanford would accompany Thompson's body. Tupper's doctor insisted that Tupper could not go; the Canadian government, notably Lord Aberdeen, were looking for ways to keep not only Tupper but Senator Sanford out of it.

There were reasons. Senator Eli Sanford was a rich and generous Conservative. But, as certain aspects of his conduct in Thompson's visit to Muskoka showed, he was apt to be obtrusive and vulgar and the Aberdeens already knew him well enough to want to keep him at arm's length. Annie was aggrieved over the prominent part already played by 'the old wretch Sir Charles Tupper' and the Sanfords. 'Do you think the Queen will think we are like the Sanfords?' was the question Annie put to Lady Aberdeen. It was delicately hinted that the Admiralty did not think there would be any real need for Tupper or Sanford to go to Canada in the *Blenheim* unless the Canadian government should insist. But Sanford got his way. Mrs Sanford and her daughter with Helena Thompson sailed for New York on RMS *Majestic*; Sanford would go in *Blenheim*. Aberdeen was a bit rueful about the outcome; 'it seemed almost like a bit of melancholy comedy,' he wrote to Ripon, 'that two very advertising persons should as it were have been so greatly advertised by this calamity.'[64]

The journey of Thompson's body from London to Portsmouth on Saturday, 22 December was almost like a British state funeral. There was a special train with a special car; even the engine was draped in black. Ships in Portsmouth harbour dipped their ensigns as the train arrived; the Roman Catholic bishop of Portsmouth met the train, followed the gun carriage, which was in turn followed by naval and military officers in full uniform. The *Blenheim*'s sides were painted black, the gangway draped in black, and on a blustery rainy day Thompson's body was brought on board and installed in the captain's stateroom.[65] Then, after a short service, the *Blenheim* slipped out of Portsmouth harbour with instructions to arrive at Halifax on midday, Tuesday, 1 January 1895. The government of Canada set Thompson's state funeral for two days later.

Extensive preparations were made, far more than Thompson or Annie would have wanted. All the late Victorian taste for funeral paraphernalia went into it.[66] Louis Coste, the chief engineer of the Department of Public Works, was put in charge and sent to Halifax to organize it. That included rearranging Thompson's little family plot in Holy Cross cemetery. The cemetery was at the corner of South Park and South streets, and the family plot had been bought years before on the north side. Three of their babies, Annie's mother, and her two brothers were already there, and would probably have to be moved to allow room for Thompson's grave in the centre.[67]

Annie with her five children left Ottawa on Friday, 28 December, in a private railway car. Helena arrived from New York in time to accompany her family to Halifax. There were three private cars on the train, for there were other guests, including the Dewdneys from Victoria and the vice-regal party picked up in Montreal. In Halifax Annie and her children stayed with her uncle, John Pugh.

Annie was not pleased at the funeral arrangements. She did not object to two thousand roses, four thousand carnations, three thousand ferns or three thousand hyacinths; but she had asked especially that heavy black coverings and black plumes be avoided especially on the funeral car that would take Thompson's body through the Halifax streets. Thompson always had a horror of such things. But late Victorian taste proved difficult to stop. By the time Annie got to Halifax much of the work had been done. Public Works and the funeral director were apparently willing to try to redo things as much as possible with only two days left but in the end Archbishop O'Brien of Halifax suggested to Annie that with so much already done it was best left alone. It was, although Annie disliked it very much.[68]

New Year's Day, 1895, was a day of mist and drenching rain; HMS *Blenheim* arrived punctually at midday; she came up the harbour, saluted in succession by the guns of York Redoubt, Point Pleasant, George's Island, and the Citadel. Everyone knew Thompson's body had come home. The city was full of people; the streets were lined with men of the 65th Halifax Rifles to control the crowds. The coffin was escorted formally off the *Blenheim*, placed on a gun carriage and covered with the Canadian flag, the red ensign with Canada's coat of arms on the fly. Four powerful black horses pulled the carriage through the rainy streets to Province House where Thompson was to lie in state. The red room, the Legislative Council chamber, was partly in purple, partly in black, though the tall brilliant portraits of George III and Queen Charlotte, and the British generals and statesmen, mostly in bright red, were mercifully left to brighten the room.

That night Louis Coste and David Pottinger opened Thompson's coffin. They had to see if the French embalmer's work was good enough to allow Annie and the children to see him. Thompson's body was preserved but his face was so discoloured by blood that the coffin was closed.

Bishop Cameron came down from Antigonish the day before the funeral. He was to be the celebrant at the requiem funeral at St Mary's Cathedral and he feared breaking down from physical as well as emotional strain. He could hardly talk to the Aberdeens about Thompson, only to say that of all the men he had known, Thompson seemed to him the man who lived most habitually with 'a sense of the presence of God about him.' The strong words were Lady Aberdeen's: the sentiment belonged to both of them.[69]

Thursday, 3 January was a beautiful day. It seemed to Lady Aberdeen almost like a blessing, the sun shining, the air mild and still. The city was crowded to overflowing; every train that arrived brought new loads of people. There were seven thousand applicants for the seven hundred seats in St Mary's Cathedral. The cathedral on the inside was draped in black, but that was relieved with white crosses, monograms, texts, and some silver. Five lieutenant-governors came: Dewdney from British Columbia, Kirkpatrick from Ontario, Chapleau from Quebec, Howlan from Prince Edward Island, Daly from Nova Scotia. There was a whole row of archbishops and bishops. Cameron performed the mass and Archbishop O'Brien, not too well himself, preached the sermon. Then the procession formed up in the late morning sun outside the church and wound slowly to the cemetery – only half a mile away, though it took an hour and a half to get there. There were huge crowds of spectators; it all looked imposing and proper; there were soldiers in red from the Citadel; sailors in blue from the dockyard and *Blenheim*; the military band played Beethoven's funeral march and Handel's dead march in *Saul*; there was the sunshine. The Halifax crowd were quiet and well behaved; it was a son of their own they were burying that day in Holy Cross cemetery, half a mile from where he was born forty-nine years before.

23

In the Service of His Country

The day Thompson was buried Lord Aberdeen had to heal wounds in cabinet created by the new premier, Sir Mackenzie Bowell. On cabinet's return to Ottawa came the decision of the Privy Council in the Brophy case; as Laurier told Fielding, it 'terribly complicates matters for them.'[1] Now more than ever they needed Thompson's quiet good sense, his controlled courtesy. C.H. Tupper represented Thompson's policies; he had not Thompson's manner. His was too hot a temper; he was always sure he was right, and to admit a mistake was impossible.[2] Very early on cracks began to open that Thompson had kept closed. It was as if the difficulties that occurred while Thompson was in Paris in 1893 had taught the party little. Too long in power perhaps, or unteachable? Was it, as J.J. Curran suggested, that Protestants would not make sufficient sacrifices? Or was it simply that the party could not stand without Thompson? Thompson's old friend in Halifax, J.T. Bulmer, used another metaphor. In the Arctic when travelling by dog-team you always hung the sled harness up at night, so the dogs would not get at it and chew it up. The difficulty of the Conservative party in 1895 and 1896 was that the sled dogs had got at the harness.[3]

Lady Aberdeen was convinced as early as March 1895 that there was no alternative to a Laurier government. She was sending Gladstone Castell Hopkins's new book on Thompson – that Canadian whom Gladstone never met. The book was hastily prepared, she said; it was off the press at Brantford in record time to meet a 'loudly expressed demand for some book of the sort.' She was unhappy with the new state of politics. The loss of Thompson was being felt not less but more. The Bowell government seemed unable to manage that hard helm; its weakness and indecision were pitiful and the country was becoming irritated by it. 'We are,' she wrote, 'in the midst of a crisis now.' It was caused by C.H. Tupper wanting to hold to Thompson's policies. Since he was the strongest man in the government, no one knew what would happen.

Sir John had so much tact as well as strength that he managed to keep the incongruous racial and religious sections in his Cabinet together but now all are working against one another ... What his loss is to us personally I can scarcely describe, and the contrast which Aberdeen finds in his official relations is very marked. Although we must have no politics yet we cannot help personally hoping that the Liberals under M. Laurier may come in at the election ... they seem to have a stronger set of men as leaders.

The Liberals were finding in Thompson's death the source of their own resurrection.[4]

Thompson often earned the esteem of those who opposed him. The Liberals fought him but they were proud of him, proud of his qualities, the uprightness of his life, his Canadian patriotism.[5] It was Martin Griffin's opinion that old-style politicians on both sides of the House were afraid of Thompson; he had the faculty of impressing himself morally on the public mind. MPs told Griffin that Thompson awed his party into submission by sheer force of character.[6]

The Thompson that Lady Aberdeen knew and admired was a man well distanced from the diffident, uncertain young man of the Halifax years. She might not even have liked the young Thompson, but she was attracted by qualities in the mature one, especially his strength and confidence. These came not from any assertiveness but from a quite different source: from the slow, layered accretion of successes, the effect of years of Thompson's own work, his testing, not always willingly, of himself. Thompson's composure, the apparent repose of that powerful mind, came from having met and surmounted most of the challenges that life had brought before him. Annie was right. He had discovered that there were few limits to his potential. The limits that did exist were mainly owing to his disregard, not to say disrespect, for mere political adroitness. Those tests he did not want and probably could not have met. Rugged honesty the Conservative party badly needed in June 1891: and what it certainly got.

Thompson broke the rules of the political game, the way Gladstone had. In England the game was played with a code of behaviour created by private gentlemen on private income. In Canada the same conventions, in a frontier society often needy, greedy, or both, became corrupt. In

Victorian England a demagogue was 'a politician who intruded conscience into politics': in North America a demagogue could be defined as one who did not. Thompson believed that in Canadian politics there was no alternative to firm moral standards. That meant, of course, a tension in Thompson and his party between what was right and what was expedient. One day when a member of cabinet was not in his seat for an important vote, Thompson asked why. 'He does not like this vote,' explained the whip. 'For Heaven's sake,' Thompson said, 'does he imagine we are taking it because we like it?'[7]

Near the root of Thompson's problem as a politician was an unwillingness to say what he did not think, profess what he could not believe. Like his father, he had few soft hypocrisies. There is a revealing letter from W.E. Jones of the *Richmond Guardian* in the Eastern Townships, an old Conservative who liked Thompson but found his frankness dangerous. Jones regretted the position Thompson had taken in speaking to a prohibition delegation in March 1894. It was difficult, Jones admitted, but prohibition was coming, and if the Conservative party did not take it up, the Liberals would.

While I greatly admired the transparent frankness of your reply to the delegation – and the thorough – indeed statesmanlike honesty of the attitude you then assumed, I do regret that you did not temporize somewhat so as to have left some chink through which a ray of hope might penetrate; for whether you meant it or not, the unanimous feeling of the delegates was that you are not disposed to take up the question, either now or in the early future.[8]

Thompson was apt to take threats badly. Threats or intimidation with him were, to use current jargon, counter-productive. Very. One clerical gentleman from Lockeport, NS, was unwise enough to use that tactic to help promote the cleric's brother. Thompson's reply was terse and unmistakable:

It [your letter] will certainly add to the difficulty in the way of your brother's advancement. The Government expect to be judged by their policy and not by the number of favours that they are able to bestow upon individual supporters. Your brother is a man of most exemplary character and I should be delighted if an opportunity were afforded to aid him, but whatever is done for him will not be facilitated by such intimations as the one which your letter conveys.[9]

One unfriendly Liberal paper in Sherbrooke remarked that while Thompson was a good minister of justice, he was a very bad tactician.[10]

That puts it too harshly but it gets at Thompson's instinctive dislike of manipulation, his dislike of hypocrisy, his belief in the sturdy principles, laid down perhaps by his father, summed up in Horace's,

Integer vitae, scelerisque purus
Non eget Mauris jaculis, neque arcu.[11]

His dislike of appeals to emotion and prejudice was rooted in these same principles. His speeches carried few people off their feet. They were not supposed to. They were appeals to good sense, rugged integrity, intellectual honesty, or reasonableness. His speeches aroused enthusiasm when he was heading the House off from indulging its prejudices, as in the Riel debate of 1886 or the Jesuits' Estates debate of 1889. His speeches were cool, logical, powerful appeals to justice and reason; they were not and could not be addressed to passions. On the campaign trail Thompson was apt to give his scruples looser rein. His mordant wit, his sarcasm, were sharpened by party struggle, by the necessity of winning, or the need simply to hold an audience. To hold crowds you had from time to time to say wicked things. Even then he tended to form these shafts as humour, not without truth – therefore they stung – but directed to making prejudice laughable.

Thompson left few monuments and few memories. A debate developed in Montreal within a week of his death over his legacy. *La Patrie*, the Liberal paper, said that although an admirable man, he had left nothing behind. *La Minerve* replied in detail, citing the Canadian Criminal Code, the Bills of Exchange Act, the creation of the Exchequer Court, developments toward prison reform.[12] *La Minerve*'s list looks meagre enough measured against the man. Thompson's energies were absorbed by a flood of administrative details, with diplomacy, and especially with the rancorous religious and educational questions so conspicuous in the 1890s. Thompson died in the middle of the Manitoba school question, in the end betrayed by the legal system he had relied on. The North-West school question was a better test of his talents; it was quiescent for a decade after 1894.

Thompson's legacy was his integrity and his hard work. He had little political genius. He did best what he knew best to do. That conclusion neglects his talents – his patience, his courtesy, his mastery of the order paper in Parliament – but in the immediate sense of what he did, what he was famous for, it has to be roughly correct. His name has been largely forgotten, writ in water as Keats said. Yet a man so distinguished by decency, intelligence, knowledge, with so strong a grasp of his duty, a man so passionately Canadian, cannot be so easily written off. He was one of the finest men the country produced; many at the time of his death sensed it though few remember him now. The Conservative party was the vehicle that carried his loyalties to colleagues, friends, that deployed his service to his country; but it was only a vehicle. Thompson would have agreed with Alexander Pope:

> For forms of government let fools contest;
> Whate'er is best administered is best;
> For modes of faith let graceless zealots fight;
> His can't be wrong whose life is in the right ...[13]

Something of that comes through in a tribute from T.F. Bayard, secretary of state in Cleveland's first administration, who had seen much of Thompson in Washington and was now American ambassador to London. 'His work, ability and patriotism were well known to me,' Bayard wrote Tupper, 'and I mourn his loss not alone for Canada but for the community of good government everywhere.'[14] Those modest words really say everything.

As to what constituted good government, Thompson's ideas, like those of most Canadian prime ministers, cannot be addressed in the expectation of coherent answers. Thompson nowhere articulated them. What ought to be the common good of society, the moral purpose of its politics, what governments ought, in short, to do, were questions hardly to be answered. Thompson might have begun by saying that man's life was not made easier or better by cynical comments on its worthlessness. Life was a fact: you began with that. Thompson distrusted the work of the literary greats of his time, Ibsen and Tolstoy in particular, for what seemed to him their perverted moral sense, or rather, the apparent absence of any at all. He liked Balzac who, though painting humanity in the sombre, bourgeois colours of *Eugénie Grandet*, conveyed such perceptive compassion for women; it was that mixture in Balzac, that powerful amalgam of observation and imagination, reality and morality, that helped Thompson confirm what was the duty of a man in and to the world.

The other element was of course Thompson's Catholicism. It is difficult to grasp. It is not obvious even in letters to Annie, and one can discern only outlines. Christianity and charity he had in common with good Protestants. The solidity of the Catholic church, the firmness of its eschatology, the certainty of its answers, appealed to him. It knew what it expected. Thompson accepted its authoritarian doctrines, and he accepted its authority when rightly deployed. But he did distinguish between what was proper authority and what was not. He was not intimidated by authority as such, not even the authority of an archbishop, as his long fight for the Sisters of Charity against Archbishop Hannan demonstrated. Bishops were men first, and of God as God's wisdom was, or was not, vouchsafed unto them. With Thompson a bishop's consecration rather established duty than enshrined authority. Those clerics who put duty ahead of ambition, like Bishop Cameron, or intellectual vitality ahead of sacerdotal conformity, like Archbishop Connolly – these were the men whom Thompson could and did admire, and this sense of duty was indisputably part of his view of the church. Much that was more questionable, the too easily accepted miracles, the tasteless or bad in decoration, Thompson eschewed or denied. He knew the church had to represent heavenly love by means of earthly love; he knew it had to touch many classes of society and absorb many different practices. Even so, the poetry and elegance of the church, the majesty of her ceremonies, the beauty of Notre Dame, may have been less important to him than its inner confidence.

Thompson had not much poetry in him at all. He recited it when young, as schoolboys did; but he did not inherit his father's passion for it. In his long correspondence with Annie there is never a line of poetry, hardly a turn of phrase that suggested a mind that loved literature. He quoted very little; whatever Thompson wrote he put through his own head, he did not import in wodges from others. His writing has its own sinewy strength, wit, and sarcastic, occasionally whimsical, humour, like the ships going aground on the Ledges at Barrington in December 1869 to celebrate his arrival. Whatever poetic instincts he had inherited gave him power to write transparent prose, limpid, strong, and smooth as a deep-running brook, serving as the effortless, translucent conveyor of his ideas. Clarity was what he aimed at: metaphors, symbolism, even poetry, cluttered prose with unnecessary ornamentation and cant. Old John S. Thompson's remark in 1831 that simplicity and strength were basic to poetry was translated by his son as basic to prose.

Thompson's mind had a distinctly judicial cast. If there were issues or problems, there ought probably to be a remedy. He would set about finding it. *Ubi causa, ibi remedium* may put it too strongly, but it gets at Thompson's thinking. Like many lawyers, he tended to distrust abstract speculation. The closest he came to it was his fascination with large legal reconstructions. These took the form of clearing away tangles of legal underbrush: open, reorder, make clarity from confusion. The charter and laws of Halifax of 1873, the Nova Scotia Judicature Act of 1884, the Bills of Exchange Act of 1890, the Criminal Code of 1892, the thick volume of Justice papers on disallowance, represent Thompson's instinct for great synthesis.

In the House of Commons Thompson could be characterized as one of its intellectuals if by that is understood a brilliant, sharply focused luminosity, rather than a protean light deployed across a wide range of interests, like David Mills, the academic of the House. Thompson respected Mills, a professor of law; on the other hand, with Edward Blake's long-winded and morally anguished positions Thompson betrayed impatience. It was as if Mills and Blake represented the good and the bad sides of the intellectual in Parliament. Thompson tended to dislike those who fussed around problems; such people acted as if to solve an issue was to spoil it. They were like Faulkland in Sheridan's *The Rivals*, who could not take even happiness unless alloyed by hesitations and 'buts.' Thompson would have said, with Jack Absolute, 'Confound your buts! ... a captious critic in love, a slave to fretfulness and whim, who has no difficulties but of his own creating, is a subject more fit for ridicule than compassion!'[15] For Thompson, to live was to decide. There were complicated, difficult issues to deal with in the world. The best one could do was to sit down and, patient and persevering, master the details; run them through that excellent computer, your own head; then, finally, decide and be done with it.

The obverse of complications of law, of life, the obverse of ditherers, was children. Thompson enjoyed their society; T.M. Daly used to walk home with him in 1894 after the House was over and was much struck by Thompson's susceptibility to children. Thompson would listen to them, talk to them in order to understand what they were trying to say and do. Daly's son Harold, then eight years old, used to drop in freely at Thompson's office at the Ministry of Justice on the ground floor of the East Block. Harold was a delightful relief from a constant stream of callers with their portentous business. When Thompson thought it was time to get back to duty, Harold would be let out through the private door into the wide East Block corridor.[16] Thompson could be moved to tears by accidents to children; nothing made him more venomous or dangerous than cruelty to children.

It was part of a tenderness more widely extended for those whom he felt were unable sufficiently to defend themselves. As minister of justice his severity was more apparent than real; but against criminals convicted of crimes that were mean, violent, or cruel Thompson was apt to be unrelenting. Even here his scrupulousness with evidence made him careful, especially with capital cases. At least one criminal and almost certainly more escaped the gallows because despite trial, judge, and jury, Thompson thought the evidence was just not strong enough.

Thompson could not have been loved as Sir John Macdonald was. He knew it. He never tried to make himself another Macdonald, imitate the inimitable. He was satisfied, a little complacently perhaps, that rectitude was wisdom, innocence was safety. He was respected on both sides of politics for it. For a man who never much liked his political métier, who preferred law's cool, articulated intricacy, that was both a triumph and an imposition. The country mourned Sir John Thompson not as a man ripe with years and experience but a man at the crown of his working life, into whose hands Canada had consigned, with an almost visible sigh of relief, its most difficult problems, and with a growing confidence that they would be resolved with wisdom, integrity, charity. So the elegy in the *St. John Daily Sun*,[17] remembered him:

> No dreams of glory dwarfed his loftier aim,
> To whom his country's good was more than fame,
> No sheen of gold obscured his clearer view
> Who saw the right, and held the balance true ...
> His country mourns – how much was fate unkind –
> The onward look of that untrammelled mind ...

Epilogue

Like his father, Sir John Thompson died without a will. He had little enough; he may not have thought it necessary or urgent to think about it. There are some twists in the story of Thompson's estate. In Ontario his estate was quite modest. The newspapers said he was worth $9,000 and they were right. Thompson owned no land in Ontario; what he had was mostly insurance. Pursuant to the Ontario Succession Duty Act of 1892 the inventory of the property, over which Letters of Administration were granted, totalled $9,727. This included his household goods ($1,000), savings in the bank ($2,493), plus three life insurance policies totalling $5,526.[1] The interest on that $9,727, even at 5 per cent, would only be $500 a year. One young person living alone and frugally might survive on that. Thompson's estate was sufficiently notorious that a public subscription was launched in December 1894 by the cabinet, much to Annie's embarrassment. Both she and the Aberdeens thought it would have been better to let Parliament decide, when it met in 1895, what it wished to do. There was a precedent: Lady Cartier and her two daughters had received an annual grant of $1,200 from Parliament ever since Cartier's death in 1873.

The national subscription was a typical action of the government that succeeded Thompson, well-meant but ill-considered. If national, then it ought to have been with consent and agreement of both political parties. It was uncomfortable for Annie to feel beholden to friends or to those whom she did not like, still more to know how much they had given. In the end Parliament was called in anyway, not only to pay the expenses of Thompson's funeral, but also because Foster, leading in the House of Commons, asked on 14 June 1895 for a parliamentary contribution of $25,000 to the Lady Thompson Fund. It was embarrassing that it was opposed. The motion to strike it out of the Estimates was defeated 76 to 39. The list of those who voted for Thompson's widow included, be it said to their everlasting credit, some MPs who had reason not always to like Thompson. Laurier voted for the grant; that would have been expected. He was joined by Cartwright, Sir Hector Langevin, J.D. Edgar, and D'Alton McCarthy.[2] The final total of the fund was $62,500, which was invested in mortgages, mostly at $4\frac{1}{2}$ per cent, and some Consumers Gas shares. The deed of trust, 12 July 1895, gave Annie the income for her lifetime. This meant about $2,800 a year. She would not be rich, especially with Frankie to look after, but she would be able to get by.[3]

The side of the story not generally known was Thompson's property in Nova Scotia. The day after Thompson's funeral, Letters of Probate were granted by Judge S.L. Shannon in Halifax to Annie as principal, and John Pugh and David Pottinger as sureties. It took some while to get an inventory of Thompson's land and property in Halifax; the appraisal was not set out until January 1896. The house and four acres of grounds at Willow Park that Thompson had valued in 1889 at $9,000 was put down at $5,000. Its market value was less than that, for it was sold by Joseph Thompson in September 1896 for only $2,000.[4] Besides the old house at Willow Park, Thompson owned some twenty-three building lots on Chebucto Road in a district then called Quinn's Field, and there were a dozen other lots scattered around the Willow Park property. There was also one piece of land at Heatherton in Antigonish County. But all those Halifax building lots totalled only $2,000. Thompson's main Halifax assets outside of real estate were eight mortgages (about $5,800) and a few promissory notes (about $1,200). Altogether Thompson's Halifax estate looked more imposing than it actually was. The valuation for probate was $14,073, but with the market price for Willow Park taken into account it was more like $11,000.[5]

After Thompson's death, Annie and her family determined to move to Toronto, and upon her return from Halifax she began to prepare for it. Lady Aberdeen found her in February 1895 feverishly packing, pulling down curtains, making her Somerset Street home into a desolation before she had even a house in Toronto to go to! Early in March the two women together found a house at the upper end of Sherbourne Street overlooking Rosedale ravine, which Annie rented for three years.[6] She later moved to a house at 18½ St Joseph Street, near St Michael's College, between Bay Street and Queen's Park and which would be her home for the rest of her life.

One consideration in choosing both houses was ample, dry storage space for what Lady Aberdeen called Annie's 'boxes of accumulations.' The core of these was some thirty trunks of Thompson's papers. Annie was seized of the importance of these long before Thompson died. She already had boxes of his letters at Willow Park in 1886. Annie had the habit of putting them by year by year. Thompson himself was a considerable accumulator of papers; according to Lady Aberdeen, he never destroyed anything.[7] Three days after Thompson's death Annie was after those papers of her husband's, asking that they be collected from his office in the East Block and turned over to her. There is an instruction to that effect from the new prime minister, Mackenzie Bowell, to Thompson's private secretary, Douglas Stewart.[8]

What papers a minister kept, and what papers were left behind in the department as official, was – and is – an awkward question. A cabinet minister can handle his correspondence in two different ways. He can use his own department's system; in the case of the Department of Justice this was set up by an elaborate series of files under individuals, issues, or subjects. Or he can use his own private filing system which, although kept at the department, is under his control. Thompson generally seems to have inclined toward the latter, a habit perhaps dating from his days as attorney general of Nova Scotia. It was a habit most fortunate in that case, for almost nothing has survived from the civil service side of the office of attorney general in Nova Scotia.

As for the Department of Justice in Ottawa, the civil service files are extensive; there are frequent pencil notations by Thompson on the documents, or notes that he scribbled in ink for his officials; but the bulk of his correspondence Annie seems to have carted home. There she put together the collection that came to be called the Thompson Papers. In the thirty trunks were also the papers of Thompson's father, letters from Thompson to his children, Annie's papers – especially Thompson's letters to her, and hers to him. It is the greatest family correspondence of any of the prime ministers. Very few were family men and those that were preserved little family correspondence. None of Macdonald's letters to Agnes Macdonald seem to have survived nor any of hers to him. There are some Mackenzie family letters and fascinating they are. Abbott had none; Tupper's correspondence with his wife seems to have largely gone, though that with his son remains. Laurier's private letters to Lady Laurier are thin and he had no children. Borden the same. King was a bachelor and so was Bennett. Meighen kept his private life private. St Laurent's papers may turn up something. Pearson's, Diefenbaker's, Trudeau's are not yet known. A man will tell his wife things he will tell no one else if he loves her and trusts her, as Thompson did Annie. If politics was the stage, Thompson's letters to Annie were the behind-the-scenes of it.

In guarding this legacy, Annie was conservative in the best sense of the word. She seems to have resisted attempts by her family to get into or 'sort' the papers, and after her death her policy was carried on by J.T.C. Thompson and perhaps too by the daughters.

Lady Annie Thompson lived on in Toronto. On 10 April 1913, in hospital for an exploratory operation, she died under the anaesthetic. She had inoperable cancer.[9]

John T.C. Thompson came back to Ottawa to practise law some years prior to his mother's death. In 1915 he joined the Princess Louise Dragoons, and emerged from the war as a colonel, with a DSO, and became head of Sir Robert Borden's Pension Commission. He proved to be even more adept at saying no than his father had been. He died in 1952, unmarried.

Joseph Thompson married Maud Temple in Toronto, was made a KC in 1927, had two children, and died in 1935.

The two elder girls married in Western Canada, probably through the Aberdeens' associations in the Okanagan valley. Babe married E.C. Wragge of Nelson, BC, in 1905, had three daughters, but died in 1917 at the age of forty-one. Helena Thompson married E.R. MacGregor of Kamloops, BC, had two daughters, and died in Toronto in September 1944. Frankie lived on in the house on St Joseph Street unmarried until her death in 1947.[10]

Thus when old Colonel Thompson came to the Public Archives in 1949 to give over the Thompson Papers, he was the last surviving member of Thompson's immediate family.

Notes

APQ	Archives publiques de Québec
DCB	*Dictionary of Canadian Biography,* University of Toronto Press
DJ Records	Department of Justice Records, Public Archives of Canada
JSDT	Sir John S.D. Thompson Papers, Public Archives of Canada
JST	J.S. Thompson Papers, Public Archives of Canada
NSR	*Nova Scotia Reports* (law cases)
PABC	Public Archives of British Columbia
PAC	Public Archives of Canada
PAM	Public Archives of Manitoba
PANS	Public Archives of Nova Scotia
PAO	Public Archives of Ontario
PRO	Public Record Office (Great Britain)
SCR	*Supreme Court Reports*

PART ONE: HALIFAX BOY AND LAWYER, 1845–1877

1 J.S. THOMPSON COMES TO HALIFAX

1 This first paragraph rides over two awkward questions. Rather than burden the text I elucidate them here.

a/ The evidence for Thompson being born at 5 Argyle Street is strong but indirect. Thompson's father was a teacher, and almost certainly taught his few pupils in a room of his own (rented) home. His advertisement in the Halifax *Nova Scotian*, Monday, 3 Nov. 1845 (and for several successive

Mondays) offered tuition at 5 Argyle Street in reading, writing, grammar, composition, shorthand (with an emphasis on the principles basic to each subject). The nearest direct evidence is thinner, a letter to Thompson from F.D. Vieth, 16 Jan. 1893 (vol. 173 in JSDT), asking if he was born in the house at the corner of Gottingen Street and Gray's Lane (now Prince William Street). This passage has been stroked through, presumably by Thompson, presumably as incorrect. J.S. Thompson only moved to this Gottingen Street house in 1851. He appears to have lived at the Argyle Street house from about 1843 to 1850.

b/ Thompson's birthdate is clear but awkward, since Thompson's own recollection, and all references since, are to 10 Nov. 1844, not 1845. But there is no specific evidence for this date. That Thompson so remembered it is no guarantee of its authenticity. Before 1900 probably about a quarter of all birth dates, as remembered by the individuals themselves, are incorrect, as to year, month, or day. The records of the Brunswick Street Methodist Church are quite clear. On 20 May 1847 John David Thompson was baptized, the date of his birth being set down as 10 Nov. 1845. That length of time, a year and a half from birth to baptism, is quite long even as it is.

2 There is an excellent article on the genealogy of the family, 'Sir J.S.D. Thompson: A Prime Minister's Family Connections,' by A.E. Marble and T.M. Punch, *Nova Scotia Historical Quarterly*, VII, 4 (Dec. 1977), 377–88.

3 JST, vol. 3, J.S. Thompson to Maria Brownrigg, 10 Dec. 1820, from London (draft); also ibid., vol. 1, J.S. Thompson to William Thompson, May 1828 (draft)

4 From Burke's speech, 'For the better security of the independence of Parliament and the economical reformation of the civil and other estimates,' in *The Works of the Right Honourable Edmund Burke* (London 1786) II, 112. Burke's speech was given 11 Feb. 1780.

5 Halifax *Morning Chronicle*, Saturday, 18 Apr. 1863. This reference has been brought to my attention by Professor David Sutherland.

6 W.M. Brown, 'Recollections of old Halifax,' Nova Scotia Historical Society, *Collections*, XIII (1908), 92

7 *Nova Scotia, Assembly Journals, 1832*, Appendix 49. See also Gwenyth Andrews, 'The Establishment of Institutional Care in Halifax in the mid 19th Century' (honours essay, Dalhousie University 1974), 5–7.

8 Halifax *Morning Journal*, 15 May 1857

9 *Revised Statutes of Nova Scotia*, 1873, c. 30

10 Halifax *British Colonist*, 26 Apr. 1866, letter from Rev. G.W. Hill. His letter was written to the mayor of Halifax in response to a request from the clerk of the Board of Health that he report any conditions apt to conduce to the spread of cholera.

11 Halifax *Morning Journal*, 16 Nov. 1860, gives a long description of the city at that time of year. I have assumed that conditions in 1830 were not that different.

12 JST, vol. 1, J.S. Thompson to William Thompson, May 1828 (draft)

13 The reference to conducting a newspaper refers to working as assistant to Howe on the *Nova Scotian*; JST, vol. 3, J.S. Thompson to Mrs Clarke, May 1829 (draft).

14 *Halifax Monthly Magazine* (Feb. 1831), 321. See Nancy Fraser, 'Two Nova Scotian Literary Periodicals of the 1830s: The *Halifax Monthly Magazine* and the *Pearl*' (MA thesis, Dalhousie University 1977).

15 *Halifax Monthly Magazine* (Aug. 1831), 138

16 JST, vol. 3, Thompson to Howe, n.d. (draft)

17 Ibid., vol. 1, Howe to Thompson, 29 Jan. [1832]

18 *Halifax Monthly Magazine* (Sept. 1830), 122. See Fraser, 'Two Nova Scotian Literary Periodicals,' 14.

19 J. Murray Beck, *Joseph Howe: Conservative Reformer, 1804–1848* (Kingston and Montreal 1982), 272

20 JST, vol. 2, Joseph S. Thompson to John S. Thompson, 14 Oct. 1844, from Waterford

21 Ibid., vol. 3, J.S. Thompson to his nephew, William, 17 Aug. 1845, from Halifax (draft)

2 FATHER AND SON

1 JST, vol. 3, J.S. Thompson to Joseph Thompson, 7 July 1853 (draft); a flageolet is a type of recorder.

2 PANS, Halifax County, Register of Deeds, Book 97, f.96; Book 98, f.211; Book 99, f.477

3 Halifax *Mail-Star*, 31 Oct. 1947, has a picture of the house.

4 JST, vol. 3, J.S. Thompson to Howe, 14 Oct. 1852 (draft)

5 JSDT, vol. 293, Memoir for Lady Thompson prepared by W.A. Hendry of Halifax, dated 10 Jan. 1895

6 JST, vol. 3, J.S. Thompson to Joseph Thompson, 7 July 1853 (draft), from Halifax

7 Ibid., vol. 2, William Brown to J.S. Thompson, 30 Jan. 1861, from Boston

8 Ibid., vol. 3, Thompson to Joseph Thompson, 7 July 1853 (draft) from Halifax

9 See J. Johnston, 'Anti-Catholicism in Nova Scotia, 1846–1860' (MA thesis, Dalhousie University 1977), 138.

10 JST, vol. 3, J.S. Thompson to Joseph Thompson, Dec. 1857 (draft)

11 PANS, Vertical File, Thompson Papers, John S. Thompson to the Attorney-General, 31 Aug. 1859

12 The sale is recorded PANS, Halifax County, Registry of Deeds, Book 129, f.332.

13 William Thompson died at Grahamstown, Cape Colony, 20 Feb. 1882, having spent the last of a £90 remittance from his brother John David on drink. JSDT, vol. 25, William Bond to Thompson, 1 Mar. 1882, from Grahamstown. A power of attorney, dated 21 Apr. 1881, was received from William Thompson the year before authorizing J.S.D. Thompson to sell or dispose of William's share of his father's estate. JSDT, vol. 20.

14 JST, vol. 3, W.M. Brown to J.S. Thompson, n.d., probably 1863

15 William Marsters Brown was born in Halifax in 1811. His uncle was William Stairs, founder of William Stairs, Son, and Morrow Ltd. Brown joined the Total Abstinence Society in 1840. He emigrated to Boston about 1860, and died in 1888 in Ontario. Ibid., vol. 2, W.M. Brown to J.S. Thompson, n.d., probably 1862

16 Ibid., vol. 3, Joseph Thompson to J.S. Thompson, 14 Feb. 1856, from Waterford

17 PAC, Aberdeen Papers, vol. 2. Griffin's memorandum on Lady Aberdeen's article on Sir John Thompson, published in *Outlook*, 26 Jan. 1895

18 PAC, Sir James Gowan Papers, J.S.D. Thompson to Gowan, 30 May 1889

19 JST, vol. 2, W.M. Brown to J.S. Thompson, 27 Mar. 1862, from Boston

20 Ibid., W.M. Brown to J.S. Thompson, 25 Oct. 1861 from Boston

21 Ibid., W.M. Brown to J.S. Thompson, 4 June 1862, from Boston

22 Ibid., W.M. Brown to J.S. Thompson, 5 Dec. 1861, from Boston

23 F.H. Vieth, *Recollections of the Crimean Campaign ... with Garrison Life in the Canadian Lower Provinces* (Montreal 1907), 2. I am grateful to T.M. Punch, MA, for having brought this to my attention. I could find no reference, however, to 'Bingen on the Rhine,' Vieth's title. A colleague, H.S. Granter, brought up in Newfoundland, solved the mystery at once. It had once been in the Royal Readers for Newfoundland and Nova Scotia, and had survived into the 1920s in Newfoundland.

The reference to the Campbell poem is in JSDT, vol. 168, John Erwin to Thompson, n.d. [1892], from Bridgetown, Annapolis County. Erwin was an old Halifax schoolmate.

24 JST, vol. 3. The political reference was to the fact that William Young and J.W. Johnston, leaders of the Liberal and Conservative parties respectively at the end of the 1850s, had been rivals for the plum of the chief justiceship of Nova Scotia. Whoever won the election of 1859 would get it. William Young got it.

25 Benjamin Russell, 'The Career of Sir John Thompson,' *Dalhousie Review*, I, 2 (1921), 189
26 John Doull, 'Sir John Thompson,' *Canadian Bar Review*, XXV (1947), 451
27 There were two John George Bourinots. The first (1814–87) was MLA for Cape Breton before confederation, and was a senator afterward. The second, his son, who did the Assembly debates, later became clerk of the House of Commons (1837–1902).
28 In Halifax *Evening Mail*, 13 Dec. 1894. Power (1841–1921) became a senator in 1877, and was a contemporary of Thompson's.
29 JSDT, vol. 293, Annie Affleck's diary. This, the only volume in existence, goes from June to Dec. 1867.
30 JST, vol. 2
31 Valentine's portrait is in the Public Archives of Nova Scotia.
32 Thompson edited and introduced a book on the poetry of John McPherson (1817–45), *Harp of Acadia: Poems, Descriptive and Moral* (Halifax 1862).
33 PANS, John Allison Bell Diaries, 19 Oct. 1863; 11 Nov. 1867. John Allison Bell (1816–1901), son of Hon. Hugh Bell (1780–1860), began in the dry-goods business in Halifax in 1839, was a Liberal-Reform candidate in the 1859 election but was defeated. His father's death left him burdened with a mountain of debt and he was forced out of business. He became chief commissioner of Halifax's water supply system, 1862–72, and in 1874 was appointed city auditor, a post he retained until his death at the age of eighty-five.
34 See also the description by Edmund Gosse of his father, in *Father and Son: A Study of Two Temperaments* (London 1974), 174, a reference brought to my attention by Professor Peter Burroughs.

3 THE COURTING OF ANNIE AFFLECK

1 Martin Joseph Griffin (1847–1921) came to Nova Scotia in 1854 with his family from Newfoundland. Editor of the Halifax *Evening Express*, he moved to be editor of the new Halifax *Morning Herald*, 1875–81, and then went to the *Toronto Daily Mail*, 1881–5. He was then appointed to the Library of Parliament.
2 PAC, Martin Griffin Papers, vol. 3, Griffin to C.H. Tupper, 25 July 1888; ibid., vol. 2, Macdonald to Griffin, 11 May 1881 (private)
3 Benjamin Russell, 'The Career of Sir John Thompson,' *Dalhousie Review*, I, 2 (1921), 191
4 J.E.E. Dalberg-Acton, 1st Baron Acton (1834–1902), in *History of Freedom and Other Essays* (London 1922), 522, 533, 547

5 Thompson to J.J. Curran, 13 June 1891, in J.J. Curran, 'Reminiscences of Sir John Thompson,' *Canadian Magazine*, XXVI 3 (Jan. 1906), 220–2

6 Father Whelan of St Patrick's Church, Ottawa, in Ottawa *Citizen*, 17 Dec. 1894

7 Thompson to J.J. Curran, 13 June 1891, in Curran, 'Reminiscences of Sir John Thompson'

8 J. Castell Hopkins, *The Life and Work of the Rt. Hon. Sir John Thompson, P.C., K.C.M.G., Q.C. Prime Minister of Canada* (Brantford, Ont., 1895), 40

9 This paragraph is based on Annie Affleck's own recollections, in a letter to Sir Joseph Pope. PAC, Pope Papers, vol. 5, Annie Thompson to Pope, 6 June 1896

10 The Affleck children were, after Annie: Johanna (Joey), later Sister Mary Helena (1854–1925); John Laughlin (1894–54); James E. (1852–78); Peter B. (1854–post-1903); Francis (1856–73); Mary Helena (1860–4); Frances A. (1863–1903). See the article of A.E. Marble and T.M. Punch, 'Sir J.S.D. Thompson: A Prime Minister's Family Connections,' *Nova Scotia Historical Quarterly*, VII, 4 (DEC. 1977), 377–88.

11 JSDT, vol. 293, Annie Affleck's diary, 19 Sept. 1867; 6 July 1867; 22 Dec. 1867

12 Ibid., 11 July 1867; 21 Sept. 1867; 5, 6 Dec. 1867

13 See the editorial, 'The People's Park,' in *Halifax Evening Reporter*, 11 Aug. 1877.

14 JSDT, vol. 293, Annie Affleck's diary, 25 Aug. 1867 (her underlining)

15 Ibid., 13 Sept. 1867

16 Ibid., 9 Oct. 1867; 23 Oct. 1867; 1 Nov. 1867. In the quotations that follow I have not indicated which parts of Annie's diary were in shorthand and which were not; most are from shorthand.

17 Annie does not use the word 'passion' but that is the meaning that I derive from, 'I feel lonesome without him, is it flesh?' (4 Nov. 1867). Again, 'Now am I not flesh? Thompson has not been in to night and I spent the evening as lonesome as can be. So much for being flesh. Oh dear, will I ever learn to check a little bit ... if I could only see him for a minute it would satisfy me' (5 Nov. 1867). In these quotations I have put in punctuation, even if Annie did not.

18 Ibid., 9, 10 Dec. 1867

19 Ibid., 24 Dec. 1867

20 Ibid., 27 Dec. 1867

21 Ibid., 31 Dec. 1867

22 JSDT, vol. 283, Annie to Thompson, 24 Jan. 1886, 'I got my box of valuables and read all my pet's old letters, all the little scraps of notes of long ago before we were married ... when I used to get the smuggled notes from him.'

23 Lady Aberdeen mentions that Annie's having worked in a shop in Halifax before she was married made some difficulty in Ottawa society. J.T. Saywell, ed., *The Canadian Journal of Lady Aberdeen, 1893–1898* (Toronto 1960), 164

24 Hopkins, *Thompson*, 37

25 JSDT, vol. 1, Bacon to Rose, 5 July 1870: 'Licentiam vobis domus matrimonium celebrandi inter J.S.D. Thompson et Annie Affleck, cum illis dispensantes super impedimento temporalitatis cultus ...'

26 So I infer from a letter Thompson wrote two years later from the same hotel. Ibid., vol. 288, Thompson to Annie, 7 Dec. 1872

27 PANS, Microfilm C–709, Canada, Census of 1871, Province of Nova Scotia, District 196, Sub-District E, Ward Five, Enumeration Division No. 2, p. 12, no. 41

28 Russell, 'Sir John Thompson,' 192

29 Hopkins, *Thompson*, 43

30 St Mary's Cathedral, Halifax, baptismal registers, 1870–7, p. 45

31 Hopkins, *Thompson*, 43

32 J.J. Curran, 'Reminiscences of Sir John Thompson,' *Canadian Magazine*, XXVI, 3 (Jan. 1906), 221, quoting a letter from Thompson, of 13 June 1891

33 Ottawa *Citizen*, 13 Dec. 1894, interview with George Johnson

34 PAC, Aberdeen Papers, vol. 2, Griffin's Memorandum on Lady Aberdeen's article, 'Canada's late Premier,' published in *Outlook*, 26 Jan. 1896

35 The Halifax Morning Herald Company was incorporated in 1875, *Statutes of Nova Scotia*, c. 87. Its directors included W.J. Almon, F. Allison, C.H.M. Black, T.E. Kenny, S.L. Shannon, J.S.D. Thompson, and eleven others. Capital was $20,000.

36 *Halifax Evening Reporter*, 14 May 1875

37 PANS, County of Halifax, Register of Deeds, Book 156, f.711. At $4 to the currency pound, this meant Thompson had an equity of $920 in the property. The property was offered by Charles Annand, executor of the estate of Elizabeth Troup.

38 PANS, Thompson Papers. There is a small but useful collection, donated by Sir Joseph Chisholm.

39 PANS, John Allison Bell Diaries (13 Sept. 1875), 68

40 PANS, RG 7, vol. 64, Thompson to Provincial Secretary, 31 Aug. 1868. This was brought to my attention by Allan Dunlop, assistant archivist of Nova Scotia.

41 Aberdeen Papers, vol. 2, Griffin's Memorandum on Lady Aberdeen's article on Thompson

42 Russell, 'Sir John Thompson,' 188

43 Benjamin Russell, *Autobiography* (Halifax, 1932), 111–12. For criticism of

Ritchie for the 'run on the docket,' see Halifax *Acadian Recorder*, 17 Feb. 1876; he is defended in the *Halifax Evening Reporter*, 18 Feb. 1876.

44 Russell, *Autobiography*, 90

45 Russell, 'Sir John Thompson,' 188; JSDT, vol. 15, Russell to Thompson, 25 Feb. 1880. Some pressure was put on Russell by Simon Holmes, the premier, to appoint James Oxley as his assistant. Russell demurred, saying he wanted an assistant in whom he, Russell, had confidence.

46 PBW Archive, Thompson to Daniel Sargent, 4 Sept. 1871, from Halifax. This letter has been given to me by Mr H.R. Banks, of Barrington Passage, NS, to whom I am greatly indebted.

47 PANS, County of Halifax, Registry of Deeds, Book 180, ff. 142–6. The property was registered in both their names.

48 The Halifax *Mail-Star*, 3 Mar. 1949, reproduced an early drawing of the house by J.N. Meagher. From this drawing it was possible to identify a picture in PAC said, incorrectly, to be an Ottawa house. It was actually a photograph of Willow Park, found in the Thompson Papers, and taken probably in the late 1870s. See also, JSDT, vol. 288, Thompson to Annie, 7 Oct. 1884, from Annapolis Royal; vol. 289, Thompson to Annie, 8 Nov. 1886, from Ottawa; vol. 283, Annie to Thompson, 12 Jan. 1886, from Halifax; Annie to Thompson, 1 Feb. 1886, from Halifax.

49 St Mary's Cathedral, Halifax, baptismal registers, 1870–7, p. 45

4 THE HALIFAX OF ALDERMAN THOMPSON

1 Halifax *Morning Chronicle*, 2, 3, 4 Oct. 1871

2 For this development, see Phyllis Blakeley, *Glimpses of Halifax, 1867–1900* (Halifax 1949), 104; Nova Scotia Provincial Museum, *Report, 1935–1936*; Halifax *Evening Express*, 29 Sept. 1871; *Halifax Evening Reporter*, 13 Mar. 1873; Halifax *Acadian Recorder*, 2 Jan. 1872, 11 Sept. 1872.

3 For the history of lighting, see Blakeley, *Glimpses of Halifax*, 113–15.

4 City of Halifax, *Annual Report, 1872–1873*, 24–27 especially. The report is dated 22 May, 1873. It is discussed and paraphrased at length in the Halifax *Evening Express*, 17 Aug. 1874.

5 *Halifax Evening Reporter*, 3 Oct. 1872

6 Ibid., 11 May 1875; Halifax *Morning Herald*, 8 Jan. 1879

7 Ibid., 7 Mar. 1877

8 Halifax *Evening Express*, 4 Nov. 1873

9 *Halifax Evening Reporter*, 10 Sept. 1876; Halifax *Evening Express*, 16 Jan. 1874; PANS, John Allison Bell Diaries, 1 Nov. 1876

10 Halifax *Evening Express*, 29 Oct. 1873

11 *Halifax Evening Reporter*, 9 June 1873
12 PANS, Halifax, City Council, *Minutes*, 21 Nov. 1871, 8, 11 Mar. 1872
13 Ibid., 9 Sept. 1872; 1 Nov. 1872; Halifax *Morning Chronicle*, 2 Nov. 1872
14 Halifax, City Council, *Minutes*, 10 Dec. 1874; John Allison Bell Diaries, 11 Dec. 1874
15 The main part of the 1871 debt was incurred for waterworks, some $670,000.
16 City of Halifax, *Annual Report, 1871–1872*, 8
17 Presented to city council 12 Aug. 1872. *Halifax Evening Reporter*, 13 Aug. 1872
18 John Allison Bell Diaries, 26 Mar. 1877
19 Blakeley, *Glimpses of Halifax*, 8, 68–9; Halifax *Acadian Recorder*, 11 Nov. 1871
20 Halifax, City Council, *Minutes*, 13, 26 Mar. 1874. Also Halifax *Evening Express*, 24, 26 Mar. 1874
21 The full story of the struggle over the Jennett site, as Thompson's northern site was called, is too massive for telling here. See *Nova Scotia, Legislative Council Journals, 1874*, 29 Apr. to 7 May 1874, pp. 74–6, 83–5, 90, 98; Halifax, City Council, *Minutes*, 15, 28 July, 4, 13 Aug., 20 Oct. 1874; Halifax *Evening Express*, 18, 23, 24 July 1874; and Halifax *Morning Chronicle*, and *Acadian Recorder* for the same dates.
22 Halifax, City Council, *Minutes*, 30 Mar. 1872; 19, 20 Mar. 1873; *Nova Scotia, Statutes, 1874*, c.14 sec.5; *Halifax Evening Reporter*, 24 Apr. 1873, argued that liquor legislation was wholly useless.
23 Halifax *Evening Express*, 6 Mar. 1874
24 JSDT, vol. 1, Thompson to Mayor M.H. Richey, 3 Nov. 1875 (draft)
25 Halifax, City Council, *Minutes*, 18 Mar., 23 May 1873; *Nova Scotia, Statutes, 1873*, c. 12; *Halifax Evening Reporter*, 24 May 1873; Halifax *Evening Express*, 28 Jan. 1874. See also, Blakeley, *Glimpses of Halifax*, 181–4.
26 Halifax, City Council, *Minutes*, 18 Aug. 1874; *Nova Scotia, Statutes, 1875*, c. 45; *Halifax Evening Reporter*, 3 Aug. 1874; Blakeley, *Glimpses of Halifax*, 174–80
27 See D.B. Flemming, 'Archbishop Connolly,' *DCB*, x, 191–3.
28 Halifax, Board of School Commissioners, *Minutes*, vol. 4, p. 419 (29 Apr. 1874); pp. 429–30 (13 May 1874). Section 15 of the 1864 School Act stated that drunkenness was to be punished by loss of licence.
29 *Nova Scotia, Statues, 1864*, c. 29. A Mary Connolly was named as one of the original founders.
30 *Halifax Evening Reporter*, 31 Aug. 1872, letter from Archbishop Connolly of 30 Aug.
31 *Nova Scotia, Assembly Journals, 1874*, Appendix 14

32 Halifax, Board of School Commissioners, *Report, 1874*, by James Thompson, dated 1 Feb. 1875, p. 11

33 Halifax *Evening Express*, 21 Feb. 1874; Halifax *Morning Chronicle*, 21 Feb. 1874

34 Halifax *Evening Express*, 24 Feb. 1874, a pro-Catholic paper

35 Ibid., letter from G.M. Grant, dated Sunday evening

36 Halifax, City Council, *Minutes*, 9, 14 Apr. 1874. The reason for the five-day delay was owing to the mayor's absence on 9 April, an absence he apologized for. There had been Catholic whispers of a Protestant conspiracy to keep him away, but it was probably nothing.

37 Halifax *Evening Express*, 14 Apr. 1874

38 Ibid., 5 May 1874

39 *Nova Scotia, Assembly Debates and Proceedings, 1874*, pp. 249–53 (May 5, 1874)

40 Halifax, Board of School Commissioners, *Minutes*, vol. 5, pp. 172–8 (23 Feb. 1876). See also *Halifax Evening Reporter*, 24 Feb. 1876.

41 Halifax, Board of School Commissioners, *Minutes*, vol. 5, pp. 384–418, *passim* (10, 31 Oct., 12 Dec. 1877)

42 Ibid., pp. 221–5 (14 June 1876)

43 *Halifax Evening Reporter*, 28 July 1876, letter from Grant of 28 July. For another opinion of Connolly's blarney, however, see John Allison Bell Diaries, 7 Aug. 1876.

44 *Halifax Evening Reporter*, 19, 22, 23 Aug., 13 Sept. 1876

45 Halifax, Board of School Commissioners, *Report, 1878*, pp. 1–23. Thompson's report is actually dated 2 Jan. 1879.

5 PRACTISING LAW

1 JSDT, vol. 289, Thompson to Annie, 17 Jan. 1886

2 Ibid., vol. 1, Thompson to E.N. Sharp, 20 Apr. 1875 (draft); Sharp to Thompson, 2 Feb. 6, 7, 22 Apr. 1875

3 Benjamin Russell *Autobiography* (Halifax 1932), 290–1. It is sad to record it did not hold him for long. He died 8 July 1886.

4 PANS, MSS. of the Nova Scotia Historical Society, N.H. Meagher, 'Sir William Young,' Part 2, p. 23

5 Halifax *Evening Express*, 12 Nov. 1874

6 See R.C. Brown, *Robert Laird Borden, Vol. I: 1854–1914* (Toronto 1975), 18.

7 JSDT, vol. 30, Wallace Graham to Thompson, 17 Nov. 1884, from Ottawa; vol. 31, Graham to Thompson, 2 Feb. 1885 [should be 1886] from Halifax; vol. 54, Graham to Thompson, 16 May 1887, from Washington

8 Ibid., vol. 246, Thompson to Thomas Hodgins, Toronto, 20 Nov. 1890 (private)

9 *NSR*, 82–92

10 *Halifax Herald*, 19 Dec. 1894, reporting Alderman McKerron's reminiscences

11 *NSR*, 469

12 Ibid., 98 et seq; judgment given 31 Mar. 1879

13 Halifax *Morning Chronicle*, 27 Dec. 1877

14 Halifax *Morning Herald*, 29 Dec. 1877

15 *SCR*, 640. Thompson did not argue the case but acted as solicitor for the appellant. The case was argued in Ottawa by James Cockburn, QC.

16 JSDT, vol. 1, M.M. Jackson to Thompson, 19 May 1877 (private). Hopkins asserts (*Thompson*, 51) that Thompson's fee was estimated to be $6,000!

17 JSDT, vol. 1, Dwight Foster to Thompson, 22 May 1877, 1 June 1877, from Boston

18 Massachusetts Historical Society, Boston, R.H. Dana Papers, Dana to his sister, Miss R.C. Dana, 5 Aug. 1877, from Halifax

19 Ibid., R.H. Dana to his father, 26 Aug. 1877, from Halifax

20 PAC, Mackenzie Papers, Mackenzie to Galt, 2 Oct. 1877 (confidential)

21 PAC, Galt Papers, vol. 8, Galt to his wife, Sunday [Nov. 1877], from Halifax; R.H. Dana Papers, R.H. Dana Sr to William Bryant, n.d. but about 15 Nov. 1877, from Boston

22 R.H. Dana Papers, R.H. Dana to W.M. Evarts, 30 Nov. 1877 (private and confidential)

23 JSDT, vol. 2, Dwight Foster to Thompson, 29 Jan. 1878, from Boston

24 Ibid., vol. 288, Thompson to Annie, 7 Dec. 1872, from Saint John; same, 13 Sept. 1874, from Amherst

25 Ibid., vol. 288, Thompson to Annie, 13, 15, 17 Sept. 1874, from Amherst; vol. 283, Annie to Thompson, 17 July 1876

26 Ibid., vol. 288, Thompson to Annie, 12 Oct. 1876, from Kentville; vol. 283, Annie to Thompson, 22 June 1881

27 Ibid., Annie to Thompson, 23 Oct. 1881

28 Ibid., vol. 288, Thompson to Annie, 14 July 1876

29 Ibid., Thompson to Annie, 21 May 1879; 9 Oct. 1879, from Truro

30 Archbishop John Joseph Lynch to Mgr. Kirby, president, Irish College, Rome, 24 Jan. 1880, from Halifax, in JSDT, vol. 15 (copy)

31 Halifax *Evening Express*, 25 July 1874

32 JSDT, vol. 15, Sister Mary de Sales Dwyer and Sister Mary Aloysia Holden to Thompson, 1 Oct. 1879, and 26 Nov. 1879, from Rome

33 Ibid., Bishop Cameron to Thompson, 9 Jan. 1879 (private); Mother Mary Francis to Archbishop of Halifax, 20 June 1879, in Sister Francis d'Assisi, *Two Mothers: Mother M. Francis Maguire and Mother M. Benedicta Harrington* (Halifax 1971), 34–6

34 D'Assisi, *Two Mothers*, 38–41; Halifax *Citizen*, 7 July 1879

35 JSDT, vol. 12, Mother Mary Francis to Thompson, 15 Sept. 1879; Sister Aloysia to Thompson, 22 Sept. 1879, from Liverpool; vol. 13, Sister Mary de Sales to Thompson, 1 Oct. 1879, from Rome

36 See d'Assisi, *Two Mothers*, 59–60.

37 JSDT, vol. 14, Sisters Aloysia and de Sales to Thompson, 26 Nov., 6 Dec. 1879, from Rome

38 Ibid., vol. 15, Cameron to Thompson, 23 Jan. 1880 (private). This long letter of Cameron's was sent probably to the sisters either at the Mount or in Rome, for underneath is written, 'Please keep this Private and return to me when read. JSDT.'

39 So reported by Sisters Aloysia and de Sales, ibid., to Thompson, 15 Jan. 1880, from Rome (underlining theirs)

40 D'Assisi, *Two Mothers*, 68–72

41 Archives of the Sacred Congregation of the Propaganda, Rome, Scritturi Referiti nei Congressi, vol. 22, f.393; also in d'Assisi, *Two Mothers*, 73

42 JSDT, vol. 15, Lynch to Mgr. Kirby, Irish College, Rome, 24 Jan. 1880, from Halifax (copy)

43 Ibid., Cameron to Thompson, 27 Jan. 1880, from Arichat

44 Ibid., Cameron to Thompson, 28 Feb. 1880, from Arichat

45 Ibid., vol. 16, Sisters Aloysia and de Sales to Thompson, 25 Apr. 1880, from Rome

46 In 1895 Annie gave the medallion to Lady Aberdeen saying, 'Many years ago it was brought to him from Rome by one of the Sisters of Charity, for whom he risked so much.' PAC, Aberdeen Papers, vol. 4, Lady Annie Thompson to Lady Aberdeen, 14 Mar. 1895

47 JSDT, vol. 15, Sisters Aloysia and de Sales to Thompson, 24 Jan. 1880, from Rome

PART TWO: POLITICIAN, ATTORNEY GENERAL, AND JUDGE, 1877–1885

6 GETTING ELECTED FOR ANTIGONISH

1 It was said that the quid pro quo for Annand's appointment to London was his paper's willingness to oppose renewal of the extra subsidy given to Nova Scotia from 1869 to 1878 (*Morning Herald*, 9 Jan. 1879).

2 See *Canada, House of Commons Debates* (14 May 1869), p. 334; ibid. (18 Feb. 1870), pp. 74–6; ibid. (21 Mar. 1870), pp. 595–6.

3 James MacDonald to William Miller, 25 Sept. 1877, from Halifax, in Senator

Miller, *Incidents in the Political Career on the Late Sir John Thompson Not Contained in Mr. J. Castell Hopkins' Book* (n.d., n.p., [1895?]), 2

4 Halifax *Evening Mail*, 15 Dec. 1894, letter from Hon. James MacDonald

5 W. Moorsom, *Letters from Nova Scotia* (London 1830), 344, cited in D. Campbell and R.A. MacLean, *Beyond the Atlantic Roar: A Study of the Nova Scotia Scots* (Toronto 1974) 63

6 Senator Miller to Father Ronald Macdonald, 26 Oct. 1877, from Arichat, in Miller, *Incidents*, 7

7 JSDT, vol. 225, Thompson to J.J. Mackinnon, Antigonish, 6 Nov. 1877 (private and confidential); PANS, Sir John Thompson Papers, Thompson to Miller, 23 Nov. 1877, from Antigonish

8 Halifax *Morning Herald*, 21 Nov. 1877

9 PANS, Sir John Thompson Papers, Thompson to Miller, 23 Nov. 1877, from Antigonish

10 Miller, *Incidents*, 10

11 JSDT, vol. 288, Thompson to Annie, 26 Nov. 1877 from Antigonish; ibid., Thompson to Annie, 3 Sept. 1878, from Antigonish

12 Antigonish *Casket*, December 1877, quoted in Halifax Morning *Herald*, 18 Dec. 1877. (The *Casket* has disappeared for this period.)

13 JSDT, vol. 288, Thompson to Annie, 27 Nov. 1877, from Antigonish

14 Ibid., Thompson to Annie, 30 Nov. 1877, from Pomquet Forks

15 Halifax *Morning Chronicle*, 29 Nov. 1877 (italics in original)

16 Ibid., 4 Dec. 1877

17 *Halifax Evening Reporter*, 20 Nov. 1877

18 The results were:

	Thompson	McDonald
Arisaig	121	39
Cape George	89	27
Morristown	69	27
Antigonish	213	127
Lochaber	42	38
Fraser Mills	53	92
St Andrews	88	45
Tracadie	73	16
Harbour Boucher	56	60
Pomquet Forks	109	46
Ohio	140	19
	1,053	536

(Halifax *Morning Chronicle*, 17 Dec. 1877)

19 Comment made as the returns were coming in to the *Chronicle* at the telegraph office in December 1877. Benjamin Russell, 'The Career of Sir John Thompson,' *Dalhousie Review*, I, 2 (1921), 192
20 Letter quoted in an editorial in the *Morning Chronicle*, 11 Dec. 1877
21 *Halifax Evening Reporter*, 19 Dec. 1877
22 The documents are printed in *Nova Scotia, Assembly Journals, 1876*, Appendix 12; *Journals, 1879*, Appendix 13; a general outline is given in G.M. Haliburton, 'A History of Railways in Nova Scotia' (MA thesis, Dalhousie University 1955), 168–213.
23 JSDT, vol. 1, P.C. Hill to Patrick Chisholm at Havre Boucher, 26 Sept. 1877
24 *Nova Scotia, Assembly Debates and Proceedings* (30 Mar. 1878), 210–11
25 JSDT, vol. 2, Tupper to Thompson, 15 Feb. 1878 (private)
26 *Nova Scotia, Assembly Debates and Proceedings* (1 Apr. 1878), 213
27 Ibid., (3 Apr. 1878), 229. What Thompson and the committee adopted had also been suggested to him by J.J. MacKinnon five weeks earlier. JSDT, vol. 2, J.J. MacKinnon to Thompson, 28 Feb. 1878
28 *Nova Scotia, Assembly Debates and Proceedings, 1878*, 250

7 ATTORNEY GENERAL OF NOVA SCOTIA

1 Dalhousie University Archives, MacMechan Papers, Private Journals, 12 Dec. 1894
2 *Halifax Herald*, 13 Dec. 1894, interview with Judge R.L. Weatherbe
3 Ibid., interview with Judge C.J. Townshend. The intimate friend is not identified.
4 For example he dined in Ottawa at Chief Justice Taschereau's, while on Supreme Court business, Wednesday, 26 Oct. 1881, and thought it nearly as good as Connolly's. JSDT, vol. 288, Thompson to Annie, 30 Oct. 1881, from Ottawa
5 Ibid., vol. 288, Thompson to Annie, 24 June 1878, from Antigonish. 'Lazzaroni' is an Italian word usually referring to the beggars who live by their wits (and other arts) in streets of Naples.
6 Ibid., vol. 5. Angus McGillivray to Thompson, 1 Aug. 1878, from Antigonish; Archibald McGillivray to Thompson, 3 Aug. 1878 (confidential and private), from Morristown; Archibald A. McGillivray to Thompson, 17 Aug. 1878, from Antigonish; Archibald A. McGillivray to Bishop Cameron, 9 Sept. 1878, from Antigonish. There were at least three McGillivrays in Antigonish who impinged on Thompson's life: Angus McGillivray (1842–1917), the Liberal lawyer; Big Archie McGillivray of Morristown; and his unlovely nephew, Archibald A. McGillivray of Antigonish (and other places).

7 Ibid., vol. 288, Thompson to Annie, 3 Sept. 1878, from Antigonish

8 Ibid., vol. 5, T.I. Daly to Thompson, 30 Sept. 1878, from Windsor

9 Ibid., vol. 2, Griffin to Thompson, n.d.; vol. 5, Father Gerroir to Thompson, 3 Oct. 1878

10 See, for example, ibid., vol. 6, Archibald McGillivray to Thompson, 11 Oct. 1878 (private), from Morristown.

11 Ibid., S.H. Holmes to Thompson, 15 Oct. 1878

12 Halifax *Morning Herald*, 11 Oct., 8 Nov. 1878

13 JSDT, vol. 6, H. Crosskill to Thompson, 19 Nov. 1878, from Halifax

14 New Glasgow *Eastern Chronicle*, 24 October, 7 Nov. 1878. Its opinion of other ministers, Thompson included, was much better. It looked to Creelman to supply the financial expertise that Holmes apparently lacked.

15 *Nova Scotia, Assembly Journals, 1882*, Appendix 14

16 *Nova Scotia, Assembly Debates and Proceedings* (16 Apr. 1879), 220

17 *Morning Herald*, 29 Jan. 1879, letter from 'Ratepayer' of 24 Jan.

18 Hopkins, *Thompson*, 60

19 PANS, Simon Holmes Papers, Townshend to Holmes, 13 Feb. 1879; see also J. Murray Beck, *The Evolution of Municipal Government in Nova Scotia 1749-1973* (Halifax 1973), ch. 4.

20 *Nova Scotia, Assembly Debates and Proceedings* (8 Apr. 1879), 136-7

21 Ibid., 155

22 Ibid. (19 Mar. 1879), 66

23 This is Thompson's estimate. JSDT, vol. 280, 'Memoranda.' J.M. Beck's is somewhat different, in *Government of Nova Scotia* 245n.

24 *Nova Scotia, Assembly Debates and Proceedings* (19 Mar. 1879), 61

25 *Nova Scotia, Legislative Council Journals* (15 Apr. 1879), 90. See J.M. Beck's excellent account of the Council in these years.

26 As late as 1920 there was ample evidence that lawyers used their role as attorney general to extend the range and heighten the fees of their private practice. *Canadian Law Times*, XL (1920), 82-3. This reference was brought to my attention by Professor James Snell, University of Guelph.

27 *Halifax Evening Reporter*, 20 Nov., 11 Dec. 1875

28 Charles Hibbert Tupper joined the firm in 1880, the result of pressure from old Sir Charles; Robert Borden joined it in 1882 when Thompson went to the Supreme Court of Nova Scotia.

29 John Doull, 'Four Attorney Generals,' Nova Scotia Historical Society, *Collections*, XXVIII (1947), 5-8

30 *Halifax Evening Reporter*, 14, 19, 21 Dec. 1876; Halifax *Morning Herald*, 27 Nov. 1877

31 PANS, RG 34/312, J.3

32 JSDT, vol. 18, William Miller to Thompson, 30 Nov. 1880

33 Ibid., vol. 13, J.H. Townshend to Thompson, 16 Oct. 1879, from Tangier
34 The law is in c. 159 of the *Revised Statutes of Nova Scotia* (1873) that prohibited any shooting, gambling, or sporting on Sunday, 'works of necessity and mercy excepted.'
35 JSDT, vol. 7, Mathilda Thorp to Thompson, 10 Dec. 1878; John U. Smith to Thompson, 30 Dec. 1878
36 Ibid., vol. 17, D. Macdonald to Simon Holmes, 2 Aug. 1880; T.M. King to Thompson, 12 Aug. 1880
37 JSDT, vol. 24, Francis Cunningham to Thompson, 26 Jan. 1882. New Brunswick had adopted a rule in 1860, incorporated in its *Revised Statutes* for 1877, that after a week in prison an insolvent debtor could ask, and a judge could order, that 5s. a week be paid *by* the creditor *to* the debtor (Cap. 124, RS 1877). This was what Cunningham was referring to. For more on Cunningham's adventures, see P.B. Waite, *John A. Macdonald: His Life and World* (Toronto 1975), 47–8; JSDT, vol. 25, Cunningham to Thompson, 13 Mar. 1882; *Nova Scotia, Legislative Assembly Journals* (4 Mar. 1882), 77.
38 JSDT, vol. 12, William Currie to Thompson, 16 Sept. 1879 from Maitland
39 *Nova Scotia, Assembly Debates and Proceedings* (17 Mar. 1879), 44
40 Ibid., (13 Mar. 1880), 70. The cost to the crown was the $30 paid to S.L. Shannon.
41 Halifax *Morning Herald*, 1 Nov. 1880
42 Both the practice, and the fact that the official overseer of the poor could not give the names of those so farmed out, shocked both lawyers and the Supreme Court judge, Robert Weatherbe. T.C. Haliburton has a comment on the practice in *The Clockmaker* (Halifax 1836) as it appeared in Parrsboro, selling the poor to the lowest bidder on town meeting day (chapter XXVII).
43 JSDT, vol. 287, Lectures on evidence, Lecture IV, 'The frailty of human recollection;' Lecture VI, 'Cross-examination,' 13 Dec. and 20 Dec. 1883 respectively
44 JSDT, vol. 287, Lecture XII, 'Circumstantial evidence,' 22 Jan. 1884
45 Halifax *Morning Chronicle*, 6 Dec. 1880, reporting the trial at Annapolis Royal. It started on 1 Dec. and finished 6 Dec. The Halifax *Chronicle* and the *Herald* carried extensive accounts of the trial. Both accounts are used here.
46 Halifax *Morning Chronicle*, 8 Dec. 1880, reporting Thompson's speech to the jury of 6 Dec.; also *Morning Herald*, 7 Dec. 1880. Thibault was hanged in Annapolis jail, 8 Feb. 1881.
47 Ibid., 9 Dec. 1880
48 Ibid., 4 Jan. 1895, recollections of J.T. Bulmer
49 JSDT, vol. 18, Bishop Cameron to Thompson, 26 Dec. 1880; vol. 19, Archibald McGillivray to Thompson, 26 Jan. 1881, from Morristown

50 Ibid., vol. 19, Townshend to Thompson, 8 Jan. 1881; vol. 18, J.S. McDonald to Thompson, 10 Dec. 1880, from Wolfville, and vol. 19, 24 Jan. 1881
51 Ibid., vol. 18, James MacDonald to Thompson, 26 Nov., 6 Dec. 1880
52 *Nova Scotia, Assembly Debates and Proceedings* (11 Mar. 1880), 64–6

8 THE FALL OF THE HOLMES–THOMPSON GOVERNMENT

1 *Nova Scotia Statutes*, 1876, 39 Vic. c. 28. See the article by Denis Healy, 'The University of Halifax, 1875–1881,' *Dalhousie Review*, LIII, 1 (Spring 1973), 39–56.
2 D.C. Harvey, *An Introduction to the History of Dalhousie University* (Halifax 1938), 96
3 JSDT, vol. 22, L.S. Ford to Thompson, 3 Aug. 1881
4 Ibid., vol. 20, Bishop Cameron to Thompson, 21 Mar. 1881
5 *Nova Scotia, Assembly Debates and Proceedings* (23 Mar. 1881), 74–6; JSDT, vol. 22, L.S. Ford to Thompson, 3 Aug. 1881, from Liverpool
6 Ibid., vol. 20, Bishop Cameron to Thompson, 24 Mar. 1881; *Nova Scotia, Legislative Council Debates and Proceedings* (9 Apr. 1881), 62–9
7 *Nova Scotia, Legislative Council Journals* (9 Apr. 1881), 61–2
8 *Nova Scotia, Legislative Council Debates and Proceedings* (30 Mar. 1881); ibid. (9 Apr. 1881), 71–7
9 *Nova Scotia, Assembly Debates and Proceedings* (31 Jan. 1882), 71
10 Ibid., (12 Apr. 1881), 182–6. JSDT, vol. 22, Ford to Thompson, 3 Aug. 1881
11 Professor Murray Beck has pointed out to me that although Holmes's long absences did not help cabinet government, the problem pre-dated his premiership and continued afterward. The Hill government's economies cut out two of the salaried portfolios by amalgamation: the duties of provincial treasurer were assumed by the provincial secretary, and those of the commissioner of crown lands were transferred to the attorney general. That left only three ministers with portfolio.
12 JSDT, vol. 17, C.A. Smith to Thompson, 13 Sept. 1880 (private); vol. 19, C.A. Smith to Thompson, 12 Jan. 1881 from Chester; vol. 21, J.S. McDonald to Thompson, 21 May 1881, from Wolfville
13 The interested reader can cut his legal teeth on this one: 250 logs were cut on land thought to be crown land. It was, however, private land, as yet unsurveyed owing to errors. The cut logs were sold. The buyer of the logs claimed that since he paid for them, they were his. The original owner of the land claimed them. Who is right and what ought to be done? JSDT, vol. 21, L.S. Ford to Thompson, 6 June 1881, from Milton, Queens County. For Thompson's reply, see vol. 225, Letterbook, pp. 680–2, Thompson to

Samuel Smith, surveyor at Brookfield, 9 June 1881; Thompson to L.S. Ford, 9 June 1881 (two letters).

14 Ibid., vol. 19, Tupper to Thompson, 18 Feb. 1881

15 Ibid., vol. 17, Bishop Cameron to Thompson, 18 Nov. 1880

16 Ibid., vol. 24, Archibald A. McGillivray to Thompson, 8 Feb. 1882; vol. 25, same, 8 Mar. 1882 (telegram). The $1,000 was secured by a mortgage.

17 Ibid., vol. 20, Bishop Cameron to Thompson, 4 Mar. 1881

18 PAC, Macdonald Papers, vol. 230, James MacDonald to John A. Macdonald, 7 Apr. 1881, from Halifax; *Nova Scotia, Assembly Debates and Proceedings* (24 Jan. 1882), 15

19 JSDT, vol. 22, Bishop Cameron to Thompson, 21 Oct. 1881, from Antigonish

20 Ibid., vol. 22, H.F. McDougall to Thompson, 2 Aug. 1881, from Grand Narrows; George Johnson to Thompson, 16 Aug. 1881, from Halifax

21 Ibid., Bishop Cameron to Thompson, 18 Aug. 1881, from Antigonish

22 Ibid., Bishop Cameron to Thompson, 21 Oct. 1881, from Antigonish

23 Ibid., vol. 288, Thompson to Annie, 20 Oct. 1881, from Ottawa

24 Ibid., Thompson to Annie, 22, 25 Oct. 1881, from Ottawa

25 Ibid., vol. 283, Annie to Thompson, 29 Oct. 1881, from Halifax

26 Ibid., vol. 288, Thompson to Annie, 27 Oct. 1881, from Ottawa; (1881) 7 *SCR*, 290

27 JSDT, vol. 283, Annie to Thompson, 31 Oct. 1881, from Halifax

28 Ibid., vol. 288, Thompson to Annie, 30 Oct., 3 Nov. 1881, from Ottawa

29 G.M. Haliburton has made a noble effort to sort out this tangled story. See his 'A History of Railways in Nova Scotia' (MA thesis, Dalhousie University 1955).

30 JSDT, vol. 19, Townshend to Thompson, 18 Jan. 1881 (private) from Amherst

31 Ibid., J.S. McDonald to Thompson, 24 Jan. 1881 (private) from Wolfville; Bishop Cameron to Thompson, 21 Jan. 1881 from Antigonish

32 Ibid., vol. 273, Memorandum in Thompson's hand, 16 Aug. 1881

33 Ibid., vol. 280, memoranda, political and miscellaneous. This is from notes for a speech or a pamphlet; I have slightly altered the punctuation in order to make it clear.

34 *Nova Scotia, Assembly Debates and Proceedings* (8 Apr. 1880), 207

35 Ibid., (26 Jan. 1882), 69; PAO, Blake Papers, general Canadian political correspondence, Fielding to Black, 23 Jan. 1882 (private); *Nova Scotia, Legislative Council Journals* (21 Feb. 1882), 35

36 JSDT, vol. 27, Holmes to Thompson, Thursday evening, n.d. (probably Thursday, 2 March 1882)

37 L.G. Power, 'Our First President, J.W. Ritchie,' Nova Scotia Historical

Society, *Collections* (1918), 15. Ritchie's resignation took effect 29 May, 1882.

38 Halifax *Acadian Recorder*, 6 Mar. 1882

39 JSDT, vol. 25, Cameron to Thompson, 14 Mar. 1882

40 Ibid., J.S. McDonald to Thompson, 5 Apr. 1882 (private and confidential)

41 Ibid., McDonald to Thompson, 17 Apr. 1882 (private); *Acadian Recorder*, 21 Apr. 1882

42 JSDT, vol. 273, Thompson to Tupper, 8 May 1882 (draft)

43 Halifax *Acadian Recorder*, 12, 13 May 1882

44 There is no extant correspondence on this subject, but some such scenario was probably in Tupper's mind.

45 Halifax *Morning Chronicle*, 27, 29 May 1882

46 JSDT, vol. 25, Cameron to Thompson, Apr., n.d., 1882

47 This was not altogether obvious to some lieutenant-governors. Matthew Richey, Archibald's successor, got into difficulty over the resignation of Premier Pipes in 1884 and consulted Sir John A. Macdonald. Macdonald was specific on this point. Macdonald Papers, vol. 525, Macdonald to Richey, 29 July 1884 (private).

48 Halifax *Morning Chronicle*, 29 May 1882. Creelman was seventy-three years old.

49 JSDT, vol. 27, Tupper to Allan, 8 June 1882, telegram (copy): Allan to Tupper, 8 June 1882 (copy)

50 Ibid., vol. 288, Thompson to Annie, 1 June 1882, from Antigonish

51 Ibid., Thompson to Annie, 6 June 1882, from Antigonish; ibid., vol. 283, Annie to Thompson, 14 June 1882, from Halifax

52 Ibid., vol. 28, Gayton to Thompson, 1 July 1882 (private and confidential), from Yarmouth; A.C. Bell to Thompson, 6 July 1882, from Port Hood; 7 July 1882, from Port Hawkesbury; A.J. White to Thompson, 10 July 1882, from Sydney

53 Halifax *Acadian Recorder*, 1 Mar. 1882; 8, 14 July 1882

54 JSDT, vol. 27, Smith to Thompson, 23 June 1882, from Chester; N.W. White to Thompson, 24 June 1882, from Shelburne; John Morrison to Thompson; 24 June 1882, from St Ann's

55 J.M. Beck, *The Evolution of Municipal Government in Nova Scotia, 1749–1973* (Halifax 1973), 27

56 JSDT, vol. 27, J.H. Hearn to Thompson, 24 June 1882 (private), from Sydney

57 Halifax *Acadian Recorder*, 7 Mar. 1882

58 Thompson deleted these opinions from his draft letter to Tupper of 8 May 1882, JSDT, vol. 273.

9 MR JUSTICE THOMPSON

1 Halifax *Herald*, 4 Jan. 1895, account of Thompson's life by J.T. Bulmer. It also necessitated Thompson and Graham giving up the crown agency, acquired only a few months before. JSDT, vol. 27, Graham to Thompson, 6, 8, 19 June 1882, from Halifax

2 *Robert Laird Borden, His Memoirs*, ed. Henry Borden (Toronto 1938), I, 8; R.C. Brown, *Robert Laird Borden: A Biography: I, 1854–1914* (Toronto 1975), 19–21

3 JSDT, vol. 288, Thompson to Annie, 6, 9 Aug. 1882, from Halifax. Thompson was paid, even though his official commission had not arrived. Because of that he did not have to go on circuit yet. His commission is dated 9 Aug. 1882 (ibid., vol. 300).

4 Ibid., vol. 28, Griffin to Thompson, 21 July 1882, from Toronto; vol. 60, Graham to Thompson, 20 Sept. 1887, from Halifax. The context of Graham's assertion was Thompson's offer to Robert Borden, Graham's partner, to become deputy minister of justice, at $3,600 a year. Graham wrote that 'neither of us I think receives anything like as much from our business as the Deputy's salary.'

5 Ibid., vol. 230, emphasized by Thompson in a letter to T.B. Akins, 2 May 1887

6 See the excellent little book by L.W. Collins, *In Halifax Town: On Going for a Walk in Halifax, Nova Scotia* (Halifax 1975), 43, 79.

7 *Halifax Evening Reporter*, 11 May 1876, 3 May 1875

8 Ibid., 7 Nov. 1876

9 Henry Cecil, *Tipping the Scales* (London 1964), 192

10 *The Times* (London), 6 Mar. 1891

11 University of British Columbia Archives, Charles Hibbert Tupper Papers, Thompson to C.H. Tupper, 19 Mar. 1885, (private), from Halifax

12 JSDT, vol. 32, Wallace Graham to Thompson, 26 Nov. 1885; vol. 82, Wallace Graham to Thompson, 6 Mar. 1889; vol. 237, Thompson to Wallace Graham, 14 Mar. 1889 (private); vol. 46, J.N. Lyons to Thompson, 25 Nov. 1886, from Halifax

13 See J.M. Beck, *The Government of Nova Scotia* (Toronto 1957), chs. VIII and XVIII.

14 JSDT, vol. 288, Thompson to Annie, 18 Aug. 1882, from Liverpool. It seems that Thompson and Annie did go on this trip.

15 Ibid., Thompson to Annie, 25 Oct. 1882, from Port Hood; Thompson to Annie, 30 May 1885, from Lunenburg

16 Ibid., Thompson to Annie, 2 Oct. 1882, from Sydney; Portia King's account

of Newfoundland was published later in *The Week* (Toronto), 29 July 5 Aug. 1886.

17 Benjamin Russell, *Autobiography* (Halifax 1932), 119. I have altered slightly the quotation; Russell's recollection fifty years afterward was wrong in that he had included DesBarres with the chief justice and Smith, forgetting that DesBarres had resigned in 1881.

18 Ibid., 120; 16 *N.S.R.*, 35

19 17 *N.S.R.*, 49. It is possible that Thompson may here have been influenced by the Privy Council decision in *Hodge* v. *the Queen* (1883) where the legislative supremacy of both the Dominion Parliament and the provincial legislatures within their own jurisdictions was held to be not less than the imperial government within its field.

20 Halifax *Herald*, 4 Jan. 1895, account by J.T. Bulmer

21 Benjamin Russell, 'The Career of Sir John Thompson,' *Dalhousie Review*, I, 2 (1921), 201, 197

22 Leon Radzinowicz, *Sir James Fitzjames Stephen*, Seldon Society Lecture (London 1957), 7

23 Toronto *Globe*, 13 Dec. 1894, quoting Magurn, as of December 1892

24 Benjamin Russell, 'Recollections of W.S. Fielding,' *Dalhousie Review*, IX (1929–30), 327. Fielding had the same regrets as Thompson.

25 See *Halifax Evening Reporter*, 26 Sept. 1876

26 Benjamin Russell, 'Legal Education,' in *Proceedings of Canadian Bar Association*, III (1918), 118–19, cited in John Willis, *A History of Dalhousie Law School* (Toronto 1979), 23; *Dalhousie Gazette*, XVI, 2, 23 Nov. 1883, quoting Thompson's speech to a newly formed Dalhousie Law School Library Committee, on 18 Aug. 1883

27 Willis, *History of Dalhousie Law School*, 21

28 JSDT, vol. 288, Thompson to Annie, 17 Apr. 1883, from Boston

29 *Dalhousie Gazette* 23 Nov. 1883, reporting Thompson's speech of 9 Aug. 1883; 7 Dec. 1883, letter from J.T. Bulmer quoting Thompson in another context

30 Benjamin Russell, 'John Thomas Bulmer,' *Dalhousie Review*, IX (1929–30), 68–78. Slade actually said 'three rods,' but it would have spoiled the story to stop and elucidate, as necessary for most readers, that three rods meant fifty feet.

31 JSDT, vol. 30, M. McLeod to Thompson, 15 Feb. 1884, from Charlottetown; Bora Laskin, *The British Tradition in Canadian Law* (London 1969), 84, cited in Willis, *History of Dalhousie Law School*, 13

32 *Dalhousie Gazette*, 14 Nov. 1885

33 JSDT, vol. 287 contains Thompson's lectures on evidence.

34 JSDT, vol. 234, Thompson to Judge Sinclair of Hamilton, 25 June 1888; vol. 287, Lecture xv, Thursday, 31 Jan. 1884

35 Ibid., Lecture xii, Tuesday, 22 Jan. 1884

36 H. Allen, ed., *The Complete Tales and Poems of Edgar Allan Poe* (New York 1938), 'The Mystery of Marie Roget,' 169–207, esp. 191. Poe at the beginning of this story quotes Prince Karl von Hardenberg (1750–1822): 'Es gibt eine Reihe idealischer Begebenheiten, die der Wirklichkeit parallel läuft. Selten fallen sie zusammen.'

37 JSDT, vol. 30, A.J. White to Thompson, 29 Jan. 1884; C.H. Tupper to Thompson, 8 Feb. 1884, from Ottawa; C.J. Townshend to Thompson, 3 May 1884, from Amherst

38 Nova Scotia, 47 Vic. c. 25

39 Ibid., vol. 30, J.J. Stewart to Thompson, 6 June 1884 (private and confidential), from Halifax

40 PAC, Macdonald Papers, vol. 282, Macdonald to Tupper, 7 Apr. 1884

41 PAC, Tupper Papers, vol. 6, Macdonald to Tupper, 28 June 1884

42 Macdonald Papers, vol. 282, J. Parsons to Macdonald, 10 May 1884. Parsons was secretary of the Liberal-Conservative Association of Halifax.

43 Ibid., vol. 281, Thompson to Macdonald, 24 May 1884, from Rimouski; vol. 282, Alpin Grant to Tupper, 21 May 1884 (private) from Halifax; Tupper Papers, vol. 6, Macdonald to Tupper, 4 June 1884

44 Macdonald Papers, vol. 283, C.J. Townshend to Tupper, 8 Jan. 1885, from Amherst, enclosed in Tupper to Macdonald, 22 Jan. 1885 from London

45 Ibid., vol. 428, Mrs Isabella Holmes to Macdonald, 11 July 1886

46 Tupper Papers, vol. 6, Tupper to Charles Hibbert Tupper, 26 Mar. 1885, from London

47 Ibid., Macdonald to Tupper, 27 Feb. 1885 (private) from Ottawa

48 University of British Columbia Archives, Charles Hibbert Tupper Papers, Thompson to Hibbert Tupper, 19 Mar. 1885, from Halifax

49 JSDT, vol. 288, Thompson to Annie, 3 June 1885, from Lunenburg; 19 June 1885, from Yarmouth

50 Sir Charles Hibbert Tupper Papers, 'Reminiscences.' Tupper gives no clear date when this happened except that it was prior to Thompson's final acceptance of office. The quotation of Macdonald is from Canto 1, line cxvii, of *Don Juan*.

51 Macdonald Papers, vol. 526, Macdonald to Thompson, 20 July 1885 (private and confidential)

52 Ibid., vol. 273, Thompson to Macdonald, 1 Aug. 1885 (private), from Halifax; Dalhousie University Archives, Archibald MacMechan Papers, Private Journals, 30 Dec. 1894. The quotation about Antigonish is allegedly

Thompson's but it comes third hand, from Hector McInnes through MacMechan.

53 JSDT, vol. 283, Annie to Thompson, 5 Nov. 1885. Two Cape Breton constituencies, Inverness and Richmond, had Catholic majorities, but much smaller than Antigonish.

54 Macdonald Papers, vol. 418, Stairs to Macdonald, 4 Aug. 1885 (private and confidential), from Dartmouth

55 Ibid., vol. 526, Macdonald to Campbell, 14 Sept. 1885; vol. 418, Stairs to Macdonald, 11 Aug. 1885, from Dartmouth

56 JSDT, vol. 31, Cameron to Thompson, 29 Aug. 1885, from Antigonish

57 Archibald MacMechan Papers, Private Journals, 30 Dec. 1894; Macdonald Papers, vol. 273, Thompson to Macdonald, 2 Sept. 1885, from Halifax; Tupper to Macdonald, 2 Sept. 1885

58 Macdonald Papers, vol. 197, Campbell to Macdonald, 9 Sept. 1885

59 Ibid., Macdonald to Campbell, 12 Sept. 1885 (private)

60 Ibid., Campbell to Macdonald, 14 Sept. 1885; vol. 526, Macdonald to Campbell, 14, 15 Sept. 1885; Ottawa *Citizen*, 13 Dec. 1894

61 Macdonald Papers, vol. 273, Thompson to Macdonald, 2 Sept. 2, 1885 (private), from Halifax

62 Ibid., vol. 526, Macdonald to C.H. Tupper, 17 Sept. 1885, enc. Macdonald to McIsaac, 17 Sept. 1885; vol. 273, Macdonald to Thompson, 21 Sept. 1885, from Ottawa

63 JSDT, vol. 288, Thompson to Annie, 25 Sept. 1885, from Ottawa

64 Ibid., Thompson to Annie, 26 Sept. 1885, from Ottawa

PART THREE: THE TRAIN TO OTTAWA: MINISTER OF JUSTICE IN MACDONALD'S CABINET, 1885–1891

10 MINISTER OF JUSTICE

1 D. Campbell and R.A. MacLean, *Beyond the Atlantic Roar: A Study of the Nova Scotia Scots* (Toronto 1974), 236. Much of this paragraph is based upon ch. 7, 'Politics.'

2 PANS, Fielding Papers, vol. 490, Fielding to A.F. McIntyre, of Ottawa, 30 Sept. 1885 (private)

3 JSDT, vol. 31, Cameron to Thompson, 29 Aug. 1885

4 *Yarmouth Herald*, 30 Sept. 1885; *The Week*, 1 Oct. 1885

5 McIsaac died in 1902 at the age of sixty.

6 In 1872 Macdonald appointed S.H. Blake, a Liberal, as chancellor of

Ontario. Alexander Mackenzie appointed a Conservative, A.W. Savary, to be county court judge in Digby County, as well as appointing McIsaac's Conservative predecessor.

7 JSDT, vol. 31, Cameron to Thompson, 9 Oct. 1885.

8 Ibid., vol. 288, Thompson to Annie, 4 Oct. 1885, from Antigonish; vol. 31, Lachlan Cameron to Thompson, 12 Oct. 1885, from St Andrews; New Glasgow *Eastern Chronicle*, 1 Oct. 1885

9 Toronto *Globe*, 28 Sept. 1885; Saint John *Daily Telegraph*, 26 Sept. 1885

10 Fielding Papers, vol. 490, Fielding to J.E.B. McCready of Saint John, 30 Sept. 1885 (private)

11 JSDT, vol. 283, Annie to Thompson, 28 Oct. 1885, from Halifax; Annie is reporting a conversation with the bishop.

12 Ibid., vol. 288, Thompson to Annie, 4 Oct. 1885, from Antigonish; Halifax *Herald*, 4 Jan. 1895, reminiscences of J.T. Bulmer; PAC, Harold Daly Papers, MG 27, F9, Part III, Observations, 1

13 P.B. Waite, *Canada 1874–1896: Arduous Destiny* (Toronto 1971), 24, 49

14 Halifax *Morning Chronicle*, 23 Oct. 1885, letter from 'x.' The authenticity of this letter was not denied by Bishop Cameron in a long letter to the *Chronicle*, published 11 Nov. 1885.

15 Ibid.

16 JSDT, vol. 288, Thompson to Annie, 9 Oct. 1885, from Antigonish

17 JSDT, vol. 31, James Purcell to Thompson, 20 Oct. 1885, from Port Mulgrave; Halifax *Morning Chronicle*, 11 Nov. 1885, letter from Bishop Cameron; JSDT, vol. 288, Thompson to Annie, 12 Oct. 1885

18 *North Sydney Herald*, 21 Oct. 1885. Thompson's own forecast, on 10 Oct., was accurate: 'in about one half the county I expect fine majorities. In the other half I believe McIntosh will have majorities and the question is which will preponderate.' JSDT, vol. 288, Thompson to Annie, 10 Oct. 1885, from Antigonish

19 Halifax *Morning Chronicle*, 19, 23 Oct. 1885

20 PAC, Macdonald Papers, vol. 273, Thompson to Macdonald, 21 Oct. 1885, from Halifax; JSDT, vol. 288, Thompson to Annie, 18 Oct. 1885, from Antigonish

21 JSDT, vol. 289, Thompson to Annie, 31 Aug. 1886, from Ottawa

22 Ibid., vol. 288, Thompson to Annie, 4 Oct. 1885, from Antigonish; vol. 283, Annie to Thompson, 28 Oct. 1885, from Halifax

23 Ibid., Annie to Thompson, 2 Nov. 1885, from Halifax

24 Ibid., vol. 288, Thompson to Annie, 30 Oct. 1885, from Ottawa. Hincks was brought into Macdonald's government in 1869 but he had once been premier in the province of Canada. Two other very young justice ministers

were Charles Hibbert Tupper (1894–6), and John Turner (1968–72). Turner was the youngest, beating Thompson by nine months.

25 *Canada, Statutes, 1868*, c. 39; *RSC* (1886), c. 21

26 JSDT, vol. 288, Thompson to Aloysia Thompson, 29 Oct. 1885

27 Ibid., Thompson to Annie, 31 Oct. 1885; vol. 283, Annie to Thompson, 5 Nov. 1885; vol. 288, Thompson to Annie, 10 Dec. 1885

28 PAC, RG 13, A2, Department of Justice Papers, Central Registry Files, vol. 89, no. 67, A. Gobeil, Deputy Minister of Public Works, to Deputy Minister of Justice, 16 Jan. 1893

29 Ibid., no. 163, a return to Parliament on the national origins, birthplace, and creed of members of the Department of Justice, dated 21 Feb. 1893, with salaries attached

30 PAC, Mackenzie Bowell Papers, vol. 4, Thompson to Bowell, 2 Nov. 1885 (private). Sargent did eventually get his raise, at end of June 1886.

31 *The Week*, 29 Sept. 1887, as editorial comment

32 JSDT, vol. 79. No. 8826 has a list of deputy ministers and their dates of appointment as of mid-1888.

33 *Globe*, 11 July 1885

34 University of Western Ontario Archives, J.H. Coyne Papers, H.J. Macdonald to Coyne, 27 Apr. 1871, from Ottawa; JSDT, vol. 288, Thompson to Aloysia Thompson, 29 Oct. 1885, from Ottawa. (Most other letters to her are in vol. 297.)

35 JSDT, vol. 30, C.H. Tupper to Thompson, n.d., from Ottawa (the letter was written about May 1883); *The Week*, 24 May 1888, 'Ottawa Letter' by Sara Jeanette Duncan

36 JSDT, vol. 283, Annie to Thompson, 25 Nov. 1883, from Halifax; vol. 288, Thompson to Annie, 12 Dec. 1885 from Ottawa

37 JSDT, vol. 288, Thompson to Annie, 3 Nov. 1885, from Ottawa; vol. 32, Griffin to Thompson, n.d.

38 Ibid., vol. 288, Thompson to Annie, 8 Nov. 1885, from Ottawa

39 Ibid., Thompson to Annie, 31 Oct. 1885

40 Ibid., Thompson to Annie, 31 Oct. 13 Dec. 1885

41 Ibid., Thompson to Annie, 30 Oct. 1885

42 For the 1884 quarrel with Sir Charles Tupper, see *supra*, p. 127; for the 1890 one with Charles Hibbert Tupper, see Waite, *Canada 1874–1896*, 221.

43 As to Bowell's scrupulousness, Thompson gave an interesting example. Some Catholics in Halifax wanted to import some statues, via Thompson, to avoid customs duties. Thompson replied that neither he nor the minister of customs himself were exempt. 'I know of his [Bowell] paying duty of some

dresses for his wife a short time ago.' JSDT, vol. 288, Thompson to Annie, 4 Feb. 1886

44 Macdonald Papers, vol. 221, Gowan to Macdonald, 10 Nov. 1885, from Barrie

45 JSDT, vol. 288, Thompson to Annie, 30, 31 Oct., 8 Nov. 1885; vol. 283, Annie to Thompson, 5, 6 Nov. 1885, from Halifax

46 RG 13, Department of Justice Records, B15, Capital case files, vol. 31

47 RG 13, A3, Department of Justice Letterbooks, vol. 619, p. 429

48 Ibid., p. 475, p. 587, 11, 28 Nov. 1885

49 The correspondence on this contretemps is JSDT, vol. 288, Thompson to Annie, 10, 11, 12, 13, 15 Nov; vol. 283, Annie to Thompson, 11, 12, 14, 16, 18 Nov., 1885. Most of the telegrams are in the new supplementary volume [vol. 301?].

50 Ibid., vol. 288, Thompson to Annie, 13, 15 Nov. 1885

51 Ibid., Thompson to Annie, 22 Nov. 1885

52 Macdonald Papers, vol. 221, Gowan to Macdonald, 18 Nov. 1885, from Barrie

53 JSDT, vol. 288, Thompson to Annie, 18 Nov. 1885

54 Ibid., Thompson to Annie, 17, 18, 22 Nov. 1885

55 Ibid., Thompson to Annie, 29 Nov. 1885; vol. 283, Annie to Thompson, 30 Nov. 1885. Thompson gave a champagne reception for Bishop Cameron and Canon O'Donnell, 27 Nov. and a dinner party at the Rideau Club for fourteen, 28 Nov.

56 Ibid., vol. 32, Cameron to Thompson, 16 Nov. 1885, from Antigonish (private)

57 'Left and right bowers' was a metaphor frequently used in Canadian politics. In euchre, the two highest cards were the jack of trumps, the right bower, and the jack of the same colour, the left bower. The name comes from the old German word for jack, *Bauer*.

58 PANS, J.J. Stewart Papers, Douglas Stewart to J.J. Stewart, 10 Nov. 1881, from Ottawa, 25 May 1882; JSDT, vol. 288, Thompson to Annie, 23 Nov. 1885; Thompson to Annie, 5 Dec. 1885

59 In 1882 Stewart had two offers to work outside the government. He went to the minister and asked him what his retiring allowance would be if he resigned. He did not even ask for an increase. The result was his promotion to first class clerk a few weeks later. J.J. Stewart Papers, D.B. Stewart to his father, 15 Feb. 1879; D.B. Stewart to his father, 25 May 1882; JSDT, vol. 289, Thompson to Annie, 13 Jan. 1886, from Ottawa

60 Thompson mentioned some of the difficulties when Annie was attempting to teach the boys shorthand in 1891. Notice the following words, he told Annie:

deed *//* ; total *ly* ; roar *✓* ; read *ŋ* ; favoured *ᴠ✓* . JSDT, vol. 291, Thompson to Annie, 7 Sept. 1891, from Ottawa

61 J.J. Stewart Papers, D.B. Stewart to his father, 26 June 1879, from Ottawa

62 JSDT, vol. 33, Bishop Cameron to Thompson, 22 Dec. 1885, from Antigonish, quoting O'Donnell's letter

63 Ibid., vol. 288, Thompson to Annie, 22, 29 Nov. 1885; vol. 283, Annie to Thompson, 25 Nov. 1885

64 Ibid., Annie to Thompson, 11 Dec. 1885; vol. 288, Thompson to Annie, 12 Dec. 1885

65 Ibid., Thompson to Annie, 6 Jan. 1885

66 Ibid., vol. 283, Annie to Thompson, 24 Nov. 1885. The reader may recall the advice of Sister Aloysia, from Rome in January 1880, to Thompson, 'that the work of the day ought to be sufficient without staying in town and doing the work of others at night –' *Supra,* p. 65

67 Ibid., Annie to Thompson, 20 Nov. 1885; ibid., Fanny Affleck to Thompson, 20 Nov. 1885

68 Ibid., Annie to Thompson, 19, 27 Nov. 1885

69 Ibid., vol. 288, Thompson to Annie, 6 Jan. 1886, from Ottawa. Whist is a game that goes back to the sixteenth century and beyond.

70 Ibid., Thompson to Annie, 17 Jan. 1886; vol. 283, Annie to Thompson, 9 Jan. 1886; 21 Jan. 1886. The reference to the train at Truro was because Annie took Joe with her to make an overnight visit to Stellarton 20 Jan. coming back the next day.

71 Ibid., Thompson to Annie, 28 Jan. 1886

72 Ibid., vol. 289, Thompson to Annie, 27 June 1886

73 JSDT, vol. 290, Thompson to Annie, 28 Mar. 1887

74 Ibid., vol. 289, Thompson to Annie, 6 Feb. 1886

11 DEFENDING THE MACDONALD GOVERNMENT

1 Norman Ward, 'The Formative Years of the House of Commons, 1867–1891,' *Canadian Journal of Economics and Political Science,* XVIII, 4 (Nov. 1952), 432–3; Paul Bilkey, *Persons, Papers and Things* (Toronto 1949), 62

2 *Montreal Daily Star,* 15 Mar. 1886. Founded by Hugh Graham (1848–1934) in 1869, the journal was conducted by him for nearly seventy years. It had probably the largest circulation in Canada, estimated by Graham in 1887 at 27,000 for the daily edition, and 115,000 for the weekly. It was not a party paper, according to its editor, not at least in these years. JSDT, vol. 54, Hugh Graham to Macdonald, 4 May 1887 (private)

3 Sir John Willison, *Reminiscences, Political and Personal* (Toronto 1919), 147–8

4 University of Toronto Library, Charlton Papers, 'Reminiscences,' 525
5 JSDT, vol. 36, Macdonald to Thompson, 16 Mar. 1886 (private). Two days later Macdonald was in such pain he had to have morphine injections for sciatica.
6 *Canada, House of Commons Debates* (11 Mar. 1886), p. 68
7 *Montreal Daily Star*, 18 Mar. 1886
8 Sir Richard Cartwright, *Reminiscences* (Toronto 1912), 265
9 Stonyhurst College Library, Lancashire, *The Stonyhurst Magazine*, 78 (February 1895), 453
10 Montreal *Gazette*, 26 Mar. 1886, reported by Ottawa correspondent 25 Mar. Also quoted again by Montreal *Gazette*, 13 Dec. 1894. Other comments on this speech are made by the Ottawa *Citizen*, 13 Dec. 1894.
11 Richardson's history is curious. He was head clerk in the Department of Justice; Blake appointed in 1875 as deputy minister of justice a friend from Toronto, Z.A. Lash. Richardson then applied for a North-West magistracy and got it (*Manitoba Free Press*, 30 Mar. 1887).
12 *House of Commons Debates* (22 Mar. 1886), pp. 267–9; *Manitoba Free Press*, 17 Dec. 1885; PAO, Blake Papers, Laurier to Blake, 31 Dec. 1885 (private)
13 Father Alexis André to F.-X. Lemieux, 31 Aug. 1885, from Regina, part of a sworn deposition of Lemieux for the medical commission, dated 28 Oct. 1885, in RG 13, B15, vol. 32, Department of Justice
14 Quoted by a correspondent in the *Toronto Daily Mail*, 3 Aug. 1885. See also G.F.G. Stanley, *Louis Riel* (Toronto 1963), 363. Riel had some peculiar ideas about digestion. If you chewed your food well, he believed, you helped to spiritualize the body; if you wolfed your food down, you increased the body's animal nature. The great cause of sin in the world was the latter. Father André to F.-X. Lemieux, cited above
15 This is from McKay's evidence at the trial. See *Queen v. Riel*, p. 61; also quoted by Stanley, *Louis Riel*, 310; *Canada, House of Commons Debates* (22 Mar. 1886), p. 276.
16 Ibid., pp. 277–8. Neither the italics nor the exclamation mark occur in the debates, but are reported that way in *Montreal Daily Star*, 23 Mar. 1886.
17 *House of Commons Debates* (22 Mar. 1886), p. 283. I have altered the wording slightly following the *Montreal Daily Star*, 23 Mar. 1886.
18 *House of Commons Debates* (22 Mar. 1886), pp. 286–7; *Toronto Daily Mail*, 23 Mar. 1886
19 *House of Commons Debates* (22 Mar. 1886), pp. 290–1. This conclusion was suggested to Thompson by his friend J.T. Bulmer.
20 Ottawa *Citizen*, 13 Dec. 1894; *Montreal Daily Star*, 23 Mar. 1886; JSDT, vol. 36, Bishop Cameron to Martin Griffin, 27 Mar. 1886, from Antigonish

21 Ibid., Campbell to Thompson, 23 Mar. [1886]; University of Toronto Library, Charlton Papers, Diary, Monday, 22 Mar. 1886

22 Willison, *Reminiscences*, 144–5; JSDT, vol. 37, Bishop Cameron to Thompson, 15 Apr. 1886, from Antigonish, and reporting Ottawa via Miss Amy Pope of Charlottetown

23 *Montreal Daily Star*, 26 Mar. 1886

24 The final tally was:

Government:	English-speaking Conservatives	97
	French-Canadian Conservatives	25
	English-speaking Liberals	24
		___
		146
Opposition:	French-Canadian Conservatives	17
	English-speaking Liberals	24
	French-speaking Liberals	11
		___
		52

25 JSDT, vol. 297, Thompson to Joe, 11 Mar. 1886; vol. 289, Thompson to Annie, 1, 8, 10 May 1886; Thompson to Annie, 3 May 1886

26 Ibid., Thompson to Annie, Sunday, 24 May 1886; Sunday, 31 May 1886

27 PAC, Sir Charles Tupper Papers, vol. 7, A.W. McLelan to Tupper, 23 Apr. 1886

28 Halifax *Morning Chronicle*, 18 May 1886. The most recent article is Colin Howell, 'W.S. Fielding and the Repeal Elections of 1886 and 1887,' *Acadiensis*, VIII, 2 (Spring 1979), 28–46.

29 JSDT, vol. 39, L.S. Ford to Macdonald, 17 May 1886, from Milton, Queen's Co., and minuted to Thompson, 'My dear Thompson, Please acknowledge this and write that you are going down. JAMD.'

30 Howell, 'W.S. Fielding,' 34

31 JSDT, vol. 40, Lachlan Cameron to Thompson, 21 June 1886, from South River, Antigonish County

32 PAC, Macdonald Papers, vol. 117, J.F. Stairs to Macdonald, 17 June 1886 (confidential), from Halifax

33 JSDT, vol. 289, Thompson to Annie, 26 June 1886

34 Ibid., Thompson to Annie, 27 June 1886

35 Ibid., Thompson to Annie, 30 June 1886

36 PAC, Department of Justice Papers, RG 13, A3, vol. 622, p. 459, Thompson to Governor General in Council, 6 July, 1886; ibid., p. 458, Thompson to Governor General in Council 7 July 1886

37 Dumont told Mercier in New York in January 1888, 'J'ai un droit à une

indemnité du Gouvernement pour les pertes que j'ai soubis.' PAC, Laurier Papers, vol. 2, Dumont to Mercier, 25 janvier 1888

38 Ibid., Thompson to Annie, 4, 5 July 1886; vol. 297, Thompson to Joe, 5 July 1886; vol. 289, Thompson to Annie, 8 July 1886

39 Ibid., vol. 289, Thompson to Annie, 10 July 1886

40 Ibid., vol. 297, Thompson to Joe, 6 Feb. 1886; vol. 289, Thompson to Annie, 26, 27 Oct. 1886

41 Ibid., Thompson to Annie, 13 Sept. 1886

42 Ibid., vol. 42, Macdonald to Thompson, 27 July 1886 (confidential)

43 Ibid., vol. 44, Macdonald to Thompson, 1 Sept. 1886 (private); 3 Sept. 1886 (private). The legal information comes from pencilled notes in Thompson's hand on the back of the second letter. The commission was issued on 9 Dec. 1886. For the text, see Greg Kealey, ed., *Canada Investigates Industrialism* (Toronto 1973), 3.

44 University of British Columbia, C.H. Tupper Papers, Tupper to McLelan, 4 Oct. 1886; JSDT, vol. 45, Tupper to Thompson, 6 Oct. 1886

45 Ibid., Thompson to Annie, 10 Nov. 1886, from Orillia

46 Ibid., Thompson to Annie, 12 Nov. 1886, from Ottawa

47 Ibid., Thompson to Annie, 28 Nov. 1886, from Toronto; vol. 289, Thompson to Annie, 6 Dec. 1886, from Ottawa; Thompson to Annie, 14 Dec. 1886, from St Thomas; I have sketched this campaign a little more fully in *Canada 1874-1896*, 189-90.

48 Sir Charles Tupper Papers, vol. 7, Macdonald to Tupper, 20 Dec. 1886 (private and confidential)

49 PAC, Lansdowne Papers (microfilm), Macdonald to Lansdowne, 17 Mar. 1886; also 29 Mar. 1886. Cameron married Emma Tupper in 1869.

50 PBW archives, Thompson to Annie, 23 Jan. 1887. This letter existed once, but was removed from the Thompson Papers about 1947 and turned up in a typed copy in St Francis Xavier University library. That copy has since disappeared; my copy is a xerox of the typed version.

51 Ibid., Thompson to Annie, 22 Sept. 1887; vol. 45, McGillivray to Thompson, 18 Oct. 1886, from North Sydney; ibid., vol. 46, McGillivray to Thompson, 13 Nov. 1886 from North Sydney

52 Ibid., vol. 47, Power to Thompson, 9 Dec. 1886, telegram; Pottinger to Thompson, 11 Dec. 1886, telegram, from Moncton

53 Ibid., vol. 48, D.H. McDonald to Thompson, 17 Jan. 1887, from Antigonish, containing copies of evidence taken under oath and forwarded to the chief superintendent

54 Power was not actually appointed until sometime after the election; ibid., vol. 52, Thompson to Pottinger, 29 May 1887 (private), endorsed Pottinger to

Thompson, n.d., in red ink, Pottinger's usual custom with his cousin's letters. As to baggage master's responsibility, see vol. 273, Miscellaneous, Pottinger to Thompson, 29 June 1888 (private).

55 Ibid., vol. 49, Dunn to Thompson, 18 Feb. 1887

56 Ibid., vol. 50, B.F. Power to Thompson, 4 Mar. 1887

57 Ibid., vol. 290, Thompson to Annie, 5, 10, 14, 17 Feb. 1887, from Central House, Antigonish

58 The text of Bishop Cameron's letter appeared in the Ottawa *Free Press*, 22 Nov. 1890. The *Free Press* said editorially that the Antigonish Liberals were taking the case to Rome. When Bishop Cameron saw the newspaper, he burst out laughing. 'I would like to see the Court that would condemn me for addressing this circular to the electorate!' JSDT, vol. 118, J.J. Cameron to Thompson, 1 Dec. 1890, from Antigonish).

59 Halifax *Morning Herald*, 25 Feb. 1887; also JSDT, vol. 49, no. 5286, has the same figures with pencilled changes by Thompson; PANS, J.J. Stewart Papers, Douglas Stewart to J.S. Stewart, 21 Mar. 1887, from Ottawa.

60 Halifax *Morning Herald*, 12 Feb. 1887

61 Ibid., 26 Feb. 1887

12 ADMINISTERING THE DEPARTMENT OF JUSTICE

1 JSDT, vol. 290, Thompson to Annie, 9 Apr. 1887, from Ottawa

2 Ibid., Thompson to Annie, 7 Oct. 1887

3 Ibid., Thompson to Annie, 11 Apr. 1887, from Montreal

4 Ibid., Thompson to Annie, 7 Oct. 1887

5 The situation was complicated. The petitions against Tupper's and McLelan's elections were intended as offsets for a Conservative petition against the election of A.G. Jones in Halifax. However, the Conservative petition against Jones was abandoned; Halifax was a two-member constituency and one Conservative had been elected. Tupper's and McLelan's petitions were not abandoned, but they both won re-election in October 1887. Thompson elaborates the reasons in ibid., Thompson to Annie, 14 Apr. 1887.

6 British Library, Gladstone Papers, Addl. MSS. 44090, Lady Aberdeen to Gladstone, 6 Nov. 1894, from Victoria, BC

7 PAC, Lansdowne Papers, Microfilm A-627, Goldwin Smith to Lansdowne, 1 Mar. 1886, from Toronto

8 *Canada, House of Commons Debates* (28 Apr. 1887), pp. 154–8

9 JSDT, vol. 290, Thompson to Annie, 30 Apr., 2, 3 May 1887

10 Ibid., vol. 238, Thompson to Judge R. Weatherbe, 15 Apr. 1889 (private)

11 *House of Commons Debates* (15 June 1887), p. 1017

12 PAC, Macdonald Papers, vol. 221, Gowan to Macdonald, 28 Aug. 1887; DJ Records, RG 13, A2, vol. 67, f. 841, Thompson to Deputy-Minister, 28 July 1887. (This reference has been brought to my attention by Professor J.G. Snell, University of Guelph.)

13 Macdonald Papers, vol. 192, Burbidge to Macdonald, 2 Oct. 1886 (personal)

14 Ibid., vol. 37, J.G. Hodgins to Thompson, 10 Apr. [1886], (private) from Toronto

15 JSDT, vol. 45, G.W. Burbidge to Thompson, 21 Oct. 1886 (private)

16 *House of Commons Debates* (31 May 1887), p. 644. The case is cited in Moore's Privy Council Reports, vol. I. In 1926 the Privy Council declared Thompson's prohibition *ultra vires*.

17 Sir W.J. Ritchie (1813–92), chief justice of the Supreme Court of Canada, and J.W. Ritchie (1808–90) of the Supreme Court of Nova Scotia were brothers, both born in Annapolis Royal.

18 JSDT, vol. 290, Thompson to Annie, 30 Sept. 1887

19 Ibid., vol. 38, Macdonald to Thompson, 27 Apr. 1886

20 *House of Commons Debates* (25, 26 May 1887), pp. 524, 590

21 JSDT, vol. 290, Thompson to Annie, 30 Sept. 1887

22 Ibid., vol. 58, Graham to Thompson, 13 July 1887, from London

23 See *Exchequer Court of Canada Reports*. Vol. 2 begins those of Burbidge's new court: *Bourget* v. *the Queen*, p. 1; *Vezina* v. *the Queen*, p. 12; *Guay* v. *the Queen*, p. 18; *Kearney* v. *the Queen*, p. 21. The relevant appeals are in 17 *Can. SCR* 1 and 17 *Can. SCR* 30.

24 JSDT, vol. 290, Thompson to Annie, 30 Sept. 1887

25 Macdonald Papers, vol. 275, Thompson to Macdonald, 16 Oct. 1889; DJ Records, RG 13, A2, vol. 89, f. 163 gives national origins, birthplace, and creed, in a report dated 21 Feb. 1893; RG 13, A3, vol. 656, ff. 293–4, gives names ranks and salaries for fiscal years 1893–4, 1894–5.

26 Macdonald Papers, vol. 273, Thompson to Macdonald, 21 Sept. 1887

27 Wallace Graham (1848–1917) was appointed puisne judge of the Supreme Court of Nova Scotia in 1889, and became chief justice in 1915.

28 JSDT, vol. 60, Graham to Thompson, 30 Sept. 1887, from Halifax; see also R.C. Brown, *Robert Laird Borden* (Toronto 1975) I, 22.

29 JSDT, vol. 290, Thompson to Annie, 4 Oct. 1887

30 Sedgewick (1848–1906) was born in Aberdeen and came to Nova Scotia as a child; he took his BA at Dalhousie (1867), studied law in Ontario with John Sandfield Macdonald, and practised law in Halifax after 1873. There was no impediment to moving between the bars of the several provinces. Thompson disallowed two NWT ordinances in August 1890 because it placed barriers

upon lawyers moving there from other provinces. DJ Records, RG 13, A3, vol. 642, Thompson to Council, 31 Aug. 1890

31 JSDT, vol. 290, Thompson to Annie, 24 Sept. 1887
32 Macdonald Papers, vol. 271, Stephen to Macdonald, 12 Jan. 1888 (private)
33 JSDT, vol. 290, Thompson to Annie, 1 July 1887
34 Ibid., Thompson to Annie, 17 June 1887
35 Ibid., Thompson to Annie, 19 July 1887
36 Ibid., vol. 297, Thompson to Joe, 4 Aug. 1887, from Ottawa
37 See, for example, *L'Etendard* (Montreal), 2 mai 1890.
38 JSDT, vol. 228, Thompson to Moylan, 15 Mar. 1887; vol. 236, Thompson to Moylan, Memorandum re Bourke, Hospital Overseer at Stony Mountain, 16 Nov. 1888
39 *Canada, Sessional Papers*, 1887, no. 4
40 *House of Commons Debates* (25 Apr., 6 June 1887), pp. 111, 806–7
41 JSDT, vol. 52 has a clutch of letters and telegrams; vol. 229, Thompson to Michaud, 15 Apr. 1887.
42 The law was Ontario 43 Vic. c.34. See Neil Sutherland, *Children in English-Canadian Society: Framing the Twentieth-Century Consensus* (Toronto 1976), 99–100.
43 JSDT, vol. 264, Thompson to Justice Rose, 28 Oct. 1893. John Edward Rose (1844–1901) was appointed to the High Court of Ontario in 1883. The paragraphing in the quotation is my own.
44 DJ Records, RG 13, A3, vol. 620, p. 637, Thompson to the Governor-General in Council, 23 Feb. 1886; RG 13, B15, vol. 35. Thompson was not always against use of circumstantial evidence; see *supra*, ch. 7, for an example of his use of it as attorney general of Nova Scotia.
45 Ibid., RG 13, A3, vol. 652, p. 400, Deputy-Minister of Justice to G.G. Dustan, 29 Nov. 1892
46 *House of Commons Debates* (6 June 1887), p. 799
47 PAC, Bowell Papers, vol. 5, Thompson to Bowell, 28 Nov. 1886, from Toronto
48 JSDT, vol. 139, N.H. Meagher to Thompson, 27 Oct. 1891. N.H. Meagher (1842–1932) was appointed Supreme Court Justice in 1890.
49 DJ Records, RG 13, A5, vol. 2040, f. 290, Thompson's memorandum for the Deputy-Minister, 21 June 1887
50 JSDT, vol. 48, Macdonald to Thompson, 3 Jan. 1887 (private)
51 Ibid., vol. 134, Thompson to ?, draft in Thompson's hand, Aug. 1891?
52 DJ Records, RG 13, A3, vol. 619, Deputy-Minister Justice to Deputy-Minister Finance, 2 Sept. 1885; JSDT, vol. 52, H.H. Bligh to Thompson, 2 Apr. 1887 (private and confidential)

53 Ibid., vol. 226, Thompson to Dewdney, 14 Dec. 1885 (confidential)

54 Ibid., vol. 35, Fitzgerald Cochrane to Thompson, 8 Feb. 1886, from Calgary; Travis to Thompson, 8 Feb. 1886; Macdonald Papers, vol. 419, A.M. Burgess to Joseph Pope, 26 Jan. 1886 (private)

55 DJ Records, RG 13, A3, vol. 620, f. 411, Burbidge to Travis, 28 Jan. 1886; JSDT, vol. 226, Thompson to Travis, 13 Feb. 1886

56 DJ Records, RG 13, A3, vol. 621, f. 131, Thompson to Governor-General in Council, 18 Mar. 1886. The Taylor report is listed in the Sessional Papers for 1887, but it was not printed. I am using Thompson's opinion of the Taylor report, JSDT, vol. 229, Thompson to Tupper, 23 Mar. 1887. The Travis affair was discussed in Parliament in 1886; see *House of Commons Debates* (27 Apr. 1886), pp. 886–9.

57 *House of Commons Debates* (9 Mar. 1888), p. 114

58 JSDT, Acton Burrows (editor of Winnipeg *Call*) to Thompson, 30 June 1887 (private), enclosing article from Winnipeg *Free Press*; vol. 290, Thompson to Annie, 15 June 1887: 'Travis has been abusing me in every number of the *Free Press* for the past week.'

59 DJ Records, RG 13, A3, vol. 622, f. 11 *et seq.*, Thompson to Governor-General in Council, 12 May 1886. For legal discussion of this question, see A.H. March, 'The right to Appoint Queen's Counsel,' in *Canadian Law Times*, X (Feb. 1890), 25–40; John Madden, 'Appointment of Queen's Counsel: opinion of Mr. Madden,' ibid., XII (Nov. 1892), 259–69; A.H. Marsh, 'Appointment of Queen's Counsel,' ibid., XIII (Jan. 1893), 1–13. For *Lenoir* v. *Ritchie*, see 3 *SCR* 624.

60 DJ Records, RG 13, A2, vol. 64, f. 610, Mowat to Thompson, 6 Apr. 1886; Thompson to Mowat, 4 May 1886; Mowat to Thompson, 26 May 1886

61 Ibid., Thompson to Mowat, 2 Aug. 1886 (draft in Thompson's hand); E.F.B. Johnston to G.W. Burbidge, 26 Aug. 26, 1886

62 JSDT, vol. 236, Thompson to Mowat, 14 Nov. 1888 (private); vol. 131, Mowat to Thompson, 29 June 1891 (private). For arrangements for discussions, see vol. 113, Mowat to Thompson, 25 Sept. 1890. The background of Dominion-Ontario relations is usefully deployed in a recent book by Christopher Armstrong, *The Politics of Federalism: Ontario's Relations with the Federal Government, 1867–1942* (Toronto 1981), 9–32.

63 DJ Records, RG 13, A3, vol. 648, f. 274–5, Thompson to Governor-General in Council, 8 Jan. 1892

64 The name was sometimes misspelled as Radcliffe. He was appointed by order-in-council, 11 Jan. 1892. Radclive lived in Toronto, at 132 Lisgar Street. DJ Records, RG 13, A3, vol. 648, f. 727

65 Hector Charlesworth, *More Candid Chronicles* (Toronto 1928), 215–16

66 Halifax *Morning Chronicle*, 30 Nov., 2 Dec. 1892

67 DJ Records, RG 13, A3, vol. 628, Memorandum for the Superintendent General of Indian Affairs, 20 July 1887, f. 81–5

68 *St Catherines Milling & Lumber Co., v. the Queen*, XIV *Appeal Cases*, p. 46. The St Catherines Lumber Co. relied on a Dominion licence given in July 1883. The case went against the company in the high court of Ontario in June 1885, which decision was affirmed in the Supreme Court of Canada, June 1887, and at the Privy Council.

69 JSDT, vol. 235, Thompson to Langevin, 23 Aug. 1888 (private); vol. 76, Whidden to Thompson, 24 Oct. 1888 (telegram); 25 Oct. 1888 (telegram); draft telegram, Thompson to Henry Hill, n.d.

70 Ibid., vol. 60, James A. Lougheed to Thompson, 2 Sept. 1887

71 Ibid., vol. 66, T.B. Maguire to Hector Langevin, 14 Mar. 1888 (private), from Battleford. This letter found its way into the Thompson papers probably because it dealt with the question of salaries for judges, a vexed issue in 1888.

72 Ibid., vol. 38, Macdonald to Thompson, 27 Apr. 1886

73 The statute is 49 Vic. c.25. See especially ss. 27 and 29.

74 JSDT, vol. 290, Thompson to Annie, 5 Oct. 1887; ibid., Thompson to Annie, 14 Oct. 1887

13 ADVENTURES IN WASHINGTON

1 PANS, John Allison Bell Diaries, Wednesday, 22 Aug. 1888, p. 270

2 Thompson makes this point with some force in the British–Canadian reply to the American memorandum at Washington of 22 Nov. 1887. See PAC, Macdonald Papers, vol. 178, f. 73668.

3 A.A. Adee to Bayard, 27 May 1886, in Bayard MS., Library of Congress, Washington, cited in C.C. Tansill, *The Foreign Policy of Thomas F. Bayard* (New York 1940), 221n

4 *Canada, House of Commons Debates* (10 Apr. 1888), p. 708. Tupper's view he put bluntly to the American commissioners in December 1887, and so too did Chamberlain, that 'Great Britain could not abate one of her Treaty rights – on this she took her stand; and she could not surrender them without equivalent.' PAC, Tupper Papers, vol. 21, Proceedings of Washington Conference, pp. 54–5 (10 Dec. 1887)

5 By Article IV St George's Bay, between Cape George and Port Hood Island was deliberately left out of the treaty, probably because it gave access to the Strait of Canso, where the Americans were given, by Article IX, the right of free passage. Thompson noted this before Parliament in April 1888. *House of Commons Debates* (10 Apr. 1888), p. 709

6 Thompson maintained that they were enforced in quite as exacting a fashion

as in 1886 and 1887, but gives no authority. House of Commons, *Debates* (10 Apr. 1888), p. 707

7 There is an extensive literature on this subject. A recent and very good general survey is C.P. Stacey, *Canada and the Age of Conflict. I: 1867–1921* (Toronto 1977), 1–39; a sound, specialized study is Robert Craig Brown, *Canada's National Policy, 1883–1900: A Study of Canadian-American Relations* (Princeton 1964), 3–41, 63–90.

8 JSDT, vol. 247, Thompson to G.G. Dustan, 24 Jan. 1891 (private)

9 Ibid., vol. 36, Macdonald to Thompson, 17 Mar. 1886

10 *The Nation* (New York), 14 Jan. 1886, no. 1072

11 *House of Commons Debates* (10 Apr. 1888), p. 711

12 The original poem is set down in a brief biography of Jonathan McCully (1809–77) for *DCB*, vol. x. I have changed the words to suit my purpose from its original railway ambiance.

13 See James Candow, 'The North Atlantic Fisheries Dispute of 1886–1888 and its Perception by the *New York Times* and the *New York Tribune* (MA thesis, Dalhousie University 1977), 23, citing O.E. Sette and A.W.H. Needler, 'Statistics of the Mackerel Fishery off the East Coast of North America 1804–1930,' in US, Department of Commerce, *Investigational Report No. 19* (Washington 1934), 21.

14 It transpired two years later that Kinney had bought the bait despite express orders of the owner against it. JSDT, vol. 235, Thompson to W.L. Putnam, 3 July 1888

15 Macdonald Papers, vol. 174, T.F. Bayard to Sackville-West, 29 May 1886 (copy)

16 This news reached Washington where it was remarked on in A.A. Adee to Bayard, 27 May 1886, cited in Tansill, *Foreign Policy of Thomas F. Bayard*, 221n.

17 JSDT, vol. 39, Graham to C.H. Tupper, 19 May 1886

18 PAC, Lansdowne Papers, Macdonald to Lansdowne, 21 May 1886

19 JSDT, vol. 40, G.E. Foster to Thompson, 5 June 1886 (telegram): 'Instruct Nova Scotia captains immediately seize no vessel for buying bait,' sent in Sir John Macdonald's cipher. Macdonald Papers, vol. 13, Macdonald to Lansdowne, 6 June 1886

20 *Canada, Sessional Papers, 1887*, no. 16, pp. 48–49; Appendix A, pp. 2–47; see also Candow, 'Fisheries Dispute,' 46–7.

21 Macdonald Papers, vol. 174, Memorandum of Minister of Justice on letter of Phelps to Granville of 2 June 1886. JSDT, vol. 39, Macdonald to Thompson, Monday, 31 [May 1886] enclosed Lansdowne to Macdonald, 30 May 1886; vol. 40, Lord Granville to Lord Lansdowne, 24 June 1886 (copy), Lord Lansdowne to Lord Granville, 26 June 1886 telegram (copy)

22 *New York Tribune*, 6 Aug. 1886; also 6 Sept. 1886, and 12 Oct. 1886; see Candow, 'Fisheries Dispute,' 50–1.

23 *New York Tribune*, 1 Sept. 1887; Candow, 'Fisheries Dispute,' 91

24 Sir Charles Tupper, *Recollections of Sixty Years in Canada* (London 1914), 176–8

25 W.C. Ford, in *The Forum* (New York), Oct. 1886, pp. 174–81, makes this point.

26 *Grip* (Toronto) 12 July 1877

27 JSDT, vol. 63, Macdonald to Thompson, 2 Dec. 1877; PAC, Sir James Gowan Papers, Macdonald to Gowan, 19 Oct. 1887 (private)

28 Willoughby Maycock, *With Mr. Chamberlain in the United States and Canada* (Toronto 1914), 6–7

29 JSDT, vol. 290, Thompson to Annie, 19 Oct. 1887

30 Macdonald Papers, vol. 527, Macdonald to Lord Lansdowne, 18 Oct. 1887; it is also quoted in Brown, *Canada's National Policy*, 61.

31 Lansdowne Papers, Macdonald to Lansdowne, 14 Sept. 1887

32 JSDT, vol. 290, Thompson to Annie, 14, 19 Oct. 1887

33 See Macdonald Papers, vol. 273, Thompson to Macdonald, 12 July 1886, on a recent despatch of Bayard on the *Adams* case, and also the Thompson memorandum on the Phelps letter to Granville, mentioned in footnote 21.

34 JSDT, vol. 290, Thompson to Annie, 21 Oct., 2 Nov. 1887

35 Ibid., Supp. vol., Thompson to Annie, 26 Oct. 1887

36 Ibid., vol. 290, Thompson to Annie, 18 Nov. 1887

37 Ibid., Thompson to Annie, 20 Nov. 1887

38 Ibid., Thompson to Annie, 19 Nov. 1887; vol. 63, Martin Griffin to Thompson, 2 Dec. 1887. There is a portrait of Frances Folsom Cleveland in Maycock, *With Mr. Chamberlain*, 34.

39 JSDT, vol. 290, Thompson to Annie, 20, 25 Nov. 1887

40 University of British Columbia Archives, Sir Charles Hibbert Tupper Papers, Tupper to Macdonald, 7 Mar. 1890, from Washington, reporting conversation with T.F. Bayard. As to Sackville-West's performance in 1887–8, see Maycock, *With Mr. Chamberlain*, 34.

41 JSDT, vol. 290, Thompson to Annie, 21 Nov. 1887

42 Baedeker's *United States* for 1904 gives the essentials of Washington geography. The Arlington Hotel was on Vermont Street, a quarter of a mile from the White House and the State Department building.

43 Maycock, *With Mr. Chamberlain*, 63; Macdonald Papers, vol. 180, Tupper to Macdonald, 24 Nov. 1887 (copy)

44 JSDT, vol. 290, Thompson to Annie, 23, 25, 26 Nov. 1887

45 Ibid., Thompson to Annie, 28 Nov., 4 Dec. 1887

46 Ibid., vol. 122, J.H. Choate to Sir Charles Tupper, 12 Feb. 1891 from New

York (the firm of Evarts, Choate and Beaman of 52 Wall Street); Tupper to Choate, 16 Feb. 1891, from Toronto (in Sir Charles's hand), vol. 126, W.M. Evarts to Tupper, 4, 7 Apr. 1891. The incident also got into the New York papers; see the New York *Morning Journal*, 6 Feb. 1891.

47 Macdonald Papers, vol. 176, Thompson to Macdonald, 28 Nov. 1887
48 Ibid., f. 73666
49 Ibid., vol. 180, Tupper to Macdonald, 30 Nov. 1887
50 JSDT, vol. 290, 2, 7 Dec. 1887
51 Brown, *Canada's National Policy*, 71–2. Chamberlain and Tupper both took credit for this suggestion; it seems more likely that Chamberlain's claim is correct.
52 JSDT, vol. 290, Thompson to Annie, 11, 12, 14, 15 Dec. 1887
53 Ibid., vol. 63, Macdonald to Thompson, 24 Dec. 1887 (telegram); ibid., vol. 290, Thompson to Annie, 20, 29 Dec. 1887
54 Ibid., Thompson to Annie, 29 Dec. 1887; 2, 3, 4 Jan. 1888
55 University of Birmingham Library, Chamberlain Papers, Salisbury to Chamberlain, 31 Dec. 1887, cited in Brown, *Canada's National Policy*, 73
56 Macdonald Papers, vol. 180, Tupper to Macdonald, 19, 22 Jan. 1888
57 JSDT, vol. 290, Thompson to Annie, 16 Jan. 1888, from Washington
58 Macdonald Papers, vol. 176, Thompson to Macdonald, 12 Jan. 1888 (confidential)
59 JSDT, vol. 290, Thompson to Annie, 25 Jan. 1888
60 For discussion of the Bering Sea question, see ch. 16, especially pp. 276–7.
61 Macdonald Papers, vol. 176, Thompson to Macdonald, 25 Jan. 1888; Thompson to Macdonald, 26 Jan. 1888 (telegram); Macdonald to Tupper, 28 Jan. 1888 (draft telegram)
62 JSDT, vol. 290, Thompson to Annie, 14, 26 Jan. 1888
63 Ibid., 14, 22 Jan. 1888
64 Ibid., Thompson to Annie, 24, 25, 26 Jan., 2 Feb. 1888
65 This occurs in *The Eustace Diamonds* (1873), ch. 28, 'Mr. Dove in his chambers.' Trollope was not, incidentally, a lawyer himself.
66 Macdonald Papers, vol. 176, Thompson to Macdonald, 11 Feb. 1888 (private)
67 JSDT, vol. 67, Putnam to Thompson, 16 Mar. 1888 (personal)
68 *House of Commons Debates* (10 Apr. 1888), pp. 704–5; ibid., (17 Apr. 1888), p. 889; *St. John Telegraph*, 27 Feb. 1888, cited in Brown, *Canada's National Policy*, 85–6
69 Ibid., 81
70 *Case and Comment* (New York), xxix, 4 (Autumn 1923), 99. J.W. Davis (1873–1955) was solicitor general in Woodrow Wilson's administration, 1913–18, and was then ambassador to Great Britain, 1918–21.

71 JSDT, vol. 238, Thompson to Dr. J.B. Angell, 6 May 1889
72 PAC, Tupper Papers, vol. 29, Chamberlain to Tupper, 2 Apr. 1888 (secret); Thompson to Tupper, 3 Sept. 1888
73 JSDT, vol. 74, Salisbury to Thompson, 7 Aug. 1888 (telegram): Macdonald to Thompson, 27 Aug. 1888 (telegram); ibid., vol. 290, Thompson to Annie, 31 Aug. 1888
74 Ibid., Thompson to Annie, 28, 31 Aug. 1888. There is a vast sheaf of congratulatory telegrams in vol. 74. See also Ottawa *Citizen*, 28 Aug. 1888, Toronto *Empire*, same date, and other papers; *Halifax Herald*, 29 Aug. 1888; *Renfrew Journal*, 30 Aug. 1888.
75 PANS, John Allison Bell Diaries, Wednesday, 22 Aug. 1888, p. 269
76 JSDT, vol. 298, Thompson to John, 22 Sept. 1888

14 OVERSEER OF PROVINCIAL LAW: THOMPSON AND DISALLOWANCE

1 JSDT, vol. 290, Thompson to Annie 27 Jan. 1888; Thompson to Annie, 2 Feb. 1888. In 1889 Thompson indicated to a possible purchaser that he did not really want to sell Willow Park, but might consider doing so if he were offered $9,000. In 1895 it was appraised at $5,000.
2 Thompson's rented houses in Ottawa were as follows:
   1 Nov. 1887 to 31 Oct. 1888, 277 Cooper Street;
   1 Nov. 1888 to 30 June 1889, 215 Metcalfe Street;
   1 July 1889 to 1 Nov. 1892, 181 Lisgar Street;
   1 Nov. 1892 to Mar. 1895, 276 Somerset Street.
3 Sara Jeanette Duncan in *The Week*, 10 May 1888, 'Ottawa Letter'
4 JSDT, vol. 290, Thompson to Annie, 24 Oct. 1887; ibid., vol. 298, Thompson to John and Joe, 31 Mar., 21 May 1888
5 Ibid., vol. 61, Macdonald to Thompson, 18 Oct. 1887 (private)
6 More detail on the history of this question is given in Waite, *Canada 1874–1896*, 205–8.
7 *Canada, House of Commons Debates* (26 Apr. 1888), p. 1003
8 PAC, Macdonald Papers, vol. 296, L. Pereira to Joseph Pope, 20 Apr. 1888 (private); JSDT, vol. 70, Fr. W. Daly to Thompson, 2 May 1888, from Windsor, NS.; Sara Jeanette Duncan in *The Week*, 26 Apr. 1888, 'Ottawa Letter'
9 Ottawa *Free Press*, 5 May 1888
10 JSDT, vol. 70, G.W. Burbidge to Thompson, 8 May 1888 (private) from Quebec; Lachlan Cameron to Thompson, 14 May 1888, from South River, Antigonish Co.
11 Ibid., vol. 92, Purcell to Thompson, 25 Sept. 1889, from Port Mulgrave
12 Ibid., vol. 72, Bishop Cameron to Thompson, 27 June 1888

13 Ibid., vol. 71, J.F. Stairs to Thompson, 16 May 1888 (confidential); PAC, Tupper Papers, vol. 8, Martin Griffin to Tupper, 25 July 1888

14 Macdonald Papers, vol. 273, Thompson to Macdonald, 20 Aug. 1888 (private) from Ottawa; JSDT, vol. 82, Graham to Thompson, 6 Mar. 1889, from Halifax; vol. 113, Barker to Thompson, 16 Sept. 1890, from Saint John. The New Brunswick judges canvassed thus by Thompson were: G.E. King (1839–1904); J.J. Fraser (1829–96); A.L. Palmer (1820–99). Two Ontario judges that were candidates were G.W. Burton (1818–1901), C.S. Patterson (1823–93), both of the Ontario Court of Appeal. Macdonald, for some reason, was uneasy about both these two candidates. JSDT, vol. 76, D'Alton McCarthy to Macdonald, 9 Oct. 1888 (private). Minute, Macdonald to Thompson, 'Neither Burton nor Patterson would be safe I think.'

15 Ibid., vol. 80, Palmer to Macdonald, 24 Jan. 1889, endorsed over to Thompson. The ancient enmity lay between Palmer and Sir Albert J. Smith. Sir W.J. Ritchie considered himself the latter's protector.

16 Ibid., supp. vol. Thompson to Annie, 3 July 1888

17 Ibid., vol. 297, Thompson to Joe, 22 Oct. 1888

18 Ibid., Thompson to Joe, 27 Aug. 1888; supp. vol., Bishop Cameron to Annie, 4 Mar. 1895

19 Ibid., vol. 298, Annie to John, 29 Nov. 1885, from Halifax

20 Ibid., vol. 297, Thompson to Joe, 10, 17 Dec. 1888; 25 Feb., 15 Apr. 1889

21 Ibid., vol. 236, Desbarats to Thompson, 5 Sept. 1888; ibid., vol. 238, Thompson to W.B. Harte, 2 Apr. 1889; Thompson to Wm. Smith, 12 Apr. 1889

22 *House of Commons Debates* (21 May 1888), p. 1658

23 See Waite, *Canada 1874–1896*, 197–8

24 Macdonald Papers, vol. 273, Thompson to Macdonald, 15 Nov. 1888

25 The text of this letter is in W.E. Hodgins, ed., *Correspondence, Reports of the Ministers of Justice and Orders in Council upon the Subject of Dominion and Provincial Legislation, 1867–1895* (Ottawa 1896), 61–2.

26 See *supra*, p. 185. The first edition appeared in 1886, the second in 1896.

27 For a brief review, see G.V. La Forest, *Disallowance and Reservation of Provincial Legislation* (Ottawa 1955), 36–43. Appendix A gives a table of disallowed statutes from 1867 to 1954.

28 Hodgins, *Dominion and Provincial Legislation*, 206. See *infra*, p. 345.

29 Macdonald Papers, vol. 275, Thompson to Macdonald, 15 July 1889

30 DJ Records, RG 13, A3, vol. 636, f. 587, Thompson to Governor General in Council, 1 June 1889. He reduced the sentence from eight years to six.

31 The Nova Scotia act was 49 Vic. c.56; the British Columbia, 50 Vic. c.27; the Manitoba, 53 Vic. c.31.

32 Thompson to Governor-General in Council, 28 Mar. 1887, in Hodgins, *Dominion and Provincial Legislation*, 314–15

33 Macdonald to Governor-General in Council, 2 Jan. 1873, on British Columbia, 35 Vic. c.35, in Hodgins, *Dominion and Provincial Legislation*, 1015

34 Thompson to Mowat, 4 Feb. 1889, in Hodgins, *Dominion and Provincial Legislation*, 2067–7

35 *Attorney General for Canada v. Attorney General of Ontario*, 20 *Ontario Reports*, 222; 23 *SCR* 458 (1894)

36 JSDT, vol. 73, Macdonald to Thompson, 18 July 1888 (private) from Dalhousie, NB.; Macdonald to Thompson, 21 July 1888 (private) from Dalhousie. It was disallowed 7 Sept. 1888. See Hodgins, *Dominion and Provincial Legislation*, 345.

37 PAM, Schultz Papers, Macdonald to Schultz, 8 Oct. 1888 (private)

38 Report to Governor-General in Council, 18 Jan. 1889, in Hodgins, *Dominion and Provincial Legislation*, 357–8, 360

39 See the excellent chapter in J.T. Saywell, *The Office of Lieutenant-Governor* (Toronto 1957), 192–227. La Forest in *Disallowance and Reservation of Provincial Legislation* gives a table of bills reserved in Appendix B, pp. 102–15.

40 Macdonald Papers, vol. 186, Thompson to Macdonald, 2 Feb. 1889. This correspondence is cited in Saywell, *Office of Lieutenant-Governor*, 204–5.

41 *La Minerve* is cited without date in R. Rumilly, *Histoire de Québec* (Montréal, n.d.), VI, *Les Nationaux*, 94. Irreverence because it is a play on two meanings of *cour*, a court and a courtyard. With the hyphen, *basse-cour* is a cul-de-sac, or something more like a robbers' roost.

42 Macdonald Papers, vol. 275, Desjardins to Thompson, 9 July 1889 (confidential), from Montreal

43 Ibid., Thompson to Desjardins, 10 July 1889 (personal); Thompson to Desjardins, 10 July 1889 (confidential). The personal letter could be shown to Mercier; the confidential one was for Desjardins alone. These letters were all copied for Sir John Macdonald. The original of the 10 July personal letter is in the Fonds Desjardins, Jesuit Archives, St Hippolyte, Quebec, file 5241/35.

44 DJ Records, RG 13, A3, vol. 639, ff. 57–59, Sedgewick to C.H. Tupper, 4 Jan. 1890

45 Thompson to Governor General in Council, 31 May 1890, in Hodgins, *Dominion and Provincial Legislation*, 753. The immediate context was a New Brunswick statute of 1889, c. 23; Thompson questioned whether s. 4, allowing the New Brunswick Executive Council to appoint justices of the peace, was constitutional. The act was not, however, disallowed.

46 The history of this question can be best studied in two books: R.C. Dalton, *The Jesuits' Estates Question 1760–1888: A Study of the Background for the Agitation of 1889* (Toronto 1968); and J.R. Miller, *Equal Rights: The Jesuits' Estates Act Controversy* (Montreal 1979). There is a short account in *Canada 1874–1896*, 209–13.

47 D.L. Kinzer, *An Episode in Anti-Catholicism: The American Protestive Association* (Seattle 1964), 21

48 John Higham, *Strangers in the Land: Patterns of American Nativism* (New Brunswick NJ, 1955), 138

49 Willoughby Maycock, *With Mr. Chamberlain in America* (London 1914), 104

50 John Ruskin, *Sesame and Lilies* (London, 1905), 66

51 *Grip* (Toronto) 6 Apr. 1889. It is reproduced in Miller, *Equal Rights*, 185.

52 *Brossard et al.* v. *Langevin*, 1 *SCR*, 145, on appeal from a decision of Judge Routhier, at La Malbaie

53 See *Derouin* v. *Archambault*, reported in *Lower Canada Jurist*, XIX (1875), 157; *Vigneux* v. *Noiseux*, reported in ibid., XXI (1877), 91.

54 R. Rumilly, *Honoré Mercier et son temps*, 2 vols. (Montréal 1975) II, 95

55 *Toronto Daily Mail*, 12 June 1889; Miller, *Equal Rights*, 99

56 *Toronto Daily Mail*, 13 July 1889; see Miller, *Equal Rights*, 108.

57 Ottawa *Citizen*, 13 Dec. 1889, reporting McCarthy's speech of 12 Dec. This speech was also published as a pamphlet and can be found in the Macdonald Papers, vol. 148.

58 Most of this came from Professor E.A. Freeman (1823–92) whom McCarthy quotes, in *House of Commons Debates* (22 Jan. 1890), p. 42. See also J.R. Miller, '"As a Politician He Is a Great Enigma;" The Social and Political Ideas of D'Alton McCarthy,' *CHR*, LVIII, 4 (Dec. 1977), 411.

59 JSDT, vol. 78, McCarthy to Thompson, 13 Dec. 1888. The decision in *St. Catherines Milling & Lumber Co.* v. *the Queen* had been given the day before.

60 Sir John Willison, *Reminiscences, Political and Personal* (Toronto 1919), 140–1; Miller, *Equal Rights*, 67

61 *House of Commons Debates* (27 Mar. 1889), p. 842 *et seq.*

62 Ibid., p. 859 *et seq.*

63 Ibid., pp. 868–9

64 JSDT, vol. 83, Griffin to Thompson, 28 Mar. 1889, reporting conversation with Wallis, Ottawa correspondent of the *Toronto Daily Mail*

65 Macdonald Papers, vol. 529, Macdonald to McLelan, 4 July 1889 (private and confidential); vol. 232, McLelan to Macdonald, 29 June 1889, from Halifax

66 *House of Commons Debates* (28 Mar. 1889), pp. 874, 898

67 *L'Etendard* (Montreal) 30 mars 1889. *L'Etendard* was generally regarded as

spokesman for the ultramontane position. It was owned and edited by Senator F.-X. Trudel to whom, incidentally, Thompson sent a brief note thanking him for the kind words. JSDT, vol. 238, Thompson to Trudel, 2 Apr. 1889

68 JSDT, vol. 298, Thompson to John and Joe, 6 May 1889

69 The poem is quoted by Miller, *Equal Rights*, 91.

70 JSDT, vol. 83, Gowan to Thompson, 28 Mar. 1889; vol. 84, Gowan to Thompson, 4 Apr. 1889 (private), from Barrie; vol. 86, Gowan to Thompson, 17 May 1889, from London; PAC, Sir James Gowan Papers, Thompson to Gowan, 30 May 1889

71 JSDT, vol. 90, Macdonald to Thompson, 2, 4 July 1889 (private) from Rivière du Loup. This letter is superscribed, 'Written in a great hurry;' vol. 91, Sedgewick to Thompson, 12 Aug. 1889, from Ottawa; Macdonald to Thompson, 14 Aug. 1889, from Rivière du Loup; Hodgins, *Dominion and Provincial Legislation*, 420–7. Graham's cheque was returned.

72 Hector Charlesworth, *Candid Chronicles: Leaves from the Notebook of a Canadian Journalist* (Toronto 1925), 108, who had it as the 'inside story' from a Roman Catholic journalist

73 See Tardivel's *La Vérité*, 20 avril 1889; *La Patrie*, 19 déc. 1889, both cited in Pierre Savard, *Jules-Paul Tardivel, la France et les États-Unis 1851–1905* (Québec 1967), 199.

74 Macdonald Papers, vol. 275, Thompson to Macdonald, 3 Aug. 1889, from Rimouski

75 Hopkins, *Thompson*, 142–3; JSDT, vol. 91, Macdonald to Thompson, 14 Aug. 1889 (private) from Rivière du Loup

76 Macdonald Papers, vol. 275, Thompson to Macdonald, 11 Aug. 1889, from Halifax

77 Ibid., vol. 208, D. Creighton to Macdonald, 11 Oct. 1889 (private)

78 Quoted by R.J. Gabel, *Public Funds for Church and Private Schools* (Washington 1937), 487

15 DRAGON'S TEETH

1 JSDT, vol. 89, Macdonald to Thompson, 4 July 1889 (private and confidential) from Rivière du Loup

2 PAC, Tupper Papers, vol. 7, Sir Charles Tupper to C.H. Tupper, 17 June 1888, from London

3 JSDT, vol. 72, Macdonald to Thompson, 13 June [1888] (private)

4 Ibid., vol. 89, Macdonald to Thompson, 4 July 1889 (private and confidential) from Rivière du Loup; PAC, Macdonald Papers, vol. 275, Thompson to

Macdonald, 11 July 1889 (private) from Ottawa; also another of this same date, not so marked

5 JSDT, vol. 89, Macdonald to Thompson, 4 July 1889 (private and confidential) from Rivière du Loup

6 Macdonald Papers, vol. 275, Thompson to Macdonald, 11 July 1889. There were three letters to Macdonald of this date; this letter has a subhead, 'American relations.' It is nine pages long, all written in Thompson's hand, from Ottawa.

7 JSDT, vol. 90, Macdonald to Thompson, 25 July 1889 (private) from Rivière du Loup

8 Macdonald Papers, vol. 275, Thompson to Macdonald, 27 July 1889, from Ottawa

9 JSDT, vol. 90, H.F. McDougall to Thompson, 26 July 1889 (private) from Grand Narrows; Macdonald Papers, vol. 275, Thompson to Macdonald, 27 July 1889, from Ottawa; 11 Aug. 1889, from Halifax; JSDT, vol. 91, C.C. Gregory to Thompson, 23 Aug. 1889, from Antigonish

10 JSDT, vol. 92, S.E. Dawson to Thompson, 28 Sept. 1889, from Montreal

11 Archibald MacMechan, 'A City by the Sea,' *The Week*, 3 Jan. 1890, pp. 75–6

12 JSDT, vol. 297, Annie to John and Joe, 27 Oct. 1890

13 Halifax *Morning Herald*, 7 Oct. 1889; T.W. Acheson, 'The National Policy and the Industrialization of the Maritimes, 1880–1910,' *Acadiensis*, I, 2 (Spring 1972), 3n

14 Halifax *Herald*, 7 Oct. 1889

15 *The Week*, 10 Jan. 1890, criticizing the Winnipeg *Free Press*'s distortion of *The Week*'s position on separate schools

16 JSDT, vol. 93, Charles Annand to Thompson, 11 Oct. 1889 (private and confidential)

17 Ibid., Griffin to Thompson, 9 Oct. 1889. Translation: 'How long, Cataline, will you continue to abuse our patience?'

18 M.R. Lupul, *The Roman Catholic Church and the North-West School Question: A Study in Church-State Relations in Western Canada 1875–1905* (Toronto 1974), 35

19 *Qu'Appelle Vidette*, 8 Dec. 1887, 19 July 1888, cited in ibid., 42

20 *La Minerve*, 25 Sept. 1888, reporting Thompson's speech of 24 Sept. Two days later *La Minerve* reported a Conservative victory, 3,829 to 3,144, which it called a majority 'écrasante.' Perhaps it can be pointed out that in thirteen Dominion by-elections held in Quebec between 1886 and 1890, the Conservatives held six seats and won two seats from the Liberals while losing one to them. The Liberals held four others.

21 Archiepiscopal Archives of St Boniface (AASt.B), Thompson to Taché, 5 Oct. 1888

22 Ibid., Taché to Thompson, 12 Oct. 1888 (draft)

23 Ibid., Taché to Thompson, 24 Nov. 1888 (draft)

24 Ibid.

25 W.E. Hodgins, ed., *Correspondence, Reports of the Ministers of Justice and Orders in Council upon the Subject of Dominion and Provincial Legislation 1867–1895* (Ottawa 1896), 1249–51, Thompson to Governor-General in Council, 10 Jan. 1890

26 Lupul, *Roman Catholic Church and the North-West*, 54. The motion for deleting French language was not exactly carried seventeen to two; an attempt by Rouleau to move the six months' hoist was defeated by that majority.

27 *Montreal Daily Star*, 19, 22 Feb. 1890

28 *Canada, House of Commons Debates* (22 Jan. 1890), cols. 50–51; ibid. (18 Feb. 1890), col. 838

29 Ibid., cols. 879–82

30 Ibid., (21 Feb. 1890), cols. 1017–18

31 Ibid., (20 Feb. 1890), col. 895

32 *The Week*, 31 Jan. 1890. Edward Blake said much the same in the debates. The *Montreal Daily Star*, 21 Feb. 1890, put a rather different gloss on the same idea: 'The surest way to perpetuate the dual language system is for the English to be continually wounding the sensitiveness of the French on this subject.'

33 PAC, J.R. Gowan Papers, Macdonald to Gowan, 10 July 1890, from Rivière du Loup

34 Macdonald Papers, vol. 335, Aikens to Macdonald, 12 Mar. 1890 (private)

35 *Brandon Mail*, 11, 18 July 1889, in D.J. Hall, *Clifford Sifton*, I (Vancouver 1981), 43

36 Macdonald Papers, vol. 275, Thompson to Macdonald, 18 Dec. 1889, enclosing Schultz to Macdonald 9 Dec. 1889 (confidential). The Schultz letter is found in Macdonald Papers, vol. 264.

37 *House of Commons, Debates* (29 Apr. 1890), cols. 4086–94

38 'An Act to authorize companies incorporated out of this province to transact business therein,' and an 'Act respecting diseases of animals' where there were clear conflicts with existing federal law. See Hodgins, *Dominion and Provincial Legislation*, 941–5, 946–7.

39 Not altogether without warrant. Martin resigned in March 1890, apparently with the intention of forcing Greenway out. Greenway hoped to get Sifton or someone else as attorney general, couldn't, and was forced to take Martin

back again. Macdonald Papers, vol. 264, Schultz to Macdonald, 31 Mar. 1890 (private); same, 9 Apr. 1890 (confidential)

40 Ibid., Schultz to Macdonald, 15 Apr. 1890 (private)

41 *United States* v. *Northern Securities Co.* (1904). Holmes was here entering a dissent against the majority judgment.

42 JSDT, vol. 103, N. Cherrier to Macdonald, 10 Mar. 1890. It is endorsed, Macdonald to Thompson, 13 Mar. 1890 (private): 'For Sir John Thompson's consideration.'

43 Ibid., Cherrier to Macdonald, 12 Mar. 1890

44 Ibid., vol. 106, Cherrier to Macdonald, 21 Apr. 1890 (private)

45 AASt.B, Taché to Thompson, 6 May 1890 (draft)

46 Thompson's point was really that in New Brunswick Roman Catholics had the rights that they had 'by law' before the union: in Manitoba, by virtue of s. 22 of the Manitoba Act of 1870, the Roman Catholics had the rights that they had 'by law or practice.' See Waite, *Canada 1874–1896*, 41, 248.

47 AASt.B, Thompson to Taché, 17 May 1890, from Montreal. This important letter is written in Thompson's secretary's hand, but is corrected by, and signed by, Thompson. It is also in his letterbooks. JSDT, vol. 245.

48 Ibid., Thompson to J.J.C. Abbott, 6 Nov. 1890, refers to a meeting of it in six days' time.

49 *House of Commons, Debates* (25 Feb. 1890), col. 1088. See also *Montreal Daily Star*, 24 Jan. 1890.

50 *House of Commons Debates* (10 Apr. 1890), cols. 3162–3

51 Ibid., (4 May 1886), col. 620. There is a brief account in *Canada 1874–1896*, p. 218; a much more comprehensive account is in P. Baskerville, 'J.C. Rykert and the Conservative Party 1882–92: Study of a Scandal,' *CHR*, LII, 2 (June 1971) 144–64.

52 *House of Commons Debates* (11 Feb. 1890), col. 450

53 Ibid. (11 March 1890) col. 1713

54 JSDT, vol. 103, Rykert to Thompson, 10 Mar. 1890

55 Griffin found one in British *Parliamentary Journals* for 1806. Ibid., vol. 103, Griffin to Thompson, 9 Mar. 1890

56 See Waite, *Canada 1874–1896*, 220.

57 *House of Commons, Debates* (17 Mar. 1890), col. 2095

58 JSDT, vol. 103, Rykert to Thompson, 14 Mar. 1890 (telegram) from St Catharines

59 Ibid., vol. 105, Girouard to Thompson, 11 Apr. 1890; Toronto *Empire*, 11 Apr. 1890, report from Ottawa of April 10

60 JSDT, vol. 106, Laidlaw to Thompson, 28 Apr. 1890

61 *House of Commons, Journals, 1890*, Appendix 4, p. xxix

62 Ibid., p. xxxiv; Toronto *Globe*, 3, 5 May 1890

63 JSDT, vol. 103, C.H. Tupper to Thompson, 13 Mar. 1890 from Washington
64 British Library, Additional MSS. 43637, Ripon Papers, Thompson to Ripon, 17 Aug. 1893, from Liverpool
65 JSDT, vol. 223, J.R. Robertson to Thompson, 25 Oct. 1894, from Toronto
66 Macdonald Papers, vol. 332, S.E. Dawson to John Lowe, Deputy Minister of Agriculture, 22 Sept. 1888 [should be 1889] (copy)
67 S.E. Dawson, *Copyright in Books: an Inquiry into its Origin, and an Account of the Present State of the Law in Canada* (Montreal 1882), 36–37; for the British side, F.R. Daldy, *The Colonial Copyright Acts* (London 1889), JSDT, vol. 282 contain a number of these pamphlets. A recent article on this subject is R.A. Shields, 'Imperial Policy and the Canadian Copyright Act of 1889,' *Dalhousie Review*, LX, 4 (Winter 1980–1), 634–58.
68 Macdonald Papers, vol. 332, Sir John Thompson's Memorandum for Sir John Macdonald, dated 26 Sept. 1889; also ibid., printed memorial of the Copyright Association of Canada, f. 150069
69 Ibid., Sir John Thompson's memorandum, p. 6 (f. 150091)
70 Hector Charlesworth, *Candid Chronicles: Leaves from the Notebook of a Canadian journalist* (Toronto 1925), 110. Hunter, Rose, it can be added, also proved rather leaky in a more famous incident in 1891.
71 Sir John Thompson's Memorandum, p. 7 (f. 150092)
72 Toronto *Evening Telegram*, 17 Aug. 1888
73 *House of Commons Debates* (20 Apr. 1889), pp. 1399–1400
74 4 *New South Wales Law Reports* (1883) 167
75 *Appeal Cases before the House of Lords and the Judicial Committee of the Privy Council*, x, 290
76 Ibid., x., 281
77 Ibid., x., 678
78 CO 42, vol, 800, Minute of 26 Sept. 1889 on a Thompson memorandum of 3 Aug. 1889. Also cited in Shields, 'Imperial Policy,' 638.
79 Macdonald Papers, vol. 332, S.E. Dawson to J. Lowe, 28 Sept. 23, 1888 [1889?] (copy)
80 PAC, Sir Charles Tupper Papers, vol. 9, Macdonald to Tupper, 5 June 1890 (private and confidential); same, 23 June 1890

16 THOMPSON'S CANADIAN DIPLOMACY

1 JSDT, vol. 297, Thompson to Babe, 5 July 1890
2 University of British Columbia Archives, Sir Charles Hibbert Tupper Papers, Thompson to C.H. Tupper, 11 July 1890 (private)

3 PAC, Macdonald Papers, vol. 275, Thompson to Macdonald, 11 July 1890; ibid., second letter, written in the afternoon of the same day
4 Brian L. Blakeley, *The Colonial Office 1868–1892* (Durham 1972), 157–8, citing Viscount Knutsford, *In Black and White* (London 1926) 211–12
5 PAC, Bowell Papers, vol. 8, Thompson to Bowell, 15 July 1890 (private) from London
6 Macdonald Papers, vol. 275, Thompson to Macdonald, 15 July 1890
7 Bowell Papers, vol. 8, Thompson to Bowell, 15 July 1890 (private)
8 APQ, Collection Chapais, Boîte 3, Langevin to Edmond Langevin, 17, 19 juin 1879
9 PAC, Caron Papers, vol. 194, Thompson to Caron, 29 July 1890 (private)
10 JSDT, vol. 297, Thompson to Helena, 17 July 1890, from London
11 Caron Papers, vol. 194, Thompson to Caron, 29 July 1890 (private)
12 JSDT, vol. 111, Knutsford to Thompson, 23 July [1890]
13 Ibid., vol. 273, Thompson to Macdonald, 25 July 1890; it is also in Macdonald Papers, vol. 275.
14 Ibid.
15 Macdonald Papers, vol. 275, Thompson to Macdonald, 4 Aug. 1890
16 R.B. Mowat, *The Life of Lord Pauncefote* (London 1929), 141–4
17 Such is the tone of Blaine's despatch to Pauncefote, 22 Jan. 1890, in *Foreign Relations of the United States, 1890*, 368.
18 Ibid., Blaine to Pauncefote, 29 May 1890, p. 420
19 F.F. Thompson, *The French Shore Question in Newfoundland* (Toronto 1961), 91, 113
20 JSDT, vol. 297, Thompson to Babe, 10 Aug. 1890
21 PAC, Stanley Papers, microfilm A 446, Macdonald to Stanley, 25 Aug. 1890 (private)
22 JSDT, vol. 297, Thompson to Babe, 22 Sept. 3 Nov. 1890
23 Ibid., vol. 291, Thompson to Annie, 11 Oct. 1890, from Antigonish
24 Ibid., vol. 298, Annie to John and Joe, 1, 14 Oct. 1890
25 Ibid., vol. 112, Tupper to Thompson, 2 Sept. 1890
26 R.M.F. Deering, 'The Federal Election of 1891 in Nova Scotia' (MA thesis, Dalhousie University, 1967), 10–11
27 Halifax *Morning Herald*, 2 Oct. 1890
28 Ibid., vol. 298, Thompson to John, 13 Nov. 1890. John did not go to either, but came to Toronto to begin law.
29 Ibid., vol. 115, Langevin to Thompson, 22 Oct. 1890; Aberdeen to Thompson, 20 Oct. 1890 (telegram) from Winnipeg
30 K. Tynan, *The Years of the Shadow* (New York 1919), 107
31 Marjorie Pentland, *A Bonnie Fechter* (London 1952), 110

32 Stanley Papers, microfilm A 673, Sir Julian Pauncefote to Lord Stanley, 27 Mar. 1891 (private). The terms were: US right to purchase bait; in return, free admission into the United States of cod, salmon, herring, lobster; the arrangement to run for ten years.

33 JSDT, vol. 115, Thompson to Tupper, 27 Oct. 1890 (draft cable in Thompson's handwriting)

34 Stanley Papers, Macdonald to Stanley, 17 Nov. 1890

35 JSDT, vol. 118, Morine to Thompson, 4 Dec. 1890 (confidential), from Halifax

36 S.J.R. Noel, *Politics in Newfoundland* (Toronto 1971), 37, citing T. Dennett, *John Hay* (New York 1933), 423

37 JSDT, vol. 246, Thompson to Morine, 18 Dec. 1890 (private)

38 Ibid., vol. 118, Morine to Thompson, 4 Dec. 1890 (confidential)

39 Ibid., vol. 119, Macdonald to Thompson, 17 Dec. 1890: 'I really think the Govt ought to help Morine. A small sum will do and some means ought to be found to do so. We ought to have a Secret Service fund[.] Mention this in Council.'

40 Ibid., vol. 118, Macdonald to Thompson, 8 Dec. 1890, enclosing Stanley to Macdonald, same date, in turn enclosing Pauncefote to Stanley, 7 Dec. 1890 (telegram). Blaine's suggestion was made about 7 Dec. in an interview with Pauncefote. Blaine wanted private discussions first. See also R.C. Brown, *Canada's National Policy* (Princeton 1967), 200–203.

41 This is reported in a long article on Thompson by Arnott Magurn, the Ottawa correspondent of the Toronto *Globe*, in the *Globe*, Saturday, 10 Dec. 1892. A letter from Macdonald to Stanley, 26 Jan. 1891 only partly confirms the *Globe*; Thompson denied however the gist of the *Globe*'s assertion. Stanley Papers, Thompson to Lord Stanley, 13 Dec. 1892

42 Brown, *Canada's National Policy*, 201

43 Ibid., 195

44 J.W. Foster, *Diplomatic Memoirs* (Boston 1909), 2 vols., I, 178. Foster succeeded Blaine as secretary of state when Blaine resigned because of ill health in June 1892.

45 Waite, *Canada, 1874–1896*, 223

46 See Blaine's *Twenty Years of Congress* (Norwich 1888), 2 vols., II, ch. 27. See also Blaine's remarkable letter to President Harrison of September 1891, cited in Alice Felt Tyler, *The Foreign Policy of James G. Blaine* (Minneapolis 1927), 351.

47 JSDT, vol. 247, Thompson to Macdonald, 28 Jan. 1891 (draft telegram)

48 Ibid., vol. 121, Stanley to Knutsford, 28 Jan. 1891 (draft telegram)

49 Ibid., vol. 122, Macdonald to Thompson 5 Feb. [1891]. The idea came from J.C. Patterson, MP Essex North, who was, incidentally, defeated in 1891.

50 Ibid., vol. 248, draft letter to the Maritime bishops, dated Halifax, 16 Feb. 1891. The Ontario bishops were: archbishops of Toronto, Kingston, and Ottawa; bishops of London, Hamilton, Peterborough, Alexandria, and Pontiac. The Maritime bishops were: Saint John, Bathurst, Yarmouth, Charlottetown, Antigonish, plus the archbishop of Halifax.

51 Ibid., vol. 123, Bishop Lorrain to Thompson, 25 Feb. 1891 (private)

52 Ibid., Bishop Macdonell to Thompson, 26 Feb. 1891

53 Ibid., vol. 119, C.H. Cahan to Thompson, 20 Dec. 1890; vol. 122, Cameron to Thompson, 3 Feb. 1891

54 Macdonald Papers, vol. 275, f. 125958, speech drafted in Thompson's hand

55 Ibid., Thompson to Macdonald, 18 Feb. 1891 (telegram)

56 PABC, O'Reilly Family Papers, Jane Dewdney to Mrs O'Reilly, 26 Feb., 4 Mar. [1891], from Ottawa. Mrs Jane Dewdney was the wife of Edgar Dewdney, minister of the interior, 1888–92.

57 JSDT, vol. 123, Angus A. McGillivray to Thompson, 22 Feb. 1891, from Dunnaglas, Antigonish County

58 Ibid., vol. 291, Thompson to Annie, 24 Feb., 1 Mar. 1891, from Antigonish

59 Ibid., Holmes to Thompson, 26 Feb. 1891, from Halifax

60 Ibid., vol. 124, L. deV. Chipman to Thompson, n.d. (private and confidential), from Kentville; vol. 125, same to same, 19 Mar. 1891 (private)

61 Ibid., vol. 124, Pope to Thompson, 1 Mar. 1891 (cipher telegram)

62 J.S. Willison, 'Reminiscences, Political and Otherwise,' in *Canadian Magazine*, LII, 6 (April 1919), 1,028

63 JSDT, vol. 126, W.C. Bill to Macdonald, Thompson and C.H. Tupper, 6 Apr. 1891 (confidential)

64 Ibid., vol. 124, F.J. Tremaine to Thompson, 18 Mar. 1891

65 Halifax *Morning Herald*, 2, 20 Feb. 1891

66 Ibid., 13 Feb. 1891

67 Ibid., 13 Mar. 1891

68 *Globe*, 9 Mar. 1891

69 JSDT, vol. 248, Thompson to Johnstone, 14 Mar. 1891

70 Ibid., vol. 248, Thompson to C.D. Randall, 30 Mar. 1891

71 Ibid., vol. 253, Thompson to W.R. Meredith, 29 Jan. 1892 (private)

72 *Canada, House of Commons Debates* (21 Sept. 1891), col. 5813, as reported by Israel Tarte

73 PAC, Angers Papers, Angers to Macdonald, 29 Dec. 1890 (confidential, copy); same, 22 Jan. 1891 (private and confidential, copy); Andrée Désilets, *Hector-*

Louis Langevin, un père de la confédération canadienne (1826–1906) (Quebec 1969), 392

74 JSDT, vol. 134, J.R. Gowan to Thompson, 12 Aug. 1891 (private), from Barrie

75 Ibid., vol. 126, Curran to Thompson, 10 Apr. 1891 (private), from Montreal, reporting events of the previous day

76 Ibid., vol. 249, Thompson to Osler, 21 or 22 May 1891, to North Bend, BC (draft telegram, private); vol. 29, Osler to Thompson, 24 May 1891 (private), from Vancouver

77 Ibid., vol. 128, Gowan to Thompson, 18 May 1891, from Barrie

78 The actual source of this quotation is J.D. Edgar, who got it from J.J.C. Abbott, reported by Edgar to his wife (PAO, Edgar Papers, Edgar to Matilda Edgar, 12 June 1891). Thompson also refers to this incident in his Hamilton speech of 1 Nov. 1893, when unveiling the statue of Macdonald. Toronto *Empire*, 2 Nov. 1893; also quoted in Joseph Pope, *Memoirs of the Right Honourable Sir John Alexander Macdonald* (Toronto 1930[?]), Appendix XXXI, 788])

79 JSDT, vol. 291, Thompson to Annie, 14 May 1891

80 Ibid., vol. 128, Boyd to Thompson, Thursday afternoon, n.d. [7 May 1891, from Montreal]

81 Ibid., vol. 291, Thompson to Annie, 22 May 1891. See also *House of Commons Debates* (21 May 1891), cols. 362–3

82 JSDT, vol. 291, Thompson to Annie, 20 May 1891

83 PAO, Edgar Papers, Edgar to his wife, Matilda, 14 June 1891; JSDT, vol. 291, Thompson to Annie, 29 May 1891

84 This story comes from C.H. Cahan, then editor of the Halifax *Herald*, who was staying in Ottawa at the time, and whom Thompson found at times 'painfully attentive.' Cahan told it to Willison (PAC, Willison Papers, C.H. Cahan to Willison, 4 Nov. 1918). See also J.T. Saywell, 'The Crown and the Politicians: the Canadian Succession Question, 1891–1895,' *CHR*, XXXVII, 4 (Dec. 1956), 310.

85 JSDT, vol. 129, R.W. Powell's Bulletin, endorsed Dewdney to Thompson, as of 6 a.m., Sunday, 31 May 1891

86 *Globe*, 15 June 1891

87 JSDT, vol. 291, Thompson to Annie, 31 May, 1, 2, and 4 June 1891

88 Ibid., vol. 130, T.C. Patteson to Thompson, 9 June 1891 (confidential)

89 R.S. White, 'Parliament and Personalities,' *Dalhousie Review*, XVI, 1 (1936–37). Robert Smeaton White (1855–1944) was the son of Thomas White, Macdonald's minister of the interior. R.S. White was MP for Cardwell, 1888–95.

90 *Montreal Daily Star*, 10 June 1891, special report to the *Star* from Ottawa, 9 June of an interview with Sir John Thompson

PART FOUR: BECOMING PRIME MINISTER, 1891–1894

17 THE WAGES OF THE MACDONALD ERA

1 JSDT, vol. 291, Thompson to Annie, 10 June 1891
2 PAC, Stanley Papers, A446, Stanley to Lord Salisbury, 4 June 1891 (very confidential); PAC, Sir Charles Tupper Papers, vol. 9, Lady Macdonald to Tupper, 24 July 1891
3 JSDT, vol. 291, Thompson to Annie, 9 June 1891
4 The precedent was cited by Laurier two weeks later in a debate on the delay. Thompson, despite his strong feelings about Lord Stanley's action at the time, played down Laurier's criticism. *Canada, House of Commons Debates* (22 June 1891), col. 1110
5 *Montreal Daily Star*, 10 June 1891; PAC, Laurier Papers, vol. 5, Stanley to Laurier, 9 June 1891
6 JSDT, vol. 130, W. Montague (MP for Haldimand) to G.E. Foster, 12 June 1891 (private), from Ottawa
7 Ibid., vol. 249, Thompson to J.J. Cameron, 8 June 1891 (private)
8 Thompson to Curran, 13 June 1891, in J.J. Curran, 'Reminiscences of Sir John Thompson,' in *Canadian Magazine*, XXVI, 13 (Jan. 1906), 220
9 JSDT, vol. 130, W.R. Meredith to C.H. Mackintosh, 12 June 1891 (private and confidential, copy)
10 *Montreal Daily Star*, 2 June 1891; Montreal *Gazette*, 12 June 1891, quoting Hamilton *Times*; Montreal *Gazette*, 25 June 1891, quoting Montreal *Witness*; Montreal *La Presse*, 25 juin 1891
11 JSDT, vol. 130, J.J. Curran to Thompson, 12 June 1891 (private and confidential), from Montreal
12 PAO, Edgar Papers, Edgar to his wife Matilda, 12 June 1891
13 JSDT, vol. 291, Thompson to Annie, 10 June 1891
14 PAO, Wallace Family Papers, Sam Hughes to Clarke Wallace, 30 May 1891, from Lindsay
15 Sir Charles Tupper Papers, vol. 23, Tupper to C.H. Tupper, 23 June 1891; vol. 17, Tupper to G.M. Grant, 20 Oct. 1891
16 JSDT, vol. 291, Thompson to Annie, 10 June 1891
17 *La Presse*, 13 juin 1891; Québec *l'Electeur*, 16 juin 1891
18 APQ, Collection Chapais, Langevin Papers, Boîte 9, Chapais to Langevin, 12 juin 1891, from Quebec
19 Stanley Papers, A673, Stanley to Langevin, 13 June 1891 (confidential). This letter appears to be the original. It is marked 'conveyed verbally.'
20 PAO, Edgar Papers, Edgar to his wife, 14 June 1891

21 *Canada, Senate Debates* (17 June 1891), p. 93. This was quoted by Thompson in the House of Commons. *Debates* (22 June 1891), col. 1118

22 Sir Charles Tupper Papers, vol. 9, MacMaster to Tupper, 14 Aug. 1891 (private)

23 PAO, Alexander Campbell Papers, Abbott to Campbell, 30 June 1891; PAM, Acton Burrows Papers, Hugh John Macdonald to Burrows, 4 June 1892 (private)

24 Maurice Pope, ed., *Public Servant: The Memoirs of Sir Joseph Pope* (Toronto 1960), 81

25 Montreal *Gazette*, 13 Dec. 1894

26 JSDT, vol. 293, Thompson to Joe, 2 Mar. 1892. This is in effect the answer to J.T. Saywell's comment that Thompson 'deliberately assumed Macdonald's old seat as striking proof of his paramountcy ...' (J.T. Saywell, 'The Canadian Succession Question, 1891–1896,' *CHR*, XXXVII, 4 [Dec. 1956] 314). It is probable that Thompson's letters to his children were not available when Saywell wrote.

27 *Globe*, 16 June 1891

28 *The Week* (Toronto), 8 May 1891, article by x

29 Montreal *La Minerve*, 20 juin 1891

30 He was writing for an opposition paper, however; Québec *l'Electeur*, 18 juin 1891.

31 *North Sydney Herald*, 14 Oct. 1891, quoting the Hamilton *Spectator*

32 JSDT, vol. 134, J.R. Gowan to Thompson, 12 Aug. 1891 (private) from Barrie

33 These figures are reported by W.C. Desbrisay, parliamentary correspondent for the Charlottetown *Examiner*, but he did not altogether trust them (Charlottetown *Examiner*, 3 Sept. 1891).

34 *House of Commons Debates* (22 June 1891), col. 1149

35 PAC, Mme Joseph Lavergne Papers, Laurier to Emilie Lavergne, 7 août 1891. Laurier's letters to her were invariably written in English, presumably so her servants (and children?) would not be able to read them.

36 *House of Commons Debates* (22 June 1891), col. 1125

37 Ibid., cols. 1161, 1150. *Taikun* became the American word 'tycoon.'

38 Montreal *Gazette*, 15 June 1891

39 JSDT, vol. 134, Gowan to Thompson, 12 Aug. 1891 (private), from Barrie

40 Ibid., Gowan to Thompson, 8 Aug. 1891 (private), from Toronto

41 Sir Charles Tupper Papers, vol. 9, Lady Macdonald to Sir Charles Tupper, 4 Nov. 1891

42 Montreal *La Minerve*, 16 juillet, 1891

43 Quoted by M.C. Cameron, MP for Huron West, in *House of Commons Debates* (20 Aug. 1891), col. 4189

44 JSDT, vol. 297, Thompson to Frankie, 17 July 1891

45 Ibid., Thompson to Babe, 17 July 1891

46 Ottawa *Journal*, 13 Dec. 1894

47 JSDT, vol. 133, J.T. Bulmer to Thompson, 31 July 1891 (private), from Halifax

48 *House of Commons Debates* (17 June 1891), col. 989

49 PAC, RG 13, A3, vol. 646, R. Sedgewick to G.E. Foster, 4 Sept. 1891

50 *Globe*, 25 July 1891

51 JSDT, vol. 291, Thompson to Annie, 9 July 1891

52 Ibid., vol. 134, Gowan to Thompson, 8 Aug. 1891 (private), from Toronto

53 Ibid., vol. 291, Thompson to Annie, 29 July 1891

54 Ibid., vol. 297, Thompson to Babe, 17 July 1891

55 Ibid., vol. 291, Thompson to Annie, 29 July 1891

56 Langevin Papers, Boîte 7, J.J.C. Abbott to Langevin, 28 July, 1891 (confidential)

57 *House of Commons Debates* (11 Aug. 1891) col. 3653

58 The Langevin papers do contain McGreevy letters. One of them, from 1887, mentions that if Langevin had $25,000, as apparently he had, ready to invest, he could get 4½ per cent for it through McGreevy's connection as director of the Union Bank. The usual rate was only 3 per cent. Boîte 18 in the Langevin Papers has McGreevy letters.

59 For example, P.V. Valin's evidence (p. 492, Appendix 1), is specifically denied by Langevin, p. 1148. P.V. Valin (1827–97) was MP for Montmorency from 1878 to 1887, and for some years was chairman of the Quebec Harbours Board.

60 Langevin Papers, Boîte 23, Langevin to Taillon, 14 nov.1891

61 *The Week*, 12 Aug. 1891

62 JSDT, vol. 291, Thompson to Annie, 18 Aug. 1891

63 PAC, Laurier Papers, vol. 5, Laurier to Beaugrand (editor of *La Patrie*), 17 août 1891 (personnelle copy)

64 Charlottetown *Examiner*, 27 Aug. 1891, report from Ottawa of 26 Aug. by W.C. Desbrisay

65 JSDT, vol. 291, Thompson to Annie, 14 Aug. 1891

66 Ibid., Thompson to Annie, 26 Aug. 1891

67 Ibid., Thompson to Annie, 2 Sept. 1891

68 JSDT, vol. 291, Thompson to Annie, 11 Sept. 1891

69 Langevin Papers, Boîte 7, Abbott to Langevin, 5 Sept. 1891 (confidential)

70 JSDT, vol. 136, Langevin to Abbott, 7 Sept. 1891 (copy); Abbott to Langevin, 7 Sept. 1891 (draft); *House of Commons Debates* (7 Sept. 1891), col. 5074

71 *Canada, House of Commons Journals, 1891*, Appendix 1, p. ivnn

72 JSDT, vol. 137, D'Alton McCarthy to Thompson, 21 Sept. 1891
73 *House of Commons Debates* (25 Sept. 1891), cols. 6121–2
74 Charlottetown *Examiner*, 25 Sept. 1891, report of W.C. Debrisay, from Ottawa, 24 Sept.; *House of Commons Debates* (24 Sept. 1891), cols. 6064–86
75 *North Sydney Herald*, 21 Oct. 1891, quoting a letter of E.M. Saunders from the Halifax *Herald*. Saunders (1829–1916) was pastor of the first Baptist church in Ottawa, and edited *Life and letters of Sir Charles Tupper*, 2 vols. (London 1916).
76 Langevin Papers, Boîte 25, F. Vanasse to Langevin, 16 sept. 1891, from Montreal
77 JSDT, vol. 156, Annie McGreevy to Thompson, 3 June 1892 (private); vol. 256, Thompson to Annie McGreevy, 8 June 1892; vol. 164, Amyot to Thompson, 6 Oct. 1892
78 One element of nastiness was a telegram from Matthew Walsh, private secretary to John Costigan, then secretary of state, to Robert McGreevy, 22 Nov. 1893: 'Possibly you are now satisfied with your handiwork inasmuch as your brother and benefactor as also your friend have both gone to prison ...' It was represented to Thompson that private secretaries of ministers had no business abusing crown witnesses, and making them pay 42 cents for the pleasure of receiving it. Thompson was very much opposed to what Walsh had done and proposed to take action. Ibid., vol. 192, G. Amyot to Thompson, 25 Nov. 1893; vol. 265, Thompson to Amyot, 2 Dec. 1893, from Antigonish
79 Ibid., vol. 193, Griffin to Thompson, 18 Dec. 1893
80 PAC, RG 13, A3, vol. 656, Thompson to H.E. in Council, n.d. but probably 26 Feb. 1894; JSDT, vol. 201, Aberdeen to Thompson, 27 Feb. 1894 (private); the full explanation of the events is in British Library, Addl. MSS 44090, Gladstone Papers, Lady Aberdeen to Gladstone, 3 Mar. 1894.
81 PAC, Pacaud Papers, vol. 2, Laurier to Pacaud, 27 déc. 1893 (personelle)
82 Charlottetown *Examiner*, 25 Sept. 1891

18 STEADYING THE HELM

1 JSDT, vol. 130, J.J. Curran to Thompson, 12 June 1891 (private and confidential), from Montreal
2 Ibid., vol. 291, Thompson to Annie, 14, 15 Aug. 1891
3 Ibid., vol. 135, D. McN. Parker to Thompson, 24 Aug. 1891
4 Ibid., vol. 137, F.J. Tremaine to Thompson, 24 Sept. 1891
5 Ibid., vol. 291, Thompson to Annie, 7 Sept. 1891
6 Ibid., Thompson to Annie, 12, 14 Sept. 1891

7 Ibid., vol. 139, J.A. Chisholm to Thompson, 22 Oct. 1891, from Halifax

8 Ibid., A. O'Donnell to Thompson, 16 Oct. 1891, from St Denis

9 Ibid., vol. 298, Thompson to John, 13 Dec. 1891

10 Ibid., vol. 155, Gowan to Thompson, 21 May 1892

11 Ibid., vol. 138, Douglas to Thompson, 13 Oct. 1891 (private) from Chatham; vol. 252, Thompson to Douglas, 21 Oct. 1891 (private); vol. 139, Douglas to Thompson, 23 Oct. 1891, from Chatham

12 The 1891 meeting with Bunting was set for Monday, 9 Nov.; ibid., vol. 140, Douglas to Thompson, 2, 5 Nov. 1891 (telegrams). Later correspondence is in vol. 177, Douglas to Thompson, 22 Feb. 1893 (private and confidential), from Chatham; vol. 260, Thompson to Douglas, 28 Feb. 1893.

13 Montreal *La Presse*, 4, 16 juin 1891

14 *Grip* (Toronto), 23 Jan. 1892

15 Montreal *Gazette*, 13 Nov. 1891, quoting Quebec *Le Canadien*

16 Hamilton *Spectator*, 31 Oct. 1891; ibid., 7 Nov. 1891, letter of Chapleau, dated Ottawa, 5 Nov. The Montreal *Gazette*, 10 Nov. 1891 reprints some of this correspondence. See also comments by W.R. Meredith to J.P. Whitney, 31 Oct. 1891 (PAO, Whitney Papers), cited in H.B. Neatby and J.T. Saywell, 'Chapleau and the Conservative party in Quebec,' *CHR*, XXXVII, 1 (Mar. 1956), 15.

17 *The Week* (Toronto), 4 Dec. 1891

18 The authority here is Thompson: '... every minister has placed his resignation in the hands of the Premier so as to give the amplest freedom for reconstruction. Not one of us knows whether he will be asked to remain or not, or what Department may be assigned to him if he should remain.' JSDT, vol. 252, Thompson to John Sharples of Quebec, 26 Nov. 1891 (private)

19 J.A. Willison, *Reminiscences, Political and Personal* (Toronto 1919), 108–10

20 JSDT, vol. 274, Meredith to Abbott, 24 June 1891 (confidential, copy); PAO, Clarke Wallace Papers, envelope 11, Meredith to Wallace, 23 June 1891 (confidential)

21 PAC, Martin Griffin Papers, Gowan to Griffin, 22 Jan. 1892. Gowan admitted, however, that he had never actually met Meredith.

22 JSDT, vol. 130, Meredith to C.H. Mackintosh, 12 June 1891 (private and confidential, copy)

23 Ibid., vol. 250, Thompson to Abbott, 17 July 1891; ibid., vol. 274, Abbott to Meredith, n.d., copy

24 Ibid., vol. 137, Cameron to Thompson, 24 Sept. 1891 (private), from Montreal

25 Ibid., vol. 141, Cameron to Thompson, 17 Nov. 1891 (personal)

26 Ibid., vol. 143, J.G. Moylan to Thompson, 20 Dec. 1891, from Kingston.

Angers was very much of the same opinion. He wrote Abbott, 'I do not see that he [Meredith] brings your cabinet any strength at all. All his friends are already your supporters, and his entry will only widen the breach between the Liberal-Conservatives and the Roman Catholic clergy of Ontario and will estrange the great majority of Conservatives in our province.' PAC, Angers Papers, Letterbooks, p. 100, Angers to Abbott, 2 Jan. 1891 [should be 1892]

27 JSDT, vol. 143, C.B. Whidden to Thompson, 22 Dec. 1891; vol. 144, Lachlan Cameron to Thompson, 24 Dec. 1891

28 Ibid., vol. 253, Thompson to J.N. Lyons, 26 Dec. 1891

29 The petition against Thompson's election in Antigonish went to the Supreme Court of Nova Scotia on appeal from Justice Weatherbe. It turned upon 'the sufficiency of orders extending the time for trial.' Both Thompson and Borden were sure Weatherbe's point was irrelevant, and that view was put before the chief justice and Justice Meagher on 28 Nov. 1891. The Supreme Court agreed with Borden and the appeals were dismissed. It affected both the Antigonish and Lunenburg petitions as well as C.H. Tupper's in Pictou. The correspondence is quite large and fairly technical, beginning with Borden to Thompson, 13 July 1891, JSDT, vol. 132; also vols. 141, 145, 151, 152, 252–3.

30 Ibid., vol. 252, Thompson to C.H. Cahan, 24 Nov. 1891

31 Ibid., vol. 146, Tupper to Thompson, 20 Jan. 1891 (telegram), Windsor Junction to Antigonish

32 Ibid., vol. 291, Thompson to Annie, 19 Jan. 1891, from Halifax

33 Ibid., vol. 147, C.H. Cahan to Thompson, 26 Jan. 1892 (two telegrams)

34 Ibid., vol. 148, Tupper to Thompson, 3 Feb. 1892 (telegram), from Liverpool, NS

35 Ibid., vol. 148, Morine to Thompson, 6 Feb. 1892 (telegram)

36 There are a dozen telegrams at the beginning of vol. 148 on the by-elections.

37 Two months later F.O.L. Patch of Liverpool claimed that Morine had got $450 from him, on promises of full ministerial authorization. Ibid., vol. 152, Patch to Thompson, 11 Apr. 1892 (private), from Liverpool. Thompson said that neither he nor Tupper gave any such guarantee as Morine had suggested. 'We subscribed all we could afford ...' he told F.O.L. Patch. Vol. 255, Thompson to Patch, 18 Apr. 1892 (private). It would appear that the problem may have originated with C.H. Tupper, and especially J.B. Mills, MP for Annapolis. See vol. 158, C.H. Cahan to Thompson, 18 July 1892.

38 Ibid., vol. 291, Thompson to Annie, 11 Feb. 1892, from Washington

39 Montreal *Herald*, 15 Feb. 1892

40 Goldwin Smith to J.W. Foster, 16 Feb. 1892, in J.W. Foster, *Diplomatic Memoirs*, 2 vols. (Boston 1909), II, 182

41 University of Toronto Archives, Charlton Papers, MS. Reminiscences, pp. 657–8

42 JSDT, vol. 148, Abbott to Thompson, 8 Feb. 1892 (confidential memorandum)

43 See the useful introduction to the subject in Alvin C. Gluek, Jr, 'Canada's Splendid Bargain: the North Pacific Fur Seal Convention of 1911,' *CHR*, LXIII, 2 (June 1982), 180–1.

44 R.C. Brown, *Canada's National Policy, 1883–1900* (Princeton 1964), 112

45 PAC, Lord Stanley Papers, A446, Stanley to Salisbury, 11 Oct. 1891 (private)

46 Ibid.

47 Ibid., A673, Stanley to Pauncefote, 9 Feb. 1892 (private), from Ottawa

48 JSDT, vol. 291, Thompson to Annie, 11 Feb. 1892; vol. 298, Thompson to John, 2 Mar. 1892

49 Ibid., vol. 254, Thompson to Abbott, 11 Feb. 1892 (in cipher); Abbott to Thompson, 12 Feb. 1892; Thompson to Abbott, same date; Abbott to Thompson, 13 Feb. 1892

50 Ibid., précis of meeting, 11 Feb. 1892; Foster, *Diplomatic Memoirs*, II, 180

51 JSDT, vol. 291, Thompson to Annie, 14 Feb. 1892

52 Brown, *Canada's National Policy*, 298

53 JSDT, vol. 291, Thompson to Annie, 13 Feb. 1892. J.W. Foster thought that Harrison had the best mind of any president since Lincoln (*Diplomatic Memoirs*, II, 253).

54 Lord Stanley Papers, A673, Pauncefote to Stanley, 1 June 1892; also *New York Sun*, 1 June 1892

55 A.F. Taylor, *The Foreign Policy of James G. Blaine* (Minnesota 1927), 357–9

56 JSDT, vol. 160, Dewdney to Thompson, 5 Aug. 1892, from Halifax

57 Montreal *Gazette*, 6 Aug. 1892

58 JSDT, vol. 160, Abbott to Thompson, 3 Aug. 1892, from Ottawa

59 *New York Sun*, 15 Aug. 1892; Toronto *Evening Telegram*, 13 Aug. 1892. Bowell sent these to Thompson, 16 Aug. 1892.

60 JSDT, vol. 161, Bowell to Thompson, 22 Aug. 1892, from Belleville

61 *The Week*, 4 Mar. 1892

62 *Canada, House of Commons Debates* (29 Feb. 1892), col. 31; ibid. (29 Mar. 1892), col. 618

63 JSDT, vol. 443, Dewdney to Thompson, 15 Dec. 1891, from Regina

64 *House of Commons Debates* (22 Mar. 1892), col. 360

65 JSDT, vol. 152, Fitzpatrick to Caron, 11 Apr. 1892 (private, copy)

66 *House of Commons Debates* (6 Apr. 1892), col. 1046

67 The government's procedure was partly of Thompson's devising, but he obtained from J.G. Bourinot, clerk of the Commons, some specific sugges-

tions. Bourinot concluded, 'If your government is not satisfied with simply voting down the original [Edgar] motion, then they should clearly pursue such a course as is supported by sound principles of constitutional and parliamentary usage and correct political ethics.' JSDT, vol. 152, Bourinot to Thompson, 14 Apr. 1892

68 Desmond Morton and R.H. Roy, *Telegrams of the North-West Campaign, 1885* (Toronto 1972), xciv–xcv, xcv n

69 JSDT, vol. 154, F.J. Walsh to Thompson, 2 May 1892 (private); Thompson to F.J. Walsh, 9 May 1892 (private)

70 *Grip*, 23 Apr. 1892; 20 Feb. 1892

71 JSDT, vol. 154, F.J. Walsh to Thompson, n.d., endorsed on Thompson to Walsh, 9 May 1892 (private)

72 PAC, Laurier Papers, vol. 6, Edgar to Laurier, 8 Sept. 1892 (private), from Toronto

73 JSDT, vol. 161, Sedgewick to Thompson, 24 Aug. 1892 (telegram)

74 PAC, RG 13, Department of Justice Papers, File 37/1892, Abbott to Sedgewick, 13 Feb. 1892

75 Chambly (Liberal) became Chambly-Verchères for the next election; Chateauguay and Rouville (both Liberal) stayed as they were; Napierville (Liberal) became Laprairie-Napierville, and where in 1896 the effect was that a Conservative seat in Laprairie was lost. Montreal *Herald*, 2 May 1892

76 *House of Commons Debates* (15 June 1892), col. 3789

77 Montreal *Herald*, 1 July 1892; PAC, Gowan Papers, M-1900, Thompson to Gowan, 1 June 1892

78 See *Grip*, 18 June 1892

79 *House of Commons Debates* (28 June 1892), col. 4354. Cartwright, perhaps deliberately, reversed the order of the lines. They are here quoted as in Pope's 'Of the character of women.'

80 Gowan Papers, M-1900, Thompson to Gowan, 5 July 1892. The quotation from Shakespeare Thompson had nearly right. I have quoted it as it is in act I, scene iii of *Hamlet*.

81 *House of Commons Debates* (28 June 1892), cols. 4354–77

82 University of British Columbia Archives, C.H. Tupper Papers, Thompson to Tupper, 18 July 1892

83 Department of Justice, File 63/1894, vol. II, J.R. Gowan to Sedgewick, 14 May 1892 (personal), from Barrie

84 JSDT, vol. 153, Gowan to Thompson, 25 Apr. 1892

85 Ibid., 21 Apr. 1892 (private), from Barrie; Gowan to Abbott, 21 Apr. 1892; Department of Justice Papers, file 63/1894, Gowan to Sedgewick, 14 May 1892 (personal)

86 G. Parker, 'The Origins of the Canadian Criminal Code' in D.H. Flaherty, ed., *Essays in the History of Canadian Law* (Osgoode Society 1981), 280, n 67

87 Thompson made these points to Justice Rose of the Ontario High Court. JSDT, vol. 242, Thompson to Rose, 8 Mar. 1890. See *House of Commons Debates* (12 Apr. 1892), cols. 1312–13

88 R.C. Macleod, 'The Shaping of the Canadian Criminal Law, 1892–1902' in *CHA, Historical Papers, 1978*, 64 and note

89 *House of Commons Debates* (19 May 1892), cols. 2839–43. It can be added on this point that Sedgewick was angry at such suggestions as Mulock's, pointing out how careful Thompson was to indicate any changes made either in statute or common law. See Department of Justice Papers, File 63/1894, Memorandum of Sedgewick, 3 Feb. 1893.

90 JSDT, vol. 154, Gowan to Thompson, 5 May 1892

91 Macleod, 'The Shaping of the Canadian Driminal Law,' 66; *House of Commons Debates* (12 Apr. 1892), col. 1316

92 Department of Justice Papers, file 63/1894, I, James Masson, MP for Grey North to Sedgewick, May 1892

93 Ibid., Gowan to Thompson, [16?] May 1892, from Barrie

94 Gowan Papers, M-1900, Thompson to Gowan 18 May, 1892, and 1 June 1892

95 Montreal *Gazette*, 17 June 1892, open letter to Sir John Thompson, signed D.A. Watt. See also Parker, 'Origins of the Canadian Criminal Code,' 268–9.

96 JSDT, vol. 155, J.K. McLennan to Thompson, 18 May 1892, from Treherne, Manitoba

97 Department of Justice Papers, File 63/1894, I

98 For the Baie des Chaleurs scandal, see Waite, *Canada 1874–1896*, 234 ff.

99 JSDT, vol. 155, Gowan to Thompson, 21 May 1892; vol. 158, Gowan to Thompson, 6 July 1892

100 *Canada, Senate Debates* (6 July 1892), pp. 464–6, 472

101 JSDT, vol. 158, Gowan to Thompson, 18 July 1892, reporting a letter from Sir John Abbott; *Senate Debates* (6 July 1892), p. 484

102 See Graham Parker, 'The Origins of the Canadian Criminal Code,' 273; JSDT, vol. 94, Taschereau to Thompson, 23 Oct. 1889; *Canadian Law Journal*, XXIX (1893), 94–5, cited in Parker, 280.

103 Department of Justice, File 63/1894, I, Sedgewick's Memorandum of 3 Feb. 1893. The sections were 133, 181, 185, 215, 266, 543, 684, 705, 735, 838.

104 JSDT, vol. 158, Gowan to Thompson, 18 July 1892

105 Ibid., vol. 157, Gowan to Thompson, 28 June 1892

106 *The Week*, 17 June 1892; see also 4 Mar. 1892.

107 JSDT, vol. 256, Thompson to Hugh Henry, 18 July 1892. Henry had been the lawyer whom Thompson had brought up in May 1891 to help Langevin.

108 C.H. Tupper Papers, Thompson to Tupper, 18 July 1892 (private); JSDT, vol. 293, Jane Dewdney to Annie, 17 July 1892, from Ottawa
109 JSDT, vol. 158, Girouard to Thompson, 12 July 1892; Sanford to Thompson, 13 July 1892; vol. 159, Caron to Thompson, 28 July 1892
110 Ibid., vol. 293, Jane Dewdney to Annie, 17 July 1892, from Ottawa
111 Ibid., vol. 160, Bowell to Thompson, 3 Aug. 1892 (private)
112 Ibid., Sedgewick to Thompson 6 Aug. 1892 (private)
113 Ibid., Abbott to Thompson, Tues. [9 Aug. 1892?], from Ste Anne de Bellevue

19 THE NEW PRIME MINISTER

1 *Grip* (Toronto), 24 Sept. 1892
2 Reported in *Saturday Night* (Toronto), 23 Sept. 1893
3 PAC, J.R. Gowan Papers, M-1900, Thompson to Gowan, 29 Dec. 1892 (private)
4 PAC, Griffin Papers, vol. 1, Cameron to Griffin, 3 June 1889
5 JSDT, vol. 297, Thompson to Frankie, 22 Aug. 1891; Thompson to Helena, 3 Dec. 1892
6 Ibid., vol. 257, Thompson to G.G. Dustan of Halifax, 13 Oct. 1892
7 PAC, Laurier Papers, vol. 6, Senator Lawrence Power to Laurier, 9 Dec. 1892 (private), from Halifax
8 J.T. Saywell, ed., *The Canadian Journal of Lady Aberdeen, 1893–1898* (Toronto 1960), 13 Dec. 1894, pp. 166–7
9 Griffin Papers, Gowan to Griffin, 8 Oct. 1892 (confidential)
10 *The Week* (Toronto), 2 Dec. 1892
11 Griffin Papers, Gowan to Griffin, 8 Oct. 1892 (confidential)
12 *Toronto World*, 6 Sept. 1892; JSDT, vol. 164, A. Boultbee to Abbott, 4 Oct. 1892
13 JSDT, vol. 167, Mowat to Thompson, 18 Nov. 1892 (confidential)
14 Laurier Papers, vol. 6, Davies to Laurier, 14 Oct. 1892
15 JSDT, vol. 257, Thompson to Perley, 14 Oct. 1892 (private). Perley had been by no means convinced that Bowell would have been a good choice; vol. 164, Perley to Thompson, 8 Oct. 1892 (private).
16 Ibid., vol. 166, Abbott to Thompson, 10 Nov. 1892
17 Ibid., vol. 171, Abbott to H. Colmer, 28 Dec. [1892], from Bordighera, Italy
18 Ibid., vol. 167, Lord Stanley to Thompson, 22 Nov. 1892 (private); 24 Nov. 1892 (private)
19 Montreal *La Presse*, 20 déc. 1892, reporting Ouimet's speech of 19 Dec.
20 There had been a long feud between the *Star* and Abbott. The *Star* alleged

that Abbott had objected to exposures of alleged boodling on Montreal city council. JSDT, vol. 167, D. MacMaster to Thompson, 28 Nov. 1892 (private)

21 Ibid., vol. 259, Thompson to F.J. Boyers, 25 Jan. 1893

22 *Globe*, 28 Nov. 1892, Ottawa report of 26 Nov.

23 Ibid., report of 27 Nov.

24 See PAC, *Guide to Canadian Ministries since Confederation* (Ottawa 1974), iv, 175. The government's proceeding was noted by the Toronto *Empire*, 28 Nov. 1892.

25 JSDT, vol. 165, D.L. Scott to Edgar Dewdney, 24 Oct. 1892 (confidential), from Regina

26 The import of these changes was debated in the Commons, where Thompson made it clear that both controllers exercised their duties under the general supervision of the minister of trade and commerce. *Canada, House of Commons Debates* (24 Feb. 1893), cols. 1245–55

27 J.L. Payne, 'Recollections of a Private Secretary,' *Montreal Daily Star*, 29 Dec. 1923, 19 Jan. 1924, cited in O. Mary Hill, *Canada's Salesman to the World: The Department of Trade and Commerce, 1892–1939* (Montreal and Toronto 1977), 17

28 *Globe*, 7 Dec. 1892

29 JSDT, vol. 167, David Creighton to Thompson, 29 Nov. 1892 (private), from Toronto

30 Ibid., Dewdney to Thompson, 26 Nov. 1892, from Victoria; vol. 166, Sam Hughes to Thompson, 7 Nov. 1892 (personal), from Lindsay

31 *Montreal Daily Star*, 1 Dec. 1892

32 PBW archives, Thompson to Carling, 2 Dec. 1892 (private and confidential). This letter is a shorthand draft intended for Thompson's secretary to transcribe. There are no Carling Papers.

33 PAC, Stanley Papers, Thompson to Stanley, 5 Dec. 1892; Stanley to Thompson, 5 Dec. [1892] (very confidential, copy); also JSDT, vol. 169, which has the original of Stanley's letter

34 Ibid., M.G. Bremner to Thompson, 3 Dec. 1892 (telegram). In 1896 three of the five seats around London went Liberal.

35 Queen's University Archives, James Williamson Papers, Hugh John Macdonald to Williamson, 19 Jan. 1893, from Winnipeg

36 Ibid., Hugh John Macdonald to Williamson, 3 July 1892. He was MP for Winnipeg.

37 PAO, Clarke Wallace Papers, Wallace to his wife Belinda, 6 June 1894; *Saturday Night*, 17 Dec. 1892

38 Griffin Papers, Gowan to Griffin, 30 Nov. 1892; Toronto *Empire*, 12 May 1894, report by Faith Fenton

39 JSDT, vol. 164, Wallace to Thompson, 7 Oct. 1892, from Woodbridge; *Saturday Night*, 1 Apr. 1893; Griffin Papers, Gowan to Griffin, 29 Dec. 1892

40 University of British Columbia Archives, Sir Charles Hibbert Tupper Papers, Thompson to Tupper, 18 July 1892; PAO, Edgar Papers, Laurier to Edgar, 14 Dec. 1894; *La Presse*, 10 déc. 1892

41 JSDT, vol. 163, R.S. White to Thompson, 19 Sept. 1892 (private), from Montreal; Archives du Ministère des Affaires étrangères, Paris, Correspondence consulaire et commerciale, Québec, 16, f. 53 v., 22 mars 1893, cited in Pierre Savard, *Le Consulat de France à Québec et à Montréal de 1859 à 1914* (Paris 1970), 46

42 JSDT, vol. 164, Chapleau to Thompson, 11 Oct. 1892 (private); vol. 167, R.S. White to Thompson, 28 Nov. 1892 (private)

43 Ibid., vol. 258, Thompson to Angers, 10 Oct. 1892 (private); vol. 166, Charles de Boucherville to Thompson, 5 nov. 1892

44 Ibid., vol. 167, Nantel to Thompson, 29 nov. 1892

45 Ibid., vol. 170, Chapleau to Thompson, 14 Dec. 1892 (private)

46 Ibid., vol. 167, A.W. Ogilvie to Thompson, 29 Nov. 1892 (private and confidential)

47 Ibid., vol. 169, C.H. Mackintosh to Thompson, 2 Dec. 1892 (private and confidential)

48 Ibid., vol. 167, R.S. White to Thompson, 30 Nov. 1892 (private); vol. 169, Hugh Graham to Thompson, 3, 5 Dec. 1892

49 Laurier Papers, vol. 6, Senator L.G. Power to Laurier, 29 Dec. 1892, replying to Laurier's of 13 Dec.

50 Montreal *Herald*, 25 Nov. 1892; also cited in the *Globe*, 28 Nov. 1892

51 Montreal *Witness*, 24 Dec. 1892; JSDT, vol. 157, J.E. Rose to Thompson, 27 June 1892 (private), from Toronto. This was in reference to another outburst of Dr Douglas.

52 *Toronto World*, 27 Dec. 1892

53 *Empire*, 10 Dec. 1892

54 *Globe*, 6 Jan. 1893, reporting the Board of Trade banquet of 5 Jan.

55 *Empire*, 14 Jan. 1893, reporting Thompson's speech of the previous evening

56 *New York Sun*, 19 Dec. 1892; JSDT, vol. 259, Thompson to Taché, 7 Feb. 1893

57 *House of Commons Debates* (11 May 1892), col. 2482; British Library, Ripon Papers, Addl MSS. 43516, Lord Ripon to Lord Rosebery, 29, 31 Oct. 1892 (copies)

58 PRO, CO 42/813, ff. 653–5, minutes by Anderson, 22 Oct. 1892, and by Meade, 24 Oct. 1892. Also London *Daily Chronicle*, 22 Oct. 1892, and *House of Commons Debates* (11 May 1892), col. 2577

59 JSDT, vol. 261, Thompson to Sandford Fleming, 3 May 1893

60 Ibid., vol. 186, Bowell to Thompson, 23 Sept. 1893, from Honolulu; British Library, Addl. MSS. 41224, Campbell-Bannerman Papers, Ripon to Bannerman, 30 May, 1894 (confidential)

61 Ripon Papers, Addl. MSS. 43516, Ripon to Rosebery, n.d. (private, copy), probably 4–9 Jan. 1893; Ripon to Rosebery, 9 Feb. 1893 (private, copy); Addl. MSS. 43559, Ripon to Stanley, 6 Mar. 1893 (copy); Stanley to Ripon, 30 Mar. 1893 (private); JSDT, vol. 171, Stanley to Thompson, 27 Dec. 1892

Important aspects of the Esquimalt difficulty are discussed in Desmond Morton, *Ministers and Generals: Politics and the Canadian Militia, 1868–1904* (Toronto 1970), 43–4, 100–1, 195–6.

62 Saywell, ed., *Journal of Lady Aberdeen*, 18 July 1894, p. 245; G.R. MacLean, 'The Canadian Offer of Troops for Hong Kong, 1894,' *CHR*, XXXVIII, 4 (Dec. 1957), 275–83; CO 42/824, ff. 379, Minute by Fairfield(?), 'General Herbert seems to have persuaded a weak Minister to telegraph without authority ...' 25 Oct. 1894

63 JSDT, vol. 140, Taché to Thompson, 10 Nov. 1891, from St Boniface; ibid., vol. 144, Taché to Thompson, 29 Dec. 1891; vol. 151, same, 21 Mar. 1892. See L.C. Clark, 'A History of the Conservative Administrations, 1891–1896' (PHD thesis, University of Toronto, 1968), 255–6

64 JSDT, vol. 143, Archbishop Fabre to Thompson, 11 Dec. 1891 (telegram): 'Ewart informs me that Davie [*sic*] is retained against us by Local Gov't how can that be true;' AAStB, Thompson to Taché, 24 Dec. 1891 (private); same, 4 Jan. 1892

65 JSDT, vol. 274, Thompson to Bompas, Bischoff, 9 June 1893, from Paris; ibid., vol. 182, Bompas, Bischoff to Thompson, 10 June 1893, from London. Bompas's reply was a mixture of sweet reasonableness and justification for their actions. Thompson's letter was written a year after the events above in connection with some other developments Thompson had been unhappy about. In the end Thompson stopped general retainers with Bompas, Bischoff as of July 1893. He was convinced they were not acting in good faith. See vol. 261, Thompson to E.L. Newcombe, 3 July 1893

66 Ibid., R.S. White to Thompson, 8 Aug. 1892 (private, enclosing N.C. Wallace to White, 6 Aug. 1892, reporting Ewart's comments)

67 Early in the 1893 session, the House of Commons asked for copies of the Privy Council decision in *Winnipeg* v. *Barrett*. David Mills added that he thought the arguments ought to be reprinted also. This was done. *Sessional Papers*, 1893, no. 33A. The reference above is pp. 124–5.

68 *Empire*, 15 Aug. 1892

69 Gowan Papers, A 1898, Thompson to Gowan, 29 Dec. 1892 (private)

70 Reported by Arnott Magurn in a biography of Thompson in the *Globe*, 10 Dec. 1892

71 Catholics in Manitoba protested against the Protestant interpretation, arguing that the subsection in the Manitoba Act with 'law or practice' in it was thought at the time sufficient to cover all eventualities. Otherwise, the words 'or is thereafter established by the legislature of the Province' in the BNA Act, would never have been omitted from the Manitoba Act. JSDT, vol. 160, La Rivière to Thompson, 9 Aug. 1892 (confidential), from St Boniface

72 *Sessional Papers*, 1893, no. 33, p. 6

73 *Globe*, 28 Nov. 1892; JSDT, vol. 170, Chapleau to Thompson, 22 Dec. 1892, from Montreal; ibid., vol. 171, same, 29 Dec. 1892, from Sherbrooke

74 *Empire*, 14 Jan. 1893, reporting Thompson's speech of 13 Jan.

75 Laurier Papers, vol. 8, T.P. Gorman to Laurier, 26 Feb. 1894 (personal), from Ottawa; PAC, Caron Papers, vol. 195, Caron to H.A. Turcotte, 5 avril 1895; Quebec *Le Courrier du Canada*, 30 mars 1895. As to Thompson's determination, this is referred to in a long letter from Bishop Cameron to Thompson, reporting the substance of the bishop's conversation with Father Lacombe and the Bishop of Sherbrooke, 27 Apr. 1894. JSDT, vol. 207, Cameron to Thompson, 30 Apr. 1894, from Antigonish

76 Archives archiépiscopales du Québec, Taché to Ouimet, 14 mars 1894, enclosed in Taché to Bégin, 18 mars 1894; JSDT, vol. 210, Taché to Thompson, 30 May 1894

77 Archives des Jésuites, St Jérome, Québec, Fonds Bernier, Thompson to Bernier, 17 Oct. 1894 (private)

78 *House of Commons Debates* (6 Mar. 1893), cols. 1757, 1778

79 Ibid., 1798

80 *Empire*, 30 Dec. 1892, edit.; 2 Jan. 1893, letter from McCarthy of 30 Dec. 1892; 3 Jan. 1893, edit.

81 JSDT, vol. 175, David Creighton to Thompson, 3 Feb. 1893 (private), from Toronto. See also Gowan Papers, M-1898, Griffin to Gowan, 5 Jan. 1893; Gowan to Griffin, 9 Jan. 1893.

82 *House of Commons Debates* (6 Mar. 1893), cols. 1806–7

83 Reported in *Empire*, 9 Mar. 1893

84 Thompson did not want to have Caron in the invidious position of being the superintendent of the judges who were reporting on the Edgar charges and reviewing the evidence. Caron Papers, vol. 195, Thompson to Caron, 8 Mar. 1893 (private)

85 JSDT, vol. 178, Chisholm to Thompson, 1 Mar. 1893 (private)

86 Stanley Papers, Thompson to Stanley, 31 Mar. 1893, from Paris; *Globe*, 10 Mar. 1893

20 THE PARIS INTERLUDE, 1893

1 PANS, Vertical MS. file, Sir John Thompson Papers, Thompson to J.A. Chisholm, 13 Apr. 1893, from Paris; PAC, Caron Papers, vol. 195, Thompson to Caron, 18 Apr. 1893; JSDT, vol. 298, Thompson to John, 13 Apr. 1893

2 PAC, Griffin Papers, vol. 4, Griffin to L.G. Power, 6 Sept. 1893; ibid., Thompson to Griffin, 18 Apr. 1893 (private). For Henry James, see Leon Edel, *Henry James: The Conquest of London 1870–1883* (London 1962), 75.

3 Historical Society of Ottawa, Alan Stewart Collection. Thompson's passport was issued by the Government of Canada, 8 Mar. 1893. For Thompson's laugh, see JSDT, vol. 192, S.D. Scott (of the *St. John Daily Sun*) to Thompson, 24 Nov. 1893 (personal, enclosing John Boyd[?] to Scott, 23 Nov. 1893)

4 British Library, Addl. MSS. 43556, Ripon Papers, Sir Robert Meade to Ripon, 28 Dec. 1892. Meade added about the sentence quoted, 'Sir C. Tupper made apology for the last sentence [of the cable] but I begged him to read it to me.'

5 Ibid., Addl. MSS. 43559, Ripon Papers, Stanley to Ripon, 29 Dec. 1892 (private)

6 Ibid., 43556, Meade to Ripon, 28 Dec. 1892

7 Ibid., 43516, Ripon to Rosebery, n.d. (private, copy, probably 4–9 Jan. 1893); same to same, 9 Feb. 1893 (private, copy); 43556, Meade to Ripon, 3, 4, 6 Jan. 1893

8 J.W. Foster, *Diplomatic Memoirs*, 2 vols. (Boston 1909), II, 32–4

9 Ibid., 37

10 PAC, Gowan Papers, M-1900, Thompson to Gowan, 20 Sept. 1893

11 PANS, Sir John Thompson Papers, Thompson to Chisholm, 13 Apr. 1893; London *Daily News*, 14 Dec. 1894. The *News* correspondent said that he had seen much of Thompson in Paris in 1893.

12 Maurice Pope, ed., *Public Servant: The Memoirs of Sir Joseph Pope* (Toronto 1960), 92

13 CO 42/815, f. 163, FO to Treasury, 24 June 1892

14 PAC, Stanley Papers, Thompson to Stanley, 31 Mar. 1893

15 *New York World*, 9 Apr. 1893; also Toronto *Empire*, 10 Apr. 1893

16 London *Daily News*, 7 Apr. 1893. This position was well stated by the *New York Sun*, 30 Mar. 1892, which criticized President Harrison in an editorial entitled, 'Giving away our rights in the Behring Sea.'

17 Foster describes how this event occurred in *Diplomatic Memoirs*, II, 40–1.

18 Griffin Papers, vol. 3, Thompson to Griffin, 18 Apr. 1893; Caron Papers, vol. 195, Thompson to Caron, 3 May 1893

19 Griffin Papers, Thompson to Griffin, 18 Apr. 1893

20 Pope, *Public Servant*, 93; JSDT, vol. 182, Griffin to Thompson, 24 June 1893;

PAC, Pope Papers, vol. 1, Diary, 13 Aug. 13, 1893; PANS, Sir John Thompson Papers, Thompson to J.A. Chisholm, 13 Apr. 1893

21 *Empire*, 12 May 1893, report from Paris of 11 May; ibid., 13 May 1893, report of 12 May

22 Ibid., 24 May 1893, report of 23 May

23 Ibid., 25 May 1893, from Paris; London *Standard*, 14 Dec. 1894, reporting interview with Sir Charles Russell (by then Lord Russell of Killowen)

24 Caron Papers, vol. 195, Thompson to Caron, 18 Apr. 1893; JSDT, vol. 180, Curran to Thompson, 25 Apr. 1893

25 Ibid., vol. 180, Chapleau to Thompson, 8 Apr. 1893

26 PAC, Tupper Papers, vol. 9, Tupper to Thompson, 17 Mar. 1893 (copy)

27 PAC, Lord Lorne Papers, Macdonald to Lorne, 2 Jan. 1879, enclosing Galt to Macdonald, 18 Dec. 1878. Lord Lyons, originally quite unhelpful, rallied round after Canadian appeals to the British Foreign Office. Macdonald to Lorne, 7 Jan. 1879, enclosing Galt to Macdonald, 20 Dec. 1878

See also R.A. Shields's article, 'Sir Charles Tupper and the Franco-Canadian Treaty of 1895: A Study of Imperial Relations,' *CHR*, XLIX, 1 (Mar. 1968), 1–23. Professor Shields did not at that time have access to the Stanley or the Ripon Papers, nor some of the newer acquisitions in the Tupper Papers.

28 PANS, Sir John Thompson Papers, Thompson to J.A. Chisholm, 13 Apr. 1893, from Paris

29 Stanley Papers, Thompson to Stanley, 31 Mar. 1893, from Paris

30 JSDT, vol. 179, Foster to Thompson, 22 Mar. 1893 (private); vol. 180, same, 3, 11 Apr. 1893

31 British Library, Addl. MSS. 43556, Ripon Papers, Meade to Ripon, 25 Mar. 1893

32 PRO, FO 27/3126, Dufferin to Rosebery, 27 Mar. 1893; PAC, Bowell Papers, vol. 11, Thompson to Bowell, 25, 28, 29 Mar. 1893 (private)

33 See Shields, 'Tupper and the Franco-Canadian Treaty,' 20–3.

34 *Saturday Night* (Toronto), 1 Apr. 1893

35 JSDT, vol. 179, Foster to Thompson, 22 Mar. 1893. A slightly different account is given by J.J. Curran in the letter cited below. A perspective from the Privy Council office is in W.C. Desbrisay to Rev. J.T. McNally, 23 Mar. 1893, in the Archiepiscopal Archives of Halifax. *Kingston News*, 11, 15 Mar. 1893, has the Wallace speech. See *Canada, House of Commons Debates* (21 Mar. 1893), col. 2709 *et seq.*

36 JSDT, Curran to Thompson, 22 Mar. 1893 (private)

37 *Toronto World*, 22 Mar. 1893; also commented on by the *Globe*, 23 Mar. 1893

38 JSDT, vol. 180, Foster to Thompson, 3 Apr. 1893

39 Ibid., Bowell to Thompson, 4 Apr. 1893 (telegram)
40 Ibid., vol. 261, Thompson to Foster, 26 June 1893; *House of Commons Journals, 1894*, app. 2; S.L. Shannon, '"Twas Fifty Years Ago,"' *Dalhousie Review*, x (1930–1), 535–40
41 JSDT, vol. 182, J.S. Hall to Thompson, 9 June 1893 (private); ibid., vol. 261, Thompson to Foster, 26 June 1893
42 The debt of the Province of Canada at Confederation was set down at $62.5 million. It was later found to be $73 million, and an act in 1873 provided for this excess, the provinces still liable for the interest on the $10.5 million between 1867 and 1873. This was eventually capitalized and remitted to the Province of Canada account in 1884, and arranged between the three governments in 1888, with recourse to arbitration to get the exact sum to be divided between Ontario and Quebec. So at least J.M. Courtney explained to Thompson. JSDT, vol. 182, Courtney to Thompson, 30 June 1893
43 Ibid., Hall to Thompson, 26 June 1893 (telegram)
44 Ibid., vol. 261, Thompson to Foster, 26 June 1893
45 Stanley Papers, Stanley to Thompson, 27 Apr. 1893 (private)
46 Ripon Papers, Ripon to Aberdeen, 9 May 1893 (confidential, copy). This letter is also in the Aberdeen Papers, and is quoted at length in J.T. Saywell, ed., *The Canadian Journal of Lady Aberdeen 1893–1898* (Toronto 1960), xxxviii.
47 See infra, ch. 23, for arrangements for a Gladstone–Thompson meeting at Hawarden.
48 JSDT, vol. 261, Thompson to Aberdeen, 1 July 1893
49 Pope, ed., *Public Servant*, 97
50 Griffin Papers, Thompson to Griffin, 18 July 1893 (private)
51 Pope, ed., *Public Servant*, 100
52 PAC, C.H. Tupper Papers, Tupper to Bowell, 20 June 1893 (copy); Toronto *Globe*, 28 Aug. 1893, quoting Thompson's speech in Ottawa of 26 Aug.
53 Pope, ed., *Public Servant*, 98
54 JSDT, vol. 182, Hébert to Thompson 19 juin 1893; 'Je serai très heureux de vous voir ce soir pour une dernière retouche à votre buste.' See also, vol. 185, Hébert to Thompson, 1 Sept. 1893; vol. 196, same, 12 jan. 1894 (privé). The bust remained in the hands of the Thompson family until 1935, when it was given to the Archives of Nova Scotia by Colonel J.T.C. Thompson, through Senator E.N. Rhodes, Conservative premier of Nova Scotia from 1925 to 1930. See *Halifax Mail*, 1 Aug. 1935. (This information was unearthed for me by Allan C. Dunlop, assistant archivist of Nova Scotia.)
55 JSDT, vol. 297, Thompson to Joe, 16 July 1893, from Paris; same, 8 Aug. 1893, from Paris; vol. 184, Abbe G. LeClère to Thompson, 6 août 1893; Griffin Papers, Thompson to Griffin, 18 July 1893 (private)

56 co 42/821, f. 295 *et seq.*

57 *Globe*, 28 Aug. 1893, and *Empire* of same date

58 co 42/823, f. 761, Aberdeen to Ripon, 14 Aug. 1894 (telegram); C.C. Tansill, *Canadian-American Relations 1875–1911* (New Haven 1943), 345–7

59 A.C. Gluek, Jr, 'Canada's Splendid Bargain: The North Pacific Fur Seal Convention of 1911,' *CHR*, LXIII, 2 (June 1982), 182–3

60 As reported in the *Globe*, 28 Aug. 1893

21 THE WEIGHT OF RESPONSIBILITY

1 PAC, Griffin Papers, vol. 4, Griffin to Power, 6 Sept. 1893

2 JSDT, vol. 298, Thompson to John, 4 July 1893, from Paris; vol. 183, Griffin to Thompson, 25 July 1893, from Ottawa; Griffin Papers, vol. 4, Thompson to Griffin, 18 July 1893, from Paris

3 Lady Aberdeen reports Tupper's words in her diary with some incredulity; J.T. Saywell, ed., *The Canadian Journal of Lady Aberdeen, 1893–1898* (Toronto 1960), 18 July 1895, p. 247. Tupper's words to C.H. Tupper are as follows; 'Thompson told me he was satisfied that A.[berdeen] went to Canada anxious to see a change of Govt. and that he had much trouble to overcome his prejudices.' PAC, Tupper Papers, vol. 10, Charles Tupper to C.H. Tupper, 7 Jan. 1895

4 Saywell, *Journal of Lady Aberdeen*, 13 Dec. 1894, p. 167

5 Ibid., p. xv

6 PAC Aberdeen Papers, vol. 4, Helena Thompson MacGregor to Lady Aberdeen, 6 June [1915]

7 Countess of Aberdeen, 'Canada's Late Premier,' in *The Outlook*, (New York), 26 Jan. 1895. Also in Aberdeen Papers, 000523–6. See also *Journal of Lady Aberdeen*, 9 Jan. 1894, p. 50.

8 PAC, National Council of Women, vol. 1, Minutes, 1–59

9 Toronto *Empire*, 4 Nov. 1893

10 Hamilton *Spectator*, 5 Dec. 1893

11 Saywell, ed., *Journal of Lady Aberdeen*, 3 Jan. 1895, p. 182

12 Ibid., 14 Apr. 1894, p. 89; 13 Dec. 1894, p. 168; Faith Fenton in the *Empire*, 21 Apr. 1894

13 Ottawa *Citizen*, 13 Apr. 1894, reporting speech of 12 Apr.

14 Saywell, ed., *Journal of Lady Aberdeen*, 14 Apr. 1894, p. 89

15 *Saturday Night* (Toronto), 16 Sept. 1893

16 *Empire*, 7 Oct. 1893, reporting Thompson's speech at Dunnville of 6 Oct.

17 *Owen Sound Times*, 12 Oct. 1893, reporting Thompson's speech of 5 Oct.

18 JSDT, vol. 193, Griffin to Thompson, 13 Dec. 1893 (personal); same, 18 Dec. 1893. Thompson's reply to the 13 Dec. letter is not extant, for Griffin

unfortunately had a habit of destroying Thompson's letters. Thompson's tone is inferred from Griffin's second letter.

19 *Grip* (Toronto), 11 July 1891
20 Ibid., 4 June 1892
21 Saywell, ed., *Journal of Lady Aberdeen*, 1 Jan. 1894, p. 47
22 *Owen Sound Times*, 12 Oct. 1893
23 The cases are: 24 *SCR* 170; *Appeal Cases*, 348; 1 *Olmstead* 343, all usually cited as *Attorney General for Ontario* v. *Attorney General for Canada*. There is a file of correspondence on this question in the Department of Justice, No 204/1893. The following are the principal letters: Mowat to Bowell, 20 Apr. 1893; Bowell to Mowat, 22 Apr. 1893; J.R. Cartwright, Deputy Attorney General of Ontario to E.L. Newcombe, 2 June 1893; Mowat to Thompson, 14 Oct. 1893.
24 *Empire*, 2 Nov. 1893, reporting Thompson's speech of 1 Nov.
25 So little newspaper comment as to be remarked. *Saturday Night*, 4 Nov. 1893
26 See *supra*, p. 357
27 JSDT, vol. 196, Creighton to Thompson, 11 Jan. 1894; vol. 197, same, 18 Jan. 1894. See also Montreal *La Minerve*, 16 fev. 1894.
28 JSDT, vol. 196, T.C. Patteson to Thompson, 7 Jan. 1894 (private); PAC, Department of Justice Records, RG 13, B7, vol. 963, 'Secret file on American annexationists,' 1893–4. File 1 consists of letters from a Canadian spy, T.B. Grant, to David Creighton of the *Empire*, in typed copies, sent weekly from New York, beginning in November 1893, and ending in October 1894. File 2 comprises letters from F.W. Glen, the working manager of the National Continental Union League, to Edward Farrer, January to April 1894.
29 Ibid., Mercier to C.A. Dana, 9 Aug. 1893 (private and confidential). Mercier admitted he was broke. He also asked Dana to be sure to seal and register every letter. The *New York Sun*, 25 Mar. 1894, carried a picture of Mercier as a Canadian hopeful. See R. Rumilly, *Mercier* (Montréal, 1975), II, 358–60. For both Jetté and Tardivel, see Pierre Savard, *J.-P. Tardivel, la France et les États-Unis 1851–1905* (Montréal, 1975), 231–2.
30 *New York Sun*, 20, 28 Mar. 1894
31 RG 13, B7, vol. 963, file 1, Grant to Creighton, 19 Apr. 1894, referring to letter of Tarte's in *New York Sun* of that date and forthcoming editorial on the subject
32 Ibid., Grant to Creighton, 26 Mar. 1894
33 Saywell, ed., *Journal of Lady Aberdeen*, 9 Jan. 1894, p. 51
34 Montreal *Gazette*, 15 Feb. 1894, reporting Thompson's speech of 14 Feb.
35 JSDT, vol. 266, Thompson to Schultz, 17 Feb. 1894. For details, see Lovell C. Clark, 'A history of the Conservative Administrations, 1891–1896' (PH.D. thesis, University of Toronto, 1968), 298–302; also the fair-minded account

by D.J. Hall, *Clifford Sifton: the Young Napoleon, 1861–1900* (Vancouver 1981), 82–4. Thompson's revised view, see *supra*, p. 365, Thompson to Bernier, 17 Oct. 1894 (private), in Archives des Jésuites, St Jérome, Québec, Fonds Bernier.

36 *Canada, House of Commons Debates* (18 Apr. 1894), col. 1611

37 M.R. Lupul, *The Roman Catholic Church and the North-West School Question: A Study of Church-State Relations in Western Canada, 1875–1905* (Toronto 1974), 70–1

38 Reported in the *Regina Standard*, 23 Dec. 1892, quoted in ibid., 78

39 Ibid., 89

40 *House of Commons Debates* (26 Apr. 1894), cols. 2051, 2058–60

41 JSDT, vol. 199, L.N. Bégin to Caron, 3 fev. 1894 (privé). Bégin was coadjutor for Cardinal Taschereau from 1891 to 1898, when he succeeded to the archdiocese.

42 Ibid., vol. 204, Caron to Thompson, 24 Mar. 1894 (private and confidential)

43 Ibid., vol. 207, Cameron to Thompson, 30 Apr. 1894, from Antigonish

44 *House of Commons Debates* (26 Apr. 1894), col. 2060

45 Father Leduc to Joseph Royal, 16 mai 1894, cited in Lupul, *The Roman Catholic Church and the North-West*, 109

46 JSDT, vol. 210, Taché to Thompson, 20 May 1894. Thompson's draft reply, in the same volume, was probably written about 7 June. Taché's letter is also in AASt.B TA 3434-3441. Lupul usefully tabulates Thompson's remarks in the House on 26 April, Taché's reply, and Thompson's marginal comments (*The Roman Catholic Church and the North-West*, 112–13).

47 Ibid., vol. 213, J.J. Curran to Thompson, 26 June 1894, from Winnipeg

48 *House of Commons Debates* (16 July 1894), cols. 6080–6153

49 Lupul, *The Roman Catholic Church and the North-West*, 115

50 *House of Commons Debates* (19 Apr. 1894), col. 1689

51 JSDT, vol. 297, Thompson to Joe, 4, 26 Mar. 1894

52 *House of Commons Debates* (16 Mar. 1894), col. 61

53 Ottawa *Journal*, 13 Dec. 1894

54 JSDT, vol. 199, Burbidge to Thompson, 9 Feb. 1894; ibid., vol. 297, Thompson to Joe, 12 Feb. 1894; *Regina Leader*, 13 Dec. 1894

55 JSDT, vol. 298, Annie to John, 23 Apr. 1894

56 Saywell, ed., *Journal of Lady Aberdeen*, 24 Mar. 1895, p. 213

57 Ibid., 13 Dec. 1894, p. 165

58 JSDT, vol. 267, Thompson to R.F. Armstrong, 11 Apr. 1894; PANS, Sir John Thompson Papers, Thompson to Chisholm, 27 Apr. 1894

59 PAC, Tupper Papers, vol. 10, Sir Charles Tupper to Sir C.H. Tupper, 9 Feb. 1895, from London

60 Reported in *Toronto World*, 18 Dec. 1894; also *Hamilton Times*, 15 Dec. 1894

61 JSDT, vol. 297, Thompson to Joe, 25 Nov. 1893
62 Ibid., vol. 195, C.H. Mackintosh to Thompson, 4 Jan. 1894, from Regina
63 PAO, Clarke Wallace Papers, Env. 27, Wallace to his wife Belinda, 28 Mar. 1894
64 JSDT, vol. 267, Thompson to Massey, 7 Apr. 1894, replying to Massey's of 30 Mar. 1894. Massey complained of the new duty of 20 per cent saying 'you have virtually given our home trade over to a foreign country without any reasonable excuse ...' The letter was written from Aiken, South Carolina, and addressed 'Dear Thompson' (vol. 204).
65 *House of Commons Debates* (27 Mar. 1894), col. 195
66 The account of budget night is based on Faith Fenton's report on the women's page in the *Empire*, 21 Apr. 1894.
67 JSDT, vol. 213, Foster to Thompson, Friday morning, n.d.
68 *Toronto World*, 8 Dec. 1893, reporting Thompson's speech of 7 Dec. at Antigonish. 'Yellow' as referring to cowardice is a meaning that dates only from about 1896.
69 *House of Commons Debates* (26 June 1894), cols. 4956 *et seq.*; Montreal *La Presse*, 28 juin 1894. Tarte raised the question of the integrity of the judges again, 12 July. Thompson wrote him directly; if Tarte would make specific his charges, Thompson would see that both charges and the judges' replies were laid before the House. JSDT, vol. 269, Thompson to Tarte, 14 July 1894. It is addressed sternly 'Sir.'
70 Montreal *La Presse*, 21 juin 1894; PAC, Gowan Papers, Thompson to Gowan, 29 June 1894
71 *House of Commons Debates* (25 June 1894), cols. 4936 *et seq.* Mackintosh, the lieutenant-governor, wrote Thompson thanking him for the defence Thompson had given. '... no more cruel or unjust charge could be made – and only such a thorough paced blackguard as Martin would assume responsibility for it. All the Liberals here are disgusted.' JSDT, vol. 214, Mackintosh to Thompson, 3 July 1894
72 *House of Commons Debates* (25 Apr. 1894), cols. 1959–61. The offender in this case was the *Ottawa Free Press*.
73 Joseph Schull, *Ontario since 1867* (Toronto 1978) 124; the *Empire*, 30 June 1894, gave a result more generous to Conservatives, but it was somewhat *parti pris*.
74 *Statutes of Canada, 1894*, 57–58 Vic. c. 58; *House of Commons Debates* (25 June 1894), col. 4940
75 JSDT, vol. 213, Starr to Thompson, 27 June 1894, from Toronto. See also Neil Sutherland, *Children in English Canadian Society: Framing the Twentieth Century Consensus* (Toronto 1976), ch. 8, especially 114–17.

76 W.A. Calder, '"The Way of the Transgressor Is Hard:" Punishment in Canada's Federal Penitentiary System, 1867–1899,' given at Canadian Historical Association, 1978, unpublished paper, p. 13
77 Parliament created the parole system in 1899 (63 Vic. c. 49).
78 JSDT, vol. 270, Thompson to Aberdeen, 4 Aug. 1894; it is also in the Aberdeen Papers, vol. 4.
79 *Annual Report of Prisoner's Aid Society*, 1893, p. 6, cited in Calder, 'Punishment in Canada's Penitentiary System,' 5
80 JSDT, vol. 191, J.G. Moylan to Douglas Stewart, 15 Nov. 1893. This was information to allow Stewart to prepare a reply to a letter of G.G. Dustan of Halifax, who would not believe that the cells at Kingston were only 2' 5" wide.
81 PAC, Sir Robert Borden Papers, vol. 294, Bishop Cameron to [D.] McMaster, 1 Mar. 1894, from Antigonish. The bishop was reporting the gist of a long interview with Thompson on his problems with the administration of the prison system. How the letter came to be in the Borden Papers is a mystery. It may have been grouped with some letters between Van Horne and Thompson about fast steamship service, given to Borden by E.W. Beatty in 1928.
82 *House of Commons Debates* (1895), col. 3142, as cited in Calder, 'Punishment in Canada's Penitentiary System,' 2
83 Ibid., 7–8
84 *House of Commons Debates* (May 7 1894), col. 2410; ibid. (19 June 1894), col. 4594
85 *Saturday Night*, 15 Dec. 1894; *Empire*, 12 May 1894
86 British Library, Addl. MSS. 43516, Ripon Papers, Ripon to Rosebery, 22 Mar. 1894 (copy); Rosebery to Ripon, 23 Mar. 1894 (private)
87 Ibid., Ripon to Rosebery, 20 May 1894 (confidential, copy); Addl. MSS. 43526, Kimberley to Ripon, 6 June 1894
88 The obstacles Thompson and Bowell meant were in two categories. First were British treaties with Belgium and Germany with most favoured nation clauses. Second was an inhibition in the constitution of the Australian colonies against intercolonial tariff reductions. See O. Mary Hill, *Canada's Salesman to the World: The Department of Trade and Commerce, 1892–1939* (Montreal and Toronto 1977), 73–4.
89 Aberdeen Papers, vol. 4, Thompson to Lady Aberdeen, 27 Oct. 1894
90 JSDT, vol. 216, J.A. Gillies (MP for Cape Breton) to Thompson, 31 July 1894, from Sydney; vol. 218, J.C. Patterson to Thompson, 11 Aug. 1894 (private and confidential), from Toronto; vol. 217, Daly to Thompson, 10 Aug. 1894 (private), from Toronto
91 Ibid., vol. 217, Daly to Thompson, 10 Aug. 1894, from Toronto

92 Ibid., vol. 218, Foster to Thompson, 18 Aug. 1894, from Aophoqui, NB; vol. 219, Provand to Thompson, 22 Aug. 1894, from London
93 Ibid., vol. 221, Sir Charles Tupper to Sir Charles Hibbert Tupper, n.d. (copy), f. 27576. This was probably copied by Tupper Jr for Thompson; *Empire*, 30 Oct. 1894; see *infra*. p. 418.
94 Ibid., 21 Aug. 1894, reporting Thompson's speech of 20 Aug.
95 See *supra*, p. 386.
96 PANS, Sir John Thompson Papers, Thompson to J.A. Chisholm, 12 Aug. 1894
97 JSDT, vol. 217, Mackintosh to Thompson, 9 Aug. 1894
98 Toronto *Empire*, 1 Sept. 1894. The photographs by great luck have been preserved. PAC, Photography Archives, C 9079 and C 10111. The snapshots appear to have been taken by Babe Thompson.

22 THE END OF THINGS

1 JSDT, vol. 291, Thompson to Annie, 2, 6 Sept. 1894, from Ottawa
2 *Toronto World*, 13 Dec. 1894, report of interview on 12 Dec. with Dr J.F.W. Ross. The *World* created a sensation in Toronto when on 6 Dec. 1894 it announced that Thompson would resign as premier owing to illness. The Toronto *Empire*, 7 Dec. 1894, then attacked the *World* for its 'shameful fabrication,' a position supported by J.C. Patterson, John Haggart, and W.H. Montague. See also the *World*, 7 Dec. 1894.
3 JSDT, vol. 291, Thompson to Annie, 9 Sept. 1894, from Montreal
4 Ibid., vol. 291, Thompson to Annie, 19 Sept. 1894, from Antigonish; ibid., vol. 222, Chisholm to Thompson, 9 Oct. 1894, from Halifax
5 *St. John Daily Sun*, 12 Sept. 1894, reporting Thompson's speech of earlier that day
6 PANS, Sir John Thompson Papers, Thompson to Chisholm, 11 Oct. 1894 from Ottawa, enclosing power of attorney to act relative to the Armstrong lots; JSDT, vol. 291, Thompson to Annie, 16 Sept. 1894, from Antigonish
7 Ibid., vol. 195, Ede & Sons to Thompson, 3 Jan. 1894
8 PANS, Sir John Thompson Papers, Thompson to Chisholm, 12 Aug. 1894, from Port Carling
9 JSDT, Cameron to Thompson, 21 Feb. 1894; sup. vol. [301?], Cameron to Thompson, 28 Sept. 1894, from St Denis; vol. 222, Cameron to Thompson, 9 Oct. 1894, from St Denis
10 Probably the most accurate source about the Ottawa diagnosis was Lady Aberdeen, who had long talks with Annie on 13 Dec. and afterward. See J.T. Saywell, ed., *The Canadian Journal of Lady Aberdeen, 1893–1898* (Toronto

1960), 13 Dec. 1894, p. 162. The Roddick Papers at the McGill University Archives contain nothing about Thompson.

There is a curious story in the Moncton *Daily Times*, 13 Dec. 1894. When Thompson was at Amherst in September a friend called to see him. Thompson invited him in, told him to take a chair, but he (Thompson) preferred to lie down. Thompson said he envied his visitor his health and felt himself definitely unwell, and was not sure where the cure lay. Thompson was alleged to have said that he was 'a done man.' Since this was published after his death one may perhaps discount it. Similar rumours appeared in several papers: the *St. John Daily Sun*, 14 Dec. 1894; *Montreal Daily Star*, 12 Dec. 1894; Bathurst *Courrier des Provinces Maritimes*, 20 déc. 1894.

11 *Toronto Daily Mail*, 13 Dec. 1894
12 *Empire*, 15 Oct. 1894; JSDT, vol. 266, Thompson to Archdeacon Kelly of Kingston, 16 Feb. 1894
13 *Toronto World*, 14 Dec. 1894
14 JSDT, vol. 223, Sir Frank Smith to Thompson, 18 Oct. 1894, from Toronto, answering Thompson's letter of 12 Oct.
15 Ibid., vol. 271, Thompson to Senator John Ferguson of Toronto, 8 Sept. 1894 (confidential); PAC, Gowan Papers, M-1897, Creighton to Gowan, 25 Oct. 1894 (confidential); 28 Oct. 1894 (private)
16 Gowan Papers, M-1900, Thompson to Gowan, 27 Oct. 1894
17 Saywell, ed., *Journal of Lady Aberdeen*, 13 Dec. 1894, pp. 165–6
18 *The Times* (London), 5 Nov. 1894. It is interesting that this editorial was carefully clipped by W.S. Fielding of Nova Scotia, and a copy of it turns up in the Fielding Papers, Box 1 (PANS).
19 *Toronto World*, 13 Oct. 1894
20 CO 42/828, Thompson to Lord Ripon, 8 Nov. 1894, ff. 491–4, and CO Minutes thereon
21 Ibid., f. 489
22 *The Times*, 21 Nov. 1894
23 CO 42/828, f. 297, F.R. Daldy to J. Bramston, 25 Nov. 1894
24 Saywell, ed., *Journal of Lady Aberdeen*, 13 Dec. 1894, p. 162
25 JSDT, vol. 224, J.G. Colmer to Thompson, 29 Nov. 1894; the itinerary in Castell Hopkins, *Thompson*, is only partly correct (p. 436), and is incorrect about the date of Thompson's arrival in London, for which Tupper gives both date and time (JSDT, vol. 292, Sir Charles Tupper to Annie Thompson, 14 Nov. [should be Dec.] 1894).

Lady Macdonald missed connections with them. See Queen's University, Williamson Papers, Agnes Macdonald to Williamson, 4 Jan. 1895, from San Remo.

26 JSDT, vol. 292, Tupper to Annie Thompson, 14 Dec. 1894 (marked 14 Nov. in error)
27 Recollection of Senator Sanford, reported in Halifax *Morning Chronicle*, 2 Jan. 1895
28 London *Standard*, 14 Dec. 1894, reporting interview with Lord Russell of Killowen
29 JSDT, vol. 224 has a number of these invitations.
30 Ibid., sup. vol. [301?], Gladstone to Thompson, 28 Nov. 1894
31 British Library, Gladstone Papers, Addl. MSS 44090, Lady Aberdeen to Gladstone, 6 Nov. 1894; Addl. MSS 44519, Thompson to Gladstone, 4 Dec. 1894, from London
32 British Library, Ripon Papers, Addl. MSS. 43516, Rosebery to Ripon, 30 Nov., 2 Dec. 1894 (private)
33 See Harvey Mitchell, 'Canada's Negotiations with Newfoundland, 1887–1895,' *CHR*, XL, 4 (Dec. 1959), 284–5.
34 PRO CO 42/814, Anderson's Minute of 17 Feb. on Pauncefote's telegram of 15 Feb. 1892 to the Foreign Office
35 See St John Chadwick, *Newfoundland: Island into Province* (Cambridge 1967), 62.
36 JSDT, vol. 233, Thompson to T.E. Kenny, 22 Feb. 1888 (private and confidential)
37 Ibid., vol. 346, Thompson to A.B. Morine, 18 Dec. 1890 (private)
38 Ibid., vol. 166, Morine to Thompson, 3 Nov. 1892, from St John's
39 Ripon Papers, Addl. MSS 43559, Sir Terence O'Brien to Ripon, 6 Dec. 1892 (private)
40 University of British Columbia Archives, C.H. Tupper Papers, Thompson to Tupper, 15 Nov. 1892 (telegram)
41 Ripon Papers, Addl. MSS. 43559, O'Brien to Ripon, 18 Nov. 1893 (private); 2 June 1894; 20 Jan. 1895 (private)
42 Chadwick, *Island into Province*, 66–9
43 See *supra*, ch. 16. London *Times*, 11 Dec. 1894 had a long, fair-minded, and comprehensive editorial on copyright, indeed one of the best short accounts of the issue available.
44 JSDT, vol. 292, Tupper to Annie Thompson, 14 Dec. 1894
45 Thompson shopped on Saville Row on 11 Dec. He was looking for a parasol for Annie, and bought for himself dress breeches and black silk stockings. The bill turns up in Annie's papers, and she asked Pope to remit the amount, £4.12s.6d. in all, to London. JSDT, vol. 299, Annie Thompson to Pope, 14 Feb. 1895
46 Halifax *Morning Chronicle*, 2 Jan. 1895, interview with Senator Sanford
47 There was a report in the *New York World*, 16 Dec. 1894, repeated in the

Empire the following day, that attributed Thompson's death to a long court ceremony, alleging that it lasted a full hour and twenty-five minutes. This is almost certainly a *canard.* Thompson's invitation says 1:15 for the commencement of the ceremony; he was sworn in, according to the court circular at 1:30 p.m. He was at lunch by about 1:35. Thompson's official invitation is in JSDT, vol. 300, dated Whitehall, 8 Dec. 1894.

48 There are many accounts, differing slightly in detail. This is based on Lord Breadalbane's sworn evidence, and reported in *St. James Gazette,* 13 Dec. 1894. Most of the London papers carried accounts of Thompson's death. A small collection is in JSDT, vol. 294. G.E. Foster made an extensive collection of Canadian obituaries. PAC, G.E. Foster Papers, vol. 83.

49 Standard time had been brought in after the International Meridan Conference in Washington in 1884, that gave international recognition, and implementation, to Sandford Fleming's idea of standard time.

50 JSDT, vol. 292, has the telegrams; *Empire,* 13 Dec., has the effect of them on the East Block offices.

51 Faith Fenton in *Empire,* 13 Dec. 1894 describes the scene.

52 Saywell, ed., *Journal of Lady Aberdeen,* 13 Dec. 1894, pp. 161–2

53 PAC, Griffin Papers, vol. 1, Gowan to Griffin, 15, 20 Dec. 1894; Chapleau reported in Halifax *Herald,* 14 Dec. 1894

54 *Montreal Daily Star,* 12 Dec. 1894

55 PAO, Edgar Papers, Laurier to Edgar, 14 Dec. 1894

56 Ottawa *Le Temps,* 13 déc. 1894; *St. John Daily Sun,* 15 Dec. 1894, special despatch from Ottawa

57 JSDT, vol. 197, Taillon to Thompson, 25 juin 1894 (personelle et confidentielle)

58 Reported in Quebec *Le Courrier du Canada,* 13 déc. 1894, and translated here from the French

59 *The Times,* 15 Dec. 1894

60 George Peabody (1795–1869) was also given a funeral service in Westminster Abbey.

61 Ripon Papers, Addl. MSS. 53532, Ripon to Harcourt, 13 Dec. 1894 (copy); Harcourt to Ripon, 13 Dec. 1894

62 PRO CO 42/824, f. 768, Ripon to Aberdeen, 13 Dec. 1894

63 Ibid., f. 773, minute of H.W. Just, Ripon's private secretary, to Robert Meade, on Aberdeen to Ripon, 16 Dec. 1894 (telegram), asking about military forces at Halifax taking part in Thompson's funeral

64 Saywell, ed., *Journal of Lady Aberdeen,* 17, 19 Dec. 1894, pp. 172, 174; CO 42/824 ff. 766–7, H.W. Just to Sir Charles Tupper, 15 Dec. 1894 (draft); British Library, Addl. MSS. 43559, Aberdeen to Ripon, 24 Dec. 1894 (private)

65 Hopkins, *Thompson,* 445–6, gives a detailed description.

66 *Canada, House of Commons Debates* (19 June 1895), cols. 2921 *et seq.* gives total costs as $21,993, plus $3,615 for trains.
67 JSDT, vol. 292, Joseph Pope to John Pugh (Annie's uncle by marriage), 14 Dec. 1894 (copy)
68 Saywell, ed., *Journal of Lady Aberdeen*, 31 Dec. 1894, p. 177
69 Ibid., 2 Jan. 1895, p. 182

23 IN THE SERVICE OF HIS COUNTRY

1 PANS, Fielding Papers, Box 1, Laurier to Fielding, 12 Jan. 1895 (private and confidential), from Arthabaskaville. Laurier was too unwell to come to Thompson's funeral.
2 J.T. Saywell, ed., *The Canadian Journal of Lady Aberdeen 1893–1898*, (Toronto 1960), 3 Jan. 1895, p. 184
3 See *supra*, p. 380; Benjamin Russell, 'J.T. Bulmer,' in *Dalhousie Review*, IX (1929–30), 76.
4 British Library, Addl. MSS. 44090, Gladstone Papers, Lady Aberdeen to Gladstone, 28 Mar. 1895, from Ottawa; Fielding Papers, Box 1, Laurier to Fielding, 31 May 1895 (confidential)
5 Montreal *Herald*, 12, 13 Dec. 1894; Montreal *La Presse*, 13 déc. 1894
6 PAC, Aberdeen Papers, vol. 2, Memorandum for Lady Aberdeen by Martin Griffin written in 1895
7 Gertrude Himmelfarb, *Victorian Minds* (New York 1968), 207; Benjamin Russell, 'The Career of Sir John Thompson,' *Dalhousie Review*, I, 2 (1921), 200
8 JSDT, vol. 205, W.E. Jones to Thompson, 2 Apr. 1894, referring to an interview on 27 Mar.
9 Ibid., vol. 272, Thompson to Rev. D. McKinnon, 23 Oct. 1894
10 *Union des Cantons de l'Est* (Sherbrooke), 22 fév. 1894
11 'The man of upright life, free from guilt, has no need of Moorish darts or bow.'
12 Montreal *La Patrie*, 13 déc. 1894; *La Minerve*, 19 déc. 1894
13 Pope's *Essay on Man*, Ep. iii, 1.303
14 JSDT, vol. 292, Bayard to Tupper, 14 Dec. 1894 (personal)
15 From act IV, scene iii. The play was produced first at Covent Garden in 1775.
16 Toronto *Empire*, 13 Dec. 1894; PAC, MG 27, III, F. 9, Harold Daly Papers, 'Memoirs,' p. 6. This reference has been given to me by Professor Craig Brown, University of Toronto.
17 *St. John Daily Sun*, 4 Jan. 1895, a poem by A.M. Belding. In order to get the sense right in the truncated version quoted here, I have had to alter slightly the fifth line.

EPILOGUE

1 PAO, Carleton County, Surrogate Court, No 2575, Letters of Administration sworn 24 Dec. 1894. The administrators were Daniel O'Connor, John Haney, and Annie Thompson.
2 *Canada, House of Commons Debates* (14 June 1895), col. 2682. Those who opposed the grant to the Lady Thompson Fund included Louis Davies, Frederick Borden, Israel Tarte, F. Langelier, G. McMullen, and F. Landerkin.
3 JSDT, vol. 294, contains details of subscribers. Sir Donald Smith gave $5,000; W.W. Ogilvy of Montreal, $2,500; Hugh Graham, $1,000; Angers, Bowell, Caron, Tuppers Sr and Jr, Patterson, Ouimet $500 each. Sir Richard Cartwright and Robert Borden gave $100 each. So also did Bishop Cameron. One curious contribution came from NWMP, 'K' Division, $73.32. A still more curious $5 came from a Rev. J.M. O'Flaherty, of St Stephen, New Brunswick. Was this Thompson's early rival for Annie's affections?
4 JSDT, vol. 279, Thompson to Mrs Barnaby, 18 July 1889, in which he says he had not intended to sell the property, and 'although the house is not in a very good condition it is very substantially built ...' For the sale, see Halifax County Deeds, Reel 1057, vol. 316, f. 373, which records the sale of Willow Park, 22 Sept. 1896 to W.B. Freeman.
5 Halifax County, Court of Probate, No 4616
6 J.T. Saywell, ed. *The Canadian Journal of Lady Aberdeen 1893–1898*, (Toronto 1960), 14 Feb. 1895, p. 196; 6 Mar. 1895, p. 208
7 Ibid., 4 Jan. 1895, p. 185
8 Historical Society of Ottawa, Alan Stewart Collection, Bowell to Douglas Stewart, 15 Dec. 1894
9 PAC Aberdeen Papers, vol. 4, Helena Thompson MacGregor to Lady Aberdeen, 22[?] Apr. 1913
10 See the excellent article by A.E. Marble and T.M. Punch, 'Sir J.S.D. Thompson: A Prime Minister's Family Connections,' *Nova Scotia Historical Quarterly*, VII, 4 (Dec. 1977), 377–88.

Picture Credits

PUBLIC ARCHIVES CANADA: Thompson in 1859 PA25801; Thompson in 1867 PA25799; Thompson aged 34 C12188; Annie Affleck C19302; Inter-colonial Railway Station C19262; Willow Park C53832; Abbott PA33933; Tupper PA27084; McCarthy PA25698; Foster PA27164; Thompson in 1891 C68645; John and Joe Thompson C70470; Frances Thompson C53834; Helena Thompson C70582; Mary Aloysia Thompson C70583; Thompson in 1894 PA12206; Lady Thompson C10107; family group C10111

PUBLIC ARCHIVES OF NOVA SCOTIA: Halifax in 1890; Thompson's funeral

ST FRANCIS XAVIER UNIVERSITY, ANTIGONISH: Bishop John Cameron

MAP: Courtney C.J. Bond

Bibliographical Essay

PERSONAL PAPERS

The Thompson Papers are organized in three broad groups. Vols. 1–224 are the letters received by Thompson; they begin in 1869 and end in 1894. They are arranged in strict chronological order. Vols. 225–72 are Thompson's letter books, 1877 to 1894, incomplete for the early years and uneven throughout. They are not always easy to read. Vols. 272–82 are miscellaneous correspondence. Vol. 283 is Annie's letters to Thompson; vols. 288–91 are Thompson's letters to her, 1869 to 1894. Other family letters, notably Thompson to his five children are in vols. 297–8. A new volume of family letters was turned up by Kaye Lamb, set aside by Norah Story in 1949 as too personal for public access. (They were not *that* personal.)

Besides this great three-hundred-volume collection of Thompson Papers at PAC, there is a small collection at PANS, from the papers of Sir Joseph Chisholm, Thompson's brother-in-law. These seem to have been carefully selected, and one misses in them the richness of the inter-family relations so characteristic of the PAC papers. A still smaller and more curious collection of papers is in the Historical Society of the Ottawa, mainly odds and ends handed down probably from Douglas Stewart, Thompson's private secretary. Thompson's passport is there, for example, and the instructions about the removal of the Thompson papers from the Department of Justice.

Important Thompson letters will be found in the manuscript collections of contemporaries, the largest group of which is in the Macdonald Papers, vols. 273–5, at PAC. But one cannot neglect the Sir James Gowan Papers, as well as those of Martin Griffin, Mackenzie Bowell, J.P.R.A. Caron, Sir Charles Tupper, all at PAC, nor the papers of Sir Hector Langevin, at APQ. Other ministers have been less generous with papers. The G.E. Foster Papers (PAC) are not very satisfying, the

Dewdney Papers at Calgary and Victoria are very thin. J.J. Curran seems to have left nothing and Chapleau's papers contain little that is useful.

Governors general also had correspondence with Thompson, notably Lord Stanley and Lord Aberdeen. These seem to have been selected from a much larger archive of originals. Lord Aberdeen specifically asked young J.T.C. Thompson to dig out from the Thompson Papers the Aberdeen letters, which were to be returned to him. These will be found, with some from Thompson, in the Aberdeen Papers at PAC.

One also cannot neglect important correspondence available in the British Library (formerly the Library of the British Museum), London. The Ripon Papers will repay attention; there are also materials in the Gladstone Papers.

What is missing for a comprehensive view of Thompson are the dozens of letters he must have written to Bishop Cameron, and which the diocese of Antigonish says have not been found. G.G. Dustan of Halifax claimed that he had five hundred Thompson letters, but they seem to have disappeared. There are no Pottinger Papers of any substance, though a tiny collection at the Hector Trust in Pictou tantalizes one.

In Nova Scotia there is very much less to go on. Thompson's colleagues in the Nova Scotian government left almost no papers at all. His own law office, and that of Robert Borden, was burned out in 1885, and their considerable legal correspondence has disappeared.

OFFICIAL RECORDS

The vast collection of the Department of Justice, Ottawa, is now at PAC, RG 13, and consists of records that date from before confederation (in the case of the Province of Canada) and going down to 1934. The incoming correspondence is RG 13, A2, called the Central Registry files and cover the period of Thompson's tenure as minister of justice from 1885 to 1894, vols. 64–99 in some thirty-five large boxes. The outgoing letter books are RG 13, A3, vols. 619–59. RG 13, B15 are the capital case files, use of which requires special permission. RG 13, B7 are the secret files on the American annexationists in Canada, 1893–4.

Some Department of Justice records were not surrendered and are still at the department, where they can be seen by permission. Some important small files turn up there, including some on individual judges, the correspondence with Mowat on the *Local Prohibition* case reference, as well as extensive correspondence with Canadian judges about the new Criminal Code of 1892.

There are a few cross-references to some of this correspondence in the Attorney General's Papers (RG 4) at PAO but they have not been explored systematically.

There are almost no useful papers in PANS on the role and functioning of the Attorney General of Nova Scotia in the late nineteenth century.

There are however official records in Halifax of the School Board, still in the custody of the commissioners in the old high school that was new in Thompson's years, at the corner of Sackville and Brunswick streets. The Minutes of City Council are available on microfilm at PANS. The Supreme Court records while Thompson was judge (1882–5) are still in a raw and unsorted condition, and did not seem to offer much of value for this book. More easily accessible are the reports of the principal law cases published as *Nova Scotia Reports*.

PUBLISHED SOURCES

The single most indispensable book for Thompson is *The Canadian Journal of Lady Aberdeen, 1893–1898*, elegantly introduced and edited by J.T. Saywell, published by the Champlain Society in 1960. Lady Aberdeen, as every reader of this book will know, was a great admirer of Sir John Thompson; she found everything about him marvellous and never hesitated to tell her diary so. The Champlain Society volume is now out of print. Sir Charles Tupper's *Recollections of Sixty Years in Canada* (London 1914) has been carefully edited, really too much so to be of use. J.S. Willison's *Reminiscences, Political and Personal* (Toronto 1919), are not directly concerned with Thompson, but when they bear upon him they are fascinating. Thompson also surfaces from time to time in Hector Charlesworth's *Candid Chronicles* (Toronto 1925) and *More Candid Chronicles* (Toronto 1928).

Newspapers are indispensable, but they are a vast ocean of good and ill. In any case one can never be at an end with them. There are certainly things about Thompson in the two hundred or so daily newspapers in Canada that I will not have seen. It is a field open to the enterprising and the valiant, and it will prove rewarding. The notes will suggest that although I have cast my net widely, the mesh has been quite large enough to let all sorts of things through.

SECONDARY LITERATURE

The secondary literature on Thompson is not large and is given sufficient attention in the notes. One must mention, however, J. Castell Hopkins's book, *The Life and Work of the Rt. Hon. Sir John Thompson P.C., K.C.M.G., Q.C., Prime Minister of Canada* (Brantford 1895). It bears a preface from Lord Aberdeen dated 25 February 1895. Written in two months, it was a work of the times intended for Canadians (and others) who admired Thompson and wanted to know more about him. Hopkins (1864–1923) was a journalist with the Toronto *Empire*. Almost certainly Annie read his manuscript before it was published, and it is known she read early chapters in draft. Hopkins's emphasis in the latter part of the book, in the fashion of the time, exaggerates Thompson's imperial feelings. Thompson spent a good deal of his life at odds with the imperial government over one issue or another, though usually, with the exception of copyright, with little bitterness.

Hopkins was young, energetic, and copious, and his getting a book out at all within two months of Thompson's death owes more to industry than to elegance. His language we would now read as flat, even flatulent; and his biography is for most purposes dead. Still, for Thompson's early life it has uses. One must however guess what Annie has seen fit to exclude: in effect, what there is between the lines.

An important and more formidable secondary source has not been published: Lovell Clark's PH D thesis for the University of Toronto in 1968, 'A History of the Conservative Administrations, 1891–1896.' J.P. Heisler's useful 'Sir John Thompson,' also for Toronto, in 1955, is unpublished.

The article literature is not large but some is very good. References have been made to it in the notes and need not be repeated here. One article could be noted, the result of J.T. Saywell's work on Thompson for the Champlain Society book: 'Sir John Thompson – the Unknown,' in *Canadian Forum* (July 1957), 79–80.

Index